SOCIAL REFORMERS

THE MACMILLAN COMPANY
NEW YORK · BOSTON · CHICAGO · DALLAS
ATLANTA · SAN FRANCISCO

MACMILLAN AND CO., Limited
LONDON · BOMBAY · CALCUTTA · MADRAS
MELBOURNE

THE MACMILLAN COMPANY
OF CANADA, Limited
TORONTO

SOCIAL REFORMERS

ADAM SMITH TO JOHN DEWEY

EDITED BY

DONALD O. WAGNER, PH.D.

INSTRUCTOR IN HISTORY
NEW YORK UNIVERSITY

WITH A FOREWORD BY

CARLTON J. H. HAYES

PROFESSOR OF HISTORY
COLUMBIA UNIVERSITY

NEW YORK
THE MACMILLAN COMPANY
1939

Published February, 1934. Reprinted May, 1935; May, 1937; March, 1939.

SET UP AND ELECTROTYPED BY T. MOREY & SON
• PRINTED IN THE UNITED STATES OF AMERICA •

FOREWORD

Everybody senses that a new social order is emerging in America and throughout Christendom and the whole world. But there is wide difference of opinion as to precisely what the new order is or should be, and little appreciation of its historic setting.

As a matter of fact, the "new social order" has been emerging for a hundred and fifty years—ever since the shift of population began, in revolutionary proportion, from field to factory, from countryside to city, from agriculture to industry, and ever since great minds began to recognize the essentially dynamic character of modern life and to speculate about its course and purpose. For the evolution of modern society depends, and for a century and a half has continuously depended, not only on material circumstances and technological advance, but also on human aspirations and the counsels of philosophers. It is significant that, contemporaneously with the early stage of the Industrial Revolution, and in the very year in which the Declaration of American Independence appeared, Adam Smith published his *Wealth of Nations* and Jeremy Bentham his *Fragment on Government.* These classics set forth a doctrine of economic and political liberalism which proved as influential as the steam-engine itself in laying the foundations for a new social order. If the steam-engine made some new order practicable and imperative, the liberalism of Smith and Bentham (and the Fathers of the American Republic) entered consciously into architects' specifications of what the new order should actually be.

Since then, the building of the new social order has proceeded apace. Every generation has discovered new structural materials or new uses for old materials; in our own day, the possibilities of construction, and likewise of destruction, have been almost infinitely extended. We must remember, however, that such possibilities have been conditioned by successive generations of architects—of social philosophers—who have obtained popular and sometimes governmental approval of this or that drawing which they have made of the imagined society of the future. The drawings and specifications are diverse: they include not only those of liberalism and "rugged individualism" but also those of socialism of different styles, utopian and "scientific," collectivist and anarchist, communist and Christian. But all of them, in greater or less degree, are part and parcel of the intellectual heritage of the present day, and consequently, if we would truly understand the latest stage in the emerging social order, it is as important to have a first-hand knowledge of the classics of modern social thought as to study contemporary statistics or mechanics.

A convenient introduction to such knowledge is afforded by the following pages. Dr. Donald Wagner, with scholarly care and great good sense, has brought together in one book particularly pertinent passages from the writings of a variety of social reformers of the past hundred and fifty years—from Adam Smith and Jeremy Bentham, through Cobbett and Owen, Proudhon and von Ketteler, Spencer and Comte, Marx and Sorel, to Sidney Webb and John Dewey. The selected passages are brief enough to be at once arresting and easily readable; and they are long enough to bring out the reasoning of each author on special points and to convey at least the flavor of his whole philosophy. The prefatory essays with which Dr. Wagner introduces his several characters are delightful as well as informing, and the attendant bibliographies constitute a useful, up-to-date guide to further reading.

The book merits a wide use in colleges and universities. It should be an indispensable companion-volume to the textbook in any course on modern history in which social and economic developments are related to political activity; in other words, in any course on modern history worth "giving" or "taking." And beyond the young men and women that receive formal instruction in institutions of higher learning, the book merits perusal and study by all persons who would be intelligent about twentieth-century society and who therefore would seek acquaintance with the social thought of modern times.

CARLTON J. H. HAYES

PREFACE

Mr. Mark Van Doren imagines a university in which the students have read only "the acknowledged masterpieces of the past. . . . None of them was read in an abridged edition. Neither was any of them approached through a digest or commentary." No one can find fault with the ideal here implied; it is certainly impossible to compress volumes into a few pages (although sometimes the only thing lost is repetitiousness). On the other hand, no matter how fertile in ideas a writer may have been, he is usually remembered for only a few of them, and if we happen to be interested less in the totality of his philosophy than in its impact on subsequent thought we are justified in making and using compendiums which keep that interest in view. The latter is the main purpose of this book, as its title indicates, and the reader will not look for an epitome of any writer's whole system of thought. Nor is it claimed that all important contributions to reformist theory have been included. Needless to say this would have required not one but many volumes.

There are a number of useful histories of reformist thought, but few collections of extracts from the original works themselves. Yet the homeopathic dose has at least one advantage over the predigested form—it is apt to retain more of the original flavor. And very often the way a thing is said largely accounts for its importance and popularity. But an inadequate impression of a writer's viewpoint is gained unless the quotations are long enough to give some idea of the range and sweep of the argument. This restricts the number of personages that can be dealt with in a single volume and makes the problem of selection a difficult one. Great figures choose themselves but the claims of others are a matter of opinion. In the present case, where claims seemed to be otherwise about equal, some weight has been given to geographical distribution and adaptability to quotation.

The biographical notes are intended to reveal something of the connection between personal experience and doctrinal tendency, and to indicate the sources and influence of doctrine.

Any method of grouping social theorists is properly subject to criticism. The one made use of here takes into account chronology, similarity of viewpoint, and the evolution of doctrine. But reformers have a habit of defying efforts to organize them, and no particular stress is laid on the arrangement adopted in this book.

Acknowledgments are due the following publishers for permission to reprint extracts from works under copyright: the D. Appleton-Century Co. (for the quotations from Spencer's *The Principles of Sociology* and *The Man versus the State*), the Viking Press, Inc. (Bernstein's *Evolutionary Socialism*, Veblen's *The Theory of the Leisure Class*, and Sorel's *Reflections on Violence*), Doubleday, Doran and Co. (Henry George's *Progress and Poverty*), and Harcourt, Brace and Co. (Tawney's *The Acquisitive Society*). I am specially obliged to the following for allowing me gratis use of copyrighted material: Professor John Dewey and Minton, Balch and Co. (Dewey's *Individualism Old and New*), the International Publishing Co. (Lenin's *State and Revolution*), Benziger Brothers (*The Great Encyclical Letters of Leo XIII*), the T. Y. Crowell Co. (Tolstoy's *What Is To Be Done?* and *The Kingdom of God Is within You*), and the Carnegie Endowment for International Peace (Rocco's *The Political Theory of Fascism*).

I also wish to thank Professor E. L. Kayser of George Washington University for help in choosing the passages from Bentham, and my colleague, Dr. Russell Pope, on whose translations the selections from von Ketteler and Wagner are based. My brother, Mr. Allan H. Wagner, assisted me with the translations from Fourier and with the typing of the manuscript. That more errors of transcription have not crept into the book is due to the vigilance of my father, Mr. J. B. Wagner. My debt to Professor Carlton Hayes of Columbia University goes far beyond his suggestions for improving this book and his aid in bringing it to press, for it was he who first aroused my interest in the whole subject of social reform.

D. O. W.

New York City
January, 1934

A second printing of this book enables me to correct certain errors and misprints in the text. I wish to thank those correspondents who have called my attention to some of them.

D. O. W.

April, 1935

CONTENTS

PART I

EARLY ECONOMIC AND POLITICAL LIBERALISM

PART III

EARLY NINETEENTH-CENTURY SOCIALISMS

PART V

"SCIENTIFIC" SOCIALISM

PART VI

STATE SOCIALISM, LIMITED AND UNLIMITED

PART VII

WORKERS' CONTROL: FUNCTIONAL THEORIES, REVOLUTIONARY AND EVOLUTIONARY

ANARCHISM

PART I

EARLY ECONOMIC AND POLITICAL LIBERALISM

I

ADAM SMITH

1723–1790

Adam Smith belonged neither by birth nor early training to that rising commercial middle class which in the end adopted him as its prophet. His father, who died in 1723 shortly before the birth of his son, had been a customs official in Kirkcaldy, Scotland, and the family thus owed its comfortable station in life to the very system of trade regulation which Adam Smith later on did so much to destroy. His mother came of a family of landed proprietors, many of whom entered the army. In the *Wealth of Nations* Smith calls the art of war "certainly the noblest of the arts."

When but three years old, the young Adam was kidnapped by gypsies, being recovered, however, almost immediately. This seems to have been the sole romantic incident that ever befell him; he never married or even (according to the best authorities) fell in love. What was more important for his career, the town of Kirkcaldy boasted several nail manufactories, and it may be that observation of their processes first taught him the importance of the division of labor in industry.

At fourteen he entered Glasgow College where he came under the influence of Francis Hutcheson. Just what he owed to this association will perhaps always be disputed. At any rate a marked resemblance exists between the precepts of Hutcheson and the later views of his pupil in regard to religion, political liberty, freedom of enterprise, and labor as the determinant of value. After three years at Glasgow the faculty awarded Smith an exhibition (equivalent to a present-day fellowship in America) at Balliol College, Oxford. At that time lecturers and tutors at Oxford were permitted to treat their positions as sinecures, and Smith had to rely on self-help and the resources of the Balliol library to complete his education. Previously he had favored mathematics; now, perhaps for want of an instructor in that subject, he read widely though with an inclination toward the Greek and Latin classics. In 1746 he left Oxford with the degree of B.A. and a satisfactory grounding in classical literature.

The next two years were spent at Kirkcaldy while he sought an appointment as travelling tutor to some young gentleman of wealth. Failing this he turned to literature for a livelihood, and with the backing of an influential friend undertook a series of public lectures at Edinburgh on that subject. These were sufficiently well received to be followed by a series advocating freedom of commerce. His success at Edinburgh won him a place on the faculty of his alma mater, Glasgow University, as professor of logic. This he soon exchanged for the chair of moral philosophy, which carried with it the duty of expounding the principles of political economy. The handsome, thriving town of Glasgow with its flourishing commerce afforded him a wealth of economic data; he became the particular friend of one of its two greatest merchant-bankers, and it was to the latter that he owed much of the information later embodied in the *Wealth of Nations*.

Meanwhile his reputation was enhanced by the publication of the *Theory of Moral Sentiments* (1759). This work so impressed Charles Townshend that in 1764 he engaged Smith to accompany his ward, the young Duke of Buccleuch, as tutor on a tour through France. Smith resigned his professorship and, accompanied by his charge, spent the next three years in travel, observation of French conditions, and intercourse with the leaders of French society and thought. He met and was influenced by members of the economic school then dominant in France, the Physiocrats, including Quesnay and Turgot. The interlude was financially as well as intellectually profitable: he received a generous salary and a pension for life from the Duke, a compensation which in the end amounted to £8,000 for three years' work.

Smith was now free to complete the economic studies which led to the *Wealth of Nations,* a work which occupied him for the next twelve years. Sections of the manuscript were submitted to the criticism of friends, and Benjamin Franklin is said to have contributed much to the part dealing with colonies. The book appeared in 1776 and by 1780 had been translated into French, German, Danish, and Italian. In Spain it was suppressed by the Inquisition on account of the "lowness of its style and the looseness of its morals."

Adam Smith's fame was now secure. Gibbon, Hume, Johnson, Burke, Reynolds, and their coterie accepted him not only as a familiar but as an equal. Charles Townshend and William Pitt became his disciples and he was consulted from time to time by other ministers of government on the practical details of fiscal policy. A grateful chancellor of the exchequer to whom Smith had suggested certain new forms of taxation appointed him in 1778 to the post of commissioner of customs in Scotland. He therefore removed to Edinburgh, where he lived, diligently performing the duties of his office, until his death in 1790. He left only a modest estate, having contributed largely to charity during his lifetime.

Smith's influence on subsequent economic and social thought can scarcely be exaggerated. The *Wealth of Nations* was the sieve through which a great part of eighteenth-century philosophy passed to posterity, for it was about the only economic work of its period that continued to be widely read. Its influence, moreover, was not confined to the school which advocated economic liberalism or laissez-faire. While this was Adam Smith's central doctrine, he so qualified and explained it as to provide its critics with what they considered adequate reasons for rejecting it entirely. This is true particularly of his explanation of rent and of his treatment of labor as the source of profit. It is not surprising, therefore, to find the early socialists and later on Karl Marx himself using statements in the *Wealth of Nations* to justify theories which Smith would have unquestionably denounced. Thus it was the comprehensiveness and even the occasional inconsistency of his book that helped to make it popular. "An economist must have peculiar theories indeed," says a recent writer, "who cannot quote from the *Wealth of Nations* to support his special purposes."

REFERENCES

The standard edition of the *Wealth of Nations* is by Edwin Cannan (1904). Besides this work and the *Theory of Moral Sentiments* Smith also wrote a *Dissertation on the Origin of Languages* and *Essays on Philosophical Subjects*. His *Lectures on Justice, Police, Revenue, and Arms*, reported by one of his students, were first published in 1896.

Among recent critical discussions of his work may be mentioned *Adam Smith, 1776–1926*, by P. H. Douglas and others (1928), and *The Tables Turned*, Essay II, by James Bonar (1926).

The fullest biography is by John Rae (1895). Shorter lives have been written by, among others, R. B. Haldane (1887) and F. W. Hirst (1904).

READINGS FROM

AN INQUIRY INTO THE NATURE AND CAUSES OF THE WEALTH OF NATIONS

Self-Interest as an Economic Motive.[1] In civilised society [man] stands at all times in need of the co-operation and assistance of great multitudes, while his whole life is scarce sufficient to gain the friendship of a few persons. In almost every other race of animals each individual, when it is grown up to maturity, is entirely independent, and in its natural state has occasion for the assistance of no other living creature. But man has almost constant occasion for the help of his brethren, and it is in vain for him to expect it from their benevolence only. He will be more likely to prevail if he can interest their self-love in his favour, and show them that it is for their own advantage to do for him what he requires of them. Whoever offers to another a bargain of any kind, proposes to do this. Give me that which I want, and you shall have this which you want, is the meaning of every such offer; and it is in this manner that we obtain from one another the far greater part of those good offices which we stand in need of. It is not from the benevolence of the butcher, the brewer, or the baker that we expect our dinner, but from their regard to their own interest. We address ourselves, not to their humanity but to their self-love, and never talk to them of our own necessities but of their advantages. Nobody but a beggar chooses to depend chiefly upon the benevolence of his fellow-citizens. . . .

Labor, Rent, and Profit, the Components of Price.[2] In that early and rude state of society which precedes both the accumulation of stock and the appropriation of land, the proportion between the quantities of labour necessary for acquiring different objects seems to be the only circumstance which can afford any rule for exchanging them for one another. If among a nation of hunters, for example, it usually costs twice the labour to kill a beaver which it does to kill a deer, one beaver should naturally exchange for or be worth two deer. It is natural that what is usually the produce of two days' or two hours' labour, should be worth double of what is usually the produce of one day's or one hour's labour.

[1] Bk. I, ch. ii (Vol. I, pp. 12–13). This and subsequent volume and page references are to the Everyman edition.

[2] Bk. I, ch. vi (Vol. I, pp. 41–44).

If the one species of labour should be more severe than the other, some allowance will naturally be made for this superior hardship; and the produce of one hour's labour in the one way may frequently exchange for that of two hours' labour in the other.

Or if the one species of labour requires an uncommon degree of dexterity and ingenuity, the esteem which men have for such talents will naturally give a value to their produce, superior to what would be due to the time employed about it. Such talents can seldom be acquired but in consequence of long application, and the superior value of their produce may frequently be no more than a reasonable compensation for the time and labour which must be spent in acquiring them. In the advanced state of society, allowances of this kind, for superior hardship and skill, are commonly made in the wages of labour; and something of the same kind must probably have taken place in its earliest and rudest period.

In this state of things the whole produce of labour belongs to the labourer; and the quantity of labour commonly employed in acquiring or producing any commodity is the only circumstance which can regulate the quantity of labour which it ought commonly to purchase, command, or exchange for.

As soon as stock has accumulated in the hands of particular persons, some of them will naturally employ it in setting to work industrious people whom they will supply with materials and subsistence, in order to make a profit by the sale of their work, or by what their labour adds to the value of the materials. In exchanging the complete manufacture either for money, for labour, or for other goods, over and above what may be sufficient to pay the price of the materials, and the wages of the workmen, something must be given for the profits of the undertaker of the work who hazards his stock in this adventure. The value which the workmen add to the materials, therefore, resolves itself in this case into two parts, of which the one pays their wages, the other the profits of their employer upon the whole stock of materials and wages which he advanced. He could have no interest to employ them, unless he expected from the sale of their work something more than what was sufficient to replace his stock to him; and he could have no interest to employ a great stock rather than a small one, unless his profits were to bear some proportion to the extent of his stock.

The profits of stock, it may perhaps be thought, are only a different name for the wages of a particular sort of labour, the labour of inspection and direction. They are, however, altogether different, are regulated by quite different principles, and bear no proportion to the quantity, the hardship, or the ingenuity of this supposed labour of inspection and direction. They are regulated altogether by the value of the stock employed, and are greater or smaller in proportion to the extent of this stock. Let us suppose, for example, that in some particular place, where the common annual profits of manufacturing stock are ten per cent., there are two different manufactures, in each of which twenty workmen are employed at the rate of fifteen pounds a year each, or at the expense of three hundred a year in each manufactory. Let us suppose, too, that the coarse materials annually wrought up in the one cost only seven hundred pounds, while the finer materials in the other cost seven thousand. The capital annually employed in the one will in this case amount only to one thousand pounds; whereas that employed in the other will amount to seven thousand three hundred pounds. At the rate of ten per cent., therefore, the undertaker of the one will expect a yearly profit of about one hundred pounds only; while that of the other will expect about seven hundred and thirty pounds. But though their profits are so very different, their labour of inspection and direction may be either altogether or very nearly the same. In many great works almost the whole labour of this kind is committed to some principal clerk. His wages properly express the value of this labour of inspection and direction. Though in settling them some regard is had commonly, not only to his labour and skill, but to the trust which is reposed in him, yet they never bear any regular proportion to the capital of which he oversees the management; and the owner of this capital, though he is thus discharged of almost all labour, still expects that his profits should bear a regular proportion to his capital. In the price of commodities, therefore, the profits of stock constitute a component part altogether different from the wages of labour, and regulated by quite different principles.

In this state of things, the whole produce of labour does not always belong to the labourer. He must in most cases share it with the owner of the stock which employs him. Neither is the quantity of labour commonly employed in acquiring or producing any commodity, the only circumstance which can regulate the quantity which it ought commonly to purchase, command, or exchange for. An additional quantity, it is evident, must be due for the profits of the stock which advanced the wages and furnished the materials of that labour.

As soon as the land of any country has all become private property, the landlords, like all other men, love to reap where they never sowed, and demand a rent even for its natural produce. The wood of the forest, the grass of the field, and all the natural fruits of the earth, which, when land was common, cost the labourer only the trouble of gathering them, come, even to him, to have an additional price fixed upon them. He must then pay for the licence to gather them; and must give up to the landlord a portion of what his labour either collects or produces. This portion, or, what comes to the same thing, the price of this portion, constitutes the rent of land, and in the price of the greater part of commodities makes a third component part.

The real value of all the different component parts of price, it must be observed, is measured by the quantity of labour which they can, each of them, purchase or command. Labour measures the value not only of that part of price which resolves itself into labour, but of that which resolves itself into rent, and of that which resolves itself into profit. . . .

Wages and the Conflict between Master and Workman.[1] What are the common wages of labour, depends everywhere upon the contract usually made between those two parties, whose interests are by no means the same. The workmen desire to get as much, the masters to give as little as possible. The former are disposed to combine in order to raise, the latter in order to lower the wages of labour.

It is not, however, difficult to foresee which of the two parties must, upon all ordinary occasions, have the advantage in the dispute, and force the other into a compliance with their terms. The masters, being fewer in number, can combine much more easily; and the law, besides, authorises, or at least does not prohibit their combinations, while it prohibits those of the workmen. We have no acts of parliament against combining to lower the price of work; but many against combining to raise it. In all such disputes the masters can hold out much longer. A landlord, a farmer, a master manufacturer, a merchant, though they did not employ a single workman, could generally live a year or two upon the stocks which they have already acquired. Many workmen could not subsist a week, few could subsist a month, and scarce any a year without employment. In the long-run the workman may be as necessary to his master as his master is to him; but the necessity is not so immediate.

We rarely hear, it has been said, of the combinations of masters, though frequently of those of workmen. But whoever imagines, upon

[1] Bk. I, chs. viii, ix (Vol. I, pp. 58–60, 70, 72–74, 88).

this account, that masters rarely combine, is as ignorant of the world as of the subject. Masters are always and everywhere in a sort of tacit, but constant and uniform combination, not to raise the wages of labour above their actual rate. To violate this combination is everywhere a most unpopular action, and a sort of reproach to a master among his neighbours and equals. We seldom, indeed, hear of this combination, because it is the usual, and one may say, the natural state of things, which nobody ever hears of. Masters, too, sometimes enter into particular combinations to sink the wages of labour even below this rate. These are always conducted with the utmost silence and secrecy, till the moment of execution, and when the workmen yield, as they sometimes do, without resistance, though severely felt by them, they are never heard of by other people. Such combinations, however, are frequently resisted by a contrary defensive combination of the workmen; who sometimes too, without any provocation of this kind, combine of their own accord to raise the price of their labour. Their usual pretences are, sometimes the high price of provisions; sometimes the great profit which their masters make by their work. But whether their combinations be offensive or defensive, they are always abundantly heard of. In order to bring the point to a speedy decision, they have always recourse to the loudest clamour, and sometimes to the most shocking violence and outrage. They are desperate, and act with the folly and extravagance of desperate men, who must either starve, or frighten their masters into immediate compliance with their demands. The masters upon these occasions are just as clamorous upon the other side, and never cease to call aloud for the assistance of the civil magistrate, and the rigorous execution of those laws which have been enacted with so much severity against the combinations of servants, labourers, and journeymen. The workmen, accordingly, very seldom derive any advantage from the violence of those tumultuous combinations, which, partly from the interposition of the civil magistrate, partly from the superior steadiness of the masters, partly from the necessity which the greater part of the workmen are under of submitting for the sake of present subsistence, generally end in nothing, but the punishment or ruin of the ringleaders. . . .

The common complaint that luxury extends itself even to the lowest ranks of the people, and that the labouring poor will not now be contented with the same food, clothing, and lodging which satisfied them in former times, may convince us that it is not the money price of labour only, but its real recompense, which has augmented.

Is this improvement in the circumstances of the lower ranks of the people to be regarded as an advantage or as an inconveniency to the society? The answer seems at first sight abundantly plain. Servants, labourers, and workmen of different kinds, make up the far greater part of every great political society. But what improves the circumstances of the greater part can never be regarded as an inconveniency to the whole. No society can be flourishing and happy, of which the far greater part of the members are poor and miserable. It is but equity, besides, that they who feed, clothe, and lodge the whole body of the people, should have such a share of the produce of their own labour as to be themselves tolerably well fed, clothed, and lodged. . . .

The liberal reward of labour, as it encourages the propagation, so it increases the industry of the common people. The wages of labour are the encouragement of industry, which, like every other human quality, improves in proportion to the encouragement it receives. A plentiful subsistence increases the bodily strength of the labourer, and the comfortable hope of bettering his condition, and of ending his days perhaps in ease and plenty, animates him to exert that strength to the utmost. Where wages are high, accordingly, we shall always find the workmen more active, diligent, and expeditious than where they are low: in England, for example, than in Scotland; in the neighbourhood of great towns than in remote country places. Some workmen, indeed, when they can earn in four days what will maintain them through the week, will be idle the other three. This, however, is by no means the case with the greater part. Workmen, on the contrary, when they are liberally paid by the piece, are very apt to over-work themselves, and to ruin their health and constitution in a few years. A carpenter in London, and in some other places, is not supposed to last in his utmost vigour above eight years. Something of the same kind happens in many other trades, in which the workmen are paid by the piece, as they generally are in manufactures, and even in country labour, wherever wages are higher than ordinary. Almost every class of artificers is subject to some peculiar infirmity occasioned by excessive application to their peculiar species of work. Ramuzzini, an eminent Italian physician, has written a particular book concerning such diseases. We do not reckon our soldiers the most industrious set of people among us. Yet when soldiers have been employed in some particular sorts of work, and liberally paid by the piece, their officers have frequently been obliged to stipulate with the undertaker, that they should not be allowed to earn above a certain sum every day, according to the rate at which they were paid. Till this stipulation was made, mutual emulation and the desire of greater gain frequently prompted them to over-work themselves, and to hurt their health by excessive labour. Excessive application during four days of the week is frequently the real cause of the idleness of the other three, so much and so loudly complained of. Great labour, either of mind or body, continued for several days together, is in most men followed by a great desire of relaxation, which, if not restrained by force or by some strong necessity, is almost irresistible. It is the call of nature, which requires to be relieved by some indulgence, sometimes of ease only, but sometimes, too, of dissipation and diversion. If it is not complied with, the consequences are often dangerous, and sometimes fatal, and such as almost always, sooner or later, bring on the peculiar infirmity of the trade. If masters would always listen to the dictates of reason and humanity, they have frequently occasion rather to moderate than to animate the application of many of their workmen. It will be found, I believe, in every sort of trade, that the man who works so moderately as to be able to work constantly not only preserves his health the longest, but, in the course of the year, executes the greatest quantity of work. . . .

Our merchants and master-manufacturers complain much of the bad effects of high wages in raising the price, and thereby lessening the sale of their goods both at home and abroad. They say nothing concerning the bad effects of high profits. They are silent with regard to the pernicious effects of their own gains. They complain only of those of other people. . . .

Economic Liberty and Its Enemies.[1] The whole of the advantages and disadvantages of the different employments of labour and stock must, in the same neighbourhood, be either perfectly equal or continually tending to equality. If in the same neighbourhood, there was any employment evidently either more or less advantageous than the rest, so many people would crowd into it in the one case, and so many would desert it in the other, that its advantages would soon return to the level of other employments. This at least would be the case in a society where things were left to follow their natural course, where there was perfect liberty, and where every man was perfectly free both to choose what occupation he thought proper, and to change it as often as he thought proper. Every man's interest would prompt him to seek the advantageous, and to shun the disadvantageous employment.

[1] Bk. I, ch. x (Vol. I, pp. 88–89, 102–103, 107–108, 110, 128–129).

Pecuniary wages and profit, indeed, are everywhere in Europe extremely different according to the different employments of labour and stock. But this difference arises partly from certain circumstances in the employments themselves, which, either really, or at least in the imaginations of men, make up for a small pecuniary gain in some, and counterbalance a great one in others; and partly from the policy of Europe, which nowhere leaves things at perfect liberty. . . .

The five following are the principal circumstances which, so far as I have been able to observe, make up for a small pecuniary gain in some employments, and counterbalance a great one in others: first, the agreeableness or disagreeableness of the employments themselves; secondly, the easiness and cheapness, or the difficulty and expense of learning them; thirdly, the constancy or inconstancy of employment in them; fourthly, the small or great trust which must be reposed in those who exercise them; and, fifthly, the probability or improbability of success in them. . . .

The five circumstances above mentioned, though they occasion considerable inequalities in the wages of labour and profits of stock, occasion none in the whole of the advantages and disadvantages, real or imaginary, in the different employments of either. The nature of those circumstances is such that they make up for a small pecuniary gain in some, and counterbalance a great one in others.

In order, however, that this equality may take place in the whole of their advantages or disadvantages, three things are requisite even where there is the most perfect freedom. First, the employments must be well known and long established in the neighbourhood; secondly, they must be in their ordinary, or what may be called their natural state; and, thirdly, they must be the sole or principal employments of those who occupy them. . . .

But the policy of Europe, by not leaving things at perfect liberty, occasions other inequalities of much greater importance.

It does this chiefly in the three following ways. First, by restraining the competition in some employments to a smaller number than might otherwise be disposed to enter into them; secondly, by increasing it in others beyond what it naturally would be; and, thirdly, by obstructing the free circulation of labour and stock, both from employment to employment and from place to place.

First, the policy of Europe occasions a very important inequality in the whole of the advantages and disadvantages of the different employments of labour and stock, by restraining the competition in some employments to a smaller number than might otherwise be disposed to enter into them.

The exclusive privileges of corporations are the principal means it makes use of for this purpose.

The exclusive privilege of an incorporated trade necessarily restrains the competition, in the town where it is established, to those who are free of the trade. To have served an apprenticeship in the town, under a master properly qualified, is commonly the necessary requisite for obtaining this freedom. The bye-laws of the corporation regulate sometimes the number of apprentices which any master is allowed to have, and almost always the number of years which each apprentice is obliged to serve. The intention of both regulations is to restrain the competition to a much smaller number than might otherwise be disposed to enter into the trade. The limitation of the number of apprentices restrains it directly. The long term of apprenticeship restrains it more indirectly, but as effectually, by increasing the expense of education. . . .

The property which every man has in his own labour, as it is the original foundation of all other property, so it is the most sacred and inviolable. The patrimony of a poor man lies in the strength and dexterity of his hands; and to hinder him from employing this strength and dexterity in what manner he thinks proper without injury to his neighbour is a plain violation of this most sacred property. It is a manifest encroachment upon the just liberty both of the workman and of those who might be disposed to employ him. As it hinders the one from working at what he thinks proper, so it hinders the other from employing whom they think proper. To judge whether he is fit to be employed may surely be trusted to the discretion of the employers whose interest it so much concerns. The affected anxiety of the law-giver lest they should employ an improper person is evidently as impertinent as it is oppressive.

The institution of long apprenticeships can give no security that insufficient workmanship shall not frequently be exposed to public sale. When this is done it is generally the effect of fraud, and not of inability; and the longest apprenticeship can give no security against fraud. Quite different regulations are necessary to prevent this abuse. The sterling mark upon plate, and the stamps upon linen and woollen cloth, give the purchaser much greater security than any statute of apprenticeship. He generally looks at these, but never thinks it worth while to inquire whether the workman had served a seven years' apprenticeship. . . .

People of the same trade seldom meet together, even for merriment and diversion, but the conversation ends in a conspiracy against the public, or in some contrivance to raise prices. It is impossible indeed to prevent such meetings, by any law which either could be executed, or would be consistent with liberty and justice. But though the law cannot hinder people of the same trade from sometimes assembling together, it ought to do nothing to facilitate such assemblies, much less to render them necessary. . . .

The pretence that corporations are necessary for the better government of the trade is without any foundation. The real and effectual discipline which is exercised over a workman is not that of his corporation, but that of his customers. It is the fear of losing their employment which restrains his frauds and corrects his negligence. An exclusive corporation necessarily weakens the force of this discipline. A particular set of workmen must then be employed, let them behave well or ill. . . .

Though anciently it was usual to rate wages, first by general laws extending over the whole kingdom, and afterwards by particular orders of the justices of peace in every particular county, both these practices have now gone entirely into disuse. "By the experience of above four hundred years," says Doctor Burn, "it seems time to lay aside all endeavours to bring under strict regulations, what in its own nature seems incapable of minute limitation; for if all persons in the same kind of work were to receive equal wages, there would be no emulation, and no room left for industry or ingenuity."

Particular acts of parliament, however, still attempt sometimes to regulate wages in particular trades and in particular places. Thus the 8th of George III. prohibits under heavy penalties all master tailors in London, and five miles round it, from giving, and their workmen from accepting, more than two shillings and seven pence halfpenny a day, except in the case of a general mourning. Whenever the legislature attempts to regulate the differences between masters and their workmen, its counsellors are always the masters. When the regulation, therefore, is in favour of the workmen, it is always just and equitable; but it is sometimes otherwise when in favour of the masters. Thus the law which obliges the masters in several different trades to pay their workmen in money and not in goods is quite just and equitable. It imposes no real hardship upon the masters. It only obliges them to pay that value in money, which they pretended to pay, but did not always really pay, in goods. This law is in favour of the workmen; but the 8th of George III. is in favour of the masters. When masters combine together in order to reduce the wages of their workmen, they commonly enter into a private bond or agreement not to give more than a certain wage under a certain penalty. Were the workmen to enter into a contrary combination of the same kind, not to accept of a certain wage under a certain penalty, the law would punish them very severely; and if it dealt impartially, it would treat the masters in the same manner. But the 8th of George III. enforces by law that very regulation which masters sometimes attempt to establish by such combinations. The complaint of the workmen, that it puts the ablest and most industrious upon the same footing with an ordinary workman, seems perfectly well founded.

In ancient times, too, it was usual to attempt to regulate the profits of merchants and other dealers, by rating the price both of provisions and other goods. The assize of bread is, so far as I know, the only remnant of this ancient usage. Where there is an exclusive corporation, it may perhaps be proper to regulate the price of the first necessary of life. But where there is none, the competition will regulate it much better than any assize. . . .

Further Examples of Governmental Interference.[1] Though the profusion of government must, undoubtedly, have retarded the natural progress of England towards wealth and improvement, it has not been able to stop it. . . . England, . . . as it has never been blessed with a very parsimonious government, so parsimony has at no time been the characteristical virtue of its inhabitants. It is the highest impertinence and presumption, therefore, in kings and ministers, to pretend to watch over the economy of private people, and to restrain their expense, either by sumptuary laws, or by prohibiting the importation of foreign luxuries. They are themselves always, and without any exception, the greatest spend-thrifts in the society. Let them look well after their own expense, and they may safely trust private people with theirs. If their own extravagance does not ruin the state, that of their subjects never will. . . .

In some countries the interest of money has been prohibited by law. But as something can everywhere be made by the use of money, something ought everywhere to be paid for the use of it. This regulation, instead of preventing, has been found from experience to in-

[1] Bk. II, chs. iii, iv; Bk. IV, Introduction and chs. i, ii; Bk. IV, ch. ix (Vol. I, pp. 309–310, 319, 375, 395–403, 406–412; Vol. II, p. 180).

crease the evil of usury; the debtor being obliged to pay, not only for the use of the money, but for the risk which his creditor runs by accepting a compensation for that use. He is obliged, if one may say so, to insure his creditor from the penalties of usury. . . .

The different progress of opulence in different ages and nations has given occasion to two different systems of political economy with regard to enriching the people. The one may be called the system of commerce, the other that of agriculture. I shall . . . begin with the system of commerce. It is the modern system, and is best understood in our own country and in our own times. . . .

[This commercial or "mercantile" system is based on the false but] popular notion that wealth consists in money, or in gold and silver. . . . Some of the best English writers upon commerce set out with observing that the wealth of a country consists, not in gold and silver only, but in its lands, houses, and consumable goods of all different kinds. In the course of their reasonings, however, the lands, houses, and consumable goods seem to slip out of their memory, and the strain of their argument frequently supposes that all wealth consists in gold and silver, and that to multiply those metals is the great object of national industry and commerce.

The two principles being established, however, that wealth consisted in gold and silver, and that those metals could be brought into a country which had no mines only by the balance of trade, or by exporting to a greater value than it imported, it necessarily became the great object of political economy to diminish as much as possible the importation of foreign goods for home consumption, and to increase as much as possible the exportation of the produce of domestic industry. Its two great engines for enriching the country, therefore, were restraints upon importation, and encouragements to exportation.

The restraints upon importation were of two kinds.

First, restraints upon the importation of such foreign goods for home consumption as could be produced at home, from whatever country they were imported.

Secondly, restraints upon the importation of goods of almost all kinds from those particular countries with which the balance of trade was supposed to be disadvantageous.

Those different restraints consisted sometimes in high duties, and sometimes in absolute prohibitions.

Exportation was encouraged sometimes by drawbacks, sometimes by bounties, sometimes by advantageous treaties of commerce with foreign states, and sometimes by the establishment of colonies in distant countries. . . .

The two sorts of restraints upon importation above-mentioned, together with these four encouragements to exportation, constitute the six principal means by which the commercial system proposes to increase the quantity of gold and silver in any country by turning the balance of trade in its favour. I shall consider each of them [1] in a particular chapter, and without taking much further notice of their supposed tendency to bring money into the country, I shall examine chiefly what are likely to be the effects of each of them upon the annual produce of its industry. According as they tend either to increase or diminish the value of this annual produce, they must evidently tend either to increase or diminish the real wealth and revenue of the country.

By restraining, either by high duties, or by absolute prohibitions, the importation of such goods from foreign countries as can be produced at home, the monopoly of the home market is more or less secured to the domestic industry employed in producing them. Thus the prohibition of importing either live cattle or salt provisions from foreign countries secures to the graziers of Great Britain the monopoly of the home market for butcher's meat. The high duties upon the importation of corn, which in times of moderate plenty amounts to a prohibition, gives a like advantage to the growers of that commodity. The prohibition of the importation of foreign woollens is equally favourable to the woollen manufacturers. The silk manufacture, though altogether employed upon foreign materials, has lately obtained the same advantage. The linen manufacture has not yet obtained it, but is making great strides towards it. Many other sorts of manufacturers have, in the same manner, obtained in Great Britain, either altogether or very nearly, a monopoly against their countrymen. The variety of goods of which the importation into Great Britain is prohibited, either absolutely, or under certain circumstances, greatly exceeds what can easily be suspected by those who are not well acquainted with the laws of the customs.

That this monopoly of the home market frequently gives great encouragement to that particular species of industry which enjoys it, and frequently turns towards that employment a greater share of the labour and stock of the society than would otherwise have gone into it, cannot be doubted. But whether it tends either to increase

[1] Only a part of the argument concerning restraints on importation is printed here.

the general industry of the society, or to give it the most advantageous direction, is not, perhaps, altogether so evident.

The general industry of the society never can exceed what the capital of the society can employ. As the number of workmen that can be kept in employment by any particular person must bear a certain proportion to his capital, so the number of those who can be continually employed by all the members of a great society must bear a certain proportion to the whole capital of that society, and never can exceed that proportion. No regulation of commerce can increase the quantity of industry in any society beyond what its capital can maintain. It can only divert a part of it into a direction into which it might not otherwise have gone; and it is by no means certain that this artificial direction is likely to be more advantageous to the society than that into which it would have gone of its own accord.

Every individual is continually exerting himself to find out the most advantageous employment for whatever capital he can command. It is his own advantage, indeed, and not that of the society, which he has in view. But the study of his own advantage naturally, or rather necessarily, leads him to prefer that employment which is most advantageous to the society.

First, every individual endeavours to employ his capital as near home as he can, and consequently as much as he can in the support of domestic industry; provided always that he can thereby obtain the ordinary, or not a great deal less than the ordinary profits of stock.

Thus, upon equal or nearly equal profits, every wholesale merchant naturally prefers the home trade to the foreign trade of consumption, and the foreign trade of consumption to the carrying trade. In the home trade his capital is never so long out of his sight as it frequently is in the foreign trade of consumption. He can know better the character and situation of the persons whom he trusts, and if he should happen to be deceived, he knows better the laws of the country from which he must seek redress. . . .

Secondly, every individual who employs his capital in the support of domestic industry, necessarily endeavours so to direct that industry that its produce may be of the greatest possible value.

The produce of industry is what it adds to the subject or materials upon which it is employed. In proportion as the value of this produce is great or small, so will likewise be the profits of the employer. But it is only for the sake of profit that any man employs a capital in the support of industry; and he will always, therefore, endeavour to employ it in the support of that industry of which the produce is likely to be of the greatest, or to exchange for the greatest quantity either of money or of other goods.

But the annual revenue of every society is always precisely equal to the exchangeable value of the whole annual produce of its industry, or rather is precisely the same thing with that exchangeable value. As every individual, therefore, endeavours as much as he can both to employ his capital in the support of domestic industry, and so to direct that industry that its produce may be of the greatest value; every individual necessarily labours to render the annual revenue of the society as great as he can. He generally, indeed, neither intends to promote the public interest, nor knows how much he is promoting it. By preferring the support of domestic to that of foreign industry, he intends only his own security; and by directing that industry in such a manner that its produce may be of the greatest value, he intends only his own gain, and he is in this, as in many other cases, led by an invisible hand to promote an end which was no part of his intention. Nor is it always the worse for the society that it was no part of it. By pursuing his own interest he frequently promotes that of the society more effectually than when he really intends to promote it. I have never known much good done by those who affected to trade for the public good. It is an affectation, indeed, not very common among merchants, and very few words need be employed in dissuading them from it.

What is the species of domestic industry which his capital can employ, and of which the produce is likely to be of the greatest value, every individual, it is evident, can, in his local situation, judge much better than any statesman or lawgiver can do for him. The statesman who should attempt to direct private people in what manner they ought to employ their capitals would not only load himself with a most unnecessary attention, but assume an authority which could safely be trusted, not only to no single person, but to no council or senate whatever, and which would nowhere be so dangerous as in the hands of a man who had folly and presumption enough to fancy himself fit to exercise it.

To give the monopoly of the home market to the produce of domestic industry, in any particular art or manufacture, is in some measure to direct private people in what manner they ought to employ their capitals, and must, in almost all cases, be either a useless or a hurtful regulation. If the produce of domestic can be brought there as cheap as that of foreign industry, the regulation is evidently useless. If it cannot, it must generally be hurtful. It is the maxim of every prudent master of a family never to make at home what it will cost him more to make than to buy. The tailor does not attempt to make his own shoes, but buys them of the shoemaker. The shoemaker does not attempt to make his own clothes, but employs a tailor. The farmer attempts to make neither the one nor the other, but employs those different artificers. All of them find it to their interest to employ their whole industry in a way in which they have some advantage over their neighbours, and to purchase with a part of its produce, or what is the same thing, with the price of a part of it, whatever else they have occasion for.

What is prudence in the conduct of every private family can scarce be folly in that of a great kingdom. If a foreign country can supply us with a commodity cheaper than we ourselves can make it, better buy it of them with some part of the produce of our own industry employed in a way in which we have some advantage. The general industry of the country, being always in proportion to the capital which employs it, will not thereby be diminished, no more than that of the above-mentioned artificers; but only left to find out the way in which it can be employed with the greatest advantage. It is certainly not employed to the greatest advantage when it is thus directed towards an object which it can buy cheaper than it can make. The value of its annual produce is certainly more or less diminished when it is thus turned away from producing commodities evidently of more value than the commodity which it is directed to produce. According to the supposition, that commodity could be purchased from foreign countries cheaper than it can be made at home. It could, therefore, have been purchased with a part only of the commodities, or, what is the same thing, with a part only of the price of the commodities, which the industry employed by an equal capital would have produced at home, had it been left to follow its natural course. The industry of the country, therefore, is thus turned away from a more to a less advantageous employment, and the exchangeable value of its annual produce, instead of being increased, according to the intention of the lawgiver, must necessarily be diminished by every such regulation.

By means of such regulations, indeed, a particular manufacture may sometimes be acquired sooner than it could have been otherwise, and after a certain time may be made at home as cheap or cheaper than in the foreign country. But though the industry of the society may be thus carried with advantage into a particular channel sooner than it could have been otherwise, it will by no means follow that the sum total, either of its industry, or of its revenue, can ever be augmented by any such regulation. The industry of the society can augment only in proportion as its capital augments, and its capital can augment only in proportion to what can be gradually saved out of its revenue. But the immediate effect of every such regulation is to diminish its revenue, and what diminishes its revenue is certainly not very likely to augment its capital faster than it would have augmented of its own accord had both capital and industry been left to find out their natural employments.

Though for want of such regulations the society should never acquire the proposed manufacture, it would not, upon that account, necessarily be the poorer in any one period of its duration. In every period of its duration its whole capital and industry might still have been employed, though upon different objects, in the manner that was most advantageous at the time. In every period its revenue might have been the greatest which its capital could afford, and both capital and revenue might have been augmented with the greatest possible rapidity.

The natural advantages which one country has over another in producing particular commodities are sometimes so great that it is acknowledged by all the world to be in vain to struggle with them. By means of glasses, hotbeds, and hot walls, very good grapes can be raised in Scotland, and very good wine too can be made of them at about thirty times the expense for which at least equally good can be brought from foreign countries. Would it be a reasonable law to prohibit the importation of all foreign wines merely to encourage the making of claret and burgundy in Scotland? But if there would be a manifest absurdity in turning towards any employment thirty times more of the capital and industry of the country than would be necessary to purchase from foreign countries an equal quantity of the commodities wanted, there must be an absurdity, though not altogether so glaring, yet exactly of the same kind, in turning towards any such employment a thirtieth, or even a three-hundredth part more of either. Whether the advantages which one country has over another be natural or acquired is in this respect of no consequence. As long as the one country has those advantages, and the other wants them, it will always be more advantageous for the latter rather to buy of the former than to make. It is an acquired advantage only, which one artificer has over his neighbour, who exercises another trade; and yet they both find it more advantageous to buy of one another than to make what does not belong to their particular trades.

Merchants and manufacturers are the people who derive the greatest advantage from this monoply of the home market. The prohibition of the importation of foreign cattle, and of salt provisions, together with the high duties upon foreign corn, which in times of moderate plenty amount to a prohibition, are not near so advantageous to the farmers and graziers of Great Britain as other regulations of the same kind are to its merchants and manufacturers. Manufactures, those of the finer kind especially, are more easily transported from one country to another than corn or cattle. It is in the fetching and carrying manufactures, accordingly, that foreign trade is chiefly employed. In manufactures, a very small advantage will enable foreigners to undersell our own workmen, even in the home market. It will require a very great one to enable them to do so in the rude produce of the soil. If the free importation of foreign manufactures were permitted, several of the home manufactures would probably suffer, and some of them, perhaps, go to ruin altogether, and a considerable part of the stock and industry at present employed in them would be forced to find out some other employment. But the freest importation of the rude produce of the soil could have no such effect upon the agriculture of the country. . . .

There seem, however, to be two cases in which it will generally be advantageous to lay some burden upon foreign for the encouragement of domestic industry.

The first is, when some particular sort of industry is necessary for the defence of the country. The defence of Great Britain, for example, depends very much upon the number of its sailors and shipping. The act of navigation, therefore, very properly endeavours to give the sailors and shipping of Great Britain the monopoly of the trade of their own country, in some cases by absolute prohibitions and in others by heavy burdens upon the shipping of foreign countries. . . .

The act of navigation is not favourable to foreign commerce, or to the growth of that opulence which can arise from it. The interest of a nation in its commercial relations to foreign nations is, like that of a merchant with regard to the different people with whom he deals, to buy as cheap and to sell as dear as possible. But it will be most likely to buy cheap, when by the most perfect freedom of trade it encourages all nations to bring to it the goods which it has occasion to purchase; and, for the same reason, it will be most likely to sell dear, when its markets are thus filled with the greatest number of buyers. The act of navigation, it is true, lays no burden upon foreign ships that come to export the produce of British industry. . . . But if foreigners, either by prohibitions or high duties, are hindered from coming to sell, they cannot always afford to come to buy, because coming without a cargo, they must lose the freight from their own country to Great Britain. By diminishing the number of sellers, therefore, we necessarily diminish that of buyers, and are thus likely not only to buy foreign goods dearer, but to sell our own cheaper, than if there was a more perfect freedom of trade. As defence, however, is of much more importance than opulence, the act of navigation is, perhaps, the wisest of all the commercial regulations of England.

The second case, in which it will generally be advantageous to lay some burden upon foreign for the encouragement of domestic industry is, when some tax is imposed at home upon the produce of the latter. In this case, it seems reasonable that an equal tax should be imposed upon the like produce of the former. This would not give the monopoly of the home market to domestic industry, nor turn towards a particular employment a greater share of the stock and labour of the country than what would naturally go to it. It would only hinder any part of what would naturally go to it from being turned away by the tax into a less natural direction, and would leave the competition between foreign and domestic industry, after the tax, as nearly as possible upon the same footing as before it. In Great Britain, when any such tax is laid upon the products of domestic industry, it is usual at the same time, in order to stop the clamorous complaints of our merchants and manufacturers that they will be undersold at home, to lay a much heavier duty upon the importation of all foreign goods of the same kind. . . .

As there are two cases in which it will generally be advantageous to lay some burden upon foreign for the encouragement of domestic industry, so there are two others in which it may sometimes be a matter of deliberation; in the one, how far it is proper to continue the free importation of certain foreign goods; and in the other, how far, or in what manner, it may be proper to restore that free importation after it has been for some time interrupted.

The case in which it may sometimes be a matter of deliberation how far it is proper to continue the free importation of certain foreign goods is, when some foreign nation restrains by high duties or prohibitions the importation of some of our manufactures into their country. Revenge in this case naturally dictates retaliation, and that we should impose the like duties and prohibitions upon the importation of some or all of their manufactures into ours. Nations, accordingly, seldom fail to retaliate in this manner. . . .

There may be good policy in retaliations of this kind, when there is a probability that they will secure the repeal of the high duties or prohibitions complained of. The recovery of a great foreign market will generally more than compensate the transitory inconvenience of paying dearer during a short time for some sorts of goods. To judge whether such retaliations are likely to produce such an effect does not, perhaps, belong so much to the science of a legislator, whose deliberations ought to be governed by general principles which are always the same, as to the skill of that insidious and crafty animal, vulgarly called a statesman or politician, whose councils are directed by the momentary fluctuations of affairs. When there is no probability that any such repeal can be procured, it seems a bad method of compensating the injury done to certain classes of our people to do another injury ourselves, not only to those classes, but to almost all the other classes of them. . . .

Every system which endeavours, either by extraordinary encouragements to draw towards a particular species of industry a greater share of the capital of the society than what would naturally go to it, or, by extraordinary restraints, force from a particular species of industry some share of the capital which would otherwise be employed in it, is in reality subversive of the great purpose which it means to promote. It retards, instead of accelerating, the progress of the society towards real wealth and greatness; and diminishes, instead of increasing, the real value of the annual produce of its land and labour.

All systems either of preference or restraint, therefore, being thus completely taken away, the obvious and simple system of natural liberty establishes itself of its own accord. Every man, as long as he does not violate the laws of justice, is left perfectly free to pursue his own interest his own way, and to bring both his industry and capital into competition with those of any other man, or order of men. The sovereign is completely discharged from a duty, in the attempting to perform which he must always be exposed to innumerable delusions, and for the proper performance of which no human wisdom or knowledge could ever be sufficient; the duty of superintending the industry of private people, and of directing it towards the employments most suitable to the interest of the society.

Some of the Proper Functions of Government.[1] According to the system of natural liberty, the sovereign has only three duties to attend to; three duties of great importance, indeed, but plain and intelligible to common understandings: first, the duty of protecting the society from the violence and invasion of other independent societies; secondly, the duty of protecting, as far as possible, every member of the society from the injustice or oppression of every other member of it, or of the duty of establishing an exact administration of justice; and, thirdly, the duty of erecting and maintaining certain public works and certain public institutions which it can never be for the interest of any individual, or small number of individuals, to erect and maintain; because the profit could never repay the expense to any individual or small number of individuals, though it may frequently do much more than repay it to a great society. . . .

Ought the public . . . to give no attention, it may be asked, to the education of the people? . . .

In the progress of the division of labour, the employment of the far greater part of those who live by labour, that is, of the great body of the people, comes to be confined to a very few simple operations, frequently to one or two. But the understandings of the greater part of men are necessarily formed by their ordinary employments. The man whose whole life is spent in performing a few simple operations, of which the effects are perhaps always the same, or very nearly the same, has no occasion to exert his understanding or to exercise his invention in finding out expedients for removing difficulties which never occur. He naturally loses, therefore, the habit of such exertion, and generally becomes as stupid and ignorant as it is possible for a human creature to become. The torpor of his mind renders him not only incapable of relishing or bearing a part in any rational conversation, but of conceiving any generous, noble, or tender sentiment, and consequently of forming any just judgment concerning many even of the ordinary duties of private life. Of the great and extensive interests of his country he is altogether incapable of judging, and unless very particular pains have been taken to render him otherwise, he is equally incapable of defending his country in war. The uniformity of his station in life naturally corrupts the courage of his mind, and makes him regard with abhorrence the irregular, uncertain, and adventurous life of a soldier. It corrupts even the activity of his body, and renders him incapable of exerting his strength with vigour and

[1] Bk. IV, ch. ix; Bk. V, ch. i (Vol. II, pp. 180–181, 263–264, 266–267, 269–270, 297–298).

perseverance in any other employment than that to which he has been bred. His dexterity at his own particular trade seems, in this manner, to be acquired at the expense of his intellectual, social, and martial virtues. But in every improved and civilised society this is the state into which the labouring poor, that is, the great body of the people, must necessarily fall, unless government takes some pains to prevent it. . . .

Though the common people cannot, in any civilised society, be so well instructed as people of some rank and fortune, the most essential parts of education, however, to read, write, and account, can be acquired at so early a period of life that the greater part even of those who are to be bred to the lowest occupations have time to acquire them before they can be employed in those occupations. For a very small expense the public can facilitate, can encourage, and can even impose upon almost the whole body of the people the necessity of acquiring those most essential parts of education.

The public can facilitate this acquisition by establishing in every parish or district a little school, where children may be taught for a reward so moderate that even a common labourer may afford it; the master being partly, but not wholly, paid by the public, because, if he was wholly, or even principally, paid by it, he would soon learn to neglect his business. In Scotland the establishment of such parish schools has taught almost the whole common people to read, and a very great proportion of them to write and account. In England the establishment of charity schools has had an effect of the same kind, though not so universally, because the establishment is not so universal. If in those little schools the books, by which children are taught to read, were a little more instructive than they commonly are, and if, instead of a little smattering of Latin, which the children of the common people are sometimes taught there, and which can scarce ever be of any use to them, they were instructed in the elementary parts of geometry and mechanics, the literary education of this rank of people would perhaps be as complete as it can be. There is scarce a common trade which does not afford some opportunities of applying to it the principles of geometry and mechanics, and which would not therefore gradually exercise and improve the common people in those principles, the necessary introduction to the most sublime as well as to the most useful sciences. . . .

A man without the proper use of the intellectual faculties of a man, is, if possible, more contemptible than even a coward, and seems to be mutilated and deformed in a still more essential part of the character of human nature. Though the state was to derive no advantage from the instruction of the inferior ranks of people, it would still deserve its attention that they should not be altogether uninstructed. The state, however, derives no inconsiderable advantage from their instruction. The more they are instructed the less liable they are to the delusions of enthusiasm and superstition, which, among ignorant nations, frequently occasion the most dreadful disorders. An instructed and intelligent people, besides, are always more decent and orderly than an ignorant and stupid one. They feel themselves, each individually, more respectable and more likely to obtain the respect of their lawful superiors, and they are therefore more disposed to respect those superiors. They are more disposed to examine, and more capable of seeing through, the interested complaints of faction and sedition, and they are, upon that account, less apt to be misled into any wanton or unnecessary opposition to the measures of government. In free countries, where the safety of government depends very much upon the favourable judgment which the people may form of its conduct, it must surely be of the highest importance that they should not be disposed to judge rashly or capriciously concerning it. . . .

The expense of defending the society, and that of supporting the dignity of the chief magistrate, are both laid out for the general benefit of the whole society. It is reasonable, therefore, that they be defrayed by the general contribution of the whole society, all the different members contributing, as nearly as possible, in proportion to their respective abilities.

The expense of the administration of justice, too, may, no doubt, be considered as laid out for the benefit of the whole society. There is no impropriety, therefore, in its being defrayed by the general contribution of the whole society. The persons, however, who give occasion to this expense are those who, by their injustice in one way or another, make it necessary to seek redress or protection from the courts of justice. The persons again most immediately benefited by this expense are those whom the courts either restore to their rights or maintain in their rights. The expense of the administration of justice, therefore, may very properly be defrayed by the particular contribution of one or other, or both, of those two different sets of persons, according as different occasions may require, that is, by the fees of court. It cannot be necessary to have recourse to the general contribution of the whole society, except for the conviction of those criminals who have not themselves any estate or fund sufficient for paying those fees.

Those local or provincial expenses of which the benefit is local or provincial (what is laid out, for example, upon the police of a particular town or district) ought to be defrayed by a local or provincial revenue, and ought to be no burden upon the general revenue of the society. It is unjust that the whole society should contribute towards an expense of which the benefit is confined to a part of the society. The expense of maintaining good roads and communications is, no doubt, beneficial to the whole society, and may, therefore, without any injustice, be defrayed by the general contribution of the whole society. This expense, however, is most immediately and directly beneficial to those who travel or carry goods from one place to another, and to those who consume such goods. The turnpike tolls in England, and the duties called peages in other countries, lay it altogether upon those two different sets of people, and thereby discharge the general revenue of the society from a very considerable burden.

The expense of the institutions for education and religious instruction is likewise, no doubt, beneficial to the whole society, and may, therefore, without injustice, be defrayed by the general contribution of the whole society. This expense, however, might perhaps with equal propriety, and even with some advantage, be defrayed altogether by those who receive the immediate benefit of such education and instruction, or by the voluntary contribution of those who think they have occasion for either the one or the other. . . .

II

JEREMY BENTHAM

1748–1832

Inherited wealth permitted Jeremy Bentham to occupy himself exclusively with the welfare of mankind. During the seventeenth and eighteenth centuries a pawnbroker and two lawyers amassed a fortune which in great part went to finance his project of a model prison (never erected) during the nineteenth. The heir and inventor was born in London in 1748.

Jeremy Bentham had great natural abilities—he entered Westminster school at seven, wrote Greek and Latin letters before he was eleven, and went to Oxford at twelve. His childhood, however—or perhaps consequently—was not a very happy one. The servants frightened him with ghost stories and his parents tried to withhold any book that might amuse him. The only reading he recalled with pleasure was Fénelon's *Télêmaque* and some fairy tales given him by his French teacher. *Télêmaque*, written for the education of a French prince, instilled the doctrine that a ruler exists only for the good of his people, and Bentham later claimed to have discerned in it the first gleams of his principle of Utility. Jeremy's father was embarrassingly alive to his son's talents. He constantly boasted of them to his friends, dreamed of seeing a future lord chancellor in the family, and urged Jeremy to push himself forward. Such experiences were distressing to a nervous and bashful child whose "earliest recollection," he said, was "the pain of sympathy." The elements of a "pleasure-pain" philosophy were already in the making.

In 1763 Bentham left Oxford with his B.A. degree and went to London to "eat his dinners" in Lincoln's Inn—the genial preliminary to a law career. But the profession was not inviting and he evaded it temporarily by returning to Oxford. There he took up chemistry and attended Blackstone's lectures on English law. These studies determined his future line of action: the one provided him with a "scientific" method, the other offered a convenient butt of criticism. He immediately detected, he said afterward, Blackstone's mistakes on the subject of "natural law." Beyond that, Oxford gave him an M.A. degree in 1766. Before leaving he also discovered in Priestley's *Essay on Government* a statement which suggested the famous phrase "the greatest happiness of the greatest number." Perhaps he was making use of this concept when, pursued by a talkative lady with a marriageable daughter, he escaped on one occasion through the window. All this occurred before he was twenty.

Bentham now turned seriously to the practice of law. It became apparent, however, that he lacked the qualities of an advocate: his advice to one prospective client was not to waste money on a lawsuit. As he contemplated the forbidding pile of legal lore which must be digested, his distaste grew, and a simple formula to dispense with such "old trash" seemed more than ever desirable. Intimations of the formula had appeared long before; it was now clarified and set to work. Beccaria supplied him with the word "utility" which he linked to the "greatest happiness" idea of Priestley, but Hume, Montesquieu, Barrington, and particularly Helvetius all had an influence on the result.

Bentham now obtained his father's grudging permission to give up active practice of the law and to proceed with his studies in chemistry and the principles of legislation; he sat down to collect stores of material for critical works on the law. Composition at this time was difficult for him—he had not yet invented what he called his "new lingo," those graphic if not very elegant words such as "minimize," "codify," and "international" which have since become indispensable. His first important work, *A Fragment on Government*, appeared anonymously in 1776. It was directed against the prevailing theory of original contract and natural right as expounded by Blackstone. The abilities displayed were such that for a time the work was attributed to Camden or Mansfield, both learned judges of the day, until Bentham's father, who could contain himself no longer, let its true source be known. The book procured Bentham the friendship of Lord Shelburne, the liberal Whig leader and future prime minister, and during the course of a long visit at Bowood, Shelburne's country seat, he met and took the measure of many of the great politicians of the age.

In 1789 the *Principles of Morals and Legislation* appeared. From then on perhaps Bentham's main energies were given to drawing up and commenting on ideal codes of law. As early as 1779 he had had the ambitious idea of interesting Catherine II of Russia in these projects. His brother, then in Russia setting up western arts and institutions on an estate of Catherine's chief minister, was directed to prostrate himself before the empress and eat dust rather than fail to communicate Jeremy's plans. The latter himself visited Russia in 1786, but about all he accomplished was the writing of a *Defense of Usury*, called forth by Pitt's proposal to reduce the legal rate of interest in Great Britain. Years later Bentham approached the Czar Alexander I with another scheme. This time he received a valuable ring—and promises. Bentham returned the ring.

In fact the governing classes in general seemed apathetic to reform. Although Bentham had always been on the "right side" —against the American rebels, against John Wilkes, loyal to George III, the "patriot king"—his proposals to eliminate corruption and inefficiency in government were steadily ignored. At first, he said, he "never suspected that the people in power were against reform. I supposed they only wanted to know what was good in order to embrace it." Gradually, however, this simple faith was destroyed.

But the French Revolution opened new vistas. He was ready now to accept reform by way of revolution, and even at last to countenance the transfer of power from kings who had misused it to the body of the people. Bentham's relations with the French revolutionists were flattering to himself if not very productive of results. He plied them with advice on parliamentary procedure, criticisms of their Declaration of Rights, thoughts on judicial reform, and arguments showing why they ought to give up their colonies. Though clinging obstinately to natural rights, colonies, and the venerable abuses of the prison system, Frenchmen were grateful for sympathy from any quarter and in 1792 conferred on "Benthom" the title of Citizen of France.

Bentham's inclination toward democracy became more marked as time passed. By 1818 he was advocating the secret ballot and manhood suffrage, putting off the vote for women merely because public opinion was unprepared for it. And meanwhile his prodigious industry was bringing its reward. A group of young and enthusiastic admirers surrounded him—economists, members of Parliament, government officials—who sowed his ideas broadcast among the ruling classes. Bentham's literary production was enormous, but his published works, though numerous, were few in comparison to the writings which he circulated privately or accumulated in his study. The principle of Utility was expounded and elaborated in every field: in law, politics, education, prison reform, economics, and even religion. Through Etienne Dumont, a Swiss clergyman, his work on law and legislation, digested and translated into French, attained a wide circulation abroad. Leaders of many South American republics consulted him on the codification of law. In 1823 appeared a *Codification Proposal* addressed to all liberal nations. It was accompanied by testimonials "to the merits of the author culled from every quarter of the globe." His last published work was an elaboration of this theme. He died in 1832, secure in the knowledge that his ideas had borne abundant fruit.

To Bentham and his followers (among whom were James Mill, Henry Brougham, Samuel Romilly the law reformer, and E. G. Wakefield the colonial theorist) can be traced, in whole or in part, most of the reforms accomplished in early nineteenth-century England. Those most characteristically Benthamite in origin occurred in the field of law: such are the reorganization of the judiciary and particularly certain changes in the penal system—Bentham was one of the first to advocate comparatively light penalties rigidly enforced instead of drastic ones which the criminal was pretty sure to escape. The new East Indian criminal code was based almost entirely upon his doctrine. Even in those fields where Bentham had nothing really original to offer he gave reformers a principle of procedure. Neglecting tradition, vested interests, and false philosophies, they were to judge an institution by its usefulness. The only difficulty was that some insisted on confounding vested interest with utility.

REFERENCES

Bentham's *Works* in eleven volumes (ed. Bowring, 1843) contain only a fragment of his writings. The controversial works on religion were designedly left out. Large quantities of unpublished manuscript on all subjects are preserved at the University of London. Current editions of some of his more important works are: *A Fragment on Government* (ed. F. C. Montague, 1891); *Introduction to the Principles of Morals and Legislation* (1907); *Plan for a Universal and Perpetual Peace* (1927); Dumont's *Theory of Legislation* (ed. C. K. Ogden, 1931).

Exhaustive discussions of Bentham's work occur in E. Halévy's *La Formation du radicalisme philosophique* (1901–04) and in L. Stephen's *The English Utilitarians*, Vol. I (1900). An admirable brief treatment is Victor Cohen's *Bentham* (1927, Fabian Tract No. 221).

Bowring's *Life of Bentham* is in Vols. X and XI of the *Works* (above). The standard modern biography is by C. M. Atkinson (1905).

READINGS FROM

VARIOUS WORKS

The Principle of Utility.[1] Nature has placed mankind under the governance of two sovereign masters, *pain* and *pleasure*. It is for them alone to point out what we ought to do, as well as to determine what we shall do. On the one hand the standard of right and wrong, on the other the chain of causes and effects, are fastened to their throne. They govern us in all we do, in all we say, in all we think: every effort we can make to throw off our subjection, will serve but to demonstrate and confirm it. In words a man may pretend to abjure their empire: but in reality he will remain subject to it all the while. The *principle of utility* [2] recognises this subjection, and assumes it for the foundation of that system, the object of which is to rear the fabric of felicity by the hands of reason and of law. Systems which attempt to question it, deal in sounds instead of sense, in caprice instead of reason, in darkness instead of light.

But enough of metaphor and declamation: it is not by such means that moral science is to be improved.

The principle of utility is the foundation of the present work: it will be proper therefore at the outset to give an explicit and determinate account of what is meant by it. By the principle of utility is meant that principle which approves or disapproves of every action whatsoever, according to the tendency which it appears to have to augment or diminish the happiness of the party whose interest is in question: or, what is the same thing in other words, to promote or to oppose that happiness. I say of every action whatsoever; and therefore not only of every action of a private individual, but of every measure of government.

[1] *Works*, Vol. I, "Principles of Morals and Legislation," pp. 1–3, 6–9.

[2] Note by the author, July, 1822—"To this denomination has of late been added, or substituted, the *greatest happiness* or *greatest felicity* principle: this for shortness, instead of saying at length *that principle* which states the greatest happiness of all those whose interest is in question, as being the right and proper, and only right and proper and universally desirable, end of human action: of human action in every situation, and in particular in that of a functionary or set of functionaries exercising the powers of Government. The word *utility* does not so clearly point to the ideas of *pleasure* and *pain* as the words *happiness* and *felicity* do; nor does it lead us to the consideration of the *number*, of the interests affected; to the *number*, as being the circumstance, which contributes, in the largest proportion, to the formation of the standard here in question; the *standard of right and wrong*, by which alone the propriety of human conduct, in every situation, can with propriety be tried. This want of a sufficiently manifest connexion between the ideas of *happiness* and *pleasure* on the one hand, and the idea of *utility* on the other, I have every now and then found operating, and with but too much efficiency, as a bar to the acceptance, that might otherwise have been given, to this principle."

By utility is meant that property in any object, whereby it tends to produce benefit, advantage, pleasure, good, or happiness (all this in the present case comes to the same thing), or (what comes again to the same thing) to prevent the happening of mischief, pain, evil, or unhappiness to the party whose interest is considered: if that party be the community in general, then the happiness of the community: if a particular individual, then the happiness of that individual.

The interest of the community is one of the most general expressions that can occur in the phraseology of morals: no wonder that the meaning of it is often lost. When it has a meaning, it is this. The community is a fictitious *body*, composed of the individual persons who are considered as constituting as it were its *members*. The interest of the community then is, what?—the sum of the interests of the several members who compose it.

It is in vain to talk of the interest of the community, without understanding what is the interest of the individual. A thing is said to promote the interest, or to be *for* the interest, of an individual, when it tends to add to the sum total of his pleasures: or, what comes to the same thing, to diminish the sum total of his pains.

An action then may be said to be conformable to the principle of utility, or, for shortness sake, to utility (meaning with respect to the community at large), when the tendency it has to augment the happiness of the community is greater than any it has to diminish it.

A measure of government (which is but a particular kind of action, performed by a particular person or persons) may be said to be conformable to or dictated by the principle of utility, when in like manner the tendency which it has to augment the happiness of the community is greater than any which it has to diminish it.

When an action, or in particular a measure of government, is supposed by a man to be conformable to the principle of utility, it may be convenient, for the purposes of discourse, to imagine a kind of law or dictate, called a law or dictate of utility: and to speak of the action in question, as being conformable to such law or dictate.

A man may be said to be a partizan of the principle of utility, when the approbation or disapprobation he annexes to any action, or to any measure, is determined by and proportioned to the tendency which he conceives it to have to augment or to diminish the happiness of the community: or in other words, to its conformity or unconformity to the laws or dictates of utility.

Of an action that is conformable to the principle of utility, one may always say either that it is one that ought to be done, or at least that it is not one that ought not to be done. One may say also, that it is right it should be done; at least that it is not wrong it should be done: that it is a right action; at least that it is not a wrong action. When thus interpreted, the words *ought,* and *right* and *wrong,* and others of that stamp, have a meaning: when otherwise, they have none.

Has the rectitude of this principle been ever formally contested? It should seem that it had, by those who have not known what they have been meaning. Is it susceptible of any direct proof? It should seem not: for that which is used to prove every thing else, cannot itself be proved: a chain of proofs must have their commencement somewhere. To give such proof is as impossible as it is needless.

Not that there is or ever has been that human creature breathing, however stupid or perverse, who has not on many, perhaps on most occasions of his life, deferred to it. By the natural constitution of the human frame, on most occasions of their lives men in general embrace this principle, without thinking of it: if not for the ordering of their own actions, yet for the trying of their own actions, as well as of those of other men. There have been, at the same time, not many, perhaps, even of the most intelligent, who have been disposed to embrace it purely and without reserve. There are even few who have not taken some occasion or other to quarrel with it, either on account of their not understanding always how to apply it, or on account of some prejudice or other which they were afraid to examine into, or could not bear to part with. For such is the stuff that man is made of: in principle and in practice, in a right track and in a wrong one, the rarest of all human qualities is consistency.

When a man attempts to combat the principle of utility, it is with reasons drawn, without his being aware of it, from that very principle itself. His arguments, if they prove any thing, prove not that the principle is *wrong,* but that, according to the applications he supposes to be made of it, it is *misapplied.* Is it possible for a man to move the earth? Yes; but he must first find out another earth to stand upon. . . .

Among principles adverse to that of utility, that which at this day seems to have most influence in matters of government, is what may be called the principle of sympathy and antipathy. By the principle of sympathy and antipathy, I mean that principle which approves or disapproves of certain actions, not on account of their tending to augment the happiness, nor yet on account of their tending to diminish the happiness of the party whose interest is in question, but merely because a man finds himself disposed to approve or disapprove of them: holding up that approbation or disapprobation as a sufficient reason for itself, and disclaiming the necessity of looking out for any extrinsic ground. Thus far in the general department of morals: and in the particular department of politics, measuring out the quantum (as well as determining the ground) of punishment, by the degree of the disapprobation.

It is manifest, that this is rather a principle in name than in reality: it is not a positive principle of itself, so much as a term employed to signify the negation of all principle. What one expects to find in a principle is something that points out some external consideration, as a means of warranting and guiding the internal sentiments of approbation and disapprobation: this expectation is but ill fulfilled by a proposition, which does neither more nor less than hold up each of those sentiments as a ground and standard for itself.

In looking over the catalogue of human actions (says a partizan of this principle) in order to determine which of them are to be marked with the seal of disapprobation, you need but to take counsel of your own feelings: whatever you find in yourself a propensity to condemn, is wrong for that very reason. For the same reason it is also meet for punishment: in what proportion it is adverse to utility, or whether it be adverse to utility at all, is a matter that makes no difference. In that same *proportion* also is it meet for punishment: if you hate much, punish much: if you hate little, punish little: punish as you hate. If you hate not at all, punish not at all: the fine feelings of the soul are not to be overborne and tyrannized by the harsh and rugged dictates of political utility.

The various systems that have been formed concerning the standard of right and wrong, may all be reduced to the principle of sympathy and antipathy. One account may serve for all of them. They consist all of them in so many contrivances for avoiding the obligation of appealing to any external standard, and for prevailing upon the reader to accept of the author's sentiment or opinion as a reason, and that a sufficient one, for itself. The phrases different, but the principle the same.

It is curious enough to observe the variety of inventions men have hit upon, and the variety of phrases they have brought forward, in order to conceal from the world, and, if possible, from themselves, this very general and therefore very pardonable self-sufficiency.

1. One man [Lord Shaftesbury, Hutchinson, Hume, &c.] says, he has a thing made on purpose to tell him what is right and what is wrong; and that it is called a *moral sense:* and then he goes to work at his ease, and says, such a thing is right, and such a thing is wrong—why? "because my moral sense tells me it is."

2. Another man [Dr. Beattie] comes and alters the phrase: leaving out *moral*, and putting in *common*, in the room of it. He then tells you, that his common sense teaches him what is right and wrong, as surely as the other's moral sense did: meaning by common sense, a sense of some kind or other, which, he says, is possessed by all mankind: the sense of those, whose sense is not the same as the author's, being struck out of the account as not worth taking. This contrivance does better than the other; for a moral sense, being a new thing, a man may feel about him a good while without being able to find it out: but common sense is as old as the creation; and there is no man but would be ashamed to be thought not to have as much of it as his neighbours. It has another great advantage: by appearing to share power, it lessens envy: for when a man gets up upon this ground, in order to anathematize those who differ from him, it is not by a *sic volo sic jubeo*, but by a *velitis jubeatis* [not as I wish but as you wish].

3. Another man [Dr. Price] comes, and says, that as to a moral sense indeed, he cannot find that he has any such thing: that however he has an *understanding*, which will do quite as well. This understanding, he says, is the standard of right and wrong: it tells him so and so. All good and wise men understand as he does: if other men's understandings differ in any point from his, so much the worse for them: it is a sure sign they are either defective or corrupt.

4. Another man says, that here is an eternal and immutable Rule of Right: that that rule of right dictates so and so: and then he begins giving you his sentiments upon any thing that comes uppermost: and these sentiments (you are to take for granted) are so many branches of the eternal rule of right.

5. Another man [Dr. Clark], or perhaps the same man (it's no matter) says, that there are certain practices conformable, and others repugnant, to the Fitness of Things; and then he tells you at his leisure, what practices are conformable and what repugnant: just as he happens to like a practice or dislike it.

6. A great multitude of people are continually talking of the Law of Nature; and then they go on giving you their sentiments about what is right and what is wrong: and these sentiments, you are to

understand, are so many chapters, and sections of the Law of Nature.

7. Instead of the phrase, Law of Nature, you have sometimes Law of Reason, Right Reason, Natural Justice, Natural Equity, Good Order. Any of them will do equally well. This latter is most used in politics. The three last are much more tolerable than the others, because they do not very explicitly claim to be any thing more than phrases: they insist but feebly upon the being looked upon as so many positive standards of themselves, and seem content to be taken, upon occasion, for phrases expressive of the conformity of the thing in question to the proper standard, whatever that may be. On most occasions, however, it will be better to say *utility: utility* is clearer, as referring more explicitly to pain and pleasure.

8. We have one philosopher [Woolaston], who says, there is no harm in any thing in the world but in telling a lie: and that if, for example, you were to murder your own father, this would only be a particular way of saying, he was not your father. Of course, when this philosopher sees any thing that he does not like, he says, it is a particular way of telling a lie. It is saying, that the act ought to be done, or may be done, when, *in truth*, it ought not to be done.

9. The fairest and openest of them all is that sort of man who speaks out, and says, I am of the number of the Elect: now God himself takes care to inform the Elect what is right: and that with so good effect, that let them strive ever so, they cannot help not only knowing it but practising it. If therefore a man wants to know what is right and what is wrong, he has nothing to do but come to me.

It is upon the principle of antipathy that such and such acts are often reprobated on the score of their being *unnatural:* the practice of exposing children, established among the Greeks and Romans, was an unnatural practice. Unnatural, when it means any thing, means unfrequent: and there it means something; although nothing to the present purpose. But here it means no such thing: for the frequency of such acts is perhaps the great complaint. It therefore means nothing; nothing, I mean, which there is in the act itself. All it can serve to express is, the disposition of the person who is talking of it: the disposition he is in to be angry at the thoughts of it. Does it merit his anger? Very likely it may: but whether it does or no is a question, which, to be answered rightly, can only be answered upon the principle of utility.

Unnatural, is as good a word as moral sense, or common sense; and would be as good a foundation for a system. Such an act is unnatural:

that is, repugnant to nature: for I do not like to practise it; and, consequently, do not practise it. It is therefore repugnant to what ought to be the nature of every body else.

The mischief common to all these ways of thinking and arguing (which, in truth, as we have seen, are but one and the same method, couched in different forms of words) is their serving as a cloke, and pretence, and aliment, to despotism: if not a despotism in practice, a despotism however in disposition: which is but too apt, when pretence and power offer, to show itself in practice. The consequence is, that with intentions very commonly of the purest kind, a man becomes a torment either to himself or his fellow-creatures. If he be of the melancholy cast [Dr. Price], he sits in silent grief, bewailing their blindness and depravity: if of the irascible [Dr. Beattie], he declaims with fury and virulence against all who differ from him; blowing up the coals of fanaticism, and branding with the charge of corruption and insincerity, every man who does not think, or profess to think as he does.

If such a man happens to possess the advantages of style, his book may do a considerable deal of mischief before the nothingness of it is understood.

These principles, if such they can be called, it is more frequent to see applied to morals than to politics: but their influence extends itself to both. In politics, as well as morals, a man will be at least equally glad of a pretence for deciding any question in the manner that best pleases him, without the trouble of inquiry. If a man is an infallible judge of what is right and wrong in the actions of private individuals, why not in the measures to be observed by public men in the direction of those actions? Accordingly (not to mention other chimeras) I have more than once known the pretended law of nature set up in legislative debates, in opposition to arguments derived from the principle of utility.

"But is it never, then, from any other considerations than those of utility, that we derive our notions of right and wrong?" I do not know: I do not care. Whether a moral sentiment can be originally conceived from any other source than a view of utility, is one question: whether upon examination and reflection it can, in point of fact, be actually persisted in and justified on any other ground, by a person reflecting within himself, is another: whether in point of right it can properly be justified on any other ground, by a person addressing himself to the community, is a third. The two first are questions of speculation: it matters not, comparatively speaking, how they are decided. The last is a question of practice: the decision of it is of as much importance as that of any can be.

"I feel in myself," say you, "a disposition to approve of such or such an action in a moral view: but this is not owing to any notions I have of its being an useful one to the community. I do not pretend to know whether it be an useful one or not: it may be, for aught I know, a mischievous one." "But is it then," say I, "a mischievous one? Examine; and if you can make yourself sensible that it is so, then, if duty means any thing, that is, moral duty, it is your *duty* at least to abstain from it: and more than that, if it is what lies in your power, and can be done without too great a sacrifice, to endeavour to prevent it. It is not your cherishing the notion of it in your bosom, and giving it the name of virtue, that will excuse you."

"I feel in myself," say you again, "a disposition to detest such or such an action in a moral view; but this is not owing to any notions I have of its being a mischievous one to the community. I do not pretend to know whether it be a mischievous one or not: it may be not a mischievous one: it may be, for aught I know, an useful one."—"May it indeed," say I, "be an useful one? but let me tell you then, that unless duty, and right and wrong, be just what you please to make them, if it really be not a mischievous one, and any body has a mind to do it, it is no duty of your's, but, on the contrary, it would be very wrong in you, to take upon you to prevent him: detest it within yourself as much as you please; that may be a very good reason (unless it be also a useful one) for your not doing it yourself: but if you go about, by word or deed, to do any thing to hinder him, or make him suffer for it, it is you, and not he, that have done wrong: it is not your setting yourself to blame his conduct, or branding it with the name of vice, that will make him culpable, or you blameless. Therefore, if you can make yourself content that he shall be of one mind, and you of another, about that matter, and so continue, it is well: but if nothing will serve you, but that you and he must needs be of the same mind, I'll tell you what you have to do: it is for you to get the better of your antipathy, not for him to truckle to it." . . .

Objections to the Principle of Utility.[1] Trifling scruples and trifling verbal difficulties may be raised in opposition to the principle of utility, but no real and distinct objection can be opposed to it. Indeed, how can it be combated, if not by reasons drawn from the

[1] *Ibid.*, pp. 11–12, 13.

principle itself? To say that it is dangerous, is to say that to consult utility *is* contrary to utility. . . .

Evil may be done, whilst it is believed that the *principle of utility* is followed. A feeble and limited mind may deceive itself, by considering only a part of the good and evil. A man under the influence of passion may deceive himself, by setting an extreme value upon one advantage which hides from him the inconveniences attending upon it. What constitutes a wicked man, is the habit of seeking pleasures hurtful to others; and even this supposes the absence of many kinds of pleasures. But we ought not to charge upon this principle the faults which are opposed to it, and which it alone can serve to remove. If a man calculate badly, it is not arithmetic which is in fault, it is himself. If the reproaches which are heaped upon Machiavel are well founded, his errors do not arise from his having made use of the principle of utility; but from his having made false applications of it. . . .

This *principle of utility*, it is said, is only the renewal of epicurism, and it is known what ravages this doctrine made in manners: it was always the doctrine of the most corrupt men.

Epicurus, it is true, is the only one among the ancients who has the merit of having known the true source of morality; but to suppose that his doctrine leads to the consequences imputed to it, is to suppose that happiness can be the enemy of happiness itself. "*Sic praesentibus utaris voluptatibus ut futuris non noceas.*" [So use present joys that you do not injure future ones.] Seneca is here in accordance with Epicurus: and what more can be desired in morals than the cutting off of every pleasure hurtful to one's self or to others. But is not this the *principle of utility?*

But it may be said, every one will be constituting himself judge of this utility: every obligation will cease when he no longer thinks he perceives in it his own interest.

Every one will constitute himself judge of his own utility; this is and this ought to be, otherwise man would not be a reasonable being. He who is not a judge of what is suitable for himself, is less than an infant, is a fool. The obligation which binds men to their engagements, is nothing but a feeling of an interest of a superior class, which outweighs an inferior interest. Men are not always held by the particular utility of a certain engagement; but in the case in which the engagement becomes burthensome to one of the parties, they are still held by the general utility of engagements—by the confidence that each enlightened man wishes to have placed in his word, that he may be considered as trustworthy, and enjoy the advantages attached to probity and esteem. It is not the engagement which constitutes the obligation by itself; for there are some void engagements; there are some unlawful. Why? Because they are considered as hurtful. It is the utility of the contract which gives it force.

The most exalted acts of virtue may be easily reduced to a calculation of good and evil. This is neither to degrade nor to weaken them, but to represent them as the effects of reason, and to explain them in a simple and intelligible manner. . . .

Utility, Not an Original Contract, the Justification of Government.[1] As to the Original Contract, . . . a few pages, perhaps, may not be ill bestowed in endeavouring to come to a precise notion about its reality and use. The stress laid on it formerly, and still, perhaps, by some, is such as renders it an object not undeserving of attention. I was in hopes, however, . . . that this chimera had been effectually demolished by Mr. Hume. I think we hear not so much of it now as formerly. The indestructible prerogatives of mankind have no need to be supported upon the sandy foundation of a fiction.

With respect to this, and other fictions, there was once a time, perhaps, when they had their use. With instruments of this temper, I will not deny but that some political work may have been done, and that useful work, which, under the then circumstances of things, could hardly have been done with any other. But the season of *Fiction* is now over: insomuch, that what formerly might have been tolerated and countenanced under that name, would, if now attempted to be set on foot, be censured and stigmatized under the harsher appellations of *encroachment* or *imposture.* To attempt to introduce any *new* one, would be *now* a crime: for which reason there is much danger, without any use, in vaunting and propagating such as have been introduced already. In point of political discernment, the universal spread of learning has raised mankind in a manner to a level with each other, in comparison of what they have been in any former time: nor is any man now so far elevated above his fellows, as that he should be indulged in the dangerous licence of cheating them for their good.

As to the fiction now before us, in the character of an *argumentum ad hominem*, coming when it did, and managed as it was, it succeeded to admiration.

[1] *Works*, Vol. I, "A Fragment on Government," pp. 268–272.

That compacts, by whomsoever entered into, *ought* to be kept;—that men are *bound* by compacts, are propositions which men, without knowing or inquiring why, were disposed universally to accede to. The observance of promises they had been accustomed to see pretty constantly enforced. They had been accustomed to see Kings, as well as others, behave themselves as if bound by them. This proposition, then, "that men are bound by *compacts;*" and this other, "that, if one party performs not his part, the other is released from his," being propositions which no man disputed, were propositions which no man had any call to prove. In theory they were assumed for axioms: and in practice they were observed as rules. If, on any occasion, it was thought proper to make a show of proving them, it was rather for form's sake than for any thing else; and that, rather in the way of momento or instruction to acquiescing auditors, than in the way of proof against opponents. On such an occasion, the common-place retinue of phrases was at hand: *Justice, Right Reason* required it; the *Law of Nature* commanded it, and so forth: all of which are but so many ways of intimating that a man is firmly persuaded of the truth of this or that moral proposition, though he either thinks he *need not*, or finds he *can't*, tell *why*. Men were too obviously and too generally interested in the observance of these rules, to entertain doubts concerning the force of any arguments they saw employed in their support. It is an old observation, how Interest smoothes the road to Faith.

A compact, then, it was said, was made by the King and People: the terms of it were to this effect:—The People, on their part, promised to the King a *general obedience:* the King, on his part, promised to *govern* the People in such a *particular* manner always, as should be *subservient* to their happiness. I insist not on the words: I undertake only for the sense; as far as an imaginary engagement, so loosely and so variously worded by those who have imagined it, is capable of any decided signification. Assuming, then, as a general rule, that promises, when made, ought to be observed; and, as a point of fact, that a promise to this effect in particular had been made by the party in question, men were more ready to deem themselves qualified to judge when it was such a promise was *broken*, than to decide directly and avowedly on the delicate question, when it was that a King acted so far in *opposition* to the happiness of his People, that it were better no longer to obey him.

It is manifest, on a very little consideration, that nothing was gained by this manoeuvre after all: no difficulty removed by it. It was still necessary, and that as much as ever, that the question men studied to avoid should be determined, in order to determine the question they thought to substitute in its room. It was still necessary to determine, whether the King in question had, or had not, acted so far in *opposition* to the happiness of his people, that it were better no longer to obey him; in order to determine, whether the promise he was supposed to have made, had or had not been broken. For what was the supposed purport of this promise? It was no other than what has just been mentioned.

Let it be said, that part at least of this promise was to govern in *subservience to Law:* that hereby a more precise rule was laid down for his conduct, by means of this supposal of a promise, than that other loose and general rule to govern in subservience to the *happiness of his people:* and that, by this means, it is the letter of the *Law* that forms the tenor of the rule.

Now true it is, that the governing in opposition to Law, is *one* way of governing in opposition to the happiness of the people: the natural effect of such a contempt of the Law being, if not actually to destroy, at least to threaten with destruction, all those rights and privileges that are founded on it: rights and privileges on the enjoyment of which that happiness depends. But still it is not this that can be safely taken for the entire purport of the promise here in question: and that for several reasons. *First,* Because the most mischievous, and under certain constitutions the most feasible, method of governing in opposition to the happiness of the people, is, by setting the Law itself in opposition to their happiness. *Second,* Because it is a case very conceivable, that a King may, to a great degree, impair the happiness of his people without violating the letter of any single Law. *Third,* Because extraordinary occasions may now and then occur, in which the happiness of the people may be better promoted by acting, for the moment, in *opposition* to the Law, than in *subservience* to it. *Fourth,* Because it is not any single violation of the Law, as such, that can properly be taken for a breach of his part of the contract, so as to be understood to have released the people from the obligation of performing theirs. For, to quit the fiction, and resume the language of plain truth, it is scarce ever any single violation of the Law that, by being *submitted to,* can produce so much mischief as shall surpass the probable mischief of *resisting* it. If every single instance whatever of such a violation were to be deemed an entire dissolution of the contract, a man who reflects at all would scarce find any where, I believe, under the sun, that Government which he could allow to subsist for twenty years together. It is plain, therefore, that to pass any sound decision upon the question which the inventors of this fiction substituted instead of the true one, the latter was still necessary to be decided. All they gained by their contrivance was, the convenience of deciding it obliquely, as it were, and by a side wind; that is, in a crude and hasty way, without any direct and steady examination.

But, after all, for what *reason* is it, that men *ought* to keep their promises? The moment any intelligible reason is given, it is this: that it is for the *advantage* of society they should keep them; and if they do not, that as far as *punishment* will go, they should be *made* to keep them. It is for the advantage of the whole number that the promises of each individual should be kept: and, rather than they should not be kept, that such individuals as fail to keep them should be punished. If it be asked, how this appears? the answer is at hand:—Such is the benefit to gain, and mischief to avoid, by keeping them, as much more than compensates the mischief of so much punishment as is requisite to oblige men to it. Whether the dependence of *benefit* and *mischief* (that is, of *pleasure* and *pain*) upon men's conduct in this behalf, be as here stated, is a question of *fact*, to be decided, in the same manner that all other questions of fact are to be decided, by testimony, observation, and experience.

This, then, and no other, being the *reason* why men should be made to keep their promises, viz. that it is for the advantage of society that they should, is a reason that may as well be given at once why *Kings*, on the one hand, in governing, should in general keep within established Laws, and (to speak universally) abstain from all such measures as tend to the unhappiness of their subjects: and, on the other hand, why *subjects* should obey Kings as long as they so conduct themselves, and no longer; why they should obey, in short, *so long as the probable mischiefs of obedience are less than the probable mischiefs of resistance:* why, in a word, taking the whole body together, it is their *duty* to obey just so long as it is their *interest*, and no longer. This being the case, what need of saying of the one, that *he* PROMISED so to *govern;* of the other, that they PROMISED so to *obey*, when the fact is otherwise?

True it is, that, in this country, according to ancient forms, some sort of vague promise of *good government* is made by Kings at the ceremony of their coronation: and let the acclamations, perhaps given, perhaps not given, by chance persons out of the surrounding multitude, be construed into a promise of *obedience* on the part of the *whole* multitude: that whole multitude itself a small drop collected together by chance out of the ocean of the state: and let the two promises thus made be deemed to have formed a perfect *compact:*—not that either of them is declared to be the *consideration* of the other.

Make the most of this concession: one experiment there is, by which every reflecting man may satisfy himself, I think beyond a doubt that it is the consideration of *utility*, and no other, that, secretly, perhaps, but unavoidably, has governed his judgment upon all these matters. The experiment is easy and decisive. It is but to reverse, in supposition, in the first place, the import of the *particular* promise thus feigned; in the next place, the effect in point of *utility* of the observance of promises *in general*. Suppose the King to promise that he would govern his subjects *not* according to Law; *not* in the view to promote their happiness:—would this be binding upon *him?* Suppose the people to promise they would obey him *at all events*, let him govern as he will; let him govern to their destruction:—would this be binding upon *them?* Suppose the constant and universal effect of an observance of promises were to produce *mischief*, would it *then* be men's *duty* to observe them? would it *then* be *right* to make Laws, and apply punishment to *oblige* men to observe them?

"No," (it may perhaps be replied); "but for this reason: among promises, some there are that, as every one allows, are void: now these you have been supposing, are unquestionably of the number. A promise that is in itself *void*, cannot, it is true, create any obligation: But allow the promise to be *valid*, and it is the promise itself that creates the obligation, and nothing else." The fallacy of this argument is easy to perceive. For what is it, then, that the promise depends on for its *validity?* what is it that being *present* makes it *valid?* what is it that being *wanting* makes it *void?* To acknowledge that any *one* promise may be void, is to acknowledge that if any *other* is *binding*, it is not merely because it is a promise. That circumstance, then, whatever it be, on which the validity of a promise depends; that circumstance, I say, and not the promise itself, must, it is plain, be the cause of the obligation which a promise is apt in general to carry with it.

But farther. Allow, for argument's sake, what we have disproved: allow that the obligation of a promise is independent of every other:

allow that a promise is binding *propriâ vi:* Binding, then, on whom? On him certainly who makes it. Admit this: For what reason is the same individual promise to be binding on those who *never* made it? The King, *fifty years ago*, promised my *Great-Grandfather* to govern him according to Law: my Great-Grandfather, *fifty years ago*, promised the King to obey him according to Law. The King, *just now*, promised my *neighbour* to govern him according to Law: my neighbour, *just now*, promised the King to obey him according to Law. Be it so: What are these promises, all or any of them, to *me?* To make answer to this question, some other principle, it is manifest, must be resorted to, than that of the *intrinsic* obligation of promises upon those who make them.

Now this *other* principle that still recurs upon us, what other can it be than the *principle of* UTILITY? The principle which furnishes us with that *reason*, which alone depends not upon any higher reason, but which is itself the sole and all-sufficient reason for every point of practice whatsoever. . . .

Particular Objects of Government.[1] Every thing which the legislator is called upon to distribute among the members of the community, may be reduced to two classes:

1*st*, Rights
2*d*, Obligations.

Rights are in themselves advantages; benefits for him who enjoys them: obligations, on the other hand, are duties; burthensome charges for him who has to fulfil them.

Rights and obligations, though distinct and opposite in their nature, are simultaneous in their origin, and inseparable in their existence. According to the nature of things, the law cannot grant a benefit to any, without, at the same time, imposing a burthen on some one else; or, in other words, a right cannot be created in favour of any one, without imposing a corresponding obligation on another. In what manner is a right of property in land conferred on me? By imposing upon every body except myself the obligation not to touch its produce. How is the right of commanding conferred on me? By imposing upon a district, or a number of persons, the obligation to obey me.

The legislator ought to confer rights with pleasure, since they are in themselves a benefit; he ought to impose obligations with repugnance, since they are in themselves an evil. In accordance with the

[1] *Works*, Vol. I, "Principles of the Civil Code," pp. 301–303, 309, 312–313, 314, 316, 317.

principle of utility, he ought never to impose a burthen but that he may confer a benefit of a greater value.

In the same proportion as it creates obligations, the law curtails liberty: it converts into offences, acts which would otherwise be permitted and unpunishable. The law creates an offence, either by a positive commandment or by a prohibition.

These curtailments of liberty are inevitable. It is impossible to create rights, to impose obligations, to protect the person, life, reputation, property, subsistence, or liberty itself, but at the expense of liberty.

But every restraint imposed upon liberty is liable to be followed by a natural feeling of pain, more or less great, independent of an infinite variety of inconveniences and sufferings which may result from the particular mode of this restraint. It follows, therefore, that no restraint should be imposed, no power conferred, no coercive law sanctioned, without a specific and satisfactory reason. There is always one reason against every coercive law, and one reason which, were there no other, would be sufficient by itself: it is, that such a law is restrictive of liberty. Whoever proposes a coercive law, ought to be ready to prove, not only that there is a specific reason in favour of this law, but also that this reason is more weighty than the general reason against every law. . . .

The sole object of government ought to be the greatest happiness of the greatest possible number of the community.

The happiness of an individual is greater, in proportion as his sufferings are lighter and fewer in number, and as his enjoyments are greater and larger in number.

The care of providing for his enjoyments ought to be left almost entirely to each individual; the principal function of government being to protect him from sufferings.

It fulfils this office by creating rights which it confers upon individuals: rights of personal security; rights of protection for honour; rights of property; rights of receiving assistance in case of need. To these rights, correspond offences of all classes. The law cannot create rights without creating the corresponding obligations. It cannot create rights and obligations without creating offences. It can neither command nor prohibit, without restraining the liberty of individuals.

The citizen, therefore, cannot acquire any right without the sacrifice of a part of his liberty. Even under a bad government, there is no proportion between the sacrifice and the acquisition. Governments approach to perfection, in proportion as the acquisition is greater, and the sacrifice less. . . .

In this distribution of rights and obligations, the legislator, we have already said, should have for his object the happiness of the body politic. In inquiring more particularly in what this happiness consists, we find four subordinate objects—

Subsistence.
Abundance.
Equality.
Security. . . .

In legislation, the most important object is security. If no direct laws are made respecting subsistence, this object will be neglected by no one. But if there are no laws respecting security, it will be useless to have made laws respecting subsistence: command production—command cultivation; you will have done nothing: but secure to the cultivator the fruits of his labour, and you most probably have done enough.

Security, we have observed, has many branches: it is necessary that one branch of security should give way to another. For example, liberty, which is one branch of security, ought to yield to general security, since it is not possible to make any laws but at the expense of liberty.

It is not possible, then, to obtain the greatest good, but by the sacrifice of some subordinate good. In distinguishing among these objects, which, on each occasion, deserves the pre-eminence, consists the difficulty of the legislative art. Each one claims pre-eminence in turn, and it sometimes requires a complex calculation to determine to which the preference is due.

Equality ought not to be favoured, except in cases in which it does not injure security; where it does not disturb the expectations to which the laws have given birth; where it does not derange the actually established distribution.

If all property were to be equally divided, the certain and immediate consequence would be, that there would soon be nothing more to divide. Every thing would be speedily destroyed. Those who had hoped to be favoured by the division, would not suffer less than those at whose expense it would be made. If the condition of the industrious were not better than the condition of the idle, there would be no reason for being industrious.

If the principle were established, that all men should possess *equal rights*, by a necessary train of consequences, all legislation would be rendered impossible. The laws never cease establishing inequalities, since they cannot bestow rights upon any, without imposing obligations upon others.

Declare that all men, that is, all the human race, have equal rights: there is an end of all subordination. The son has equal rights with his father; he has the same right to direct and to punish him; he has as much in his father's house, as his father himself. The maniac has the same right to shut up others, as they have to shut up him. The idiot has the same right to govern his family, as his family have to govern him. All this is included in the equality of rights: it means all this, or it means nothing at all. It is true, those who have maintained this doctrine of the equality of rights, have neither been fools nor idiots. They had no intention of establishing this absolute equality: they had in their minds some restrictions, some modifications, some explanations. But if they knew not how to speak in a sensible and intelligible manner, was it possible that the blind and ignorant multitude should better understand what they did not understand themselves? And if they proclaimed independence, was it not too certain that they would be listened to? . . .

The laws, in creating property, have created wealth; but with respect to poverty, it is not the work of the laws—it is the primitive condition of the human race. The man who lives only from day to day, is precisely the man in a state of nature. The savage, the poor in society, I acknowledge, obtain nothing but by painful labour; but in a state of nature, what could he obtain but at the price of his toil? Has not hunting its fatigues, fishing its dangers, war its uncertainties? And if man appear to love this adventurous life—if he have an instinct greedy of these kinds of perils—if the savage rejoice in the delights of an idleness so dearly purchased—ought it to be concluded that he is more happy than our day labourers? No: the labour of these is more uniform, but the reward is more certain: the lot of the woman is more gentle, infancy and old age have more resources; the species multiplies in a proportion a thousand times greater, and this alone would suffice to show on which side is the superiority of happiness. Hence the laws, in creating property, have been benefactors to those who remain in their original poverty. They participate more or less in the pleasures, advantages, and resources of civilized society: their industry and labour place them among the candidates for fortune: they enjoy the pleasures of acquisition: hope mingles with their labours. The security which the law gives them, is this of little importance? Those who look from above at the inferior ranks, see all objects less than they really are; but at the base of the pyramid, it is the summit which disappears in its turn. So far from making these comparisons, they dream not of them; they are not tormented with impossibilities: so that, all things considered, the protection of the laws contributes as much to the happiness of the cottage, as to the security of the palace. It is surprising that so judicious a writer as Beccaria should have inserted, in a work dictated by the soundest philosophy, a doubt subversive of the social order. *The right of property*, says he, *is a terrible right, and may not perhaps be necessary.* Upon this right, tyrannical and sanguinary laws have been founded. It has been most frightfully abused; but the right itself presents only ideas of pleasure, of abundance, and of security. It is this right which has overcome the natural aversion to labour—which has bestowed on man the empire of the earth—which has led nations to give up their wandering habits—which has created a love of country and of posterity. To enjoy quickly—to enjoy without punishment,—this is the universal desire of man; this is the desire which is terrible, since it arms all those who possess nothing, against those who possess any thing. But the law, which restrains this desire, is the most splendid triumph of humanity over itself. . . .

Must there, therefore, be constant opposition, an eternal war between the two rivals, *Security* and *Equality?* Up to a certain point they are incompatible, but with a little patience and skill they may be brought by degrees to coincide.

Time is the only mediator between these contrary interests. Would you follow the counsels of equality without contravening those of security, wait for the natural period which puts an end to hopes and fears—the period of death.

When property is vacated by the death of the proprietors, the law may intervene in the distribution to be made, either by limiting in certain respects the power of disposing of it by will, with the design of preventing too great an accumulation of property in the hands of a single person, or by making the right of succession subservient to the purposes of equality, in case the deceased should not leave a husband, or wife, or relations, in the direct line, and should not have made use of his power of disposing of it by will. It passes then to new possessors, whose expectations are not formed, and equality may produce good to all, without deceiving the expectations of any. The principle only is indicated here: it will be more largely developed in the second Book.

When it regards the correction of a species of civil inequality such as slavery, the same attention ought to be paid to the rights of property; the operation should be gradual, and the subordinate object should be pursued without sacrificing the principal object. The men whom you would render free by these gradations, will be much more fitted for its enjoyment, than if you had led them to trample justice under foot, in order to introduce them to this new social condition.

We may observe, that in a nation which prospers by agriculture, manufactures, and commerce, there is a continual progress towards equality. If the laws do not oppose it—if they do not maintain monopolies—if they do not restrain trade and its exchanges—if they do not permit entails—large properties will be seen, without effort, without revolutions, without shock, to subdivide themselves by little and little, and a much greater number of individuals will participate in the advantage of moderate fortunes. This will be the natural result of the different habits formed by opulence and poverty. The first, prodigal and vain, seeks only to enjoy without creating: the second, accustomed to obscurity and to privations, finds its pleasures in its labours and its economy. From this arises the change which is going on in Europe, from the progress of arts and commerce, notwithstanding the obstacles of the laws. The ages of feudality are not long since passed by, in which the world was divided into two classes—a few great proprietors who were every thing, and a multitude of slaves who were nothing. These lofty pyramids have disappeared or have been lowered, and their debris has been spread abroad: industrious men have formed new establishments, of which the infinite number proves the comparative happiness of modern civilization. Hence we may conclude, that *security*, by preserving its rank as the supreme principle, indirectly conducts to the establishment of *equality;* whilst this latter, if taken as the basis of the social arrangement, would destroy security in establishing itself. . . .

Ought provision for the poor, for public worship, and the cultivation of the arts and sciences, to be ranked among the wants of the state for which provision ought to be made by forced contributions? . . .

It appears, that it may be laid down as a general principle of legislation, that a regular contribution should be established for the wants of indigence; it being well understood that those only ought to be regarded as indigent, who are in want of necessaries. But from this definition it follows, that the title of the indigent, as indigent, is stronger than the title of the proprietor of a superfluity, as proprietor; since the pain of death, which would finally fall upon the neglected indigent, will always be a greater evil than the pain of disappointed expectation, which falls upon the rich when a limited portion of his superfluity is taken from him.

With regard to the amount of a legal contribution, it ought not to exceed simple necessaries: to exceed this would be to punish industry for the benefit of idleness. Establishments which furnish more than necessaries, are only good when supported at the expense of individuals, because they can use discretion in the distribution of their assistance, and apply it to specific classes. . . .

If the ministers of religion are considered as charged with the maintenance of one of the sanctions of morality (the religious sanction), the expense of their support ought to be referred to the same head as the expenses of police and justice—to that of internal security. They are a body of inspectors and teachers of morals, who form, so to speak, the advanced guard of the law; who possess no power over crime, but who combat with the vices out of which crimes spring; and who render the exercise of authority more rare, by maintaining good conduct and subordination. If they were charged with all the functions which might suitably be assigned to them, such as the education of the inferior classes, the promulgation of the laws, the promulgation of different public acts, the utility of their services would be more manifest. . . .

With regard to the cultivation of the fine arts, of the embellishment of a country, of buildings of luxury, of objects of ornament and pleasure—in a word, for these works of supererogation, ought forced contributions to be levied? Can the imposition of taxes, which have no other than this brilliant but superfluous destination, be justified?

I would not plead here, for that which is agreeable, in opposition to what is useful,[1] nor justify the starving of the people, to give feasts to a court, or pensions to buffoons. But one or two reflections may be presented, by way of apology:—

1. The amount expended, and which can be expended, upon these objects, is commonly but little, compared with the mass of necessary contributions. If any one should advise that his portion of this super-

[1] I do not mean that there is a real opposition between the useful and the agreeable: every thing which gives pleasure is useful; but in ordinary language, that is exclusively called *useful* which possesses a distant utility; that *agreeable*, which has an immediate utility, or is limited to present pleasure. Very many things, whose utility is contested, have therefore a more certain utility than those to which this denomination is appropriated.

fluous expense should be returned to each person, would it not be an impalpable object?

2. This supererogatory part of the taxes, being confounded with the mass of those which are necessary, its collection is imperceptible: it does not excite any distinct sensation, which can give rise to any distinct complaint; and the evil of the first order, being limited to so trifling an amount, is not sufficient to produce an evil of the second order.

3. This luxury of pleasure may have a palpable utility, by attracting a concourse of foreigners, who will spend their money in the country, and thus other nations will by degrees, be made tributary to that which sways the sceptre of fashion. A country fertile in amusements, may be considered as a great theatre, which is supported in part at the expense of a crowd of spectators attracted from all parts. . . .

A Proposed Reform of the Suffrage.[1] *Universal suffrage*, *Annual Parliaments*, and *Election by Ballot:*—at public meetings, these are the words commonly (it is believed) employed, for expressing the essential features of Radical Reform.

Another expression, however, there is, which in some respects seems to afford a promise of being more apposite. This is—*secret*, *universal*, *equal*, *and annual suffrage*. . . .

I. Secresy is of the very first importance: because where there is no secresy, there can be no assurance of *genuineness*. The vote may be bribed or forced, the vote is the expression of the wish—not of the voter, but of him by whom he is either bribed or forced. So far as this state of things has place, the wishes, by which the choice is determined, will be—not the wishes of the *many*, governed by the interests of the many, but the wishes of the few, governed by the interests of the few—by that comparatively narrow body of interest which is in a state of continual opposition to the universal interest, and to which, in so far as the opposition has place, or by the ruling few is thought to have place, the universal happiness will be made a constant sacrifice. . . .

II. *Universality* we say for shortness, instead of *Virtual Universality*. No man means that children that can but just speak, should vote: no man appears to mean that females should vote.

To some it has appeared necessary to exclude from voting *persons insane*, and *criminals:* to exclude them by special exception. No won-

[1] *Works*, Vol. III, pp. 558, 559, 560, 561, 562. Probably written late in 1819.

der:—yet nothing can be more needless. Such as are lawfully under confinement, would no more be let out to vote than for any other purpose. As to those who are not under confinement,—*criminality*, if it means anything to the purpose, means *mischievousness*. But the most mischievous among criminals, adjudged and denominated such after legal conviction, could not set his foot in either House, without finding himself in company with men in numbers—not to say in a vast majority—more mischievous than himself: men, whose principal differences from himself, consist in impunity derived from situation and confederacy—in impunity added to greater mischievousness: men whose mischievousness was acting on the largest scale, while his was acting on a petty scale. Exclude criminals? *How* will you exclude criminals? Exclude criminals convict? Yes, *that* you may: but, even in this class, in which mischievousness is not secured from the imputation of criminality by high-handed impunity,—of those convicted, how small is the proportion to those not convicted! . . .

Property, it is continually said, is the only bond and pledge of attachment to country.—Not it indeed. Want of property is a much stronger one. He who has property, can change the shape of it, and carry it with him to another country, whenever he pleases: he who has no property, can do no such thing. In the eyes of those who live by the labour of others, the existence of those by whose labour they live, is indeed of no value: not so in the eyes of the labourers themselves. Life is not worth more to yawners than to labourers: and their own country is the only country in which they can so much as hope to live. Among a hundred of them, not ten exceptions to this will you find.

Now as to the qualification by *reading*.—At first blush, it seems to involve exclusion:—it does no such thing in effect. From two to three months' social pastime, at the hours of repose from work, would give it to all adults in whose eyes the privilege were worth that price: and he, in whose eyes it were not worth that price, could not, with much justice, complain at the not having it. Qualification by householdership does involve exclusion: for it is not in every man's power to pay rent and taxes for a house. Householdership is evidence of property; it is for this cause that it is required by those who stipulate for it. Qualification by payment of taxes—*that* too involves exclusion: if by payment of taxes be meant that which is anything to the purpose. Qualification by payment to [of] indirect taxes, if those be the taxes meant, is *universality of suffrage:* for where is the human being that pays not to taxes on consumption? to the taxes called *indirect* taxes? . . . Qualification by reading involves no exclusion. . . .

An elector is a trustee: a trustee ought not to be unfit for his trust.

It is to reading that the people owe all their strength: that strength at which, even thus early, tyrants tremble.

III. By *equality of suffrage*, is meant equality of effect and value, as between the suffrage of one man and the suffrage of another. The greater the number of votes to each seat, the smaller is the effect of each vote. . . .

What should never be out of mind is—that without the reduction universally made in the marketable value of votes by this equality as between suffrage and suffrage,—without the reduction made in the value of a seat by annuality of suffrage,—without the defalcation made, from the effective force of corruption, by the greatest practicable reduction made by the exclusion of placemen, in the quantity of money and money's worth applicable to the purpose of corruption,—without these aids, secresy of suffrage would not suffice to insure exclusion of effective corruption. . . .

IV. Of *annuality of suffrage*, the main uses seem to be as follows:—

1. The faculty of divesting of their power all unfit representatives, before they have had time to produce any lasting mischief.

2. The keeping them out of the way of temptation, by rendering their breach of trust not worth purchasing by the corrupter-general, at any price for which it would be worth the while of a man in his situation to sacrifice his good name. . . .

Secresy, universality, equality, and annuality—behold in them the four cardinal points of the constitutional compass: secresy is the polar star.

Without secresy of suffrage, universality, equality, and annuality, altogether, would be worse than nothing. Even without universality, without equality, without annuality, secresy would of itself do much. . . . Secresy would be a strong pledge for complete reform, and of itself no inconsiderable step to it. It would of itself be a great part of the reform, and might engage men to wait with thankfulness and patience for the rest. . . .

All cry of danger—danger to property—would be here without pretext. If in radicalism there were any real danger, it might be excluded by *graduality*. Yes, by graduality. But by what graduality? Not assuredly by that which Lord Erskine, and his clients, have so plainly shown *they* mean—a gradual progress in doing nothing. No:

but a gradual introduction of members really chosen by those by whom they pretend to be chosen:—really chosen by those whose interest is the universal interest. The proportion—say a fourth at a time; say a fifth; say a sixth. France, which under its newly simplified and improved mode of election lets in a fifth at a time has in that particular shown us an example. I mention this—not as necessary—not as eligible—but as that which a Whig, if there were any sincerity in him, could not object to. . . .

III

THOMAS ROBERT MALTHUS
1766–1834

Malthus was the second son in a family of eight children, six of whom were girls. His father after a short career as a lawyer had retired to a small estate in Surrey, where Robert (as he was known in the family) was born in 1766. It has been surmised that life in the country, where families were large and poverty was the rule, helped to produce the famous theory of population. The elder Malthus followed the modes of his time: he botanized, made the acquaintance of Rousseau (in due time becoming his executor), admired Condorcet and Godwin, and looked forward to an age of human perfection.

At thirteen Robert met a perhaps more acrid nature when he was sent to study with Richard Graves, a clergyman of parts and author of a coarse satirical novel on the Methodists. Graves remarked the lad's love of "fighting for fighting's sake" though without ill-will, and his keen sense of humor. Three years under Graves's tuition and a further period at the academy of Gilbert Wakefield, a churchman turned dissenter, fitted him for Cambridge. Wakefield practiced the educational doctrines of Rousseau; that is, he subordinated discipline to encouraging the boy's natural abilities. Entering Jesus College, Cambridge, in 1784, Malthus probably tasted heterodoxy again as the pupil of William Frend, who was later deposed from his fellowship for irregular religious views. But neither this association nor a marked impediment of speech shook Malthus's determination to enter the Church; he finished the university course with credit in 1788 and took orders two years later. He then seems to have continued his studies at home and at Cambridge. These covered a broad range, and in 1793 he was elected to a fellowship at Cambridge. It was not until 1797 that he began active duties as a parish priest in his native Surrey.

Father and son delighted to argue, and one of their debates became an incident of history. The dispute was as to the perfectibility of man; Malthus senior upheld the doctrine of Godwin, Robert preferred to be original and pessimistic. So struck was the latter with the force of his own arguments that he presented them to the world in 1798 as *An Essay on the Principle of Population as It Affects the Future Improvement of Society*. Though published anonymously the book at once focussed upon itself the attention of enlightened Englishmen. Like many difficult books since, it was said—doubtless with some exaggeration—that everyone discussed it but almost no one read it. The very defects of the work were what gave it its amazing prominence. The book gained in impact by its narrowness—if the argument had taken the shape (and bulk) it assumed in the second edition, Malthus's views might have caused scarcely a ripple. As it was he returned a direct and almost unqualified negative to the current faith in social improvement by asserting (with a qualification apt to be overlooked) that the generative powers of the human race were sufficient to inundate the world unless checked ultimately by misery and vice.

Malthus had his followers, but at first his opponents were much more vociferous. A controversy with Godwin dating from the first appearance of the *Essay* gradually became embittered as the popularity of Godwin's social viewpoint waned and that of his younger rival increased. Criticism and further study caused Malthus somewhat to moderate his pessimism. His first opinion had been based chiefly on the incidental remarks of Adam Smith, Robert Wallace, and Richard Price—indeed the only originality he claimed lay in having appreciated the force of their statements and worked them out in detail. First-hand inquiry in many European countries between 1798 and 1802 confirmed him in his main contentions, but in the vastly enlarged second edition of the *Essay* in 1803 he was more ready to admit the efficacy of a "preventive check" on population. This however heightened the attack from a different quarter. The religious community saw in it a meddling with the designs of Providence, which enjoined men, in the words of the Bible, to "go forth and populate the world." Malthus replied with equally well-chosen texts, but the objectors refused to be silenced; Southey, Coleridge, Hazlitt, and Cobbett sided with Godwin.

The influence of Malthus, however, continued to increase. His study of population had led him into the field of economics, the *Essay* showed Utilitarian leanings, and he at once took his place along with James Mill and Ricardo as a leading member of the classical school of economists. In course of time he made several noteworthy contributions to economic theory which were summed up in the *Political Economy* (1820).

Malthus married in 1804. In 1805 he was appointed professor of history and political economy in the new college at Haileybury established by the East India Company as a training school for its employees in the Indian civil service. Success did not desert him as a schoolmaster: he was noted for the quality of his lectures, which his hearers "not only understood but 'did not even find dull.'" He remained at Haileybury until his death, which occurred suddenly in 1834. Two children survived him.

The most opposite effects have been attributed to the work of Malthus. It is charged that his doctrine of population made the propertied classes indifferent to reform and forgetful of their social obligations, for if the only result of improving social conditions was to encourage the poor to breed faster, philanthropy was useless. His leading interpreter, however, while admitting that Malthus's treatment of labor problems was not, on the whole, a happy one, contends that the proper inference from his central doctrine is that the standard of living must be raised in order that workingmen may imitate other classes in limiting their families. However this may be, a steady decline in the British birth-rate—beginning it is true shortly before the publication of the *Essay*—may be partly due to its teaching. And while Malthus condemned (on moral grounds) the "artificial" restriction of births, he actually laid the foundation for the birth-control movement. The widespread influence of his great book even outside the field of social relations is illustrated by the fact that both Alfred Russel Wallace and Charles Darwin found in it a clue to their own theory of the origin of species.

REFERENCES

The most recent complete edition of the *Essay* is that of 1890 (ed. G. T. Bettany). The first edition was reprinted with notes by J. Bonar in 1926. *Parallel Passages from the First and Second Editions . . .* (1895) is useful for purposes of comparison. Malthus wrote a final and summary statement of his views, notable for certain important revisions, for the 1824 supplement to the *Encyclopedia Britannica* (art. "Population").

For critical discussions of Malthus see J. Bonar, *Malthus and His Work* (2nd ed., 1924) and *The Tables Turned* (1931), essay iii; G. Talbot Griffith, *Population Problems in the Age of Malthus* (1926), especially ch. iv; Ezra Bowen, "Malthus, a Revaluation" (*Scientific Monthly*, May, 1930, pp. 465–471).

The fullest biography is in Bonar, *Malthus and His Work* (above), book v.

READINGS FROM

AN ESSAY ON THE PRINCIPLE OF POPULATION [1]

Statement of the Subject. Ratios of the Increase of Population and Food.[2] In an inquiry concerning the improvement of society, the mode of conducting the subject which naturally presents itself, is,

1. To investigate the causes that have hitherto impeded the progress of mankind towards happiness; and,
2. To examine the probability of the total or partial removal of these causes in future.

To enter fully into this question, and to enumerate all the causes that have hitherto influenced human improvement, would be much beyond the power of an individual. The principal object of the present essay is to examine the effects of one great cause intimately united with the very nature of man; which, though it has been constantly and powerfully operating since the commencement of society, has been little noticed by the writers who have treated this subject. The facts which establish the existence of this cause have, indeed, been repeatedly stated and acknowledged; but its natural and necessary effects have been almost totally over-looked; though probably among these effects may be reckoned a very considerable portion of that vice and misery, and of that unequal distribution of the bounties of nature, which it has been the unceasing object of the enlightened philanthropist in all ages to correct.

The cause to which I allude, is the constant tendency in all animated life to increase beyond the nourishment prepared for it.

It is observed by Dr. Franklin, that there is no bound to the prolific nature of plants or animals, but what is made by their crowding and interfering with each other's means of subsistence. Were the face of the earth, he says, vacant of other plants, it might be gradually sowed and overspread with one kind only, as for instance with fennel: and were it empty of other inhabitants, it might in a few ages be replenished from one nation only, as for instance with Englishmen.

This is incontrovertibly true. Through the animal and vegetable kingdoms Nature has scattered the seeds of life abroad with the most profuse and liberal hand; but has been comparatively sparing in the room and the nourishment necessary to rear them. The germs of existence contained in this earth, if they could freely develop themselves,

[1] The page references are to G. T. Bettany's edition (1890).

[2] Bk. I, ch. i (pp. 2–7).

would fill millions of worlds in the course of a few thousand years. Necessity, that imperious, all-pervading law of nature, restrains them within the prescribed bounds. The race of plants and the race of animals shrink under this great restrictive law; and man cannot by any efforts of reason escape from it.

In plants and irrational animals, the view of the subject is simple. They are all impelled by a powerful instinct to the increase of their species; and this instinct is interrupted by no doubts about providing for their offspring. Wherever therefore there is liberty, the power of increase is exerted; and the superabundant effects are repressed afterwards by want of room and nourishment.

The effects of this check on man are more complicated. Impelled to the increase of his species by an equally powerful instinct, reason interrupts his career, and asks him whether he may not bring beings into the world, for whom he cannot provide the means of support. If he attend to this natural suggestion, the restriction too frequently produces vice. If he hear it not, the human race will be constantly endeavouring to increase beyond the means of subsistence. But as, by that law of our nature which makes food necessary to the life of man, population can never actually increase beyond the lowest nourishment capable of supporting it, a strong check on population, from the difficulty of acquiring food, must be constantly in operation. This difficulty must somewhere, and must necessarily be severely felt in some or other of the various forms of misery, or the fear of misery, by a large portion of mankind.

That population has this constant tendency to increase beyond the means of subsistence, and that it is kept to its necessary level by these causes, will sufficiently appear from a review of the different states of society in which man has existed. But, before we proceed to this review, the subject will, perhaps, be seen in a clearer light, if we endeavour to ascertain what would be the natural increase of population, if left to exert itself with perfect freedom; and what might be expected to be the rate of increase in the productions of the earth under the most favourable circumstances of human industry.

It will be allowed that no country has hitherto been known, where the manners were so pure and simple, and the means of subsistence so abundant, that no check whatever has existed to early marriages from the difficulty of providing for a family, and that no waste of the human species has been occasioned by vicious customs, by towns, by unhealthy occupations, or too severe labour. Consequently in no state that we have yet known, has the power of population been left to exert itself with perfect freedom.

Whether the law of marriage be instituted, or not, the dictate of nature and virtue seems to be an early attachment to one woman; and where there were no impediments of any kind in the way of an union to which such an attachment would lead, and no causes of depopulation afterwards, the increase of the human species would be evidently much greater than any increase which has been hitherto known.

In the northern states of America, where the means of subsistence have been more ample, the manners of the people more pure, and the checks to early marriages fewer, than in any of the modern states of Europe, the population has been found to double itself, for above a century and a half successively, in less than twenty-five years. Yet, even during these periods, in some of the towns, the deaths exceeded the births, a circumstance which clearly proves that, in those parts of the country which supplied this deficiency, the increase must have been much more rapid than the general average.

In the back settlements, where the sole employment is agriculture, and vicious customs and unwholesome occupations are little known, the population has been found to double itself in fifteen years. Even this extraordinary rate of increase is probably short of the utmost power of population. Very severe labour is requisite to clear a fresh country; such situations are not in general considered as particularly healthy; and the inhabitants, probably, are occasionally subject to the incursions of the Indians, which may destroy some lives, or at any rate diminish the fruits of industry.

According to a table of Euler, calculated on a mortality of 1 in 36, if the births be to the deaths in the proportion of 3 to 1, the period of doubling will be only 12 years and 4-5ths. And this proportion is not only a possible supposition, but has actually occurred for short periods in more countries than one.

Sir William Petty supposes a doubling possible in so short a time as ten years.

But, to be perfectly sure that we are far within the truth, we will take the slowest of these rates of increase, a rate in which all concurring testimonies agree, and which has been repeatedly ascertained to be from procreation only.

It may safely be pronounced, therefore, that population, when unchecked, goes on doubling itself every twenty-five years, or increases in a geometrical ratio.

The rate according to which the productions of the earth may be supposed to increase, it will not be so easy to determine. Of this, however, we may be perfectly certain, that the ratio of their increase in a limited territory must be of a totally different nature from the ratio of the increase of population. A thousand millions are just as easily doubled every twenty-five years by the power of population as a thousand. But the food to support the increase from the greater number will by no means be obtained with the same facility. Man is necessarily confined in room. When acre has been added to acre till all the fertile land is occupied, the yearly increase of food must depend upon the melioration of the land already in possession. This is a fund, which, from the nature of all soils, instead of increasing, must be gradually diminishing. But population, could it be supplied with food, would go on with unexhausted vigour; and the increase of one period would furnish the power of a greater increase the next, and this without any limit.

From the accounts we have of China and Japan, it may be fairly doubted, whether the best-directed efforts of human industry could double the produce of these countries even once in any number of years. There are many parts of the globe, indeed, hitherto uncultivated, and almost unoccupied; but the right of exterminating, or driving into a corner where they must starve, even the inhabitants of these thinly-peopled regions, will be questioned in a moral view. The process of improving their minds and directing their industry would necessarily be slow; and during this time, as population would regularly keep pace with the increasing produce, it would rarely happen that a great degree of knowledge and industry would have to operate at once upon rich unappropriated soil. Even where this might take place, as it does sometimes in new colonies, a geometrical ratio increases with such extraordinary rapidity, that the advantage could not last long. If the United States of America continue increasing, which they certainly will do, though not with the same rapidity as formerly, the Indians will be driven further and further back into the country, till the whole race is ultimately exterminated, and the territory is incapable of further extension.

These observations are, in a degree, applicable to all the parts of the earth, where the soil is imperfectly cultivated. To exterminate the inhabitants of the greatest part of Asia and Africa, is a thought that could not be admitted for a moment. To civilise and direct the industry of the various tribes of Tartars and Negroes, would certainly be a work of considerable time, and of variable and uncertain success.

Europe is by no means so fully peopled as it might be. In Europe there is the fairest chance that human industry may receive its best direction. The science of agriculture has been much studied in England and Scotland; and there is still a great portion of uncultivated land in these countries. Let us consider at what rate the produce of this island might be supposed to increase under circumstances the most favourable to improvement.

If it be allowed that by the best possible policy, and great encouragements to agriculture, the average produce of the island could be doubled in the first twenty-five years, it will be allowing, probably, a greater increase than could with reason be expected.

In the next twenty-five years, it is impossible to suppose that the produce could be quadrupled. It would be contrary to all our knowledge of the properties of land. The improvement of the barren parts would be a work of time and labour; and it must be evident to those who have the slightest acquaintance with agricultural subjects, that in proportion as cultivation extended, the additions that could yearly be made to the former average produce must be gradually and regularly diminishing. That we may be the better able to compare the increase of population and food, let us make a supposition, which, without pretending to accuracy, is clearly more favourable to the power of production in the earth, than any experience we have had of its qualities will warrant.

Let us suppose that the yearly additions which might be made to the former average produce, instead of decreasing, which they certainly would do, were to remain the same; and that the produce of this island might be increased every twenty-five years, by a quantity equal to what it at present produces. The most enthusiastic speculator cannot suppose a greater increase than this. In a few centuries it would make every acre of land in the island like a garden.

If this supposition be applied to the whole earth, and if it be allowed that the subsistence for man which the earth affords might be increased every twenty-five years by a quantity equal to what it at present produces, this will be supposing a rate of increase much greater than we can imagine that any possible exertions of mankind could make it.

It may be fairly pronounced, therefore, that, considering the present average state of the earth, the means of subsistence, under circumstances the most favourable to human industry, could not possibly be made to increase faster than in an arithmetical ratio.

The necessary effects of these two different rates of increase, when brought together, will be very striking. Let us call the population of this island eleven millions; and suppose the present produce equal to the easy support of such a number. In the first twenty-five years the population would be twenty-two millions, and the food being also doubled, the means of subsistence would be equal to this increase. In the next twenty-five years the population would be forty-four millions, and the means of subsistence only equal to the support of thirty-three millions. In the next period the population would be eighty-eight millions, and the means of subsistence just equal to the support of half that number. And, at the conclusion of the first century, the population would be a hundred and seventy-six millions, and the means of subsistence only equal to the support of fifty-five millions, leaving a population of a hundred and twenty-one millions totally unprovided for.

Taking the whole earth, instead of this island, emigration would of course be excluded; and, supposing the present population equal to a thousand millions, the human species would increase as the numbers, 1, 2, 4, 8, 16, 32, 64, 128, 256, and subsistence as 1, 2, 3, 4, 5, 6, 7, 8, 9. In two centuries the population would be to the means of subsistence as 256 to 9; in three centuries as 4096 to 13, and in two thousand years the difference would be almost incalculable.

In this supposition no limits whatever are placed to the produce of the earth. It may increase for ever and be greater than any assignable quantity; yet still the power of population being in every period so much superior, the increase of the human species can only be kept down to the level of the means of subsistence by the constant operation of the strong law of necessity, acting as a check upon the greater power.

The General Checks to Population, and the Mode of Their Operation.[1] The ultimate check to population appears then to be a want of food, arising necessarily from the different ratios according to which population and food increase. But this ultimate check is never the immediate check, except in cases of actual famine.

The immediate check may be stated to consist in all those customs, and all those diseases, which seem to be generated by a scarcity of the means of subsistence; and all those causes, independent of this scarcity, whether of a moral or physical nature, which tend prematurely to weaken and destroy the human frame.

These checks to population, which are constantly operating with

[1] Bk. I, ch. ii; Bk. II, ch. xiii (pp. 7–14, 297).

more or less force in every society, and keep down the number to the level of the means of subsistence, may be classes under two general heads—the preventive, and the positive checks.

The preventive check, as far as it is voluntary, is peculiar to man, and arises from that distinctive superiority in his reasoning faculties, which enables him to calculate distant consequences. The checks to the indefinite increase of plants and irrational animals are all either positive, or, if preventive, involuntary. But man cannot look around him, and see the distress which frequently presses upon those who have large families; he cannot contemplate his present possessions or earnings, which he now nearly consumes himself, and calculate the amount of each share, when with very little addition they must be divided, perhaps, among seven or eight, without feeling a doubt whether, if he follow the bent of his inclinations, he may be able to support the offspring which he will probably bring into the world. In a state of equality, if such can exist, this would be the simple question. In the present state of society other considerations occur. Will he not lower his rank in life, and be obliged to give up in great measure his former habits? Does any mode of employment present itself by which he may reasonably hope to maintain a family? Will he not at any rate subject himself to greater difficulties and more severe labour, than in his single state? Will he not be unable to transmit to his children the same advantages of education and improvement that he had himself possessed? Does he even feel secure that, should he have a large family, his utmost exertions can save them from rags and squalid poverty, and their consequent degradation in the community? And may he not be reduced to the grating necessity of forfeiting his independence, and of being obliged to the sparing hand of Charity for support?

These considerations are calculated to prevent, and certainly do prevent, a great number of persons in all civilised nations from pursuing the dictate of nature in an early attachment to one woman.[1] If this restraint do not produce vice, it is undoubtedly the least evil that can arise from the principle of population. Considered as a restraint on a strong natural inclination, it must be allowed to produce a certain degree of temporary unhappiness; but evidently slight, compared with the evils which result from any of the other checks to population; and merely of the same

[1] [This statement is followed in the first edition (1798) by: "And this restraint almost necessarily, though not absolutely so, produces vice. Yet in all societies, even those that are most vicious, the tendency to a virtuous attachment is so strong, that there is a constant effort towards an increase of population. This constant effort as constantly tends to subject the lower classes of the society to distress, and to prevent any great amelioration of their condition."]

nature as many other sacrifices of temporary to permanent gratification, which it is the business of a moral agent continually to make.

When this restraint produces vice, the evils which follow are but too conspicuous. A promiscuous intercourse to such a degree as to prevent the birth of children, seems to lower, in the most marked manner, the dignity of human nature. It cannot be without its effect on men, and nothing can be more obvious than its tendency to degrade the female character, and to destroy all its most amiable and distinguishing characteristics. Add to which, that among those unfortunate females, with which all great towns abound, more real distress and aggravated misery are, perhaps, to be found, than in any other department of human life.

When a general corruption of morals, with regard to the sex, pervades all the classes of society, its effects must necessarily be, to poison the springs of domestic happiness, to weaken conjugal and parental affection, and to lessen the united exertions and ardour of parents in the care and education of their children:—effects which cannot take place without a decided diminution of the general happiness and virtue of the society; particularly as the necessity of art in the accomplishment and conduct of intrigues, and in the concealment of their consequences necessarily leads to many other vices.

The positive checks to population are extremely various, and include every cause, whether arising from vice or misery, which in any degree contributes to shorten the natural duration of human life. Under this head, therefore, may be enumerated all unwholesome occupations, severe labour and exposure to the seasons, extreme poverty, bad nursing of children, great towns, excesses of all kinds, the whole train of common diseases and epidemics, wars, plague, and famine.

On examining these obstacles to the increase of population which I have classed under the heads of preventive and positive checks, it will appear that they are all resolvable into moral restraint, vice, and misery.

Of the preventive checks, the restraint from marriage which is not followed by irregular gratifications may properly be termed moral restraint.[1]

[1] It will be observed, that I here use the term moral in its most confined sense. By *moral* restraint I would be understood to mean a restraint from marriage, from prudential motives, with a conduct strictly moral during the period of this restraint; and I have never intentionally deviated from this sense. When I have wished to consider the restraint from marriage unconnected with its consequences, I have either called it prudential restraint, or a part of the preventive check, of which indeed it forms the principal branch.

In my review of the different stages of society, I have been accused of not allowing sufficient weight in the prevention of population to moral restraint; but when the confined sense of the term, which I have here explained, is adverted to, I am fearful that I shall not be found to have erred much in this respect. I should be very glad to believe myself mistaken.

Promiscuous intercourse, unnatural passions, violations of the marriage bed, and improper arts to conceal the consequences of irregular connexions, are preventive checks that clearly come under the head of vice.

Of the positive checks, those which appear to arise unavoidably from the laws of nature, may be called exclusively misery; and those which we obviously bring upon ourselves, such as wars, excesses, and many others which it would be in our power to avoid, are of a mixed nature. They are brought upon us by vice, and their consequences are misery.

The sum of all these preventive and positive checks, taken together, forms the immediate check to population; and it is evident that, in every country where the whole of the procreative power cannot be called into action, the preventive and the positive checks must vary inversely as each other; that is, in countries either naturally unhealthy, or subject to a great mortality, from whatever cause it may arise, the preventive check will prevail very little. In those countries, on the contrary, which are naturally healthy, and where the preventive check is found to prevail with considerable force, the positive check will prevail very little, or the mortality be very small.

In every country some of these checks are, with more or less force, in constant operation; yet, notwithstanding their general prevalence, there are few states in which there is not a constant effort in the population to increase beyond the means of subsistence. This constant effort as constantly tends to subject the lower classes of society to distress, and to prevent any great permanent melioration of their condition.

These effects, in the present state of society, seem to be produced in the following manner. We will suppose the means of subsistence in any country just equal to the easy support of its inhabitants. The constant effort towards population, which is found to act even in the most vicious societies, increases the number of people before the means of subsistence are increased. The food, therefore, which before supported eleven millions, must now be divided among eleven millions and a half. The poor consequently must live much worse, and many of them be reduced to severe distress. The number of labourers also being above the proportion of work in the market, the price of labour must tend to fall, while the price of provisions would at the same time tend to rise. The labourer therefore must do more work, to earn the same as he did before. During this season of distress, the discouragements to marriage and the difficulty of rearing a family are so great, that the progress of population is retarded. In the mean time, the cheapness of labour, the plenty of labourers, and the necessity of an increased industry among them, encourage cultivators to employ more labour upon their land, to turn up fresh soil, and to manure and improve more completely what is already in tillage, till ultimately the means of subsistence may become in the same proportion to the population, as at the period from which we set out. The situation of the labourer being then again tolerably comfortable, the restraints to population are in some degree loosened; and, after a short period, the same retrograde and progressive movements, with respect to happiness, are repeated.

This sort of oscillation will not probably be obvious to common view; and it may be difficult even for the most attentive observer to calculate its periods. Yet that, in the generality of old states, some alternation of this kind does exist though in a much less marked, and in a much more irregular manner, than I have described it, no reflecting man, who considers the subjects deeply, can well doubt.

One principal reason why this oscillation has been less remarked, and less decidedly confirmed by experience than might naturally be expected, is, that the histories of mankind which we possess are, in general, histories only of the higher classes. We have not many accounts that can be depended upon, of the manners and customs of that part of mankind, where these retrograde and progressive movements chiefly take place. A satisfactory history of this kind, of one people and of one period, would require the constant and minute attention of many observing minds in local and general remarks on the state of the lower classes of society, and the causes that influenced it; and to draw accurate inferences upon this subject, a succession of such historians for some centuries would be necessary. This branch of statistical knowledge has, of late years, been attended to in some countries, and we may promise ourselves a clearer insight into the internal structure of human society from the progress of these inquiries. But the science may be said yet to be in its infancy, and many of the objects, on which it would be desirable to have information, have been either omitted or not stated with sufficient accuracy. Among these, perhaps, may be reckoned the proportion of the number of adults to the number of marriages; the extent to which vicious customs have prevailed in consequence of the restraints upon matrimony; the comparative mortality among the children of the most distressed part of the community, and of those who live rather more at their ease; the variations in the real price of labour; the observable difference in the state of the lower classes of society, with respect to ease and happiness, at different times during a certain period; and very accurate registers of births, deaths, and marriages, which are of the utmost importance in this subject.

A faithful history, including such particulars, would tend greatly to elucidate the manner in which the constant check upon population acts; and would probably prove the existence of the retrograde and progressive movements that have been mentioned; though the times of their vibration must necessarily be rendered irregular from the operation of many interrupting causes; such as, the introduction or failure of certain manufactures; a greater or less prevalent spirit of agricultural enterprise; years of plenty, or years of scarcity; wars, sickly seasons, poor-laws, emigrations, and other causes of similar nature.

A circumstance which has, perhaps, more than any other, contributed to conceal this oscillation from common view, is the difference between the nominal and real price of labour. It very rarely happens that the nominal price of labour universally falls; but we well know that it frequently remains the same, while the nominal price of provisions has been gradually rising. This, indeed, will generally be the case, if the increase of manufactures and commerce be sufficient to employ the new labourers that are thrown into the market, and to prevent the increased supply from lowering the money-price. But an increased number of labourers receiving the same money-wages will necessarily, by their competition, increase the money-price of corn. This is, in fact, a real fall in the price of labour; and, during this period, the conditions of the lower classes of the community must be gradually growing worse. But the farmers and capitalists are growing rich from the real cheapness of labour. Their increasing capitals enable them to employ a greater number of men; and, as the population had probably suffered some check from the greater difficulty of supporting a family, the demand for labour, after a certain period, would be great in proportion to the supply, and its price would of course rise, if left to find its natural level; and thus the wages of labour, and consequently the condition of the lower classes of society, might have progressive and retrograde movements, though the price of labour might never nominally fall.

In savage life, where there is no regular price of labour, it is little to be doubted that similar oscillations took place. When population has increased nearly to the utmost limits of the food, all the preventive and the positive checks will naturally operate with increased force. Vicious habits with respect to the sex will be more general, the exposing of children more frequent, and both the probability and fatality of wars and epidemics will be considerably greater; and these causes will probably continue their operation till the population is sunk below the level of the food; and then the return to comparative plenty will again produce an increase, and, after a certain period, its further progress will again be checked by the same causes.[1]

But without attempting to establish these progressive and retrograde movements in different countries, which would evidently require more minute histories than we possess, and which the progress of civilisation naturally tends to counteract, the following propositions are intended to be proved:—

1. Population is necessarily limited by the means of subsistence.
2. Population invariably increases where the means of subsistence increase, unless prevented by some very powerful and obvious checks.[2]
3. These checks, and the checks which repress the superior power of population, and keep its effects on a level with the means of subsistence, are all resolvable into moral restraint, vice and misery. . . .

Proposed Systems for Improving Society.[3] To a person who views the past and present states of mankind in the light in which they have appeared in the two preceding books, it cannot but be a matter of astonishment, that all the writers on the perfectibility of man and of society, who have noticed the argument of the principle

[1] Sir James Stuart very justly compares the generative faculty to a spring loaded with a variable weight (*Polit. Econ.*, Vol. I, b. i, c. 4, p. 20) which would of course produce exactly that kind of oscillation which has been mentioned. In the first book of his *Political Economy*, he has explained many parts of the subject of population very ably.

[2] I have expressed myself in this cautious manner, because I believe there are some instances, where population does not keep up to the level of the means of subsistence. But these are extreme cases; and, generally speaking, it might be said that,

2. Population always increases where the means of subsistence increase.
3. The checks which repress the superior power of population, and keep its effects on a level with the means of subsistence, are all resolvable into moral restraint, vice and misery.

It should be observed, that, by an increase in the means of subsistence, is here meant such an increase as will enable the mass of the society to command more food. An increase might certainly take place, which in the actual state of a particular society would not be distributed to the lower classes, and consequently would give no stimulus to population.

[3] Bk. III, chs. i, ii (pp. 296, 307–308, 309, 310, 311–312, 313–314, 317).

of population, treat it always very lightly, and invariably represent the difficulties arising from it as at a great and almost immeasurable distance. . . . The system of equality, which Mr. Godwin proposes, is, on a first view of it, the most beautiful and engaging of any that has yet appeared. A melioration of society to be produced merely by reason and conviction gives more promise of permanence than any change effected and maintained by force. The unlimited exercise of private judgment is a doctrine grand and captivating, and has a vast superiority over those systems, where every individual is in a manner the slave of the public. The substitution of benevolence, as the master-spring and moving principle of society, instead of self-love appears at first sight to be a consummation devoutly to be wished. In short, it is impossible to contemplate the whole of this fair picture without emotions of delight and admiration, accompanied with an ardent longing for the period of its accomplishment. But alas! that moment can never arrive. . . .

The great error under which Mr. Godwin labours throughout his whole work is, the attributing of almost all the vices and misery that prevail in civil society to human institutions. Political regulations and the established administration of property are, with him, the fruitful sources of all evil, the hotbeds of all the crimes that degrade mankind. Were this really a true state of the case, it would not seem an absolutely hopeless task, to remove evil completely from the world: and reason seems to be the proper and adequate instrument for effecting so great a purpose. But the truth is, that though human institutions appear to be, and indeed often are, the obvious and obtrusive causes of much mischief to society, they are, in reality, light and superficial, in comparison with those deeper-seated causes of evil, which result from the laws of nature and the passions of mankind. . . .

But let us imagine for a moment Mr. Godwin's system of equality realized, and see how soon this difficulty might be expected to press, under so perfect a form of society. A theory that will not admit of application cannot possibly be just.

Let us suppose all the causes of vice and misery in this island removed. War and contention cease. Unwholesome trades and manufactories do not exist. Crowds no longer collect together in great and pestilent cities for purposes of court intrigue, of commerce, and of vicious gratification. Simple, healthy and rational amusements take the place of drinking, gaming and debauchery. There are no towns sufficiently large to have any prejudicial effects on the human constitution.

The greater part of the happy inhabitants of this terrestrial Paradise live in hamlets and farm-houses scattered over the face of the country. All men are equal. The labours of luxury are at an end; and the necessary labours of agriculture are shared amicably among all. The number of persons and the produce of the island we suppose to be the same as at present. The spirit of benevolence, guided by impartial justice, will divide this produce among all the members of society according to their wants. Though it would be impossible that they should all have animal food every day, yet vegetable food, with meat occasionally, would satisfy the desires of a frugal people, and would be sufficient to preserve them in health, strength and spirits.

Mr. Godwin considers marriage as a fraud and a monopoly. Let us suppose the commerce of the sexes established upon principles of the most perfect freedom. Mr. Godwin does not think himself, that this freedom would lead to a promiscuous intercourse; and in this I perfectly agree with him. The love of variety is a vicious, corrupt and unnatural taste, and could not prevail in any great degree in a simple and virtuous state of society. Each man would probably select for himself a partner, to whom he would adhere, as long as that adherence continued to be the choice of both parties. It would be of little consequence, according to Mr. Godwin, how many children a woman had or to whom they belonged. Provisions and assistance would spontaneously flow from the quarter in which they abounded to the quarter in which they were deficient. And every man, according to his capacity, would be ready to furnish instruction to the rising generation.

I cannot conceive a form of society so favourable upon the whole to population. The irremediableness to marriage, as it is at present constituted, undoubtedly deters many from entering into this state. An unshackled intercourse on the contrary would be a most powerful incitement to early attachments; and as we are supposing no anxiety about the future support of children to exist, I do not conceive that there would be one woman in a hundred, of twenty-three years of age, without a family.

With these extraordinary encouragements to population, and every cause of depopulation, as we have supposed, removed, the numbers would necessarily increase faster than in any society that has ever yet been known. I have before mentioned that the inhabitants of the back settlements of America appear to double their numbers in fifteen years. England is certainly a more healthy country than the back settlements of America; and as we have supposed every house in the island to be airy and wholesome, and the encouragements to have a family greater even than in America, no probable reason can be assigned, why the population should not double itself in less, if possible, than fifteen years. But to be quite sure, that we do not go beyond the truth, we will only suppose the period of doubling to be twenty-five years; a ratio of increase, which is slower than is known to have taken place throughout all the United States of America. . . .

Alas! what becomes of the picture, where men lived in the midst of plenty, where no man was obliged to provide with anxiety and pain for his restless wants; where the narrow principle of selfishness did not exist; where the mind was delivered from her perpetual anxiety about corporal support, and free to expatiate in the field of thought which is congenial to her? This beautiful fabric of the imagination vanishes at the severe touch of truth. The spirit of benevolence, cherished and invigorated by plenty, is repressed by the chilling breath of want. The hateful passions that had vanished re-appear. The mighty law of self-preservation expels all the softer and more exalted emotions of the soul. The temptations to evil are too strong for human nature to resist. The corn is plucked up before it is ripe, or secreted in unfair proportions; and the whole black train of vices that belong to falsehood are immediately generated. Provisions no longer flow in for the support of a mother with a large family. The children are sickly from insufficient food. The rosy flush of health gives place to the pallid cheek and hollow eye of misery. Benevolence, yet lingering in a few bosoms, makes some faint expiring struggles, till at length self-love resumes his wonted empire, and lords it triumphant over the world. . . .

It may be curious to observe, in the case that we have been supposing, how some of the principal laws, which at present govern civilised society, would be successively dictated by the most imperious necessity. As man, according to Mr. Godwin, is the creature of the impressions to which he is subject, the goadings of want could not continue long, before some violations of public or private stock would necessarily take place. As these violations increased in number and extent, the more active and comprehensive intellects of the society would soon perceive that, while the population was fast increasing, the yearly produce of the country would shortly begin to diminish. The urgency of the case would suggest the necessity of some immediate measures being taken for the general safety. Some kind of convention would be then called, and the dangerous situation of the country stated in the strongest terms. It would be observed that while they lived in the midst of plenty, it was of little consequence who laboured the least, or who possessed the least, as every man was perfectly willing and ready to supply the wants of his neighbour. But that the question was no longer, whether one man should give to another that which he did not use himself; but whether he should give to his neighbour the food which was absolutely necessary to his own existence. It would be represented that the number of those who were in want very greatly exceeded the number and means of those who should supply them; that these pressing wants, which from the state of the produce of the country could not all be gratified, had occasioned some flagrant violations of justice; that these violations had already checked the increase of food, and would, if they were not by some means or other prevented, throw the whole community into confusion; that imperious necessity seemed to dictate that a yearly increase of produce should, if possible, be obtained at all events; that in order to effect this first great and indispensable purpose, it would be advisable to make a more complete division of land, and to secure every man's property against violation by the most powerful sanctions. . . .

And thus it appears that a society constituted according to the most beautiful form that imagination can conceive, with benevolence for its moving principle instead of self-love, and with every evil disposition in all its members corrected by reason, not force, would, from the inevitable laws of nature, and not from any fault in human institutions, degenerate in a very short period into a society constructed upon a plan not essentially different from that which prevails in every known state at present; a society, divided into a class of proprietors and a class of labourers, and with self-love for the main-spring of the great machine. . . .

The Poor Laws.[1] To remedy the frequent distresses of the poor, laws to enforce their relief have been instituted; and in the establishment of a general system of this kind England has particularly distinguished herself. But it is to be feared, that, though it may have alleviated a little the intensity of individual misfortune, it has spread the evil over a much larger surface. . . .

The poor-laws of England tend to depress the general condition of the poor in these two ways. Their first obvious tendency is to in-

[1] Bk. III, chs. v, vi (pp. 332, 342–343).

crease population without increasing the food for its support. A poor man may marry with little or no prospect of being able to support a family without parish assistance. They may be said, therefore, to create the poor which they maintain: and as the provisions of the country must, in consequence of the increased population, be distributed to every man in smaller proportions, it is evident that the labour of those who are not supported by parish assistance, will purchase a smaller quantity of provisions than before, and consequently more of them must be driven to apply for assistance.

Secondly, the quantity of provisions consumed in workhouses, upon a part of the society that cannot in general be considered as the most valuable part, diminishes the shares that would otherwise belong to more industrious and more worthy members, and thus, in the same manner, forces more to become dependent. If the poor in the workhouses were to live better than they do now, this new distribution of the money of the society would tend more conspicuously to depress the condition of those out of the workhouses by occasioning an advance in the price of provisions.

Fortunately for England, a spirit of independence still remains among the peasantry. The poor-laws are strongly calculated to eradicate this spirit. They have succeeded in part; but had they succeeded as completely as might have been expected, their pernicious tendency would not have been so long concealed.

Hard as it may appear in individual instances, dependent poverty ought to be held disgraceful. Such a stimulus seems to be absolutely necessary to promote the happiness of the great mass of mankind; and every general attempt to weaken this stimulus, however benevolent its intention, will always defeat its own purpose. If men be induced to marry from the mere prospect of parish provision, they are not only unjustly tempted to bring unhappiness and dependence upon themselves and children, but they are tempted, without knowing it, to injure all in the same class with themselves.

The poor-laws of England appear to have contributed to raise the price of provisions, and to lower the real price of labour. They have therefore contributed to impoverish that class of people whose only possession is their labour. It is also difficult to suppose that they have not powerfully contributed to generate that carelessness and want of frugality observable among the poor, so contrary to the disposition generally to be remarked among petty tradesmen and small farmers. The labouring poor, to use a vulgar expression, seem always to live from hand to mouth. Their present wants employ their whole attention; and they seldom think of the future. Even when they have an opportunity of saving they seldom exercise it; but all that they earn beyond their present necessities goes, generally speaking, to the ale-house. The poor-laws may therefore be said to diminish both the power and the will to save, among the common people; and thus to weaken one of the strongest incentives to sobriety and industry, and consequently to happiness. . . .

The Only Effective Mode of Improving the Conditions of the Poor.[1] In the first edition of this essay I observed, that as from the laws of nature it appeared, that some check to population must exist, it was better that this check should arise from a foresight of the difficulties attending a family and the fear of dependent poverty, than from the actual presence of want and sickness. This idea will admit of being pursued farther; and I am inclined to think that, from the prevailing opinions respecting population, which undoubtedly originated in barbarous ages, and have been continued and circulated by that part of every community which may be supposed to be interested in their support, we have been prevented from attending to the clear dictates of reason and nature on this subject. . . .

However powerful may be the impulses of passion, they are generally in some modified by reason. And it does not seem entirely visionary to suppose that, if the true and permanent cause of poverty were clearly explained and forcibly brought home to each man's bosom, it would have some, and perhaps not an inconsiderable influence on his conduct; at least the experiment has never yet been fairly tried. Almost everything, that has been hitherto done for the poor, has tended, as if with solicitous care, to throw a veil of obscurity over this subject, and to hide from them the true cause of their poverty. When the wages of labour are hardly sufficient to maintain two children, a man marries, and has five or six; he of course finds himself miserably distressed. He accuses the insufficiency of the price of labour to maintain a family. He accuses his parish for their tardy and sparing fulfilment of their obligation to assist him. He accuses the avarice of the rich, who suffer him to want what they can so well spare. He accuses the partial and unjust institutions of society, which have awarded him an inadequate share of the produce of the earth. He accuses perhaps the dispensations of Providence which have assigned to

[1] Bk. IV, chs. i, iii, ix (pp. 440–441, 457–458, 459, 494–495).

him a place in society so beset with unavoidable distress and dependence. In searching for objects of accusation, he never adverts to the quarter from which his misfortunes originate. The last person that he would think of accusing is himself, on whom in fact the principal blame lies, except so far as he has been deceived by the higher classes of society. He may perhaps wish that he had not married, because he now feels the inconveniences of it; but it never enters into his head that he can have done any thing wrong. He has always been told, that to raise up subjects for his king and country is a very meritorious act. He has done this, and yet is suffering for it; and it cannot but strike him as most extremely unjust and cruel in his king and country, to allow him thus to suffer, in return for giving them what they are continually declaring that they particularly want. . . .

The object of those who really wish to better the condition of the lower classes of society, must be to raise the relative proportion between the price of labour and the price of provisions, so as to enable the labourer to command a larger share of the necessaries and comforts of life. We have hitherto principally attempted to attain this end by encouraging the married poor, and consequently increasing the number of labourers, and overstocking the market with a commodity which we still say that we wish to be dear. It would seem to have required no great spirit of divination to foretell the certain failure of such a plan of proceeding. There is nothing however like experience. It has been tried in many different countries, and for many hundred years, and the success has always been answerable to the nature of the scheme. It is really time now to try something else. . . .

If, among the higher classes of society, the object of securing the operation of the prudential check to marriage to a sufficient degree appear to be attainable without much difficulty, the obvious mode of proceeding with the lower classes of society, where the point is of the principal importance, is to endeavour to infuse into them a portion of that knowledge and foresight, which so much facilitates the attainment of this object in the educated part of the community.

The fairest chance of accomplishing this end would probably be by the establishment of a system of parochial education upon a plan similar to that proposed by Adam Smith. In addition to the usual subjects of instruction, and those which he has mentioned, I should be disposed to lay considerable stress on the frequent explanation of the real state of the lower classes of society, as affected by the principle of population, and their consequent dependence on themselves for the chief part of their happiness or misery. It would be by no means necessary or proper in these explanations to underrate, in the smallest degree, the desirableness of marriage. It should always be represented as, what it really is, a state peculiarly suited to the nature of man, and calculated greatly to advance his happiness and remove the temptations to vice; but, like property or any other desirable object, its advantages should be shewn to be unattainable, except under certain conditions. And a strong conviction in a young man of the great desirableness of marriage, with a conviction at the same time that the power of supporting a family was the only condition which would enable him really to enjoy its blessings, would be the most effectual motive imaginable to industry and sobriety before marriage, and would powerfully urge him to save that superfluity of income which single labourers necessarily possess, for the accomplishment of a rational and desirable object, instead of dissipating it, as is now usually done, in idleness and vice. . . .

Subordinate Methods of Improving the Conditions of the Poor.[1] It may indeed be affirmed with the most perfect confidence that there is only one class of causes from which any approaches towards a remedy can be rationally expected; and that consists of whatever has a tendency to increase the prudence and foresight of the labouring classes. This is the touchstone to which every plan proposed for the improvement of the condition of the poor should be applied. If the plan be such as to co-operate with the lessons of Nature and Providence, and to encourage and promote habits of prudence and foresight, essential and permanent benefit may be expected from it; if it has no tendency of this kind, it may possibly still be good as a temporary measure, and on other accounts, but we may be quite certain that it does not apply to the source of the specific evil for which we are seeking a remedy. . . .

I have already observed, however, and I here repeat it again, that the general principles on these subjects ought not to be pushed too far, though they should always be kept in view; and that many cases may occur, in which the good resulting from the relief of the present distress may more than overbalance the evil to be apprehended from the remote consequence.

All relief in instances of distress, not arising from idle and improvident habits, clearly comes under this description; and in general it

[1] Bk. IV, chs. xii, xiii, xiv (pp. 524–525, 531–532, 540), Appendix (p. 567).

may be observed, that it is only that kind of *systematic* and *certain* relief, on which the poor can confidently depend, whatever may be their conduct, that violates general principles in such a manner as to make it clear that the general consequence is worse than the particular evil.

Independently of this discriminate and occasional assistance, the beneficial effects of which I have fully allowed in a preceding chapter, I have before endeavoured to shew, that much might be expected from a better and more general system of education. Everything that can be done in this way has indeed a very peculiar value; because education is one of those advantages, which not only all may share without interfering with others, but the raising of one person may actually contribute to the raising of others. If, for instance, a man by education acquires that decent kind of pride and those juster habits of thinking, which will prevent him from burdening society with a family of children which he cannot support, his conduct, as far as an individual instance can go, tends evidently to improve the condition of his fellow-labourers; and a contrary conduct from ignorance would tend as evidently to depress it.

I cannot help thinking also, that something might be done towards bettering the situation of the poor by a general improvement of their cottages, if care were taken, at the same time, not to make them so large as to allow of two families settling in them; and not to increase their number faster than the demand for labour required. One of the most salutary and least pernicious checks to the frequency of early marriages in this country is the difficulty of procuring a cottage, and the laudable habits which prompt a labourer rather to defer his marriage some years in the expectation of a vacancy, than to content himself with a wretched mud cabin, like those in Ireland.[1]

Even the cow system, upon a more confined plan, might not be open to objection. With any view of making it a substitute for the poor-laws, and of giving labourers a right to demand land and cows in proportion to their families; or of taking the common people from the consumption of wheat, and feeding them on milk and potatoes; it appears to me, I confess, truly preposterous: but if it were so or-

[1] Perhaps, however, this is not often left to his choice, on account of the fear which every parish has of increasing its poor. There are many ways by which our poor-laws operate in counteracting their first obvious tendency to increase population, and this is one of them. I have little doubt that it is almost exclusively owing to these counteracting causes, that we have been able to persevere in this system so long, and that the condition of the poor has not been so much injured by it as might have been expected.

dered as merely to provide a comfortable situation for the better and more industrious labourers, and to supply at the same time a very important want among the poor in general, that of milk for their children; I think that it would be extremely beneficial, and might be made a very powerful incitement to habits of industry, economy and prudence. With this view, however, it is evident that only a certain portion of labourers in each parish could be included in the plan; that good conduct, and not mere distress, should have the most valid claim to preference; that too much attention should not be paid to the number of children; and that universally, those who had saved money enough for the purchase of a cow, should be preferred to those who required to be furnished with one by the parish. . . .

It is less the object of the present work to propose new plans of improving society, than to inculcate the necessity of resting contented with that mode of improvement which already has in part been acted upon as dictated by the course of nature, and of not obstructing the advances which would otherwise be made in this way. . . .

Many persons, whose understandings are not so constituted that they can regulate their belief or disbelief by their likes or dislikes, have professed their perfect conviction of the truth of the general principles contained in the Essay; but, at the same time, have lamented this conviction, as throwing a darker shade over our views of human nature, and tending particularly to narrow our prospects of future improvement. In these feelings I cannot agree with them. If, from a review of the past, I could not only believe that a fundamental and very extraordinary improvement in human society was possible, but feel a firm confidence that it would take place, I should undoubtedly be grieved to find, that I had overlooked some cause, the operation of which would at once blast my hopes. But if the contemplation of the past history of mankind, from which alone we can judge of the future, renders it almost impossible to feel such a confidence, I confess that I had much rather believe that some real and deeply-seated difficulty existed, the constant struggle with which was calculated to rouse the natural inactivity of man, to call forth his faculties, and invigorate and improve his mind; a species of difficulty, which it must be allowed is most eminently and peculiarly suited to a state of probation; than that nearly all the evils of life might with the most perfect facility be removed, but for the perverseness and wickedness of those who influence human institutions.

A person who held this latter opinion must necessarily live in a constant state of irritation and disappointment. The ardent expectations, with which he might begin life, would soon receive the most cruel check. The regular progress of society, under the most favourable circumstances, would to him appear slow and unsatisfactory; but instead even of this regular progress, his eye would be more frequently presented with retrograde movements, and the most disheartening reverses. The changes, to which he had looked forward with delight, would be found big with new and unlooked-for evils; and the characters, on which he has reposed the most confidence, would be seen frequently deserting his favourite cause, either from the lessons of experience or the temptations of wealth and power. In this state of constant disappointment, he would be but too apt to attribute every thing to the worst motives; he would be inclined to give up the cause of improvement in despair; and judging of the whole from a part, nothing but a peculiar goodness of heart and amiableness of disposition could preserve him from that sickly and disgusting misanthropy, which is but too frequently the end of such characters.

On the contrary, a person who held the other opinion, as he would set out with more moderate expectations, would of course be less liable to disappointment. A comparison of the best with the worst states of society, and the obvious inference from analogy, that the best were capable of further improvement, would constantly present to his mind a prospect sufficiently animating to warrant his most persevering exertions. But aware of the difficulties with which the subject was surrounded, knowing how often in the attempt to attain one object some other had been lost, and that, though society had made rapid advances in some directions, it had been comparatively stationary in others, he would be constantly prepared for failures. These failures instead of creating despair, would only create knowledge; instead of checking his ardour, would give it a wiser and more successful direction; and, having founded his opinion of mankind on broad and general grounds, the disappointment of any particular views would not change this opinion; but even in declining age he would probably be found believing as firmly in the reality and general prevalence of virtue as in the existence and frequency of vice; and to the last, looking forward with a just confidence to those improvements in society, which the history of the past, in spite of all the reverses with which it is accompanied, seems clearly to warrant.

It may be true that, if ignorance is bliss, 'tis folly to be wise; but if ignorance be not bliss, as in the present instance; if all false views of society must not only impede decidedly the progress of improvement, but necessarily terminate in the most bitter disappointments to the individuals who formed them; I shall always think that the feelings and prospects of those, who make the justest estimates of our future expectations, are the most consolatory; and that the characters of this description are happier themselves, at the same time that they are beyond comparison more likely to contribute to the improvement and happiness of society. . . .

IV

DAVID RICARDO

1772–1823

The father of Ricardo traced his descent from the Jews who were exiled from Spain during the reign of Ferdinand and Isabella. Abraham Ricardo himself was a native of Holland whence he migrated to England some time between 1760 and 1770. He prospered as a broker and merchant, reared a large family, and as a man of strict integrity had the esteem of the Jewish community, whose charitable funds he administered.

David, the third child, was born in 1772. He was put to school in Amsterdam under the care of an uncle and trained for a purely commercial career. At fourteen he entered his father's business where his talent and judgment won general confidence.

But sympathy between father and son was lacking, and their relations grew more and more difficult. Patriarchal discipline at home and by proxy even in Amsterdam was irksome when it discouraged David's interest in natural science and Shakespeare, intolerable when it threatened to limit his choice in religion and marriage. Ricardo dissented from the Hebrew faith, but the final breach with his religion and his father came when he married a Quaker in 1793. Thereafter he had to make his own way. The task was not too difficult, however. A number of his father's associates on the stock exchange, impressed with his ability, were shrewd enough to give him liberal backing.

Within five years perhaps, by the time he was twenty-six, Ricardo became financially independent. But he was not content with moderate success; a combination of genius and opportunity speedily transformed him from a stockbroker into a financier. He took part in underwriting government loans and built up a fortune of some £2,000,000, which he thought sufficient to retire upon in 1816. The Napoleonic wars had been profitable to Ricardo, but they also brought sacrifices: his patriotism on one occasion extended to advising the government to borrow twelve millions instead of twenty-four. In order to devote more time to study he became a country gentleman;

land, just at that time, also seemed to be a better investment than securities.

Long before this he had resumed his early studies in natural science; to these he now added mathematics. A chance reading of Adam Smith in 1799, however, had also turned his attention to economics. The first fruit of this new interest was two pamphlets on monetary theory (1810 and 1811). These brought him the favorable notice and friendship of Malthus and James Mill. In 1815 he published a tract opposing the Corn Laws in which his characteristic doctrines concerning wages and profits were first enunciated. Having now gained a considerable reputation as an economist, he feared to endanger it by publishing the longer treatise on which he was engaged. Friends persuaded him, however, and in 1817 it appeared as the *Principles of Political Economy and Taxation*. Ricardo's hesitation seemed at first to be justified. His literary style was lame, the language involved; Ricardo himself declared that not more than twenty-five persons in England understood him and these found many of his ideas heterodox. But the work gained steadily in favor, in the end becoming a classic in its field.

According to his contemporary and chief propagandist, McCulloch, Ricardo now "determined to extend the sphere of his usefulness by entering the House of Commons." For a man with the proper credentials this was by no means difficult. The electors of a certain borough in Ireland dutifully chose Ricardo in return for a loan of £20,000 (without interest) to their proprietor and the economist took his seat for Portarlington in 1819. He proved to be an active member of Parliament "for his time." Although he voted with the opposition, his reputation for lucidity as a speaker and the prestige of his wealth insured him the respect of the entire House of Commons, and he is said to have influenced Peel's free-trade policy. At the height of his reputation he died suddenly in 1823.

Ricardo is described as a modest and generous man. He supported an almshouse and two schools in the country and contributed to almost every charitable institution in London. James Mill eulogized him, not quite accurately perhaps, as a brilliant example of the self-made man—so dear to the hearts of liberal economists.

Justly or unjustly, Ricardo came to be regarded as the chief exponent of indefeasible economic law and the leading advocate of a laissez-faire policy. As such he was the butt of much criticism when that viewpoint began to decline in favor. Yet his elaboration of the idea that labor regulates value was seized upon by socialists as one of the principal vindications of their system, while his doctrine of wages afforded them (or so they thought) a blasting argument against capitalism. In fact, a group of early reformers (William Thompson, John Gray, Thomas Hodgskin, and J. F. Bray) came to be known as "Ricardian Socialists," although the epithet seems to be on the whole misapplied. Ricardo's description of the conflict of interest between the landlords and the rest of the community is also significant. He became a country gentleman, but his sympathies remained firmly anchored in the marts of industry and trade.

REFERENCES

The collected *Works*, in one volume, edited with a sketch of Ricardo's life by J. R. McCulloch, were published in 1846. The standard edition of the *Principles*, with commentary, is by E. C. K. Gonner (1891, reprinted 1927). Gonner has also edited the *Economic Essays* (1923). The most complete biography is that of Jacob H. Hollander: *Ricardo, a Centenary Estimate* (1910). A very favorable evaluation of Ricardo's work is given in J. M. Robertson's "Ricardo" (*Contemporary Review*, 1917, Vol. CXII, pp. 500–508).

READINGS FROM

PRINCIPLES OF POLITICAL ECONOMY AND TAXATION [1]

The Problem of Political Economy.[2] The produce of the earth—all that is derived from its surface by the united application of labour, machinery, and capital, is divided among three classes of the community; namely, the proprietor of the land, the owner of the stock or capital necessary for its cultivation, and the labourers by whose industry it is cultivated.

But in different stages of society, the proportions of the whole produce of the earth which will be allotted to each of these classes, under the names of rent, profit, and wages, will be essentially different; depending mainly on the actual fertility of the soil, on the accumulation of capital and population, and on the skill, ingenuity, and instruments employed in agriculture.

To determine the laws which regulate this distribution is the principal problem in Political Economy: much as the science has been

[1] The page references are to E. C. K. Gonner's edition (1891, reprinted 1927).
[2] Preface (p. 1).

improved by the writings of Turgot, Stuart, Smith, Say, Sismondi, and others, they afford very little satisfactory information respecting the natural course of rent, profit, and wages. . . .

Labor Regulates Value.[1] *The value of a commodity, or the quantity of any other commodity for which it will exchange, depends on the relative quantity of labour which is necessary for its production, and not on the greater or less compensation which is paid for that labour.*

It has been observed by Adam Smith, that "the word Value has two different meanings, and sometimes expresses the utility of some particular object, and sometimes the power of purchasing other goods which the possession of that object conveys. The one may be called *value in use;* the other *value in exchange. . . .*" Water and air are abundantly useful; they are indeed indispensable to existence, yet, under ordinary circumstances, nothing can be obtained in exchange for them. Gold, on the contrary, though of little use compared with air or water, will exchange for a great quantity of other goods.

Utility then is not the measure of exchangeable value, although it is absolutely essential to it. If a commodity were in no way useful,—in other words, if it could in no way contribute to our gratification,—it would be destitute of exchangeable value, however scarce it might be, or whatever quantity of labour might be necessary to procure it.

Possessing utility, commodities derive their exchangeable value from two sources: from their scarcity, and from the quantity of labour required to obtain them.

There are some commodities, the value of which is determined by their scarcity alone. No labour can increase the quantity of such goods, and therefore their value cannot be lowered by an increased supply. Some rare statues and pictures, scarce books and coins, wines of a peculiar quality, which can be made only from grapes grown on a particular soil, of which there is a very limited quantity, are all of this description. Their value is wholly independent of the quantity of labour originally necessary to produce them, and varies with the varying wealth and inclinations of those who are desirous to possess them.

These commodities, however, form a very small part of the mass of commodities daily exchanged in the market. By far the greatest part of those goods which are the objects of desire, are procured by labour;

[1] Ch. i, sec. 1 (pp. 5–7).

and they may be multiplied, not in one country alone, but in many, almost without any assignable limit, if we are disposed to bestow the labour necessary to obtain them.

In speaking then of commodities, of their exchangeable value, and of the laws which regulate their relative prices, we mean always such commodities only as can be increased in quantity by the exertion of human industry, and on the production of which competition operates without restraint.

In the early stages of society, the exchangeable value of these commodities, or the rule which determines how much of one shall be given in exchange for another, depends almost exclusively on the comparative quantity of labour expended on each. . . .

That this is really the foundation of the exchangeable value of all things, excepting those which cannot be increased by human industry, is a doctrine of the utmost importance in political economy; for from no source do so many errors, and so much difference of opinion in that science proceed, as from the vague ideas which are attached to the word value.

If the quantity of labour realized in commodities, regulate their exchangeable value, every increase of the quantity of labour must augment the value of that commodity on which it is exercised, as every discrimination must lower it. . . .

Labor and Profit.[1] There can be no rise in the value of labour without a fall of profits. If the corn is to be divided between the farmer and the labourer, the larger the proportion that is given to the latter, the less will remain for the former. So if cloth or cotton goods be divided between the workman and his employer, the larger the proportion given to the former, the less remains for the latter. . . .

Rent.[2] It remains however to be considered, whether the appropriation of land, and the consequent creation of rent, will occasion any variation in the relative value of commodities, independently of the quantity of labour necessary to production. In order to understand this part of the subject, we must enquire into the nature of rent, and the laws by which its rise or fall is regulated.

Rent is that portion of the produce of the earth, which is paid to the landlord for the use of the original and indestructible powers of the soil. . . .

[1] Ch. i, sec. 4 (pp. 28–29).
[2] Ch. ii, secs. 24, 25, 27 (pp. 44, 46–48, 49–50, 51–52).

On the first settling of a country, in which there is an abundance of rich and fertile land, a very small proportion of which is required to be cultivated for the support of the actual population, or indeed can be cultivated with the capital which the population can command, there will be no rent; for no one would pay for the use of land, when there was an abundant quantity not yet appropriated, and, therefore, at the disposal of whosoever might choose to cultivate it.

On the common principles of supply and demand, no rent could be paid for such land, for the reason stated why nothing is given for the use of air and water, or for any other of the gifts of nature which exist in boundless quantity. With a given quantity of materials, and with the assistance of the pressure of the atmosphere, and the elasticity of steam, engines may perform work, and abridge human labour to a very great extent; but no charge is made for the use of these natural aids, because they are inexhaustible, and at every man's disposal. In the same manner the brewer, the distiller, the dyer, make incessant use of the air and water for the production of their commodities; but as the supply is boundless, they bear no price. If all land had the same properties, if it were unlimited in quantity, and uniform in quality, no charge could be made for its use, unless where it possessed peculiar advantages of situation. It is only, then, because land is not unlimited in quantity and uniform in quality, and because in the progress of population, land of an inferior quality, or less advantageously situated, is called into cultivation, that rent is ever paid for the use of it. When in the progress of society, land of the second degree of fertility is taken into cultivation, rent immediately commences on that of the first quality, and the amount of that rent will depend on the difference in the quality of these two portions of land.

When land of the third quality is taken into cultivation, rent immediately commences on the second, and it is regulated as before, by the difference in their productive powers. At the same time, the rent of the first quality will rise, for that must always be above the rent of the second, by the difference between the produce which they yield with a given quantity of capital and labour. With every step in the progress of population, which shall oblige a country to have recourse to land of a worse quality, to enable it to raise its supply of food, rent, on all the more fertile land, will rise.

Thus suppose land—No. 1, 2, 3—to yield, with an equal employment of capital and labour, a net produce of 100, 90, and 80 quarters of corn. In a new country, where there is an abundance of fertile land compared with the population, and where therefore it is only necessary to cultivate No. 1, the whole net produce will belong to the cultivator, and will be the profits of the stock which he advances. As soon as population had so far increased as to make it necessary to cultivate No. 2, from which ninety quarters only can be obtained after supporting the labourers, rent would commence on No. 1; for either there must be two rates of profit on agricultural capital, or ten quarters, or the value of ten quarters must be withdrawn from the produce of No. 1, for some other purpose. Whether the proprietor of the land, or any other person, cultivated No. 1, these ten quarters would equally constitute rent; for the cultivator of No. 2 would get the same result with his capital, whether he cultivated No. 1, paying ten quarters for rent, or continued to cultivate No. 2, paying no rent. In the same manner it might be shown that when No. 3 is brought into cultivation, the rent of No. 2 must be ten quarters, or the value of ten quarters, whilst the rent of No. 1 would rise to twenty quarters; for the cultivator of No. 3 would have the same profits whether he paid twenty quarters for the rent of No. 1, ten quarters for the rent of No. 2, or cultivated No. 3 free of all rent. . . .

The most fertile, and most favourably situated, land will be first cultivated, and the exchangeable value of its produce will be adjusted in the same manner as the exchangeable value of all other commodities, by the total quantity of labour necessary in various forms from first to last, to produce it, and bring it to market. When land of an inferior quality is taken into cultivation, the exchangeable value of raw produce will rise, because more labour is required to produce it.

The exchangeable value of all commodities, whether they be manufactured, or the produce of the mines, or the produce of the land, is always regulated, not by the less quantity of labour that will suffice for their production under circumstances highly favourable, and exclusively enjoyed by those who have peculiar facilities of production; but by the greater quantity of labour necessarily bestowed on their production by those who have no such facilities; by those who continue to produce them under the most unfavourable circumstances; meaning—by the most unfavourable circumstances, the most unfavourable under which the quantity of produce required, renders it necessary to carry on the production. . . .

It is true, that on the best land, the same produce would still be obtained with the same labour as before, but its value would be enhanced in consequence of the diminished returns obtained by those who employed fresh labour and stock on the less fertile land. Notwithstanding, then, that the advantages of fertile over inferior lands are in no case lost, but only transferred from the cultivator, or consumer, to the landlord, yet, since more labour is required on the inferior lands, and since it is from such land that we are enabled to furnish ourselves with the additional supply of raw produce, the comparative value of that produce will continue permanently above its former level, and make it exchange for more hats, cloth, shoes, etc., etc., in the production of which no such additional quantity of labour is required.

The reason then, why raw produce rises in comparative value, is because more labour is employed in the production of the last portion obtained, and not because a rent is paid to the landlord. The value of corn is regulated by the quantity of labour bestowed on its production on that quality of land, or with that portion of capital, which pays no rent. Corn is not high because a rent is paid, but a rent is paid because corn is high; and it has been justly observed, that no reduction would take place in the price of corn, although landlords should forego the whole of their rent. Such a measure would only enable some farmers to live like gentlemen, but would not diminish the quantity of labour necessary to raise raw produce on the least productive land in cultivation. . . .

Natural and Market Price.[1] In making labour the foundation of the value of commodities, and the comparative quantity of labour which is necessary to their production, the rule which determines the respective quantities of goods which shall be given in exchange for each other, we must not be supposed to deny the accidental and temporary deviations of the actual or market price of commodities from this, their primary and natural price.

In the ordinary course of events, there is no commodity which continues for any length of time to be supplied precisely in that degree of abundance, which the wants and wishes of mankind require, and therefore there is none which is not subject to accidental and temporary variations of price.

It is only in consequence of such variations, that capital is apportioned precisely, in the requisite abundance and no more, to the production of the different commodities which happen to be in demand. With the rise or fall of price, profits are elevated above, or depressed

[1] Ch. iv, sec. 33 (p. 65).

below their general level, and capital is either encouraged to enter into, or is warned to depart from the particular employment in which the variation has taken place. . . .

The Natural Rate of Wages.[1] Labour, like all other things which are purchased and sold, and which may be increased or diminished in quantity, has its natural and its market price. The natural price of labour is that price which is necessary to enable the labourers, one with another, to subsist and to perpetuate their race. without either increase or diminution.

The power of the labourer to support himself, and the family which may be necessary to keep up the number of labourers, does not depend on the quantity of money which he may receive for wages, but on the quantity of food, necessaries, and conveniences become essential to him from habit, which that money will purchase. The natural price of labour, therefore, depends on the price of the food, necessaries, and conveniences required for the support of the labourer and his family. With a rise in the price of food and necessaries, the natural price of labour will rise; with the fall in their price, the natural price of labour will fall.

With the progress of society the natural price of labour has always a tendency to rise, because one of the principal commodities by which its natural price is regulated, has a tendency to become dearer, from the greater difficulty of producing it. As, however, the improvements in agriculture, the discovery of new markets, whence provisions may be imported, may for a time counteract the tendency to a rise in the price of necessaries, and may even occasion their natural price to fall, so will the same causes produce the correspondent effects on the natural price of labour. . . .

The market price of labour is the price which is really paid for it, from the natural operation of the proportion of the supply to the demand; labour is dear when it is scarce, and cheap when it is plentiful. However much the market price of labour may deviate from its natural price, it has, like commodities, a tendency to conform to it.

It is when the market price of labour exceeds its natural price, that the condition of the labourer is flourishing and happy, that he has it in his power to command a greater proportion of the necessaries and enjoyments of life, and therefore to rear a healthy and numerous family.

[1] Ch. v, secs. 35, 36, 37, 38, 40, 41 (pp. 70–71, 74, 77, 82, 84).

When, however, by the encouragement which high wages give to the increase of population, the number of labourers is increased, wages again fall to their natural price, and indeed from a re-action sometimes fall below it.

When the market price of labour is below its natural price, the condition of the labourers is most wretched: then poverty deprives them of those comforts which custom renders absolute necessaries. It is only after their privations have reduced their number, or the demand for labour has increased, that the market price of labour will rise to its natural price, and that the labourer will have the moderate comforts which the natural rate of wages will afford.

Notwithstanding the tendency of wages to conform to their natural rate, their market rate may, in an improving society, for an indefinite period, be constantly above it; for no sooner may the impulse, which an increased capital gives to a new demand for labour, be obeyed, than another increase of capital may produce the same effect; and thus, if the increase of capital be gradual and constant, the demand for labour may give a continued stimulus to an increase of people. . . .

It is not to be understood that the natural price of labour, estimated even in food and necessaries, is absolutely fixed and constant. It varies at different times in the same country, and very materially differs in different countries.[1] It essentially depends on the habits and customs of the people. An English labourer would consider his wages under their natural rate, and too scanty to support a family, if they enabled him to purchase no other food than potatoes, and to live in no better habitation than a mud cabin; yet these moderate demands of nature are often deemed sufficient in countries where "man's life is cheap," and his wants easily satisfied. Many of the conveniences now enjoyed in an English cottage, would have been thought luxuries at an earlier period of our history. . . .

The friends of humanity cannot but wish that in all countries the labouring classes should have a taste for comforts and enjoyments, and that they should be stimulated by all legal means in their exertions to procure them. There cannot be a better security against a

[1] "The shelter and the clothing which are indispensable in one country may be no way necessary in another; and a labourer in Hindostan may continue to work with perfect vigour, though receiving, as his natural wages, only such a supply of covering as would be insufficient to preserve a labourer in Russia from perishing. Even in countries situated in the same climate, different habits of living will often occasion variations in the natural price of labour, as considerable as those which are produced by natural causes."—P. 68, "An Essay on the External Corn Trade," by R. Torrens, Esq. [Author's note.]

superabundant population. In those countries, where the labouring classes have the fewest wants, and are contented with the cheapest food, the people are exposed to the greatest vicissitudes and miseries. They have no place of refuge from calamity; they cannot seek safety in a lower station; they are already so low, that they can fall no lower. On any deficiency of the chief article of their subsistence, there are few substitutes of which they can avail themselves, and dearth to them is attended with almost all the evils of famine. . . .

These then are the laws by which wages are regulated, and by which the happiness of far the greatest part of every community is governed. Like all other contracts, wages should be left to the fair and free competition of the market, and should never be controlled by the interference of the legislature. . . .

It is a truth which admits not a doubt, that the comforts and well-being of the poor cannot be permanently secured without some regard on their part, or some effort on the part of the legislature, to regulate the increase of their numbers, and to render less frequent among them early and improvident marriages. The operation of the system of poor laws has been directly contrary to this. They have rendered restraint superfluous, and have invited imprudence, by offering it a portion of the wages of prudence and industry. . . .

Opposition of Interest between the Landlord and the Consumer and Manufacturer.[1] Corn can be permanently at an advanced price, only because additional labour is necessary to produce it; because its cost of production is increased. The same cause invariably raises rent; it is therefore for the interest of the landlord that the cost attending the production of corn should be increased. This, however, is not the interest of the consumer; to him it is desirable that corn should be low relatively to money and commodities, for it is always with commodities or money that corn is purchased. Neither is it the interest of the manufacturer that corn should be at a high price, for the high price of corn will occasion high wages, but will not raise the price of his commodity. Not only, then, must more of his commodity, or, which comes to the same thing, the value of more of his commodity, be given in exchange for the corn which he himself consumes, but more must be given, or the value of more, for wages to his workmen, for which he will receive no remuneration. All classes, therefore, except the landlords, will be injured by the increase in the price of corn.

[1] Ch. xxiv, sec. 117 (pp. 321–322).

The dealings between the landlord and the public are not like dealings in trade, whereby both the seller and buyer may equally be said to gain, but the loss is wholly on one side, and the gain wholly on the other; and if corn could by importation be procured cheaper, the loss in consequence of not importing is far greater on one side, than the gain is on the other. . . .

V

THOMAS PAINE

1737–1809

Thomas Paine was by birth as well as sympathy a man of the people. The only thing his ancestors bequeathed him was, his enemies might have said, a strangely appropriate name—"Paine" is derived from *païen*, or pagan. *Païen*, however, also means "peasant" and in this sense is less inaccurate, for Paine was reared in a provincial town where his father practiced farming in a small way. The elder Paine's chief business was stay- or corset-making. In religion he was a Quaker.

Thomas was born in Thetford, England, in 1737. The town at this time was a rotten borough controlled by the Duke of Grafton, and it is believed that Thetford's institutions served as a horrible example to Paine when he came to deal with the abuses of charters and corporations in *The Rights of Man.* More intimate influences also left their mark. The somber aspects of Quakerism oppressed him, and as a child he persisted in believing that "God was too good" to sacrifice His Son even to redeem mankind. Nevertheless the Quaker's bent toward democracy and hatred of slavery colored Paine's own views later on.

Thomas's parents could afford him only a grammar-school education. He showed great aptitude for mathematics and a turn for science and poetry, but was removed from school at thirteen to learn the business of stay-making. After an apprenticeship of five years he ran away to sea and joined a privateer, the war with France having just broken out (1756). The adventure was brief; he soon returned to England.

The next eighteen years of Paine's life, until his departure for America, were checkered and obscure. He lived in half a dozen towns of southern England, returning once to Thetford, with short intervals in London. His first wife, whom he married in 1759, died within a year; a second marriage lasted three years, the parties separating in 1774. Paine at first followed the trade of stay-making but this proved unremunerative and he obtained employment as a revenue officer or exciseman. After three years he was discharged for certain irregularities in his records. The offense, however, was a venial one; the authorities accepted his humble apology and after a suitable period he was again employed to gauge beer casks and watch for smugglers. In the interim he had taught English at starvation wages in a London academy.

These years were not spent merely in marrying and getting a rather precarious living. At the very beginning Paine had attended philosophic lectures in London. Later on an argumentative disposition and tenacious opinions kept his wits sharp and educated him for future controversies. From time to time he gathered an audience and preached religion "as an independent, or Methodist." Once, oddly enough, he sought ordination as a preacher in the Church of England, but was rejected.

When the excisemen decided to ask Parliament for higher wages, Paine was chosen to present their petition. While in London on this mission he met and seems to have favorably impressed Benjamin Franklin. The next year (1774) Paine was discharged from the government service, ostensibly for having left his post to escape troublesome creditors. Penniless, he returned to London apparently a failure. As a last resort he decided to try his fortune in America.

Paine arrived in Philadelphia in 1774 and on Franklin's recommendation obtained a position on the staff of the *Pennsylvania Magazine.* The event proved that Paine had at last found his true vocation. Within a year his fame as a pamphleteer had spread throughout the colonies. His first object of attack was the slavery system, but as the relations between England and her colonies approached a crisis he took up the cause of his adopted country. *Common Sense*, published anonymously in 1775, definitely established Paine as a propagandist of the first order. The argument for independence was invested with a brilliance that struck the entire country. Perhaps 500,000 copies of the pamphlet were ultimately sold and Paine contributed the entire proceeds (a fortune in itself) to the American colonies.

When war finally broke out—an event for which Paine was in no small degree responsible—he immediately joined the American forces. His military exploits were insignificant, however, compared with the effect of such writings as *The Crisis*, which enormously strengthened the morale of both soldiers and civilians. He gained the friendship and esteem of Washington, Jefferson, Monroe, and other leaders of the Revolution.

Before the end of the war Paine held several official positions, culminating in the important secretaryship of the Foreign Affairs Committee. This office he was compelled to resign as a result of disagreement with Congress. But Paine's fortunes lagged far behind his reputation. On several occasions he applied to influential friends for more adequate recognition of his public services. Ultimately the state of New York granted him a farm at New Rochelle, Pennsylvania added £500 in cash, and Congress voted him $3,000.

The American Revolution ended, Paine's career as an international prophet of liberty had no more than fairly begun. At odd moments his active mind had evolved a number of mechanical inventions ranging from a smokeless candle to an iron arch-bridge. It was during a visit to England undertaken in 1787 to promote his bridge that he plunged once more into the cauldron of revolutionary politics. His arrival in England was greeted with enthusiasm. In fifteen years affairs had changed—and were to change still further in a much shorter time. Colonial sympathizers (including Edmund Burke) lionized him; the prospects of the bridge advanced. Then, in 1789–90, came the first stages of revolution in France and with them, Burke's denunciation of the innovators: *Reflections on the Revolution in France.* At a bound the writer's fame became European. His pamphlet was a masterpiece; its effect could be neutralized only by a master.

Meanwhile Paine had visited France several times on the business of his bridge and had watched the Revolution mature. His reaction was exactly the opposite of Burke's. When the *Reflections* appeared therefore, Paine rapidly composed his answer, and the first part of *The Rights of Man* was published early in 1791. The best praise of the pamphlet is to say that it was entirely worthy of the occasion which produced it. The sale was enormous and though Paine was almost bankrupt at the time he donated the entire proceeds to the Society for Constitutional Information, a group sympathetic to France. But the forces of order and patriotism were slowly gathering. He had outraged most Englishmen by constant agitation for reform of their constitution, and when the second part of *The Rights of Man* was issued in 1792 the government started a prosecution for high treason.

Before the trial occurred Paine was in France. His popularity there was immense: every cottage displayed his portrait and in 1792 three *départements* chose him to represent them in the Constitutional Convention. But except during the American Revolution Paine seemed fated to suffer with minorities. It was so in England, now it happened in France. From motives of humanity and in the belief that it would provoke foreign invasion, he resisted the execution of Louis XVI. Whether this was the real reason for Paine's downfall is uncertain: at any rate he was eventually denounced by Robespierre and imprisoned. An order was even issued for his execution, but for some obscure reason it was not carried out.

On his release in 1794 (after Robespierre's overthrow) Paine appeared once more in the Convention to protest (ineffectually) against the reactionary measure which disfranchised half the French electorate. After the Convention dissolved he continued to reside for some years in France, writing pamphlets on democracy, agrarian reform, and other subjects. His hopes for the English had fallen so low that he advocated an invasion of England to help the masses establish liberal government. Napoleon Bonaparte, just returned from his first Italian campaign, heard of the proposal. On a visit to Paine he discussed and adopted it, remarking that he slept with a copy of *The Rights of Man* under his pillow—a practice which, judging by later events, must have had small effect.

In 1802 Paine returned to America. He was received with mingled praise and obloquy. The latter sentiment rose from a pamphlet he had written while anticipating imprisonment and execution in France. *The Age of Reason* contained his religious views; it was a rationalistic attack on the less comprehensible portions of Christian tradition, which he ridiculed mercilessly. Critics disregarded the fact that he also proclaimed his belief in God and accepted much of Christian ethics. And these latter opinions were utterly sincere. In fact Paine had helped to found a religious sect in France—"Theophilanthropy" —which obtained a considerable following and only disappeared with the reëstablishment of Catholicism.

The religious issue clouded Paine's last years. His friends were numerous, but the professional Christians were more so. Even pamphlets failed him: eight "Letters to the Citizens of the United States" did not shake their belief that they knew an atheist when they saw one. When Paine's health began to fail and death seemed near, strange happenings were reported: he had recanted—his friends were keeping him stupefied with liquor so that he would not recant. The credulous were determined to make Paine's death as eventful as his life. But his adventures did not cease even when, in 1809, he was underground at last: ten years later William Cobbett, once his bitter enemy, reverently dug up the bones and took them back to England.

Paine is perhaps the only philosophic writer of his time whose works still remain in the broadest sense popular. This is due, no doubt, as much to the vigor and lucidity of his style as to the cogency of his argument. He appealed to common men in language they could understand. As a result he is credited with having inspired the first really working-class movement in England for democratic reform. He insisted, above all, on political liberty, but he also had very positive ideas as to the need and manner of social change. In his writings, laissez-faire sometimes appears to conflict with a decided bias in favor of state socialism. It has been suggested that in supporting economic liberalism he was, in some cases at least, trying to protect the property interests of workingmen against the encroachments of the new industrial capitalism. Paine's religious views alienated that large section of the working class which clung to orthodox beliefs. His destructive and negative opinions created a far greater impression than the positive side of his doctrines, and this fact still further limited his influence. Many of Paine's contemporaries, however, believed that the abuses of the time were numerous and glaring enough to stand a good deal of plain, unqualified destruction.

REFERENCES

Paine's continuing popularity is attested by the multitude of cheap reprints of his works that constantly appear. Inclusive editions of his writings have been published by M. D. Conway (4 vols., 1894–96) and by the Thomas Paine National Historical Society (10 vols., 1925).

Recent estimates of his work are given in Kingsley Martin's *Thomas Paine* (1925, Fabian Tract No. 217) and in Norman Sykes's chapter on Paine in *Social and Political Ideas of the Revolutionary Era* (ed. F. J. C. Hearnshaw, 1931).

The fullest biography is by M. D. Conway (1892). Of several recent *Lives* M. A. Best's (1927) is the most thorough.

READINGS FROM

THE RIGHTS OF MAN

The Source of Good Government.[1] Every history of the creation, and every traditionary account, whether from the lettered or unlettered world, however they may vary in their opinion or belief of certain particulars, all agree in establishing one point, the *unity*

[1] Part I (pp. 42–49, 130, 134–135). Page references are to the Everyman edition.

of man; by which I mean that men are all of *one degree,* and consequently that all men are born equal, and with equal natural rights, in the same manner as if posterity had been continued by *creation* instead of *generation,* the latter being only the mode by which the former is carried forward; and consequently every child born into the world must be considered as deriving its existence from God. The world is as new to him as it was to the first man that existed, and his natural right in it is of the same kind.

The Mosaic account of the creation, whether taken as divine authority or merely historical, is fully up to this point, *the unity or equality of man.* The expressions admit of no controversy. "And God said, Let us make man in our own image. In the image of God created he him; male and female created he them." The distinction of sexes is pointed out, but no other distinction is even implied. If this be not divine authority it is at least historical authority, and shows that the equality of man, so far from being a modern doctrine, is the oldest upon record.

It is also to be observed that all the religions known in the world are founded, so far as they relate to man, on the *unity of man,* as being all of one degree. Whether in heaven or in hell, or in whatever state man may be supposed to exist hereafter, the good and the bad are the only distinctions. Nay, even the laws of Governments are obliged to slide into this principle, by making degrees to consist in crimes and not in persons.

It is one of the greatest of all truths, and of the highest advantage to cultivate. By considering man in this light, and by instructing him to consider himself in this light, it places him in a close connection with all his duties, whether to his Creator or to the creation, of which he is a part; and it is only when he forgets his origin, or, to use a more fashionable phrase, his *birth and family,* that he becomes dissolute. It is not among the least of the evils of the present existing Governments in all parts of Europe that man, considered as man, is thrown back to a vast distance from his Maker, and the artificial chasm filled up by a succession of barriers, or sort of turnpike gates, through which he has to pass. I will quote Mr. Burke's catalogue of barriers that he has set up between Man and his Maker. Putting himself in the character of a herald, he says: *We fear God—we look with* AWE *to kings—with affection to Parliaments—with duty to magistrates—with reverence to priests, and with respect to nobility.* Mr. Burke has forgotton to put in "*chivalry.*" He has also forgotten to put in Peter.

The duty of man is not a wilderness of turnpike gates through which he is to pass by tickets from one to the other. It is plain and simple, and consists but of two points. His duty to God, which every man must feel; and with respect to his neighbour, to do as he would be done by. If those to whom power is delegated do well they will be respected; if not, they will be despised; and with regard to those to whom no power is delegated, but who assume it, the rational world can know nothing of them.

Hitherto we have spoken only (and that but in part) of the natural rights of man. We have now to consider the civil rights of man, and to show how the one originates from the other. Man did not enter into society to become *worse* than he was before, not to have fewer rights than he had before, but to have those rights better secured. His natural rights are the foundation of all his civil rights. But in order to pursue this distinction with more precision, it will be necessary to mark the different qualities of natural and civil rights.

A few words will explain this. Natural rights are those which appertain to man in right of his existence. Of this kind are all the intellectual rights, or rights of the mind, and also all those rights of acting as an individual for his own comfort and happiness, which are not injurious to the natural rights of others. Civil rights are those which appertain to man in right of his being a member of society. Every civil right has for its foundation some natural right pre-existing in the individual, but to the enjoyment of which his individual power is not, in all cases, sufficiently competent. Of this kind are all those which relate to security and protection.

From this short view it will be easy to distinguish between that class of natural rights which man retains after entering into society and those which he throws into the common stock as a member of society.

The natural rights which he retains are all those in which the *power* to execute it is as perfect in the individual as the right itself. Among this class, as is before mentioned, are all the intellectual rights, or rights of the mind; consequently religion is one of those rights. The natural rights which are not retained, are all those in which, though the right is perfect in the individual, the power to execute them is defective. They answer not his purpose. A man, by natural right, has a right to judge in his own cause; and so far as the right of the mind is concerned, he never surrenders it. But what availeth it him to judge, if he has not power to redress? He therefore deposits this right in the common stock of society, and takes the arm of society, of which he is a part, in preference and in addition to his own. Society *grants* him nothing. Every man is a proprietor in society, and draws on the capital as a matter of right.

From these premisses two or three certain conclusions will follow:

First, *That every civil right grows out of a natural right; or, in other words, is a natural right exchanged.*

Secondly, *That civil power properly considered as such is made up of the aggregate of that class of the natural rights of man, which becomes defective in the individual in point of power, and answers not his purpose, but when collected to a focus becomes competent to the purpose of every one.*

Thirdly, *That the power produced from the aggregate of natural rights, imperfect in power in the individual, cannot be applied to invade the natural rights which are retained in the individual, and in which the power to execute is as perfect as the right itself.*

We have now, in a few words, traced man from a natural individual to a member of society, and shown, or endeavoured to show, the quality of the natural rights retained, and of those which are exchanged for civil rights. Let us now apply these principles to Governments.

In casting our eyes over the world, it is extremely easy to distinguish the Governments which have arisen out of society, or out of the social compact, from those which have not; but to place this in a clearer light than what a single glance may afford, it will be proper to take a review of the several sources from which Governments have arisen and on which they have been founded.

They may be all comprehended under three heads—

First, *Superstition.*

Secondly, *Power.*

Thirdly, *The common interest of society and the common rights of man.*

The first was a Government of Priestcraft, the second of Conquerors, and the third of Reason.

When a set of artful men pretended, through the medium of oracles, to hold intercourse with the Deity, as familiarly as they now march up the back-stairs in European Courts, the world was completely under the government of superstition. The oracles were consulted, and whatever they were made to say became the law; and this sort of Government lasted as long as this sort of superstition lasted.

After these a race of conquerors arose, whose Government, like that of William the Conqueror, was founded in power, and the sword assumed the name of a sceptre. Governments thus established last as long as the power to support them lasts; but that they might avail themselves of every engine in their favour, they united fraud to force, and set up an idol which they called *Divine Right*, and which, in imitation of the Pope, who affects to be spiritual and temporal, and in contradiction to the Founder of the Christian religion, twisted itself afterwards into an idol of another shape, called *Church and State*. The key of St. Peter and the key of the Treasury became quartered on one another, and the wondering cheated multitude worshipped the invention.

When I contemplate the natural dignity of man, when I feel (for Nature has not been kind enough to me to blunt my feelings) for the honour and happiness of its character, I become irritated at the attempt to govern mankind by force and fraud, as if they were all knaves and fools, and can scarcely avoid disgust at those who are thus imposed upon.

We have now to review the governments which arise out of society, in contradistinction to those which arose out of superstition and conquest.

It has been thought a considerable advance towards establishing the principles of Freedom to say that Government is a compact between those who govern and those who are governed; but this cannot be true, because it is putting the effect before the cause; for as man must have existed before Governments existed, there necessarily was a time when Governments did not exist, and consequently there could originally exist no governors to form such a compact with. The fact therefore must be that the *individuals themselves*, each in his own personal and sovereign right, *entered into a compact with each other* to produce a Government: and this is the only mode in which Governments have a right to arise, and the only principle on which they have a right to exist.

To possess ourselves of a clear idea of what Government is, or ought to be, we must trace it to its origin. In doing this we shall easily discover that Governments must have arisen either *out* of the people or *over* the people. Mr. Burke has made no distinction. He investigates nothing to its source, and therefore he confounds everything; but he has signified his intention of undertaking, at some future opportunity, a comparison between the Constitutions of England and France. As he thus renders it a subject of controversy by throwing the gauntlet, I take him up on his own ground. It is in high challenges that high truths have the right of appearing; and I accept it with the more readiness because it affords me, at the same time, an opportunity of pursuing the subject with respect to Governments arising out of society.

But it will be first necessary to define what is meant by a *Constitution*. It is not sufficient that we adopt the word; we must fix also a standard signification to it.

A Constitution is not a thing in name only, but in fact. It has not an ideal, but a real existence; and wherever it cannot be produced in a visible form, there is none. A Constitution is a thing *antecedent* to a Government, and a Government is only the creature of a Constitution. The Constitution of a country is not the act of its Government, but of the people constituting a Government. It is the body of elements, to which you can refer, and quote article by article; and which contains the principles on which the Government shall be established, the manner in which it shall be organised, the powers it shall have, the mode of elections, the duration of Parliaments, or by what other name such bodies may be called; the powers which the executive part of the Government shall have; and in fine, everything that relates to the complete organisation of a civil Government, and the principles on which it shall act, and by which it shall be bound. A Constitution, therefore, is to a Government what the laws made afterwards by that Government are to a Court of Judicature. The Court of Judicature does not make the laws, neither can it alter them; it only acts in conformity to the laws made: and the Government is in like manner governed by the Constitution.

Can, then, Mr. Burke produce the English Constitution? If he cannot, we may fairly conclude that though it has been so much talked about, no such thing as a Constitution exists, or ever did exist, and consequently that the people have yet a Constitution to form.

Mr. Burke will not, I presume, deny the position I have already advanced—namely, that Governments arise either *out* of the people or *over* the people. The English Government is one of those which arose out of a conquest, and not out of society, and consequently it arose over the people; and though it has been much modified from the opportunity of circumstances since the time of William the Conqueror, the country has never yet regenerated itself, and is therefore without a Constitution. . . .

Reason and Ignorance, the opposite to each other, influence the great bulk of mankind. If either of these can be rendered sufficiently extensive in a country, the machinery of Government goes easily on. Reason obeys itself; and Ignorance submits to whatever is dictated to it.

The two modes of Government which prevail in the world, are—

First, Government by election and representation

Secondly, Government by hereditary succession.

The former is generally known by the name of Republic; the latter by that of Monarchy and Aristocracy.

Those two distinct and opposite forms erect themselves on the two distinct and opposite bases of Reason and Ignorance.

As the exercise of Government requires talents and abilities, and as talents and abilities cannot have hereditary descent, it is evident that hereditary succession requires a belief from man to which his reason cannot subscribe, and which can only be established upon his ignorance; and the more ignorant any country is, the better it is fitted for this species of Government.

On the contrary, Government, in a well-constituted Republic, requires no belief from man beyond what his reason can give.

He sees the *rationale* of the whole system, its origin and its operation; and as it is best supported when best understood, the human faculties act with boldness, and acquire under this form of Government a gigantic manliness. . . .

When men think of what Government is, they must necessarily suppose it to possess a knowledge of all the objects and matters upon which its authority is to be exercised. In this view of Government, the Republican system, as established by America and France, operates to embrace the whole of a Nation; and the knowledge necessary to the interest of all the parts, is to be found in the centre, which the parts by representation form; but the old Governments are on a construction that excludes knowledge as well as happiness; Government by monks, who know nothing of the world beyond the walls of a convent, is as inconsistent as Government by Kings.

What we formerly called Revolutions, were little more than a change of persons, or an alteration of local circumstances. They rose and fell like things of course, and had nothing in their existence or their fate that could influence beyond the spot that produced them. But what we now see in the world, from the Revolutions of America and France, are a renovation of the natural order of things, a system of principles as universal as truth and the existence of man, and combining moral with political happiness and national prosperity.

"I. *Men are born, and always continue, free and equal in respect of their rights. Civil distinctions, therefore, can be founded only on public utility.*

II. *The end of all political associations is the preservation of the natural and imprescriptible rights of man; and these rights are liberty, property, security, and resistance of oppression.*

III. *The Nation is essentially the source of all sovereignty; nor can* ANY INDIVIDUAL, *or* ANY BODY OF MEN, *be entitled to any authority which is not expressly derived from it. . . .*" [1]

The General Sphere of Government.[2] Government is no farther necessary than to supply the few cases to which society and civilisation are not conveniently competent; and instances are not wanting to show, that everything which Government can usefully add thereto, has been performed by the common consent of society, without Government. . . .

Formal Government makes but a small part of civilised life; and when even the best that human wisdom can devise is established, it is a thing more in name and idea than in fact. It is to the great and fundamental principles of society and civilisation—to the common usage universally consented to, and mutually and reciprocally maintained—to the unceasing circulation of interest, which, passing through its million channels, invigorates the whole mass of civilised man—it is to these things, infinitely more than to anything which even the best instituted Government can perform, that the safety and prosperity of the individual and of the whole depends.

The more perfect civilisation is, the less occasion has it for Government, because the more it does regulate its own affairs, and govern itself; but so contrary is the practice of old Governments to the reason of the case, that the expences of them increase in the proportion they ought to diminish. It is but few general laws that civilised life requires, and those of such common usefulness, that whether they are enforced by the forms of government or not, the effect will be nearly the same. If we consider what the principles are that first condense men into society, and what the motives that regulate their mutual intercourse afterwards, we shall find, by the time we arrive at what is called Government, that nearly the whole of the business is performed by the natural operation of the parts upon each other.

Man, with respect to all those matters, is more a creature of consistency than he is aware, or than Governments would wish him to believe. All the great laws of society are laws of nature. Those of

[1] These are the first three articles of the "Declaration of the Rights of Man and of Citizens" enacted by the French National Assembly in 1789. (Editor.)

[2] Part II, chs. i, iv (pp. 158–160, 198).

trade and commerce, whether with respect to the intercourse of individuals or of nations, are laws of mutual and reciprocal interests. They are followed and obeyed, because it is the interest of the parties so to do, and not on account of any formal laws their Governments may impose or interpose. . . .

Government is nothing more than a national association; and the object of this association is the good of all, as well individually as collectively. Every man wishes to pursue his occupation, and to enjoy the fruits of his labours and the produce of his property in peace and safety, and with the least possible expence. When these things are accomplished, all the objects for which Government ought to be established are answered. . . .

The Particular Objects of Government—with Special Reference to Great Britain.[1] Having in all the preceding parts of this work endeavoured to establish a system of principles as a basis on which Governments ought to be erected, I shall proceed in this to the ways and means of rendering them into practice. But in order to introduce this part of the subject with more propriety and stronger effect, some preliminary observations, deducible from, or connected with those principles, are necessary.

Whatever the form or Constitution of Government may be, it ought to have no other object than the *general* happiness. When instead of this it operates to create and increase wretchedness, in any of the parts of society, it is on a wrong system and reformation is necessary. . . .

If commerce were permitted to act to the universal extent it is capable, it would extirpate the system of war, and produce a Revolution in the uncivilized state of Governments. The invention of commerce has arisen since those Governments began, and it is the greatest approach towards universal civilization that has yet been made by any means not immediately flowing from moral principles. . . .

No question has arisen within the records of history that pressed with the importance of the present. It is not whether this or that party shall be in or not, or Whig or Tory, or high or low shall prevail; but whether man shall inherit his rights, and universal civilization take place? Whether the fruits of his labours shall be enjoyed by himself or consumed by the profligacy of Governments? Whether robbery shall be banished from Courts, and wretchedness from countries?

[1] Part II, ch. v (pp. 212, 215, 221–222, 235–236, 238–239, 242, 245–256, 258–260, 262–263, 265–266, 274).

When, in countries that are called civilized, we see age going to the workhouse and youth to the gallows, something must be wrong in the system of Government. It would seem, by the exterior appearances of such countries, that all was happiness; but there lies hidden from the eye of common observation, a mass of wretchedness that has scarcely any other chance, than to expire in poverty or infamy. Its entrance into life is marked with the presage of its fate; and until this is remedied, it is in vain to punish.

Civil Government does not consist in executions; but in making that provision for the instruction of youth and the support of age, as to exclude, as much as possible, profligacy from the one and despair from the other. Instead of this, the resources of a country are lavished upon kings, upon Courts, upon hirelings, imposters and prostitutes; and even the poor themselves, with all their wants upon them, are compelled to support the fraud that oppresses them.

Why is it that scarcely any are executed but the poor? The fact is a proof, among other things, of a wretchedness in their condition. Bred up without morals, and cast upon the world without a prospect, they are the exposed sacrifice of vice and legal barbarity. The millions that are superfluously wasted upon Governments are more than sufficient to reform those evils, and to benefit the condition of every man in a Nation, not included within the purlieus of a Court. . . .

Before I proceed to the means of rendering Governments more conducive to the general happiness of mankind than they are at present, it will not be improper to take a review of the progress of taxation in England. . . . The people of England of the present day, have a traditionary and historical idea of the bravery of their ancestors; but whatever their virtues or their vices might have been, they certainly were a people who would not be imposed upon, and who kept Government in awe as to taxation, if not as to principle. Though they were not able to expel the monarchical usurpation, they restricted it to a republican economy of taxes. . . .

[During the four hundred years after the Norman Conquest national taxation sank from £400,000 to £100,000. In the last three hundred years it has risen to £17,000,000.] The difference between the first four hundred years and the last three is so astonishing, as to warrant an opinion that the national character of the English has changed. It would have been impossible to have dragooned the former English into the excess of taxation that now exists; and when it is considered that the pay of the army, the navy, and of all the revenue officers, is the same now as it was above a hundred years ago, when the taxes were not above a tenth part of what they are at present, it appears impossible to account for the enormous expenditure on any other ground than extravagance, corruption and intrigue. . . .

Since the year 1788 upwards of one million of new taxes have been laid on, besides the produce from the lotteries, and as the taxes have in general been more productive since than before, the amount may be taken in round numbers at £17,000,000. . . .

This sum of seventeen millions is applied to two different purposes, the one to pay the interest of the national debt, the other to the current expences of each other. About nine millions are appropriated to the former, and the remainder, being nearly eight millions, to the latter. As to the million said to be applied to the reduction of the debt, it is so much like paying with one hand and taking out with the other as not to merit much notice. . . .

All circumstances, . . . taken together, arising from the French Revolution, from the approaching harmony and reciprocal interest of the two nations, the abolition of our Court intrigue on both sides, and the progress of knowledge in the science of Government, the annual expenditure might be put back to one million and a half, viz.:—

Navy	£500,000
Army	500,000
Expences of government . . .	500,000
	£1,500,000 . . .

Taking, therefore, one million and a half as a sufficient peace establishment for all the honest purposes of Government, which is three hundred thousand pounds more than the peace establishment in the profligate and prodigal time of Charles the Second (notwithstanding, as has been already observed, the pay and salaries of the army, navy, and revenue officers continue the same as at that period), there will remain a surplus of upwards of six millions out of the present current expences. The question then will be, how to dispose of this surplus? . . .

In the first place, . . . the poor-rates are a direct tax which every housekeeper feels, and who knows also, to a farthing, the sum which he pays. . . . The first step, therefore, of practical relief, would be to abolish the poor-rates entirely and in lieu thereof, to make a remission of taxes to the poor of double the amount of the present poor-rates, viz., four millions annually, out of the surplus taxes. By this measure, the poor will be benefited two millions, and the housekeepers two millions. . . .

It will then remain to be considered, which is the most effectual mode of distributing this remission of four millions.

It is easily seen, that the poor are generally composed of large families of children, and old people past their labour. If these two classes are provided for, the remedy will so far reach to the full extent of the case, that what remains will be incidental, and in a great measure, fall within the compass of benefit clubs, which, though of humble invention, merit to be ranked among the best of modern institutions. . . .

Allowing five children (under fourteen years) to every two families,[1]

The number of children would be . .	630,000
The number of parents, were they all living, would be	504,000

It is certain, that if the children are provided for, the parents are relieved of consequence, because it is from the expence of bringing up children that their poverty arises.

Having thus ascertained the greatest number that can be supposed to need support on account of young families, I proceed to the mode of relief or distribution, which is,

To pay as a remission of taxes to every poor family, out of the surplus taxes, and in room of poor-rates, four pounds a year for every child under fourteen years of age; enjoining the parents of such children to send them to school, to learn reading, writing, and common arithmetic; the ministers of every parish, of every denomination to certify jointly to an office, for that purpose, that this duty is performed. . . .

By adopting this method, not only the poverty of the parents will be relieved, but ignorance will be banished from the rising generation, and the number of poor will hereafter become less, because their abilities, by the aid of education, will be greater. Many a youth, with good natural genius, who is apprenticed to a mechanical trade, such as a carpenter, joiner, millwright, shipwright, blacksmith, etc., is prevented getting forward the whole of his life from the want of a little common education when a boy.

[1] The calculations by which Paine arrives at his figures have in this and most subsequent cases been omitted. (Editor.)

I now proceed to the case of the aged.

I divide age into two classes. First, the approach of age, beginning at fifty. Secondly, old age commencing at sixty.

At fifty, though the mental faculties of man are in full vigour, and his judgment better than at any preceding date, the bodily powers for laborious life are on the decline. He cannot bear the same quantity of fatigue as at an earlier period. He begins to earn less, and is less capable of enduring wind and weather; and in those retired employments where much sight is required, he fails apace, and sees himself, like an old horse, beginning to be turned adrift.

At sixty his labour ought to be over, at least from direct necessity. It is painful to see old age working itself to death, in what are called civilized countries, for daily bread. . . .

The persons to be provided for . . . will be husbandmen, common labourers, journeymen of every trade and their wives, sailors, and disbanded soldiers, worn-out servants of both sexes, and poor widows.

There will be also a considerable number of middling tradesmen, who having lived decently in the former part of life, begin, as age approaches, to lose their business, and at last fall to decay.

Besides these there will be constantly thrown off from the revolutions of that wheel which no man can stop nor regulate, a number from every class of life connected with commerce and adventure. . . .

I [now] proceed to the mode of rendering [the] condition [of the aged] comfortable, which is,

To pay every such person of the age of fifty years, and until he shall arrive at the age of sixty, the sum of six pounds per annum out of the surplus taxes, and ten pounds per annum during life after the age of sixty. . . .

This support . . . is not of the nature of charity but of a right. Every person in England, male and female, pays on an average in taxes two pounds eight shillings and sixpence per annum from the day of his (or her) birth; and if the expence of collection be added, he pays two pounds eleven shillings and sixpence; consequently, at the end of fifty years he has paid one hundred and twenty-eight pounds fifteen shillings, and at sixty one hundred and fifty-four pounds ten shillings. Converting, therefore, his (or her) individual tax into a tontine, the money he shall receive after fifty years is but little more than the legal interest of the nett money he has paid; the rest is made up from those whose circumstances do not require them to draw such support, and the capital in both cases defrays the expences of Government. . . .

The sum thus remitted to the poor will be,

To two hundred and fifty-two thousand poor families, containing six hundred and thirty thousand children	£2,520,000
To one hundred and forty thousand aged persons	1,120,000
	£3,640,000

There will then remain three hundred and sixty thousand pounds out of the four millions, part of which may be applied as follows:—

After all the above cases are provided for there will still be a number of families who, though not properly of the class of poor, yet find it difficult to give education to their children; and such children, under such a case, would be in a worse condition than if their parents were actually poor. A Nation under a well-regulated Government should permit none to remain uninstructed. It is monarchical and aristocratical Government only that requires ignorance for its support.

Suppose, then, four hundred thousand children to be in this condition, which is a greater number than ought to be supposed after the provisions already made, the method will be:

To allow for each of those children ten shillings a year for the expence of schooling for six years each, which will give them six months' schooling each year, and half-a-crown a year for paper and spelling books.

The expence of this will be annually £250,000.

There will then remain one hundred and ten thousand pounds.

Notwithstanding the great modes of relief which the best instituted and best principled Government may devise, there will still be a number of smaller cases, which it is good policy as well as beneficence in a Nation to consider.

Were twenty shillings to be given immediately on the birth of a child, to every woman who should make the demand, and none will make it whose circumstances do not require it, it might relieve a great deal of instant distress.

There are about two hundred thousand births yearly in England, and if claimed by one-fourth,

The amount would be . . £50,000.

And twenty shillings to every new-married couple who should claim in like manner. This would not exceed the sum of £20,000.

Also twenty thousand pounds to be appropriated to defray the funeral expences of persons, who, travelling for work, may die at a distance from their friends. By relieving parishes from this charge, the sick stranger will be better treated.

I shall finish this part of the subject with a plan adapted to the particular condition of a metropolis, such as London.

Cases are continually occurring in a metropolis different to those which occur in the country, and for which a different, or rather an additional, mode of relief is necessary. In the country, even in large towns, people have a knowledge of each other, and distress never arises to that extreme height it sometimes does in a metropolis. There is no such thing in the country as persons, in the literal sense of the word, starved to death, or dying with cold from the want of a lodging. Yet such cases, and others equally as miserable, happen in London.

Many a youth comes up to London full of expectations, and with little or no money, and unless he get immediate employment he is already half-undone; and boys bred up in London without any means of a livelihood, and as it often happens of dissolute parents, are in a still worse condition; and servants long out of place are not much better off. In short, a world of little cases is continually arising, which busy or affluent life knows not of, to open the first door to distress. Hunger is not among the postponeable wants, and a day, even a few hours, in such a condition is often the crisis of a life of ruin.

These circumstances which are the general cause of the little thefts and pilferings that lead to greater, may be prevented. There yet remain twenty thousand pounds out of the four millions of surplus taxes, which with another fund hereafter to be mentioned, amounting to about twenty thousand pounds more, cannot be better applied than to this purpose. The plan then will be:

First,—To erect two or more buildings, or take some already erected, capable of containing at least six thousand persons, and to have in each of these places as many kinds of employment as can be contrived, so that every person who shall come may find something which he or she can do.

Secondly,—To receive all who shall come, without inquiring who or what they are. The only condition to be, that for so much, or so many hours' work each person shall receive so many meals of wholesome food and a warm lodging, at least as good as a barrack. That a certain portion of what each person's work shall be worth shall be reserved, and given to him or her, on their going away; and that each person shall stay as long or as short a time, or come as often as he chuse, on these conditions.

If each person stayed three months, it would assist by rotation twenty-four thousand persons annually, though the real number, at all times, would be but six thousand. By establishing an asylum of this kind, persons to whom temporary distresses occur would have an opportunity to recruit themselves, and be enabled to look out for better employment.

Allowing that their labour paid but one half the expence of supporting them, after reserving a portion of their earnings for themselves, the sum of forty thousand pounds additional would defray all other charges for even a greater number than six thousand.

The fund very properly convertible to this purpose, in addition to the twenty thousand pounds remaining of the former fund, will be the produce of the tax upon coals, so iniquitously and wantonly applied to the support of the Duke of Richmond. It is horrid that any man, more especially at the price coals now are, should live on the distresses of a community; and any Government permitting such an abuse deserves to be dismissed. This fund is said to be about twenty thousand pounds per annum.

I shall now conclude this plan with enumerating the several particulars, and then proceed to other matters.

The enumeration is as follows:—

First—Abolition of two million poor-rates.

Secondly—Provision for two hundred and fifty-two thousand poor families.

Thirdly—Education for one million and thirty thousand children.

Fourthly—Comfortable provision for one hundred and forty thousand aged persons.

Fifthly—Donation of twenty shillings each for fifty thousand births.

Sixthly—Donation of twenty shillings each for twenty thousand marriages.

Seventhly—Allowance of twenty thousand pounds for the funeral expences of persons travelling for work, and dying at a distance from their friends.

Eighthly—Employment, at all times, for the casual poor in the cities of London and Westminster.

By the operation of this plan, the poor laws, those instruments of civil torture, will be superseded, and the wasteful expence of litigation prevented. The hearts of the humane will not be shocked by ragged and hungry children, and persons of seventy or eighty years of age, begging for bread. The dying poor will not be dragged from place to place to breathe their last, as a reprisal of parish upon parish. Widows will have a maintenance for their children, and not be carted away, on the death of their husbands, like culprits and criminals; and children will no longer be considered as increasing the distresses of their parents. The haunts of the wretched will be known, because it will be to their advantage, and the number of petty crimes, the offspring of distress and poverty, will be lessened. The poor, as well as the rich, will then be interested in the support of Government, and the cause and apprehension of riots and tumults will cease. Ye who sit in ease, and solace yourselves in plenty—and such there are in Turkey and Russia, as well as in England—and who say to yourselves, "Are we not well off?" have ye thought of these things? When ye do, ye will cease to speak and feel for yourselves alone.

The plan is easy in practice. It does not embarrass trade by a sudden interruption in the order of taxes, but effects the relief by changing the application of them; and the money necessary for the purpose can be drawn from the excise collections, which are made eight times a year in every market town in England. . . .

[The remainder of the excess taxation should go to increase the salaries of revenue officers and the lower clergy and to provide compensation for soldiers who will be mustered out if an alliance with France is arranged.]

The tax on houses and windows is one of those direct taxes which, like the poor rates, is not confounded with trade, and when taken off, the relief will be instantly felt. This tax falls heavy on the middling class of people.

The amount of this tax by the returns of 1788 was—

Houses and windows, by the Act of 1766	£385,459	11	7
Ditto, by the Act of 1779 . . .	130,739	14	5½
Total	£516,199	6	0½

If this tax be struck off, there will then remain about one million of surplus taxes; and as it is always proper to keep a sum in reserve for incidental matters, it may be best not to extend reductions further in the first instance, but to consider what may be accomplished by other modes of reform.

Among the taxes most heavily felt is the commutation tax. I shall therefore offer a plan for its abolition, by substituting another in its place, which will effect three objects at once.

First, That of removing the burthen to where it can best be borne.

Secondly, Restoring justice among families by a distribution of property.

Thirdly, Extirpating the overgrown influence arising from the unnatural law of primogeniture, and which is one of the principal sources of corruption at elections. . . .

When taxes are proposed, the country is amused by the plausible language of taxing luxuries. One thing is called a luxury at one time, and something else at another; but the real luxury does not consist in the article, but in the means of procuring it, and this is always kept out of sight.

I know not why any plant or herb of the field should be a greater luxury in one country than another; but an overgrown estate in either is a luxury at all times, and, as such, is the proper object of taxation. It is, therefore, right to take those kind tax-making gentlemen upon their own word, and argue on the principle themselves have laid down, that of *taxing luxuries*. If they or their champion, Mr. Burke, who, I fear, is growing out of date, like the man in armour, can prove that an estate of twenty, thirty, or forty thousand pounds a year is not a luxury, I will give up the argument.

Admitting that any annual sum, say, for instance, a thousand pounds, is necessary for the support of a family, consequently the second thousand is of the nature of a luxury, the third still more so, and by proceeding on we shall at last arrive at a sum that may not improperly be called a prohibitable luxury. It would be impolitic to set bounds to property acquired by industry, and therefore it is right to place the prohibition beyond the probable acquisition to which industry can extend; but there ought to be a limit to property or the accumulation of it by bequest. It should pass in some other line. The richest in every Nation have poor relations, and those often very near in consanguinity.

The following table of progressive taxation is constructed on the above principles, and as a substitute for the commutation tax. It will reach the point of prohibition by a regular operation, and thereby supersede the aristocratical law of primogeniture.

[A progressive tax on incomes over £50 is proposed, the rate on successive increments of income rising from 1¼ to 100 per cent. An income of £1000 would pay £21 tax, an income of £2000, £59, etc. The maximum possible income after the deduction of the tax would be £12370.]

On small and middling estates [the tax] is lighter (as it is intended to be) than the commutation tax. It is not till after seven or eight thousand a year that it begins to be heavy. The object is not so much the produce of the tax as the justice of the measure. The Aristocracy has screened itself too much, and this serves to restore a part of the lost equilibrium.

As an instance of its screening itself, it is only necessary to look back to the first establishment of the excise laws, at what is called the Restoration, or the coming of Charles the Second. The aristocratical interest then in power commuted the feudal services itself was under, by laying a tax on beer brewed for *sale;* that is, they compounded with Charles for an exemption from those services for themselves and their heirs by a tax to be paid by other people. The Aristocracy do not purchase beer brewed for sale, but brew their own beer free of the duty; and if any commutation at that time were necessary, it ought to have been at the expence of those for whom the exemptions from those services were intended; instead of which, it was thrown on an entire different class of men.

But the chief object of this progressive tax (besides the justice of rendering taxes more equal than they are), is, as already stated, to extirpate the overgrown influence arising from the unnatural law of primogeniture, and which is one of the principal sources of corruption at elections.

It would be attended with no good consequences to inquire how such vast estates as thirty, forty, or fifty thousand a year could commence, and that at a time when commerce and manufactures were not in a state to admit of such acquisitions. Let it be sufficient to remedy the evil by putting them in a condition of descending again to the community, by the quiet means of apportioning them among all the heirs and heiresses of those families. This will be the more necessary, because hitherto the Aristocracy have quartered their younger children and connections upon the public, in useless posts, places and offices, which when abolished will leave them destitute, unless the law of primogeniture be also abolished or superseded. . . .

There are two classes of people to whom the laws of England are particularly hostile, and those the most helpless: younger children and the poor. Of the former I have just spoken; of the latter I shall mention one instance out of the many that might be produced, and with which I shall close this subject.

Several laws are in existence for regulating and limiting workmen's wages. Why not leave them as free to make their own bargains as the law-makers are to let their farms and houses? Personal labour is all the property they have. Why is that little, and the little freedom they enjoy, to be infringed? But the injustice will appear stronger if we consider the operation and effect of such laws. When wages are fixed by what is called a law, the legal wages remain stationary, while everything else is in progression; and as those who make that law still continue to lay on new taxes by other laws, they increase the expence of living by one law and take away the means by another.

But if those gentlemen law-makers and tax-makers thought it right to limit the poor pittance which personal labour can produce, and on which a whole family is to be supported, they certainly must feel themselves happily indulged in a limitation on their own part of not less than twelve thousand a year, and that of property they never acquired (nor probably any of their ancestors), and of which they have made so ill a use. . . .

When it shall be said in any country in the world my poor are happy; neither ignorance nor distress is to be found among them; my jails are empty of prisoners, my streets of beggars; the aged are not in want; the taxes are not oppressive; the rational world is my friend, because I am the friend of its happiness: When these things can be said, then may that Country boast its Constitution and its Government. . . .

A Way to Promote the Peace and Happiness of the World.[1] In the preceding part of this work I have spoken of an alliance between England, France and America for purposes that were to be afterwards mentioned. Though I have no direct authority on the part of America I have good reason to conclude that she is disposed to enter into a consideration of such a measure, provided that the Governments with which she might ally acted as national Governments, and not as Courts enveloped in intrigue and mystery. That France as a Nation, and a national Government, would prefer an alliance with England, is a matter of certainty. Nations, like individuals, who have long been enemies without knowing each other, or knowing why, become the better friends when they discover the errors and impositions under which they had acted.

Admitting, therefore, the probability of such a connection, I will

[1] Part II, ch. v (pp. 276–279).

state some matters by which such an alliance, together with that of Holland, might render service, not only to the parties immediately concerned, but to all Europe.

It is, I think, certain, that if the fleets of England, France and Holland were confederated they could propose, with effect, a limitation to, and a general dismantling of, all the navies in Europe, to a certain proportion to be agreed upon.

First, That no new ship of war shall be built by any power in Europe, themselves included.

Secondly, That all the navies now in existence shall be put back, suppose to one-tenth of their present force. This will save to France and England at least two millions sterling annually to each, and their relative force be in the same proportion as it is now. If men will permit themselves to think, as rational beings ought to think, nothing can appear more ridiculous and absurd, exclusive of all moral reflections, than to be at the expence of building navies, filling them with men, and then hauling them into the ocean, to try which can sink each other fastest. Peace, which costs nothing, is attended with infinitely more advantage than any victory with all its expence. But this, though it best answers the purpose of Nations, does not that of Court Governments, whose habited policy is pretence for taxation, places and offices.

It is, I think, also certain, that the above confederated powers, together with that of the United States of America, can propose with effect, to Spain, the independence of South America, and the opening those countries of immense extent and wealth to the general commerce of the world, as North America now is.

With how much more glory and advantage to itself does a Nation act when it exerts its powers to rescue the world from bondage and to create itself friends, than when it employs those powers to encrease ruin, desolation and misery. The horrid scene that is now acting by the English Government in the East Indies, is fit only to be told of Goths and Vandals, who, destitute of principle, robbed and tortured the world they were incapable of enjoying.

The opening of South America would produce an immense field of commerce, and a ready money market for manufactures, which the eastern world does not. The east is already a country full of manufactures, the importation of which is not only an injury to the manufactures of England, but a drain upon its specie. The balance against England by this trade is regularly upwards of half a million annually sent out in the East India ships in silver; and this is the reason, together with German intrigue and German subsidies, there is so little silver in England.

But any war is harvest to such Governments, however ruinous it may be to a nation. It serves to keep up deceitful expectations, which prevent a people looking into the defects and abuses of Government. It is the *lo here!* and the *lo there!* that amuses and cheats the multitude.

Never did so great an opportunity offer itself to England, and to all Europe, as is produced by the two Revolutions of America and France. By the former, freedom has a national champion in the western world; and by the latter, in Europe. When another Nation shall join France, despotism and bad Government will scarcely dare to appear. To use a trite expression, the iron is becoming hot all over Europe. The insulted German and the enslaved Spaniard, the Russ and the Pole, are beginning to think. The present age will hereafter merit to be called the Age of Reason, and the present generation will appear to the future as the Adam of a new world.

When all the Governments of Europe shall be established on the representative system, Nations will become acquainted, and the animosities and the prejudices fomented by the intrigue and artifice of Courts will cease. The oppressed soldier will become a freeman; and the tortured sailor, no longer dragged along the streets like a felon, will pursue his mercantile voyage in safety. It would be better that Nations should continue the pay of their soldiers during their lives, and give them their discharge, and restore them to freedom and their friends, and cease recruiting, than retain such multitudes at the same expence in a condition useless to society and themselves. As soldiers have hitherto been treated in most countries they might be said to be without a friend. Shunned by the citizens on an apprehension of being enemies to liberty, and too often insulted by those who commanded them, their condition was a double oppression. But where general principles of liberty pervade a people everything is restored to order; and the soldier, civilly treated, returns the civility. . . .

PART II

CRITICS OF THE NEW SOCIAL ORDER

VI

WILLIAM COBBETT

1763–1835

William Cobbett was born a countryman and to the end of his days remained one at heart. He sang the virtues of rural life, clung steadfastly to many of the beliefs and prejudices which it implanted, and as a critic of society placed the grievances of the peasant uppermost. The "improvements" of the new industrial age left him cold. Compromise, he found, was often necessary, but he idealized the institutions of the past and imagined that if recent abuses could be pruned away an earlier and purer society might be restored.

Cobbett was born in 1763, the son of a farmer-innkeeper of Surrey, England. Bred to farm work, at fourteen he rose to clipping hedges on the Bishop of Winchester's nearby estate, Farnham Castle. On hearing of the king's wondrous gardens at Kew, Cobbett set out incontinently for that place. On the way he saw in a shop window and purchased Swift's *Tale of a Tub*. The book engrossed him, and through its direct and vigorous language is said to have formed his own literary style. He obtained work at Kew and even had the honor of being noticed—and laughed at for his countrified appearance—by the Prince of Wales. After a time he returned home.

Cobbett's father differed somewhat from the rest of his class. He possessed enough learning to teach William the three R's (about all the instruction the latter ever received) and held decidedly unpatriotic views on the subject of the American Revolution. This, however, did not prevent William from entering the British army a year after the conclusion of the war. The act itself was a means of escape. He had gone to London and fallen into a monotonous and confining situation as an attorney's clerk. Joining the army seemed to be the only way out.

Cobbett's regiment was detailed for service in New Brunswick, where he remained for six years. Before leaving England he was given clerical work to do, and having skill and industry (rare qualities in the English army at that time) he achieved the rank of regimental sergeant-major. While in America he also found time to study grammar and composition and to win a wife. But army life was hard for the ordinary soldier, the systematic oppression of his officers made it more so, and as Cobbett's position gave him access to the inner workings of the military system he returned to England in 1791 with a burning desire to expose it. After prudently quitting the army he brought charges of corruption against several officers of his regiment. The resources of the War Office, however, amply sufficed to thwart an ex-sergeant-major, no matter how strong his case happened to be. For Cobbett had overlooked one trifling fact: the practices he objected to were not only tolerated—they were regarded in the highest circles as essential to the conduct of military affairs. He relieved his feelings by writing a pamphlet.

Perhaps to escape the attention of the government (his pamphlet had become embarrassingly popular) Cobbett travelled to France in 1792. He kept himself aloof from the currents of revolution and applied himself to learning French. When war between France and England threatened, he sailed for America.

Cobbett arrived in the United States in 1793 armed with a letter of recommendation from the American minister at Paris. He at first sought an appointment in the civil service, but when no opening presented itself, turned for a livelihood to translating French and teaching English to French émigrés. But the state of affairs disgusted him. He made some friends, but found the generality of Americans a "cheating, sly, roguish gang." As a patriotic Englishman he resented their anti-British sentiments. The situation undoubtedly called for a pamphlet. His first venture was so successful in irritating the Americans that under the appropriate pseudonym of "Peter Porcupine" he issued one tract after another dealing with "malicious attacks upon the monarchy and the monarch of England," the shortcomings of such popular idols as Tom Paine, and the horrors of the French Revolution.

Nothing was better calculated to restore his credit with the home government. When he returned to England in 1800, therefore, the authorities offered to give him a newspaper outright in return for his support. This he declined. He was willing, however (after an unsuccessful venture of his own) to accept the backing of a member of the government, William Windham, and others, in setting up a weekly paper. But it was stipulated that he should have complete freedom of expression.

The *Political Register*, which was the result of these transactions, turned out to be a bad investment for those in authority. At first the line it took was unexceptionable; Cobbett proclaimed his loyalty to the established order in Church and State, opposed reform of the suffrage, and denounced radical ideas imported from France. He even upheld bull-baiting as an ancient and manly sport, and the slave trade as a mainstay of British commerce.

Gradually, however, Cobbett became more alive to the defects of British institutions. The aristocratic Church and State were admirable in theory, in practice they were shot through with corruption. Cobbett therefore turned his guns on sinecures and unjustifiable pensions. The fiscal policy of the government seemed designed to enrich the vulgar race of stock-jobbers, and on this subject Cobbett was equally violent. His career, in fact, was becoming a study in progressive disillusionment.

As Cobbett grew more critical of the governing classes, the influence of his *Political Register* among the mass of the population steadily mounted. He had not forgotten the British soldier, and when in 1810 he attacked the authorities for crushing a mutiny with German troops the government seized upon it as a pretext for accusing him of sedition. He was convicted, fined, and sentenced to two years in prison.

The Luddite riots of 1811–12 opened Cobbett's eyes still further. So far as he had considered social abuses at all, he had up to this time viewed them from the standpoint of the agricultural worker. Now the grievances of industrial labor were made painfully clear. In future, therefore, attempts of the factory workers to defend themselves by the organization of trade unions had Cobbett's unqualified support.

When the Napoleonic wars ended in 1815, the English government, unduly terrified by labor agitation, set about repressing somewhat imaginary revolutions at home. One of its first acts was to limit the freedom of the press, Cobbett's paper being a principal object of attack. Anticipating another prosecution, Cobbett in 1817 withdrew to America, where he remained for two years. The virtues—and vices—of Americans were probably much what they had been twenty years before, but he now found a great deal to admire. "To see a free country for once, and to see every labourer with plenty to eat and drink! Think of that! . . . No packed juries of tenants. . . . No hangings and rippings-up. . . . No Cannings, Liverpools, Castlereaghs, Eldons, Ellenboroughs, or Sidmouths. . . . No Wilberforces. Think of *that!* No Wilberforces!"

Even before his second journey to America Cobbett had reached the conclusion that no essential reform could be won by further appeals to the English ruling class. Placing the initiative in the hands of the people seemed to be the only alternative. After 1816 therefore Cobbett, the ancient enemy of parliamentary reform, became one of its leading champions. But he was not enamored of his fellow Radicals. The optimistic laissez-faire philosophy and middle-class affiliations of Benthamite democrats aroused his outspoken disgust. If a choice must be made, he still preferred an aristocracy of birth to one of wealth and brains.

During the campaign for parliamentary reform Cobbett continued his agitation, by pen and tongue, for many of the causes with which he had earlier been identified. He attacked the government's policy of deflation which played into the hands of wealthy bond-holders, and urged his own scheme of monetary and fiscal reform (borrowed mainly from Thomas Paine, whose admirer he had long since become). Though deprecating working-class violence, he condemned the savage methods used in putting down the agrarian rising of 1830, and bore witness to its beneficent effect on labor conditions. This brought upon him a prosecution for inciting to violence, but the government was unable to obtain his conviction even with a packed jury.

Cobbett supported the very moderate Reform Bill of 1832 merely because he regarded it as an entering wedge. On his election to the reformed Parliament in 1832 therefore he called for further increments of democracy. But a middle-class Parliament had gotten enough of this commodity for the present and had other objects in view. One of these was the "reform" of the poor law. In this project Cobbett detected the keen odor of privilege. Proponents of the measure glossed it with the most profound philosophical arguments and appealed to the sacred authority of Malthus, but Cobbett saw in it only an attempt to relieve the rich at the expense of the poor. His resistance, however, though never more determined, was useless and the New Poor Law went into effect in 1834. This proved to be Cobbett's last great contest. He died in 1835.

The writings of Cobbett were more popular and influential among the mass of Englishmen than those of any other writer of his time—except perhaps Thomas Paine's. His broad sympathy for every section of the working class enabled him to promote harmony and solidarity among them. His chief significance, it has been said, is that he helped to create in workingmen the confidence and class consciousness which equipped them for future progress. More than that, he was himself a striking example of the talent which, people began to suspect, existed even among the "lower orders" of society.

REFERENCES

Files of the *Political Register* are preserved in a number of the larger libraries. Many of Cobbett's other works have been reprinted; among the current editions are *Advice to Young Men* (1930); *Life and Adventures of Peter Porcupine* (Cobbett's autobiography up to 1796, reprinted 1927); *Rural Rides in . . . England, . . . Tours in Scotland and . . . England, and Letters from Ireland* (ed. G. D. H. and Margaret Cole, 3 vols., 1930); *Journal of the Last Hundred Days of English Freedom* (1921).

Lives have been written by G. D. H. Cole (1927; extremely full as to social and political background); Lewis Melville (1913; based chiefly on Cobbett's correspondence); E. I. Carlyle (1904); G. K. Chesterton (1925). For a short sketch see G. D. H. Cole, *William Cobbett* (Fabian Tract No. 215, 1925).

READINGS FROM

COBBETT'S POLITICAL REGISTER [1]

Slavery in the West Indies Compared with "Free Labor" in England.[2]

TO

WILLIAM WILBERFORCE

On the state of the Cotton Factory Labourers . . .

Kensington, 27 *August*, 1823.

WILBERFORCE,

I have you before me in a canting pamphlet; and, upon your conduct and character, as developed in that pamphlet, it is my intention to remark fully, at some future time. At present, I shall use it only thus: to ask you what need there was, or what propriety there was, in spending your time in writing and publishing, "An Appeal to the religion, justice and humanity of the Inhabitants of the British Empire, in behalf of the Negro slaves in the West Indies;" to ask you what propriety, what sense, what sincerity, there could be in your putting forth this thing, in the present state of this country? It is to the in-

[1] The title of this publication was slightly changed from time to time, as appears in the succeeding footnotes.

[2] *Cobbett's Weekly Register*, Vol. XLVII, Aug. 30, 1823, col. 513–514, 514–516, 520–522.

habitants of the "British Empire" that you appeal, in this heap of shameless cant. . . .

Now, WILBERFORCE, what do you want these people to do; you appeal to them for *something*. It is hardly to be believed that you do not want them to do something in consequence of your appeal. You call upon them in behalf of the slaves in the West Indies. In short, this is what you appeal to them for, to cause the "transmuting the wretched Africans into the condition of *free British labourers*." There is a great deal of canting trash; a great deal of lying; a great deal of that cool impudent falsehood for which the Quakers are famed; a monstrous quantity of hypocrisy is there evident in these seventy-seven pages of yours; but this would appear to be the substance; this would appear to be what you want; namely, to make the West India Negro slaves *as well off as the labourers in this kingdom*. As to "*transmuting the wretched Africans into the condition*," and so forth, that is nonsense too beastly to be used by any one but a son of cant. To put your meaning into plain English, it comes to this, that you want the inhabitants of this country and of Scotland and Ireland, to do something that shall make the West India Blacks *as well off* as the working part of the Whites in these countries.

Now, this being your meaning, there is no man who knows any thing at all of the real situation of the Blacks, who will not declare you to be totally ignorant of the subject on which you are writing; or to be a most consummate hypocrite. Why do you not give us something of a description of the labours, the lodging, the food, the drink, the state of health, and particularly, of the nature and quantity of the food, and the nature and quantity of the labour, in the West Indies. You do not give us any account of these. You pretend to want the Blacks to be *as free* as British labourers; but you do not tell us what you mean by the word *freedom*. The devil a bit do you make any *comparison* between the lives which the Blacks lead, and the lives which the White labourers lead. . . .

You make your appeal in Piccadilly, London, amongst those who are wallowing in luxuries, proceeding from the labour of the people. You should have gone to the gravel-pits, and made your appeal to the wretched creatures with bits of sacks round their shoulders, and with hay-bands round their legs: You should have gone to the road-side, and made your appeal to the emaciated, half-dead things who are there cracking stones to make roads as level as a die for the tax-eaters to ride on. What an insult it is, and what an unfeeling, what a cold-blooded hypocrite must he be that can send it forth; what an insult to call upon people under the name of free British labourers; to appeal to them in behalf of Black slaves, when these free British labourers; these poor mocked, degraded wretches would be happy to lick the dishes and bowls, out of which the Black slaves have breakfasted, dined or supped. What! while it is notorious that millions of human beings in these wretched countries never taste of food other than that which is not sufficient to nourish even a poor pig; when it is in evidence before the House of Commons itself, that English labourers, once so well fed, carry even to the field with them cold potatoes instead of meat and bread! Talk, indeed, of "*transmuting* the wretched Africans into this condition." If the West India planters were to attempt such transmutation, they would speedily have to repent of it. If they were to attempt to give their Black slaves potatoes instead of the Indian meal and pork and rice, which they do give them; if they were to attempt such transmutation, they would soon find, that, to submit quietly to the eating of cold potatoes, men must be under that THING which is called the "*envy of surrounding nations, and the admiration of the world!*" . . .

Motives of English Manufacturers in Desiring the Independence of the Spanish Colonies.[1]

TO THE

COTTON-LORDS

On their petition to the honourable house, praying that illustrious and pure assembly to take measures for causing an acknowledgment, by England, of the freedom and independence of the Spanish colonies in America: and also on the complaints of the cotton-lords against the corn bill.

Kensington, 7th July, 1824.

MY LORDS,

SEIGNEURS of the Twist, sovereigns of the Spinning-Jenny, great yeomen of the Yarn, give me leave to approach you with some remarks on your Petition to that House which is so well worthy of receiving your prayers. It seems to have been made for you, and you for it. . . .

What, my Lords, do you talk about "*the cause of freedom*"! Are *you* become supporters of that cause? Why, then, it is not the cause of freedom. The devil can be for holiness before you can be for real free-

[1] *Ibid.*, Vol. LI, July 10, 1824, col. 65, 88–91.

dom. Oh, no! And it is not *freedom* that you want given to Spanish America. It is robbery, it is plunder, it is bloodshed; and all for the sake of *a market for your calicoes*. When I petitioned for the acknowledgment, the insurgents had not attempted to sell their country to, and to make the people the slaves of, the Jews and Jobbers of London. Their "*Bonds*" were not then "*in the market*," that infernal den of roguery. *Freedom*, indeed! *Liberty* to be stripped of their clothes, and to be starved to death by tax-gatherers, with military uniform on their backs and bayonets in their hands! *Liberty* to be exposed to the *extreme unction!* The *liberty* which you would give to the Catholics of Spanish America would *hardly be better* than that which is given to other *Catholics*. What reason have I to suppose that you intend any thing *better* for the people of Spanish America, who are all Catholics? If you intend anything *better* for them, you are most unnatural dogs; and, if you do not, ought not a Spanish American, who wishes success to your "*Liberty*" projects, to suffer all the torments that can, even by divine wrath, be inflicted on him in this world and in the world to come? The man who wishes, for no matter what purpose, to see the Mexicans, or the Peruvians, or any body else, reduced to such a state as the people of Ireland are reduced to, must be a *monster*. What must he be, then, if he wish to see them thus reduced for the purpose of *securing a market for your calicoes!* The cause of the insurgents is not *now* "the cause of *freedom:*" it is the cause of *robbery*, *plunder*, *slavery*. Let the people of those countries once be well fastened down by *loans* and *debts;* let them once see the *bayonet* brought to take their clothes and their food from them, in order that they may be sent away for the use of Jews and Jobbers; let them once see the hook-nosed and round-eyed race, who, unfortunately for the world, escaped from Pharaoh's midwives; let them once see this accursed race sending the bayonet into their houses and plantations to take away the fruit of their earnings; let the Spanish Americans once suffer themselves to be brought into this state, and they and their children's children will curse the hour that loan-jobbing villains were suffered to set up the cry of liberty and independence. But, as for *you*, the Lords of the spinning-jenny, your audacity surpasses even that of these loan-jobbing "*patriots*." You see the state in which Ireland is, and you say nothing about Ireland, while you cross the equinoctial line, in search of objects of your tenderness. You must think the people of Ireland *free enough*, or your conduct is very inconsistent. However, there are your own poor creatures, who work in your factories, where you keep the heat at *eighty-four degrees*. You can look with an eye perfectly calm on the poor souls that are thus toiling for you. You can see the poor children pining away their lives in these hells upon earth; you can see them actually gaping for breath, swallowing the hot and foul air, and sucking the deadly *cotton-fuz* into their lungs: you can, with all the delight of greediness gratified, behold scenes like these in your own country, under your own roofs; aye, and invented and put in practice by yourselves: and, at the very moment when you are thus engaged, you are pouring forth your souls in the cause of Spanish American "*freedom*"! Yes, and abusing me, because I do not think, that it would be for the good of England, that Spaniards should be enslaved by loan-jobbing, for the purpose of enabling you to add to the numbers of the poor creatures, who are condemned to lead a miserable life, and to die at a premature age, with their lungs choked up with cotton-fuz! . . .

Distress Not Caused by Machinery.[1]

Letter to the Luddites [2]

. . . However enlarged our views may be; however impartial we may feel towards our countrymen; still, there will be some particular part of them whose conduct we view with more than ordinary approbation, and for whom we feel more than ordinary good will. It is impossible for me, as a native of these Islands, not to feel proud at beholding the attitude which my countrymen are now taking; at hearing the cause of freedom so ably maintained by men who seem to have sprung up, all at once, out of the earth, from the North of Scotland to the Banks of the Thames. At Glasgow, at Paisley, at Bridgeton, throughout the noble counties of York and Lancaster, and in many other parts besides the Metropolis, we now behold that which to behold almost compensates us for a life of persecution and misery. But, still, amidst this crowd of objects of admiration, Nottingham always attracts my particular attention. I have before me the history of the conduct of Nottingham in the worst of times. I have traced its conduct down to the present hour. It has been foremost in all that is public-spirited and brave; and, I shall be very nearly returned to the earth when my blood ceases to stir more quickly than usual at the bare sound of the name of Nottingham.

[1] *Cobbett's Weekly Political Register*, Nov. 30, 1816, col. 563–564, 572–575.

[2] The term applied to bands of workmen, who, in protest against social conditions, were destroying machinery in various parts of England.

Judge you, then, my good friends, what pain it must have given me to hear you accused of acts, which I was not only unable to justify, but which, in conscience and in honour, I was bound to condemn! I am not one of those, who have the insolence to presume, that men are *ignorant* because they are *poor*. If I myself have more knowledge and talent than appears to have fallen to the lot of those who have brought us into our present miserable state, it ought to convince me, that there are thousands and thousands, now unknown to the public, possessed of greater talent, my education having been that of the common soldier grafted upon the ploughboy. Therefore, I beg you not to suppose, that I address myself to you as one who pretends to any superiority in point of rank, or of natural endowments. I address you as a friend who feels most sincerely for your sufferings; who is convinced that you are in error as to the cause of those sufferings; who wishes to remove that error; and, I do not recollect any occasion of my whole life when I have had so ardent a desire to produce conviction.

As to the *particular* ground of quarrel between you and your employers, I do not pretend to understand it very clearly. There must have been faults or follies on their side, at some time or other, and there may be still; but, I think, that we shall see, in the sequel, that those circumstances which appear to you to have arisen from their *avarice*, have in fact arisen from their want of the *means*, more than from their want of *inclination*, to afford you a competence in exchange for your labour; and, I think this, because it is their *interest* that you should be happy and contented. . . .

The notion of our Labourers in agriculture is, that Thrashing Machines, for instance, *injure* them, because, they say, if it were not for those machines, we should have *more work* to do. This is a great error. For, if, in consequence of using a machine to beat out his corn, the farmer does not expend *so much* money on *that sort* of labour, he has so much *more money* to expend on some *other sort* of labour. If he saves twenty pounds a year in the article of thrashing, he has that twenty pounds a year to expend in draining, fencing, or some other kind of work; for, you will observe, that he does not take the twenty pounds and put it into *a chest* and lock it up, but lays it out in his business; and his business is to improve his land and to add to the quantity and amount of his produce. Thus, in time, he is enabled to feed more mouths in consequence of his machine, and, to buy, and cause others to buy, more clothes than were bought before; and, as in the case of the ten sailors, the skill of the mechanic tends to produce *ease* and *power* and *happiness*.

The thrashing machines employ women and children in a dry and comfortable barn, while the men can be spared to go to work in the fields. Thus the weekly income of the labourer, who has a large family, is, in many cases, greatly augmented, and his life rendered so much the less miserable. But, this is a trifle compared with the great *principle*, upon which I am arguing, and which is applicable to all *manufactories* as well as to farming; for, indeed, what is a farmer other than *a manufacturer of Corn and Cattle?*

That the using of machinery, *generally speaking*, can do the journeyman manufacturer *no harm*, you will be satisfied of in one moment, if you do but reflect, that it is the *quantity of the demand* for goods that must always regulate the *price*, and that the price of the goods must regulate the *wages* for making the goods. I shall show by and by how the *demand*, or *market*, may be affected by an alteration in the currency or money of a country.

The quantity of demand for *Lace*, for instance, must depend upon the quantity of money which the people of the country have to expend. When the means of expending are abundant, then a great quantity of Lace will be bought; but, as those means diminish, so will the purchases of Lace diminish in amount. But, in every state of a country, in this respect, the effect of *machinery* must be the same. There will always be a quantity of money to spare to expend in Lace. Sometimes, as we have seen, the quantity of this money will be greater, and sometimes it will be less; but, in no case do I see, that machinery can possibly do the journeyman lace-maker any harm. Suppose, for instance, that the sum which the whole nation have to expend in Lace, be 100,000 pounds a year; that the number of yards of Lace be 500,000; and that the making of the Lace, at 40*l*. a family, give employment to 2,500 families. The Lace by the means of *machinery* can be made, it is supposed, at 4*s*. a yard. But, destroy all machinery, and then the Lace cannot be made, perhaps, under 20*s*. a yard. What would the effect of this be? No advantage to you; because, as there is only 100,000*l*. a year to spare to be expended in Lace, there would be a demand for only *one hundred thousand yards* instead of *five hundred thousand yards*. There would still be 2,500 families employed in Lace-making, at 40*l*. a year for each family; but, at any rate, no *advantage* could possibly arise to you from the change, because the whole quantity of money expended in Lace must remain the same.

Precisely the same must it be with regard to the *Stocking* and all other manufactures. But, while the destruction of machinery would produce *no good* to you with regard to the *home* trade, it would produce a great deal of *harm* to you with regard to the foreign trade; because it would make your goods so *high in price*, that other nations, who would very soon have the machinery, would be able to make the same goods at a much *lower price*.

I think, then, that it is quite clear, that the existence of machinery to its present extent cannot possibly do the journeyman manufacturer *any harm;* but, on the contrary, that he must be injured by the destruction of machinery. And, it appears to me equally clear, that if machines could be invented so as to make Lace, Stockings, &c. for half or a quarter the present price, such an improvement could not possibly be injurious to you. Because, as the *same sum of money* would still, if the country continued in the same state, be laid out in Lace, Stockings, &c. there would be a *greater quantity* of those goods sold and used, and the sum total of your wages would be exactly the same as it is now.

But, if machinery were injurious to you now, it must *always* have been injurious to you; and there have been times, when you had no great reason to complain of want of employment at any rate. So that it is evident, that your distress must have arisen from *some other cause* or *causes*. Indeed, I know that this is the case; and, as it is very material that you should have a clear view of these causes, I shall enter into a full explanation of them; because, until we come at the nature of the *disease*, it will be impossible for us to form any opinion as to the *remedy*.

Your distress, that is to say, that which you now more immediately feel, arises from want of employment with wages sufficient for your support. The want of such employment has arisen from the want of a sufficient demand for the goods you make. The want of a sufficient demand for the goods you make has arisen from the want of means in the nation at large to purchase your goods. This want of means to purchase your goods has arisen from the weight of the taxes coöperating with the bubble of paper-money. The enormous burden of taxes and the bubble of paper-money have arisen from the war, the sinecures, the standing army, the loans, and the stoppage of cash payments at the Bank; and, it appears very clearly to me, that these never would have existed, if the Members of the House of Commons had been chosen annually by the people at large. . . .

How to Achieve Reform.[1]

TO THE

JOURNEYMEN AND LABOURERS OF ENGLAND, WALES, SCOTLAND, AND IRELAND . . .

FRIENDS AND FELLOW COUNTRYMEN,

Whatever the Pride of rank, of riches or of scholarship may have induced some men to believe, or to affect to believe, the real strength and all the resources of a country, ever have sprung and ever must spring, from the *labour* of its people; and hence it is, that this nation, which is so small in numbers and so poor in climate and soil compared with many others, has, for many ages, been the most powerful nation in the world: it is the most industrious, the most laborious, and therefore, the most powerful. Elegant dresses, superb furniture, stately buildings, fine roads and canals, fleet horses and carriages, numerous and stout ships, warehouses teeming with goods; all these, and many other objects that fall under our view, are so many marks of national wealth and resources. But all these spring from *labour*. Without the Journeyman and the labourer none of them could exist; without the assistance of their hands, the country would be a wilderness, hardly worth the notice of an invader.

As it is the labour of those who toil which makes a country abound in resources, so it is the same class of men, who must, by their arms, secure its safety and uphold its fame. Titles and immense sums of money have been bestowed upon numerous Naval and Military Commanders. Without calling the justice of these in question, we may assert that the victories were obtained by *you* and your fathers and brothers and sons in co-operation with those Commanders, who, with *your* aid have done great and wonderful things; but, who, without that aid, would have been as impotent as children at the breast.

With this correct idea of your own worth in your minds, with what indignation must you hear yourselves called the Populace, the Rabble, the Mob, the Swinish Multitude; and with what greater indignation, if possible, must you hear the projects of those cool and cruel and insolent men, who, now that you have been, without any fault of yours, brought into a state of misery, propose to narrow the limits of parish relief, to prevent you from marrying in the days of your youth, or to thrust you out to seek your bread in foreign lands, never

[1] *Ibid.* Nov. 2, 1816, Vol. 31, col. 433–435, 455–458.

more to behold your parents or friends? But suppress your indignation, until we return to this topic, after we have considered the *cause* of your present misery and the measures which have produced that cause.

The times in which we live are full of peril. The nation, as described by the very creatures of the government, is fast advancing to that period when an important change must take place. It is the lot of mankind, that some shall labour with their limbs and others with their minds; and, on all occasions, more especially on an occasion like the present, it is the duty of the latter to come to the assistance of the former. We are all equally interested in the peace and happiness of our common country. It is of the utmost importance, that in the seeking to obtain those objects, our endeavours should be uniform, and tend all to the same point. Such an uniformity cannot exist without an uniformity of sentiment as to public matters, and to produce this latter uniformity amongst you is the object of this address.

As to the *cause* of our present miseries, it is the *enormous amount of the taxes*, which the government compels us to pay for the support of its army, its placemen, its pensioners, &c. and for the payment of the interest of its debt. That this is the *real* cause has been a thousand times proved; and, it is now so acknowledged by the creatures of the government themselves. *Two hundred and five* of the Correspondents of the Board of Agriculture ascribe the ruin of the country to *taxation*. Numerous writers, formerly the friends of the Pitt System, now declare, that taxation has been the cause of our distress. Indeed, when we compare our present state to the state of the country previous to the wars against France, we must see that our present misery is owing to no other cause. The taxes then annually raised amounted to about 15 millions: they amounted last year to 70 millions. The nation was then happy: it is now miserable. . . .

I know of no enemy of reform and of the happiness of the country so great as that man, who would persuade you that we possess *nothing good*, and that *all* must be torn to pieces. There is no principle, no precedent, no regulations (except as to mere matter of detail), favourable to freedom, which is not to be found in the Laws of England or in the example of our Ancestors. Therefore, I say, we may ask for, and we want *nothing new*. We have great constitutional laws and principles, to which we are immoveably attached. We want *great alteration*, but we want *nothing new*. Alteration, modification to suit the times and circumstances; but the great principles ought to be and must be, the same, or else confusion will follow.

It was the misfortune of the French people, that they had no great and settled principles to refer to in their laws or history. They sallied forth and inflicted vengeance on their oppressors; but, for want of settled principles, to which to refer, they fell into confusion; they massacred *each other;* they next flew to a military chief to protect them even *against themselves;* and the result has been what we too well know. Let us, therefore, congratulate ourselves, that we have great constitutional principles and laws, to which we can refer, and to which we are attached.

That *Reform* will come I know, if the people do their duty; and all that we have to guard against is *confusion*, which cannot come if Reform take place *in time.* I have before observed to you, that when the friends of corruption in France saw that they could not prevent *a change*, they bent their endeavours to produce *confusion*, in which they fully succeeded. They employed numbers of unprincipled men to go about the country proposing all sorts of mad schemes. They produced, first a confusion in men's minds, and next a civil war between provinces, towns, villages, and families. The tyrant ROBESPIERRE, who was exceeded in cruelty only by some of the Bourbons, was proved to have been in league with the open enemies of France. He butchered all the real friends of freedom whom he could lay his hands on, except PAINE, whom he shut up in a dungeon till he was reduced to a skeleton. This monster was, at last, put to death himself; and his horrid end ought to be a warning to any man, who may wish to walk in the same path. But I am, for my part, in little fear of the influence of such men. They cannot cajole *you*, as Robespierre cajoled the people of Paris. It is, nevertheless, necessary for you to be on your guard against them, and, when you hear a man talking big and hectoring about projects which *go farther than a real and radical reform of the Parliament*, be you well assured, that that man would be a second Robespierre if he could, and that he would make use of you, and sacrifice the life of the very last man of you; that he would ride upon the shoulders of some through rivers of the blood of others, for the purpose of gratifying his own selfish and base and insolent ambition.

In order effectually to avoid the rock of confusion, we should keep steadily in our eye, not only what we *wish* to be done, but what *can* be done *now*. We know that such a reform as would send up a Parliament, chosen by all the payers of direct taxes, is not only just and reasonable, but *easy of execution.* I am, therefore, for accomplishing that object first; and I am not at all afraid, that a set of men who would really hold the purse of the people, and who had been just chosen freely by the people, would very soon do every thing that the warmest friend of freedom could wish to see done.

While, however, you are upon your guard against false friends, you should neglect no opportunity of doing all that is within your power to give support to the cause of Reform. *Petition* is the channel for your sentiments, and there is no village so small that its petition would not have some weight. You ought to attend at every public meeting within your reach. You ought to read to, and to assist each other in coming at a competent knowledge of all public matters. Above all things, you ought to be unanimous in your object, and not to suffer yourselves to be *divided.*

The subject of *religion* has nothing to do with this great question of reform. A reformed parliament would soon do away all religious distinctions and disabilities. In their eyes, a Catholic and a Protestant would both appear in the same light.

The COURIER, the TIMES, and other emissaries of Corruption, are constantly endeavouring to direct your wrath against Bakers, Brewers, Butchers, and other persons, who deal in the necessaries of life. But, I trust, that you are not to be stimulated to such a species of violence. These tradesmen are as much in distress as you. They cannot help their malt and hops and beer and bread and meat being too dear for you to purchase. They all sell as cheap as they can without being absolutely ruined. The beer you drink is more than half *tax*, and when the tax has been paid by the seller, he must have payment back again from you who drink, or he must be ruined. The Baker has numerous taxes to pay, and so has the Butcher, and so has the Miller, and the Farmer. Besides all men are *eager to sell*, and, if they could sell *cheaper*, they certainly would, because that would be the sure way of *getting more custom.* It is the weight of the taxes, which presses us *all* to the earth, *except those who receive their incomes out of those taxes.* Therefore I exhort you most earnestly not to be induced to lay violent hands on those, who really suffer as much as yourselves.

On the subject of *lowering wages*, too, you ought to consider, that your employers cannot give to you, that which they have not. At present corn is *high in price*, but that high price is no benefit to the farmer, because it has arisen from that *badness of the crop*, which Mr. HUNT foretold at the Common Hall, and for the foretelling of which he was so much abused by the hirelings of the press, who, almost up to this very moment, have been boasting and thanking God for the goodness of *the crop!* The farmer, whose corn is half destroyed, gains nothing by selling the remaining half for *double* the price at which he would have sold the whole. If I grow 10 quarters of wheat, and, if I save it all, and sell it for 2 pounds a quarter, I receive as much money as if I sold the one half of it for four pounds a quarter. And, I am better off in the former case, because I want wheat for *seed* and because I want some to *consume myself*. These matters I recommend to your serious consideration; because, it being *unjust* to fall upon your employers to force them to give that which they have not to give, your conduct in such cases must tend to weaken the great cause, in which we ought all now to be engaged; namely, *the removal of our burdens through the means of a reformed parliament*. It is the interest of vile men of all descriptions to set one part of the people against the other part; and, therefore, it becomes you to be constantly on your guard against their allurements. . . .

VII

JEAN CHARLES LÉONARD SIMONDE DE SISMONDI

1773–1842

The aristocratic Italian family of the Sismondi were victims of the sixteenth-century Florentine conquest of their native Pisa. In 1524 they took refuge in France, whence, having adopted the Protestant religion, they were again compelled to remove, settling finally in Geneva, Switzerland. The family name also had its vicissitudes, so that Jean Charles Léonard was born a Simonde in 1773. Later on he revived the ancient patronymic Sismondi.

Sismondi's aptitudes and education pointed to a career as a scholar. His father, however, had jeopardized the family's moderate fortune by investing in French bonds just before the Revolution, and it seemed desirable to recoup these losses by placing the son in business. Sismondi, who as a student had been noted for his "uncommon docility," submitted to the unwelcome prospect and entered a Genevese mercantile house at Lyons, France. He rose rapidly in the firm, and the training proved to be an excellent foundation for his later economic studies. In 1792 repercussions of the French Revolution were felt in Geneva. Sismondi's father was imprisoned as an aristocrat, and when the son returned to Geneva he shared the same fate.

In 1793 the family were able to escape to England where they remained for eighteen months. As a child Sismondi had displayed a keen interest in political ideas. When only ten years old he had founded a model republic with his playmates (among whom was Benjamin Constant, the later political theorist), Sismondi being the "Solon" of the group. Now he seized the opportunity to study the institutions of another, if less ideal, state. These, it appears, impressed him greatly. In after life he spoke with admiration of "the noble English liberty, the habeas corpus, the trial by jury, and fixed laws."

After their sojourn in England the Sismondis (or Simondes) returned to Geneva, only to be driven out again after another clash with the authorities. This time they retreated to Tuscany where they purchased a farm. Even here Sismondi was not free from political persecution. His father returned to Geneva, but he himself underwent several short periods of imprisonment during a four or five years' residence in the country. The stay, however, was not unfruitful. Besides cultivating the farm he wrote a treatise on the agriculture of Tuscany and laid the foundation for works on politics and Italian history. All of these were published after his return to Geneva, which occurred in 1800 on his appointment as secretary of the chamber of commerce of the province of Leman.

Sismondi had conceived an admiration not only for the political arrangements of England but also for the philosophy of its leading economist. When he wrote a *Treatise on Commercial Wealth*, therefore, the book was keyed to the doctrines of Adam Smith. This work, which appeared in 1803, greatly advanced his reputation, bringing an offer of a post in the University of Vilna. This he refused however as likely to hamper his freedom of expression, and he returned to historical writing. From 1803 to 1818 Sismondi was occupied with his sixteen-volume *History of the Italian Republics*. The period almost coincided with Napoleon's ascendancy in Europe. Until the emperor's downfall in 1814 Sismondi was disposed to criticize him for his ambition and love of power. But with the restoration of the Bourbons and their reactionary policy with regard to the distribution of the land his sentiments quickly changed and he welcomed Napoleon on his return from Elba as the defender of revolutionary principles and the chosen of the people. "I am not a friend to democracy," he wrote at the time, "but I should be ashamed to call myself an aristocrat." Napoleon sought to reward his unexpected defender with the Legion of Honor, but the distinction was refused. In 1841, however, he accepted it at the hands of Louis Philippe.

Meanwhile researches into history and observation of commercial events led him to doubt the inerrancy of Adam Smith, whose doctrines he had so confidently retailed in 1803. A brief statement of Sismondi's recast opinions on economic matters appeared in his article "Political Economy," written for the *Edinburgh Encyclopedia* in 1818. This was expanded and published the next year as *New Principles of Political Economy, or Wealth in Its Relation to the Population*. The book seems to have created no particular stir at the time, although its influence in the end was, as we shall see, far from negligible.

In 1819 also Sismondi married a sister-in-law of Sir James Mackintosh, the Scottish philosopher. But marriage had no effect in checking his almost incredible literary output. A host of books and articles, chiefly on historical but also on governmental and economic subjects, flowed from his pen. He even wrote a novel, "more exact than interesting," which dealt with the state of Gaul in 492. The volumes of his magnum opus, the *History of the French*, reached a score and still the task was far from done.

In 1841 he was elected to an assembly for revising the constitution of Geneva. For a long time he had suffered from cancer, and his struggle against the democratic party in the assembly sapped his last remaining strength. The *History of the French* had to be left unfinished—"he could continue it only to the twenty-ninth volume"—when death intervened in 1842.

Sismondi is remembered chiefly as a historian, and the extent of his influence as a social and economic writer is still a matter of doubt. It is true that in a most remarkable way he anticipated many of the criticisms which were levelled at the laissez-faire school later on in the century and suggested numerous social enactments which have since gained general acceptance. Yet it would be wrong to attribute these later developments exclusively or even principally to his writings. On the other hand his influence is clearly traceable in the work of certain of his successors, particularly in that of the socialist group. Villeneuve-Bargemont, the Christian Socialist, borrowed many of his ideas, Louis Blanc was also in his debt, and Marx and Engels, while condemning as "petty-bourgeois" Sismondi's views on patriarchal agriculture and the corporate organization of industry, accepted his ideas as to the concentration of wealth. The germ of Marx's economic interpretation of history may exist in Sismondi's analysis of economic evolution into three stages: slavery, feudalism, and modern industry.

REFERENCES

No modern edition of Sismondi's economic works exists, and with the exception of a short group of extracts (*Political Economy and the Philosophy of Government*, 1847) none have been translated into English.

There is no full-length biography of Sismondi. The book just mentioned contains F. A. M. Mignet's sketch of his life—brief and generally inadequate.

Among the works dealing with Sismondi's social and economic theories are Mao-lan Tuan's *Simonde de Sismondi as an Economist* (1927), Antony Babel's *Sismondi et les origines de la législation du travail* (1927), and René Jeandeau's *Sismondi précurseur de la législation sociale contemporaine* (1913).

READINGS FROM

NEW PRINCIPLES OF POLITICAL ECONOMY [1]

Twofold Object of the Science of Government.[2] The science of government has, or ought to have, for its object the happiness of men in society. Its aim is to assure them the greatest felicity compatible with their nature. Likewise its aim is to secure the participation of the greatest possible number in that felicity. In none of the political sciences should the legislator lose sight of this twofold object: the highest degree of happiness attainable through social organization and the equitable participation of all in that happiness. His task is not complete if in order to afford equal enjoyments to all he prevents the complete development of distinguished individuals, and permits no one to rise above his kind or to become an example to humanity and a leader in discoveries beneficial to all. No more will the legislator have attained his object if, having no purpose but the development of these privileged beings, he raises a few of them above their fellow-citizens at the expense of the misery and degradation of all the rest. A nation in which no one suffers but in which no one enjoys sufficient leisure or comfort to feel intensely or to think deeply is only half civilized, even though it affords its lower class a fair chance to be happy. A nation in which the great mass of the population is exposed to constant privation, bitter anxiety as to its livelihood, and everything that can bend its will, deprave its morals, and blight its character, is in a state of servitude, even though its upper class contains men who have achieved the utmost human felicity: men, that is, whose talents are fully developed, whose rights are completely guaranteed, and whose enjoyments are fully insured.

The association of men in a body politic could not have occurred in former times and cannot be maintained to-day except on the basis of common advantage. No right can exist which is not founded on mutual confidence inspired by a common goal. Order subsists because the immense majority of those united in a body politic see in order their security; and government exists only to secure, in the name of all, that common advantage which all expect from it.

Thus society protects private property of various kinds even though it is unequally distributed, if this inequality redounds to the advantage

[1] *Nouveaux principes d'économie politique*, 2nd ed. (1827). Translation by the present editor.

[2] Vol. I, pp. 1–3, 5–6.

of all. The various objects of governmental science—namely, enabling individuals to attain the highest possible distinction, using that individual distinction for the greatest advantage of all, preserving all citizens equally from suffering, and preventing any one from being injured by the play of passions or the pursuit of selfish interest on the part of his associates—all these objects are of equal importance, for all are equally essential to the national happiness.

Criticism of the Laissez-faire Doctrine.[1] Our doctrine is that of Adam Smith. The light that his genius cast upon the field of science showed his followers the right path, and all our progress since then has been due to him. . . .

Having professed our deep admiration for that creative genius and our lively gratitude for an illumination which we owe to him alone, it will doubtless occasion surprise that the practical conclusions we draw from his doctrine seem often diametrically opposed to his own and that the experience of half a century during which his theory has been more or less put into practice makes it possible, we believe, to demonstrate that in more than one case entirely different conclusions must be drawn from it.

We hold, with Adam Smith, that labor is the sole source of wealth and thrift the only means of accumulating it, but we add that enjoyment is the sole object of that accumulation, and that there is an increase of national wealth only when there is an increase of national enjoyment.

Adam Smith, looking only at wealth, and seeing that all those who possess it have an interest in increasing it, concluded that this increase could best be encouraged by abandoning society to the exercise of each individual interest. He said to the government: The sum of private fortunes forms the wealth of the nation; every rich man strives to become still richer: let him do it; by enriching himself he will enrich the nation.

We estimate wealth in relation to the population which it should support or render happy. In our opinion, a nation does not progress in wealth merely because it accumulates more capital: it does so only if the increased capital distributes more comfort among the population which it sustains. . . .

The rich can augment their wealth either by new production or by taking a greater part of what was formerly reserved for the poor. To regularize this division, to make it equitable, we invoke almost constantly that governmental intervention which Adam Smith rejected.

[1] Vol. I, pp. 50–54, 55–56, 200–201.

Experience seems to justify this new attitude. Although the authority of Adam Smith has by no means completely transformed all departments of economic legislation, the basic dogma of free and universal competition has made great progress in all civilized countries. The result has been a prodigious development of industrial power, but for some classes of the population it has often meant frightful suffering also. Experience has made us feel the need of that protective authority which we invoke; such authority is necessary to prevent men from being sacrificed to the progress of an opulence which profits them nothing. The State alone can rise above materialistic calculations which envisage merely the increase of production and suffice to determine the actions of individuals. It can also take into account the enhancement of the general happiness and comfort—the goal toward which nations should strive.[1]

We feel it necessary to forewarn the reader of this important difference in conclusions, though we refuse to make it a subject of controversy. We shall not stop to combat those opinions of Adam Smith which we do not share, or to point out the occasions when we part company with him and his numerous commentators. The principles of political science should form a single whole and proceed one from another. We have presented them in what seems to be their natural concatenation without pretending to distinguish our own ideas from those of our predecessors. If in fact these principles support each other and form a well-knit whole, we shall have attained our object, for we do not mean to raise a new system in opposition to that of the master, but simply to show how experience should modify it. . . .

Adam Smith regarded political economy as a science based on experience. He strove to examine each fact in its social environment, and never to lose sight of the diverse circumstances to which it was related or the various effects it might have on human happiness. In criticizing him to-day we may observe that he was not always faithful to this synthetic method of reasoning, that he did not always keep in view his essential purpose, namely, to discover the relationship of wealth to population or to national enjoyment. His new disciples in England have plunged even further into abstractions, abstractions that make us completely lose sight of man, to whom wealth belongs

[1] [Author's note.]—Others have noticed that experience did not completely bear out Adam Smith's doctrine. . . . In general Adam Smith considered political economy as too exclusively subject to calculation, although it is, in several connections, within the domain of the feelings and imagination, which are incalculable.

and who ought to enjoy it. At first one would think that by disengaging theory from all accessory circumstances, one might make it clearer and easier to grasp. The contrary has occurred: the new English economists are extremely obscure and difficult to understand because our minds revolt at accepting the abstractions they ask of us. But this repugnance is itself a warning that by attempting to segregate a principle and view it in isolation we are getting away from the truth, for in the moral sciences everything is linked together.

The ingenious work of Mr. D. Ricardo seems to be a remarkable example of this new tendency of English economists. . . .

It is a truth much dwelt upon by economists that each person understands his own interest better than the government can understand it, whence they argue that every law which attempts to direct him in the care of his fortune is always useless and often harmful. But they too lightly affirm that the interest of the individual which consists in avoiding the greater of two evils is always beneficial to society. The interest of a robber lies in despoiling his neighbor, and it is to the latter's interest to let him do it if yielding to superior force is the only way to avoid destruction; but society has no interest in permitting the one to use force or in allowing the other to succumb to it. Now the entire social order constantly displays just such coercion, not always accompanied by the same types of violence but involving the same danger to those who resist it. Social institutions have almost always given rise to such coercion, but society ought not to go on supporting it with all its influence. Very frequently society compels the poor man to submit to more and more burdensome conditions on pain of starving to death; having placed him in this position it ought to undertake his defense. Doubtless the interest of the mass of métayers [farmers on shares] does not consist in accepting less than half the harvest as the price of their labor, but the interest of the métayer who has lost his place and cannot find another lies in accepting a third part or less than a third, and thus endangering the subsistence of his fellows. Doubtless the personal interest of day-laborers requires that the wages of a ten-hour day should be enough to live on and support their children until the latter are fully developed physically: indeed, the interest of society requires it. But the unemployed day-laborer must find bread at any cost; he will work fourteen hours a day, he will make his children enter a factory at the age of six, and by risking his health in order to escape the pressure of present want he will jeopardize the existence of his whole class. . . .

Industrial Crises: the Result of Laissez-faire.[1] It is of some consequence to the happiness of citizens whether every one's share of comfort and enjoyment approaches equality or whether a few have all the superfluity, while the masses are reduced to the bare necessaries of life. Whether the national income is distributed in one manner or in the other is also of some consequence to the progress of national wealth. Equality of enjoyments must result in affording producers a constantly expanding market; their inequality a constantly diminishing one. . . .

When large-scale farming replaces small-scale farming more capital is perhaps absorbed by the land and reproduced by it, and more capital than before may be divided among the whole farming population. But the consumption of one family of rich farmers plus that of fifty families of miserable day-laborers is not as valuable to the nation as the consumption of fifty peasant families in moderate circumstances. Likewise, in the towns the consumption of a millionaire manufacturer who employs a thousand poorly paid workmen is not as valuable to the nation as the consumption of a hundred less wealthy masters each of whom employ only ten workmen who are much less poor. . . . The concentration of fortunes in the hands of a few men narrows the domestic market, and industry is more and more reduced to seek an outlet in foreign markets, where it is threatened with the greatest convulsions.

All states whose production exceeds their consumption turn their eyes toward this foreign market, and as its bounds are unknown its extent seems unlimited. But with the perfection of navigation, the opening of routes and better assurance of protection it becomes apparent that the market of the universe is quite as limited as that of each nation was formerly, and that the reliance of all producers upon the foreign market has everywhere raised production above demand. It becomes plain also that, as the great reduction in price offered by the producers of one country to the consumers of another is a decree of death to the producers of the latter country, the resistance to this commercial aggression, though violent and disorderly, is almost always popular, however contrary it may appear to be to the interest of the consumers. The latter comprise, however, all the inhabitants of the country. . . .

When one scans the reports of trade, the newspapers, and the accounts of travellers, one sees everywhere proofs of this superabundant

[1] Vol. 1, pp. 357–358, 361–362, 364, 367–370, 371–372.

production which outstrips consumption and is regulated not by demand but by the amount of capital seeking employment. One sees proof also of this activity of the merchants which leads them to rush *en masse* into every new market and exposes them by turns to ruinous losses in every trade from which they anticipated profit. . . .

Seven years have passed since the first publication of this work,[1] and the commercial revolutions which have succeeded each other in the interval have in my opinion increasingly confirmed the doctrine that among opulent nations production is often determined not by requirements but by the abundance of capital, the consequence being that it quickly outstrips consumption and produces cruel distress.

The crisis which afflicted English commerce in 1819 quieted down, and the reviving prosperity of manufacturing was several times represented to me as proof of my errors. I might have answered that a free, industrious, enlightened nation like England almost always has the strength to recover from its disasters; that an immense amount of capital had been lost in 1819 and numerous families ruined, but that the wealth of the rest of the world had increased in peace-time, and that a new and considerable revenue exchanged for English products had revived the industry of the latter. Another and much more powerful cause, however, was operating; it is worth some comment.

The opening of the immense market which Spanish America offered to industrious producers seemed to me the event which might do most to relieve English manufactures. The British government was of the same opinion, and in the seven years which passed after the commercial crisis of 1819 an unheard-of effort was put forth to introduce English commerce into the most distant parts of Mexico, Colombia, Brazil, Rio de la Plata, Chili and Peru. . . . But however large the market presented by free America, it would not have sufficed to absorb all the merchandise that England had produced in excess of consumption if the borrowing of the new republics had not suddenly augmented immeasurably their means of buying English merchandise. Each American state borrowed from England a sum sufficient to put its government in operation, and although this was capital funds, it was spent immediately within the year like revenue; that is to say, the entire loan was used to buy English merchandise. . . . As long as this strange commerce lasted, as long as Englishmen asked only

[1] It was first published in 1819, when the industrial crisis in England was at its height.

that Americans be good enough to buy English merchandise with English capital and consume it for love of them, the prosperity of English manufacturing seemed glittering. . . . But when the capital was spent and the time for payment arrived, the veil suddenly dropped, the illusion vanished, and distress, even more severe than it had been in 1818, began once more.

The crisis therefore has returned more sharply than ever: no orders in the factories; no sales; insufficient wages for the workers, a large number of whom can find no work; the capital of the manufacturers tied up in finished goods which tax all their warehouses: such are the signs of the existing distress and of the growing disproportion between production and consumption. . . .

However, I am far from saying that the evil is irremediable: the nation has great resources and the ministry is very skillful. But an experience so dearly bought should at last spread enlightenment; it should cause the fact to be recognized that consumption is not the necessary consequence of production; that the glutting of the market is, on the contrary, the inevitable result of the system into which we have precipitated ourselves.

Machinery and the Division of Labor.[1] The division of labor requires that business be conducted on a very large scale, since each workman who is restricted to a single operation must find a means of keeping himself constantly occupied. More circulating capital is therefore required. Moreover the multiplication of machines which displace or reduce human labor requires an expensive establishment to begin with, a first cost which is only returned piecemeal: it therefore presupposes the possession of unemployed capital which can be spared from present use in order to establish a kind of perpetual rent.

The increasing division of labor is, as we have seen, the principal cause of the increase of the powers of production. Each person does better the thing he is confined to; and when finally his work is reduced to the simplest operation, he comes to do it with so much ease and rapidity that the eye cannot follow him and one scarcely comprehends how the hand of man can attain such a degree of dexterity and speed.

Frequently this division of labor makes it apparent that the worker is no longer even the equal of a machine—a machine can in fact replace him. Several great inventions in mechanics as applied to the arts have been the result of such observation on the part of the worker or his

[1] Vol. I, pp. 394–396, 397, 398; Vol. II, pp. 330–334.

employer. But by this division man loses in intelligence, health, and good humor everything that he gains in the ability to produce wealth.

It is through the variety of its operations that the mind develops; a nation desires men in order to make citizens of them, not to turn them into machines almost like those propelled by fire and water. The division of labor has given a value to such simple operations that the youngest children are capable of performing them; and children, before developing any of their faculties or knowing any of the joys of life, are in effect condemned to turn a wheel, twist a cock, wind a bobbin. More lace, more pins, more thread, more silk and cotton fabric are the fruit of this great division of labor; but at what a hateful price are they purchased, if it is by the moral sacrifice of so many thousands of persons! . . .

Although the uniformity of operations to which all the activity of workers in such a factory is reduced seems harmful to their intellect, it is only fair to say that according to the observations of the best judges the factory operatives in England are superior in intelligence, education, and morality to the farm laborers. They owe these advantages to the numerous means of instruction which in that country are placed within reach of all classes of the people. Since they live together constantly, are less spent by fatigue, and are more able to indulge in conversation, ideas circulate more rapidly amongst them. Once they are aroused, emulation puts them far ahead of the workers of every other country. This moral advantage is important entirely aside from the increase of wealth, while on the other hand the moral degradation that appears to have followed the establishment of several manufactures is an evil for which no increase of wealth can compensate. . . .

When a technical invention augments the productive powers of man, doubtless it should not be employed to the disadvantage of those whom it ought to serve. If it is not called forth by any new demand for labor, if it does not put the goods produced within the reach of new consumers, it should not at the very least displace or render useless a certain number of producers whether native or foreign. But there is no way of directly checking the revolution which the invention produces. It would be both useless and dangerous to suppress the invention itself. If we were to prevent the adoption of a new machine in our own workshops our neighbors would not be so scrupulous: they would make war on our workmen with their steam engines, their spinning machines, and all their new inventions. It is a war to the death in which one is forced to defend oneself but which one is imprudent to commence.

No spectacle is more amazing, more terrifying perhaps, than that presented by England in the midst of an opulence which at first is so dazzling to the eye. If one is not content to consider merely the colossal wealth of the peers of the realm to whom £20,000 is only a moderate income, if one estimates their luxury at its true value and according to the enjoyment it procures—an insulting luxury which displays itself in sumptuous carriages, numerous lackeys running through the streets with raised staffs, and fox-hunting turn-outs of a score of horses and two-score dogs that cost two thousand pounds a year—one feels some indignation in comparing such prodigality with the suffering of the poor. The highways are traversed alternately by troops of beggars discharged from the factories and by bands of ragged Irishmen who apply at farm after farm for any kind of agricultural work at a greatly reduced wage. The former like the latter ask alms only when work is denied them; but all the places are filled. The farm laborer, the cottager, sees with bitterness these strangers competing with him for work which before was hardly sufficient to support himself. In the cities, in the capital, at Hyde Park Corner, where the most splendid carriages follow each other with the speed of light, groups of ten or twenty factory workers, sitting motionless with despair in their eyes and their limbs exhausted with fear, fail to excite even a moment's notice. A third of the factories are closed, still another third will have to close soon, and all the stores are over-stocked. Merchandise is everywhere offered for sale at a price so low as not to pay half the cost of making it; and all the letters from South America announce that the immense cargoes sent there in the course of trade can be sold for scarcely enough to cover the freight. Amidst this universal distress, when the workman is everywhere turned away and the English nation has yielded its place to steam engines that do everything men used to do, rewards are still offered to the inventor of new machines which would render useless the workers who still find a livelihood. Certainly it seems that in the midst of so much suffering one might avoid encouraging the things which, now at least, can only increase distress still more. Abolishing the patents granted to inventors of new technical processes would not perhaps change very much the progress of *scientific power*, as it has been well named, but it would remove the feeling among poverty-stricken workers that, in their distress, the government is also leagued against them. . . .

The Road to Social Justice.[1] I confess that having indicated where in my opinion principle and justice are to be found, I do not feel able to set forth the means of attaining them. The way in which the fruits of labor are distributed amongst those who combine to produce them seems vicious to me; but it appears almost beyond human power to devise a state of property absolutely different from the one to which we have become accustomed. The suffering of the class most numerous and perhaps most essential to society has been recently so excessive that in the most civilized countries the minds of several philanthropists have been struck with the necessity of finding a remedy for it. Men, perhaps more full of zeal for humanity than of experience or knowledge of the human heart, have proposed under the name of coöperation a completely new organization of society which would substitute corporate for personal interest, in bodies organized for the purpose of performing all the work that society requires. Mr. Owen of New Lanark is the best known writer of this sect, which has a great number of partisans in England, France, and America. It would be useless however to combat his principles: up to the present they have not been explained in such a way as to make much impression, and one always feels a kind of remorse in exposing all the errors and inconsistencies of people whose writings express so much good will toward their fellow-men and whose motives are so pure.

But as a relationship exists between the system developed in the writings of Messrs. Owen, Thompson, Fournier [Fourier?], and Muiron and the reform toward which I think we ought to move, I feel obliged to declare definitely that we agree only on a single point and that on all others we have nothing in common. Like them I desire instead of competition an association among those who coöperate in producing the same things. But I do not regard the means they have proposed for arriving at that end as ever capable of attaining it.

I desire urban as well as rural industry to be divided amongst a great number of independent workshops and not combined under a single head who commands hundreds or thousands of workers. I desire manufacturing capital to be divided amongst a great number of middling capitalists and not united in the possession of one man who is master of several millions; I want the industrious workman to have the prospect, almost the certainty, of becoming the partner of his master, so that he will marry only when he has a share in the business instead of growing old without hope of advancement as he

[1] Vol. II, pp. 364–367.

does to-day. But to bring about these reforms I ask only the slow and indirect means of legislation, only the execution of complete justice between master and workman. This would require the former to assume all the responsibility for the evil he does the latter. Let the law constantly favor the division and not the accumulation of inheritances; let it compel the master to find a pecuniary and political advantage in binding his workmen more closely to himself, in hiring them for longer periods, in sharing his profits with them, and perhaps private interest, being better directed, will itself repair the evil it has done society. The heads of industry would then exert their intelligence to find a way to raise the workmen to their own plane, to interest them in property and thrift, and finally to make men and citizens of them, instead of laboring incessantly, as they do at present, to turn them into machines.

Unfortunately it does not depend entirely on legislation to free the poor man from anxiety, suffering and even unjust dependence. But perhaps a great deal will already have been done for his happiness when his hopes are restored and when, instead of the precarious condition to which he is condemned nowadays, there is presented to him as the object of his aspirations a period of rest and comfort to which by good conduct he may attain. . . .

VIII

THOMAS CARLYLE

1795–1881

Thomas Carlyle was born in 1795 at Ecclefechan, a town of five hundred people on the southern border of Scotland. His fellow townsmen looked beyond their community: they were accustomed to gather out-of-doors on summer evenings to discuss theology, politics, and other matters, and as a boy "Tom" listened eagerly at these sessions. Carlyle's father, though not given to argument, had decided and somewhat unorthodox ideas, especially on religion; he believed the Bible to be "quite true" but relied on his own interpretation of it.

It was a time of rapid industrial change. The elder Carlyle, himself in fairly comfortable circumstances, being a master mason, retained the workingman's point of view. "The lot of a poor man is growing daily worse," his son reported him as saying. "The world cannot and will not last as it is. Mighty changes of which none can see the end are on the way." The local weavers customarily employed someone to read to them while working and Tom at the age of seven was shouting heroic ballads above the clatter of the looms. It was his first contact with the labor problem.

More than ordinary pains were taken with the boy's education, for it was recognized that he had exceptional gifts. Before he was eight he could translate Virgil and Horace. As a student at a nearby academy, however, he made himself rather obnoxious to his school-fellows, talking a great deal and protesting against cruelty to beggars and animals. The fact that he had conscientious scruples against fighting was no protection whatever, and he had to give up pacifism. Meanwhile he read a good deal of Shakespeare, the *Arabian Nights*, and ordinary fiction. He worshipped Robert Burns as a hero, and the humanitarian strain in Burns's poetry made itself heard in his own later writings.

At fourteen Carlyle entered the University of Edinburgh. His studies were at first chiefly Latin and Greek; later, mathematics. A religious if unconforming background, and indeed his own inclinations, suggested the Church as a career and on completing the arts course in 1813 he set about preparing for the ministry. Gradually the plan was abandoned. Doubts had first assailed him when he read Hume's *Essays*, and in the end he gave up Christianity as a creed without, however, losing a strong sense of religion.

A period of teaching followed the university, first at £70 then at £80 a year. But the stipend and prestige of the position were too narrow—they failed to meet the requirements of a young lady Carlyle was just then pursuing. Dissatisfied with his "paltry trade" he returned to Edinburgh in 1818 with some vague notion of studying engineering.

At Edinburgh he lived precariously by translating scientific books, tutoring, writing reviews, and doing biographical articles for the new *Edinburgh Encyclopedia*. The difficulties of his own situation increased his sympathy for the laboring class; he looked forward hopefully to an upheaval of society. "Mutiny, revolt" is "a light matter to the young," he wrote in old age—and in easier circumstances. At this time also he learned German and began to familiarize himself with the philosophers and poets of Germany, whose writings were to have such a profound effect on his later career. Meanwhile in casting about for a profession he encountered the law. The experience was brief—a year of study sufficed to unveil its trickery and the tedious road that lay before an impatient candidate. The prospect was further darkened by a chronic dyspepsia which from that time, says his biographer, was "at the background of all he said or did."

In 1821 a ray of light appeared in the person of Jane Welsh. He found her beautiful: she was certainly intelligent, and after a courtship of five years they were married. In the interval Carlyle's circumstances had materially improved. An influential friend had thrown two wealthy young men in his way (one of them Charles Buller, the future colonial statesman) who engaged him as a tutor. He had also published a life of Schiller. Now, rather reluctantly, being aware of the uncertainties, he admitted that literature was to be his profession.

Carlyle's first manifesto on the social question appeared in 1829. It was an article called "Signs of the Times." Among the Signs which Carlyle discerned were a widening gulf between rich and poor and a growing subjection, not only of artisans, but of philosophy, art, and literature, to the machine. The utilitarian philosophy which overhung it all quite naturally drew his satire.

The article, reprinted in France, brought a sympathetic response from the followers of Saint-Simon, and Carlyle presently received a packet containing various works of that reformer. As early as 1827 he had read of and marvelled at Saint-Simon's proposed priesthood of savants. The religious inventions of the sect he still thought queer, but he professed to agree with most of their social opinions. He even translated Saint-Simon's *New Christianity* with the expectation that James Bowring, the disciple of Bentham, would publish it. But Bowring was unresponsive.

A close affinity to Saint-Simonism was seen in Carlyle's next important work. *Sartor Resartus*, printed first serially in 1833–34, summed up his criticism of society in allegorical and rather cryptic fashion. It also displayed all his familiar idiosyncracies of style. These no doubt help to explain Carlyle's success, but to some they were not attractive. Later on when an admirer proposed a pension for Carlyle a kindly but harassed statesman remarked "that a man who wrote such a style ought to starve." For some years before the work appeared, Carlyle had been steeping himself in German literature and had also been writing a good deal on the subject. *Sartor* recalls the point of view of certain German philosophers—that of Fichte among others. What, if anything, he owed either to the Saint-Simonians or to the Germans is not clear, however. In the former case his leading biographer regards the similarity rather as a matter of chance than of borrowing.

"Carlyle had said his say in *Sartor*"—not very clearly, perhaps—at least not in language for the multitude. Nor was there a marked improvement in this respect when he set his philosophy to a historical theme. *The French Revolution* (1837) thrust obliquely at the folly of governors and money-masters. As a work of art it was a resounding triumph and in that sense its appearance may have been more important "than Jena or Waterloo." But the social gospel was still clouded by the prophet's language.

Carlyle could speak directly enough when he chose. Events of the late '30's—starvation and unrest in Ireland which spread to Scotland and England, and the rise of Chartism among the workers—gave him a text which he drove home with muscular force. *Chartism* (1839) for the first time raised the "condition of England" question. It epitomized the social philosophy of *Sartor* and *The French Revolution.*

In 1840 he followed up *Chartism* with a series of lectures on

"Heroes," in which he dwelt on the prime importance of leadership in social movements. His next project was a work on Cromwell but the woes of the time deflected him temporarily into social propaganda. *Past and Present* repeated at length his characteristic philosophy, again in less highly wrought style than was customary with him. It was this straightforwardness which helped to make the book the literary sensation of 1843. Once more, in *Latter-Day Pamphlets* (1850), he battered at the stupidities of society. The ideas were the same but the language had never been so violent.

In 1845 Carlyle had published the letters and speeches of Cromwell. This and the life of Frederick the Great (1858–65) were the great works of his later career. Ever since *The French Revolution* he had been an acknowledged leader of English literature; honors and adulation flowed upon him. But the death of his wife in 1866 and the onset of physical decay checked the stream of his writing. He published comparatively little from that time until his death in 1881.

As a great literary figure Carlyle carried the tidings of reform to multitudes who perhaps would not otherwise have listened to them. He excelled as a propagandist rather than as an originator of ideas. One might, with reservations, call him the Cobbett of the middle and upper classes. Mastery of language, breadth of appeal, nostalgia for the past, belief in the virtue of steadfast labor were common to both. They even shared a prejudice against the anti-slavery agitators: "Nigger-Philanthropists," Carlyle called them, who forgot "the *green* and *yellow* slaves" at home for the black ones abroad. There were as many differences, of course. Cobbett finally embraced democracy, but Carlyle looked for—even tried to create—the heroes who would save humanity in spite of itself. Not the least of Carlyle's achievements was that his social doctrine inspired a propagandist as successful as himself; namely, John Ruskin.

REFERENCES

Carlyle's works have been much reprinted. His mainly social writings are available in many cheap editions.

The social doctrine of Carlyle is analyzed in Emery Neff's *Carlyle and Mill* (2nd ed., 1926) and in F. W. Roe's *The Social Philosophy of Carlyle and Ruskin* (1921).

The most extensive biography is by David A. Wilson (1923 sq.). Among the numerous shorter lives one of the most recent and authoritative is by L. Cazamian (1932).

READINGS FROM

PAST AND PRESENT[1]

Riches and Want.[2] The condition of England, on which many pamphlets are now in the course of publication, and many thoughts unpublished are going on in every reflective head, is justly regarded as one of the most ominous, and withal one of the strangest, ever seen in this world. England is full of wealth, of multifarious produce, supply for human want in every kind; yet England is dying of inanition. With unabated bounty the land of England blooms and grows; waving with yellow harvests; thick-studded with workshops, industrial implements, with fifteen millions of workers, understood to be the strongest, the cunningest and the willingest our Earth ever had; these men are here; the work they have done, the fruit they have realised is here, abundant, exuberant on every hand of us: and behold, some baleful fiat as of Enchantment has gone forth, saying, "Touch it not, ye workers, ye master-workers, ye master-idlers; none of you can touch it, no man of you shall be the better for it; this is enchanted fruit!" On the poor workers such fiat falls first, in its rudest shape; but on the rich master-workers too it falls; neither can the rich master-idlers, nor any richest or highest man escape, but all are like to be brought low with it, and made "poor" enough, in the money sense or a far fataler one.

Of these successful skilful workers some two millions, it is now counted, sit in Workhouses, Poor-law Prisons; or have "out-door relief" flung over the wall to them,—the workhouse Bastille being filled to bursting, and the strong Poor-law broken asunder by a stronger. They sit there, these many months now; their hope of deliverance as yet small. In workhouses, pleasantly so-named, because work cannot be done in them. Twelve-hundred-thousand workers in England alone; their cunning right-hand lamed, lying idle in their sorrowful bosom; their hopes, outlooks, share of this fair world, shut-in by narrow walls. They sit there, pent up, as in a kind of horrid enchantment; glad to be imprisoned and enchanted, that they may not perish starved. The picturesque Tourist, in a sunny autumn day, through this bounteous realm of England, descries the Union Workhouse on his path. "Passing by the Workhouse of St. Ives in

[1] First published in 1843. Page references are to the Modern Readers' edition (Macmillan, 1927) which contains an interesting introduction and notes by Julia Patton.

[2] Pp. 1–3, 177–178.

Huntingdonshire, on a bright day last autumn," says the Picturesque Tourist, "I saw sitting on wooden benches, in front of their Bastille, and within their ring-wall and its railings, some half-hundred or more of these men. Tall robust figures, young mostly or of middle age; of honest countenance, many of them thoughtful and even intelligent-looking men. They sat there, near by one another; but in a kind of torpor, especially in a silence, which was very striking. In silence: for, alas, what word was to be said? An Earth all lying round, crying, Come and till me, come and reap me;—yet we here sit enchanted! In the eyes and brows of these men hung the gloomiest expression, not of anger, but of grief and shame and manifold inarticulate distress and weariness; they returned my glance with a glance that seemed to say, 'Do not look at us. We sit enchanted here, we know not why. The Sun shines and the Earth calls; and, by the governing Powers and Impotences of this England, we are forbidden to obey. It is impossible, they tell us!' There was something that reminded me of Dante's Hell in the look of all this; and I rode swiftly away!" . . .

But what will reflective readers say of a Governing Class, such as ours, addressing its Workers with an indictment of "Over-production"! Over-production: runs it not so? "Ye miscellaneous, ignoble manufacturing individuals, ye have produced too much! We accuse you of making above two-hundred thousand shirts for the bare backs of mankind. Your trousers too, which you have made, of fustian, of cassimere, of Scotch-plaid, of jane, nankeen and woollen broadcloth, are they not manifold? Of hats for the human head, of shoes for the human foot, of stools to sit on, spoons to eat with—Nay, what say we hats or shoes? You produce gold-watches, jewelries, silver-forks, and epergnes, commodes, chiffoniers, stuffed sofas—Heavens, the Commercial Bazaar and multitudinous Howel-and-Jameses cannot contain you. You have produced, produced;—he that seeks your indictment, let him look around. Millions of shirts, and empty pairs of breeches, hang there in judgment against you. We accuse you of over-producing: you are criminally guilty of producing shirts, breeches, hats, shoes and commodities, in a frightful over-abundance. And now there is a glut, and your operatives cannot be fed!"

Never surely, against an earnest Working Mammonism was there brought, by Game-preserving aristocratic Dilettantism, a stranger accusation, since this world began. My lords and gentlemen,—why, it was *you* that were appointed, by the fact and by the theory of your position on the Earth, to "make and administer Laws,"—that is to say, in a world such as ours, to guard against "gluts;" against honest operatives, who had done their work, remaining unfed! I say, *you* were appointed to preside over the Distribution and Apportionment of the Wages of Work done; and to see well that there went no labourer without his hire, were it of money-coins, were it of hemp gallows-ropes: that function was yours, and from immemorial time has been; yours, and as yet no other's. These poor shirt-spinners have forgotten much, which by the virtual unwritten law of their position they should have remembered: but by any written recognised law of their position, what have they forgotten? They were set to make shirts. The Community with all its voices commanded them, saying, "Make shirts;"—and there the shirts are! Too many shirts? Well, that is a novelty, in this intemperate Earth, with its nine-hundred millions of bare backs! But the Community commanded you, saying, "See that the shirts are well apportioned, that our Human Laws be emblem of God's Laws;"—and where is the apportionment? Two million shirtless or ill-shirted workers sit enchanted in Workhouse Bastilles, five million more (according to some) in Ugolino Hunger-cellars; and for remedy you say,—what say you?—"Raise *our* rents!" I have not in my time heard any stranger speech, not even on the Shores of the Dead Sea. You continue addressing those poor shirt-spinners and over-producers in really a *too* triumphant manner! . . .

False Philosophies: Laissez-faire and Democracy.[1] One thing I do know: Never, on this Earth, was the relation of man to man long carried on by Cash-payment alone. If, at any time, a philosophy of Laissez-faire, Competition and Supply-and-demand, start up as the exponent of human relations, expect that it will soon end.

Such philosophies will arise: for man's philosophies are usually the "supplement of his practice"; some ornamental Logic-varnish, some outer skin of Articulate Intelligence, with which he strives to render his dumb Instinctive Doings presentable when they are done. Such philosophies will arise; be preached as Mammon-Gospels, the ultimate Evangel of the World; be believed, with what is called belief, with much superficial bluster, and a kind of shallow satisfaction real in its way:—but they are ominous gospels! They are the sure, and even swift, forerunner of great changes. Expect that the old System of Society is done, is dying and fallen into dotage, when it begins to rave in that fashion. Most Systems that I have watched the death of,

[1] Pp. 195–196, 197, 223–224, 226–230.

for the last three thousand years, have gone just so. The Ideal, the True and Noble that was in them having faded out, and nothing now remaining but naked Egoism, vulturous Greediness, they cannot live; they are bound and inexorably ordained by the oldest Destinies, Mothers of the Universe, to die. Curious enough: they thereupon, as I have pretty generally noticed, devise some light comfortable kind of "wine-and-walnuts philosophy" for themselves, this of Supply-and-demand or another; and keep saying, during hours of mastication and rumination, which they call hours of meditation: "Soul, take thy ease; it is all *well* that thou art a vulture-soul;"—and pangs of dissolution come upon them, oftenest before they are aware!

Cash-payment never was, or could except for a few years be, the union-bond of man to man. Cash never yet paid one man fully his deserts to another; nor could it, nor can it, now or henceforth to the end of the world. I invite his Grace of Castle-Rackrent to reflect on this;—does he think that a Land Aristocracy when it becomes a Land Auctioneership can have long to live? Or that Sliding-scales will increase the vital stamina of it? The indomitable Plugson too, of the respected Firm of Plugson, Hunks and Company, in St. Dolly Undershot, is invited to reflect on this; for to him also it will be new, perhaps even newer. Book-keeping by double entry is admirable, and records several things in an exact manner. But the Mother-Destinies also keep their Tablets; in Heaven's Chancery also there goes on a recording; and things, as my Moslem friends say, are "written on the iron leaf." . . .

For all human things do require to have an Ideal in them; to have some Soul in them, as we said, were it only to keep the Body unputrefied. And wonderful it is to see how the Ideal or Soul, place it in what ugliest Body you may, will irradiate said Body with its own nobleness; will gradually, incessantly, mould, modify, new-form or reform said ugliest Body, and make it at last beautiful, and to a certain degree divine!—Oh, if you could dethrone that Brute-god Mammon, and put a Spirit-god in his place! One way or other, he must and will have to be dethroned. . . .

To what extent Democracy has now reached, how it advances irresistible with ominous, ever-increasing speed, he that will open his eyes on any province of human affairs may discern. Democracy is everywhere the inexorable demand of these ages, swiftly fulfilling itself. From the thunder of Napoleon battles, to the jabbering of Open-vestry in St. Mary Axe, all things announce Democracy. A distinguished man, whom some of my readers will hear again with pleasure, thus writes to me what in these days he notes from the Wahngasse of Weissnichtwo, where our London fashions seem to be in full vogue. Let us hear the Herr Teufelsdröckh [1] again, were it but the smallest word!

"Democracy, which means despair of finding any Heroes to govern you, and contented putting-up with the want of them,—alas, thou too, mein Lieber, seest well how close it is of kin to *Atheism*, and other sad *Isms:* he who discovers no God whatever, how shall he discover Heroes, the visible Temples of God?—Strange enough meanwhile it is, to observe with what thoughtlessness, here in our rigidly Conservative Country, men rush into Democracy with full cry. Beyond doubt, his Excellenz the Titular-Herr Ritter Kauderwälsch von Pferdefuss-Quacksalber, he our distinguished Conservative Premier himself, and all but the thicker-headed of his Party, discern Democracy to be inevitable as death, and are even desperate of delaying it much!" . . .

But truly, as I had to remark in the meanwhile, "the liberty of not being oppressed by your fellow man" is an indispensable, yet one of the most insignificant fractional parts of Human Liberty. No man oppresses thee, can bid thee fetch or carry, come or go, without reason shown. True; from all men thou art emancipated: but from Thyself and from the Devil—? No man, wiser, unwiser, can make thee come or go: but thy own futilities, bewilderments, thy false appetites for Money, Windsor Georges and suchlike? No man oppresses thee, O free and independent Franchiser: but does not this stupid Porter-pot oppress thee? No Son of Adam can bid thee come or go; but this absurd Pot of Heavy-wet, this can and does! Thou art the thrall not of Cedric the Saxon, but of thy own brutal appetites and this scoured dish of liquor. And thou pratest of thy "liberty"? Thou entire blockhead!

Heavy-wet and gin: alas, these are not the only kinds of thraldom. Thou who walkest in a vain show, looking out with ornamental dilettante sniff and serene supremacy at all Life and all Death; and amblest jauntily; perking up thy talk into crotchets, thy poor conduct into fatuous somnambulisms;—and *art* as an "enchanted Ape" under God's sky, where thou mightest have been a man, had proper Schoolmasters and Conquerors, and Constables with cat-o'-nine tails, been vouchsafed thee; dost thou call that "liberty"? Or your unreposing

[1] Carlyle's imaginary philosopher.

Mammon-worshipper again, driven, as if by Galvanisms, by Devils and Fixed-Ideas, who rises early and sits late, chasing the impossible; straining every faculty to "fill himself with the east wind,"—how merciful were it, could you, by mild persuasion, or by the severest tyranny so-called, check him in his mad path, and turn him into a wiser one! All painful tyranny, in that case again, were but mild "surgery"; the pain of it cheap, as health and life, instead of galvanism and fixed-idea, are cheap at any price.

Sure enough, of all paths a man could strike into, there *is*, at any given moment, a *best path* for every man; a thing which, here and now, it were of all things *wisest* for him to do;—which could he be but led or driven to do, he were then doing "like a man," as we phrase it; all men and gods agreeing with him, the whole Universe virtually exclaiming Well-done to him! His success, in such case, were complete; his felicity a maximum. This path, to find this path and walk in it, is the one thing needful for him. Whatsoever forwards him in that, let it come to him even in the shape of blows and spurnings, is liberty: whatsoever hinders him, were it wardmotes, open-vestries, poll-booths, tremendous cheers, rivers of heavy-wet, is slavery.

The notion that a man's liberty consists in giving his vote at election-hustings, and saying, "Behold, now I too have my twenty-thousandth part of a Talker in our National Palaver; will not all the gods be good to me?"—is one of the pleasantest! Nature nevertheless is kind at present; and puts it into the heads of many, almost of all. The liberty especially which has to purchase itself by social isolation, and each man standing separate from the other, having "no business with him" but a cash-account: this is such a liberty as the Earth seldom saw;—as the Earth will not long put up with, recommend it how you may. This liberty turns out, before it have long continued in action, with all men flinging up their caps round it, to be, for the Working Millions a liberty to die by want of food; for the Idle Thousands and Units, alas, a still more fatal liberty to live in want of work; to have no earnest duty to do in this God's-World any more. What becomes of a man in such predicament? Earth's Laws are silent; and Heaven's speak in a voice which is not heard. No work, and the ineradicable need of work, give rise to new very wondrous life-philosophies, new very wondrous life-practices! Dilettantism, Pococurantism, Beau-Brummelism, with perhaps an occasional, half-mad, protesting burst of Byronism, establish themselves: at the end of a certain period,—if you go back to "the Dead Sea," there is, say our Moslem friends, a very strange "Sabbath-day" transacting itself there!—Brethren, we know but imperfectly yet, after ages of Constitutional Government, what Liberty and Slavery are.

Democracy, the chase of Liberty in that direction, shall go its full course; unrestrainable by him of Pferdefuss-Quacksalber, or any of *his* household. The Toiling Millions of Mankind, in most vital need and passionate instinctive desire of Guidance, shall cast away False-Guidance; and hope, for an hour, that No-Guidance will suffice them: but it can be for an hour only. The smallest item of human Slavery is the oppression of man by his Mock-Superiors; the palpablest, but I say at bottom the smallest. Let him shake-off such oppression, trample it indignantly under his feet; I blame him not, I pity and commend him. But oppression by your Mock-Superiors well shaken off, the grand problem yet remains to solve: That of finding government by your Real-Superiors!—Alas, how shall we ever learn the solution of that, benighted, bewildered, sniffing, sneering, godforgetting unfortunates as we are? It is a work for centuries; to be taught us by tribulations, confusions, insurrections, obstructions; who knows if not by conflagration and despair! It is a lesson inclusive of all other lessons; the hardest of all lessons to learn.

One thing I do know: Those Apes, chattering on the branches by the Dead Sea, never got it learned; but chatter there to this day. To them no Moses need come a second time; a thousand Moseses would be but so many painted Phantasms, interesting Fellow-Apes of new strange aspect,—whom they would "invite to dinner," be glad to meet with in lion-soirées. To them the voice of Prophecy, of heavenly monition, is quite ended. They chatter there, all Heaven shut to them, to the end of the world. The unfortunates! Oh, what is dying of hunger, with honest tools in your hand, with a manful purpose in your heart, and much real labour lying round you done, in comparison? You honestly quit your tools; quit a most muddy confused coil of sore work, short rations, of sorrows, dispiritments and contradictions, having now honestly done with it all;—and await, not entirely in a distracted manner, what the Supreme Powers, and the Silences and the Eternities may have to say to you.

A second thing I know: This lesson will have to be learned,—under penalties! England will either learn it, or England also will cease to exist among Nations. England will either learn to reverence its Heroes, and discriminate them from its Sham-Heroes and Valets and gas-lighted Histrios; and to prize them as the audible God's-voice, amid all inane jargons and temporary market-cries, and say to them with heart-loyalty, "Be ye King and Priest, and Gospel and Guidance for us:" or else England will continue to worship new and ever-new forms of Quackhood,—and so, with what resiliences and reboundings matters little, go down to the Father of Quacks! Can I dread such things of England? Wretched, thick-eyed, gross-hearted mortals, why will ye worship lies, and "Stuffed Clothes-suits created by the ninth-parts of men"! It is not your purses that suffer: your farm-rents, your commerces, your mill-revenues, loud as ye lament over these; no, it is not these alone, but a far deeper than these: it is your souls that lie dead, crushed down under despicable Nightmares, Atheisms, Brain-fumes; and are not souls at all, but mere succedanea for *salt* to keep your bodies and their appetities from putrefying! Your cotton-spinning and thrice-miraculous mechanism, what is this too, by itself, but a larger kind of Animalism? Spiders can spin, Beavers can build and show contrivance; the Ant lays-up accumulation of capital, and has, for aught I know, a Bank of Antland. If there is no soul in man higher than all that, did it reach to sailing on the cloud-rack and spinning sea-sand; then I say, man is but an animal, a more cunning kind of brute: he has no soul, but only a succedaneum for salt. Whereupon, seeing himself to be truly of the beasts that perish, he ought to admit it, I think;—and also straightway universally to kill himself; and so, in a manlike manner at least *end*, and wave these brute-worlds *his* dignified farewell!— . . .

Wanted—a True Philosophy.[1] If the convulsive struggles of the last Half-Century have taught poor struggling convulsed Europe any truth, it may perhaps be this as the essence of innumerable others: That Europe requires a real Aristocracy, a real Priesthood, or it cannot continue to exist. Huge French Revolutions, Napoleonisms, then Bourbonisms with their corollary of Three Days, finishing in very unfinal Louis-Philippisms: all this ought to be didactic! All this may have taught us, That False Aristocracies are insupportable; that No-Aristocracies, Liberty-and-Equalities are impossible; that true Aristocracies are at once indispensable and not easily attained.

Aristocracy and Priesthood, a Governing Class and a Teaching Class: these two, sometimes separate, and endeavouring to harmonise themselves, sometimes conjoined as one, and the King a Pontiff-King: —there did no Society exist without these two vital elements, there

[1] Pp. 250–251, 253–254, 254–255, 280–282, 283–284, 285–287, 289–290.

will none exist. It lies in the very nature of man: you will visit no remotest village in the most republican country of the world, where virtually or actually you do not find these two powers at work. Man, little as he may suppose it, is necessitated to obey superiors. He is a social being in virtue of this necessity; nay he could not be gregarious otherwise. He obeys those whom he esteems better than himself, wiser, braver; and will forever obey such and even be ready and delighted to do it. . . .

Sorrowful, phantasmal as this same Double Aristocracy of Teachers and Governors now looks, it is worth all men's while to know that the purport of it is and remains noble and most real. Dryasdust, looking merely at the surface is greatly in error as to those ancient Kings. William Conqueror, William Rufus, or Redbeard, Stephen Curthose himself, much more Henry Beauclerc and our brave Plantagenet Henry: the life of these men was not a vulturous Fighting; it was a valorous Governing,—to which occasionally Fighting did, and alas must yet, though far seldomer now, superadd itself as an accident, a distressing impedimental adjunct. The fighting too was indispensable, for ascertaining who had the might over whom, the right over whom. By much hard fighting, as we once said, "the unrealities, beaten into dust, flew gradually off"; and left the plain reality and fact, "Thou stronger than I; thou wiser than I; thou king, and subject I," in a somewhat clearer condition.

Truly we cannot enough admire, in those Abbot-Samson and William-Conqueror times, the arrangement they had made of their Governing Classes. Highly interesting to observe how the sincere insight, on their part, into what did, of primary necessity, behove to be accomplished, had led them to the way of accomplishing it, and in the course of time to get it accomplished! No imaginary Aristocracy would serve their turn; and accordingly they attained a real one. The Bravest men, who, it is ever to be repeated and remembered, are also on the whole the Wisest, Strongest, everyway Best, had here, with a respectable degree of accuracy, been got selected; seated each on his piece of territory, which was lent him, then gradually given him, that he might govern it. These Vicekings, each on his portion of the common soil of England, with a Head King over all, were a "Virtuality perfected into an Actuality" really to an astonishing extent. . . .

That Feudal Aristocracy, I say, was no imaginary one. To a respectable degree, its *Jarls*, what we now call Earls, were *Strong-Ones* in fact as well as etymology; its Dukes *Leaders;* its Lords *Law-wards.* They did all the Soldiering and Police of the country, all the Judging, Law-making, even the Church-Extension; whatsoever in the way of Governing, of Guiding and Protecting could be done. It was a land Aristocracy; it managed the Governing of this English People, and had the reaping of the Soil of England in return. It is, in many senses, the Law of Nature, this same Law of Feudalism;—no right Aristocracy but a Land one! The curious are invited to meditate upon it in these days. Soldiering, Police and Judging, Church-Extension, any real Government and Guidance, all this was actually *done* by the Holders of the Land in return for their Land. How much of it is now done by them; done by anybody? . . .

If I believed that Mammonism with its adjuncts was to continue henceforth the one serious principle of our existence, I should reckon it idle to solicit remedial measures from any Government, the disease being insusceptible of remedy. Government can do much, but it can in no wise do all. Government, as the most conspicuous object in Society, is called upon to give signal of what shall be done; and, in many ways, to preside over, further, and command the doing of it. But the Government cannot do, by all its signaling and commanding, what the Society is radically indisposed to do. In the long-run every Government is the exact symbol of its People, with their wisdom and unwisdom; we have to say, Like People like Government.—The main substance of this immense Problem of Organising Labour, and first of all of Managing the Working Classes, will, it is very clear, have to be solved by those who themselves work and preside over work. Of all that can be enacted by any Parliament in regard to it, the germs must already lie potentially extant in those two Classes, who are to obey such enactment. A Human Chaos *in* which there is no light, you vainly attempt to irradiate by light shed *on* it: order never can arise there.

But it is my firm conviction that the "Hell of England" will *cease* to be that of "not making money"; that we shall get a nobler Hell and a nobler Heaven! I anticipate light *in* the Human Chaos, glimmering, shining more and more; under manifold true signals from without That light shall shine. Our deity no longer being Mammon,—O Heavens, each man will then say to himself: "Why such deadly haste to make money? I shall not go to Hell, even if I do not make money! There is another Hell, I am told!" Competition, at railway-speed, in all branches of commerce and work will then abate:—good felt-hats for the head, in every sense, instead of seven-feet lath-and-plaster hats on wheels, will then be discoverable! Bubble-periods, with their panics and commercial crises, will again become infrequent; steady modest industry will take the place of gambling speculation. To be a noble Master, among noble Workers, will again be the first ambition with some few; to be a rich Master only the second. How the Inventive Genius of England, with the whirr of its bobbins and billy-rollers shoved somewhat into the backgrounds of the brain, will contrive and devise, not cheaper produce exclusively, but fairer distribution of the produce at its present cheapness! By degrees, we shall again have a Society with something of Heroism in it, something of Heaven's Blessing on it; we shall again have, as my German friend asserts, "instead of Mammon-Feudalism with unsold cotton-shirts and Preservation of the Game, noble just Industrialism and Government by the Wisest!"

It is with the hope of awakening here and there a British man to know himself for a man and divine soul, that a few words of parting admonition, to all persons to whom the Heavenly Powers have lent power of any kind in this land, may now be addressed. And first to those same Master-Workers, Leaders of Industry; who stand nearest and in fact powerfulest, though not most prominent, being as yet in too many senses a Virtuality rather than an Actuality.

The Leaders of Industry, if Industry is ever to be led, are virtually the Captains of the World; if there be no nobleness in them, there will never be an Aristocracy more. . . .

Love of men cannot be bought by cash-payment; and without love men cannot endure to be together. You cannot lead a Fighting World without having it regimented, chivalried: the thing, in a day, becomes impossible; all men in it, the highest at first, the very lowest at last, discern consciously, or by a noble instinct, this necessity. And can you any more continue to lead a Working World unregimented, anarchic? I answer, and the Heavens and Earth are now answering, No! The thing becomes not "in a day" impossible; but in some two generations it does. Yes, when fathers and mothers, in Stockport hunger-cellars, begin to eat their children, and Irish widows have to prove their relationship by dying of typhus-fever; and amid Governing "Corporations of the Best and Bravest," busy to preserve their game by "bushing," dark millions of God's human creatures start up in mad Chartisms, impracticable Sacred-Months, and Manchester Insurrections;—and there is a virtual Industrial Aristocracy as yet only half-alive, spell-bound amid money-bags and ledgers; and an actual Idle Aristocracy seemingly near dead in somnolent delusions, in trespasses and double-barrels; "sliding," as on inclined-planes, which every new year they *soap* with new Hansard's-jargon under God's sky, and so are "sliding," ever faster, towards a "scale" and balance-scale whereon is written *Thou art found Wanting:*—in such days, after a generation or two, I say, it does become, even to the low and simple, very palpably impossible! No Working World, any more than a Fighting World, can be led on without a noble Chivalry of Work, and laws and fixed rules which follow out of that,—far nobler than any Chivalry of Fighting was. As an anarchic multitude on mere Supply-and-demand, it is becoming inevitable that we dwindle in horrid suicidal convulsion and self-abrasion, frightful to the imagination, into *Chactaw* Workers. With wigwams and scalps,—with palaces and thousand-pound bills; with savagery, depopulation, chaotic desolation! Good Heavens, will not one French Revolution and Reign of Terror suffice us, but must there be two? There will be two if needed; there will be twenty if needed; there will be precisely as many as are needed. The Laws of Nature will have themselves fulfilled. That is a thing certain to me. . . .

Awake, ye noble Workers, warriors in the one true war: all this must be remedied. It is you who are already half-alive, whom I will welcome into life; whom I will conjure, in God's name, to shake off your enchanted sleep, and live wholly! Cease to count scalps, gold-purses; not in these lies your or our salvation. Even these, if you count only these, will not long be left. Let bucaniering be put far from you; alter, speedily abrogate all laws of the bucaniers, if you would gain any victory that shall endure. Let God's justice, let pity, nobleness and manly valour, with more gold-purses or with fewer, testify themselves in this your brief Life-transit to all the Eternities, the Gods and Silences. It is to you I call; for ye are not dead, ye are already half-alive: there is in you a sleepless dauntless energy, the prime-matter of all nobleness in man. Honour to you in your kind. It is to you I call: ye know at least this, That the mandate of God to His creature man is: Work! The future Epic of the World rests not with those that are near dead, but with those that are alive, and those that are coming into life.

Look around you. Your world-hosts are all in mutiny, in confusion, destitution; on the eve of fiery wreck and madness! They will not march farther for you, on the sixpence a day and supply-and-demand principle: they will not; nor ought they, nor can they. Ye shall reduce them to order, begin reducing them. To order, to just subordination; noble loyalty in return for noble guidance. Their souls are driven nigh mad; let yours be sane and ever saner. Not as a bewildered bewildering mob; but as a firm regimented mass, with real captains over them, will these men march any more. All human interests, combined human endeavours, and social growths in this world, have, at a certain stage of their development, required organising: and Work, the grandest of human interests does now require it.

God knows, the task will be hard: but no noble task was ever easy. This task will wear away your lives, and the lives of your sons and grandsons: but for what purpose, if not for tasks like this, were lives given to men? Ye shall cease to count your thousand-pound scalps, the noble of you shall cease! Nay the very scalps, as I say, will not long be left if you count only these. Ye shall cease wholly to be barbarous vulturous Chactaws, and become noble European Nineteenth-Century Men. Ye shall know that Mammon, in never such gigs and flunky "respectabilities," is not the alone God; that of himself he is but a Devil, and even a Brute-god.

Difficult? Yes, it will be difficult. The short-fibre cotton; that too was difficult. The waste cotton-shrub, long useless, disobedient, as the thistle by the wayside,—have ye not conquered it: made it into beautiful bandana webs; white woven shirts for men; bright-tinted air-garments wherein fit goddesses? Ye have shivered mountains asunder, made the hard iron pliant to you as soft putty: the Forest-giants, Marsh-jötuns bear sheaves of golden-grain; Ægir the Sea-demon himself stretches his back for a sleek highway to you, and on Firehorses and Windhorses ye career. Ye are most strong. Thor red-bearded, with his blue sun-eyes, with his cheery heart and strong thunder-hammer, he and you have prevailed. Ye are most strong, ye Sons of the icy North, of the Far East,—far marching from your rugged Eastern Wildernesses, hitherward from the grey Dawn of Time! Ye are Sons of the *Jötun*-land; the land of Difficulties Conquered. Difficult? You must try this thing. Once try it with the understanding that it will and shall have to be done. Try it as ye try the paltrier thing, making of money! I will bet on you once more, against all Jötuns, Tailor-gods, Double-barrelled Law-wards, and Denizens of Chaos whatsoever! . . .

In a Printed Sheet of the assiduous, much-abused, and truly useful Mr. Chadwick's, containing queries and responses from far and near as to this great question, "What is the effect of education on working-men, in respect of their value as mere workers?" the present Editor, reading with satisfaction a decisive unanimous verdict as to Education, reads with inexpressible interest this special remark, put in by way of marginal incidental note, from a practical manufacturing Quaker, whom, as he is anonymous, we will call Friend Prudence. Prudence keeps a thousand workmen; has striven in all ways to attach them to him; has provided conversational soirées; play-grounds, bands of music for the young ones; went even "the length of buying them a drum:" all which has turned out to be an excellent investment. For a certain person, marked here by a black stroke, whom we shall name Blank, living over the way,—he also keeps somewhere about a thousand men; but has done none of these things for them, nor any other thing, except due payment of the wages by supply-and-demand. Blank's workers are perpetually getting into mutiny, into broils and coils: every six months, we suppose, Blank has a strike; every one month, every day and every hour, they are fretting and obstructing the shortsighted Blank; pilfering from him, wasting and idling for him, omitting and committing for him. "I would not," says Friend Prudence, "exchange my workers for his *with seven thousand pounds to boot.*"

Right, O honourable Prudence; thou art wholly in the right: Seven thousand pounds even as a matter of profit for this world, nay for the mere cash-market of this world! And as a matter of profit not for this world only, but for the other world and all worlds, it outweighs the Bank of England!—Can the sagacious reader descry here, as it were the outmost inconsiderable rock-ledge of a universal rock-foundation, deep once more as the Centre of the World, emerging so, in the experience of this good Quaker, through the Stygian mud-vortexes and general Mother of Dead Dogs, whereon, for the present, all sways and insecurely hovers, as if ready to be swallowed? . . .

Portents of a New Age.[1] Certainly it were a fond imagination to expect that any preaching of mine could abate Mammonism; that Bobus of Houndsditch will love his guineas less, or his poor soul more, for any preaching of mine! But there is one Preacher who does preach with effect, and gradually persuade all persons: his name is Destiny, is Divine Providence, and his Sermon the inflexible Course of Things. Experience does take dreadfully high school-wages; but he teaches like no other!

[1] Pp. 304–308.

I revert to Friend Prudence the good Quaker's refusal of "seven thousand pounds to boot." Friend Prudence's practical conclusion will, by degrees, become that of all rational practical men whatsoever. On the present scheme and principle, Work cannot continue. Trades' Strikes, Trades' Unions, Chartisms: mutiny, squalor, rage and desperate revolt, growing ever more desperate, will go on their way. As dark misery settles down on us, and our refuges of lies fall in pieces one after one, the hearts of men, now at last serious, will turn to refuges of truth. The eternal stars shine out again, so soon as it is dark *enough*.

Begirt with desperate Trades' Unionism and Anarchic Mutiny, many an Industrial *Law-ward*, by and by, who has neglected to make laws and keep them, will be heard saying to himself: "Why have I realised five hundred thousand pounds? I rose early and sat late, I toiled and moiled, and in the sweat of my brow and of my soul I strove to gain this money, that I might become conspicuous, and have some honour among my fellow-creatures. I wanted them to honour me, to love me. The money is here, earned with my best lifehood: but the honour? I am encircled with squalor, with hunger, rage, and sooty desperation. Not honoured, hardly even envied; only tools and the flunky-species so much as envy me. I am conspicuous,—as a mark for curses and brickbats. What good is it? My five hundred scalps hang here in my wigwam: would to Heaven I had sought something else than the scalps; would to Heaven I had been a Christian Fighter, not a Chactaw one! To have ruled and fought not in a Mammonish but in a God-like spirit; to have had the hearts of the people bless me, as a true ruler and captain of my people; to have felt my own heart bless me, and that God above instead of Mammon below was blessing me,—this had been something. Out of my sight, ye beggarly five hundred scalps of banker's-thousands: I will try for something other, or account my life a tragical futility!"

Friend Prudence's "rock-ledge," as we called it, will gradually disclose itself to many a man; to all men. Gradually, assaulted from beneath and from above, the Stygian mud-deluge of Laissez-faire, Supply-and-demand, Cash-payment the one Duty, will abate on all hands; and the everlasting mountain-tops, and secure rock-foundations that reach to the centre of the world, and rest on Nature's self, will again emerge, to found on, and to build on. When Mammon-worshippers here and there begin to be God-worshippers, and bipeds-of-prey become men, and there is a Soul felt once more in the huge-pulsing elephantine mechanic Animalism of this Earth, it will be again a blessed Earth.

"Men cease to regard money?" cries Bobus of Houndsditch: "What else do all men strive for? The very Bishop informs me that Christianity cannot get on without a minimum of Four thousand five hundred in its pocket. Cease to regard money? That will be at Doomsday in the Afternoon!"—O Bobus, my opinion is somewhat different. My opinion is, that the Upper Powers have not yet determined on destroying this Lower World. A respectable, ever-increasing minority, who do strive for something higher than money, I with confidence anticipate; ever-increasing, till there be a sprinkling of them found in all quarters, as salt of the Earth once more. The Christianity that cannot get on without a minimum of Four thousand five hundred, will give place to something better that can. Thou wilt not join our small minority, thou? Not till Doomsday in the afternoon? Well; *then*, at least, thou wilt join it, thou and the majority in mass!

But truly it is beautiful to see the brutish empire of Mammon cracking everywhere; giving sure promise of dying, or of being changed. A strange, chill, almost ghastly dayspring strikes up in Yankeeland itself: my Transcendental friends announce there, in a distinct, though somewhat lankhaired, ungainly manner, that the Demiurgus Dollar is dethroned; that new unheard-of Demiurgusships, Priesthoods, Aristocracies, Growths and Destructions, are already visible in the gray of coming Time. Chronos is dethroned by Jove; Odin by St. Olaf: the Dollar cannot rule in Heaven forever. No; I reckon, not. Socinian Preachers quit their pulpits in Yankeeland, saying, "Friends, this is all gone to coloured cob-web, we regret to say!"—and retire into the fields to cultivate onion-beds, and live frugally on vegetables. It is very notable. Old godlike Calvinism declares that its old body is now fallen to tatters, and done; and its mournful ghost, disembodied, seeking new embodiment, pipes again in the winds;—a ghost and spirit as yet, but heralding new Spirit-worlds, and better Dynasties than the Dollar one.

Yes, here as there, light is coming into the world; men love not darkness, they do love light. A deep feeling of the eternal nature of Justice looks out among us everywhere,—even through the dull eyes of Exeter Hall; an unspeakable religiousness struggles, in the most helpless manner, to speak itself, in Puseyisms and the like. Of our Cant, all condemnable, how much is not condemnable without pity;

we had almost said, without respect! The *in*articulate worth and truth that is in England goes down yet to the Foundations.

Some "Chivalry of Labour," some noble Humanity and practical Divineness of Labour, will yet be realised on this Earth. Or why *will;* why do we pray to Heaven, without setting our own shoulder to the wheel? The Present, if it will have the Future accomplish, shall itself commence. Thou who prophesiest, who believest, begin thou to fulfil. Here or nowhere, now equally as at any time! That outcast help-needing thing or person, trampled down under vulgar feet or hoofs, no help "possible" for it, no prize offered for the saving of it,—canst not thou save it, then, without prize? Put forth thy hand, in God's name; know that "impossible," where Truth and Mercy and the everlasting Voice of Nature order, has no place in the brave man's dictionary. That when all men have said "Impossible," and tumbled noisily elsewhither, and thou alone art left, then first thy time and possibility have come. It is for thee now; do thou that, and ask no man's counsel, but thy own only, and God's. Brother, thou hast possibility in thee for much: the possibility of writing on the eternal skies the record of a heroic life. That noble downfallen or yet unborn "Impossibility," thou canst lift it up, thou canst, by thy soul's travail, bring it into clear being. That loud inane Actuality, with millions in its pocket, too "possible" that, which rolls along there, with quilted trumpeters blaring round it, and all the world escorting it as mute or vocal flunky,—escort it not thou; say to it, either nothing, or else deeply in thy heart: "Loud-blaring Nonentity, no force of trumpets, cash, Long-acre art, or universal flunkyhood of men, makes thee an Entity; thou art a *Non*entity, and deceptive Simulacrum, more accursed than thou seemest. Pass on in the Devil's name, unworshipped by at least one man, and leave the thoroughfare clear!" . . .

PART III

EARLY NINETEENTH-CENTURY SOCIALISMS

IX

ROBERT OWEN

1771–1858

Robert Owen was born in Wales, made his fortune in Scotland, and became a major prophet in England. In 1771, when Owen was born, Newtown, his native place, was untouched by the industrial changes then sweeping over Britain, and his father pursued the ancient trades of saddler and ironmonger. Robert was the sixth of seven children. Parental discipline was not severe: indeed there seems to have been little occasion to exercise it, for the Owens encouraged their son to think for himself, and the latter repaid them by sensible behavior. Before the age of seven he was an omnivorous reader. Three Methodist ladies of the neighborhood lent him books and further incited him to think independently. As a child he was deeply religious; indeed he remained so throughout life, although in a more and more unorthodox fashion.

The primary and only school he ever attended gave him nothing beyond the three R's. The master, however, thought so well of his abilities that he employed him as an assistant at the age of seven. Owen thus acquired the habit of teaching others which he used to such good purpose later on.

At nine Robert was taken out of school to enter the dry-goods trade. He remained in it for nine years, being employed first in Newtown and then successively in Stamford, London, and Manchester. During his apprenticeship at Stamford he lived with his employer and was treated almost as one of the family. There was plenty of leisure for reading and reflection; he observed the clash of religious doctrine in his master's household: the husband being a Presbyterian and the wife an Anglican, Robert had to attend these churches alternately. By the age of thirteen he had come to believe that all sects were wrong and had even (if his later reminiscences can be trusted) reached a conclusion that pervaded his whole future thought. "My reason taught me . . . that my language, religion and habits were forced upon me by society—that nature gave the qualities, and society directed them." His orthodox religious sentiments were "immediately replaced by the spirit of universal charity."

But the philosophical apprentice did not lose himself in speculation; he became an excellent judge of textiles, especially cottons, and the opportunity arose of going into business for himself. Manchester, where he was now employed, was the center of the rapidly expanding cotton trade, and when a mechanic experienced in making spinning machinery suggested a partnership for this purpose Owen unhesitatingly agreed. He borrowed £100 of his brother and at the age of eighteen became a full-fledged entrepreneur. But the venture was not a success; the partner proved to be a poor manager and Owen was glad to sell his interest at the end of a year. With the proceeds of the sale—six spinning machines and a few other pieces of equipment—he set up shop for himself. This time the business prospered modestly. He did not hesitate to give it up, however, when he was offered a position as manager in one of the largest cotton mills in England.

Though not yet twenty, Owen made a brilliant record in his new post; he was soon promised a partnership and had every prospect of becoming a captain of industry. At the end of five years, however, his employer thought better of taking him into the business; Owen promptly resigned. He now formed a partnership with two other capitalists of the trade and resumed his upward march. When the New Lanark mills in Scotland came on the market Owen induced his associates to buy them.

With the acquisition of the New Lanark mills Owen's public career began. In a few years he was to be known in England and Europe as the benevolent employer *par excellence*, the more admirable because he made benevolence pay. During his years of commercial striving Owen had pondered on other things besides success in business. At Manchester he had discussed human problems with Coleridge and with John Dalton the chemist. He also doubtless observed the paternalism of Samuel Oldknow's establishment, where agriculture, quarrying, and cotton manufacture were carried on under the kindly eye of the master. At New Lanark Owen had a more direct precedent in the humane régime of David Dale, the previous owner, some of whose practices he continued. But Owen's innovations went far beyond these earlier examples. He mended the streets, enlarged old houses and built new ones, improved the sanitation, and dispensed better and cheaper food and drink in company-owned stores. Above all he ceased to employ pauper apprentices below ten years of age and reduced the working day to less than eleven hours. Such changes may seem mild enough—he would have gone farther along these lines if his partners had permitted it.

Owen had succeeded in creating something like a community at New Lanark. To unify the group completely required something more, and Owen now brought forward the proposal which in his opinion was essential not only to the success of New Lanark but to social progress in general. He would reconstitute society by way of education. The plan was announced in *A New View of Society, or Essays on the Formation of Character*, first published in parts in 1813–14. Owen's earlier views, as we have seen, foreshadowed its basic doctrine, that environment is all-important in the life of the community if not in that of the individual, and that a proper type of education will destroy national, religious, and also class prejudices. The book contained in essence the socialistic and religious philosophy which he advocated later on, but this was not at once apparent. It is not clear even yet what he owed to other thinkers in the field. At this time, however, he was on terms of friendship with William Godwin who held similar views, and before publishing the *Essays* he had submitted them for criticism to James Mill, Francis Place, and other friends. He may also have been influenced by Pestalozzi as well as other continental writers on education.

Meanwhile Owen was attempting to put his theories into practice. There was little difficulty in establishing at New Lanark an "Institution for the Formation of Character"—in other words, a school—but other projects moved more slowly. An agitation for reducing the hours of children's labor, which he started, resulted in an extremely mild act of Parliament in 1819—so mild in fact that Owen had lost interest in it before it reached the statute book. During the depression which followed the peace of 1815 he came forward with a plan to relieve unemployment by colonizing workers in "villages of coöperation." The great ones of the land did not perceive that this was communism in embryo—perhaps Owen himself was unconscious of it—and they gave the scheme much verbal support. But adequate funds were not forthcoming and Owen was kept dangling for years in vain expectation.

Owen's appeal to the governing class was a failure for more than one reason. In 1817 he had weakened his influence with "respectable" people by denouncing religion as a bar to social improvement, and from then on the charge of atheism was used more and more frequently as a means of blackening his character and discrediting his projects. But the scope of the latter only became more daring as time passed. His *Report to the County of Lanark* (1821) embodied the plan of a new social order.

Although the aristocracy had not as yet completely deserted him, his real support was coming from the working class. William Lovett, the future Chartist leader, preached Owenism, retail coöperative societies sprang up, a fund was started to establish a model community: the future of Owen's schemes seemed to rest with the proletariat.

While most of these events were taking place Owen himself was in America organizing a coöperative community at his own private expense. In 1825 he purchased a 30,000-acre estate in Indiana from a religious group who had operated it and set up his establishment under the name of "New Harmony." The settlement, however, belied its name; dissension arose over ownership, organization, and education, and Owen withdrew in 1828 with the loss of £40,000—four-fifths of his entire fortune.

He returned to England in 1829 a dominant figure in the working-class world. By 1830 there were some three hundred coöperative societies throughout the country and in 1831 the first Coöperative Congress assembled. The next year Owen carried out one of his most original ideas: he set up a "National Equitable Labor Exchange," or bank, in which workmen deposited articles of their own manufacture and received "labor notes" in exchange. For a time the enterprise was successful and the notes circulated widely in London.

Owen's personal influence in the labor movement culminated in 1833. Disillusioned by the Reform Act of 1832 which excluded them from the suffrage, the working class abandoned politics and turned to direct action as a means of redressing their grievances. General trade unions had been attempted before without success, but in 1833 the agitation recommenced. Owen travelled up and down the country preaching a union of all workingmen as the way to achieve a coöperative state. The new order, he assured them, could be erected within five years. Optimism ran high. Owen was at last in his proper rôle—the dominant figure in labor politics, the prophet of working-class solidarity.

At a meeting of delegates in 1833 he proposed a "Grand National Moral Union of the Productive and Useful Classes." A subsequent congress dropped the Moral attribute but drew up a constitution for a "Grand National Consolidated Trades Union." Individual unions adhered to the new body, large numbers of agricultural laborers came in, and within a few weeks more than half a million workers had enrolled.

Almost from the beginning signs of disruption appeared. Owen and his lieutenants planned a series of concerted strikes, but individual groups persistently involved themselves in local disputes and so weakened the general organization. Employers added to the difficulties of the Grand National when they penalized workingmen who entered it. The government itself took a hand by prosecuting members for administering illegal oaths. But dissension sprang up at the very seat of authority: Owen accused his subordinates of stirring up class hatred—they responded by charging him with atheism and autocracy. Weakened by outside attacks and internal divisions, its finances drained, the pretentious fabric of the Union gradually crumbled away. Toward the end of 1834 Owen called together a congress of Owenite societies and persuaded them to form a "British and Foreign Consolidated Association of Industry, Humanity, and Knowledge." The congress resolved that "effective measures should be adopted to reconcile the masters and operatives throughout the kingdom," but this itself was a confession that militant unionism had failed.

For the rest of his life Owen was continually elaborating his system. He took part in founding another coöperative settlement in Ireland. But Owenism was becoming more and more a religion with him; he withdrew from the labor movement and devoted his energy to propagating the new faith. In process of time his immediate following was converted into a sect; it became the "Society of Rational Religionists"—the parent of the modern secularist and ethical movements. But Owen himself did not stop there; at eighty-two he turned spiritualist and conversed on intimate terms with Shakespeare, the prophet Daniel, and Napoleon. A restless and rather pathetic figure, he died in 1858 almost forgotten by his contemporaries.

The theory and practice of Robert Owen worked powerfully toward humanizing the capitalist system of Great Britain and also toward laying the foundations of a new order of society. As a highly successful manufacturer he showed that one might conduct a profitable business and still consult the welfare of the employees, or, to put it more cynically, that philanthropy could be combined with exploitation. The economic argument has always been considered one of the most effective ways to promote reform from above; if it can be proved that profits will not suffer and may even be increased under a milder régime, the battle is already half won. Social legislation doubtless received a powerful stimulus from Owen's precept and example.

But his appeal to reformers and workingmen who demanded more fundamental measures was perhaps no less effective than his appeal to the ruling class. One of the practical results in that direction was the coöperative movement which developed ultimately into the huge modern organization of British consumers. Owen has also been called the first systematic exponent of socialism in Great Britain. The peculiar type of socialism he professed no doubt became rapidly outmoded, but his ideas contain intimations of modern state socialism, syndicalism, and guild socialism. If he did not plant the seed of these movements, he at least broke the ground for its reception.

REFERENCES

There is no collected edition of Owen's works. A selection of his shorter (and more important) writings has been edited by G. D. H. Cole (1927).

Owen's autobiography (with an introduction by M. Beer) was reprinted in 1920. Short sketches of his life and thought are given in two Fabian Tracts, No. 166 (1912) by B. L. Hutchins and No. 182 (1917) by C. E. M. Joad. The most detailed life is by F. Podmore (1906, reprinted 1923). An excellent critical biography is that of G. D. H. Cole (2nd ed., 1930).

READINGS FROM

REPORT

To the County of Lanark, of a Plan for relieving Public Distress and Removing Discontent, by giving permanent, productive Employment to the Poor and Working Classes, under Arrangements which will essentially improve their Character, and ameliorate their Condition, diminish the Expenses of Production and Consumption, and create Markets co-extensive with Production. By Robert Owen. May 1st, 1820.

The following Report was submitted, at the request of a Committee of Gentlemen of the Upper Ward of Lanarkshire, to a General Meeting of the County, held at Lanark on the 1st May, 1820 . . .

General Principles.[1] The evil for which your Reporter has been required to provide a remedy, is the general want of employment at wages sufficient to support the family of a working man beneficially for the community.

After the most earnest consideration of the subject he has been compelled to conclude that such employment cannot be procured through the medium of trade, commerce, or manufactures, or even of agriculture, until the Government and the Legislature, cordially supported by the country, shall previously adopt measures to remove obstacles which, without their interference, will now permanently keep the working classes in poverty and discontent, and gradually deteriorate all the resources of the empire.

Your Reporter has been impressed with the truth of this conclusion by the following considerations:

First.—That manual labour, properly directed, is the source of all wealth, and of national prosperity.

Second.—That, when properly directed, labour is of far more value to the community than the expense necessary to maintain the labourer in considerable comfort.

Third.—That manual labour, properly directed, may be made to continue of this value in all parts of the world, under any supposable increase of its population, for many centuries to come.

Fourth.—That, under a proper direction of manual labour, Great Britain and its dependencies may be made to support an incalculable increase of population, most advantageously for all its inhabitants.

Fifth.—That when manual labour shall be so directed, it will be found that population cannot, for many years, be stimulated to advance as rapidly as society might be benefited by its increase.

These considerations, deduced from the first and most obvious principles of the science of political economy, convinced your Reporter that some formidable artificial obstacle intervened to obstruct the natural improvement and progress of society.

It is well known that, during the last half-century in particular, Great Britain, beyond any other nation, has progressively increased its powers of production, by a rapid advancement in scientific improvements and arrangements, introduced, more or less, into all the departments of productive industry throughout the empire.

The amount of this new productive power cannot, for want of

[1] Pp. 245–248, 248–249, 250. References are to G. D. H. Cole's edition (Everyman's Library, 1927).

proper data, be very accurately estimated; but your Reporter has ascertained, from facts which none will dispute, that its increase has been enormous;—that, compared with the manual labour of the whole population of Great Britain and Ireland, it is, at least, as *forty to one*, and may be easily made as 100 *to one;* and that this increase may be extended to other countries; that it is already sufficient to saturate the world with wealth, and that the power of creating wealth may be made to advance perpetually in an accelerating ratio.

It appeared to your Reporter that the natural effect of the aid thus obtained from knowledge and science should be to add to the wealth and happiness of society in proportion as the new power increased and was judiciously directed; and that, in consequence, all parties would thereby be substantially benefited. All know, however, that these beneficial effects do not exist. On the contrary, it must be acknowledged that the working classes, which form so large a proportion of the population, cannot obtain even the comforts which their labour formerly procured for them, and that no party appears to gain, but all to suffer, by their distress.

Having taken this view of the subject, your Reporter was induced to conclude that the want of beneficial employment for the working classes, and the consequent public distress, were owing to the rapid increase of the new productive power, for the advantageous application of which, society had neglected to make the proper arrangements. Could these arrangements be formed, he entertained the most confident expectation that productive employment might again be found for all who required it; and that the national distress, of which all now so loudly complain, might be gradually converted into a much higher degree of prosperity than was attainable prior to the extraordinary accession lately made to the productive powers of society.

Cheered by such a prospect, your Reporter directed his attention to the consideration of the possibility of devising arrangements by means of which the whole population might participate in the benefits derivable from the increase of scientific productive power; and he has the satisfaction to state to the meeting, that he has strong grounds to believe that such arrangements are practicable.

His opinion on this important part of the subject is founded on the following considerations:

First.—It must be admitted that scientific or artificial aid to man increases his productive powers, his natural wants remaining the same; and in proportion as his productive powers increase he becomes less dependent on his physical strength and on the many contingencies connected with it.

Second.—That the direct effect of every addition to scientific, or mechanical and chemical power is to increase wealth; and it is found, accordingly, that the immediate cause of the present want of employment for the working classes is an excess of production of all kinds of wealth, by which, under the existing arrangements of commerce, all the markets of the world are overstocked.

Third.—That, could markets be found, an incalculable addition might yet be made to the wealth of society, as is most evident from the number of persons who seek employment, and the far greater number who, from ignorance, are inefficiently employed, but still more from the means we possess of increasing, to an unlimited extent, our scientific powers of production.

Fourth.—That the deficiency of employment for the working classes cannot proceed from a want of wealth or capital, or of the means of greatly adding to that which now exists, but from some defect in the mode of distributing this extraordinary addition of new capital throughout society, or, to speak commercially, from the want of a market, or means of exchange, co-extensive with the means of production.

Were effective measures devised to facilitate the distribution of wealth after it was created, your Reporter could have no difficulty in suggesting the means of beneficial occupation for all who are unemployed, and for a considerable increase to their number. . . .

It is urgent necessity alone that will effect the changes which our present situation demands; one of which respects the mode of distributing the enormous supply of new wealth or capital which has been lately created, and which may be now indefinitely increased. To the ignorance which prevails on this and other subjects connected with the science of political economy may be attributed the present general stagnation of commerce, and the consequent distress of the country.

Your Reporter, undismayed by any opposition he may excite, is determined to perform his duty, and to use his utmost exertions to induce the Public to take into calm consideration those practical measures which to him appear the only remedy adequate to remove this distress.

One of the measures which he thus ventures to propose, *to let prosperity loose on the country* (if he may be allowed the expression), is *a change in the standard of value.*

It is true that in the civilized parts of the world gold and silver have long been used for this purpose; but these metals have been a mere artificial standard, and they have performed the office very imperfectly and inconveniently.

Their introduction as a standard of value altered the *intrinsic* values of all things into *artificial* values; and, in consequence, they have materially retarded the general improvement of society. So much so, that, in this sense, it may well be said, "Money is the root of all evil." It is fortunate for society that these metals cannot longer perform the task which ignorance assigned to them. The rapid increase of wealth, which extraordinary scientific improvements had been the means of producing in this country prior to 1797, imposed upon the Legislature in that year an overwhelming necessity to declare virtually by Act of Parliament that gold ceased to be the British standard of value. Experience then proved that gold and silver could no longer practically represent the increased wealth created by British industry aided by its scientific improvements.

A temporary expedient was thought of and adopted, and Bank of England paper became the British legal standard of value;—a convincing proof that society may make any artificial substance, whether possessing intrinsic worth or not, a legal standard of value. . . .

Your Reporter, then, after deeply studying these subjects, practically and theoretically, for a period exceeding thirty years, and during which his practice without a single exception has confirmed the theory which practice first suggested, now ventures to state, as one of the results of this study and experience,

THAT THE NATURAL STANDARD OF VALUE IS, IN PRINCIPLE, HUMAN LABOUR, OR THE COMBINED MANUAL AND MENTAL POWERS OF MEN CALLED INTO ACTION. . . .

Spade Cultivation as a Remedy for Unemployment.[1] It is admitted that under the present system no more hands can be employed advantageously in agriculture or manufactures; and that both interests are on the eve of bankruptcy.

It is also admitted that the prosperity of the country, or rather that which ought to create prosperity, the improvement in mechanical and chemical science, has enabled the population to produce more than the present system permits to be consumed.

In consequence, new arrangements become necessary, by which

[1] Pp. 253–254, 255–256, 257, 259.

consumption may be made to keep pace with *production*, and the following are recommended:

First.—To cultivate the soil with the spade instead of the plough.

Second.—To make such changes as the spade cultivation requires, to render it easy and profitable to individuals, and beneficial to the country.

Third.—To adopt a standard of value by means of which the exchange of the products of labour may proceed without check or limit, until wealth shall become so abundant that any further increase to it will be considered useless, and will not be desired.

We proceed to give the reasons for recommending these arrangements in preference to all others.

And first, those for preferring the spade to the plough for the universal cultivation of the soil.

Practical cultivators of the soil know, that the most favourable circumstance for promoting the growth of vegetation is a due supply of moisture, and that when this is provided for, a good general crop seldom, if ever, fails.

Water enters so largely into the food of all plants that if its gradual supply can be secured, the farmer and horticulturist feel assured of a fair return for their labour. Whatever mode of cultivation, therefore, can best effect the object of drawing off from the seed or plant an excess of water, and retaining this surplus as a reservoir from which a gradual supply of moisture may be obtained as required, must possess decided advantages.

It is also known to all practical agriculturists, that to obtain the best crops, the soil ought to be well broken and separated; and that the nearer it is brought to a garden mould, the more perfect is the cultivation. . . .

These facts being incontrovertible, few perhaps will hesitate to admit them.

But it may be said that, "admitting the statement to be true to the full extent, yet the plough, with a pair of horses and one man, performs so much work in a given time that, with all its imperfections, it may be a more economical instrument for the purpose required."

Such has been the almost universal impression for ages past, and, in consequence, the plough has superseded the spade, and is considered to be an improved machine for ordinary cultivation.

All this is plausible, and is sanctioned by the old prejudices of the world; but your Reporter maintains that it is not true that the plough is, or has ever been, in any stage of society, the most economical instrument for the cultivation of the soil. It has been so in appearance only, not in reality.

Cultivated as the soil has been hitherto, the direct expense of preparing it by the plough (in the manner in which the plough prepares it) has been in many cases less per acre than it would have been by the spade. The increased crop which the latter implement would have produced, all other circumstances being the same, does not seem to have been taken into account, or to have been accurately ascertained, except by Mr. Falla, of Gateshead, near Newcastle, who, for many years, has had a hundred acres under spade cultivation, chiefly for nursery purposes, and who, by his practical knowledge of the subject, has realized, as your Reporter is informed, a large fortune. He has satisfactorily proved, by the experiments of four successive years, that although the expense of cultivation by the spade exceeds that of the plough per acre, yet the increased value of the crop greatly overbalances the increased expense of cultivation, and that even with "things as they are" the spade is a much better, and also a much more economical instrument with which to cultivate the soil, than the plough.

Why, then, your Reporter may be asked, is not the spade more generally used, and why is there now so much reluctance, on the part of those who cultivate the soil for profit, to its introduction?

A little will explain this.

Hitherto, those who have cultivated the soil for profit have generally been men trained to be tenacious of old-established practices, all their ideas have been confined within a very narrow range; they have not been taught to think about anything, till lately, except that which was in the common routine of their daily practice. Their minds were uncultivated; yet, having naturally the use of their senses, they could not fail gradually to acquire by experience a useful knowledge of their domestic animals, of pigs, sheep, cattle, and horses. These they could treat and manage well; but, taught as men have ever yet been instructed, they could acquire no knowledge of themselves, and must have consequently remained ignorant of human nature and of the means by which the powers of *men* could be applied more advantageously to the soil than the powers of *animals*. . . .

They must acquire as accurate a knowledge of *human* nature as they now possess of common *animal* nature. Agriculture, instead of being, as heretofore, the occupation of the mere peasant and farmer, with minds as defective in their cultivation as their soils, will then become the delightful employment of a race of men trained in the best habits and dispositions, familiar with the most useful practice in arts and sciences, and with minds fraught with the most valuable information and extensive general knowledge,—capable of forming and conducting combined arrangements in agriculture, trade, commerce, and manufactures, far superior to those which have yet existed in any of these departments, as they have been hitherto disjointed and separately conducted.

It will be readily perceived that this is an advance in civilization and general improvement that is to be effected solely *through the science of the influence of circumstances over human nature, and the knowledge of the means by which those circumstances may be easily controlled*. . . .

It is estimated that in Great Britain and Ireland there are now under cultivation upwards of *sixty millions* of acres; and of these, *twenty millions* are arable, and *forty millions* in pasture;—that, under the present system of cultivation by the plough and of pasturing, about *two millions*, at most, of *actual labourers* are employed on the soil, giving immediate support to about *three times* that number, and supplying food for a population of about *eighteen millions*. *Sixty millions* of acres, under a judicious arrangement of spade cultivation, with manufactures as an appendage, might be made to give healthy advantageous employment to *sixty millions* of labourers at the least, and to support in high comfort a population greatly exceeding *one hundred millions*. But in the present low state of population in these islands not more than *five or six millions* of acres could be properly cultivated by the spade, although all the operative manufacturers were to be chiefly employed in this mode of agriculture. Imperfect, therefore, as the plough is for the cultivation of the soil, it is probable that, in this country, for want of an adequate population, many centuries will elapse before it can be entirely superseded by the spade; yet under the plough system Great Britain and Ireland are even now supposed to be greatly over-peopled.

It follows from this statement, that we possess the means of supplying the labouring poor, however numerous they may be, with permanent beneficial employment for many centuries to come. . . .

Labor as the Standard of Value.[1] Having given the outline of the considerations which show the superiority in principle of the spade over the plough as a scientific and economical instrument of cultiva-

[1] Pp. 261–263.

tion;—having also described briefly the objects to be attended to in forming economical arrangements for the change proposed:—it now remains that the principle should be generally explained by which an advantageous interchange and exchange may be made of the greatly increased products of labour which will be created by the spade cultivation aided by the improved arrangements now contemplated.

These incalculably increased products will render gold, the old artificial standard of value, far more unfit for the task which is to be performed than it was in 1797, when it ceased to be the British legal standard of value, or than it is now, when wealth has so much increased.

Your Reporter is of the opinion that *the natural standard of human labour*, fixed to represent its natural worth, or power of creating new wealth, will alone be found adequate to the purposes required.

To a mind coming first to this subject, innumerable and apparently insurmountable difficulties will occur; but by the steady application of that fixed and persevering attention which is alone calculated successfully to contend against and overcome difficulties, every obstacle will vanish, and the practice will prove simple and easy.

That which can create new wealth is, of course, worth the wealth which it creates. Human labour, whenever common justice shall be done to human beings, can now be applied to produce, advantageously for all ranks in society, many times the amount of wealth that is necessary to support the individual in considerable comfort. Of this new wealth, so created, the labourer who produces it is justly entitled to his fair proportion; and the best interests of every community require that the producer should have a fair and fixed proportion of all the wealth which he creates. This can be assigned to him on no other principle than by forming arrangements by which the *natural* standard of value shall become the *practical* standard of value. To make labour the standard of value it is necessary to ascertain the amount of it in all articles to be bought and sold. This is, in fact, already accomplished, and is denoted by what in commerce is technically termed "the prime cost," or the net value of the whole labour contained in any article of value,—the material contained in or consumed by the manufacture of the article forming a part of the whole labour.

The great object of society is, to obtain wealth, and to enjoy it.

The genuine principle of barter was, to exchange the supposed prime cost of, or value of labour in, one article, against the prime cost of, or amount of labour contained in any other article. This is the only equitable principle of exchange; but, as inventions increased and human desires multiplied, it was found to be inconvenient in practice. Barter was succeeded by commerce, the principle of which is, to produce or procure every article at the *lowest*, and to obtain for it, in exchange, the *highest* amount of labour. To effect this, an artificial standard of value was necessary; and metals were, by common consent among nations, permitted to perform the office.

This principle, in the progress of its operation, has been productive of important advantages, and of very great evils; but, like barter, it has been suited to a certain stage of society.

It has stimulated invention; it has given industry and talent to the human character; and has secured the future exertion of those energies which otherwise might have remained dormant and unknown.

But it has made man ignorantly, individually selfish; placed him in opposition to his fellows; engendered fraud and deceit; blindly urged him forward to create, but deprived him of the wisdom to enjoy. In striving to take advantage of others he has over-reached himself. The strong hand of necessity will now force him into the path which conducts to that wisdom in which he has been so long deficient. He will discover the advantages to be derived from uniting in practice the best parts of the principles of barter and commerce, and dismissing those which experience has proved to be inconvenient and injurious.

This substantial improvement in the progress of society may be easily effected by exchanging all articles with each other at their prime cost, or with reference to the amount of labour in each, which can be equitably ascertained, and by permitting the exchange to be made through a convenient medium to represent this value, and which will thus represent a real and unchanging value, and be issued only as substantial wealth increases.

The profit of production will arise, in all cases, from the value of the labour contained in the article produced, and it will be for the interest of society that this profit should be most ample. Its exact amount will depend upon what, by strict examination, shall be proved to be the present real value of a day's labour; calculated with reference to the amount of wealth, in the necessaries and comforts of life, which an average labourer may, by temperate exertions, be now made to produce.

It would require an accurate and extended consideration of the existing state of society to determine the exact value of the unit or day's labour which society ought now to fix as a standard of value:—but a more slight and general view of the subject is sufficient to show, that this unit need not represent a less value than the wealth contained in the necessaries and comforts of life which may now be purchased with five shillings.

The landholder and capitalist would be benefited by this arrangement in the same degree with the labourer; because labour is the foundation of all values, and it is only from labour, liberally remunerated, that high profits can be paid for agricultural and manufactured products.

Depressed as the value of labour now is, there is no proposition in Euclid more true, than that society would be immediately benefited, in a great variety of ways, to an incalculable extent, by making labour the standard of value.

By this expedient all the markets in the world, which are now virtually closed against offering a profit to the producers of wealth, would be opened to an unlimited extent; and in each individual exchange all the parties interested would be sure to receive ample remuneration for their labour.

Before this change can be carried into effect, various preparatory measures will be necessary; the explanatory details of which will naturally succeed the development of those arrangements which your Reporter has to propose, to give all the advantages to the spade cultivation, of which that system of husbandry is susceptible. . . .

The Coöperative Community. [1] This part of the Report naturally divides itself under the following heads, each of which shall be considered separately, and the whole, afterwards, in connexion, as forming an improved practical system for the working classes, highly beneficial, in whatever light it may be viewed, to every part of society.

First.—The number of persons who can be associated to give the greatest advantages to themselves and to the community.

Second.—The extent of the land to be cultivated by such association.

Third.—The arrangements for feeding, lodging, and clothing the population, and for training and educating the children.

Fourth.—Those for forming and superintending the establishments.

Fifth.—The disposal of the surplus produce, and the relation which will subsist between the several establishments.

Sixth.—Their connexion with the Government of the country and with general society.

The first object, then, of the political economist, in forming these arrangements, must be, to consider well *under what limitation of num-*

[1] Pp. 264–268.

bers, individuals should be associated to form the first nucleus or division of society.

All his future proceedings will be materially influenced by the decision of this point, which is one of the most difficult problems in the science of political economy. It will affect essentially the future character of individuals, and influence the general proceedings of mankind.

It is, in fact, the corner-stone of the whole fabric of human society. The consequences, immediate and remote, which depend upon it, are so numerous and important, that to do justice to this part of the arrangement alone would require a work of many volumes.

To form anything resembling a rational opinion on this subject, the mind must steadily survey the various effects which have arisen from associations which accident has hitherto combined in the history of the human species; and it should have a distinct idea of the results which other associations are capable of producing.

Thus impressed with the magnitude and importance of the subject, after many years of deep and anxious reflection, and viewing it with reference to an improved spade cultivation, and to all the purposes of society, your Reporter ventures to recommend the formation of such arrangements as will unite about 300 men, women, and children, in their natural proportions, as the *minimum*, and about 2,000 as the *maximum*, for the future associations of the cultivators of the soil, who will be employed also in such additional occupations as may be advantageously annexed to it.

In coming to this conclusion your Reporter never lost sight of that only sure guide to the political economist, the principle, *that it is the interest of all men, whatever may be their present artificial station in society, that there should be the largest amount of intrinsically valuable produce created, at the least expense of labour, and in a way the most advantageous to the producers and society.*

Whatever fanciful notions may govern the mere closet theorist, who so often leads the public mind astray from its true course, the practical economist will never come to any one conclusion that is inconsistent with the foregoing fundamental principle of his science, well knowing that where there is inconsistency there *must be* error.

It is with reference to this principle that the minimum and maximum above stated (viz. 300 and 2,000) have been fixed upon, as will be more particularly developed under the subsequent heads.

Within this range more advantages can be given to the individuals and to society than by the association of any greater or lesser number.

But from 800 to 1,200 will be found the most desirable number to form into agricultural villages; and unless some very strong local causes interfere, the permanent arrangements should be adapted to the complete accommodation of that amount of population only.

Villages of this extent, in the neighbourhood of others of a similar description, at due distances, will be found capable of combining within themselves all the advantages that city and country residences now afford, without any of the numerous inconveniences and evils which necessarily attach to both those modes of society.

But a very erroneous opinion will be formed of the proposed arrangements and the social advantages which they will exhibit, if it should be imagined from what has been said that they will in any respect resemble any of the present agricultural villages of Europe, or the associated communities in America, except in so far as the latter may be founded *on the principle of united labour, expenditure, and property, and equal privileges.*

Recommending, then, from 300 to 2,000, according to the localities of the farm or village, as the number of persons who should compose the associations for the new system of spade husbandry, we now proceed to consider—

Second,—*The extent of land to be cultivated by such association.*

This will depend upon the quality of the soil and other local considerations.

Great Britain and Ireland, however, do not possess a population nearly sufficient to cultivate our *best* soils in the most advantageous manner. It would therefore be nationally impolitic to place these associations upon *inferior* lands, which, in consequence, may be dismissed from present consideration.

Society, ever misled by closet theorists, has committed almost every kind of error in practice, and in no instance perhaps a greater, than in separating the workman from his food, and making his existence depend upon the labour and uncertain supplies of others, as is the case under our present manufacturing system; and it is a vulgar error to suppose that a single individual more can be supported by means of such a system than without it; on the contrary, a whole population engaged in agriculture, with manufactures as an appendage, will, in a given district, support many more, and in a much higher degree of comfort, than the same district could do with its agricultural separate from its manufacturing population.

Improved arrangements for the working classes will, in almost all cases, place the workman in the midst of his food, which it will be as beneficial for him to create as to consume.

Sufficient land, therefore, will be allotted to these cultivators, to enable them to raise an abundant supply of food and the necessaries of life for themselves, and as much additional agricultural produce as the public demands may require from such a portion of the population.

Under a well-devised arrangement for the working classes they will all procure for themselves the necessaries and comforts of life in so short a time, and so easily and pleasantly, that the occupation will be experienced to be little more than a recreation, sufficient to keep them in the best health and spirits for rational enjoyment of life.

The surplus produce from the soil will be required only for the higher classes, those who live without manual labour, and those whose nice manual operations will not permit them at any time to be employed in agriculture and gardening.

Of the latter, very few, if any, will be necessary, as mechanism may be made to supersede such operations, which are almost always injurious to health.

Under this view of the subject, the quantity of land which it would be the most beneficial for these associations to cultivate, with reference to their own well-being and the interests of society, will probably be from half an acre to an acre and a half for each individual.

An association, therefore, of 1,200 persons, would require from 600 to 1,800 statute acres, according as it may be intended to be more or less agricultural.

Thus, when it should be thought expedient that the chief surplus products should consist in manufactured commodities, the lesser quantity of land would be sufficient; if a large surplus from the produce of the soil were deemed desirable, the greater quantity would be allotted; and when the localities of the situation should render it expedient for the association to create an equal surplus quantity of each, the medium quantity, or 1,200 acres, would be most suitable.

It follows that land under the proposed system of husbandry would be divided into farms of from 150 to 3,000 acres, but generally perhaps from 800 to 1,500 acres. This division of the land will be found to be productive of incalculable benefits in practice; it will give all the advantages, without any of the disadvantages of small and large farms.

The next head for consideration is—

Third,—*The arrangement for feeding, lodging, and clothing the population, and for training and educating the children.*

It being always most convenient for the workman to reside near to his employment, the site for the dwellings of the cultivators will be chosen as near to the centre of the land, as water, proper levels, dry situation, &c., &c., may admit; and as courts, alleys, lanes, and streets create many unnecessary inconveniences, are injurious to health, and destructive to almost all the natural comforts of human life, they will be excluded, and a disposition of the buildings free from these objections and greatly more economical will be adopted.

As it will afterwards appear that the food for the whole population can be provided better and cheaper under one general arrangement of cooking, and that the children can be better trained and educated together under the eye of their parents than under any other circumstances, a large square, or rather parallelogram, will be found to combine the greatest advantages in its form for the domestic arrangements of the association.

This form, indeed, affords so many advantages for the comfort of human life, that if great ignorance respecting the means necessary to secure good conduct and happiness among the working classes had not prevailed in all ranks, it must long ago have become universal.

It admits of a most simple, easy, convenient, and economical arrangement for all the purposes required.

The four sides of this figure may be adapted to contain all the private apartments or sleeping and sitting rooms for the adult part of the population; general sleeping apartments for the children while under tuition; store-rooms, or warehouses in which to deposit various products; an inn, or house for the accommodation of strangers; an infirmary; &c., &c.

In a line across the centre of the parallelogram, leaving free space for air and light and easy communication, might be erected the church, or places for worship; the schools; kitchen and apartments for eating; all in the most convenient situation for the whole population, and under the best possible public superintendence, without trouble, expense, or inconvenience to any party.

The advantages of this general domestic arrangement can only be known and appreciated by those who have had great experience in the beneficial results of extensive combinations in improving the condition of the working classes, and whose minds, advancing beyond the petty range of individual party interests, have been calmly directed to consider what may now be obtained by a well-devised association of human powers for the benefit of all ranks. It is such individuals only who can detect the present total want of foresight in the conduct of society, and in its gross misapplication of the most valuable and abundant means of securing prosperity. They can distinctly perceive that the blind are leading the blind from difficulties to dangers, which they feel to increase at every step. . . .

Community Dining as Training in Coöperation.[1] Arrangements are now proposed for the new agricultural villages, by which the food of the inhabitants may be prepared in one establishment, where they will eat together as one family.

Various objections have been urged against this practice; but they have come from those only who, whatever may be their pretensions in other respects, are mere children in the knowledge of the principles and economy of social life.

By such arrangements the members of these new associations may be supplied with food at far less expense and with much more comfort than by any individual or family arrangements; and when the parties have been once trained and accustomed, as they easily may be, to the former mode, they will never afterwards feel any inclination to return to the latter.

If a saving in the quantity of food,—the obtaining of a far superior quality of prepared provisions from the same materials,—and the operation of preparing them being effected in much less time, with far less fuel, and with greater ease, comfort, and health to all the parties employed,—be advantages, these will be obtained in a remarkable manner by the new arrangements proposed.

And if to partake of viands so prepared, served up with every regard to comfort, in clean, spacious, well-lighted, and pleasantly-ventilated apartments, and in the society of well-dressed, well-trained, well-educated, and well-informed associates, possessing the most benevolent dispositions and desirable habits, can give zest and proper enjoyment to meals, then will the inhabitants of the proposed villages experience all this in an eminent degree.

When the new arrangements shall become familiar to the parties, this superior mode of living may be enjoyed at far less expense and with much less trouble than are necessary to procure such meals as the poor are now compelled to eat, surrounded by every object of discomfort and disgust, in the cellars and garrets of the most unhealthy courts,

[1] P. 275.

alleys, and lanes, in London, Dublin, and Edinburgh, or Glasgow, Manchester, Leeds, and Birmingham.

Striking, however, as the contrast is in this description, and although the actual practice will far exceed what words can convey, yet there are many closet theorists and inexperienced persons, probably, who will still contend for individual arrangements and interests, in preference to that which they cannot comprehend.

These individuals must be left to be convinced by the facts themselves.

Housing.[1] We now proceed to describe the interior accommodations of the private lodging-houses, which will occupy three sides of the parallelogram.

As it is of essential importance that there should be abundance of space within the line of the private dwellings, the parallelogram, in all cases, whether the association is intended to be near the maximum or the minimum in numbers, should be of large dimensions; and to accommodate a greater or less population, the private dwellings should be of one, two, three, or four stories, and the interior arrangements formed accordingly.

These will be very simple.

No kitchen will be necessary, as the public arrangements for cooking will supersede the necessity for any.

The apartments will be always well-ventilated, and, when necessary, heated or cooled on the improved principles lately introduced in the Derby Infirmary.

The expense and trouble, to say nothing of the superior health and comforts which these improvements will give, will be very greatly less than attach to the present practice.

To heat, cool, and ventilate their apartments, the parties will have no further trouble than to open or shut two slides, or valves, in each room, the atmosphere of which, by this simple contrivance, may always be kept temperate and pure.

One stove of proper dimensions, judiciously placed, will supply the apartments of several dwellings, with little trouble and at very little expense, when the buildings are originally adapted for this arrangement.

Thus will all the inconveniences and expense of separate fires and fire-places, and their appendages, be avoided, as well as the trouble and disagreeable effects of mending fires and removing ashes, &c., &c.

[1] P. 276.

Good sleeping apartments looking over the gardens in the country, and sitting-rooms of proper dimensions fronting the square, will afford as much lodging-accommodation as, with the other public arrangements, can be useful to, or desired by, these associated cultivators.

Dress.[1] Food and lodging being thus provided for, the next consideration regards dress.

This, too, is a subject, the utility and disadvantages of which seem to be little understood by the Public generally; and, in consequence, the most ridiculous and absurd notions and practices have prevailed respecting it.

Most persons take it for granted, without thinking on the subject, that to be warm and healthy it is necessary to cover the body with thick clothing and to exclude the air as much as possible; and first appearances favour this conclusion. Facts, however, prove, that under the same circumstances, those who from infancy have been the most lightly clad, and who, by their form of dress, have been the most exposed to the atmosphere, are much stronger, more active, in better general health, warmer in cold weather, and far less incommoded by heat, than those who from constant habit have been dressed in such description of clothing as excludes the air from their bodies. The more the air is excluded by clothing, although at first the wearer feels warmer by each additional covering he puts on, yet in a few weeks, or months at most, the less capable he becomes of bearing cold than before.

The Romans and the Highlanders of Scotland appear to be the only two nations who adopted a national dress on account of its utility, without, however, neglecting to render it highly becoming and ornamental. The form of the dress of these nations was calculated first to give strength and manly beauty to the figure, and afterwards to display it to advantage. The time, expense, thought, and labour now employed to create a variety of dress, the effects of which are to deteriorate the physical powers, and to render the human figure an object of pity and commiseration, are a certain proof of the low state of intellect among all classes in society. The whole of this gross misapplication of the human faculties serves no one useful or rational purpose. On the contrary, it essentially weakens all the physical and mental powers, and is, in all respects, highly pernicious to society. . . .

[1] Pp. 276–277.

Education.[1] Your Reporter has now to enter upon the most interesting portion of this division of the subject, and, he may add, the most important part of the economy of human life, with reference to the science of the influence of circumstances over the well-being and happiness of mankind, and to the full power and control which men may now acquire over those circumstances, and by which they may direct them to produce among the human race, with ease and certainty, either universal good or evil.

No one can mistake the application of these terms to the training and education of the children. . . .

Before any rational plan can be devised for the proper training and education of the children, it should be distinctly known what capabilities and qualities infants and children possess, or, in fact, what they really are by nature.

If this knowledge is to be attained, as all human knowledge has been acquired, through the evidence of our senses, then is it evident that infants receive from a source and power over which they have no control, all the natural qualities they possess, and that from birth they are continually subjected to impressions derived from the circumstances around them; which impressions, combined with their natural qualities (whatever fanciful speculative men may say to the contrary), do truly determine the character of the individual through every period of life. . . .

From what has been said it is obvious that to produce such a total change among men as the one now contemplated by your Reporter will require the arrangement of new circumstances, that, in each part, and in their entire combinations, shall be so consistent with the known laws of nature, that the most acute mind shall fail to discover the slightest deviation from them.

It is upon these grounds that your Reporter, in educating the rising generation within his influence, has long adopted principles different from those which are usually acted upon.

He considers all children as beings whose dispositions, habits, and sentiments are to be formed *for* them; that these can be well formed only by excluding all notions of reward, punishment, and emulation; and that, if their characters are not such as they ought to be, the error proceeds from their instructors and the other circumstances which surround them. He knows that principles as certain as those upon which the science of mathematics is founded may be applied to

[1] Pp. 278–279, 282–284.

the forming of any given general character, and that by the influence of other circumstances, not a few individuals only but the whole population of the world, may in a few years be rendered a very far superior race of beings to any now upon the earth, or which has been made known to us by history.

The children in these new schools should be therefore trained systematically to acquire useful knowledge through the means of sensible signs, by which their powers of reflection and judgment may be habituated to draw accurate conclusions from the facts presented to them. This mode of instruction is founded in nature, and will supersede the present defective and tiresome system of book learning, which is ill calculated to give either pleasure or instruction to the minds of children. When arrangements founded on these principles shall be judiciously formed and applied to practice, children will with ease and delight to themselves, acquire more real knowledge in a day than they have yet attained under the old system in many months. They will not only thus acquire valuable knowledge, but the best habits and dispositions will be at the same time imperceptibly created in every one; and they will be trained to fill every office and to perform every duty that the well-being of their associates and the establishments can require. It is only by education, rightly understood, that communities of men can ever be well governed, and by means of such education every object of human society will be attained with the least labour and the most satisfaction.

It is obvious that training and education must be viewed as intimately connected with the employments of the association. The latter, indeed, will form an essential part of education under these arrangements. Each association, generally speaking, should create for itself a full supply of the usual necessaries, conveniences, and comforts of life.

The dwelling-houses and domestic arrangements being placed as near the centre of the land to be cultivated as circumstances will permit, it is concluded that the most convenient situation for the gardens will be adjoining the houses on the outside of the square; that these should be bounded by the principal roads; and that beyond them, at a sufficient distance to be covered by a plantation, should be placed the workshops and manufactory.

All will take their turn at *some one or more* of the occupations in this department, aided by every improvement that science can afford, alternately with employment in agriculture and gardening.

It has been a popular opinion to recommend a minute division of labour and a division of interests. It will presently appear, however, that this minute division of labour and division of interests are only other terms for poverty, ignorance, waste of every kind, universal opposition throughout society, crime, misery, and great bodily and mental imbecility.

To avoid these evils, which, while they continue, must keep mankind in a most degraded state, each child will receive a general education, early in life, that will fit him for the proper purposes of society, make him the most useful to it, and the most capable of enjoying it.

Before he is twelve years old he may with ease be trained to acquire a correct view of the outline of all the knowledge which men have yet attained.

By this means he will early learn what he is in relation to past ages, to the period in which he lives, to the circumstances in which he is placed, to the individuals around him, and to future events. *He will then only have any pretensions to the name of a rational being.*

His physical powers may be equally enlarged in a manner as beneficial to himself as to those around him. As his strength increases he will be initiated in the practice of all the leading operations of his community, by which his services, at all times and under all circumstances, will afford a great gain to society beyond the expense of his subsistence; while at the same time he will be in the continual possession of more substantial comforts and real enjoyments than have ever yet appertained to any class in society.

The new wealth which one individual, by comparatively light and always healthy employment, may create under the arrangements now proposed is indeed incalculable. They would give him giant powers compared with those which the working class or any other now possesses. There would at once be an end of all mere animal machines, who could only follow a plough, or turn a sod, or make some insignificant part of some insignificant manufacture or frivolous article which society could better spare than possess. Instead of the unhealthy pointer of a pin,—header of a nail,—piecer of a thread—or clodhopper, senselessly gazing at the soil or around him, without understanding or rational reflection, there would spring up a working class full of activity and useful knowledge, with habits, information, manners, and dispositions that would place the lowest in the scale many degrees above the best of any class which has yet been formed by the circumstances of past or present society. . . .

Establishment of the Coöperative Community.[1] The next object of attention is—

Fourth,—*The formation and superintendence of these establishments.*

These new farming and general working arrangements may be formed by one or any number of landed proprietors or large capitalists; by established companies having large funds to expend for benevolent and public objects; by parishes and counties, to relieve themselves from paupers and poor's-rates; and by associations of the middle and working classes of farmers, mechanics, and tradesmen, to relieve themselves from the evils of the present system.

As land, capital, and labour may be applied *to far greater pecuniary advantage* under the proposed arrangements than under any other at present known to the public, all parties will readily unite in carrying them into execution as soon as they shall be so plainly developed in principle as to be generally understood, and as parties who possess sufficient knowledge of the practical details to direct them advantageously can be found or trained to superintend them.

The chief difficulty lies in the latter part of the business. The principles may be made plain to every capacity. They are simply principles of nature, in strict unison with all we see or know from facts to be true. But the practice of everything new, however trifling, requires time and experience to perfect it. It cannot be expected that arrangements which comprehend the whole business of life, and reduce to practice the entire science of political economy, can at once be combined and executed in the best manner. Many errors will be at first committed; and, as in every other attempt by human means to unite a great variety of parts to produce one grand general result, many partial failures may be anticipated. . . .

The same class of minds that can be trained to direct any of the usual complicated business of life, may be with ease rendered competent to take a part in the management and superintendence of these new establishments.

The principal difficulty will be to set the first establishment in motion; and much care and circumspection will be requisite in bringing each part into action at the proper time, and with the guards and checks which a change from one set of habits to another renders necessary.

Yet, the principles being understood, a man of fair ordinary capacity would superintend such arrangements with more ease than most large commercial or manufacturing establishments are now conducted.

[1] Pp. 284–285, 286–288.

In these there is a continual opposition of various interests and feelings, and extensive principles of counteraction, among the parties themselves, and between the parties and the public.

On the contrary, in the new arrangements each part will give facility to all the others, and unity of interest and design will be seen and felt in every one of the operations. The mental, manual, and scientific movements will all harmonise, and produce with ease results which must appear inexplicable to those who remain ignorant of the principles which govern the proceedings.

In the first instance men must be sought who, in addition to a practical knowledge of gardening, agriculture, manufactures, the ordinary trades, &c., &c., can comprehend the principles on which these associations are formed, and, comprehending them, can feel an interest and a pleasure in putting them into execution. Such individuals may be found; for there is nothing new in the separate parts of the proposed practice—the arrangements alone can be considered new.

When one establishment shall have been formed, there will be no great difficulty in providing superintendents for many other establishments. All the children will be trained to be equal to the care of any of the departments, more particularly as there will be no counteraction between those who direct and those who perform the various operations.

Let the business be at once set about in good earnest, and the obstacles which now seem so formidable will speedily disappear.

The peculiar mode of governing these establishments will depend on the parties who form them.

Those founded by landowners and capitalists, public companies, parishes, or counties will be under the direction of the individuals whom these powers may appoint to superintend them, and will, of course, be subject to the rules and regulations laid down by their founders.

Those formed by the middle and working classes, upon a complete reciprocity of interests, should be governed by themselves, upon principles that will *prevent* divisions, opposition of interests, jealousies, of any of the common and vulgar passions which a contention for power is certain to generate. Their affairs should be conducted by a committee, composed of all the members of the association between certain ages—for instance, of those between thirty-five and forty-five, or between forty and fifty. Perhaps the former will unite more of the activity of youth with the experience of age than the latter; but it is of little moment which period of life may be fixed upon. In a short time the ease with which these associations will proceed in all their operations will be such as to render the business of governing a mere recreation; and as the parties who govern will in a few years again become the governed, they must always be conscious that at a future period they will experience the good or evil effects of the measures of their administration.

By this equitable and natural arrangement all the numberless evils of elections and electioneering will be avoided.

As all are to be trained and educated together and without distinction, they will be delightful companions and associates, intimately acquainted with each other's inmost thoughts. There will be no foundation for disguise or deceit of any kind; all will be as open as the hearts and feelings of young children before they are trained (as they necessarily are under the present system) in complicated arts of deception. At the same time their whole conduct will be regulated by a sound and rational discretion and intelligence, such as human beings trained and placed as they have hitherto been will deem it visionary to expect, and impossible to attain, in every-day practice.

The superior advantages which these associations will speedily possess, and the still greater superiority of knowledge which they will readily acquire, will preclude on their parts the smallest desire for what are now called honours and peculiar privileges.

They will have minds so well informed—their power of accurately tracing cause and effect will be so much increased, that they must clearly perceive that to be raised to one of the privileged orders would be to themselves a serious evil, and to their posterity would certainly occasion an incalculable loss of intellect and enjoyment, equally injurious to themselves and to society.

They will therefore have every motive not to interfere with the honours and privileges of the existing higher orders, but to remain well satisfied with their own station in life.

The only distinction which can be found of the least utility in these associations is that of age or experience. It is the only just and natural distinction; and any other would be inconsistent with the enlarged and superior acquirements of the individuals who would compose these associations. The deference to age or experience will be natural, and readily given; and many advantageous regulations may be formed in consequence, for apportioning the proper employments to the period of life best calculated for them, and diminishing the labour of the individual as age advances beyond the term when the period of governing is concluded.

Disposal of the Surplus Produce; the Connection between Communities.[1] Fifth,—*The disposal of the surplus produce, and the connexion which will subsist between the several establishments.*

Under the proposed system the facilities of production, the absence of all the counteracting circumstances which so abundantly exist in common society, with the saving of time and waste in all the domestic arrangements, will secure, other circumstances being equal, *a much larger amount of wealth at a greatly reduced expenditure.* The next question is, in what manner is this produce to be disposed of?

Society has been hitherto so constituted that all parties are afraid of being over-reached by others, and, without great care to secure their individual interests, of being deprived of the means of existence. This feeling has created a universal selfishness of the most ignorant nature, for it almost *ensures* the evils which it means to prevent.

These new associations can scarcely be formed before it will be discovered that by the most simple and easy regulations all the natural wants of human nature may be abundantly supplied; and the principle of selfishness (in the sense in which that term is here used) will cease to exist for want of an adequate motive to produce it.

It will be quite evident to all, that wealth of that kind which will alone be held in any estimation amongst them may be so easily created to exceed all their wants, that every desire for individual accumulation of wealth will appear as irrational as to bottle up or store water in situations where there is more of this invaluable fluid than all can consume.

With this knowledge, and the feelings which will arise from it, the existing thousand counteractions to the creation of new wealth will also cease, as well as those innumerable motives to deception which now pervade all ranks in society. A principle of equity and justice, openness and fairness, will influence the whole proceedings of these societies. There will, consequently, be no difficulty whatever in the exchange of the products of labour, mental or manual, among themselves. The amount of labour in all products, calculated on the present principle of estimating the prime cost of commodities, will be readily ascertained and the exchange made accordingly. There will be no inducement to raise or manufacture an inferior article, or to deteriorate, by deceptious practices, any of the necessaries, comforts, or luxuries of life. Every one will distinctly see it to be the immediate interest of all, that none of these irrational proceedings shall take

[1] Pp. 288–289.

place; and the best security against their occurrence will be the entire absence of all motives to have recourse to them. As the easy, regular, healthy, rational employment of the individuals forming these societies will create a very large surplus of their own products, beyond what they will have any desire to consume, each may be freely permitted to receive from the general store of the community whatever they may require. This, in practice, will prove to be the greatest economy, and will at once remove all those preconceived insurmountable difficulties that now haunt the minds of those who have been trained in common society, and who necessarily view all things through the distorted medium of their own little circle of local prejudices.

It may be safely predicted that one of these new associations cannot be formed without creating a general desire throughout society to establish others, and that they will rapidly multiply. The same knowledge and principles which unite the interests of the individuals within each establishment, will as effectually lead to the same kind of enlightened union between the different establishments. They will each render to the others the same benefits as are now given, or rather much greater benefits than are now given to each other by the members of the most closely united and affectionate families. . . .

The State and the Coöperative Community.[1] Sixth,—*The connexion of the new establishments with the Government of the country and with old society.*

Under this head are to be noticed, the amount and collection of the revenue, and the public or legal duties of the associations in peace and war.

Your Reporter concludes that whatever taxes are paid from land, capital, and labour, under the existing arrangements of society, the same amount for the same proportion of each may be collected with far more ease under those now proposed. The Government would, of course, require its revenue to be paid in the legal circulating medium, to obtain which, the associations would have to dispose of as much of their surplus produce to common society for the legal coin or paper of the realm as would discharge the demands of Government.

In time of peace these associations would give no trouble to Government; their internal regulations being founded on principles of prevention, not only with reference to public crimes, but to the private evils and errors which so fatally abound in common society. Courts

[1] Pp. 291–292, 296–297.

of law, prisons, and punishments would not be required. These are requisite only where human nature is greatly misunderstood; where society rests on the demoralizing system of individual competition, rewards, and punishments;—they are necessary only in a stage of existence previous to the discovery of the science of the certain and overwhelming influence of circumstances over the whole character and conduct of mankind. . . .

In reference to war also, [the associations] will be equally beneficial. Bodily exercises, adapted to improve the dispositions and increase the health and strength of the individual, will form part of the training and education of the children. . . .

But the knowledge of the science of the influence of circumstances over mankind will speedily enable all nations to discover, not only the evils of war, but the folly of it. Of all modes of conduct adopted by mankind to obtain advantages in the present stage of society, this is the most certain to defeat its object. It is, in truth, a system of direct demoralization and of destruction; while it is the highest interest of all individuals and of all countries to *remoralize and conserve*. Men surely cannot with truth be termed rational beings until they shall discover and put in practice the principles which shall enable them to conduct their affairs without war. The arrangements we are considering would speedily show how easily these principles and practices may be introduced into general society. . . .

What, then, to sum up the whole in a few words, does your Reporter now propose to his fellow-creatures?

After a life spent in the investigation of the causes of the evils with which society is afflicted, and of the means of removing them,—and being now in possession of facts demonstrating the practicability and the efficacy of the arrangements now exhibited, which have been the fruit of that investigation, aided by a long course of actual experiments,—he offers to exchange their poverty for wealth, their ignorance for knowledge, their anger for kindness, their divisions for union. He offers to effect this change without subjecting a single individual even to temporary inconvenience. No one shall suffer by it for an hour; all shall be essentially benefited within a short period from its introduction; and yet not any part of the existing system shall be prematurely disturbed. . . .

UTOPIAN SOCIALISM

X

CHARLES FOURIER
1772–1837

The middle-class background of Fourier left its traces in the ideal society which he depicted with such careful—almost pathetic—precision in after-life. His father was a prosperous business man of Besançon, France, where Charles was born in 1772. Parental authority in those days was part of the natural order. Young Fourier must go to the University of Besançon and study the classics, he must give up dreams of becoming a military engineer, worst of all he must enter business like his father. He was a boy of delicate perceptions, loving flowers and music from childhood, and his moral sense was no less refined. Business practices inspired in him a profound disgust. "In the catechism and at school," he said, "I was taught that one must never lie; then I was put into the shop so as to train me early in that noble profession of lying, the art of salesmanship." But he submitted to family pressure and until middle life was tied to a calling which he loathed. At the age of eighteen he became a commercial traveller with headquarters at Lyon.

Fourier's father had died in 1781 leaving him a considerable fortune. During the revolutionary disturbances, however, it was almost wiped out and he himself was twice imprisoned. After this he served for two years in the army. Somewhat later, in 1797, the first fruit of an interest in public questions appeared. He addressed two projects to the French government, one on the subject of army organization, the other on commercial agreements with enemy countries. In 1800, desiring to spread his ideas, he asked the authorities for permission to establish a newspaper which, it was promised, would be ruled "by a love of order and respect for government." The request was refused and Fourier had to unburden himself in the existing journals. In leisure moments he wrote a number of pieces in prose and verse—some in a humorous vein—for the rather emancipated women readers of a local paper called the *Bulletin*.

Meanwhile Fourier's mind was being prepared for more serious efforts. Observation of conditions in Lyon and elsewhere sharpened his early distaste for existing business practices and, on the other hand, sometimes furnished him with ideas for amending them. No better place than Lyon could have been chosen as a field of study. The most highly industrialized town of France, Lyon also exhibited the most violent forms of class conflict. Strikes, which had always been frequent, were now succeeded by armed encounters; master workmen operating domestic workshops ranged themselves against the master merchants who controlled industry. The town was subject to commercial crises, chronic unemployment, and widespread poverty. In contrast with this competitive régime Fourier could observe the numerous rural organizations outside Lyon which had been formed on a coöperative basis for the making of cheese, production of fruit, etc. Something had been done to alleviate conditions even in Lyon: a reforming, philanthropic sentiment had grown up and some experiments in insurance had been made.

Familiarity with local conditions rather than extensive borrowing from previous writers lay at the root of Fourier's theory, which he was now on the point of setting forth. It is true that wide but desultory reading and ideas then "in the air" gave him some general concepts traceable to eighteenth-century philosophy. He believed, for example, that happiness depends on satisfying the passions, that man in a state of nature is better than man in corrupt civilization, and so on. But it is not easy to perceive closer connections. Fourier stoutly maintained his own originality and later on even wrote a book to prove it. Perhaps somewhat dramatizing actual events, he said that like Newton he had gotten his original idea from an apple: a companion who had purchased one in Paris paid a hundred times what it would have cost in the provinces. Struck with this fact, Fourier built up from it the theory of industrial groups.

In 1803 he outlined his new system in "Universal Harmony," a two-page article in the *Bulletin*. This was soon followed by other contributions on the subject. He then began a period of further study and speculation, publishing nothing for three years, but writing at great length on the ramifications of his theory and holding meetings to gain publicity for it. In 1808 his first great work, the *Theory of the Four Movements*, was ready. He called the book a "prospectus" or "announcement"—most of it was abstract theory. Nevertheless he expected that society would speedily adopt the new régime and calculated that if some "prince" would back it the project could be put in operation within the year. He had taken care (in conformity with his theory) to appeal to the imagination and appetites as well as to the reason. But unfortunately nothing happened. The book was badly written (as indeed were almost all of his social works): it was vague and confused, and he waited in vain for the revolution. In fact not until eight years afterward did he gain his first disciple.

Fourier's material circumstances had not improved during his years in business. Until 1812, when he inherited a pension from his mother, he lived on the verge of actual want. The industrial depression of 1814–15 determined him to give up business: being unmarried he went to live with his sisters. The new leisure was spent in writing further expositions of the doctrine and in 1820 a second long work was finally published with the assistance of his first convert. The *Treatise on Domestic Agricultural Association* carried out the *Four Movements* in much greater and more practical detail. Yet it repeated the latter's defects of style and arrangement, and in spite of every resource of advertising—meetings held to discuss the doctrine, copies sent to prominent persons, monitions to newspaper men—the book fell almost as flat as its predecessor. Fourier even went back to commercial work, this time as agent for a New York firm.

Gradually, however, he was building up a following, small but secure. For the purpose of increasing it he began work in 1826 on another treatise. This appeared three years later as the *New Industrial and Associative World*, the cost being met by one of his more recent disciples. Propaganda was the prime object of the book; Fourier introduced few new principles, but the writing was clearer and more orderly. As a result the *New Industrial World* received favorable notice from at least one important journal and publicity, though unfriendly publicity, from the others. Fourier craved renown, but he still had to content himself with the adulation of a small circle of followers.

The latter found it difficult to preserve the proper attitude of respect. Difficulties over doctrine arose. Fourier was inclined to be dictatorial. His followers complained that his later articles—which he insisted on contributing to the journal of the sect—were harming the movement. At last they were able to divert his attention by encouraging him to compose further volumes on associative theory. His last published work seemed to vindicate their judgment: *False Industry* (1835–36) added little to the previous doctrine and was the most disorderly of his writings. By that time an intellectual decline had certainly set in. The question, indeed, is whether Fourier was not always a little mad. He seemed mentally isolated even in the midst of friends; he never knew the day, the month, or the season of the year; the grotesque images he conjured up in what were supposed to be serious works: visions of "anti-lions" and "anti-whales," appear to spring naturally enough from a demented brain. Nevertheless his loyal followers vehemently asserted his rationality, and when the end came, in 1837, contemporary opinion tardily pronounced him a great man.

Yet Fourier's doctrines spread slowly even after his death. They readily created antagonism—Catholic opinion, for example, remained thoroughly hostile. Passions being sacred with him, he saw no reason for curbing the sexual instinct; this attitude was bound to cause difficulties. Yet his teaching had at least three considerable results: it produced a sect, led to the establishment of experimental communities in Europe and America, and contributed certain elements to later varieties of socialism. The sect declined after the French Revolution of 1848 and disappeared during the Bonapartist régime. The Fourierist communities—forty or more of them were founded—also decayed, except for a certain number which departed from his more radical principles.

As for his influence on other types of socialism, the record is more notable. Before his death he had won important converts from Saint-Simonism; indeed the ability of these new followers accounts for the prestige which Fourierism temporarily enjoyed. Fragments of his philosophy, especially the criticisms which he levelled at capitalist society, passed into other schools of socialist thought. Thus his discussion of wage slavery and social disorganization made a distinct impression on German socialism, while his criticism of certain types of commerce as parasitic and unproductive, his portrayal of the defects of disaggregated industry, and his theory of the breach between town and country were incorporated, one or all, into the systems of Louis Blanc, Karl Marx, and others. As for the permanence of his influence in France, "the ideas of Fourier," wrote Georges Sorel in 1895, "have remained very much alive in our country. One may say that nine out of every ten Frenchmen concerned with social questions are incomplete or illogical Fourierists."

REFERENCES

The *Œuvres complètes* of Fourier were published in 1845. In English there is a volume of *Selections from the Works of Fourier* by Charles Gide (Julia

Franklin, trans., 1901). Several of the separate works have also been translated, none however within recent times.

An exhaustive study of Fourier's life and writings, valuable for its examination of the source and influence of his ideas, is Hubert Bourgin's *Fourier, contribution à l'étude du socialisme français* (1905).

The standard though rather old biography is by C. Pellarin (5th ed., 1871). An English translation was published in 1848.

READINGS FROM

THE NEW INDUSTRIAL AND ASSOCIATIVE WORLD [1]

Preliminary Ideas.[2] No desire is more general than that of doubling one's income by a stroke of fortune such as a rich marriage, an inheritance, or a sinecure; and if a means not merely of doubling but of quadrupling the real income of each person were found, certainly such a discovery would highly deserve the general attention.

The natural associative method will produce such a result. In France, the annual income, estimated at six billions, will be raised to twenty-four billions in the first year of the associative régime; in the other countries the proportionate increase will be similar.

The most colossal wealth would be illusory, however, if it were not supplemented by a system of distribution guaranteeing:

Proportional distribution and the participation of the poorer classes in this increased income.

Equilibrium of population, the unlimited increase of which would otherwise quickly neutralize a four-fold or even a ten-fold increase of real wealth.

These problems, the stumbling-blocks of modern science, are completely solved by the discovery of the natural associative method. . . .

The most accurate designation for this noble associative order appeared to me to be New Industrial World, which among other properties possesses that of creating industrial attraction: we shall see idle persons, even dandies, afoot at four o'clock in the morning, winter and summer, devoting themselves to useful work—to the care of gardens, to the business of the household, manufacturing, etc.—work which, performed under the mechanism of civilization, inspires the rich only with disgust.

[1] *Œuvres complètes,* Vol. VI. Translated for the present volume.
[2] *Ibid.*, pp. 1–7.

All these tasks will become attractive through the operation of a very little known principle of distribution, which I shall call the Passional Series, or Series of Contrasted Groups; it is the mechanism toward which all passions tend, the only order comformable to the will of nature. The savage will never embrace industry so long as he does not see it carried on in Passional Series.

Under such a régime the pursuit of truth and justice becomes the way to fortune, and most of the vices which we look upon as degrading—such as epicurism—the way to industrial emulation. Thus gastronomic refinements will be encouraged as the height of wisdom. Such a system is opposite to that of "civilization," in which fortune is the result of imposture, and wisdom consists in self-denial. To pursue this contrast: the "civilized" state, where falsehood and distasteful industry are the rule, will be regarded as the "looking-glass" world and the associative state, founded on truth and attractive industry, as the normal world. . . .

The study of passional attraction leads directly to the discovery of the mechanism of association, but if the subject of association is investigated before that of attraction, there is a risk of wasting centuries in the pursuit of false methods, a risk of disappointment and of belief in an impossibility. This is happening to-day, when the problem of association, which has been neglected for three thousand years, is finally beginning to fix the attention of the learned world.

For some years the word association has been written about without the thing itself being known, without the object of the associative bond itself being determined, the forms and methods it must adopt, the conditions it must fulfil, the results it must produce. The subject has been treated so confusedly that no one has even thought of discussing the method of studying the new project. This discussion would have shown that success cannot be attained by any of the known methods, and that it must be sought for in principles still virgin and untouched, particularly in that of passional attraction, which even Newton missed although he approached it closely. We shall demonstrate that the latter is the only way to make association succeed.

If the poor, the working class, are unhappy in an associative State they will disturb it by ill-will, robbery, and rebellion; such a régime will therefore fail to attain its object, which is to associate the passional as well as the material—to reconcile passions, characters, tastes, instincts and any inequalities whatever.

On the other hand, if in order to conciliate the poor their welfare is guaranteed, if a copious supply of food, clothing, etc., is advanced to them, the result will be to encourage idleness among them. The proof of this is seen in England, where two hundred millions in poor relief only serve to multiply the number of mendicants.

The remedy for idleness and other vices which would disorganize an association, is therefore a mechanism of industrial attraction, which would transform work into pleasure and guarantee the recovery of the supplies advanced. . . .

In addition to writings on the subject, there have been some practical attempts at association, some trials in America and England. A sect directed by Mr. Owen claims to have founded the associative state. The facts are all to the contrary. His group, by false methods which are in every respect contrary to nature or attraction, is working to discredit the idea of association. Moreover the Owenite sect has attracted neither savage nor civilized neighbors; not a tribe or province of the United States has been willing to adopt this monastic régime of community of goods, this semi-atheism or avoidance of religion, and other monstrosities which Mr. Owen dignifies by the name of association. . . .

None of the writers or leaders gets to the bottom of the question—the problem of associating in agricultural and domestic labors not only the pecuniary and industrial faculties, but of associating the passions, characters, tastes and instincts, developing them in each individual without injury to the mass, encouraging from earliest childhood the industrial aptitudes which are numerous among children, placing each one in the different posts to which nature calls him, and frequently varying the tasks and fortifying them by attractions sufficient to create industrial attraction. . . .

The more the word [association] has been abused, the more important it is to give some preliminary ideas on the subject. . . .

Let us fix our attention on the most salient result of the associative régime, the quadruple product. A large community in its different functions would use only a hundredth part of the hands and machines which our complicated system of small households requires. Instead of three hundred kitchens and three hundred housewives, there would be only four or five large kitchens preparing meals suited to four or five degrees of wealth—for the associative state admits of no equality. About one-tenth the number of experts would suffice to replace three hundred women employed in a "civilized" régime not possessing the numerous mechanical devices which would be used in a kitchen serving eighteen hundred people (the most suitable number). This group, without interfering with individual liberty, would provide tables and services at different prices for each person.

The people in this case would spend much less to live well than to live poorly as they do at present. The saving in fuel would be immense and would assure the restoration of forests and climatic conditions much better than a hundred inexecutable forest codes.

Household work would be so simplified that seven-eighths of the housewives and servants would become free and available for productive functions.

Our century claims to be distinguished by the spirit of association; how is it then that in agriculture it adopts distribution by families—the smallest possible combination? Smaller groupings cannot be imagined than those in our towns, anti-economic and anti-social as they are, and confined to married couples or families of five or six people. Cities which now build three hundred granaries, three hundred cellars, badly located and poorly tended, would find sufficient, in association, a single granary, a single cellar, well located, well provided with implements and occupying only one-tenth the agents which the dispersed management or family régime requires.

Agriculturists have sometimes inserted in the newspapers articles on the enormous benefits that agriculture would derive from large associative groups, if the passions of two or three hundred families working in concert could be reconciled, and their association *in passional as well as in material things* achieved.

They offer nothing but vain wishes on this subject, complaining that such a régime is impossible because of inequalities of wealth, dissimilarities of character, etc. These inequalities, far from being an obstacle, are on the contrary the essential need: passional Series cannot be organized without great inequality of wealth, characters, tastes, and instincts. If this scale of inequalities did not exist it would be necessary to create it, to establish it thoroughly, before the passions could be associated.

In the "civilized" régime we see traces of association—*but only in a material sense*, germs which are due to instinct and not to science. Instinct teaches a hundred village families that a common oven will cost much less in masonry and fuel than a hundred small household ovens, and that it would be better directed by two or three experienced bakers than the hundred small ovens tended by a hundred women who will miss two times out of three the correct degree of oven heat for bread-baking.

Good sense has taught the inhabitants of the north that if each family wishes to make its beer it will cost more than good wines. A monastic group or a military mess knows by instinct that a single kitchen serving thirty people will be better and less costly than thirty separate kitchens.

The peasants of the Jura combined, seeing that they could not make Gruyère cheese with the milk of a single household. Every day they bring milk to a common dairy where, on wooden tallies, they note the contributions of each. Thus by combining these small quantities of milk they are able to make at little expense a large cheese in one great kettle.

Why is it that our century, which has lofty economic pretensions, has not dreamed of developing these germs of association, of forming a complete system for the entire seven industrial functions, namely,

1. Domestic work
2. Agricultural work
3. Manufacturing work
4. Commercial work
5. Educational work
6. Study and utilization of the sciences
7. Study and utilization of the fine arts,

functions which must be exercised cumulatively in the greatest possible group. We shall see that according to the following theory there is to be a group of eighteen hundred people. With more than two thousand it would degenerate into a mob, become complicated; with less than sixteen hundred it would be weakly held together, subject to failures of mechanism, to interruptions of industrial attraction.

However, at little expense a reduced test could be made with a third of the number—six or seven hundred people. The results would be less brilliant, less lucrative, but would prove sufficiently that a group raised to the proper number, eighteen hundred, would realize in full the benefits and harmonies described in the following theory.

As soon as it has been proved by this trial that the mechanism, called phalanstery of passional Series, creates industrial attraction, it will be imitated with lightning rapidity. All savage peoples, all the negroes of Africa, will embrace industry: after two or three years there will be sugar to barter, weight for weight, against wheat, and other commodities of the torrid zone in proportion. . . .

Groups and Their Organization.[1] The term group is applied to any assembly whatever, even to a troop of nincompoops united by boredom, without passion or aim; empty-headed people occupied with killing time and waiting for news. In the theory of passions a group is understood to be a mass bound together by identity of taste for an exercised function. Three men dine together: they are served a soup which pleases two and displeases a third. At this moment they do not form a group as they are discordant on the function which occupies them—the soup creates no identity of passional taste.

The two whom this soup pleases form a false group. To be a true one, susceptible to passional equilibrium, a group must consist of at least three persons—just as scales are composed of three forces, of which the means maintain the equilibrium between the two extremes. Briefly, no group can consist of less than three people homogeneous in taste on the exercised function. . . .

I have spoken only of *sub-groups*, of which the minimum is three persons. A *full group* in associative mechanics, must have at least SEVEN, because it must contain three sub-divisions, called sub-groups, of which the middle one must be stronger than the extremes, so as to hold them in balance. The group of seven furnishes three sub-divisions, —2, 3, 2,—applied to three portions of one function. In this case the groups of 2, although false in isolated action, become admissible by alliance with the others.

If the center, formed of three persons, is in balance with the sub-groups, two and two, forming the extremes, then the center is always drawn to the most attractive function. Accordingly, it has a numerical superiority of one, and an attractive superiority of one. . . . A group of seven is sufficient, but nine is more perfect.

The Passions as Factors of Organization.[2] [A] distribution establishes itself naturally in every industrial or social group if free rein is given to passions and instincts. Man being by instinct the enemy of equality and inclined towards hierarchies, this graduated scale will establish itself in a series of nine groups, as in a group of nine individuals, if complete liberty is established. . . .

The most redoubtable obstacle is the play of certain Passions which the moralists would like to shackle. The best formed Series would lose all its properties of industrial Attraction, direct Agreement of inequalities, indirect Agreement of antipathies, etc., if one should

[1] *Ibid.*, pp. 55, 57–59.

[2] *Ibid.*, pp. 59, 66, 69–70, 74–76.

neglect to develop in combination with them the three resources which I have called Provocative or Distributive Passions. If one of these three is suppressed in a series, the series will be perverted; agreements and industrial attraction will be likewise warped and reduced to shadows. This would frustrate the principal equilibrium—that of distribution.

Let us define these three Passions:

I shall start with the Butterfly Passion, meaning the desire for periodic variety, contrasted situations, changes of scene, piquant incidents, novelties capable of creating illusion and stimulating both the senses and the mind.

This desire is felt moderately every hour and vigorously every two hours. If it is not satisfied man falls into indifference and boredom.

The happiness attributed to sybaritic Parisians—that is, the art of *living so well and so rapidly,* variety and concatenation of pleasures: in fine, rapidity of movement—depends in part on allowing full scope to this passion, a happiness from which Parisians are infinitely remote. . . .

I pass on to the other two Provocative Passions. The Intriguing Passion and the Composite Passion are in perfect contrast: the first is a speculative and reflective passion; the second is a blind, intoxicating passion, an impulse born of the accumulation of many pleasures of the senses and mind, simultaneously experienced.

The *Intriguing* Passion, or party spirit, is the mania for intrigue. This passion burns fiercely in ambitious people, courtiers, trade-guilds, merchants, and social life. . . .

The human spirit has such an imperative need for the Intriguing Passion that, in default of real intrigues, it eagerly seeks artificial ones: at play, in the theatre, in novels. Whenever a group is assembled there must be created for it an artificial intrigue, either by putting cards in its hands, or by hatching an electoral cabal in it. There is no one more unhappy than a courtier exiled in the country, or in a small middle-class town where no intrigue exists. A retired merchant isolated suddenly from numerous and active mercantile cabals finds himself, in spite of his wealth, the unhappiest of men.

The principal property of the Intriguing Passion in mechanical series is to excite discord or emulation between groups sufficiently similar to compete for prizes and balance votes.

Groups will not join in cultivating the early white pear, the late white, and the green spotted variety; although cultivating pears contiguous in color, these groups are essentially jealous and discordant. The same will be true concerning the three groups cultivating yellow, brown, and green pippins. . . .

The *Composite* or *Exhilarating* Passion creates enthusiastic agreements. The Intriguing Passion, or party spirit, alone would not be enough to stimulate groups to labor: there must be put in play the two contrasting Passions, the Intriguing or reflective, and the Composite or blind, the latter being the most romantic of passions, the most opposed to reason. I have said that the Composite Passion is born of the union of many pleasures of the senses and mind, experienced simultaneously. It is illegitimate Composite when it is formed of many pleasures of a single order, all sensual or all intellectual. This passion must be applied to all associative labor so that the Composite and Intriguing Passions may replace the vile forces found in "civilized" industry—forces such as the necessity of caring for children, the fear of starvation or of being confined in the poorhouse. . . .

To sum up these three Provocative Passions, these three organic forces of an industrial Series, we may observe that if they are not all three developed together industrial Attraction will not arise. If it does appear it will gradually die away and vanish completely.

Thus the condition which must be fulfilled in order to produce attractive industry is first to form series of groups subordinated to the play of these three Passions:

The Intriguing or reflective Passion which engenders discords and creates rivalry between contiguous groups, provided the groups are closely related in tastes and functions;

The Composite or blind Passion arising from the pleasures of sense and mind, which produces exaltation . . . ;

The Butterfly Passion which produces coördination and supports the other two Passions, sustaining their activity by short sessions and by the choice of new pleasures which it presents periodically before either satiety or even indifference arises.

I insist upon the importance of the Butterfly Passion which has such an evil reputation; I insist, that is, upon the necessity of short and varied sessions, a principle which condemns all "civilized" industry. Let us observe the effects of this method in the material and passional realm.

In the material realm it produces sanitary equilibrium: health is necessarily injured if one works at the same task twelve hours a day, such as weaving, sewing, writing, or other work which does not successively exercise all parts of the body and mind. In this case there is injury even in active agricultural labor as well as in office work. The one tires the limbs and vital organs, the other corrupts the solids and liquids. . . .

In the Passional realm, the Butterfly Passion produces agreement of characters, even of contraries. For example: A and B are two people of incompatible humor. It happens that of sixty groups which A frequents, he finds a third of them, twenty, in which his interests coincide with those of B, but in which he finds he must share some of B's tastes although opposed to his own. The same thing applies to B's tastes with regard to A; hence without loving each other they have mutual respect, consideration, and an interest in protecting each other.

Thus the interest which disunites friends in the "civilized" state, unites even enemies in the associative state. It conciliates repugnant characters by indirect coöperation born of the coördination of functions which short sessions produce. . . .

It is by this brevity of sessions that a series, even if it consists of only thirty persons, can introduce its members into a hundred other series and form with them bonds of friendship and interest. It will be seen that this coöperation is indispensable if two principal objects are to be attained. These are, (1) Equitable division of the triple dividend assigned to capital, labor and talent. (2) Perfect agreement in interest through the operation of cupidity which is to-day the most fertile source of discord. . . .

Organization of the Phalanstery.[1] I must state at the beginning and I shall recall frequently, that in order to operate an associative approximation, or phalanstery of reduced scale, it is necessary to know the mechanism of the phalanstery of full scale for eighteen hundred people. The operation on reduced scale will employ only one-fourth the capital which the other would require. The reductions which each branch can undergo on a small scale cannot be estimated if the full mechanism of harmony on a large scale is not known. . . .

I separate the material preparations into three parts:

1. The formation of the stock company
2. Construction, provisioning, planting
3. Coördination and successive installations.

[1] *Ibid.*, pp. 99–107.

1. *Formation of the company.* As it will be necessary in this regard to take a step quite contrary to the usual methods, that is, to shun the crowd of small stock-holders, *pauci sed boni*, I believe it is proper to defer this subject to the article *Candidature* [1] in the epilogue. Let us suppose this company completely formed and the necessary capital provided to found a large-scale phalanstery, since in order to know how to found one on a small scale we must study the theory of the large one.

2. *Material distributions of the trial canton.* These will be fully explained in this part as well as their relative dispositions in the mechanism of attraction, a point on which a company of stock-holders would fall into grave errors at every step if it was guided by prevalent prejudice.

3. *Liabilities, admissions and consecutive installations.* In this connection we shall pursue a method contrary to that of "civilized" establishments, in which the coöperators are installed brusquely and all at once. The installation of the trial phalanstery (supposing it complete) ought to be effected in five steps, namely:

The wage-earning group, subsidiary cohort		100
Root	(1) The nucleus and governing body	300
Quarter operation	(2) The preparatory class	400
Half operation	(3) The mixed class	600
Three-quarter operation	(4) The well-to-do class	400
Full operation	(5) The rich class	200
And for the approximative foundation only 900		2000 . .

A methodical treatment would require me to deal next with buildings and lands, but I shall defer these rather dry details. Let us start with the order to be followed in progressive installations of members of the community.

If buildings and lands could be found already prepared, the phalanstery might be installed in the space of nine months, namely: the first group in August, the second in September, the third in October, the fourth in March, the fifth in May.

Work could not progress so rapidly in the large-scale phalanstery, for it would be necessary first to build and plant, and then to occupy portions of the building as they are ready. I estimate then that the installation would require from twenty-one to twenty-four months.

[1] Not included in this selection. (Editor.)

The small-scale phalanstery will be limited to three groups, the first installed in August, the second in October, the third in March. First of all, one hundred wage-earners (laborers), two-thirds men and one-third women, will be employed in rough work and in functions which would weaken industrial Attraction. These hundred wage-earners will be the prop of the trial phalanstery, which will be greatly impeded by deficiencies of Attraction, and obliged to rely on such a support whether on a large or small scale.

If the company of stock-holders wished to engage immediately 1900 persons, or the 800 of reduced-scale, they would fail. At first they would be imposed upon by the working class who, unaware of the nature of their employment, would be very exacting about conditions. On the other hand, the well-to-do and rich classes would lack confidence, and would refuse every arrangement. The point is for each group to solicit admission as a mark of favor; and to succeed in this, it will be sufficient to work judiciously on the first group.

Negotiations will be entered into with the working class by stipulating that a fixed sum may be set which the contracting party can exact in case of misunderstanding as to the associative division of the profit. (I regretfully omit important details as to these arrangements.) The governing body will not anticipate disagreement about the distribution; but as the contracting parties will expect it, it will be necessary to satisfy them with this option of a fixed sum.

If the land contains some large building, a rented château or monastery, the nucleus, or primary group of about 300 plus the governing body, will be installed first. It will be composed in large measure of gardeners who will prepare orchards, do transplanting and all work which necessitates long preparation: the introduction of animals, fruit and vegetable preserving, planting of vegetables like asparagus and artichokes which do not bear the first year.

The first task will be to mold beginners in the development of Attraction, to stimulate their passions, tastes and instincts. Both fathers and children will be extremely astonished at an authority which, without moralizing and instead of mistreating them, will only be exercised to favor their tastes, shed charm on their labors by short and varied sessions, and classify them in groups and sub-groups; striving, meanwhile, to infuse them with an intriguing passion for such and such meats, such and such preparations, by graduating and scaling the distinctly different tastes of the three sexes.[1]

[1] *I.e.*, men, women, and children.

A company of stock-holders would not fail to disapprove of this procedure, and pretend that they must discipline this assemblage according to the wholesome doctrines of commerce and morality. Let us more properly envisage the goal. It will not be a question of molding "civilized" people, but "Harmonious" people, in order to promote industrial Attraction among them by the prompt formation of the passional Series. The sooner these are formed, the sooner this Attraction will arise; but the quickest way is by encouraging refined and graduated epicurism. This will create first a series in consumption, after which the scale of passional Series will extend itself to the preparation of food. Such a mechanism, once organized at the dining table and in the kitchen, will establish itself as a consequence in fruit-growing and in canning workshops. This theme must be treated in the third and fourth sections: I merely indicate it here.

Graduated gastronomy, which is easily understood, is the resource provided by God to make the mechanism of Attraction work promptly, surely, and from the very first month of trial. Such a wise provision will charm all beginners. It will not be very productive amongst the first group of 300 people, since the benefits of the Series' organization can be fully realized only in a group of 600; but the former will be a necessary seed-time for the régime of industrial Attraction. This will be established with the entrance of the second group, and will create the quadruple product.

On this subject let us note that, as to gastronomy, the culture of flowers, the employment of opera and other so-called frivolous or vicious functions, I shall be obliged incessantly to contradict "civilized" doctrines. I do not deny that these functions are obnoxious in the present state, but I visualize them as applied to the régime of passional Series, in which they become a means of benefit.

As soon as people of the neighboring villages and towns know the kind of life which the 300 beginners lead—how they choose their labors and work in short periods with change of employment at least four times a day, how meals are served with a choice of various kinds of food, and how the leaders carefully vary the pleasures of men, women and children—all this will be a subject of wide-spread discussion amongst the industrial class of the neighborhood. The welfare of the beginners will be the sole consideration; every family of workers, artisans and small cultivators will earnestly cling to its position, and whoever will have hesitated over his engagement will come to solicit it as a high favor.

I assume that by this time a wing of the phalanstery will be already constructed and habitable. The second group of 400 people will then be engaged, one part of which will be composed of instructor-workmen: carpenters, wheelwrights, shoemakers, locksmiths. Another part will consist of small cultivators, another of primary-school teachers, for the passional-Series régime quickly incites adults and children to demand instruction which they only passively accept in "civilized" society.

In engaging this second group the governing body will have their choice of the best workers who, charmed with the manner of life of the participants, will present themselves in ten-fold the necessary number.

The nucleus, increased to 700 by this recruitment, will pass from rough work to work more closely approximating its real function (*i.e.*, to one-quarter operation).

Then will begin the trial of the Series' mechanism, which cannot be attempted by less than 600 persons. The governing body will furnish working clothes and parade dress to all those engaged, and the groups will set out for work with flags, hymns, and fanfares. Three degrees at table will also be established—two for the first group and one for the governing body.

Only after this Series' mechanism has been at least roughly established shall we be able to glimpse the properties of Attraction: geometric justice, prevention of excess by alternating pleasures, perfection of work and of industrial ardor (increased by reason of gastronomic refinements), love of riches becoming the pathway of virtue, encouragement of children in productive work, use of discords in general harmony, and indirect agreement of antipathies. All these marvels, the germs of which can be seen in a group of 700 persons, could not manifest themselves in the nucleus of 300; but one of 700 or even 600 will give results that will leave no doubt as to the speedy downfall of "civilization."

Then all eyes will be fixed on this embryo of harmony. Its stock will be sought for at twice the original price; many of the rich class will ask to be included in the third group, which the governing body will set to work to assemble, or rather to accept.

Admission will be all the more in demand because there will shine forth one of the finest features of the Series régime: the relative twenty-fold increase of wealth, quadrupling the effective product and making possible with four thousand francs a standard of living which it would cost twenty thousand to maintain in "civilization."

Admission to the third group will be difficult, for this must be composed of tutors, skilled artisans, experienced cultivators, expert agriculturists: specialists charged with giving higher education to the plebeians of the phalanstery, particularly to the children.

As for choosing aspirants, rich or poor, various qualities should be looked for which are esteemed vicious or useless in "civilization," such as:

A good ear for music,
Politeness in the family circle,
Aptitude for fine arts.

In making the selection one should also follow various rules opposed to current philosophical ideas,

Preferring families having few children,
Introducing one-third unmarried people,
Seeking so-called "capricious" characters,
Establishing a graduated scale as to age, fortune, and intelligence.

Associative industry reaps great advantage from certain faculties, such as an appreciative ear, which the sophists condemn according to their principle that whoever sings and dances well advances little. This is a very false principle in associative mechanics, and above all in the trial phalanstery, which will advance very far if it has an extremely polite people, singing and dancing well.

At first the large-scale phalanstery will raise a great sum from curious visitors: this single branch of profit will triple the stockholders' capital. A large part of this harvest would be missed if the phalanstery presented to the curious only an unpolished people, unskilled in material evolutions of harmony and in the management of passions which demand much refinement.

There must be an assortment of instructor-workmen, at least three in each trade, in order to establish a competition of methods. If each of these workmen, taken from the city, brought a considerable family, almost half the fathers and children would be unaccustomed to agriculture. This would pervert the associative mechanism, in which agriculture should hold the highest rank.

In credits and charge accounts relating to advances of subsistence, garments, lodging, etc., the phalanstery never recognizes families, but only individuals, each of whom has his separate account. A man cannot enter into agreements on behalf of his wife and children; each one makes agreements individually, except children of the poor class under three years, who are kept at the expense of the phalanstery.

Consequently, every workman over-burdened by children will seek admittance; but the governing body only accepts children in suitable numbers. . . .

With the entry of the third group the phalanstery should have at least two-thirds of its plantings productive; or ought then to bear the expense of transplanting fruit trees by packing solid earth around the roots. . . . Thus there will be no risk of straining the mechanism of the phalanstery for two or three years by disagreeable labors and evil intrigues, as would be the case with young orchards which would not impassionate the groups as long as there was no fruit produced.

The trial phalanstery, even on a reduced scale, must provide for the well-being of about one hundred wage-earners whom it will employ. It will lead them to the happiness which is the outcome of association, by varying their tasks and by other means; and will guarantee them admittance either into the next phalanstery to be founded or into the present one, if it is only on a reduced scale and extensible from 900 to 1800. Everyone must be happy in this group, even the animals; their well-being is an essential branch of associative harmony and one of the sources of its wealth. It would grow poor and its mechanism become distorted if it succumbed to the egoism of Plato who, instead of looking for a remedy for the miseries of humanity, thanked the gods for having escaped the common woe; for being born a man and not a woman, Greek and not barbarian, free and not slave. I shall return to this egoism of Plato and his colleagues: is it any wonder that with such characters philosophers have overlooked the calculation of Attraction, which tends toward the happiness of all?

It is easy to foresee that each artisan and each peasant, on entering the phalanstery, will wish to subscribe for inferior places at table for his wife and children, and place them in the third degree if he himself subscribes for the second. He will also want to take for himself the entire fixed amount, or optional sum agreed upon when he was engaged, giving only the leavings to his wife and children. Such is the tender "civilized" father; the tender peasant wants everything for himself under the pretext of keeping morality sweet and pure. These marital and paternal tyrannies are inadmissible in the associative régime. Besides, after a month has passed, all society will despise this "civilized" rapacity and will be well satisfied to be exempt from keeping wives and children who as a result of industrial Attraction will be earning much more than their expenses.

The phalanstery, supplied with its third group, could be raised to *the grand approximation or half strength*, which demands 1300 people. Then the operations of high harmony will be inaugurated, such as *attractive or natural education*, which need only be sketched in the quarter-strength phalanstery of 700 persons.

Natural education in the phalanstery of one-third strength will be the most powerful bait for the wealthy class. They will be convinced after having seen the children of the phalanstery that even a monarch with all his treasures and salaried tutors is unable to give his children a quarter of the material and intellectual advantages which the poorest child will receive from the phalanstery. Accordingly, all rich people who have precious heirs whom they want well cared for, will compete for admission to the last two bodies, numbers four and five, or they will ask to have their children admitted, on condition of purchasing shares at the current price, which will already be three times that of the original capital.

I have said that the most striking property of harmonial education is that it develops in the child at the early age of three to four years a score of industrial vocations. Even a child who would be an obstinate sluggard in "civilized" households would be so affected. His taste for science and art, and his material and intellectual refinement would be cultivated without any other effort than allowing free play to attraction, nature, and all his fancies. A child reared from birth in passional Series would be more vigorous at four years of age than a child of six years in "civilized" society, and more advanced in intelligence than most children of ten years.

To add lustre to these properties of the natural method one must reserve places for children outside the phalanstery, since the great ones of the land will apply for these places in large numbers. Plebeians overburdened with families must not be admitted into the first three groups, for this would mean an excessive number of children. There must be enough children between the ages of five and thirteen to organize a dancing group consisting of 144 children of both sexes or, with their leaders, say 160. Now the number of children from five to thirteen in "civilized" families would amount to at least 220 for each 1300 individuals. The natural proportion of children in the first three groups of the phalanstery should therefore be reduced so as to admit the numerous outside children who will apply for board and lodging.

I assume that the third group will have been admitted at the beginning of Autumn; during the Winter the 1300 members will have been able to form enough bonds to make a brilliant display in the Spring.

The phalanstery will then plan to enroll its numerical complement, the last (fourth and fifth) groups, thus striking the final blow and effecting in six weeks of full operation the abandonment and ending of "civilization." Already "civilization" will have been condemned by all; the Winter during which the phalanstery is in half operation will be a season of passional calm due to the absence of the two higher classes, but after their entry "civilization" will be scornfully condemned and discredited by its most obstinate defenders.

Let us omit the details concerning the installation of the fourth and fifth groups since we are merely considering a small phalanstery of only three groups. Even this will be sufficient to attract an immense crowd of curious peasants. They will come from all parts to see whether it is true that the destiny of man, the associative mechanism of passions, is discovered, and that natural law will succeed to "moral" fancies which tend to repress, moderate and change nature, and to substitute for God's wisdom the wisdom of Cato and Target. . . .

Government of the Phalanstery.[1] The governing body [of the phalanstery], charged with directing current affairs and attending to general service, is only the delegate of the areopagus which is an authority of opinion. It [the areopagus] is composed of: first, the heads of each industrial series or pleasure (pleasures being also utilities in harmony with labors); second, the three tribes of reverends, venerables, and patriarchs; third, the principal stockholders who have a vote according to their shares, and the small stockholders who have obtained their shares by small cumulative economies; fourth, the men and women magnates of the phalanstery.

The areopagus neither makes nor enforces any statutes, everything being regulated by attraction, by the esprit-de-corps of tribes, choirs and series. It makes pronouncements upon important affairs, harvest, vintage, building, etc. Its opinions are welcomed passionally as a barometer of industry, but are not obligatory: one group would be free to change its crop despite the opinion of the areopagus.

It [the areopagus] has no influence on the principal operation, which is the proportional division of dividends among capital, labor and talent. Attraction alone is the arbiter of justice in this matter.

Neither the areopagus nor the governing body is charged with responsibilities leading to deception, as is the case with "civilized"

[1] *Ibid.*, pp. 113–115.

finance which knows how to mask all its thievery in a rubbish of figures. Accounting, in associative harmony, is the work of a special series whose bookkeeping can be inspected by everyone.

Moreover, accounts are very uncomplicated in this new order. Daily payments, the "civilized" custom of always having money in hand, are unknown here. Everyone has an open credit in proportion to his known fortune or to his presumptive profits *in attractive industry*. The neighboring phalansteries do not make daily payments for what they sell to each other: cattle, poultry, vegetables, fruits, butter, dairy products, fodder, wine, oil, wood, etc. It is written down and balanced at agreed times after clearings or compensatory payments between the cantons and regions. Individual accounts for the advance of subsistence and other furnishings are regulated only at the end of the year, at the time of inventory and division [of profits]. . . .

Litigation is reduced to a few arbitrations. Everyone can instantly withdraw the amount of his stock, except the current dividend which is regulated at the time of inventory.

Wardship for children is unnecessary. One cannot bequeath them a penny, since their inheritance consists of shares of stock which are registered in the ledger of each phalanstery and bear fixed interest, or of a dividend regulated each year after the inventory. Thus a pupil is exposed to no temptations, and his funds in each phalanstery where he has stock accumulate with interest until he comes of age (twenty years), at which time he assumes responsibility for them.

Three classes must be provided for at table, differentiated according to fortune and expenditure. This is an indispensable gradation in a harmonious community where any kind of equality is political poison. Some of the coöperators will possess a little capital from land, cattle and implements of husbandry which they have sold, or a demolished cabin for which they have been paid. For these payments they will obtain a share of stock or part of a share. They will form a class already superior to the multitude and can be admitted, if they so desire, to the tables of the second order where those also will be received who are thoroughly acquainted industrially.

A first class will be created, composed of the principal workers, instructors enrolled in the city, and creditors of a considerable optional sum. Cultivators who furnish extensive lands or a suitable house will be considered principal stockholders. These three degrees will be necessary even in the small phalanstery of reduced scale.

The governing body, or committee of managing stockholders, will form a fourth class which can really be identified with the phalanstery only when the last groups enter. . . .

Industries of the Phalanstery.[1] A phalanstery working its territory on the combinative system begins by deciding on two or three suitable employments for each portion. Mixed cultivation can always be carried on with success, except in the case of very valuable vineyards, which, however, permits the growing of fruits and vegetables as accessories to the pivotal culture. The object of the mixed cultivation is to bring in various groups and encourage competition among them. This interests them in tasks related to their own and leaves a group as little isolated as possible in its functions. . . .

Let us consider the variety of series from which can be chosen those capable of producing the *maximum amount* of harmony in the trial phalanstery under those circumstances, and of organizing in it at least 135 or even 150 to 200 series of proper mechanical structure. The choice must include:

1. Preference for the animal kingdom over the vegetable, because the animal kingdom keeps the series permanently occupied during the winter.

2. Preference for the vegetable kingdom over manufactures, because the former is more attractive and directly encourages harmony.

3. Kitchen work, because it involves permanent and ceaseless labor, labor which leads in industrial attraction, is related to production and consumption, and is most likely to further the intriguing spirit.

4. Finally, manufactures: attractive rather than profitable, for the policy of the founders must be to create an excellent equilibrium of passions and not to speculate on profits, which are out of place in the associative system. Profit would be deceptive if it did not conduce to the main object, which is to promptly display the mechanism of industrial attraction, astound "civilization" from the beginning of the campaign (the second month of full operation), and obtain by a brilliant success the recompense and profits of foundation, the tribute of the curious, etc. . . .

Manufacturing, so much extolled in the modern political system which puts it on a level with agriculture, figures in the associative state only as an accessory and complement of the agricultural system, a function subordinated to the convenience of the latter.

I do not pretend to say that it will be lightly considered in the new

[1] *Ibid.*, pp. 120, 130, 131, 248.

order, because each phalanstery will carry on manufacturing, and each individual, rich or poor, who has been reared from infancy in harmony will be a passional coöperator in half a score of manufactures. But they will hold only the second rank in industry and despite opportunity for profit will be abandoned when, in alliance with the agriculture of the territory, they fail to encourage the intriguing spirit.

He who would propose to establish a cotton-spinning mill in the trial phalanstery would commit a shocking mistake, for this phalanstery (which I suppose to be founded in France, Germany, or England) would not produce cotton nor would its neighbors produce it: it would therefore be adopting a manufacture destitute of any bond with its agriculture and local passions.

Such a manufacture will be quite admissible when the phalansteries have been fortified by several years of operation, by bonds and rivalries with neighboring phalansteries, by a mechanism of true commerce, etc. It will then be proper to have a factory in each phalanstery working up exotic products. This will be a bond with remote regions. . . .

The phalanstery pays for each service by a dividend allowed to the group. No one receives individual wages—this would be shameful. . . .

Division of the Income of the Phalanstery.[1] We finally arrive at the principal object, the terrifying problem of establishing a strikingly just and completely harmonious distribution of profits and a recompense satisfactory to everyone in accordance with his three industrial faculties: *labor, talent and capital.* . . .

We now see the triumph of that cupidity so much defamed by moralists. God would not have given us this passion if He had not foreseen a useful means of employing it for the general equilibrium. I have already proven that epicurism, likewise outlawed by philosophers, becomes the road to wisdom and industrial concord in the passional Series. It will be seen that cupidity produces the same effect, becoming a road to distributive justice, and that in creating our passions *God does well all that He does.* . . .

I distinguish between the general and particular impulsions which lead every harmonian towards equity.

1. *General impulsions* applied to the three faculties, capital, labor and talent: Alcippus is one of the rich stockholders. Such a sum as

[1] *Ibid.*, pp. 308–312, 314.

would yield him three to four per cent interest in "civilization," in the phalanstery will produce twelve to fifteen per cent, at a rough estimate, if agreement is reached in regard to the distribution. This means that he will favor distributive justice and reject every measure which would wrong one of the three faculties. If by right of strength the capitalist wished to allow *capital* half the income (for example: capital six-twelfths, labor four-twelfths, talent two-twelfths), the two numerous classes which receive an income only on the other two faculties, labor and talent, will be dissatisfied: attraction will slacken, productivity and concord will diminish, and with the third year the associative bond will be dissolved. Alcippus sees that for his own interest he must fix distribution as follows: capital four-twelfths, labor five-twelfths, talent three-twelfths. Calculated on this basis the distribution will still give Alcippus an income quadruple that which he had in "civilization"; in addition it will guarantee the contentment of the two less fortunate classes and the maintenance of the associative bond. Alcippus is the more inclined towards justice because he himself has a good number of shares to collect from in different series for capital and talent; and because pleasures, such as hunting, fishing, music, dramatic art, horticulture and bird-keeping, are paid for like work in the fields and vineyards. In addition, he has formed many friendly connections with the class of non-capitalists; he protects them, he is desirous that justice be rendered them.

In this case cupidity, which would have impelled him to vote a share of one-half for capital, is counterbalanced by two honorable impulsions. These are: his affection for various associative series which he frequents and in which moreover he has some shares of labor and talent to collect on. He also has the conviction of finding his interest in the collective interest, in the contentment of the entire phalanstery, and in the progress of industrial attraction which is the source of future riches.

Thus the violent impulse of cupidity, which to-day encourages exaggerated pretensions, encounters two balancing-forces which keep it in bounds, preserve the proper equilibrium, and guarantee justice to the three faculties and to different individuals. This beautiful agreement of passions is based on the fundamental property of a mathematical series: *the sum of the extremes is equal to double the middle term.* (In the series 2, 4, 6, 2×4 is equivalent to 2 plus 6.)

Let us analyze the same balancing-forces, the same equilibrium, in the impulsions of the poor class.

Jeannot has no capital, no stock; will he vote to favor labor at the expense of capital or talent? to fix the proportion at:

labor seven-twelfths, capital three-twelfths, talent two-twelfths?

Here the dominant impulsion is to favor labor to the detriment of the two other faculties, capital and talent. Such would be the opinion of every "civilized" poor man; the peasant says: It is I who produce everything. He believes he is entitled to everything he can steal from the lord who, for his part, thinks he has a right to take everything from the peasant. Such is the equilibrium of passions in the "civilized" state, a struggle of pillage and cunning called "perfectibility."

In a harmonious community the poor Jeannot will think very differently. His strongest impulse is to favor labor since he has no pretensions to the dividends allowed to capital. But two other impulses come to counterbalance this brutish impulse of cupidity. Jeannot has some claims on the share allotted to talent; he shines at certain tasks, therefore it is desirable for him that talent should maintain its rights. On the other hand, he knows the importance of capitalists in a phalanstery, the advantages which the poor receive from all their expenditures on free shows, carriages and horses, public meals, desserts at rich tables, and industrial adoption of his own children. Even if he could not appreciate all these opportunities of profit he would learn it in the company of the forty groups which he frequents, for the corporate bodies never misunderstand their own interests.

These two impulsions dispose Jeannot to protect the interests of talent and capital, and reduce the share of labor from seven-twelfths to five-twelfths. This reduction, all things considered, is to his advantage, for his only happiness consists in maintaining the phalanstery and attraction, which would be in jeopardy immediately if capital and talent were badly rewarded. Here gross cupidity, which would be completely dominant in our society, is balanced by two counterweights, two impulsions favorable to talent and capital, although Jeannot has only the slightest claim to either talent or capital. As in Alcippus' case it is the influence of the two extremes balancing twice the influence of the middle term. The harmonians of the three classes, rich, middling, or poor, are constantly impelled towards these just views by the impulsion of two collective interests struggling against unreasoning rapacity. Among "civilized" people this rapacity encounters no balancing-force and presents no opportunity of profiting from the maintenance of the general interest or of distributive justice.

I shall insist, in the two chapters following,[1] upon this tendency for every poor harmonian to uphold the rich class and the allotment to capital; I shall give irrefutable proofs of this impulsion. Meanwhile, let us observe that the poor man in the harmonious community has numerous chances of making his fortune; he is not discouraged as are our wage-earners who can see no way of raising themselves to the position of master. He has the hope of seeing his children attain high dignities through learning, talent, beauty, aristocratic alliances; he has a small fortune, increasing as the result of his economies, which the savings-bank receives shilling by shilling. He spends no money because he is well nourished and well clad at the charge of the phalanstery, which furnishes him all work-clothes and three dress uniforms for the three seasons. He does not dream of frequenting the public house and cabaret as do our workers, for he finds excellent fare, choice of wines and happy companionship at his five repasts. Therefore he economizes and invests in stock certificates all the profit which remains to him after payment of his expense account. He is a small proprietor; he has the spirit of property, the right to vote in various councils and the suffrage in all elections. He cannot feel aversion towards the rich men with whom he associates, with whom he is always on good terms, and whose equal he hopes to become. Without this hope of attaining fortune life becomes a burden to man. . . .

The allotment to talent, limited to three-twelfths and perhaps to two-twelfths, is, after all, very plentiful, because in each branch of industry there is a mass of novices without title to the share allotted to talent. They number at least a third in each undertaking, often a half; this assures a large portion to the other half who alone are rewarded for talent. The allotments to labor do not present this opportunity, because each member of a group working in it to a greater or less degree, has a right to participate. For that reason labor merits at least five-twelfths of the profit, and it is doubtful whether it should not be raised higher, according to the relationship: *Labor three-sixths, Capital two-sixths, Talent one-sixth*. . . .

[1] Omitted here. (Editor.)

XI

LOUIS BLANC

1811–1882

The family of Louis Blanc had been directly involved in the first French Revolution, and he himself was to carry on the tradition during subsequent upheavals of the nineteenth century. Up to 1816, when Louis was born, the Blancs had figured as victims rather than as gainers in these disturbances. His grandfather, a merchant of Lyon, was imprisoned in the Bastille during the Reign of Terror and executed as a counter-revolutionist. His father, imprisoned at the same time, managed to escape. The escape seems to have about exhausted the elder Blanc's initiative; he reappears as a ship-owner in the early years of the Empire, but it was through his wife's connections that he once more became temporarily prosperous. They obtained a place for him in the entourage of Joseph Bonaparte, and he acted as a treasury official during the latter's brief régime in Spain. His son Louis was born in Madrid in 1811. After Joseph's downfall Blanc seemed quite incapable of further exertions, even abandoning his wife and children—who fortunately were cared for by Marshal Jourdan. In 1821 Louis XVIII granted him a pension and tuition for his two sons out of respect for the Blanc who had been guillotined in 1794.

The two children accordingly entered the College of Rodez. Louis distinguished himself in the classics, particularly in rhetoric and philosophy. In 1830 the brothers completed their studies at Rodez, and being almost without resources decided to try their luck in Paris. Louis obtained work as a copyist and found it a hard struggle to live. He appealed to a friend of the family, but pride kept him from taking the kind of assistance which was offered. The brothers later accepted a gift of 600 francs a year tendered by another friend.

Louis Blanc now tried his hand at various occupations: lawyer's clerk (he "quickly abandoned chicanery"), schoolmaster, and finally tutor in the household of an iron-master at Arras. The last situation gave him plenty of leisure for self-improvement. He had already been drawn to history and now also studied the pre-revolutionary philosophers: Rousseau, Mably, Morelly, and Montesquieu. Mindful of his own recent struggles he began to mingle with the workingmen of Arras, discussing their needs with them and sharing their visions of a better society.

But Louis Blanc longed for fame. Having no political experience himself he declared that it was a detriment to leadership. For some time he had cherished journalistic ambitions and had attained some local success in that line. He now gave up his tutorship and returned to Paris where his talents might have freer range. Paris this time was not too difficult: he became a contributor to *Good Sense* and then its editor, thus securing a pulpit from which he preached democracy and opposition to the repressive government of Louis Philippe. He endeavored to win over a part of the bourgeoisie.

A disagreement with the proprietor of *Good Sense* over government operation of the railroads caused Blanc's resignation from that journal. In 1839 he joined in founding the *Review of Progress*, whose object was to promote opposition to the bourgeois monarchy. Louis Blanc announced a program of reform which included universal suffrage, a single-chamber legislature, supremacy of the legislative authority, strong local government in the communes (balanced by sufficient authority in the central government to deal with matters of national interest), and, lastly, reorganization of industry. The political reforms constituted in many essentials his definition of "the Republic," which he advocated from that time forward. In the *Organization of Labor* he elaborated the last point of the platform. This pamphlet, first published in the *Review of Progress* in 1839, contained nothing new so far as its individual ideas were concerned. Mably and Morelly, especially the latter, supplied much of the underlying philosophy, while something that resembled the independent phalanstery of Fourier was fitted to something that resembled the authoritarian state of Saint-Simon. Even the famous dictum "from each according to his capacity, to each according to his needs" had appeared in Morelly almost word for word. Nevertheless the synthesis at least was new, while the brevity of the tract and its incisive popular language gave it a value as propaganda beyond that of most of its predecessors.

The *Organization of Labor* and the later *History of Ten Years* (1841) definitely established Blanc's reputation as a popular leader, a man to be reckoned with in future political and social readjustments. The *History of Ten Years* (from 1830 to 1840) was a brightly written work which contrasted the harshness and egoism of the bourgeoisie with the noble qualities of the people, and glorified the republican party at the expense of Louis Philippe's oppressive machine.

But the old order still had some years of life in it. Republican agitation continued, but not until the end of 1847 could Louis Blanc assert—the application was obvious—that when the fruit is spoiled a breath will detach it. The breath came in February, 1848. It wafted away Guizot, the king's minister, and then the king. The moderate reformers in the legislature thereupon set up a provisional government—from which Louis Blanc was pointedly excluded. But the latter used oratory to good effect; the populace supported him, and he seized office by what amounted to a little *coup d'état*.

The mode of Louis Blanc's arrival at power did not increase his popularity with his colleagues of the provisional government. Nor were they impressed with his socialistic opinions. For the time being, however, it was necessary to humor public sentiment by granting his projects a hearing and even pretending to put them into effect. A commission headed by Louis Blanc was accordingly installed in the Luxembourg Palace to work out the details of the social millennium. Reformers, employers, and workingmen were called before it to present their ideas. Some little progress was made toward setting up the industrial régime favored by the president. The commission organized several coöperative workshops, fed them with government contracts for army uniforms, saddles, flags, and epaulettes, and went on to recommend the creation of a Ministry of Progress and the formation of a state fund for loans to workingmen.

But Louis Blanc's downfall was at hand. His enemies in the government sought to discredit his theories by foisting on him responsibility for the so-called "national workshops." These were workshops only in name; the term was applied to the manual work—costly and rather useless except as charity—dealt out by the government to relieve unemployment. Elections to the National Assembly in April, 1848, showed that the tide had turned against Blanc and his friends. The Assembly passed him over in choosing its executive committee and he immediately resigned from the Luxembourg commission. But it was his alliance with the working class that finally proved his undoing. He had encouraged popular demonstrations to impress the government with the workers' point of view. On one occasion (15 May, 1848) the crowd invaded the Assembly itself, shouting for Louis Blanc. It happened that he had been quite guiltless of inciting this particular movement and had even tried to suppress it, but the opposition seized upon it as a pretext for extinquishing him and all his works. To avoid prosecution he fled to Belgium and then to England. The bourgeoisie were again in complete control of France.

Louis Blanc remained in England for over twenty years. When he first arrived, Louis Napoleon Bonaparte was also in England waiting to make his second bid for power in France. Blanc had at one time tried to convert Louis to republicanism and for a moment his effort had seemed to succeed. Now the future emperor visited and condoled with his fellow exile. But circumstances were soon to make them inveterate opponents. Bonaparte became president and then emperor of the French, but to Louis Blanc the Second Empire was merely a second bourgeois monarchy. For the rest of his exile he ceaselessly attacked the Napoleonic régime and conspired to restore the republic. Meanwhile he made a living in England by writing and lecturing on political subjects. During this period he also finished a *History of the French Revolution*.

Three days after Napoleon surrendered to the Prussians at Sédan (1870) Louis Blanc was again in Paris, where he upheld Gambetta's policy of continuing the war to the bitter end. When hostilities ceased he was elected to the National Assembly at the head of the Paris list and strove to avert warfare between the Assembly and the commune of Paris. The effort failed and in the civil war he adhered to the Assembly. The commune accordingly denounced him as a traitor. Long exile had apparently kept him from understanding the social basis of the Paris uprising. Nevertheless when the revolt was crushed he vigorously opposed a policy of retaliation.

Louis Blanc retained his seat in the legislature until his death in 1882. He supported the republic during its critical years not as an end in itself but as a necessary instrument of social reform, and continued to advocate a variety of social measures with which his name had long been connected. Among these were state loans to producers' coöperative associations, government ownership of railroads and mines, a shorter working day, etc. He also aligned himself with the anticlericals, perhaps chiefly because he identified the Church with reaction. He was mainly responsible for founding the Democratic Socialist party in 1876.

But the career of Louis Blanc had really culminated in 1848. Before his death his doctrine had been superseded by the more fashionable communism of Proudhon and Bakunin; his oratory, a little outmoded, was listened to impatiently; and such power as he still exercised rested on the memory of a brilliant past. But although his personal reputation and authority declined markedly in later years, his ideas were absorbed into more modern socialist doctrines. Thus his federated social workshops reappear in syndicalism, while, oddly enough, the rôle he assigned to the state identifies him with the state socialists. His work, moreover, forms a link between Utopian and Marxian socialism. Finally he introduced a new tactic in propaganda: he was one of the first socialists to appeal directly to the masses.

REFERENCES

The first edition of *Organization of Labor* has been translated by M. P. Dickoré (1911).

La Vie et l'œuvre de Louis Blanc (1922), by Edouard Renard, is a scholarly biography. See also Donald C. McKay, *The National Workshops* (1933).

READINGS FROM

ORGANIZATION OF LABOR

Reasons for Organizing Labor.[1] We want . . . labor to be organized so as to bring about the suppression of misery, not only in order that the physical suffering of the people may be relieved, but also—and especially—that every one may recover his self respect; that excess of misfortune may no longer stifle in anyone the noble aspirations of the mind and the satisfactions of a legitimate pride; that there may be a place for all in the domain of education and at the springs of knowledge; that there may no longer exist either a man enslaved, absorbed in tending a revolving wheel, or a child transformed for the benefit of its family into a supplement to wages, or a mother who turns against the fruit of her womb because of the inability to live, or a young girl who is reduced, for the sake of bread, "to sell the sweet name of love!" We want labor to be organized so that the soul of the people—its soul, hark you—may not stay repressed and corrupted beneath the tyranny of things! . . .

The emancipation of the proletarians is too complicated a work, it involves too many questions, upsets too many habits, thwarts too many interests (not in realty but in appearance), for anyone to be foolish enough to believe that it can be accomplished by a series of partial and isolated efforts. All the power of the state must be applied

[1] Pp. 4–5, 14–16. Page references are to the 5th ed. (1848), reprinted with an introduction by (Sir) J. A. R. Marriott in Vol. I of his *The French Revolution of 1848 in Its Economic Aspects* (1913). Translation by the present editor.

to it. What the proletarians need to emancipate themselves are the instruments of labor; the function of the government is to furnish them with these. If we had to define the State as we conceive it we should say: the State is the banker of the poor.

Now is it true, as M. Lamartine was not afraid to assert in a recent manifesto,—is it true that this conception "consists in taking possession, in the name of the State, of the ownership and control of industry and labor; in suppressing all free will in citizens who own, sell, buy, or consume; in making or distributing products arbitrarily; in fixing maximum prices; in regulating wages; in completely replacing the proprietary and industrial State with a dispossessed citizenry?"

We have, please God, never proposed anything like this! . . . As will be seen below, we ask only that the State—when it is democratically constituted—shall create social workshops which will gradually and peacefully replace individual workshops; we ask only that the social workshops be controlled by statutes embodying the principle of association and having the form and force of law. But once founded and set in motion, the social workshop would be self-sufficient and would no longer depend on anything but its principle; the associated workmen would, after the first year, choose administrators and chiefs freely for themselves. They would distribute the profits amongst themselves; they would apply themselves to enlarging the enterprise that had been started.—Where does it appear that such a system opens the way to arbitrariness or tyranny? The State would found the social workshop, it would give it laws, it would oversee the execution of them on behalf of, in the name and to the profit of, all; but there its rôle would end: is such a rôle—can it be—tyrannous? To-day, when the government has thieves arrested for entering a house, is it on that account accused of tyranny? Is it reproached for having invaded the domain of personal life, of having penetrated the internal régime of the family? Well! In our system the State would be with reference to the social workshops only what it is to-day with reference to the whole of society. It would watch over the inviolability of the statutes in question as it does to-day over the inviolability of the laws. It would be the supreme protector of the principle of association, without being entitled or able to absorb the action of the associated workers, just as to-day it is the supreme protector of the principle of property, although it does not absorb the action of the proprietors.

Failure of the Competitive System.[1] But would we have the State intervene in the economic reform of society, at least by taking the initiative? Is it our purpose to undermine competition, to remove industry from the régime of laissez-faire? Without a doubt; and far from denying it we loudly proclaim it. Why? Because we desire liberty.

Yes, liberty! That is what we must win; but it must be true liberty, liberty for all, the liberty which is sought in vain wherever equality and fraternity, her immortal sisters, are absent.

If we were to ask why the liberty of a state of savagery was adjudged false and so destroyed, any child could give the right answer. The liberty of the savage state was, in *fact*, only detestable oppression, because it was combined with inequality of power, because it made the weak man the victim of the powerful man, and the infirm the prey of the active. Now in the present social régime we have, instead of inequality of muscular power, inequality of the means of development; instead of bodily conflict, the strife between capital and capital; instead of the abuse of physical superiority, the abuse of a superiority established by custom; instead of the weak man, the ignorant one; instead of the cripple, the poor man. Where then is liberty?

Assuredly it exists, along with even the means of easily abusing it, for those who are provided with the means of enjoying it and making it fruitful: for those who are in possession of the soil, the currency, the credit, and the thousand resources which a cultivated intellect gives. But is it the same for that class, so interesting and numerous, who have neither land, capital, credit, nor education, nothing, that is to say, which allows the individual to be self-sufficient or to develop his faculties? And then after society finds itself divided in such a way that there is great strength on one side and great weakness on the other, competition is unleashed in its midst, competition which pits the rich man against the poor man, the clever speculator against the simple workman, the banker's client against the serf of the usurer, the athlete armed to the teeth against the unarmed combatant, the agile man against the paralytic! And this disorderly, continual strife between power and impotence, this anarchy in oppression, this invisible tyranny of things, which was never surpassed in harshness by visible, palpable tyrannies of men over other men—that is what they dare to call liberty! . . .

Who, I ask, is really interested in maintaining the social order as it exists to-day? No one; no, not one. As for myself, I am readily

[1] Pp. 16–17, 24–27, 101.

persuaded that the calamities which an imperfect civilization creates spread in various forms throughout society. Consider the existence of this rich man: it is completely embittered. And for what reason? Has he not health, youth, flatterers? Does he not believe he has friends? But he is no longer capable of enjoyment—that is his wretchedness; he has exhausted desire—that is his misfortune. Impotence in satiety is the poverty of the rich, the poverty without hope! . . .

Thank heaven, in [human] societies, there is neither partial progress nor partial decay. *All* of society rises or *all* of it declines. If the laws of justice are better understood, *all* ranks profit from it. If the ideas of justice grow dim, *all* suffer. A nation in which one class is oppressed is like a man with a wound in the leg: the injured leg prevents all use of the sound one. Thus, however paradoxical this proposition may seem, oppressor and oppressed gain if oppression is destroyed; they lose equally if it is maintained. Is a very striking proof of this desired? The bourgeoisie has established its domination on unlimited competition, a tyrannical principle. Well, it is by unlimited competition that we are seeing the bourgeoisie perish to-day. I have two millions, you say; my rival has only one: in the lists of industry, with the weapon of cheap prices, I shall certainly ruin him. Cowardly and insensate man! Do you not know that to-morrow some pitiless Rothschild, using your own weapons, will ruin you? Will you then have the impudence to complain of it? In this detestable system of perpetual conflicts, medium-sized industry has devoured small industry. Pyrrhic victories! For the former is devoured in turn by large-scale industry which, forced to pursue unknown consumers to the ends of the earth, will itself soon be no more than a game of chance. Like all games of chance this one will end in knavery for some and suicide for others. Tyranny is not merely odious, it is blind. There are no brains where there are no bowels of compassion. . . .

The social order is bad. How is it to be changed?

Let us state what remedy, in our opinion, would be possible. The reader is warned in advance, however, that we regard as merely transitional the social order whose bases we shall indicate.

The Remedy.[1] The government would be considered as the supreme regulator of production and invested with great power to accomplish its task.

[1] Pp. 102–111, 115, 117–118.

This task would consist in making use of competition itself in order to put an end to competition.

The government would raise a loan whose proceeds would be applied to the creation of *social workshops* in the most important branches of national industry.

As this would require a considerable outlay of funds, the number of workshops initiating the new order would be rigorously limited; but by virtue of their very organization, as will be seen later, they would be endowed with an immense power of expansion.

The government being considered the sole founder of the *social workshops*, it would be the one to draw up the articles of association. This draft, deliberated upon and voted by the national representatives, would have the form and force of law.

All workers who offered guaranties of their responsibility would be called to labor in the *social workshops*—as many workers, that is, as could be employed by the capital first assembled for the purchase of the instruments of labor.

Although [1] the false and anti-social education of the present generation makes it difficult to seek a motive for emulation and encouragement elsewhere than in higher rewards for the laborer, wages would be equal. An entirely new education would be necessary to change ideas and habits.

[1] This paragraph is omitted in the 9th ed. (1850) and the following statement is added (p. 72):

"In the preceding edition of this book I proposed the system of equal wages—or, at least, the equal division of profits—without concealing the fact that it was only an approach toward a higher conception.

"All men are not equal in physical strength, or in intelligence; all do not have the same tastes, the same inclinations, the same habits, any more than they have the same face or figure; but it is just, it is in the general interest, it is in conformity with the principle of solidarity laid down above and with the laws of nature, that everyone should be enabled to turn to account, as completely as is consistent with the welfare of others, the faculties with which nature has endowed him. For the same reason he should be enabled to satisfy, as completely as is consistent with his own welfare, the needs which nature has given him. Thus, for example, the human body is neither vigorous nor healthy unless each member receives what will keep it entirely free from pain, and permit it to achieve its particular object expediently. Equality is therefore only proportionality, and it will not truly exist unless each person—in accordance with the law in some sort written into his constitution by God himself—PRODUCES ACCORDING TO HIS ABILITIES AND CONSUMES ACCORDING TO HIS NEEDS. . . ."

Blanc denies that he has changed his views on this point and quotes a work published some ten years previously. Then he continues:

"My opinion, then, is and has remained, I repeat, absolutely unalterable:

1. That equality of wages is not a system applicable to the present régime of individualism and competition.

2. That it is applicable to the régime of association and solidarity only as a transitional procedure.

3. Finally, that true equality, whose immortal sister is fraternity, is the equality which apportions work to ability and recompense to needs."

For the first year following the establishment of the social workshops, the government would determine the respective duties of the members. After the first year it would no longer do so. The workers having had time to estimate each other's ability and being all equally interested, as we shall see, in the success of the association, their duties would be determined on the elective principle.

Every year there would be drawn up a statement of the net profit. This would be separated into three parts, one of which would be divided equally amongst the members of the association. Another would be set aside (1) for the care of the aged, sick and infirm and (2) for the alleviation of crises in other industries (since industries would owe each other aid and succor). The third part, finally, would be devoted to furnishing the instruments of labor to those who wished to join the association, so that it might expand indefinitely.

To each of these associations, formed for industries which can operate on a large scale, would be admitted persons in occupations which would naturally be dispersed and localized. Thus each social workshop might be composed of various occupations grouped about a great industry—different parts of the same whole, obeying the same laws and participating in the same advantages.

Each member of the social workshop would have the right to dispose of his wages as he saw fit, but it would not be long before the evident economy and undeniable excellence of commercial life would cause association in labor to produce voluntary association in obtaining the necessaries and enjoyments of life.

Capitalists would be invited into the association and would receive interest on capital deposited by them. This interest would be guaranteed by the budget, but they would share in profits only if they became workers.

Once the social workshop is established on these principles, one may conceive what the result would be.

In each principal industry—in the engineering industry, for example, or in the cotton or printing trade—there would be a social workshop competing with private industry. Would the struggle be very long? No, because the social workshop would have an advantage over every individual workshop—the advantage which results from communal life and from a mode of organization in which all the workers, without exception, have an interest in producing quickly and well. Would the struggle be destructive? No, because the government would always be in a position to moderate the effects of it by preventing the price of goods produced in the social workshops from falling too low. To-day when an extremely rich individual enters the arena against others less wealthy, the unequal struggle can only be disastrous—if the individual seeks merely his personal interest—; if he can sell twice as cheaply as his competitors in order to ruin them and remain master of the field he does so. But when this individual is replaced by governmental authority itself, the question changes its aspect. . . .

Thus, instead of being the master and tyrant of the market as the big capitalist is to-day, the state would be its regulator. It would use the weapon of competition not to overthrow individual industry violently—it would be interested above all in avoiding this—but to lead it gradually toward capitulation. Soon, in fact, in every sphere of industry where a social workshop had been established, one would see workers and capitalists hastening toward that institution on account of the advantages it offered to the associates. . . .

As an industry is not always carried on in one place, as it has different centers, it would be necessary to establish, as between all the workshops belonging to the same kind of industry, the system established in each individual workshop. For it would be absurd, after having killed competition among individuals, to let it exist among corporations. Therefore in each sphere of industry which the government had succeeded in dominating there would be a central workshop upon which all the others, as supplemental workshops, would depend. Just as M. Rothschild possesses houses not only in France but in various parts of the world which are in communication with the one where the principal seat of his business is fixed, so each industry would have a principal center and branch establishments. . . .

From the solidarity of all workmen in the same workshop we have proceeded to the solidarity of workshops in the same industry. To complete the system it would be necessary to sanction the solidarity of different industries. It is for that purpose that we have deducted from the quota of profit gained by each industry a sum by means of which the State could come to the aid of any industry suffering from unforeseen or extraordinary occurrences. Moreover, in the system which we propose, crises would be much more rare. Whence do they arise nowadays in great part? From the truly atrocious conflict to which all interests devote themselves. . . . By killing competition, the evils it generates would be suppressed. No more victories, therefore no more defeats. Crises from then on could only come from outside. They are the only things it would become necessary to guard against. Doubtless treaties of peace and alliance would not suffice for that purpose, yet how many disasters would be averted if that shameful diplomacy, which is a contest in hypocrisy, lies, and baseness and whose object is the division of peoples among certain fortunate brigands—if such diplomacy were replaced by a system of alliance founded on the needs of industry and the mutual convenience of workers in all parts of the world! . . .

What we have just said regarding industrial reform is sufficient to indicate the principles and bases on which we should like to see agricultural reform operate. The abuse of collateral inheritances is universally recognized. These would be abolished and the values they were found to consist of would be declared communal property. Each commune would in this way succeed in forming a domain for itself which would be rendered inalienable, and which, since it could only expand, would lead without broils or usurpations to an immense agricultural revolution. Moreover, the communal domain would have to be exploited on a grand scale and in accordance with the rules governing industry. . . .

Let us sum up. A social revolution should be attempted:

1. Because the present social order is too full of iniquity, distress, and baseness to be capable of enduring.

2. Because there is no one, whatever his position, rank, or fortune, who has no interest in inaugurating a new social order.

3. Finally, because it is possible, even easy, to accomplish this revolution peacefully.

In the new world it would lead us into, something would still have to be done, perhaps, to realize completely the principle of fraternity. But everything would at least be prepared for that realization, which would be accomplished by education. Humanity has gotten too far away from its goal for us to be able to attain it in a day. The corrupt civilization whose yoke we still bear has disturbed all interests, but it has at the same time agitated all minds and poisoned the springs of human intelligence. Iniquity has become justice, falsehood has become truth, and in the midst of the gloom men have torn each other to pieces.

Many false ideas must be destroyed: they will disappear, we may be certain of it. So, for example, the day will come when it will be recognized that the more strength or intelligence God gives to a man, the more he owes to his fellow citizens. Then the legitimate ascendancy of genius will be proved, and worthily proved, not by the size of the tribute which it levies on society, but by the services which it renders to society. For the inequality of talents ought not to produce inequality of rights, but inequality of duties.

XII

CHARLES KINGSLEY

1819–1875

Charles Kingsley was born in 1819, the son of a country clergyman of Devonshire, England. His father had passed through Harrow and Oxford with the prospect and means of settling down to a life of aristocratic leisure. But his inheritance soon melted away—the fault was only in part his own—and in order to make a living respectably he entered the Church. Although he discharged his clerical duties faithfully he still retained a keen interest in sport, and besides being a good linguist was something of an artist and a natural historian. The mother of Kingsley is said to have been a remarkable woman. Of enthusiastic temperament, she transmitted a love of literature, science, and travel as well as a keen sense of humor to her son. With all these endowments added to his own native talent Charles was a little surfeited with encouragements to fame. He stammered badly—it was the one defect which told against him—and partly as a result of this affliction he was excessively shy and sensitive to ridicule.

At school, though active and venturesome, he lacked skill at games, but his schoolmates were quick—perhaps too quick—to detect an attitude of conscious intellectual superiority. About this superiority there was little doubt; he had written poems and sermons from the time he was four years old, and at school continued to follow the poetical bent which helped to make his later reputation. Two other things contributed to Kingsley's social education during his childhood. The travels of his family from one parish to another brought him in contact with the life of the people and the character of various parts of the country. The riots at Bristol which he witnessed as an incident of the contest over the First Reform Bill awakened in him a feeling of horror, although he is said to have gotten rid of a certain timidity in the process.

Later on Kingsley's parents moved to London where he entered King's College, later going on to Cambridge. The stiffness of grammar-school days disappeared: he was a popular figure among all classes of his fellow-students; so much so, in fact, that in order to finish the university course with honor he had to work himself into a state of collapse during the last six months. In college and afterward the works of Carlyle had a powerful effect upon his mind: the *French Revolution* even helped to intensify his belief in a righteous God. For Kingsley had been depressed by religious uncertainty and had once thought of losing himself in the wilds of America as a "prairie hunter." His doubts had not entirely cleared up when he decided that the way to dispose of them finally was to enter the ministry.

On leaving the university Kingsley therefore took orders in 1842 and accepted a curacy at Eversley, a neglected parish in Hampshire. Conditions in Eversley rapidly changed. Kingsley's physical and mental powers attracted the young men of the parish and he used all the familiar devices for improving the lot of the poor: shoe and coal clubs, a mothers' society, a loan fund, a school for adults, and a lending library. "What is the use," he wrote in 1844, "of talking to hungry paupers about heaven?"

A wider field for social effort was opened by the Chartist agitation of 1848. In 1844 Kingsley had formed the acquaintance and become an eager admirer of Frederick Denison Maurice, the liberal or "Broad Church" theologian who had helped him to resolve his religious doubts. Maurice and the group of young, enthusiastic churchmen who surrounded him were fully conscious of the social question. At this moment their interest took an important new turn. Kingsley went up to London when news of the Chartist proceedings arrived and with J. M. Ludlow, a lawyer and fellow churchman, witnessed the demonstration which accompanied the attempted Chartist petition to Parliament. Kingsley and his friends were shocked at the near approach to violence and at the same time impressed with the grievances of the demonstrators. They issued a proclamation to the "Workmen of England" written by Kingsley and signed "A Working Parson." The manifesto was a declaration of sympathy and a warning against violence. It assured the workers that "all men who have heads and hearts" knew their wrongs to be real and their complaints to be justified. But, it added, "do not humbug yourself into meaning 'license' when you cry for 'liberty.'" There was "no true freedom without virtue" and "no true industry without the fear of God and love to your fellow men." Thus the Christian Socialist movement was born.

Maurice and his friends soon made it plain that their sympathy with the working class was more than verbal. They set up a night school in London and eventually a "college" (which still exists), and contributed large sums toward starting a number of producers' coöperative establishments in the tailoring, boot, hat, and many other trades. Their activities affected almost every phase of the working-class movement and eventually helped to awaken the Church of England to a new sense of social responsibility.

Kingsley, however, had comparatively little part in these later developments. His important work was done early and in the field of propaganda; in fact he was the literary genius of Christian Socialism. Under the name of "Parson Lot" he contributed articles and tracts to the various publications of the movement; *Cheap Clothes and Nasty* was perhaps the most effective of these. In two novels, *Yeast* (1848) and *Alton Locke* (1850) he attacked the problems of industry and agriculture. Christian Socialism established his literary reputation. From then on a steady stream of novels, poems, and essays issued from his pen. Honors descended upon him: a professorship at Cambridge, a chaplaincy to the queen, a canonry of Chester and then of Westminster. But he continued to reside at Eversley, his first charge, where he died, not yet old, in 1875.

The source of Kingsley's social ideas is not far to seek. It was the revolt of a sensitive nature against conditions as he found them in parish work, stimulated by religious conviction and contact with intellectual leaders such as Maurice and Carlyle, both of whom he knew personally. The coöperative ideas which he advocated came from other members of the Christian Socialist group, who in turn borrowed them mainly from Buchez, the promoter of coöperation in France. Being essentially a poet, Kingsley appealed to the emotions and his work lost nothing in effectiveness by that fact. His social writings not only contributed to the success of Christian Socialism in his own time, they helped to keep the movement alive among a younger generation. As a popular author and lecturer he aided materially in creating the social conscience which was to transform the economic viewpoint of the generality of Englishmen.

REFERENCES

The social side of Kingsley's career is dealt with in C. W. Stubbs' *Charles Kingsley and the Christian Socialist Movement* (1900) and in M. Kaufmann's *Charles Kingsley, Christian Socialist and Social Reformer* (1892).

The standard biography is by Mrs. F. E. Kingsley (1878).

For English Christian Socialism as a whole, see C. E. Raven, *Christian Socialism* (1920) and Donald O. Wagner, *The Church of England and Social Reform since 1854* (1930).

READINGS FROM

CHEAP CLOTHES AND NASTY

AND

THE CHRISTIAN SOCIALIST

Abuses in the Clothing Trade.[1] King Ryence, says the legend of Prince Arthur, wore a paletot trimmed with kings' beards. In the first French Revolution (so Carlyle assures us) there were at Meudon tanneries of human skins. Mammon, at once tyrant and revolutionary, follows both these noble examples—in a more respectable way, doubtless, for Mammon hates cruelty; bodily pain is his devil—the worst evil which he, in his effeminacy, can conceive. So he shrieks benevolently when a drunken soldier is flogged; but he trims his paletots, and adorns his legs, with the flesh of men and the skins of women, with degradation, pestilence, heathendom, and despair; and then chuckles self-complacently over the smallness of his tailors' bills. Hypocrite!—straining at a gnat and swallowing a camel! What is flogging, or hanging, King Ryence's paletot or the tanneries of Meudon, to the slavery, starvation, waste of life, year-long imprisonment in dungeons narrower and fouler than those of the Inquisition, which goes on among thousands of free English clothes-makers at this day?

"The man is mad," says Mammon, smiling supercilious pity. Yes, Mammon; mad as Paul before Festus; and for much the same reason, too. Much learning has made us mad. From two articles in the *Morning Chronicle* of Friday, Dec. 14th, and Tuesday, Dec. 18th, on the Condition of the Working Tailors, we learnt too much to leave us altogether masters of ourselves. But there is method in our madness; we can give reasons for it—satisfactory to ourselves, perhaps also to Him who made us, and you, and all tailors likewise. Will you, freshly bedizened, you and your footmen, from Nebuchadnezzar and Co.'s "Emporium of Fashion," hear a little about how your finery is made? You are always calling out for facts, and have a firm belief in salvation by statistics. Listen to a few.

The Metropolitan Commissioner of the *Morning Chronicle* called two meetings of the Working Tailors, one in Shadwell, and the other at the Hanover Square Rooms, in order to ascertain their condition from their own lips. Both meetings were crowded. At the Hanover

[1] *Cheap Clothes and Nasty* (1849), pp. 75–83, 90–92. (Page references are to the reprint of 1881 which prefaces *Alton Locke*, Vol. I.)

Square Rooms there were more than one thousand men; they were altogether unanimous in their descriptions of the misery and slavery which they endured. It appears that there are two distinct tailor trades—the "honourable" trade, now almost confined to the West End, and rapidly dying out there, and the "dishonourable" trade of the show-shops and slop-shops—the plate-glass palaces, where gents—and, alas! those who would be indignant at that name—buy their cheap-and-nasty clothes. The two names are the tailors' own slang; slang is true and expressive enough, though, now and then. The honourable shops in the West End number only sixty; the dishonourable, four hundred and more; while at the East End the dishonourable trade has it all its own way. The honourable part of the trade is declining at the rate of one hundred and fifty journeymen per year; the dishonourable increasing at such a rate that, in twenty years it will have absorbed the whole tailoring trade, which employs upwards of twenty-one thousand journeymen. At the honourable shops the work is done, as it was universally thirty years ago, on the premises and at good wages. In the dishonourable trade, the work is taken home by the men, to be done at the very lowest possible prices, which decrease year by year, almost month by month. At the honourable shops, from 36*s.* to 24*s.* is paid for a piece of work for which the dishonourable shop pays from 22*s.* to 9*s.* But not to the workmen; happy is he if he really gets two-thirds, or half of that. For at the honourable shops, the master deals directly with his workmen; while at the dishonourable ones, the greater part of the work, if not the whole, is let out to contractors, or middle-men—"*sweaters*," as their victims significantly call them—who, in their turn, let it out again, sometimes to the workmen, sometimes to fresh middle-men; so that out of the price paid for labour on each article, not only the workmen, but the sweater, and perhaps the sweater's sweater, and a third, and a fourth, and a fifth, have to draw their profit. And when the labour price has been already beaten down to the lowest possible, how much remains for the workmen after all these deductions, let the poor fellows themselves say!

One working tailor (at the Hanover Square Rooms Meeting) "mentioned a number of shops, both at the east and west ends, whose work was all taken by sweaters; and several of these shops were under royal and noble patronage. There was one notorious sweater who kept his carriage. He was a Jew, and, of course, he gave a preference to his own sect. Thus, another Jew received it from him second-hand and at a lower rate; then it went to a third—till it came to the unfortunate Christian at perhaps the eighth rate, and he performed the work at barely living prices; this same Jew required a deposit of £5 in money before he would give out a single garment to be made. He need not describe the misery which this system entailed upon the workmen. It was well known, but it was almost impossible, except for those who had been at the two, to form an idea of the difference between the present meeting and one at the East-end, where all who attended worked for slop-shops and sweaters. The present was a highly respectable assembly; the other presented no other appearance but those of misery and degradation."

Another says—"We have all worked in the honourable trade, so we know the regular prices from our own personal experience. Taking the bad work with the good work we might earn 11*s.* a week upon an average. Sometimes we do earn as much as 15*s.*; but, to do this, we are obliged to take part of our work home to our wives and daughters. We are not always fully employed. We are nearly half our time idle. Hence, our earnings are, upon an average throughout the year, not more than 5*s.* 6*d.* a week." "Very often I have made only 3*s.* 4*d.* in the week," said one. "That's common enough with us all, I can assure you," said another. "Last week my wages was 7*s.* 6*d.*," declared one. "I earned 6*s.* 4*d.*," exclaimed the second. "My wages came to 9*s.* 2*d.* The week before I got 6*s.* 3*d.*" "I made 7*s.* 9*d.*," and "I 7*s.* or 8*s.*, I can't exactly remember which." "This is what we term the best part of our winter season. The reason why we are so long idle is because more hands than are wanted are kept on the premises, so that in case of a press of work coming in, our employers can have it done immediately." Under the day work system no master tailor had more men on the premises than he could keep continually going; but since the change to the piece-work system, masters make a practice of engaging double the quantity of hands that they have any need for, so that an order may be executed "at the shortest possible notice," if requisite. A man must not leave the premises when unemployed,—if he does, he loses his chance of work coming in. "I have been there four days together, and had not a stitch of work to do." "Yes; that is common enough." "Ay, and then you're told, if you complain, you can go, if you don't like it. I am sure twelve hands would do all they have done at home, and yet they keep forty of us. It's generally remarked that, however strong and healthy a man may be when he goes to work at that shop, in a month's time he'll be a complete shadow, and have almost all his clothes in pawn. By Sunday morning, he has no money at all left, and he has to subsist till the following Saturday upon about a pint of weak tea, and four slices of bread and butter per day!!!"

"Another of the reasons for the sweaters keeping more hands than they want is, the men generally have their meals with them. The more men they have with them the more breakfasts and teas they supply, and the more profit they make. The men usually have to pay 4*d*., and very often 5*d*. for their breakfast, and the same for their tea. The tea or breakfast is mostly a pint of tea or coffee, and three to four slices of bread and butter. *I worked for one sweater who almost starved the men; the smallest eater there would not have had enough if he had got three times as much. They had only three thin slices of bread and butter, not sufficient for a child, and the tea was both weak and bad. The whole meal could not have stood him in 2d. a head, and what made it worse was, that the men who worked there couldn't afford to have dinners, so that they were starved to the bone.* The sweater's men generally lodge where they work. A sweater usually keeps about six men. These occupy two small garrets; one room is called the kitchen, and the other the workshop; and here the whole of the six men, and the sweater, his wife, and family, live and sleep. *One sweater I worked with had four children and six men, and they, together with his wife, sister-in-law, and himself, all lived in two rooms, the largest of which was about eight feet by ten. We worked in the smallest room and slept there as well—all six of us. There were two turn-up beds in it, and we slept three in a bed. There was no chimney, and, indeed, no ventilation whatever. I was near losing my life there—the foul air of so many people working all day in the place, and sleeping there at night, was quite suffocating. Almost all the men were consumptive, and I myself attended the dispensary for disease of the lungs. The room in which we all slept was not more than six feet square. We were all sick and weak, and loth to work.* Each of the six of us paid 2*s*. 6*d*. a week for our lodging, or 15*s*. altogether, and I am sure such a room as we slept and worked in might be had for 1*s*. a week; you can get a room with a fireplace for 1*s*. 6*d*. a week. The usual sum that the men working for sweaters pay for their tea, breakfasts, and lodging is 6*s*. 6*d*. to 7*s*. a week, and they seldom earn more money in the week. Occasionally at the week's end they are in debt to the sweaters. This is seldom for more than 6*d*., for the sweater will not give them victuals if he has no work for them to do. Many who live and work at the sweater's are married men, and are obliged to keep their wives and children in lodgings by themselves. Some send them to the workhouse, others to their friends in the country. Besides the profit of the board and lodging, the sweater takes 6*d*. out of the price paid for every garment under 10*s*.; some take 1*s*., and I do know of one who takes as much as 2*s*. This man works for a large show-shop at the West End. The usual profit of the sweater, over and above the board and lodging, is 2*s*. out of every pound. Those who work for sweaters soon lose their clothes, and are unable to seek for other work, because they have not a coat to their back to go and seek it in. *Last week, I worked with another man at a coat for one of her Majesty's ministers, and my partner never broke his fast while he was making his half of it.* The minister dealt at a cheap West End show-shop. All the workman had the whole day-and-a-half he was making the coat was a little tea. But sweaters' work is not so bad as Government work after all. At that, we cannot make more than 4*s*. or 5*s*. a week altogether—that is, counting the time we are running after it, of course. *Government contract work is the worst of all, and the starved-out and sweated-out tailor's last resource.* But still, Government does not do the regular trade so much harm as the cheap show and slop-shops. These houses have ruined thousands. They have cut down the prices, so that men cannot live at the work; and the masters who did and would pay better wages, are reducing the workmen's pay every day. They say they must either compete with the large show-shops or go into the 'Gazette.'"

Sweet competition! Heavenly maid!—Now-a-days hymned alike by penny-a-liners and philosophers as the ground of all society—the only real preserver of the earth! Why not of Heaven, too? Perhaps there is competition among the angels, and Gabriel and Raphael have won their rank by doing the maximum of worship on the minimum of grace? We shall know some day. In the meanwhile, "these are thy works, thou parent of all good!" Man eating man, eaten by man, in every variety of degree and method! Why does not some enthusiastic political economist write an epic on "The Consecration of Cannibalism?". . .

In short, the condition of these men is far worse than that of the wretched labourers of Wilts or Dorset. Their earnings are as low and often lower; their trade requires a far longer instruction, far greater skill and shrewdness; their rent and food are more expensive; and their hours of work, while they have work, more than half as long again. Conceive sixteen or eighteen hours of skilled labour in a stifling and fetid chamber, earning not much more than 6*s*. 6*d*. or 7*s*. a week! And, as has been already mentioned in one case, the man who will earn even that, must work all Sunday. He is even liable to be thrown out of his work for refusing to work on Sunday. Why not? Is there anything about one idle day in seven to be found among the traditions of Mammon? When the demand comes, the supply must come; and will, in spite of foolish auld-warld notion about keeping days holy—or keeping contracts holy either, for, indeed, Mammon has no conscience —right and wrong are not words expressible by any commercial laws yet in vogue; and therefore it appears that to earn this wretched pittance is by no means to get it. "For," says one, and the practice is asserted to be general, almost universal, "there is at our establishment a mode of reducing the price of our labour even lower than we have mentioned. The prices we have stated are those *nominally* paid for making the garments; but it is not an uncommon thing in our shop for a man to make a garment, and receive nothing at all for it. I remember a man once having a waistcoat to do, the price of making which was 2*s.*, and when he gave the job in he was told that he owed the establishment 6*d.* The manner in which this is brought about is by a system of fines. We are fined if we are behind time with our job, 6*d.* the first hour, and 3*d.* for each hour that we are late." "I have known as much as 7*s.* 6*d.* to be deducted off the price of a coat on the score of want of punctuality," one said; "and, indeed, very often the whole money is stopped. It would appear, as if our employers themselves strove to make us late with our work, and so have an opportunity of cutting down the price paid for our labour. They frequently put off giving out the trimmings to us till the time at which the coat is due has expired. If to the trimmer we return an answer that is considered 'saucy,' we are fined 6*d.* or 1*s.*, according to the trimmer's temper." "I was called a thief," another of the three declared, "and because I told the man I would not submit to such language, I was fined 6*d.* These are the principal of the in-door fines. The out-door fines are still more iniquitous. There are full a dozen more fines for minor offences; indeed, we are fined upon every petty pretext. We never know what we have to take on a Saturday, for the meanest advantages are taken to reduce our wages. If we object to pay these fines, we are told that we may leave; but they know full well that we are afraid to throw ourselves out of work."

Responsibility for These Conditions.[1] Folks are getting somewhat tired of the old rodomontade that a slave is free the moment he sets foot on British soil! Stuff!—are these tailors free? Put any con-

[1] *Ibid.*, pp. 92–93, 95–101.

ceivable sense you will on the word, and then say—are they free? We have, thank God, emancipated the black slaves; it would seem a not inconsistent sequel to that act to set about emancipating these white ones. Oh! we forgot; there is an infinite difference between the two cases—the black slaves worked for our colonies; the white slaves work for *us*. But, indeed, if, as some preach, self-interest is the mainspring of all human action, it is difficult to see who will step forward to emancipate the said white slaves; for all classes seem to consider it equally their interest to keep them as they are; all classes, though by their own confession they are ashamed, are yet not afraid to profit by the system which keeps them down. . . .

But of course the men most interested in keeping up the system are those who buy the clothes of these cheap shops. And who are they? Not merely the blackguard gent—the butt of Albert Smith and Punch, who flaunts at the Casinos and Cremorne Gardens in vulgar finery wrung out of the souls and bodies of the poor; not merely the poor lawyer's clerk or reduced half-pay officer who has to struggle to look as respectable as his class commands him to look on a pittance often no larger than that of the day labourer—no, strange to say—and yet not strange, considering our modern eleventh commandment—"Buy cheap and sell dear," the richest as well as the poorest imitate the example of King Ryence and the tanners of Meudon. At a great show establishment—to take one instance out of many—the very one where, as we heard just now, "however strong and healthy a man may be when he goes to work at that shop, in a month's time he will be a complete shadow, and have almost all his clothes in pawn"—

"We have also made garments for Sir —— ——, Sir —— ——, Alderman ——, Dr. ——, and Dr. ——. We make for several of the aristocracy. We cannot say whom, because the tickets frequently come to us as Lord —— and the Marquis of ——. This could not be a Jew's trick, because the buttons on the liveries had coronets upon them. And again, we know the house is patronised largely by the aristocracy, clergy, and gentry, by the number of court-suits and liveries, surplices, regimentals, and ladies' riding-habits that we continually have to make up. *There are more clergymen among the customers than any other class, and often we have to work at home upon the Sunday at their clothes, in order to get a living.* The customers are mostly ashamed of dealing at this house, for the men who take the clothes to the customers' houses in the cart have directions to pull up at the corner of the street. We had a good proof of the dislike of gentlefolks to have it known that they dealt at that shop for their clothes, for when the trousers buttons were stamped with the name of the firm, we used to have the garments returned, daily, to have other buttons put on them, and now the buttons are unstamped"!!!

We shall make no comment on this extract. It needs none. If these men know how their clothes are made, they are past contempt. Afraid of man, and not afraid of God! As if His eye could not see the cart laden with the plunder of the poor, because it stopped around the corner? If, on the other hand, they do *not* know these things, and doubtless the majority do not,—it is their sin that they do not know it. Woe to a society whose only apology to God and man is, "Am I my brother's keeper?" Men ought to know the condition of those by whose labour they live. Had the question been the investment of a few pounds in a speculation, these gentlemen would have been careful enough about good security. Ought they to take no security when they invest their money in clothes, that they are not putting on their backs accursed garments, offered in sacrifice to devils, reeking with the sighs of the starving, tainted—yes, tainted, indeed, for it comes out now that diseases numberless are carried home in these same garments from the miserable abodes where they are made. Evidence to this effect was given in 1844; but Mammon was too busy to attend to it. These wretched creatures, when they have pawned their own clothes and bedding, will use as substitutes the very garments they are making. So Lord ——'s coat has been seen covering a group of children blotched with small-pox. The Rev. D—— finds himself suddenly unpresentable from a cutaneous disease, which it is not polite to mention on the south of Tweed, little dreaming that the shivering dirty being who made his coat has been sitting with his arms in the sleeves for warmth while he stitched at the tails. The charming Miss C—— is swept off by typhus or scarlatina, and her parents talk about "God's heavy judgment and visitation"—had they tracked the girl's new riding-habit back to the stifling undrained hovel where it served as a blanket to the fever-stricken slopworker, they would have seen *why* God had visited them, seen that His judgments are true judgments, and given His plain opinion of the system which "speaketh good of the covetous whom God abhorreth"—a system, to use the words of the *Morning Chronicle's* correspondent, "unheard of and unparalleled in the history of any country—a scheme so deeply laid for the introduction and supply of under-paid labour to the market, that it is impossible for the working man not to sink and be degraded by it into the lowest depths of wretchedness and infamy—a system which is steadily and gradually increasing, and sucking more and more victims out of the honourable trade, who are really intelligent artisans, living in comparative comfort and civilisation, into the dishonourable or sweating trade in which the slopworkers are generally almost brutified by their incessant toil, wretched pay, miserable food, and filthy homes."

But to us, almost the worst feature in the whole matter is, that the Government are not merely parties to, but actually the originators of this system. The contract system, as a working tailor stated, in the name of the rest, "had been mainly instrumental in destroying the living wages of the working man. Now, the Government were the sole originators of the system of contracts and of sweating. Forty years ago, there was nothing known of contracts, except Government contracts; and at that period the contractors were confined to making slops for the navy, the army, and the West India slaves. It was never dreamt of then that such a system was to come into operation in the better classes of trade, till ultimately it was destructive of masters as well as men. The Government having been the cause of the contract system, and consequently of the sweating system, he called upon them to abandon it. The sweating system had established the show-shops and the ticket system, both of which were countenanced by the Government, till it had become a fashion to support them.

"Even the Court assisted to keep the system in fashion, and the royal arms and royal warrants were now exhibited common enough by slopsellers."

"Government said, its duty was to do justice. But was it consistent with justice to pay only 2*s.* 6*d.* for making navy jackets, which would be paid 10*s.* for by 'honourable' tradesmen? Was it consistent with justice for the Government to pay for Royal Marine clothing (private's coat and epaulettes) 1*s.* 9*d.*? Was it consistent with justice for the Government to pay for making a pair of trousers (four or five hours' work) only 2*s.* ½*d.*? And yet, when a contractor, noted for paying just wages to those he employed, brought this under the consideration of the Admiralty, they declared they had nothing to do with it. Here is their answer:—

ADMIRALTY, *March* 19, 1847.

SIR—Having laid before my Lords Commissioners of the Admiralty your letter of the 8th inst., calling their attention to the extremely low prices paid for making up articles of clothing, provided for her Majesty's naval service, I am commanded by their lordships to acquaint you that they have no control whatever over the wages paid for making up contract clothing. Their duty is to take care that the articles supplied are of good quality, and well made: the cost of the material and the workmanship are matters which rest with the contractor; and if the public were to pay him a higher price than that demanded, it would not ensure any advantage to the men employed by him, as their wages depend upon the amount of competition for employment amongst themselves.

I am, Sir, your most obedient servant,

H. G. Ward.

W. Shaw, Esq."

Oh most impotent conclusion, however officially cautious, and "philosophically" correct! Even if the wages did depend entirely on the amount of competition, on whom does the amount of competition depend? Merely on the gross numbers of the workmen? Somewhat, too, one would think, on the system according to which the labour and the wages are distributed. But right or wrong, is it not a pleasant answer for the poor working tailors, and one likely to increase their faith, hope, and charity towards the present commercial system, and those who deny the possibility of any other? . . .

The Way Out.[1] And now comes the question—What is to be done with these poor tailors, to the number of between fifteen and twenty thousand? Their condition, as it stands, is simply one of ever-increasing darkness and despair. The system which is ruining them is daily spreading, deepening. While we write, fresh victims are being driven by penury into the slop-working trade, fresh depreciations of labour are taking place. Like Ulysses' companions in the cave of Polyphemus, the only question among them is, to scramble so far back as to have *a chance of being eaten last.* Before them is ever-nearing slavery, disease, and starvation. What can be done?

First—this can be done. That no man who calls himself a Christian—no man who calls himself a man—shall ever disgrace himself by dealing at any show-shop or slop-shop. It is easy enough to know them. The ticketed garments, the impudent puffs, the trumpery decorations, proclaim them,—every one knows them at first sight. He who pretends not to do so is simply either a fool or a liar. Let no man enter them—they are the temples of Moloch—their thresholds are rank with human blood. God's curse is on them, and on those who, by supporting them, are partakers of their sins. Above all, let no clergyman deal at them. Poverty—and many clergymen are poor—doubly

[1] *Ibid.*, pp. 102–109.

poor, because society often requires them to keep up the dress of gentlemen on the income of an artisan; because, too, the demands on their charity are quadruple those of any other class—yet poverty is no excuse. The thing is damnable—not Christianity only, but common humanity cries out against it. Woe to those who dare to outrage in private the principles which they preach in public! God is not mocked; and his curse will find out the priest at the altar, as well as the nobleman in his castle.

But it is so hard to deprive the public of the luxury of cheap clothes! Then let the public look out for some other means of procuring that priceless blessing. If that, on experiment, be found impossible—if the comfort of the few be for ever to be bought by the misery of the many—if civilisation is to benefit every one except the producing class—then this world is truly the devil's world, and the sooner so ill-constructed and infernal a machine is destroyed by that personage, the better.

But let, secondly, a dozen, or fifty, or a hundred journeymen say to one another: "It is competition that is ruining us, and competition is division, disunion, every man for himself, every man against his brother. The remedy must be in association, coöperation, self-sacrifice for the sake of one another. We can work together at the honourable tailor's workship—we can work and live together in the sweater's den for the profit of our employers; why should we not work and live together in our own workshops, or our own homes, for our own profit? The journeymen of the honourable trade are just as much interested as the slopworkers in putting down sweaters and slopsellers, since their numbers are constantly decreasing, so that their turn must come some day. Let them, if no one else does, lend money to allow us to set up a workshop of our own, a shop of our own. If the money be not lent, still let us stint and strain ourselves to the very bone, if it were only to raise one sweater's security-money, which one of us should pay into the slopseller's hands, in his own name, but on behalf of all: that will at least save one sweater's profit out of our labour, and bestow it upon ourselves; and we will not spend that profit, but hoard it, till we have squeezed out all the sweaters one by one. Then we will open our common shop, and sell at as low a price as the cheapest of the show-shops. We *can* do this,—by the abolition of sweaters' profits,—by the using, as far as possible, of one set of fires, lights, rooms, kitchens, and washhouses,—above all, by being true and faithful to one another, as all partners should be. And, then, all that the master slopsellers had better do, will be simply to vanish and become extinct."

And again, let one man, or half-a-dozen men arise, who believe that the world is not the devil's world at all, but God's: that the multitude of the people is not, as Malthusians aver, the ruin, but as Solomon believed, "the strength of the rulers"; that men are not meant to be beasts of prey, eating one another up by competition, as in some confined pike pond, where the great pike having despatched the little ones, begin to devour each other, till one overgrown monster is left alone to die of starvation. Let a few men who have money, and believe that, arise to play the man.

Let them help and foster the growth of association by all means. Let them advise the honourable tailors, while it is time, to save themselves from being degraded into slopsellers by admitting their journeymen to a share in profits. Let them encourage the journeymen to compete with Nebuchadnezzar and Co. at their own game. Let them tell those journeymen that the experiment is even now being tried, and, in many instances successfully, by no less than one hundred and four associations of journeymen in Paris. Let them remind them of that Great Name which the Parisian *ouvrier* so often forgets—of Him whose everlasting Fatherhood is the sole ground of all human brotherhood, whose wise and loving will is the sole source of all perfect order and government. Let them, as soon as an association is formed, provide for them a properly ventilated workshop, and let it out to the associate tailors at a low, fair rent. I believe that they will not lose by it—because it is right. God will take care of their money. The world, it comes out now, is so well ordered by Him, that model lodging-houses, public baths, wash-houses, insurance offices, all pay a reasonable profit to those who invest money in them—perhaps associate workshops may do the same. At all events, the owners of these show-shops realise a far higher profit than need be, while the buildings required for a tailoring establishment are surely not more costly than those absurd plate-glass fronts, and brass scroll-work chandeliers, and puffs, and paid poets. A large house might thus be taken, in some central situation, the upper floors of which might be fitted up as model lodging-rooms for the tailor's trade alone. The drawing-room floor might be the work-room; on the ground floor the shop; and, if possible, a room of call or registration office for unemployed journeymen, and a reading-room. Why should not this succeed, if the owners of the house and the workers who rent it are only true to one another? Every tyro in political economy knows that association involves a saving both of labour and of capital. Why should it not succeed, when every one connected with the establishment, landlords and workmen, will have an interest in increasing its prosperity, and none whatever in lowering the wages of any party employed?

But above all, so soon as these men are found working together for common profit, in the spirit of mutual self-sacrifice, let every gentleman and every Christian, who has ever dealt with, or could ever have dealt with, Nebuchadnezzar and Co., or their fellows, make it a point of honour and conscience to deal with the associated workmen, and get others to do the like. *It is by securing custom, far more than by gifts or loans of money, that we can help the operatives.* We should but hang a useless burthen of debt round their necks by advancing capital, without affording them the means of disposing of their produce.

Be assured, that the finding of a tailors' model lodging-house, work-rooms, and shop, and the letting out of the two latter to an association, would be a righteous act to do. If the plan does not pay, what then? only a part of the money can be lost; and to have given that to an hospital or an almshouse would have been called praiseworthy and Christian charity; how much more to have spent it not in the cure, but in the prevention of evil—in making almshouses less needful, and lessening the number of candidates for the hospital!

Regulations as to police order, and temperance, the workmen must, and, if they are worthy of the name of free men, they can organise for themselves. Let them remember that an association of labour is very different from an association of capital. The capitalist only embarks his money on the venture; the workman embarks his time—that is, much at least of his life. Still more different is the operatives' association from the single capitalist, seeking only to realise a rapid fortune, and then withdraw. The association knows no withdrawal from business; it must grow in length and in breadth, outlasting rival slop-sellers, swallowing up all associations similar to itself, and which might end by competing with it. "Monopoly!" cries a free-trader, with hair on end. Not so, good friend; there will be no real free trade without association. Who tells you that tailors' associations are to be the only ones?

Some such thing, as I have hinted, might surely be done. Where there is a will there is a way. No doubt there are difficulties—Howard and Elizabeth Fry, too, had their difficulties. Brindley and Brunel did not succeed at the first trial. It is the sluggard only who is always crying, "There is a lion in the streets." Be daring—trust in God, and He will fight for you; man of money, whom these words have touched, godliness has the promise of this life, as well as of that to come. The thing must be done, and speedily; for if it be not done by fair means, it will surely do itself by foul. The continual struggle of competition, not only in the tailors' trade, but in every one which is not, like the navigator's or engineer's, at a premium from its novel and extraordinary demand, will weaken and undermine more and more the masters, who are already many of them speculating on borrowed capital, while it will depress the workmen to a point at which life will become utterly intolerable; increasing education will serve only to make them the more conscious of their own misery; the boiler will be strained to bursting pitch, till some jar, some slight crisis, suddenly directs the imprisoned forces to one point, and then—

What then?

Look at France,[1] and see.

PARSON LOT.

The Principles of Christian Socialism.[2] A new idea has gone abroad into the world. That Socialism, the latest-born of the forces now at work in modern society, and Christianity, the eldest born of those forces, are in their nature not hostile, but akin to each other, or rather that the one is but the development, the outgrowth, the manifestation of the other, so that even the strangest and most monstrous forms of Socialism are at bottom but Christian heresies. That Christianity, however feeble and torpid it may seem to many just now, is truly but as an eagle at moult, shedding its worn-out plumage; that Socialism is but its livery of the nineteenth century (as Protestantism was its livery of the sixteenth) which it is even now putting on, to spread ere long its mighty wings for a broader and heavenlier flight. That Socialism without Christianity, on the one hand, is as lifeless as the feathers without the bird, however skilfully the stuffer may dress them up into an artificial semblance of life; and that therefore every socialist system which has endeavoured to stand alone has hitherto in practice either blown up or dissolved away; whilst almost every socialist system which has maintained itself for any time has endeavoured to stand, or unconsciously to itself has stood, upon those moral grounds of righteousness, self-sacrifice, mutual affection, common brotherhood, which Christianity vindicates to itself for an everlasting heritage. That Christianity on the other hand, in

[1] It will be remembered that this was written just after the French Revolution of 1848.

[2] *The Christian Socialist,* 2 Nov., 1850, Vol. I, p. 1. This article is signed "J. T." but the author was J. M. Ludlow.

this nineteenth century of ours, becomes in its turn chilly and helpless when stripped of its social influences, or in other words, when divorced from Socialism; when cramped up within the four walls of its churches or chapels, and forbidden to go forth into the wide world, conquering and to conquer, to assert God's rightful dominion over every process of trade and industry, over every act of our common life, and to embody in due forms of organization every deepest truth of that faith committed to its charge. That, therefore, if Christ's gospel speaks true, and "ye cannot serve God and Mammon," that gospel is wholly incompatible with a political economy which proclaims self-interest to be the very pivot of social action. That if Christ's gospel speaks true, and "thou shalt love thy neighbour as thyself," that gospel cannot stand with a system of trade based wholly on the idea of Profit, *i.e.*, of taking more from our neighbour than we give to him, and which has adopted for its maxim to "buy cheap, and sell dear." But, finally, that if Christ's gospel be true, then it is compatible with those theories or systems which, however mistaken in their means, yet have for common object to bind up into fellowship, and not to divide by selfishness and rivalry, to substitute fair prices and living wages for a false cheapness and starvation its child, and which have adopted for their watchwords "Association" and "Exchange," instead of "Competition" and "Profit."

Such is the idea which this paper is intended to express; such is the idea which has given birth to the "Society for Promoting Working Men's Associations," of which it is intended to be the organ, and which has assigned for function to the Council of Promoters of that Society "to diffuse the principles of co-operation *as the practical application of Christianity to the purposes of trade and industry*." Do not let us be misunderstood. The members of those associations, nor even the writers of this paper, are required to make in words a profession of Christianity. The men who, claiming for themselves as their dearest privilege the title of "Christians," have yet, on the common ground of coöperative principles, of Socialism in a word, gladly accepted the fellowship of those for whom that title may have seemed hitherto but an insult or a mockery, these men have done so with their eyes open. They have done so, we repeat it, because they maintain Socialism to be essentially Christian, even when struggling against that blessed name; because they are taught by their Christianity, and many of them by their church, to recognise in every sceptic and infidel, a brother for whom Christ died. The fellowship which they have entered into, the common work in which they are engaged, involves for them no sacrifice of principle. It is their right to enter into that fellowship; it is their duty to carry on that work.

But more. The writers of this paper, we have said, need not all be professed Christians; still less need they be professed Churchmen. And yet, for many of those writers, to be members of the Church of England is but a lesser privilege than to be members of the Church of Christ. They too, as Churchmen, feel it their right and their duty to join this work. If others see in the marriage of Christianity with Socialism, the sole remedy for the present evils of society, they see in the Church of England the sole agent by which that remedy can be successfully applied. They are therefore Socialists by a double title,—as Christians and as Churchmen. They believe the formularies of the Church of England, whether of worship or of doctrine, to be alone adequate to the expression of those new feelings which are agitating the hearts of the masses, from one end of the British Isles,—ay, or of the Christian world,—to the other. They believe the constitution of the Church of England, even if overlaid here and there by the excrescences of State-tyranny, to be alone adaptable to the regular and organic embodiment of those new tendencies. They believe that no social reform can be thorough and practical without the help of the Church; they believe that no Church-reform can be living and permanent, which is not in harmony with social wants. . . .

XIII

WILHELM EMMANUEL VON KETTELER

1811–1877

The name of Wilhelm Emmanuel Baron von Ketteler has an honorable place in the list of aristocrats who have given fruitful thought to the social question. Von Ketteler was born in Münster in 1811 when that German city was temporarily within the boundaries of Napoleon's empire. The elder Baron von Ketteler and his wife presided over a modest, economical, and Catholic household with a severity which at least in the Baron's case amounted to harshness. Such discipline, however, did not produce the desired effect on Wilhelm, the third of six sons. The boy attended local schools until the age of thirteen, when his violent, unruly disposition became so difficult a problem to his parents that they sent him away to a Jesuit college at Briez, Switzerland. For a time even the science of the Jesuits was taxed, but in the end it triumphed and after four years in Switzerland Wilhelm returned to Münster in a more orderly frame of mind. His spirit was not broken, however, and a pugnacious streak cropped out frequently in later life. In 1829 he began a university career which took him to Göttingen, Berlin, Heidelberg, and Munich. His studies were law and finance. At Göttingen, incidentally, he lost the tip of his nose in a duel.

On leaving the university in 1834 von Ketteler entered the legal profession as a minor (unpaid) court official of the Prussian government. Three years later the Prussian authorities arrested the aged Archbishop of Cologne for what they considered conspiracy against the state. The incident was decisive for von Ketteler's career. He viewed it as an act of religious persecution and felt that his position as a servant of Prussia had become morally untenable. Up to this time he had had no intention of entering the priesthood. Even now he said that to make him change his profession "would take a greater miracle than raising the dead." But the Bishop of Eichstädt, whom he consulted, performed the necessary miracle and he reëntered Munich to study theology in 1841.

Von Ketteler was admitted to the priesthood of the Catholic church in 1844. While still a government official he had said that his ideal was the moral and social improvement of the people, and he now worked toward it by zealously carrying out the duties of a village pastorate. A wider horizon was opened to him with the assembly of the Frankfort Parliament in 1848.

Von Ketteler sought election to that body in order to defend the interests of the Catholic church, but it was his activities outside Parliament which first aroused public interest. In a funeral speech eulogizing two conservative deputies who had been killed in conflict with the revolutionists he proclaimed himself the servant of the people but denounced the evil passions, the competition, and the avarice of society. About the same time he surprised the first German Catholic Congress by calling its attention to the social question, and in a series of six discussions in the cathedral of Mainz outlined his view of Catholic social doctrine. The Communist Manifesto of Marx and Engels having recently appeared, the discourses were looked upon as an answer to that formidable document.

Meanwhile von Ketteler had been rising in the Church. Invested with several important offices he removed to Berlin where he continued his charitable work. He also displayed his zeal for religion by helping to convert a countess. Next year (1850) he was appointed Bishop of Mainz by Pope Pius IX who had rejected the candidate of the local clergy.

As Bishop of Mainz von Ketteler was drawn into the conflict between Church and State. Elected to the Reichstag after the formation of the German Empire in 1870, he continued to uphold the claims of the Church, and although violent controversies, which he thought inconsistent with the dignity of a bishop, compelled him to resign his seat in Parliament he remained a principal leader of the opposition to Bismarck's anti-Catholic policy. Yet his devotion to the cause of social reform was unflagging. A long list of books, pamphlets, and addresses bore witness to his interest in the subject. Perhaps the most important of these works was *The Labor Question and Christianity* (1864), but his demands became steadily more far-reaching as time went on.

Von Ketteler's social theory was inspired by the guild organization of the Middle Ages and he himself was instrumental in promoting associations of journeymen and all sorts of fraternal and religious corporations. Individualism and laissez-faire drew his severest criticism; certain Liberal journals even accused him of inflaming the masses against the existing order. As for current socialism, von Ketteler condemned it as irreligious. But he was obviously more sympathetic toward its aspirations than toward those of its great competitor. Indeed he consulted the socialist Lassalle as to founding a number of coöperative societies, while Lassalle repaid the compliment by quoting *The Labor Question and Christianity* with approval.

Von Ketteler remained Bishop of Mainz until his death in 1877. His life was ascetic, and the discipline which he had rebelled against as a child he visited upon his subordinates as their father in God. His social propaganda won him the name of "the fighting bishop." For a moment in 1870 he even resisted the known wishes of the Pope by opposing, as inopportune, the doctrine of papal infallibility.

To von Ketteler belongs the credit of initiating the social trend in German Catholicism. By direct appeal as well as by his writings he admonished churchmen to study and act upon the social question. In 1869 he put forward a "labor catechism" in a speech whose anniversary was celebrated forty years afterward. Before his death a Christian Social party had been founded in Germany. The movement as a whole was continued and extended by his followers, among whom two of the most prominent were Canons Christopher Moufang and Franz Hitze. The great Catholic Center party, until the Hitler régime a powerful force in German politics, was itself profoundly influenced by the doctrines of von Ketteler and his group.

REFERENCES

The only study of Ketteler in English is by J. J. Laux (pseud. George Metlake), *Christian Social Reform* (1912), which contains long extracts from von Ketteler's writings.

In German the most extensive work is Otto Pfülf's *Bischof von Ketteler* (1899). A more recent and shorter (though still voluminous) life is Fritz Vigener's *Ketteler* (1924). The article on von Ketteler in the *Allgemeine deutsche Biographie* (Vol. XV, pp. 670 sqq.) gives a rather unfavorable view of its subject.

READINGS FROM

THE LABOR QUESTION AND CHRISTIANITY [1]

Should a Bishop Intervene? [2] Voices rise from all sides discussing the condition of the workers and suggesting ways of improving it. There exist widely scattered societies which have as their aim "the

[1] Translated for this volume.

[2] Pp. 1–3.

betterment of the moral and economic condition of the working classes." Newspaper articles and pamphlets appear entitled "Friend of the Worker," "The Worker's Reader," etc., etc.

Now if amidst all these voices and suggestions I as a Catholic bishop undertake to express my opinion on the present situation, if I also claim for myself the title "friend of the workers," if I ask all Christian men who have at heart an interest in the worker's condition also to listen to and weigh my words on this situation, then assuredly I ought first to say a few words about the propriety of expressing my opinion as well as about my aim in doing so. Many believe, perhaps, that I as a bishop have no justification or at any rate no sufficient reason for mingling in such matters; others will think that I ought, as a Catholic bishop, to turn my attention at most to Catholics. I am of a different opinion.

I believe I have a right to express my opinion on the question of the workers in so far as that question is concerned with the material needs of Christian people. In this respect it is also a question of Christian love. Our divine Redeemer has for all time inextricably bound up the Christian religion with everything that relates to the alleviation of the spiritual and bodily woe of mankind. Everywhere and at all times the church has acted in accordance with this tendency. The exercise of Christian love in works of Christian compassion has been steadily a prominent feature of the life of the Christian church. From it has proceeded the marvellous care for all the needs of men. Every question relating to the relief of the needy is therefore essentially a Christian question, a religious question in which the church and all its living members should take fervent part. . . .

My conviction, however, goes much further. I not only believe that the affairs of the working class have a deep inner relationship to Christianity, but I believe that all proposals which for the most part have heretofore been made without any regard to Christianity—yes, often in a certain discord with and scorn of it—will bring help to the working class only when and in so far as they join with Christianity. Christ is not only the savior of the world because he has redeemed our souls—he has also brought salvation for all the other relationships of men: civic, political, and social. He is also especially the Redeemer of the working class. The prosperity or the ruin of the working class depend on Christ. He has raised the working class from its condition of slavery to its present height; *without him all the humanitarian efforts of its so-called friends cannot prevent this class from sinking back again into the conditions of the old paganism*. . . .

The Labor Problem and Why It Exists.[1] The so-called labor question is essentially a question of food for the worker. It is therefore, in the first place, as important as nourishment—that is, the procuring of the necessaries of life: food, clothing, shelter. Secondly, the question is important because of the large number of workers as compared to all other classes.[2] In subject matter, then, this question is concerned with the most elemental needs of men; in scope, it embraces by far the greater part of the human race. . . .

The labor question is, we repeat, the question of feeding labor; it is the question of food for the great majority of mankind. Whoever can give good advice for its solution we wholeheartedly recognize as the benefactor of the working class. . . .

In order, however, to be able to test the methods which have been proposed to better the condition of the working class, we must first have a clear idea of the position into which they have been led with regard to income and sustenance and into the reasons which have brought about this position. . . .

The modern principles of political economy have not been uniformly carried out in all lands; still less have they permeated as yet all working-class conditions and made evident all their effects. But what we are about to say concerning the living conditions of the worker has unfortunately already become an actual fact among many working groups and in many regions; it forms at the same time the common basis toward which the entire working class has been moving, and therefore from an inner necessity will gradually produce the same phenomena everywhere.

The material existence of the working class, the procurement of all the necessaries of life for the worker and his family, depends, namely (with so few exceptions that they do not alter the rule), upon the wages of the worker; and the wages of the worker are fixed, in our time, strictly according to the necessity of existence, that is, according to what a man absolutely needs in the way of food, clothing, and shelter if his physical existence is not to be wiped out. The truth of this proposition has been made so evident by the controversies between Lassalle and his opponents that only those who wish to de-

[1] Pp. 7, 10, 16–20.

[2] We understand here by "worker" not merely "worker" in its actual meaning—one who is paid by the day, one who works for wages—but also those who carry on their own business, but with such small capital that they are in a situation similar to that of those working for pay: for example, the small artisan, tradesman, etc., as well as the small property owner who lives chiefly on a daily wage.

ceive the people can dispute it. In it lies, as is truly asserted, the entire labor question; on the one hand it explains the need of the worker, on the other it forms the touchstone for the value of all proposals for assisting the working class.

The evidence of this state of affairs is made most comprehensible to us if we consider that labor, with us, has become a commodity and is therefore subject to all the laws of commodities. Just as the price of commodities is fixed solely by supply and demand, so also is the rate of wages. The law of the price of goods lies ultimately in their necessary cost of production. Competition however makes every one who produces goods strive to produce them as cheaply as possible so as to be able to sell them more cheaply. If he can offer goods more cheaply he will gradually crowd out of the market all those who can produce their wares only at a higher price. Hence it will happen that here and there goods will be sold below their cost of production, and as a result concerns that are going down will keep alive for a while although they are incapable of survival. Their ruin is assured. Now all this applies to labor and wages also. Just as the price of goods is determined by cost of production, so also the price of labor is set by the most necessary requirements of men in the way of food, clothing, and shelter. Moreover, just as the producer of goods strives to keep down the costs of production in order to be able to withstand competition successfully, so there necessarily arises a tendency amongst the workers to underbid the essential minimum in order just to maintain life. They will accept a somewhat lower minimum where there is a certain excess labor supply. Those who offer employment stand in the world's market-place and ask "Who will work for the smallest pay?" and the workers outbid each other, demanding wages that are less and less in accord with their respective needs. Hence it occurs that finally, as in the case of goods, here and there that frightful condition arises in which these human wares are offered below the cost of their production—that is (translated into terms of men and human language), the poor worker must out of necessity accept wages below the limit of minimum subsistence for himself and all his family. This finally leads them naturally to deprive themselves of the necessary food, clothing, and shelter, which he must barter for pay. The deprivation of these necessary things—if but for a few days—is fraught with grief and misery. . . .

What a situation! Even though the consequences of it may not have developed completely everywhere they will not fail to show how lacking in love for the people were those who have evoked these consequences by their false theories. There is no longer any possible doubt about it: the entire material existence of the whole working class (by far the greater portion of the modern state), the existence of their families, the daily problem of the necessary bread for man, wife, and children—all these are exposed to the variations of the market and of the price of goods. I know nothing more lamentable than this fact. What feelings must it arouse in these poor men who, with all they need and love, are daily handed over to the contingencies of the market price! That is the slave market of our Liberal Europe, cut according to the pattern of our humane, enlightened, anti-Christian Liberalism and Free Masonry. . . .

The Basis of Property Rights.[1] We know that many regard the right to property as so assured in itself that they are disgruntled at an examination into the bases of this right, and therefore avoid taking any account of the question. But this is a fatal delusion. Many in recent times have also held authority for so certain a thing that they have never become clear as to the bases of it. Being themselves in possession of authority they ruthlessly pronounce it to be valid as a self-sufficient right, and on account of their pernicious beliefs often unconsciously do more to destroy the true bases of authority than their greatest enemies. *Nothing is in and of itself unshakeable except God and His holy will alone. Everything else has but a conditional existence and a conditional authorization.* So it is with authority, so it is with property. The latter too has only a conditional right, a right which rests solely on God and religion. Property, like authority, has its deepest and its only secure roots in religion, in the living belief in God and Christianity which teaches us the true and everlasting belief in God. Let these roots be cut and it fares with property and authority as with the tree whose roots have been cut: externally it looks the same but it has lost its strength; the first blast of wind overthrows it. This inner weakness when the deep root of God-grounded truth has been consumed has already made itself plain enough in the case of authority. Perhaps it will not fail to appear in the case of property also. If the principles of the modern state which disregards all religion and considers the denial of God as a right of education are true, then right is what the majorities of legislatures decide, and there can be no more talk of an unjustifiable attack of the popular will upon the right to property.

[1] Pp. 68–69, 74–75.

If . . . there is no personal God, or if it is true that the existence of God is still a scientific question; if therefore the standpoint of the collective European governments which permit this to be questioned as a postulate of science before our German youth upon all the rostrums of the high schools, if the great Liberal party and all those who pay homage to the free community, are right—then the whole right to private property together with all the laws governing it are solely and completely the will of men, and I do not see how any well-founded objection can be offered if the mass of people decide by a majority vote that its possessors shall hand over a part of it to them as a loan. In any case it cannot but happen that they will go further later on and demand a portion of it for good, instead of as a loan. That can happen even without thereby disputing the natural law of property rights; it will be, indeed, the consequence of a very popular interpretation of that law. Everything depends then upon the majority, and that majority has also the right to decide upon the question of the inheritance of property; that is, whether and how far the natural law includes within itself the recognition of inheritance rights to property. . . .

We must drain the consequences of our principles to the last drop, however bitter that drop may be. If these Liberal majorities can by their sovereign will scornfully decree away the thousand-year status of the church, and offend our Christian conscience in every fiber, then other majorities will soon follow who will demand on exactly the same ground and with the same majority not only millions as subsidies for labor unions but quite different things as well. . . .

Matters are very different with those who believe in God and Christ and who are therefore convinced that men ought not to *make* laws arbitrarily but should rather *find* and express justice resting on the divinely established order: who are convinced that law derives binding force from the eternal will of God. Thus they do not merely ask what the majority have decided, but *what they were entitled to decide.* We believe, namely, that the decision to help the working classes with such a subsidy exceeds the divinely established, legitimate bounds of effective state legislation, and encroaches on a province in which state authority has no further right. . . .

The Limits of Property Rights.[1] In order to establish our argument we wish first to express a few thoughts on the natural boundaries of property rights as Christian knowledge discloses them. Ac-

[1] Pp. 77–79.

cording to the unanimous opinion of Catholic theologians the rights of private property never go so far as to be valid against a fellow man in extreme need. Here emerges, in very decisive fashion, the influence which theology and religion exert upon the rights of private property. Religion cannot concede to any man in any situation an absolute, unlimited right; it proceeds from God, in Whom it finds the source and measure of all things. According to this rule, then, it measures all things and decides their position. . . . From this viewpoint, God alone is the absolute owner of property, man being but a limited owner in the degree that God has ordained. Now God has sent all men to nature, from which they are to receive their necessary wants in life; at the same time, however, He has established a law in nature's order that only by means of private property can the supremacy of man over nature and her ordered usefulness take place—a supremacy which leads to the true higher culture. While, therefore, theology holds fast to the right to private property, it insists at the same time that this right must not oppose that higher right according to which all are dependent upon the gifts of nature, and that therefore each one who finds himself in extreme need is justified, if no other available means remains, in satisfying this extreme need where and how he can. On this ground the power of the state may, as it everywhere does, obligate communities—*i.e.*, the property owners in the community—to care for the needy, that is, to give as much of their property as is necessary to provide these poor people with the necessaries of life.

Beyond this limit, however, theology really recognizes no obligations except a moral duty to assuage the need of one's fellows, a duty of Christian love for one's neighbor. The property owner can be compelled to fulfill all his lawful duties, he can be compelled by means of taxation to bear the general community-tax and the state levies, but I do not believe that he can be required to turn over more of his property to his neighbor than has been previously suggested for the purpose of bettering the latter's condition. This is where the difference between the duties of *justice* and those of Christian love for one's neighbor enters in. . . .

Human Needs and How Christianity Has Met Them.[1] In Mühlhausen, Alsace, the mortality amongst the year-old children of weavers and spinners during the years 1823 to 1834 was twice as great as amongst the children of manufacturers and merchants. Half the

[1] Pp. 99, 100, 101.

children of these workers died before reaching the age of one year. Out of 100 manufacturers and merchants 32 attained an age of over 50, while out of 100 weavers only 8, and out of 100 spinners only 3, lived to be more than 50. . . .

Must we allow our German people to move toward this new slavery, and quietly look on while, in addition, some people offer to the race the delusion that this situation is progress, freedom, enlightenment, and happiness?

Surely not. With its creative spirit Christianity since it came upon earth from heaven in the person of the Son of God has solved all great questions, including those—so far as is possible on earth—which are connected with the needs and subsistence of men. God permits Christianity, on its beneficent pathway through the world, to find ever new tasks to perform, and in solving them to reveal its heavenly origin and godlike strength. Christianity broke the spirit of the old slavery. . . .

The Greek recognized none but the free Greek as possessing complete human worth, the Roman none but the Roman citizen, the *civis Romanus*. The idea that the slave also possesses a human soul which, considering its origin and destiny, has the same value as their own, lay entirely beyond their comprehension. The slave was regarded as an animal and was not treated as a human being. *Christianity gave back its manhood to this great portion of the human race.* . . .

The Social Program of the Church.[1] The *first aid* which the church will henceforth offer to the working class is the founding and conduct of *institutions for the worker who is incapable of working*. . . .

The second aid which the church offers to the working class, also designed to meet their material need, is the Christian family together with its foundation, Christian marriage.

Christian marriage, the Christian family, affects the economic condition of the working class: it affords him, for the protection of his existence, the most necessary union, founded by God, without which all others, whatever they may be called, have no value for him. It protects the worker from the results of unchastity, even before his birth, in the life of his parents and throughout his youth and age; it puts him under the protection of that child of heaven, pure morality; finally, it multiplies his poor wages through the love and careful economy of a good wife. . . .

[1] Pp. 106, 111, 118–119, 120.

The *third aid* whereby Christianity helps the working class consists in its *truths and teachings*, which likewise give the working class *true culture*. . . .

Christianity gives to man the conscious possession and the full use of all his powers. Christianity alone has restored to him his full personality. Paganism did not know the worth of the individual man. The real worth of the human race (except themselves) was entirely unknown to the Greeks and Romans. But even among their own people they did not know the value of mankind. Fully half the people, the women, stood on a lower plane of human worth. Likewise the value of the child was unknown to them; the child could be sold and killed for a variety of reasons. The human being was swallowed up in the citizen, and his entire value depended upon his usefulness to the community. The human being scarcely existed as a personality. Paganism did not know of any working class with equal birthrights. Personal worth was first restored by the teachings of Christianity. . . .

Christianity and Workers' Associations.[1] The fourth way in which Christianity helps to improve the material condition of the working class consists in its social power. . . .

If the worker and society help themselves as much as they can, not claiming outside aid as a pretext for personal inertia, they have a natural and reasonable right to accept help from every quarter and source that offers it and is useful in furthering their interests. But all social effort is a basic natural law of human life, and Christianity therefore cannot but lend the most joyful support to all present endeavors to help the working class through nurturing their associations. It would be a great piece of foolishness if we desired to hold ourselves aloof from these efforts merely because at this moment the exhortation comes from men who are hostile to Christianity. The air remains God's air even though he who denies God breathes it, and the bread that we enjoy also remains the nourishment granted to us by God even if the baker who bakes it is a godless man. Thus it is with the association movement. The latter is based upon divine ordinance even though the men who uphold it do not recognize in it the heavenly will and often even abuse it.

The association movement however is not only justified in itself and therefore worthy our attention, but Christianity alone has those

[1] Pp. 130, 131–133, 135, 136.

higher powers over it which are required in order to bring it to completion and make it truly rich in blessings for the working class. Here again it turns out as we saw previously in the case of the education of the workers by the Liberals. What the great Liberal party offers us in this respect as its own is crumbs which have fallen from the table of Christianity. Just as the great truths which mold the worker (his individuality and personality) lie in Christianity, so also Christianity possesses the true and great ideas and the living power which have made the workers' associations living and vital corporations or bodies. It is significant that we call certain associations "bodies." The body is indeed the most complete union of the parts, which are brought together by the highest life-principle, the soul. Therefore we call such fellowships "corporations" which to a certain extent bear a soul within them and thereby unite the parts of the union. But that is the striking thing about the whole Christian order of society. Even though the direct aim of the association is entirely earthly, dedicated to daily life, nevertheless it receives a higher binding power if it is formed by Christian elements. . . .

The immeasurable difference between associations lies in whether they abide by Christianity or by the modern spirit. In the latter case the associations are organizations which have no bond other than the immediate aim of the societies. The consumers' association gives its members cheaper bread, the loan society lends capital at a lower rate of interest, the raw-material society sells goods at a cheaper price, and so on. This aim of the society is its whole essence and beyond the limit of this goal there exists amongst the members no other bond. At this point selfishness, with all its intrusion upon the rights of one's neighbors, rather threatens the attainment of this common purpose. On the other hand, when men unite in the spirit of Christianity there arises amongst them, consciously or unconsciously, a different, a higher, more sublime unity which casts its light over all the members like a beaming, warming sun. . . .

The future of this whole movement in the realm of social life belongs, therefore, to Christianity. People have torn down the old Christian guilds and they are still busy casting aside the last remnants, the last stones of this magnificent structure; they want to put up a new edifice. But this is a miserable hut—a building built upon sand. Christianity must begin this structure anew and thus restore to the workers' associations their true meaning, their real usefulness. . . .

Christian Producers' Associations.[1] Finally, as a *fifth means* of aiding the working class through Christianity we mention the promotion of *producers' associations* by the special means available only to Christianity. We ourselves have recognized the existence of producers' associations as a means of protecting the interests of the workers in the operation of the business. The worker in them is both worker and employer and hence has a double interest in their revenue—his wages as a worker and his share in the actual profits.

It is not necessary here to insist further upon the great value of producers' associations for the improvement of working-class conditions. We do not know whether it will ever be possible to afford all or even most of the workers the advantages of these societies. A splendid idea is embodied in them however which deserves our most active interest and support. It presents—so far as is feasible—the most direct and comprehensible solution of the question at issue, for it offers to the workman a new source of income in addition to the wages which he now receives and which have been reduced by the market price to the lowest possible level. Lassalle wishes to carry out this plan by advancing capital from the public treasury. We have expressed the opinion that such assistance—at least if adopted as a general principle (funds being raised from the wealthy for the purpose of providing the working class with necessary capital)—such assistance would be an intrusion upon the rights of property and an overstepping of the well-established limits of the state's taxing rights. We have also stated that it is doubtful whether such measures could be carried out so as to promote a peaceful, orderly civic development. The celebrated Professor Huber wishes to put this idea into effect partly through the efforts of the workers themselves, partly through voluntary effort; he proposes to begin with associations on a very small scale everywhere. The difficulty in establishing producers' associations lies in procuring the necessary capital. The big business figures are the rich capitalists or the companies which possess millions. These rich companies or capitalists however make the competition of other similar companies impossible if sufficient capital is not at the disposal of the latter. Business undertakings of poor workers with little or no capital are therefore stamped out and suppressed by these giant concerns which arise everywhere in ever-growing colossal forms. Where, then, are the workers to get capital? If the Lassalle plan is unfair and impracticable, as we thoroughly believe, and if there are no other means

[1] Pp. 138–139, 140–144, 148.

than those suggested by Professor Huber, then one is tempted to give up the dream of producers' associations as a fine but sterile phantasm or at any rate to renounce the hope of its being realized to such an extent that any appreciable percentage of poor workers would be helped by it. . . .

But whenever I have pondered on these problems and difficulties I have been inspired with the confidence and hope that the strength which moves Christian hearts will hasten to the aid of the working class in this realm and will cause the idea of producers' associations to bear fruit over a wider area. Large capital is essential for this purpose and I by no means believe that this aid for the working class will be suddenly forthcoming everywhere; but I do see this accomplishment in the distance and hope that the initial movements in this direction will be initiated here and there by Christian souls. Christianity in all that it undertakes is a power working from within, proceeding slowly but never failing in the end to achieve the most productive and unexpected benefits for mankind. Many incidental events may intervene before this activity of Christianity secures the necessary advance. The spirit of Christianity was also at work centuries before the great Roman families of antiquity emancipated their slaves by the thousands. Perhaps many a Schulze-Delitzsch [1] will still emerge and announce salvation to the working class before the tower built by the last of them collapses and sadly demonstrates to the poor working people anew that they have been deceived and that their hopes were vain. Perhaps the world must even try out the Lassalle program and learn its own lesson after experiencing all the great troubles which can arise from this dangerous scheme (especially if it should fall into the hands of evil demagogues)—learn, that is, that even the democrats cannot help them if they build their philosophical ideas on the mere shifting sands of human doctrine instead of on the rock of Christianity. How and when Christianity will help the working class in this respect we cannot know. But undoubtedly whatever is true, good, and practicable in the idea of producers' associations will be brought to pass by Christianity. To be sure, that class which could do a great deal in this matter, the class of rich merchants, manufacturers and capitalists is, generally speaking, at the moment rather removed from Christianity; it now forms in particular the promoting, paying, employing power of the great Liberal party. But even here Christianity

[1] F. H. Schulze-Delitzsch (1808–83), promoter of coöperative societies which spread among the artisans and small tradesmen but gained little headway among the workers. (Editor.)

has its adherents; and as for the other element, it need not always remain opposed. There was a time when the wealthy old patrician families of Rome—in which the Roman matron had herself waited upon by several hundred slave women merely to dress up her body—stood aloof from Christianity. Yet the time came when the children of these families emancipated their slaves, spent their entire fortunes to cover Italy with charitable institutions for the poor slaves, and even gave their lives in service for the love of Christ. Christianity is so marvellous! He who to-day is its enemy, to-morrow falls prostrate before the Cross, and the son of the man who cursed Christ gives his blood for love of Christ. Be that as it may: Christianity is so rich in means that it will not be hard, God willing, to guide the hearts of Christians into this activity and also to bring together the greatest capitalists who may be needed for the creation of producers' associations. There are two systems of taxation, one of which is employed by the state, the other by Christianity. The state imposes taxes through the external compulsion of tax laws, tax lists, and tax collectors. Christianity taxes through the inner law of love; the compulsion to pay taxes, the taxes, and the tax collector are free will and conscience. Under their system of taxation all the great states of Europe are going steadily down hill, and from these embarrassed financial conditions has proceeded that secret iniquity and corruption, that world-girdling net of stock-exchange speculation with all its moral corruption, which rises from the morass. Under the Christian system of taxation, on the other hand, Christianity has continued to find the most abundant means imaginable for all its great undertakings. What capital has not Christianity already collected through voluntary taxation which appeals to the conscience and heart of good Christians? When we think of all the churches, all the monasteries, all the institutions of Christian love for relieving every conceivable human need and weakness, all the parsonages and bishoprics that have been founded, and all the funds collected for the poor in the entire world, all the schools and institutions of learning founded throughout Christendom, and when we realize that almost all of this has been created and established by voluntary gifts, what conception must we then form of the vitality of Christianity? And this is true of Christianity not only in the old days; it is the same to-day. If we add together the beneficent institutions which have been built during our lives by free-will gifts, what would the total be? In the last five years this voluntary taxation of the Christian spirit has yielded the Holy Father 23 millions. Our opponents may think what they please about the use to which these gifts are put; they must at least admit that a church which reveals such a sense of reality has a corresponding inner strength which they do not possess. How then can Christianity lack means to create the institutions needed by the working class? . . .

Certain classes in our time feel the impulse to benefit their fellow men. The nobleman in earlier times contributed toward the great monastic endowments as his gift to the church. It seems to me that there could be scarcely anything more Christ-like and more pleasing to God than for a corporation to come forward and establish, on a Christian basis, one of these producers' associations in a place where the need of the workers is particularly great.

In preparation for this great opportunity it is indispensable that the idea of producers' associations itself, and the ways and means of carrying it out should first be discussed and made clear on all points. Only when it is very generally perceived, both among the working class and outside it, how important these associations are to the workers, only when a great many people are firmly convinced of their great utility and at the same time see how and by what means these associations can be established—only then can we hope that efforts to call them into being will increase and multiply. . . .

XIV

WILLIAM GODWIN

1756–1836

The father of William Godwin was a dissenting minister of conservative views: he cherished a deep-seated hostility toward the Church of England and reared a family of thirteen children. William, the seventh child, was born at Wisbeach, England, in 1756. The full force of paternal discipline often descended upon him. His father was "extremely affectionate, yet at least to me, who was never his favorite, his rebukes had a painful tone of ill-humor and asperity." At such times William turned to his mother, "the qualifier and moderator of his [father's] austerities," to whom he remained affectionately attached during the rest of her long life. The Godwins themselves possessed little learning, but a note of literary culture was supplied by a cousin who came to live with the family when William was only two years old. She singled out the boy for special attention. Being a woman of strong Calvinist convictions, she also fortified the peculiar type of religious influence which already surrounded him. It has been said indeed that the anarchism, the denial of all authority, of Godwin's later works sprang originally from his early Calvinism and his Protestant antipathy toward the dominant English Church. Even after he had abandoned most of the conventional theology and morality which went with them and had become, so he declared, an atheist, these elements still remained.

But no rebellious thoughts on the subject of religion had as yet entered his mind. The dame school (presided over by a very old lady) to which he was first sent, put him through the Bible before he was eight; a period at another nearby school followed; and the religious note was struck sharply again when he was placed under the tuition of a dissenting minister at Norwich. The latter was a stern Calvinist and an admirer of John Wilkes. "Ductility," said Godwin in after-days, "is a leading feature of my mind." Aside from this his school days brought out several other characteristics: a precocious talent, a love of reading, keen sensitiveness to injustice (which caused him to rebel against the brutalities of his tutor), and an insatiable ambition that displayed itself in rather absurd vanity.

At fifteen Godwin left Norwich and for a time acted as assistant in his old school near Wisbeach. Rejected as a student at one academy on account of his religious views, he entered Hoxton College where he remained for five years, reading deeply in theology and metaphysics in preparation for a ministerial career. Doubts of the Calvinist dispensation began to trouble him toward the end of his college course, but in 1777 he settled at Ware as a Nonconformist minister. Then or a little later he met the Rev. Joseph Fawcet, the first of four men—one being Samuel Taylor Coleridge—to whom he attributed a supreme personal influence in molding his ideas. Fawcet seems to have been chiefly notable for the vehemence with which he assailed the domestic affections.

Godwin left Ware in 1779, and although he received two more ministerial appointments his religious views became steadily more unorthodox. A reading of the French philosophers shook his belief in Christianity; for a short time in 1782 he was a deist; but Priestley's writings again converted him to Christian beliefs of the Socinian variety. In 1783 his career as a preacher was definitely at an end.

Meanwhile he had dabbled in literature and in 1783 had published a life of Chatham. After quitting the ministry he thought of starting a school, but the project failed and he turned to writing for a livelihood. Most of his productions at this time were of a political character in the partisan sense of the word. He wrote controversial pamphlets (thus gaining a reputation with the eminent Whig politicians whose views he espoused), magazine articles, and historical summaries for the *Annual Register*. He proved his versatility by turning out a novel in three weeks; another took him only ten days. By 1785 he was "fairly started" as a writer, with an entrée to the political and literary world.

Into Godwin's so far rather undistinguished life suddenly burst the French Revolution. In 1786 he had met Thomas Holcroft, the second of his intellectual godfathers. Holcroft, a former shoemaker turned playwright and translator, violently espoused the ideas of the revolution and Godwin was swept along on the tempest. As the revolution progressed, one Englishman after another rose to the occasion. Burke presented his adverse *Reflections*, Paine countered it with his *Rights of Man*, and in 1791 Godwin began to put his own ideas into shape. As the work went forward he discussed it in detail with his friends.

An Enquiry concerning Political Justice appeared in two large volumes in 1793. It immediately raised the author to the heights of literary fame. Talk of suppression arose on account of its dangerous opinions, but the prime minister brushed the objections aside with the remark that a three-guinea book could not do much harm among people who did not have three shillings for it. Nevertheless the sale was large considering the price, and there is evidence that the book circulated widely even among the poorer classes. Clubs, often composed almost entirely of laborers and mechanics, were formed to purchase the book and read it aloud.

It is perhaps impossible to discover a single basic concept in *Political Justice* that is really new. Locke and others supplied the principle that innate ideas do not exist, that the mind at birth is a blank tablet upon which society writes what it pleases. The idea that political institutions and education produce social conflict came from Helvetius and Holbach. The criticism of private property was inspired by many writers from Plato to Mably. That a practice is to be accounted good in proportion to the happiness it disseminates was a maxim derived from the school of Bentham.

The novelty of the book consisted rather in the way these various elements (and many others) were combined, and in the logic with which Godwin pushed them to their extreme limits. The work was a complete philosophy: William Hazlitt called it the first full-length system of Utilitarianism.

The next few years were perhaps the pleasantest of Godwin's life. He worked only enough to earn a modest living, being unwilling to pile up wealth which in justice to humanity he could not spend on himself and which he did not know how to give away with benefit to the recipients. Nevertheless he published two successful novels and a series of essays. He also found time to assist in defending many of his radical friends who were being persecuted by the government.

Godwin's later years were harassed by financial and domestic troubles which arose principally from his two marriages. In 1797 he married Mary Wollstonecraft, the eccentric and gifted author of *A Vindication of the Rights of Woman.* The marriage itself was happy but his wife died shortly afterward in giving birth to a daughter. Godwin was left with two infants on his incompetent hands (one being the child of Mary Wollstonecraft by a previous connection).

Expenses mounted and by 1800 he was laboring at the trade of writing not for love but for money. He added to his difficulties in 1801 by marrying a handsome but plaintive widow with two children.

Most of Godwin's later works bore the mark of servitude. They were voluminous but not of very high quality. He set great store by at least one book, *Of Population* (1820), a careful answer to Malthus, but it failed to strike the popular taste. On two occasions his friends raised subscriptions to pay his debts. He attained financial security only in 1833 when the government granted him a sinecure post as Yeoman Usher of the Exchequer. He died in 1836.

Politically Godwin is classified as an anarchist, but he had only one important follower in this tradition: Thomas Hodgskin. His influence on socialism was much more pronounced. English socialists borrowed his criticism of private property, and the Utopian Robert Owen who adopted his communistic and environmental theories transmitted the doctrine to Charles Hall, William Thompson, the Chartist leaders, and even, perhaps, ultimately to Karl Marx. Godwin has in fact been called "the first scientific socialist of modern times." One other item of influence must be noted: Percy Bysshe Shelley became a disciple of Godwin and married his daughter; much of the poet's didactic verse was inspired by Godwin.

REFERENCES

Political Justice, abridged and edited by R. A. Preston, was reprinted in 1926.

For an exposition of Godwin's ideas see H. N. Brailsford's *Shelley, Godwin, and Their Circle* (1913).

The standard biography is by C. Kegan Paul (1876). More recent lives have been written by Ford K. Brown (1926) and H. Roussin (1913, French). The latter emphasizes the psychological angle and is particularly helpful in tracing the source of Godwin's ideas and their influence on later thought.

READINGS FROM

ENQUIRY CONCERNING POLITICAL JUSTICE

Summary of Principles.[1] *The reader who would form a just estimate of the reasonings of these volumes, cannot perhaps proceed more judiciously, than by examining for himself the truth of these principles, and the support they afford to the various inferences interspersed through the work.*

[1] Vol. I, pp. xiv–xvi. References are to the 4th ed. (1842).

I

The true object of moral and political disquisition, is pleasure or happiness.

The primary, or earliest, class of human pleasures, is the pleasures of the external senses.

In addition to these, man is susceptible of certain secondary pleasures, as the pleasures of intellectual feeling, the pleasures of sympathy, and the pleasures of self-approbation.

The secondary pleasures are probably more exquisite than the primary:

Or, at least,

The most desirable state of man, is that, in which he has access to all these sources of pleasure, and is in possession of a happiness the most varied and uninterrupted.

This state is a state of high civilisation.

II

The most desirable condition of the human species, is a state of society.

The injustice and violence of men in a state of society, produced the demand for government.

Government, as it was forced upon mankind by their vices, so has it commonly been the creature of their ignorance and mistake.

Government was intended to suppress injustice, but it offers new occasions and temptations for the commission of it.

By concentrating the force of the community, it gives occasion to wild projects of calamity, to oppression, despotism, war, and conquest.

By perpetuating and aggravating the inequality of property, it fosters many injurious passions, and excites men to the practice of robbery and fraud.

Government was intended to suppress injustice, but its effect has been to embody and perpetuate it.

III

The immediate object of government, is security.

The means employed by government, is restriction, an abridgment of individual independence.

The pleasures of self-approbation, together with the right cultivation of all our pleasures, require individual independence.

Without independence men cannot become either wise, or useful, or happy.

Consequently, the most desirable state of mankind, is that which maintains general security, with the smallest encroachment upon individual independence.

IV

The true standard of the conduct of one man towards another, is justice.

Justice is a principle which proposes to itself the production of the greatest sum of pleasure or happiness.

Justice requires that I should put myself in the place of an impartial spectator of human concerns, and divest myself of retrospect to my own predilections.

Justice is a rule of the utmost universality, and prescribes a specific mode of proceeding, in all affairs by which the happiness of a human being may be affected.

V

Duty is that mode of action, which constitutes the best application of the capacity of the individual, to the general advantage.

Right is the claim of the individual, to his share of the benefit arising from his neighbour's discharge of their several duties.

The claim of the individual, is either to the exertion or the forbearance of his neighbours.

The exertions of men in society should ordinarily be trusted to their discretion; their forbearance, in certain cases, is a point of more pressing necessity, and is the direct province of political superintendence, or government.

VI

The voluntary actions of men are under the direction of their feelings.

Reason is not an independent principle, and has no tendency to excite us to action; in a practical view, it is merely a comparison and balancing of different feelings.

Reason, though it cannot excite us to action, is calculated to regulate our conduct, according to the comparative worth it ascribes to different excitements.

It is to the improvement of reason, therefore, that we are to look for the improvement of our social condition.

VII

Reason depends for its clearness and strength upon the cultivation of knowledge.

The extent of our progress in the cultivation of knowledge, is unlimited.

Hence it follows,

1. That human inventions, and the modes of social existence, are susceptible of perpetual improvement.

2. That institutions calculated to give perpetuity to any particular mode of thinking, or condition of existence, are pernicious.

VIII

The pleasures of intellectual feeling, and the pleasures of self-approbation, together with the right cultivation of all our pleasures, are connected with soundness of understanding.

Soundness of understanding is inconsistent with prejudice: consequently, as few falsehoods as possible, either speculative or practical, should be fostered among mankind.

Soundness of understanding is connected with freedom of enquiry; consequently, opinion should, as far as public security will admit, be exempted from restraint.

Soundness of understanding is connected with simplicity of manners, and leisure for intellectual cultivation: consequently, a distribution of property extremely unequal, is adverse to the most desirable state of man. . . .

The Right of Private Judgment.[1] To a rational being there can be but one rule of conduct, justice; and one mode of ascertaining that rule, the exercise of his understanding.

If in any instance I am made the mechanical instrument of absolute violence, in that instance I fall under a pure state of external slavery. If on the other hand, not being under the influence of absolute compulsion, I am wholly prompted by something that is frequently called by that name, and act from the hope of reward or the fear of punishment, the subjection I suffer is doubtless less aggravated, but the effect upon my moral habits may be in a still higher degree injurious.

In the mean time, with respect to the conduct I should observe upon such occasions, a distinction is to be made. Justice . . . is coinci-

[1] Vol. I, pp. 81–86.

dent with utility. I am myself a part of the great whole, and my happiness is a part of that complex view of things by which justice is regulated. The hope of reward, therefore, and the fear of punishment, however wrong in themselves, and inimical to the improvement of the mind, are motives which, so long as they are resorted to in society, must and ought to have some influence with my mind.

There are two descriptions of tendency that may belong to any action, the tendency which it possesses by the necessary and unalterable laws of existence, and the tendency which results from the arbitrary interference of some intelligent being. The nature of happiness and misery, pleasure and pain, is independent of positive institution. It is immutably true, that whatever tends to procure a balance of the former is to be desired, and whatever tends to procure a balance of the latter is to be rejected. In like manner there are certain features and principles inseparable from such a being as man; there are causes which, in their operation upon him, are in their own nature generative of pleasure, and some of a pleasure more excellent than others. Every action has a result which may be said to be peculiarly its own, and which will always follow upon it, unless so far as it may happen to be superseded by the operation of other and extrinsical causes.

The tendency of positive institution is of two sorts, to furnish an additional motive to the practice of virtue or right; and to inform the understanding, as to what actions are right, and what actions are wrong. Much cannot be said in commendation of either of these tendencies.

First, positive institutions may furnish an additional motive to the practice of virtue. I have an opportunity of essentially contributing to the advantage of twenty individuals; they will be benefited, and no other persons will sustain a material injury. I ought to embrace this opportunity. Here let us suppose positive institution to interfere, and to annex some great personal reward to the discharge of my duty. This immediately changes the nature of the action. Before, I preferred it for its intrinsic excellence. Now, so far as the positive institution operates, I prefer it, because some person has arbitrarily annexed to it a great weight of self-interest. But virtue, considered as the quality of an intelligent being, depends upon the disposition with which the action is accompanied. Under a positive institution then, this very action, which is intrinsically virtuous, may, so far as relates to the agent, become vicious. The vicious man would before have neglected the advantage of these twenty individuals, because he would not bring a certain inconvenience or trouble upon himself. The same man, with the same disposition, will now promote their advantage, because his own welfare is concerned in it. Twenty, other things equal, is twenty times better than one. He that is not governed by the moral arithmetic of the case, or acts from a disposition directly at war with that arithmetic, is unjust. In other words, moral improvement will be forwarded, in proportion as we are exposed to no other influence, than that of the tendency which belongs to an action by the necessary and unalterable laws of existence. This is probably the meaning of the otherwise vague and obscure principle, "that we should do good, regardless of the consequences;" and by that other, "that we may not do evil, from the prospect of good to result from it." The case would have been rendered still more glaring, if, instead of the welfare of twenty, we had supposed the welfare of millions to have been concerned. In reality, whether the disparity be great or small, the inference must be the same.

Secondly, positive institution may inform the understanding, as to what actions are right, and what actions are wrong. Here it may be of advantage to us to reflect upon the terms understanding and information. Understanding, particularly as it is concerned with moral subjects, is the percipient of truth. This is its proper sphere. Information, so far as it is genuine, is a portion detached from the great body of truth. You inform me, "that Euclid asserts the three angles of a plane triangle to be equal to two right angles." Still I am unacquainted with the truth of this proposition. "But Euclid has demonstrated it. His demonstration has existed for two thousand years, and, during that term, has proved satisfactory to every man by whom it has been understood." I am nevertheless uninformed. The knowledge of truth, lies in the perceived agreement or disagreement of the terms of a proposition. So long as I am unacquainted with the middle term by means of which they may be compared, so long as they are incommensurate to my understanding, you may have furnished me with a principle from which I may reason truly to further consequences; but, as to the principle itself, I may strictly be said to know nothing.

Every proposition has an intrinsic evidence of its own. Every consequence has premises from which it flows; and upon them, and not upon anything else, its validity depends. If you could work a miracle to prove, "that the three angles of a triangle were equal to two right angles," I should still know, that the proposition had been either true or false previously to the exhibition of the miracle; and that there was no necessary connection between any one of its terms and the miracle exhibited. The miracle would take off my attention from the true question, to a question altogether different, that of authority. By the authority adduced I might be prevailed on to yield an irregular assent to the proposition; but I could not properly be said to perceive its truth.

But this is not all. If it were, it might perhaps be regarded as a refinement foreign to the concerns of human life. Positive institutions do not content themselves with requiring my assent to certain propositions, in consideration of the testimony by which they are inforced. This would amount to no more than advice flowing from a respectable quarter, which, after all, I might reject, if it did not accord with the mature judgment of my own understanding. But in the very nature of these institutions there is included a sanction, a motive either of punishment or reward, to induce me to obedience.

It is commonly said, "that positive institutions ought to leave me free in matters of conscience, but may properly interfere with my conduct in civil concerns." But this distinction seems to have been very lightly taken up. What sort of moralist must he be, whose conscience is silent as to what passes in his intercourse with other men? Such a distinction proceeds upon the supposition, "that it is of great consequence whether I bow to the east or the west; whether I call the object of my worship Jehovah or Allah; whether I pay a priest in a surplice or a black coat. These are points in which an honest man ought to be rigid and inflexible. But as to those other, whether he shall be a tyrant, a slave, or a free citizen; whether he shall bind himself with multiplied oaths impossible to be performed, or be a rigid observer of truth; whether he shall swear allegiance to a king *de jure*, or a king *de facto*, to the best or the worst of all possible governments: respecting these points he may safely commit his conscience to the keeping of the civil magistrate." In reality, by as many instances as I act contrary to the unbiassed dictate of my own judgment, by so much I abdicate the most valuable part of the character of man.

I am satisfied at present, that a certain conduct, suppose it be a rigid attention to the confidence of private conversation, is incumbent on me. You tell me, "there are certain cases of such peculiar emergency as to supersede this rule." Perhaps I think there are not. If I admit your proposition, a wide field of enquiry is opened, respecting what cases do or do not deserve to be considered as exceptions. It is little likely that we should agree respecting all these cases. How then does the law treat me, for my conscientious discharge of what I conceive to be my duty? Because I will not turn informer (which, it may be, I think an infamous character) against my most valued friend, the law accuses me of misprision of treason, felony, or murder, and perhaps hangs me. I believe a certain individual to be a confirmed villain and a most dangerous member of society, and feel it to be my duty to warn others, perhaps the public, against the effect of his vices. Because I publish what I know to be true, the law convicts me of libel, *scandalum magnatum*, and crimes of I know not what complicated denomination.

If the evil stopped here, it would be well. If I only suffered a certain calamity, suppose death, I could endure it. Death has hitherto been the common lot of men, and I expect, at some time or other, to submit to it. Human society must, sooner or later, be deprived of its individual members, whether they be valuable, or whether they be inconsiderable. But the punishment acts, not only retrospectively upon me, but prospectively upon my contemporaries and countrymen. My neighbour entertains the same opinion respecting the conduct he ought to hold, as I did. The executioner of public justice however interposes with a powerful argument, to convince him that he has mistaken the path of abstract rectitude.

What sort of converts will be produced by this unfeeling logic? "I have deeply reflected," suppose, "upon the nature of virtue, and am convinced that a certain proceeding is incumbent on me. But the hangman, supported by an act of parliament, assures me I am mistaken." If I yield my opinion to his *dictum*, my action becomes modified, and my character also. An influence like this, is inconsistent with all generous magnanimity of spirit, all ardent impartiality in the discovery of truth, and all inflexible perseverance in its assertion. Countries, exposed to the perpetual interference of decrees, instead of arguments, exhibit within their boundaries the mere phantoms of men. We can never judge from an observation of their inhabitants, what men would be, if they knew of no appeal from the tribunal of conscience, and if, whatever they thought, they dared to speak, and dared to act.

At present there will perhaps occur to the majority of readers, but few instances of laws which may be supposed to interfere with the conscientious discharge of duty. A considerable number will occur in the course of the present enquiry. More would readily offer themselves to a patient research. Men are so successfully reduced to a common standard by the operation of positive law, that, in most countries, they are capable of little more than, like parrots, repeating what others have said. This uniformity is capable of being produced in two ways, by energy of mind and indefatigableness of enquiry, enabling a considerable number to penetrate with equal success into the recesses of truth; and by pusillanimity of temper, and a frigid indifference to right and wrong, produced by the penalties which are suspended over such as shall disinterestedly enquire, and communicate, and act upon the result of their enquiries. It is easy to perceive which of these, is the cause of the uniformity that prevails in the present instance.

One thing more in enforcement of this important consideration. "I have done something," suppose, "which though wrong in itself, I believe to be right; or I have done something which I usually admit to be wrong; but my conviction upon the subject is not so clear and forcible, as to prevent my yielding to a powerful temptation." There can be no doubt, that the proper way of conveying to my understanding a truth of which I am ignorant, or of impressing upon me a firmer persuasion of a truth with which I am acquainted, is by an appeal to my reason. Even an angry expostulation with me upon my conduct, will but excite similar passions in me, and cloud, instead of illuminate, my understanding. There is certainly a way of expressing truth, with such benevolence as to command attention, and such evidence as to enforce conviction in all cases whatever.

Punishment inevitably excites in the sufferer, and ought to excite, a sense of injustice. Let its purpose be, to convince me of the truth of a position, which I at present believe to be false. It is not, abstractedly considered, of the nature of an argument, and therefore it cannot begin with producing conviction. Punishment is a comparatively specious name; but is in reality nothing more than force put upon one being by another who happens to be stronger. But strength apparently does not constitute justice. The case of punishment, in the view in which we now consider it, is the case of you and me differing in opinion, and your telling me that you must be right, since you have a more brawny arm, or have applied your mind more to the acquiring skill in your weapons, than I have.

But let us suppose, "that I am convinced of my error, but that my conviction is superficial and fluctuating, and the object you propose is to render it durable and profound." Ought it to be thus durable and profound? There are no doubt arguments and reasons calculated to render it so. Is the subject in reality problematical, and do you wish by the weight of your blows, to make up for the deficiency of your logic? This can never be defended. An appeal to force must appear to both parties, in proportion to the soundness of their understanding, to be a confession of imbecility. He that has recourse to it, would have no occasion for this expedient, if he were sufficiently acquainted with the powers of that truth it is his office to communicate. If there be any man who, in suffering punishment, is not conscious of injury, he must have had his mind previously debased by slavery, and his sense of moral right and wrong blunted by a series of oppressions.

If there be any truth more unquestionable than the rest, it is, that every man is bound to the exertion of his faculties in the discovery of right, and to the carrying into effect all the right with which he is acquainted. It may be granted, that an infallible standard, if it could be discovered, would be considerably beneficial. But this infallible standard itself would be of little use in human affairs, unless it had the property of reasoning as well as deciding, of enlightening the mind as well as constraining the body. If a man be in some cases obliged to prefer his own judgment, he is in all cases obliged to consult that judgment before he can determine whether the matter in question be of the sort provided for or no. So that from this reasoning it ultimately appears, that the conviction of a man's individual understanding, is the only legitimate principle, imposing on him the duty of adopting any species of conduct.

Such are the genuine principles of human society. Such would be the unconstrained condition of its members, in a state, where every individual within the society, and every neighbour without, was capable of listening with sobriety to the dictates of reason. We shall not fail to be impressed with considerable regret, if, when we descend to the present mixed characters of mankind, we find ourselves obliged in any degree to depart from so simple and grand a principle. The universal exercise of private judgment is a doctrine so unspeakably beautiful, that the true politician will certainly feel infinite reluctance in admitting the idea of interfering with it. . . .

A Project of Government.[1] The only legitimate object of political institution, is the advantage of individuals. All that cannot be brought home to them, national wealth, prosperity and glory,

[1] Vol. II, pp. 91–93, 94–96.

can be advantageous only to those self-interested impostors, who, from the earliest accounts of time, have confounded the understandings of mankind, the more securely to sink them in debasement and misery.

The desire to gain a more extensive territory, to conquer or to hold in awe our neighbouring states, to surpass them in arts or arms, is a desire founded in prejudice and error. Usurped authority is a spurious and unsubstantial medium of happiness. Security and peace are more to be desired, than a national splendour that should terrify the world. Mankind are brethren. We associate in a particular district, or under a particular climate, because association is necessary to our internal tranquillity, or to defend us against the wanton attacks of a common enemy. But the rivalship of nations is a creature of the imagination. If riches be our object, riches can only be created by commerce; and the greater is our neighbour's capacity to buy, the greater will be our opportunity to sell. The prosperity of all is the interest of all.

The more accurately we understand our own advantage, the less shall we be disposed to disturb the peace of our neighbour. The same principle is applicable to him in return. It becomes us therefore to desire that he may be wise. But wisdom is the growth of equality and independence, not of injury and oppression. If oppression had been the school of wisdom, the improvement of mankind would have been inestimable, for they have been in that school for many thousand years. We ought therefore to desire that our neighbour should be independent. We ought to desire that he should be free; for wars do not originate in the unbiassed propensities of nations, but in the cabals of government and the propensities that governments inspire into the people at large. If our neighbour invade our territory, all we should desire is to repel him from it; and, for that purpose, it is not necessary we should surpass him in prowess, since upon our own ground his match is unequal. Not to say that to conceive a nation attacked by another, so long as its own conduct is sober, equitable and moderate, is an exceedingly improbable supposition.

Where nations are not brought into avowed hostility, all jealousy between them is an unintelligible chimera. I reside upon a certain spot, because that residence is most conducive to my happiness or usefulness. I am interested in the political justice and virtue of my species, because they are men, that is, creatures eminently capable of justice and virtue; and I have perhaps additional reason to interest myself for those who live under the same government as myself, because I am better qualified to understand their claims, and more capable of exerting myself in their behalf. But I can certainly have no interest in the infliction of pain upon others, unless so far as they are expressly engaged in acts of injustice. The object of sound policy and morality is to draw men nearer to each other, not to separate them; to unite their interests, not to oppose them.

Individuals ought, no doubt, to cultivate a more frequent and confidential intercourse with each other than at present subsists; but political societies of men, as such, have no interests to explain and adjust, except so far as error and violence may render explanation necessary. This consideration annihilates, at once, the principal objects of that mysterious and crooked policy, which has hitherto occupied the attention of governments. Before this principle, officers of the army and the navy, ambassadors and negociators, all the train of artifices that has been invented to hold other nations at bay, to penetrate their secrets, to traverse their machinations, to form alliances and counter-alliances, sink into nothing. The expence of government is annihilated, and, together with its expence, the means of subduing and undermining the virtues of its subjects. . . .

Government can have no more than two legitimate purposes, the suppression of injustice against individuals within the community, and the common defence against external invasion. The first of these purposes, which alone can have an uninterrupted claim upon us, is sufficiently answered, by an association, of such an extent, as to afford room for the institution of a jury, to decide upon the offences of individuals within the community, and upon the questions and controversies, respecting property, which may chance to arise. It might be easy indeed for an offender, to escape from the limits of so petty a jurisdiction; and it might seem necessary, at first, that the neighbouring parishes, or jurisdictions, should be governed in a similar manner, or at least should be willing, whatever was their form of government, to coöperate with us, in the removal or reformation of an offender, whose present habits were alike injurious to us and to them. But there will be no need of any express compact, and still less of any common centre of authority, for this purpose. General justice, and mutual interest, are found more capable of binding men, than signatures and seals. In the mean time, all necessity for causing the punishment of the crime to pursue the criminal, would soon, at least, cease, if it ever existed. The motives to offence would become rare: its aggravations few: and rigour superfluous. The principal object of punishment, is restraint upon a dangerous member of the community; and the end of this restraint would be answered, by the general inspection, that is exercised by the members of a limited circle, over the conduct of each other, and by the gravity and good sense that would characterise the censures of men, from whom all mystery and empiricism were banished. No individual would be hardy enough in the cause of vice, to defy the general consent of sober judgment that would surround him. It would carry despair to his mind, or, which is better, it would carry conviction. He would be obliged, by a force not less irresistible than whips and chains, to reform his conduct.

In this sketch is contained the rude outline of political government. Controversies between parish and parish, would be, in an eminent degree, unreasonable, since, if any question arose, about limits, for example, the obvious principles of convenience could scarcely fail to teach us, to what district any portion of land should belong. No association of men, so long as they adhered to the principles of reason, could possibly have an interest in extending their territory. If we would produce attachment in our associates, we can adopt no surer method, than that of practising the dictates of equity and moderation; and, if this failed in any instance, it could only fail with him who, to whatever society he belonged, would prove an unworthy member. The duty of any society to punish offenders, is not dependent, upon the hypothetical consent of the offender to be punished, but upon the duty of necessary defence.

But however irrational might be the controversy of parish with parish in such a state of society, it would not be the less possible. For such extraordinary emergencies therefore, provision ought to be made. These emergencies are similar in their nature, to those of foreign invasion. They can only be provided against by the concert of several districts, declaring and, if needful, enforcing the dictates of justice.

One of the most obvious remarks that suggests itself, upon these two cases, of hostility between district and district, and of foreign invasion which the interest of all calls upon them jointly to repel, is, that it is their nature to be only of occasional recurrence, and that therefore the provisions to be made respecting them, need not be, in the strictest sense, of perpetual operation. . . .

Private Property.[1] The subject of property is the key-stone that completes the fabric of political justice. According as our ideas respecting it are crude or correct, they will enlighten us as to the consequences of a *simple form of society without government*, and remove the prejudices that attach us to complexity. There is nothing that more powerfully tends to distort our *judgment* and *opinions*, than erroneous notions concerning the goods of fortune. Finally, the period that must put an end to the system of *coercion* and *punishment*, is intimately connected with the circumstance of property's being placed upon an equitable basis. . . .

The subject to which the doctrine of property relates, is, all those things which conduce, or may be conceived to conduce, to the benefit or pleasure of man, and which can no otherwise be applied to the use of one or more persons, than by a permanent or temporary exclusion of the rest of the species. Such things in particular are food, clothing, habitation and furniture.

Upon this subject two questions unavoidably arise. Who is the person entitled to the use of any particular article of this kind? Who is the person, in whose hands the preservation and distribution of any number of these articles, will be most justly and beneficially vested? . . .

Every man has a right to that, the exclusive possession of which being awarded to him, a greater sum of benefit or pleasure will result, than could have arisen from its being otherwise appropriated. This is the same principle as that just delivered, with a slight variation of form. If man have a right to anything, he has a right to justice. These terms, as they have ordinarily been used in moral enquiry, are, strictly and properly speaking, convertible terms.

Let us see how this principle will operate in the inferences it authorises us to make. Human beings are partakers of a common nature; what conduces to the benefit or pleasure of one man, will conduce to the benefit or pleasure of another. Hence it follows, upon the principles of equal and impartial justice, that the good things of the world are a common stock, upon which one man has as valid a title as another to draw for what he wants. It appears in this respect, as formerly it appeared in the case of our claim to the forbearance of each other, that each man has a sphere, the limit and termination of which is marked out, by the equal sphere of his neighbour. I have a right to the means of subsistence; he

[1] Vol. II, pp. 202, 203, 205–206, 207, 230, 232.

has an equal right. I have a right to every pleasure I can participate without injury to myself or others; his title, in this respect, is of similar extent. . . .

It must be admitted indeed, that the love of distinction appears, from experience and the past history of mankind, to have been their ruling passion. But the love of distinction is capable of different directions. At present, there is no more certain road to the general deference of mankind, than the exhibition of wealth. The poet, the wit, the orator, the saviour of his country, and the ornament of his species, may upon certain occasions be treated with neglect and biting contempt; but the man who possesses and disburses money in profusion, can scarcely fail to procure the attendance of the obsequious man and the flatterer. But let us conceive this erroneous and pernicious estimate of things to be reversed. Let us suppose the avaricious man, who is desirous of monopolising the means of happiness, and the luxurious man, who expends without limitation, in pampering his appetites, that which, in strict justice, is the right of another, to be contemplated with as much disapprobation, as they are now beheld by a mistaken world with deference and respect. Let us imagine the direct and unambiguous road to public esteem, to be the acquisition of talent, or the practice of virtue, the cultivation of some species of ingenuity or the display of some generous and expansive sentiment; and that the persons who possess these talents were as conspicuously treated with affection and esteem, as the wealthy are now treated with slavish attention. This is merely, in other words, to suppose good sense, and clear and correct perceptions, at some time to gain the ascendancy in the world. But it is plain that, under the reign of such sentiments, the allurements that now wait upon costly gratification, would be, for the most part, annihilated. If, through the spurious and incidental recommendations it derives from the love of distinction, it is now rendered to many a principal source of agreeable sensation, under a different state of opinion, it would not merely be reduced to its intrinsic value in point of sensation, but, in addition to this, would be connected with ideas of injustice, unpopularity, and dislike. . . .

"If you show yourself deserving, you shall have the essence of a hundred times more food than you can eat, and a hundred times more clothes than you can wear. You shall have a patent for taking away from others the means of a happy and respectable existence, and for consuming them in riotous and unmeaning extravagance."

Is this the reward that ought to be offered to virtue, or that virtue should stoop to take? . . .

Having considered at large the question of the person entitled to the use of the means of benefit or pleasure, it is time that we proceed to the second question of the person, in whose hands the preservation and distribution of any of these means will be most justly and beneficially vested. An interval must inevitably occur, between the production of any commodity, and its consumption. Those things which are necessary for the accommodation of man in society, cannot be obtained without the labour of man. When fit for his use, they do not admit of being left at random, but require that some care and vigilance should be exerted to preserve them, for the period of actual consumption. They will not, in the first instance, fall into the possession of each individual, in the precise proportion necessary for his consumption. Who then is to be the factor or warehouseman, that is to watch over their preservation, and preside at their distribution?

This is strictly speaking the question of property. We do not call the person who accidentally takes his dinner at my table, the proprietor of what he eats, though it is he, in the direct and obvious sense, who receives the benefit of it. Property implies some permanence of external possession, and includes in it the idea of a possible competitor.

Of property there are three degrees.

The first and simplest degree is that of my permanent right in those things, the use of which being attributed to me, a greater sum of benefit or pleasure will result, than could have arisen from their being otherwise appropriated. It is of no consequence in this case, how I came into possession of them, the only necessary conditions being their superior usefulness to me, and that my title to them is such as is generally acquiesced in by the community in which I live. Every man is unjust who conducts himself in such a manner respecting these things, as to infringe, in any degree, upon my power of using them, at the time when the using them will be of real importance to me.

It has already appeared that one of the most essential rights of man, is my right to the forbearance of others; not merely that they shall refrain from every thing that may, by direct consequence, affect my life, or the possession of my powers, but that they shall refrain from usurping upon my understanding, and shall leave me a certain equal sphere for the exercise of my private judgment. This is necessary, because it is possible for them to be wrong, as well as for me to be so, because the exercise of the understanding is essential to the improvement of man, and because the pain and interruption I suffer are as real, when they infringe, in my conception only, upon what is of importance to me, as if the infringement had been in the utmost degree palpable. Hence it follows, that no man may, in ordinary cases, make use of my apartment, furniture, or garments, or of my food, in the way of barter or loan, without having first obtained my consent.

The second degree of property is, the empire to which every man is entitled, over the produce of his own industry, even that part of it the use of which ought not to be appropriated to himself. It has been repeatedly shown that all the rights of man which are of this description, are passive. He has no right of option in the disposal of any thing which may fall into his hands. Every shilling of his property, and even every, the minutest, exertion of his powers, have received their destination from the decrees of justice. He is only the steward. But still he is the steward. These things must be trusted to his award, checked only by the censorial power that is vested, in the general sense, and favourable or unfavourable opinion of that portion of mankind among whom he resides. Man is changed from the capable subject of illimitable excellence, into the vilest and most despicable thing that imagination can conceive, when he is restrained from acting upon the dictates of his understanding. All men cannot individually be entitled to exercise compulsion on each other, for this would produce universal anarchy. All men cannot collectively be entitled to exercise unbounded compulsion, for this would produce universal slavery: the interference of government, however impartially vested, is, no doubt, only to be resorted to upon occasions of rare occurrence, and indispensable urgency.

It will readily be perceived, that this second species of property is in a less rigourous sense fundamental than the rest. It is, in one point of view, a sort of usurpation. It vests in me the preservation and dispensing of that which, in point of complete and absolute right, belongs to you.

The third degree of property is, that which occupies the most vigilant attention in the civilised states of Europe. It is a system, in whatever manner established, by which one man enters into the faculty of disposing of the produce of another man's industry. There is scarcely any species of wealth, expenditure, or splendour existing in any civilised country, that is not, in some way, produced by the express manual labour and corporal industry of the inhabitants of that country. The spontaneous productions of the earth are few, and contribute little to wealth, expenditure, or splendour. Every man may calculate, in every glass of wine he drinks, and every ornament he annexes to his person, how many individuals have been condemned to slavery and sweat, incessant drudgery, unwholesome food, continual hardships, deplorable ignorance, and brutal insensibility, that he may be supplied with these luxuries. It is a gross imposition that men are accustomed to put upon themselves, when they talk of the property bequeathed to them by their ancestors. The property is produced by the daily labour of men who are now in existence. All that their ancestors bequeathed to them was a mouldy patent, which they show, as a title to extort from their neighbours what the labour of those neighbours has produced. . . .

Another objection which has been urged against the system which counteracts the accumulation of property, is, "that it would put an end to industry." . . .

In reply to this objection, the reader must again be reminded, that the equality for which we are pleading, is an equality which would succeed to a state of great intellectual improvement. So bold a revolution cannot take place in human affairs, till the general mind has been highly cultivated. Hasty and undigested tumults, may be produced by a superficial idea of equalisation; but it is only a clear and calm conviction of justice, of justice mutually to be rendered and received, of happiness to be produced by the desertion of our most rooted habits, that can introduce an invariable system of this sort. Attempts, without this preparation, will be productive only of confusion. Their effect will be momentary, and a new and more barbarous inequality will succeed. Each man, with unaltered appetite, will watch the opportunity, to gratify his love of power or of distinction, by usurping on his inattentive neighbours. . . .

This argument will be strengthened, if we reflect on the amount of labour that a state of equality will require. What is this quantity of exertion from which the objection supposes many individuals to shrink? It is so light as rather to assume the guise of agreeable relaxation and gentle exercise, than of labour. In such a community scarcely any one can be expected, in consequence of his situation or avocations, to consider himself as exempted from the obligation to manual industry. There will be no rich man to recline in indolence, and fatten upon the labour of his fellows. The mathematician, the poet, and the philosopher, will derive a new stock of cheerfulness and energy from the recurring labour that makes them feel they are men. There will be no persons devoted to the manufacture of trinkets and luxuries; and none whose office it should be to keep in motion the complicated machine of government, tax-gatherers, beadles, excise-men, tide-waiters, clerks, and secretaries. There will be neither fleets nor armies, neither courtiers nor lacqueys. It is the unnecessary employments that at present occupy the great mass of every civilised nation, while the peasant labours incessantly to maintain them in a state more pernicious than idleness. . . .

How Reform Will Arrive.[1] It will not be right to pass over a question that will inevitably suggest itself to the mind of the reader. "If an equalisation of conditions be to take place, not by law, regulation or public institution, but only through the private conviction of individuals, in what manner shall it begin?" In answering this question it is not necessary to prove so simple a proposition, as that all republicanism, all reduction of ranks and immunities, strongly tends towards an equalisation of conditions. If men go on to improve in discernment, and this they certainly will with peculiar rapidity, when the ill-constructed governments which now retard their progress are removed, the same arguments which showed them the injustice of ranks, will show them the injustice of one man's wanting that which, while it is in the possession of another, conduces in no respect to his well-being.

It is a common error to imagine "that this injustice will be felt only by the lower orders who suffer from it;" and from thence to conclude "that it can only be corrected by violence." But in answer to this it may, in the first place, be observed that all suffer from it, the rich who engross, as well as the poor who want. Secondly, it has been endeavoured to be shown in the course of the present work, that men are not so entirely governed by self-interest, as has frequently been supposed. It appears, if possible, still more clearly, that the selfish are not governed solely by sensual gratification or the love of gain, but that the desire of eminence and distinction is, in different forms, an universal passion. Thirdly and principally, the progress of truth is the most powerful of all causes. Nothing can be more improbable than to imagine, that theory, in the best sense of the word,

[1] Vol. II, pp. 262–264.

is not essentially connected with practice. That which we can be persuaded clearly and distinctly to approve, will inevitably modify our conduct. When men shall habitually perceive the folly of individual splendour, and when their neighbours are impressed with a similar disdain, it will be impossible they should pursue the means of it with the same avidity as before.

It will not be difficult to trace, in the progress of modern Europe from barbarism to refinement, a tendency towards the equalisation of conditions. In the feudal times, as now in India and other parts of the world, men were born to a certain station, and it was nearly impossible for a peasant to rise to the rank of a noble. Except the nobles, there were no men that were rich; for commerce, either external or internal, had scarcely an existence. Commerce was one engine for throwing down this seemingly impregnable barrier, and shocking the prejudices of nobles, who were sufficiently willing to believe that their retainers were a different species of beings from themselves. Learning was another and more powerful engine. In all ages of the church we see men of the basest origin rising to the highest eminence. Commerce proved that others could rise to wealth beside those who were cased in mail; but learning proved that the low-born were capable of surpassing their lords. The progressive effect of these ideas may easily be traced. Long after learning began to unfold its powers, its votaries still submitted to those obsequious manners and servile dedications, which no man reviews at the present day without astonishment. It is but lately that men have known that intellectual excellence can accomplish its purposes without a patron. At present, among the civilised and well informed, a man of slender income, but of great intellectual powers and a firm and virtuous mind, is constantly received with attention and deference; and his purse-proud neighbour who should attempt to treat him superciliously, is sure to encounter a general disapprobation. The inhabitants of distant villages, where long established prejudices are slowly destroyed, would be astonished to see how comparatively small a share wealth has in determining the degree of attention with which men are treated in enlightened circles. . . .

XV

PIERRE-JOSEPH PROUDHON

1809–1865

Fourier and Proudhon came from the same neighborhood in France, and (as will later appear) there proved to be a proximity of ideas as well as of birth. Pierre-Joseph Proudhon was born near Besançon in 1809, the child of a working-class family. His parents, according to his own description, were of an "enterprising, contentious, unsubmissive, sarcastic humor." Through the efforts of his mother he obtained an education somewhat above his normal expectations, entering the college of Besançon at eleven years of age. As a child he had done field work and tended the cows—a rather undisciplined life in which his main amusement was his own thoughts. At college he carried off many prizes; too poor to buy books, he managed to win some of them in scholastic competition. When only sixteen the religious questions raised by a local preaching mission and a reading of Fénelon began to disturb him; with the discovery that atheism existed he determined to learn "how one went about denying God."

At eighteen Proudhon left college to earn his living in the printing trade. He worked as a proofreader and then as a compositor, picking up some knowledge of Hebrew and theology in this way, and travelling from one town to another in France and Switzerland—always, however, living in the bitterest poverty. Paris, where he stayed for a time, he found detestable, its literature frivolous and its politics mere jugglery. He left the city when the resources of a friend with whom he was living gave out. In 1832 he returned to Besançon and a few years afterward went into partnership in a printing establishment at that place. The business lasted until 1843.

Meanwhile Proudhon was beginning his literary career. The first effort was an anonymous *Essay on General Grammar*. In 1838 he competed for a prize of 1,500 francs which was to run for three years; it was offered by the Academy of Besançon to the holder of a bachelor's degree who showed the most promise in the field of literature and science, the stipulation being that contestants must be without resources of their own. Proudhon won the prize with an outline of a projected treatise on philosophy. He professed to be astonished that the "sheep" who congratulated him did not admonish him concerning his duty to the poor and oppressed.

With the prize (or part of it) in his pocket Proudhon once more essayed Paris; he obtained work on a Bourbonist newspaper and did articles on grammar, logic, and philosophy for a Catholic encyclopedia. But these enterprises failed him: he got into difficulties with the newspaper, and the encyclopedia suspended publication. Again the Academy of Besançon came to the rescue. A prize was offered for an essay "On the Utility of Celebrating Sunday, with Reference to Hygiene, Morals, and Family and Urban Relations." Proudhon submitted a composition but this time received only a bronze medal.

The reward was scarcely in proportion to the events which the paper set in train, for out of it Proudhon developed and published next year (1840) his most famous work, *What Is Property?* "If I do not deceive myself," he wrote, "my first work [*What Is Property?*] will be the most remarkable event of 1840." Modesty was never one of Proudhon's failings; he owed much of his success to a proper self-esteem, and in this case his prediction was not far wrong. The Academy had borne with his first essay, although it had discussed the utility of private property rather than that of Sunday; they were outraged beyond measure when he dedicated his second and more alarming effort to their respectable body: "If by an infallible method of investigation I establish the dogma of equality of conditions, . . . if I destroy property forever, it is to you, gentlemen, that all the glory belongs; to your succor and inspiration I owe it." The effect can be imagined: the reaction was so violent that Proudhon judged it prudent to write a second installment (1841) to moderate the effect of the first. After all, he was still receiving the stipend from the Academy's prize of 1838.

The origins of Proudhon's ideas on the subject of property and social organization in general were various. "I have run through a whole encyclopedia of systems," he said. But he never forgave Louis Blanc for pointing out the fact that he had borrowed his most famous phrase, "Property is theft," from Brissot de Warville, the revolutionary orator. Most of all, perhaps, he was indebted to Fourier. He accepted virtually all the critical parts of Fourier's work and approved the object at which the latter aimed, namely, freeing the individual and safeguarding his rights while at the same time protecting those of the group. But Proudhon rejected Fourier's method of attaining these ends; in his opinion it was an illogical combination of collectivism and individualism, and although he made free use of Fourier's terminology, such ideas as he borrowed were used merely as the elements of a new creative synthesis.

The second and more suave part of *What Is Property?* was only a mild success and Proudhon went back to violent tactics with a *Warning to Proprietors* (1842). This had the desired effect: the *Warning* was seized and its author prosecuted for attacking property, inciting to hatred of government, and offending against religion. The harassed Academy of Besançon demanded a sentence of ten years in irons. When the trial took place Proudhon himself admitted that it was sensational. He confounded the jury with learned economic explanations and drew their laughter by ridiculing priests, magistrates, and members of the legislature. The verdict of acquittal was accompanied by applause.

Proudhon's reputation was spreading outside France; his tracts achieved foreign translations, and while he remained almost as poor as ever, his opinion of his own powers more than compensated for any lack of material comfort. For a time he was employed as agent for an inland boat-transport company and wrote brochures in the interest of the firm. This did not interrupt the flow of his social publications. The latter, however, were sometimes disconcerting even to his admirers. Since 1840 he had called himself an anarchist, but his *Economic Contradictions, or Philosophy of Poverty* (1846) drew criticism from all parties. It contained, he said, the elements of a synthesis which he would one day make. When this was not forthcoming, a party of interested readers, armed with guns, invaded his apartment and called his attention to the delay. They offered to help finance a paper which he should direct. The offer was accepted and Proudhon began a stormy journalistic career. The promised synthesis appeared in 1848. It embodied among other things the plan of a national bank resembling that of Louis Blanc. Proudhon also proposed to reduce, by legislative authority, all wages, interest, and prices, and to stabilize the last. In 1849 he sketched out his theory of anarchism in the *Confessions of a Revolutionist* which had an immediate success and a lasting influence.

Meanwhile the Revolution of 1848 had thrust out Louis Philippe and installed (temporarily) a republic. Proudhon was neither a revolutionist nor a republican on principle. Revolution, he objected to Karl Marx in 1846, was merely an arbitrary appeal to force; republics should be judged by their results. Nevertheless he assisted the movement of 1848 and was elected to the legislature—only to wonder, when all was over, whether anything had been gained by it. The change, he saw clearly enough, was superficial; society remained very much the same. He opposed the popular election of a president on the ground that one so chosen would be, in fact, a king, and predicted that the popular choice would fall upon Louis Napoleon Bonaparte, whose background and principles he criticized unsparingly. The prediction was verified; Proudhon signified his disapproval by describing the president as the "personification of reaction" and the "bastard of universal suffrage." Quite naturally a prosecution was started. Proudhon fled to Brussels, but returning surreptitiously, was discovered and consigned to prison for the next three years. There he found means to continue his writing, to marry, and even to revise his opinion regarding Louis Napoleon. The latter, he thought, might be used to further his own schemes.

Proudhon was released in 1852. But another conflict with the authorities remained in store. *Justice in the Revolution and the Church*, called his capital work, was published in 1858. Justice, Proudhon held, was a human thing, not a transcendent principle; the revolution expressed this idea. Progress, therefore, would consist in the "expurgation of the absolute." The book also attacked the Church for its tendency to amass wealth. Again he was prosecuted—this time for outraging public morals and religion—but he removed to Brussels and escaped the penalty. During his sojourn at Brussels (1858–62) Proudhon made two notable pronouncements. He broke definitely with the revolutionary party, dismissing the tactics of Mazzini, Garibaldi, Kossuth, and the rest as "the old Robespierre style" and characterizing the group as a set of "humbugs." In *War and Peace* and elsewhere he seemed to justify war as natural and necessary and to uphold the dictum that might makes right. The consequence was that just before he returned to France in 1862 (he had been pardoned in 1860) the Belgians organized a demonstration against him as the enemy of weak states.

During his last years in Paris, Proudhon displayed greater facility than ever in offending his contemporaries. Nevertheless he was able to organize a group of deputies who abstained from the legislature as a protest against the Napoleonic régime. In Proudhon's opinion democracy in France was being crushed by too much centralization and by the growing number of office-seekers. The workers, he further contended, had a right to representation not only as citizens but as workers also. Thus before his death (which occurred in 1865) he had helped to resurrect the Socialist party, supposedly destroyed at the downfall of the second republic in 1851.

Prince Kropotkin, the Russian anarchist, called Proudhon the "father of anarchism." But Proudhon's great influence among the working class was superseded by that of Karl Marx, especially after the publication of *Capital* in 1867. Yet in spite of his violent attacks on Proudhon's theories Marx himself had been affected by them. In more recent times a revival of interest in Proudhon's writings has occurred, notably in the case of Georges Sorel, the exponent of French syndicalism.

REFERENCES

Proudhon's *Œuvres complètes* in thirty-seven volumes were published in 1866–83. A new French edition with copious notes is now in progress (1923 sqq.).

Proudhon, sociologue et moraliste (1929), by Jeanne Duprat, expounds his doctrine and relates it to those of his predecessors and successors. P. Armand's *P.-J. Proudhon et le fouriérisme* (1929) is a comparative study. *The Political Theories of P.-J. Proudhon* are dealt with by S. Y. Lu (1922).

There is a very full biography (in French) by A. A. Desjardins (1896). C.-A. Sainte-Beuve's *P.-J. Proudhon* (5th ed., 1875) deals with ten important years of Proudhon's life (1838–48).

READINGS FROM

WHAT IS PROPERTY? [1]

What Property Is.[2] If I were asked to answer the following question: *What is slavery?* and I should answer in one word, *It is murder*, my meaning would be understood at once. No extended argument would be required to show that the power to take from a man his thought, his will, his personality, is a power of life and death; and that to enslave a man is to kill him. Why, then, to this other question: *What is property?* may I not likewise answer, *It is robbery*, without the certainty of being misunderstood; the second proposition being no other than a transformation of the first?

I undertake to discuss the vital principle of our government and our institutions, property: I am in my right. I may be mistaken in

[1] Benjamin R. Tucker, trans. (1876). One or two mistranslations have been corrected by the present editor.

[2] Pp. 11–14.

the conclusion which shall result from my investigations: I am in my right. I think best to place the last thought of my book first: still am I in my right.

Such an author teaches that property is a civil right, born of occupation and sanctioned by law; another maintains that it is a natural right, originating in labor,—and both of these doctrines, totally opposed as they may seem, are encouraged and applauded. I contend that neither labor, nor occupation, nor law, can create property; that it is an effect without a cause: am I censurable?

But murmurs arise!

Property is robbery! That is the war-cry of '93! That is the signal of revolutions!

Reader, calm yourself: I am no agent of discord, no firebrand of sedition. I anticipate history by a few days; I disclose a truth whose development we may try in vain to arrest; I write the preamble of our future constitution. This proposition which seems to you blasphemous—*property is robbery*—would, if our prejudices allowed us to consider it, be recognized as the lightning-rod to shield us from the coming thunderbolt; but how many interests, how many prejudices, stand in the way! . . .[1] Alas! philosophy will not change the course of events: destiny will fulfill itself regardless of prophecy. Besides, must not justice be done and our education be finished?

Property is robbery! . . . What a revolution in human ideas! *Proprietor* and *robber* have been at all times expressions as contradictory as the beings whom they designate are hostile; all languages have perpetuated this opposition. On what authority, then, do you venture to attack universal consent, and give the lie to the human race? Who are you, that you should question the judgment of the nations and the ages?

Of what consequence to you, reader, is my obscure individuality? I live, like you, in a century in which reason submits only to fact and to evidence. My name, like yours, is TRUTH-SEEKER. My mission is written in these words of the law: *Speak without hatred and without fear; tell all that which thou knowest.* * * *

Others offer you the spectacle of genius wresting Nature's secrets from her, and unfolding before you her sublime messages; you will find here only a series of experiments upon *justice* and *right*, a sort of verification of the weights and measures of your conscience. The

[1] Author's punctuation. In this selection asterisks will be used to designate editor's omissions.

operations shall be conducted under your very eyes; and you shall weigh the result.

Nevertheless I build no system. I ask an end to privilege, the abolition of slavery, equality of rights, and the reign of law. Justice, nothing else; that is the alpha and omega of my argument; to others I leave the business of governing the world. * * *

The Justification of Property.[1] The Declaration of Rights has placed property on its list of the natural and inalienable rights of man, four in all: *liberty, equality, property, security.* What rule did the legislators of '93 follow in compiling this list? None. They laid down principles, just as they discussed sovereignty and the laws; from a general point of view, and according to their own opinion. They did everything in their own blind way. * * *

Nevertheless, if we compare these three or four rights with each other, we find that property bears no resemblance whatever to the others; that for the majority of citizens it exists only potentially, and as a dormant faculty without exercise; that for the others, who do enjoy it, it is susceptible of certain compromises and modifications which do not harmonize with the idea of a natural right; that, in practice, governments, tribunals, and laws do not respect it; and finally that everybody, spontaneously and with one voice, regards it as chimerical. * * *

Liberty is an absolute right, because it is to man what impenetrability is to matter,—a *sine qua non* of existence; equality is an absolute right, because without equality there is no society; security is an absolute right, because in the eyes of every man his own liberty and life are as precious as another's. These three rights are absolute; that is, susceptible of neither increase or diminution; because in society each associate receives as much as he gives—liberty for liberty, equality for equality, body for body, soul for soul, in life and in death.

But property, in its derivative sense, and by the definitions of law, is a right outside of society; for it is clear that, if the wealth of each was social wealth, the conditions would be equal for all, and it would be a contradiction to say: *Property is a man's right to dispose at will of social property.* Then if we are associated for the sake of liberty, equality, and security, we are not associated for the sake of property; then if property is a *natural* right, this natural right is not social, but *anti-social.* Property and society are utterly irreconcilable institutions. It is as im-

[1] Pp. 45, 52–53.

possible to associate two proprietors as to join two magnets by their similar poles. Either society must perish, or it must destroy property.

If property is a natural, absolute, imprescriptible, and inalienable right, why, in all ages, has there been so much speculation as to its origin?—for this is one of its distinguishing characteristics. The origin of a natural right! Good God! who ever inquired into the origin of the rights of liberty, security, or equality? They exist by the same right that we exist; they are born with us, they live and die with us. With property it is very different, indeed. By law, property can exist without a proprietor, like a quality without a subject. It exists for the human being who as yet is not, and for the octogenarian who is no more. And yet, in spite of these wonderful prerogatives which savor of the eternal and the infinite, they have never found the origin of property; the doctors still disagree. In one point only are they in harmony: namely, that the validity of the right of property depends upon the authenticity of its origin. But this harmony is their condemnation. Why have they acknowledged the right before settling the question of origin?

Certain classes do not relish investigations into the pretended titles to property, and its fabulous and perhaps scandalous history. They wish to hold to this proposition: that property is a fact; that it always has been, and always will be. * * *

The titles on which they pretend to base the right of property are two in number: *occupation* and *labor*. I shall examine them successively, under all their aspects and in detail; and I remind the reader that, to whatever authority we appeal, I shall prove beyond a doubt that property, to be just and possible, must necessarily have equality for its condition. * * *

Occupation as a Basis for Property Rights.[1] Not only does occupation lead to equality, it *prevents* property. For, since every man, from the fact of his existence, has the right of occupation, and, in order to live, must have material for cultivation on which he may labor; and since, on the other hand, the number of occupants varies continually with the births and deaths,—it follows that the quantity of material which each laborer may claim varies with the number of occupants; consequently, that occupation is always subordinate to population. Finally, that, inasmuch as possession, in right, can never remain fixed, it is impossible, in fact, that it can ever become property.

[1] Pp. 82–83.

Every occupant is, then, necessarily a possessor or usufructuary; he cannot therefore be a proprietor; he is responsible for the thing entrusted to him; he must use it in conformity with general utility, with a view to its preservation and development; he has no power to transform it, to diminish it, or to change its nature; he cannot so divide the usufruct that another shall perform the labor while he receives the product. In a word, the usufructuary is under the supervision of society, submitted to the condition of labor and the law of equality.

Thus is annihilated the Roman definition of property—*the right of use and abuse*—an immorality born of violence, the most monstrous pretension that the civil laws ever sanctioned. Man receives his usufruct from the hands of society, which alone is the permanent possessor. The individual passes away, society is deathless.

What a profound disgust fills my soul while discussing such simple truths! Do we doubt these things to-day? Will it be necessary to again take up arms for their triumph? And can force, in default of reason, alone introduce them into our laws?

All have equal right of occupancy.

The amount occupied being measured, not by the will, but by the variable conditions of space and number, property cannot exist.

This no code has ever expressed; this no constitution can admit! These are axioms which the civil law and the law of nations deny! . . .

Labor as a Basis for Property Rights.[1] But I hear the exclamations of the partisans of another system: "Labor, labor! that is the basis of property!"

Reader, do not be deceived. This new basis of property is worse than the first, and I shall soon have to ask your pardon for having demonstrated things clearer, and refuted pretensions more unjust, than any which we have yet considered. * * *

Admit, however, that labor gives a right of property in material. Why is not this principle universal? Why is the benefit of this pretended law confined to a few and denied to the mass of laborers? A philosopher, arguing that all animals sprang up formerly out of the earth warmed by the rays of the sun, almost like mushrooms, on being asked why the earth no longer yielded crops of that nature, replied: "Because it is old, and has lost its fertility." Has labor, once so fecund, likewise become sterile? Why does the tenant no

[1] Pp. 83, 110–113, 115.

longer acquire through his labor the land which was formerly acquired by the labor of the proprietor?

"Because," they say, "it is already appropriated." That is no answer. A farm yields fifty bushels per *hectare;* the skill and labor of the tenant double this product: the increase is created by the tenant. Suppose the owner, in a spirit of moderation rarely met with, does not go to the extent of absorbing this product by raising the rent, but allows the cultivator to enjoy the results of his labor; even then justice is not satisfied. The tenant, by improving the land, has imparted a new value to the property; he, therefore, has a right to a part of the property. If the farm was originally worth 100,000 francs, and if by the labor of the tenant its value has risen to 150,000 francs, the tenant, who produced this extra value, is the legitimate proprietor of one-third of the farm. M. Ch. Comte could not have pronounced this doctrine false, for it was he who said:—

"Men who increase the fertility of the earth are no less useful to their fellow-men, than if they create new land."

Why, then, is not this rule applicable to the man who improves the land, as well as to him who clears it? The labor of the former makes the land worth 1; that of the latter makes it worth 2: both create equal values. Why not accord to both equal property? I defy any one to refute this argument, without again falling back on the right of first occupancy.

"But," it will be said, "even if your wish should be granted, property would not be distributed much more evenly than it is now. Land does not go on increasing in value forever; after two or three seasons it attains its maximum fertility. That which is added by the agricultural art results rather from the progress of science and the diffusion of knowledge, than from the skill of the cultivator. Consequently, the addition of a few laborers to the mass of proprietors would be no argument against property."

This discussion would, indeed, prove a well-nigh useless one, if our labors culminated in simply extending land-privilege and industrial monopoly; in emancipating only a few hundred laborers out of the millions of proletarians. But this also is a misconception of our real thought, and does but prove the general lack of intelligence and logic.

If the laborer, who adds to the value of a thing, has a right of property in it, he who maintains this value acquires the same right. For what is maintenance? It is incessant addition,—continuous creation.

What is it to cultivate? It is to give the soil its value every year: it is, by annually renewed creation, to prevent the diminution or destruction of the value of a piece of land. Admitting, then, that property is rational and legitimate,—admitting that rent is equitable and just,—I say that he who cultivates acquires property by as good a title as he who clears, or he who improves; and that every time a tenant pays his rent, he obtains a fraction of property in the land entrusted to his care, the denominator of which is equal to the proportion of rent paid. Unless you admit this, you fall into absolutism and tyranny; you recognize class privileges; you sanction slavery.

Whoever labors becomes a proprietor—this is an inevitable deduction from the acknowledged principles of political economy and jurisprudence. And when I say proprietor, I do not mean simply (as do our hypocritical economists) proprietor of his allowance, his salary, his wages,—I mean proprietor of the value which he creates, and by which the master alone profits.

As all this relates to the theory of wages and of the distribution of products,—and as this matter never has been even partially cleared up,—I ask permission to insist on it: this discussion will not be useless to the work in hand. Many persons talk of admitting working-people to a share in the products and profits; but in their minds this participation is pure benevolence: they have never shown—perhaps never suspected—that it was a natural, necessary right, inherent in labor, and inseparable from the function of producer, even in the lowest forms of his work.

This is my proposition: *The laborer retains, even after he has received his wages, a natural right of property in the thing which he has produced.* * * *

The labor of the workers has created a value; now this value is their property. But they have neither sold nor exchanged it; and you, capitalist, you have not earned it. That you should have a partial right to the whole, in return for the materials that you have furnished and the provisions that you have supplied is perfectly just. You contributed to the productions, you ought to share in the enjoyment. But your right does not annihilate that of the laborers, who, in spite of you, have been your colleagues in the work of production. Why do you talk of wages? The money with which you pay the wages of the laborers remunerates them for only a few years of the perpetual possession which they have abandoned to you. Wages is the cost of the daily maintenance and refreshment of the laborer. You are wrong in calling it the price of a sale. The workingman has sold nothing; he knows neither his right, nor the extent of the concession which he has made to you, nor the meaning of the contract which you pretend to have made with him. On his side, utter ignorance; on yours, error and surprise, not to say deceit and fraud. * * *

In this century of bourgeois morality, in which I have had the honor to be born, the moral sense is so debased that I should not be at all surprised if I were asked, by many a worthy proprietor, what I see in this that is unjust and illegitimate. Debased creature! galvanized corpse! how can I expect to convince you, if you cannot tell robbery when I show it to you? A man, by soft and insinuating words, discovers the secret of taxing others that he may establish himself; then, once enriched by their united efforts, he refuses, on the very conditions which he himself dictated, to advance the well-being of those who made his fortune for him: and you ask how such conduct is fraudulent! Under the pretext that he has paid his laborers, that he owes them nothing more, that he has nothing to gain by putting himself at the service of others, while his own occupations claim his attention,—he refuses, I say, to aid others in getting a foothold, as he was aided in getting his own; and when, in the impotence of their isolation, these poor laborers are compelled to sell their birthright, he—this ungrateful proprietor, this knavish upstart—stands ready to put the finishing touch to their deprivation and ruin. And you think that just? Take care! I read in your startled countenance the reproach of a guilty conscience, much more clearly than the innocent astonishment of involuntary ignorance. * * *

Injurious Kinds of Property and Their Consequences.[1] AXIOM.—*Property is the Right of Increase claimed by the Proprietor over anything which he has stamped as his own.* * * *

Increase receives different names according to the thing by which it is yielded: if by land, *farm-rent;* if by houses and furniture, *rent;* if by life-investments, *revenue;* if by money, *interest;* if by exchange, *advantage, gain, profit* (three things which must not be confounded with the wages or legitimate price of labor).

Increase—a sort of royal prerogative, of tangible and consumable homage, is due to the proprietor on account of his nominal and metaphysical occupancy. His seal is set upon the thing; that is enough to prevent any one else from occupying it without *his* permission. * * *

[1] Pp. 153–155, 193–194.

Property is the right of increase; that is, the power to produce without labor. Now, to produce without labor is to make something from nothing; in short, to create. Surely it is no more difficult to do this than to moralize matter. The jurists are right, then, in applying to proprietors this passage from the Scriptures,—*Ego dixi: Dii estis et filii Excelsi omnes,*—"I said, Ye are gods, and all of you sons of the Most High." * * *

The primary cause of commercial and industrial stagnation is * * * interest on capital, that interest which the ancients with one accord branded with the name of *usury,* whenever it was paid for the use of money, but which they did not dare to condemn in the form of house-rent, farm-rent, or profit: as if the nature of the thing lent could ever warrant a charge for the lending; that is, robbery.

In proportion to the increase received by the capitalist will be the frequency and intensity of commercial crises,—the first being given, we always can determine the two others; and *vice versa.* Do you wish to know the regulator of a society? Ascertain the amount of active capital; that is, the capital bearing interest, and the legal rate of this interest. The course of events will be a series of overturns, whose number and violence will be proportional to the activity of capital.

In 1839, the number of failures in Paris alone was 1,064. This proportion was kept up in the early months of 1840; and as I write these lines, the crisis is not yet ended. It is said, further, that the number of houses which have wound up their business is greater than the number of declared failures. By this flood, we may judge of the waterspout's power of suction. * * *

In a country where the property is pretty evenly distributed, and where little business is done,—the rights and claims of each being balanced by those of others,—the power of invasion is destroyed. There—it may be truly said—property does not exist, since the right of increase is scarcely exercised at all. The condition of the laborers—as regards security of life—is almost the same as if absolute equality prevailed among them. They are deprived of all the advantages of full and free association, but their existence is not endangered in the least. With the exception of a few isolated victims of the right of property—of this misfortune whose primary cause no one perceives—the society appears to rest calmly in the bosom of this sort of equality. But have a care; it is balanced on the edge of a sword: at the slightest shock, it will fall and meet with death! * * *

Fallacious Methods of Establishing Equality.[1] But, some half-converted proprietor will observe, "Would it not be possible, by suppressing the bank, incomes, farm-rent, house-rent, usury of all kinds, and finally property itself, to proportion products to capacities? That was Saint-Simon's idea; it was also Fourier's; it is the desire of the human conscience; and no decent person would dare maintain that a minister of state should live no better than a peasant."

O Midas! your ears are long! What! will you never understand that disparity of wages and the right of increase are one and the same? Certainly, Saint-Simon, Fourier, and their respective flocks committed a serious blunder in attempting to unite, the one, inequality and communism; the other, inequality and property: but you, a man of figures, a man of economy,—you, who know by heart your logarithmic tables,—how can you make so stupid a mistake? Does not political economy itself teach you that the product of a man, whatever be his individual capacity, is never worth more than his labor, and that a man's labor is worth no more than his consumption? * * *

Listen, proprietor. Inequality of talent exists in fact; in right it is inadmissible, it goes for nothing, it is not thought of. One Newton in a century is equal to 30 millions of men; the psychologist admires the rarity of so fine a genius, the legislator sees only the rarity of the function. Now, rarity of function bestows no privilege upon the functionary; and that for several reasons, all equally forcible.

1. Rarity of genius was not, in the Creator's design, a motive to compel society to go down on its knees before the man of superior talents, but a providential means for the performance of all functions to the greatest advantage of all.

2. Talent is a creation of society rather than a gift of Nature; it is an accumulated capital, of which the receiver is only the guardian. Without society,—without the education and powerful assistance which it furnishes,—the finest nature would be inferior to the most ordinary capacities in the very respect in which it ought to shine. The more extensive a man's knowledge, the more luxuriant his imagination, the more versatile his talent,—the more costly has his education been, the more remarkable and numerous were his teachers and his models, and the greater is his debt. The farmer produces from the time that he leaves his cradle until he enters his grave: the fruits of art and science are late and scarce; frequently the tree dies before the fruit ripens. Society, in cultivating talent, makes a sacrifice to hope.

[1] Pp. 197–200, 248–249.

3. Capacities have no common standard of comparison: the conditions of development being equal, inequality of talent is simply speciality of talent.

4. Inequality of wages, like the right of increase, is economically impossible. Take the most favorable case,—that where each laborer has furnished his maximum production; that there may be an equitable distribution of products, the share of each must be equal to the quotient of the total production divided by the number of laborers. This done, what remains wherewith to pay the higher wages? Nothing whatever.

Will it be said that all laborers should be taxed? But, then, their consumption will not be equal to their production, their wages will not pay for their productive service, they will not be able to purchase their product, and we shall once more be afflicted with the calamities of property. I do not speak of the injustice done to the defrauded laborer, of rivalry, of excited ambition, and burning hatred,—these may all be important considerations, but they do not hit the point.

On the one hand, each laborer's task being short and easy, and the means for its successful accomplishment being equal in all cases, how could there be large and small producers? On the other hand, all functions being equal, either on account of the equivalence of talents and capacities, or on account of social coöperation, how could a functionary claim a salary proportional to the worth of his genius?

But, what do I say? In equality wages are always proportional to talents. What is the economical meaning of wages? The reproductive consumption of the laborer. The very act by which the laborer produces constitutes, then, this consumption, exactly equal to his production, of which we are speaking. When the astronomer produces observations, the poet verses, or the *savant* experiments, they consume instruments, books, travels, &c., &c.; now, if society supplies this consumption, what more can the astronomer, the *savant*, or the poet demand? We must conclude, then, that in equality, and only in equality, Saint-Simon's adage—*To each according to his capacity, to each capacity according to its results*—finds its full and complete application. * * *

Here my task should end. I have proved the right of the poor; I have shown the usurpation of the rich. I demand justice; it is not my business to execute the sentence. If it should be argued—in order to prolong for a few years an illegitimate privilege—that it is not enough to demonstrate equality, that it is necessary also to organize it, and above all to establish it peacefully, I might reply: The welfare of the oppressed is of more importance than official composure. Equality of conditions is a natural law upon which public economy and jurisprudence are based. The right to labor, and the principle of equal distribution of wealth, cannot give way to the anxieties of power. It is not for the proletarian to reconcile the contradictions of the codes, still less to suffer for the errors of the government. On the contrary, it is the duty of the civil and administrative power to reconstruct itself on the basis of political equality. An evil, when known, should be condemned and destroyed. The legislator cannot plead ignorance as an excuse for upholding a glaring iniquity. Restitution should not be delayed. Justice, justice! recognition of right! Reinstatement of the proletarian!—when these results are accomplished, then, judges and consuls, you may attend to your police, and provide a government for the Republic! * * *

The Defects of Communism.[1] I ought not to conceal the fact that property and communism have been considered always the only possible forms of society. This deplorable error has been the life of property. The disadvantages of communism are so obvious that its critics never have needed to employ much eloquence to thoroughly disgust men with it. The irreparability of the injustice which it causes, the violence which it does to attractions and repulsions, the yoke of iron which it fastens upon the will, the moral torture to which it subjects the conscience, the debilitating effect which it has upon society; and, to sum it all up, the pious and stupid uniformity which it enforces upon the free, active, reasoning, unsubmissive personality of man, have shocked common sense, and condemned communism by an irrevocable decree.

The authorities and examples cited in its favor disprove it. The communistic republic of Plato involved slavery; that of Lycurgus employed Helots, whose duty it was to produce for their masters, thus enabling the latter to devote themselves exclusively to athletic sports and to war. Even J. J. Rousseau—confounding communism and equality—has said somewhere that, without slavery, he did not think equality of conditions possible. The communities of the early Church did not last the first century out, and soon degenerated into monasteries. In those of the Jesuits of Paraguay, the condition of the blacks is said by all travellers to be as miserable as that of slaves; and it is a

[1] Pp. 259–262.

fact that the good Fathers were obliged to surround themselves with ditches and walls to prevent their new converts from escaping. The followers of Baboeuf—guided by a lofty horror of property rather than by any definite belief—were ruined by exaggeration of their principles; the Saint-Simonians, lumping communism and inequality, passed away like a masquerade. The greatest danger to which society is exposed to-day is that of another ship-wreck on this rock.

Singularly enough, systematic communism—the deliberate negation of property—is conceived under the direct influence of the proprietary prejudice; and property is the basis of all communistic theories.

The members of a community, it is true, have no private property; but the community is proprietor, and proprietor not only of the goods, but of the persons and wills. In consequence of this principle of absolute property, labor, which should be only a condition imposed upon man by Nature, becomes in all communities a human commandment, and therefore odious. Passive obedience, irreconcilable with a reflecting will, is strictly enforced. Fidelity to regulations, which are always defective, however wise they may be thought, allows of no complaint. Life, talent, and all the human faculties are the property of the State, which has the right to use them as it pleases for the common good. Private associations are sternly prohibited, in spite of the likes and dislikes of different natures, because to tolerate them would be to introduce small communities within the large one, and consequently private property; the strong work for the weak, although this ought to be left to benevolence, and not enforced, advised, or enjoined; the industrious work for the lazy, although this is unjust; the clever work for the foolish, although this is absurd; and, finally, man—casting aside his personality, his spontaneity, his genius, and his affections—humbly annihilates himself at the feet of the majestic and inflexible Commune!

Communism is inequality, but not as property is. Property is the exploitation of the weak by the strong. Communism is the exploitation of the strong by the weak. In property, inequality of conditions is the result of force, under whatever name it be disguised; physical and mental force; force of events, chance, *fortune;* force of accumulated property, &c. In communism, inequality springs from placing mediocrity on a level with excellence. This damaging equation is repellent to the conscience, and causes merit to complain; for, although it may be the duty of the strong to aid the weak, they prefer to do it out of generosity,—they never will endure a comparison. Give them equal opportunities of labor, and equal wages, but never allow their jealousy to be awakened by mutual suspicion of unfaithfulness in the performance of the common task.

Communism is oppression and slavery. Man is very willing to obey the laws of duty, serve his country, and oblige his friends; but he wishes to labor when he pleases, where he pleases, and as much as he pleases. He wishes to dispose of his own time, to be governed only by necessity, to choose his friendships, his recreation, and his discipline; to act from judgment, not by command; to sacrifice himself through selfishness, not through servile obligation. Communism is essentially opposed to the free exercise of our faculties, to our noblest desires, to our deepest feelings. Any plan which could be devised for reconciling it with the demands of the individual reason and will would end only in changing the thing while preserving the name. Now, if we are honest truth-seekers, we shall avoid disputes about words.

Thus communism violates the sovereignty of the conscience, and equality: the first, by restricting spontaneity of mind and heart, and freedom of thought and action; the second, by placing labor and laziness, skill and stupidity, and even vice and virtue on an equality in point of comfort. For the rest, if property is impossible on account of the desire to accumulate, communism would soon become so through the desire to shirk.

Property, in its turn, violates equality by the rights of exclusion and increase, and freedom by despotism. * * *

Anarchism the Solution.[1] By means of self-instruction and the acquisition of ideas, man finally acquires the idea of *science*,—that is, of a system of knowledge in harmony with the reality of things, and inferred from observation. He searches for the science, or the system, of inanimate bodies,—the system of organic bodies, the system of the human mind, and the system of the universe: why should he not also search for the system of society? But, having reached this height he comprehends that political truth, or the science of politics, exists quite independently of the will of sovereigns, the opinion of majorities, and popular beliefs,—that kings, ministers, magistrates, and nations, as wills, have no connection with the science, and are worthy of no consideration. He comprehends, at the same time, that if man is born a sociable being, the authority of his father over him ceases on the day when, his mind being formed and his education finished, he becomes the

[1] Pp. 276–279.

associate of his father; that his true chief and his king is the demonstrated truth; that politics is a science, not a stratagem; and that the function of the legislator is reduced, in the last analysis, to the methodical search for truth.

Thus, in a given society, the authority of man over man is inversely proportional to the stage of intellectual development which that society has reached; and the probable duration of that authority can be calculated from the more or less general desire for a true government,—that is, for a scientific government. And just as the right of force and the right of artifice retreat before the steady advance of justice, and must finally be extinguished in equality, so the sovereignty of the will yields to the sovereignty of the reason, and must at last be lost in scientific socialism. Property and royalty have been crumbling to pieces ever since the world began. As man seeks justice in equality, so society seeks order in anarchy.

Anarchy,—the absence of a master, of a sovereign [1]—such is the form of government to which we are every day approximating, and which our accustomed habit of taking man for our rule, and his will for law, leads us to regard as the height of disorder and the expression of chaos. The story is told, that a citizen of Paris, in the seventeenth century, having heard it said that in Venice there was no king, the good man could not recover from his astonishment, and nearly died from laughter at the mere mention of so ridiculous a thing. So strong is our prejudice. As long as we live, we want a chief or chiefs; and at this very moment I hold in my hand a brochure, whose author—a zealous communist—dreams, like a second Marat—of the dictatorship. The most advanced among us are those who wish the greatest possible number of sovereigns,—their most ardent wish is for the royalty of the National Guard. Soon, undoubtedly, some one, jealous of the citizen militia, will say, "Everybody is king." But, when he has spoken, I will say, in my turn, "Nobody is king; we are, whether we will or no, associated." Every question of domestic politics must be decided by departmental statistics; every question of foreign politics is an affair of international statistics. The science of government rightly belongs to one of the sections of the Academy of Sciences, whose permanent secretary is necessarily prime minister; and, since every citizen may address a memoir to the Academy, every citizen

[1] The meaning ordinarily attached to the word "anarchy" is absence of principle, absence of rule; consequently it has been regarded as synonymous with disorder. [Proudhon's note.]

is a legislator. But, as the opinion of no one is of any value until its truth has been proven, no one can substitute his will for reason,—nobody is king.

All matters of legislation and politics are matters of science, not of opinion. The legislative power belongs only to the reason, methodically recognized and demonstrated. To attribute to any power whatever the right of veto or of sanction, is the last degree of tyranny. Justice and legality are two things as independent of our approval as is mathematical truth. To compel, they need only to be known; to be known, they need only to be considered and studied. What, then, is the nation, if it is not the sovereign,—if it is not the source of the legislative power? The nation is the guardian of the law—the nation is the *executive power*. Every citizen may assert: "This is true; that is just;" but his opinion controls no one but himself. That the truth which he proclaims may become a law, it must be recognized. Now, what is it to recognize a law? It is to verify a mathematical or a metaphysical calculation; it is to repeat an experiment, to observe a phenomenon, to establish a fact. Only the nation has the right to say, "Be it known and decreed."

I confess that this is an overturning of received ideas, and that I seem to be attempting to revolutionize our political system; but I beg the reader to consider that, having begun with a paradox, I must, if I reason correctly, meet with paradoxes at every step, and must end with paradoxes. For the rest, I do not see how the liberty of citizens would be endangered by entrusting to their hands, instead of the pen of the legislator, the sword of the law. The executive power, belonging properly to the will, cannot be confided to too many proxies. That is the true sovereignty of the nation. * * *

PART IV

ECONOMIC LIBERALISM JUSTIFIED AND REVISED

XVI

HERBERT SPENCER

1820–1903

Nonconformity appeared on both sides of Spencer's family. Among his mother's ancestors were Huguenot refugees and a Wesleyan preacher. His father gradually detached himself from orthodox religion, becoming first an attendant at Quaker services and at last finding himself in agreement with his son. Herbert Spencer was born at Derby, England, in 1820, the son of a teacher of science and mathematics. The family life seems to have been rather trying. Both parents were subject to ill health with its consequent anxieties, and Herbert's self-will was more than a match for the fitful control it encountered. Nevertheless the father knew how to encourage a faculty for observing nature and a taste for science: at the age of eleven Herbert was attending lectures on phrenology and helping his father to prepare experiments in physics and chemistry. But the problem of discipline became acute and at thirteen the lad was placed under the stricter tutelage of his uncle, a minister residing near Bath. The Reverend Mr. Spencer was an advanced radical; that is, he opposed slavery and the Corn Laws, and collaborated with Joseph Sturge, the advocate of universal suffrage, in founding the *Nonconformist*. He was also an adept in promoting all the humble devices which were supposed to encourage self-help, thrift, and industry among the poor. What the latter appreciated more, perhaps, was the fact that he also secured them a local rise in wages. The influence of this uncle, added to that of his father, largely determined Herbert Spencer's point of view.

His education completed after three years at Bath, Spencer returned to Derby where he was employed for a few months as a schoolmaster's assistant. His father then obtained a post for him in the engineering department of a railway. This lasted four years; although he returned to railway service for a short time in 1844–46 his career as a civil engineer was probably hampered by the old self-assertiveness. Between 1836 and 1848 Spencer found time for many activities outside the engineering profession. He wrote several technical papers, perfected an invention (on which he made a little profit), and helped to edit *The Pilot*. The last was an organ of universal suffrage, a movement which was closely allied with Chartism. He also took part in the agitation against slavery and the Corn Laws and in favor of the separation of Church and State. Like his uncle he was a "radical all over." An article on *The Proper Sphere of Government*, published in 1843, shows that although not yet twenty-three he was already possessed by the faith in extreme individualism which from then on permeated his social thought.

In 1848 Spencer joined the staff of *The Economist* as sub-editor. The new position brought him into a circle of eminent persons, including Carlyle (uncongeniality of temperaments ended this acquaintance), George Henry Lewes, the philosopher, and Mary Ann Evans (George Eliot) whose intellect Spencer admired and whom he might have sought as a wife but for her lack of physical charm. The duties of a sub-editor were not exacting and Spencer continued to write independently, publishing his *Social Statics* in 1851. This book was an immediate success due to its emphasis on individual freedom and on the need of narrowly limiting the power of the state, both of which were popular doctrines at the time. It was followed by an article on *The Development Hypothesis* (1852), expounding the theory of organic evolution. These two ideas—individualism and organic evolution—later on constituted the theme of Spencer's fully developed philosophy.

In 1857 the thought of rounding out a complete philosophical system took shape in Spencer's mind. He had already (with little preparation) tossed off a *Principles of Psychology* (1855) and in two articles had dealt with the *Theory of Population* and *Progress: Its Law and Cause*. In 1860, therefore, the plan of the philosophy was announced; the installments were to be financed by subscription.

Almost all the remainder of a long life Spencer consecrated to rearing the huge fabric of his "Synthetic Philosophy." He had already resigned from *The Economist*, but with the help of a small legacy and gifts from American admirers he was able to bridge the financial gap until his writings became remunerative. As the parts of his philosophy appeared—the *First Principles*, the *Education*, the *Principles of Biology*, the *Descriptive Sociology*, the *Principles of Sociology*, *The Data of Ethics*, the *Ecclesiastical Institutions*, the *Political Institutions*—as these were published they met with greater or less acclaim, but their total effect was to make Spencer one of the acknowledged interpreters of the age.

In his later years, however, the world was moving away from individualism; and war (his special aversion) showed no tendency to disappear. Spencer had never been submissive or wanting in respect for his own achievements. With the publication of the last volume of the *Sociology* in 1896, his life work had been virtually finished; until his death (in 1903) therefore, he was absorbed in vigorously and bitterly resisting trends he disapproved of and in defending, with some asperity, the originality of his own ideas.

Many of these were undoubtedly far from new. On the subject of social evolution he probably owed something to Comte, while his doctrine of individualism was part of the intellectual currency of the time. Nevertheless merely as a compendium of late nineteenth-century thought his philosophy had its virtues, and from Japan to America the Spencerian library made its way.

Nor was Spencer's social influence confined to popularizing and fortifying the principle of individual liberty. Evolutionary socialists were also in his debt—the "gradualness" of Beatrice Webb, for example, derived something from her acquaintance with Spencer and his doctrines. Moreover in spite of his strong anti-socialist bias Spencer held that equity demanded nationalization of the land even in an individualist society. Late in life, however, he appears to have modified his opinion on this point, and Henry George, who had made it the central feature of his own system, denounced Spencer in bitter terms for the seeming recantation. But even so the weight of Spencer's authority must have helped materially to popularize a program which was a long step toward the socialism he so much abhorred.

REFERENCES

For an exposition of one side of Spencer's theory see W. C. Owen's *The Economics of Herbert Spencer* (1891). An interesting contrast between the social theory of Spencer and that of Thorstein Veblen is given in "The Satire of Thorstein Veblen's *Theory of the Leisure Class*," by Joseph Dorfman (*Political Science Quarterly*, September, 1932).

Aside from Spencer's autobiography, the fullest account of his career is David Duncan's *Life and Letters of Herbert Spencer* (1908).

READINGS FROM

THE PRINCIPLES OF SOCIOLOGY

AND

THE MAN VERSUS THE STATE

Social Evolution.[1] There are two ways in which men's actions, individual or social, may be regarded. We may consider them as groups of phenomena to be analyzed, and the laws of their dependence ascertained; or, considering them as causing pleasures or pains, we may associate with them approbation or reprobation. Dealing with its problems intellectually, we may regard conduct as always the result of certain forces; or, dealing with its problems morally, and recognizing its outcome as in this case good and in that case bad, we may allow now admiration and now indignation to fill our consciousness. Obviously, it must make a great difference in our conclusions whether, as in the one case, we study men's doings as those of alien creatures, which it merely concerns us to understand; or whether, as in the other case, we contemplate them as the doings of creatures like ourselves, with whose lives our own lives are bound up, and whose behaviour arouses in us, directly and sympathetically, feelings of love or hate.

In an ancillary work, *The Study of Sociology*, I have described the various perversions produced in men's judgments by their emotions. Examples are given showing how fears and hopes betray them into false estimates; how impatience prompts unjust condemnations; how in this case antipathy, and in that case sympathy, distorts belief. The truth that the bias of education and the bias of patriotism severally warp men's convictions, is enforced by many illustrations. And it is pointed out that the more special forms of bias—the class bias, the political bias, the theological bias—each originates a predisposition towards this or that view of public affairs.

Here let me emphasize the conclusion that in pursuing our sociological inquiries, and especially those on which we are now entering, we must, as much as possible, exclude whatever emotions the facts are calculated to excite, and attend solely to the interpretation of the facts. There are several groups of phenomena in contemplating which either contempt, or disgust, or indignation, tends to arise but must be restrained. . . .

[1] *The Principles of Sociology* (1897, preface dated 1881. Copyright by D. Appleton-Century Co., New York), Vol. II, pp. 229–235, 237–242.

Knowledge of the miseries which have for countless ages been everywhere caused by the antagonisms of societies, must not prevent us from recognizing the all-important part these antagonisms have played in civilization. Shudder as we must at the cannibalism which all over the world in early days was a sequence of war—shrink as we may from the thought of those immolations of prisoners which have, tens of thousands of times, followed battles between wild tribes—read as we do with horror of the pyramids of heads and the whitening bones of slain peoples left by barbarian invaders—hate, as we ought, the militant spirit which is even now among ourselves prompting base treacheries and brutal aggressions; we must not let our feelings blind us to the proofs that inter-social conflicts have furthered the development of social structures. . . .

In brief, trustworthy interpretations of social arrangements imply an almost passionless consciousness. Though feeling cannot and ought not to be excluded from the mind when otherwise contemplating them, yet it ought to be excluded when contemplating them as natural phenomena to be understood in their causes and effects.

Maintenance of this mental attitude will be furthered by keeping before ourselves the truth that in human actions the absolutely bad may be relatively good. . . .

Another of our ordinary conceptions has to be much widened before we can rightly interpret political evolution. The words "civilized" and "savage" must have given to them meanings differing greatly from those which are current. That broad contrast usually drawn wholly to the advantage of the men who form large nations, and to the disadvantage of the men who form simple groups, a better knowledge obliges us profoundly to qualify. Characters are to be found among rude peoples which compare well with those of the best among cultivated peoples. With little knowledge and but rudimentary arts, there in some cases go virtues which might shame those among ourselves whose education and polish are of the highest.

Surviving remnants of some primitive races in India, have natures in which truthfulness seems to be organic. Not only to the surrounding Hindoos, higher intellectually and relatively advanced in culture, are they in this respect far superior; but they are superior to Europeans. . . .

Similarly in respect of honesty, some of these peoples classed as inferior read lessons to those classed as superior. Of the Todas just named, ignorant and degraded as they are in some respects, Harkness says, "I never saw a people, civilized or uncivilized, who seemed to have a more religious respect for the rights of *meum* and *tuum*." . . .

Nor need we seek in remote regions or among alien races for proofs that there does not exist a necessary connexion between the social types classed as civilized and those higher sentiments which we commonly associate with civilization. The mutilations of prisoners exhibited on Assyrian sculptures are not surpassed in cruelty by any we find among the most bloodthirsty of wild races; and Rameses II., who delighted in having himself sculptured on temple-walls throughout Egypt as holding a dozen captives by the hair, and striking off their heads at a blow, slaughtered during his conquests more human beings than a thousand chiefs of savage tribes put together. The tortures inflicted on captured enemies by Red Indians are not greater than were those inflicted of old on felons by crucifixion, or on suspected rebels by sewing them up in the hides of slaughtered animals, or on heretics by smearing them over with combustibles and setting fire to them. The Damaras, described as so heartless that they laugh on seeing one of their number killed by a wild beast, are not worse than were the Romans, who gratified themselves by watching wholesale slaughters in their arenas. If the numbers destroyed by the hordes of Attila were not equalled by the numbers which the Roman armies destroyed at the conquest of Seleucia, and by the numbers of the Jews massacred under Hadrian, it was simply because the occasions did not permit. The cruelties of Nero, Gallienus, and the rest, may compare with those of Zingis and Timour; and when we read of Caracalla, that after he had murdered twenty thousand friends of his murdered brother, his soldiers forced the Senate to place him among the gods, we are shown that in the Roman people there was a ferocity not less than that which deifies the most sanguinary chiefs among the worst of savages. Nor did Christianity greatly change matters. Throughout mediæval Europe, political offences and religious dissent brought on men carefully-devised agonies equalling if not exceeding any inflicted by the most brutal of barbarians.

Startling as the truth seems, it is yet a truth to be recognized, that increase of humanity does not go on *pari passu* with civilization; but that, contrariwise, the earlier stages of civilization necessitate a relative inhumanity. Among tribes of primitive men, it is the more brutal rather than the more kindly who succeed in those conquests which effect the earliest social consolidations; and through many subsequent stages unscrupulous aggression outside of the society and cruel coercion within, are the habitual concomitants of political development. The men of whom the better organized societies have been formed, were at first, and long continued to be, nothing else but the stronger and more cunning savages; and even now, when freed from those influences which superficially modify their behaviour, they prove themselves to be little better. If, on the one hand, we contemplate the utterly uncivilized Wood-Veddahs, who are described as "proverbially truthful and honest," "gentle and affectionate," "obeying the slightest intimation of a wish, and very grateful for attention or assistance," and of whom Pridham remarks—"What a lesson in gratitude and delicacy even a Veddah may teach!" and then if, on the other hand, we contemplate our own recent acts of international brigandage, accompanied by the slaughter of thousands who have committed no wrong against us—accompanied, too, by perfidious breaches of faith and the killing of prisoners in cold blood; we must admit that between the types of men classed as uncivilized and civilized, the differences are not necessarily of the kinds commonly supposed. Whatever relation exists between moral nature and social type, is not such as to imply that the social man is in all respects emotionally superior to the pre-social man.

"How is this conclusion to be reconciled with the conception of progress?" most readers will ask. "How is civilization to be justified if, as is thus implied, some of the highest of human attributes are exhibited in greater degrees by wild people who live scattered in pairs in the woods, than by the members of a vast, well-organized nation, having marvellously-elaborated arts, extensive and profound knowledge, and multitudinous appliances to welfare?" The answer to this question will best be conveyed by an analogy.

As carried on throughout the animate world at large, the struggle for existence has been an indispensable means to evolution. Not simply do we see that in the competition among individuals of the same kind, survival of the fittest, has from the beginning furthered production of a higher type; but we see that to the unceasing warfare between species is mainly due both growth and organization. Without universal conflict there would have been no development of the active powers. The organs of perception and of locomotion have been little by little evolved during the inter-action of pursuers and pursued. Improved limbs and senses have furnished better supplies to the viscera, and improved visceral structures have ensured a better supply of aerated blood to the limbs and senses; while a higher nervous system has at each stage been called into play for coördinating the actions of these more complex structures. Among predatory animals death by starvation, and among animals preyed upon death by destruction, have carried off the least-favourably modified individuals and varieties. Every advance in strength, speed, agility, or sagacity, in creatures of the one class, has necessitated a corresponding advance in creatures of the other class; and without never-ending efforts to catch and to escape, with loss of life as the penalty for failure, the progress of neither could have been achieved.

Mark now, however, that while this merciless discipline of Nature, "red in tooth and claw," has been essential to the progress of sentient life, its persistence through all time with all creatures must not be inferred. The high organization evolved by and for this universal conflict, is not necessarily for ever employed to like ends. The resulting power and intelligence admit of being far otherwise employed. Not for offence and defence only are the inherited structures useful, but for various other purposes; and these various other purposes may finally become the exclusive purposes. The myriads of years of warfare which have developed the powers of all lower types of creatures, have bequeathed to the highest type of creature the powers now used by him for countless objects besides those of killing and avoiding being killed. His limbs, teeth, and nails are but little employed in fight; and his mind is not ordinarily occupied in devising ways of destroying other creatures, or guarding himself from injury by them.

Similarly with social organisms. We must recognize the truth that the struggles for existence between societies have been instrumental to their evolution. Neither the consolidation and re-consolidation of small groups into large ones; nor the organization of such compound and doubly compound groups; nor the concomitant developments of those aids to a higher life which civilization has brought; would have been possible without inter-tribal and inter-national conflicts. Social coöperation is initiated by joint defence and offence; and from the coöperation thus initiated, all kinds of coöperations have arisen. Inconceivable as have been the horrors caused by this universal antagonism which, beginning with the chronic hostilities of small hordes tens of thousands of years ago, has ended in the occasional vast battles of immense nations, we must nevertheless admit that without it the world would still have been inhabited only by men of feeble types, sheltering in caves and living on wild food.

But now observe that the inter-social struggle for existence which has been indispensable in evolving societies, will not necessarily play in the future a part like that which it has played in the past. Recognizing our indebtedness to war for forming great communities and developing their structures, we may yet infer that the acquired powers, available for other activities, will lose their original activities. While conceding that without these perpetual bloody strifes, civilized societies could not have arisen, and that an adapted form of human nature, fierce as well as intelligent, was a needful concomitant; we may at the same time hold that such societies having been produced, the brutality of nature in their units which was necessitated by the process, ceasing to be necessary with the cessation of the process, will disappear. While the benefits achieved during the predatory period remain a permanent inheritance, the evils entailed by it will decrease and slowly die out.

Thus, then, contemplating social structures and actions from the evolution point of view, we may preserve that calmness which is needful for scientific interpretation of them, without losing our powers of feeling moral reprobation or approbation. . . .

Private Property.[1] The fact . . . that even intelligent animals display a sense of proprietorship, negatives the belief propounded by some, that individual property was not recognized by primitive men. When we see the claim to exclusive possession understood by a dog, so that he fights in defence of his master's clothes if left in charge of them, it becomes impossible to suppose that even in their lowest state men were devoid of those ideas and emotions which initiate private ownership. All that may be fairly assumed is that these ideas and sentiments were at first less developed than they have since become. . . .

While in early stages it is difficult, not to say impossible, to establish and mark off individual claims to parts of the area wandered over in search of food, it is not difficult to mark off the claims to movable things and to habitations; and these claims we find habitually recognized. The following passage from Bancroft concerning certain North American savages, well illustrates the distinction:—"Captain Cook found among the Ahts very 'strict notions of their having a right to the exclusive property of everything that their country produces,' so that they claimed pay for even wood, water, and grass. The limits of tribal property are very clearly defined, but individuals rarely claim

[1] *Ibid.*, Vol. II, pp. 538–542, 546, 553–556.

any property in land. Houses belong to the men who combine to build them. Private wealth consists of boats and implements for obtaining food, domestic utensils, slaves, and blankets." . . . Dr. Rink's account of the Esquimaux shows that among them, too, while there is joint ownership of houses made jointly by the families inhabiting them, there is separate ownership of weapons, fishing boats, tools, etc. Thus it is made manifest that private right, completely recognized where recognition of it is easy, is partially recognized where partial recognition only is possible—where the private rights of companions are entangled with it. . . .

Recognition of this truth at once opens the way to explanation of primitive land-ownership; and elucidates the genesis of those communal and family tenures which have prevailed so widely.

While subsistence on wild food continues, the wandering horde inhabiting a given area, must continue to make joint use of the area; both because no claim can be shown by any member to any portion, and because the marking out of small divisions, if sharing were agreed upon, would be impracticable. Where pastoral life has arisen, ability to drive herds hither and thither within the occupied region is necessary. In the absence of cultivation, cattle and their owners could not survive were each owner restricted to one spot: there is nothing feasible but united possession of a wide tract. And when there comes a transition to the agricultural stage, either directly from the hunting stage or indirectly through the pastoral stage, several causes conspire to prevent, or to check, the growth of private land-ownership.

There is first the traditional usage. Joint ownership continues after circumstances no longer render it imperative, because departure from the sacred example of forefathers is resisted. Sometimes the resistance is insuperable; as with the Rechabites and the people of Petra, who by their vow "were not allowed to possess either vineyards or cornfields or houses" but were bound "to continue the nomadic life." And obviously, where the transition to a settled state is effected, the survival of habits and sentiments established during the nomadic state, must long prevent possession of land by individuals. Moreover, apart from opposing ideas and customs, there are physical difficulties in the way. Even did any member of a pastoral horde which had become partially settled, establish a claim to exclusive possession of one part of the occupied area, little advantage could be gained before there existed the means of keeping out the animals belonging to others. Common use of the greater part of the surface must long continue from mere inability to set up effectual divisions. Only small portions can at first be fenced off. Yet a further reason why land-owning by individuals, and land-owning by families, establish themselves very slowly, is that at first each particular plot has but a temporary value. The soil is soon exhausted; and in the absence of advanced arts of culture becomes useless. Such tribes as those of the Indian hills show us that primitive cultivators uniformly follow the practice of clearing a tract of ground, raising from it two or three crops, and then abandoning it: the implication being that whatever private claim had arisen, lapses, and the surface, again becoming wild, reverts to the community. . . .

Induction and deduction uniting to show, as they do, that at first land is common property, there presents itself the question—How did possession of it become individualized? There can be little doubt as to the general nature of the answer. Force, in one form or other, is the sole cause adequate to make the members of a society yield up their joint claim to the area they inhabit. Such force may be that of an external aggressor or that of an internal aggressor; but in either case it implies militant activity. . . .

At first sight it seems fairly inferable that the absolute ownership of land by private persons, must be the ultimate state which industrialism brings about. But though industrialism has thus far tended to individualize possession of land, while individualizing all other possession, it may be doubted whether the final stage is at present reached. Ownership established by force does not stand on the same footing as ownership established by contract; and though multiplied sales and purchases, treating the two ownerships in the same way, have tacitly assimilated them, the assimilation may eventually be denied. The analogy furnished by assumed rights of possession over human beings, helps us to recognize this possibility. For while prisoners of war, taken by force and held as property in a vague way (being at first much on a footing with other members of a household), were reduced more definitely to the form of property when the buying and selling of slaves became general; and while it might, centuries ago, have been thence inferred that the ownership of man by man was an ownership in course of being permanently established; yet we see that a later stage of civilization, reversing this process, has destroyed ownership of man by man. Similarly, at a stage still more advanced it may be that private ownership of land will disappear. As that primitive freedom of the individual which existed before war established coercive institutions and personal slavery, comes to be reëstablished as militancy declines; so it seems possible that the primitive ownership of land by the community, which, with the development of coercive institutions, lapsed in large measure or wholly into private ownership, will be revived as industrialism further develops. The *régime* of contract, at present so far extended that the right of property in movables is recognized only as having arisen by exchange of services or products under agreements, or by gift from those who had acquired it under such agreements, may be further extended so far that the products of the soil will be recognized as property only by virtue of agreements between individuals as tenants and the community as landowner. Even now, among ourselves, private ownership of land is not absolute. In legal theory landowners are directly or indirectly tenants of the Crown (which in our day is equivalent to the State, or, in other words, the Community); and the Community from time to time resumes possession after making due compensation. Perhaps the right of the Community to the land, thus tacitly asserted, will in time to come be overtly asserted; and acted upon after making full allowance for the accumulated value artificially given.

The rise and development of arrangements which fix and regulate private possession, thus admit of tolerably clear delineation.

The desire to appropriate, and to keep that which has been appropriated, lies deep, not in human nature only, but in animal nature: being, indeed, a condition to survival. The consciousness that conflict, and consequent injury, may probably result from the endeavour to take that which is held by another, ever tends to establish and strengthen the custom of leaving each in possession of whatever he has obtained by labour; and this custom takes among primitive men the shape of an overtly-admitted claim.

This claim to private ownership, fully recognized in respect of movables made by the possessor, and fully or partially recognized in respect of game killed on the territory over which members of the community wander, is not recognized in respect to this territory itself, or tracts of it. Property is individualized as far as circumstances allow individual claims to be marked off with some definiteness; but it is not individualized in respect of land, because, under the conditions, no individual claims can be shown, or could be effectually marked off were they shown.

With the passage from a nomadic to a settled state, ownership of land by the community becomes qualified by individual ownership;

but only to the extent that those who clear and cultivate portions of the surface have undisturbed enjoyment of its produce. Habitually the public claim survives; and either when, after a few crops, the cleared tract is abandoned, or when, after transmission to descendants, it has ceased to be used by them, it reverts to the community. And this system of temporary ownership, congruous with the sentiments and usages inherited from ancestral nomads, is associated also with an undeveloped agriculture: land becoming exhausted after a few years.

Where the patriarchal form of organization has been carried from the pastoral state into the settled state, and, sanctified by tradition, is also maintained for purposes of mutual protection, possession of land partly by the clan and partly by the family, long continues; at the same time that there is separate possession of things produced by separate labour. And while in some cases the communal land-ownership, or family land-ownership, survives, it in other cases yields in various modes and degrees to qualified forms of private ownership, mostly temporary, and subject to supreme ownership by the public.

But war, both by producing class-differentiations within each society, and by effecting the subjugation of one society by another, undermines or destroys communal proprietorship of land; and partly or wholly substitutes for it, either the unqualified proprietorship of an absolute conqueror, or proprietorship by a conqueror qualified by the claims of vassals holding it under certain conditions, while their claims are in turn qualified by those of dependents attached to the soil. That is to say, the system of status which militancy develops, involves a graduated ownership of land as it does a graduated ownership of persons.

Complete individualization of ownership is an accompaniment of industrial progress. From the beginning, things identified as products of a man's own labour are recognized as his; and throughout the course of civilization, communal possession and joint household living, have not excluded the recognition of a *peculium* obtained by individual effort. Accumulation of movables privately possessed, arising in this way, increases as militancy is restrained by growing industrialism; because this pre-supposes greater facility for disposing of industrial products; because there come along with it measures of quantity and value, furthering exchange; and because the more pacific relations implied, render it safer for men to detach themselves from the groups in which they previously kept together for mutual protection. The individualization of ownership, extended and made more definite by trading transactions under contract, eventually affects the ownership of land. Bought and sold by measure and for money, land is assimilated in this respect to the personal property produced by labour; and thus becomes, in the general apprehension, confounded with it. But there is reason to suspect that while private possession of things produced by labour, will grow even more definite and sacred than at present; the inhabited area, which cannot be produced by labour, will eventually be distinguished as something which may not be privately possessed. As the individual, primitively owner of himself, partially or wholly loses ownership of himself during the militant *régime*, but gradually resumes it as the industrial *régime* develops; so, possibly, the communal proprietorship of land, partially or wholly merged in the ownership of dominant men during evolution of the militant type, will be resumed as the industrial type becomes fully evolved. . . .

Government and the Individual.[1] Be it or be it not true that Man is shapen in iniquity and conceived in sin, it is unquestionably true that Government is begotten of aggression and by aggression. In small undeveloped societies where for ages complete peace has continued, there exists nothing like what we call Government: no coercive agency, but mere honorary headship, if any headship at all. In these exceptional communities, unaggressive and from special causes unaggressed upon, there is so little deviation from the virtues of truthfulness, honesty, justice, and generosity, that nothing beyond an occasional expression of public opinion by informally-assembled elders is needful. Conversely, we find proofs that, at first recognized but temporarily during leadership in war, the authority of a chief is permanently established by continuity of war; and grows strong where successful war ends in subjection of neighbouring tribes. And thence onwards, examples furnished by all races put beyond doubt the truth, that the coercive power of the chief, developing into king, and king of kings (a frequent title in the ancient East), becomes great in proportion as conquest becomes habitual and the union of subdued nations extensive. Comparisons disclose a further truth which should be ever present to us—the truth that the aggressiveness of the ruling power inside a society increases with its aggressiveness outside the

[1] *The Man versus the State* (published with *Social Statics*, 1914; preface dated 1892 indicates slight changes since the original edition of 1884. Copyright by D. Appleton-Century Co., New York), pp. 334–335, 357–369.

society. As, to make an efficient army, the soldiers must be subordinate to their commander; so, to make an efficient fighting community, must the citizens be subordinate to their government. They must furnish recruits to the extent demanded, and yield up whatever property is required.

An obvious implication is that political ethics, originally identical with the ethics of war, must long remain akin to them; and can diverge from them only as warlike activities and preparations become less. Current evidence shows this. At present on the Continent, the citizen is free only when his services as a soldier are not demanded; and during the rest of his life he is largely enslaved in supporting the military organization. Even among ourselves a serious war would, by the necessitated conscription, suspend the liberties of large numbers and trench on the liberties of the rest, by taking from them through taxes whatever supplies were needed—that is, forcing them to labour so many days more for the State. Inevitably the established code of conduct in the dealings of Governments with citizens, must be allied to their code of conduct in their dealings with one another. . . .

Among men's desires seeking gratifications, those which have prompted their private activities and their spontaneous coöperations, have done much more towards social development than those which have worked through governmental agencies. That abundant crops now grow where once only wild berries could be gathered, is due to the pursuit of individual satisfactions through many centuries. The progress from wigwams to good houses has resulted from wishes to increase personal welfare; and towns have arisen under the like promptings. Beginning with traffic at gatherings on occasions of religious festivals, the trading organization, now so extensive and complex, has been produced entirely by men's efforts to achieve their private ends. Perpetually, governments have thwarted and deranged the growth, but have in no way furthered it; save by partially discharging their proper function and maintaining social order. So, too, with those advances of knowledge and those improvements of appliances, by which these structural changes and these increasing activities have been made possible. It is not to the State that we owe the multitudinous useful inventions from the spade to the telephone; it was not the State which made possible extended navigation by a developed astronomy; it was not the State which made the discoveries in physics, chemistry, and the rest, which guide modern manufacturers; it was not the State which devised the machinery for producing fabrics of every kind, for transferring men and things from place to place, and for ministering in a thousand ways to our comforts. The world-wide transactions conducted in merchants' offices, the rush of traffic filling our streets, the retail distributing system which brings everything within easy reach and delivers the necessaries of life daily at our doors, are not of governmental origin. All these are results of the spontaneous activities of citizens, separate or grouped. Nay, to these spontaneous activities governments owe the very means of performing their duties. Divest the political machinery of all those aids which Science and Art have yielded it—leave it with those only which State-officials have invented; and its functions would cease. The very language in which its laws are registered and the orders of its agents daily given, is an instrument not in the remotest degree due to the legislator; but is one which has unawares grown up during men's intercourse while pursuing their personal satisfactions.

And then a truth to which the foregoing one introduces us, is that this spontaneously-formed social organization is so bound together that you cannot act on one part without acting more or less on all parts. We see this unmistakably when a cotton-famine, first paralyzing certain manufacturing districts and then affecting the doings of wholesale and retail distributors throughout the kingdom, as well as the people they supply, goes on to affect the makers and distributors, as well as the wearers, of other fabrics—woollen, linen, &c. Or we see it when a rise in the price of coal, besides influencing domestic life everywhere, hinders many of our industries, raises the prices of the commodities produced, alters the consumption of them, and changes the habits of consumers. What we see clearly in these marked cases happens in every case, in sensible or in insensible ways. And manifestly, Acts of Parliament are among those factors which, beyond the effects directly produced, have countless other effects of multitudinous kinds. As I heard remarked by a distinguished professor, whose studies give ample means of judging—"When once you begin to interfere with the order of Nature there is no knowing where the results will end." And if this is true of that sub-human order of Nature to which he referred, still more is it true of that order of Nature existing in the social arrangements of human beings.

And now to carry home the conclusion that the legislator should bring to his business a vivid consciousness of these and other such broad truths concerning the society with which he proposes to deal, let me present somewhat more fully one of them not yet mentioned.

The continuance of every higher species of creature depends on conformity, now to one, now to the other, of two radically-opposed principles. The early lives of its members, and the adult lives of its members, have to be dealt with in contrary ways. We will contemplate them in their natural order.

One of the most familiar facts is that animals of superior types, comparatively slow in reaching maturity, are enabled when they have reached it, to give more aid to their offspring than animals of inferior types. The adults foster their young during periods more or less prolonged, while yet the young are unable to provide for themselves; and it is obvious that maintenance of the species can be secured only by this parental care. It requires no proving that the blind unfledged hedge-bird, or the young puppy even after it has acquired sight, would forthwith die if it had to keep itself warm and obtain its own food. The gratuitous aid must be great in proportion as the young one is of little worth, either to itself or to others; and it may diminish as fast as, by increasing development, the young one acquires worth, at first for self-sustentation, and by-and-by for sustentation of others. That is to say, during immaturity, benefits received must vary inversely as the power or ability of the receiver. Clearly if during this first part of life benefits were proportioned to merits, or rewards to deserts, the species would disappear in a generation.

From this *régime* of the family-group, let us turn to the *régime* of that larger group formed by adult members of the species. Ask what happens when the new individual, acquiring complete use of its powers and ceasing to have parental aid, is left to itself. Now there comes into play a principle just the reverse to that above described. Throughout the rest of its life, each adult gets benefit in proportion to merit—reward in proportion to desert: merit and desert in each case being understood as ability to fulfil all the requirements of life—to get food, to find shelter, to escape enemies. Placed in competition with members of its own species and in antagonism with members of other species, it dwindles and gets killed off, or thrives and propagates, according as it is ill-endowed or well-endowed. Manifestly an opposite *régime*, could it be maintained, would, in course of time, be fatal. If the benefits received by each individual were proportionate to its inferiority—if, as a consequence, multiplication of the inferior was furthered, and multiplication of the superior hindered, progressive degradation would result; and eventually the degenerate species would fail to hold its ground in presence of antagonistic species and competing species.

The broad fact then, here to be noted, is that Nature's modes of treatment inside the family-group and outside the family-group are diametrically opposed to one another; and that the intrusion of either mode into the sphere of the other, would be destructive either immediately or remotely.

Does any one think that the like does not hold of the human species? He cannot deny that within the human family, as within any inferior family, it would be fatal to proportion benefits to merits. Can he assert that outside the family, among adults, there should not be, as throughout the animal world, a proportioning of benefits to merits? Will he contend that no mischief will result if the lowly endowed are enabled to thrive and multiply as much as, or more than, the highly endowed? A society of men, standing towards other societies in relations of either antagonism or competition, may be considered as a species, or, more literally, as a variety of a species; and it must be true of it as of other species or varieties, that it will be unable to hold its own in the struggle with other societies, if it disadvantages its superior units that it may advantage its inferior units. Surely none can fail to see that were the principle of family life to be adopted and fully carried out in social life—were reward always great in proportion as desert was small, fatal results to the society would quickly follow; and if so, then even a partial intrusion of the family *régime* into the *régime* of the State, will be slowly followed by fatal results. Society in its corporate capacity, cannot without immediate or remoter disaster interfere with the play of these opposed principles under which every species has reached such fitness for its mode of life as it possesses, and under which it maintains that fitness.

I say advisedly—society in its corporate capacity; not intending to exclude or condemn aid given to the inferior by the superior in their individual capacities. Though when given so indiscriminately as to enable the inferior to multiply, such aid entails mischief; yet in the absence of aid given by society, individual aid, more generally demanded than now, and associated with a greater sense of responsibility, would, on the average, be given with the effect of fostering the unfortunate worthy rather than the innately unworthy: there being always, too, the concomitant social benefit arising from culture of the sympathies. But all this may be admitted while asserting that the radical distinction between family-ethics and State-ethics must be maintained; and that while generosity must be the essential principle of the one, justice must be the essential principle of the other—

a rigorous maintenance of those normal relations among citizens under which each gets in return for his labour, skilled or unskilled, bodily or mental, as much as is proved to be its value by the demand for it: such return, therefore, as will enable him to thrive and rear offspring in proportion to the superiorities which make him valuable to himself and others.

And yet, notwithstanding the conspicuousness of these truths, which should strike everyone who leaves his lexicons, and his law-deeds, and his ledgers, and looks abroad into that natural order of things under which we exist, and to which we must conform, there is continual advocacy of paternal government. The intrusion of family-ethics into the ethics of the State, instead of being regarded as socially injurious, is more and more demanded as the only efficient means to social benefit. So far has this delusion now gone, that it vitiates the beliefs of those who might, more than all others, be thought safe from it. In the essay to which the Cobden Club awarded its prize in 1880, there occurs the assertion that "the truth of Free Trade is clouded over by the *laissez-faire* fallacy;" and we are told that "we need a great deal more parental government—that bugbear of the old economists."

Vitally important as is the truth above insisted upon, since acceptance or rejection of it affects the entire fabric of political conclusion formed, I may be excused if I emphasize it by here quoting certain passages contained in a work I published in 1851: premising, only, that the reader must not hold me committed to such teleological implications as they contain. After describing "that state of universal warfare maintained throughout the lower creation," and showing that an average of benefit results from it, I have continued thus:—

> Note further, that their carnivorous enemies not only remove from herbivorous herds individuals past their prime, but also weed out the sickly, the malformed, and the least fleet or powerful. By the aid of which purifying process, as well as by the fighting so universal in the pairing season, all vitiation of the race through the multiplication of its inferior samples is prevented; and the maintenance of a constitution completely adapted to surrounding conditions, and therefore most productive of happiness, is ensured.
>
> The development of the higher creation is a progress towards a form of being capable of a happiness undiminished by these drawbacks. It is in the human race that the consummation is to be accomplished. Civilization is the last stage of its accomplishment. And the ideal man is the man in whom all the conditions of that accomplishment are fulfilled.

Meanwhile, the well-being of existing humanity, and the unfolding of it into this ultimate perfection, are both secured by that same beneficent, though severe discipline, to which the animate creation at large is subject: a discipline which is pitiless in the working out of good: a felicity-pursuing law which never swerves for the avoidance of partial and temporary suffering. The poverty of the incapable, the distresses that come upon the imprudent, the starvation of the idle, and those shoulderings aside of the weak by the strong, which leave so many "in shallows and in miseries," are the decrees of a large, far-seeing benevolence.

. . . .

To become fit for the social state, man has not only to lose his savageness, but he has to acquire the capacities needful for civilized life. Power of application must be developed; such modification of the intellect as shall qualify it for its new tasks must take place; and, above all, there must be gained the ability to sacrifice a small immediate gratification for a future great one. The state of transition will of course be an unhappy state. Misery inevitable results from incongruity between constitution and conditions. All these evils which afflict us, and seem to the uninitiated the obvious consequences of this or that removable cause, are unavoidable attendants on the adaptation now in progress. Humanity is being pressed against the inexorable necessities of its new position—is being moulded into harmony with them, and has to bear the resulting unhappiness as best it can. The process *must* be undergone, and the sufferings *must* be endured. No power on earth, no cunningly-devised laws of statesmen, no world-rectifying schemes of the humane, no communist panaceas, no reforms that men ever did broach or ever will broach, can diminish them one jot. Intensified they may be, and are; and in preventing their intensification, the philanthropic will find ample scope for exertion. But there is bound up with the change a *normal* amount of suffering, which cannot be lessened without altering the very laws of life.

. . . .

Of course, in so far as the severity of this process is mitigated by the spontaneous sympathy of men for each other, it is proper that it should be mitigated; albeit there is unquestionably harm done when sympathy is shown, without any regard to ultimate results. But the drawbacks hence arising are nothing like commensurate with the benefits otherwise conferred. Only when this sympathy prompts to a breach of equity—only when it originates an interference forbidden by the law of equal freedom—only when, by so doing, it suspends in some particular department of life the relationship between constitution and conditions, does it work pure evil. Then, however, it defeats its own end. Instead of diminishing suffering, it eventually increases it. It favors the multiplication of those worst fitted for existence, and, by consequence, hinders the multiplication of those best fitted for existence—leaving, as it does, less room for them. It tends to fill the world with those to whom life will bring most pain, and tends to keep out of it those to whom life will bring most pleasure. It inflicts positive misery, and prevents positive happiness.—*Social Statics*, pp. 322–325 and pp. 380–381 (edition of 1851).

The lapse of a third of a century since these passages were published, has brought me no reason for retreating from the position taken up in them. Contrariwise, it has brought a vast amount of evidence strengthening that position. The beneficial results of the survival of the fittest prove to be immeasurably greater than those above indicated. The process of "natural selection," as Mr. Darwin called it, co-operating with a tendency to variation and to inheritance of variations, he has shown to be a chief cause (though not, I believe, the sole cause) of that evolution through which all living things, beginning with the lowest and diverging and re-diverging as they evolved, have reached their present degrees of organization and adaptation to their modes of life. So familiar has this truth become that some apology seems needed for naming it. And yet, strange to say, now that this truth is recognized by most cultivated people—now that the beneficent working of the survival of the fittest has been so impressed on them that, much more than people in past times, they might be expected to hesitate before neutralizing its action—now more than ever before in the history of the world, are they doing all they can to further survival of the unfittest!

But the postulate that men are rational beings, continually leads one to draw inferences which prove to be extremely wide of the mark.

"Yes truly; your principle is derived from the lives of brutes, and is a brutal principle. You will not persuade me that men are to be under the discipline which animals are under. I care nothing for your natural-history arguments. My conscience shows me that the feeble and the suffering must be helped; and if selfish people won't help them, they must be forced by law to help them. Don't tell me that the milk of human kindness is to be reserved for the relations between individuals, and that Governments must be the administrators of nothing but hard justice. Every man with sympathy in him must feel that hunger and pain and squalor must be prevented; and that if private agencies do not suffice, then public agencies must be established."

Such is the kind of response which I expect to be made by nine out of ten. In some of them it will doubtless result from a fellow-feeling so acute that they cannot contemplate human misery without an impatience which excludes all thought of remote results. Concerning the susceptibilities of the rest, we may, however, be somewhat sceptical. Persons who are angry if, to maintain our supposed national "interests" or national "*prestige*," those in authority do not send out thousands of men to be partially destroyed while destroying other thousands of men because we suspect their intentions, or dislike their institutions, or want their territory, cannot after all be so tender in feeling that contemplating the hardships of the poor is intolerable to them. Little admiration need be felt for the professed sympathies of people who urge on a policy which breaks up progressing societies; and who then look on with cynical indifference at the weltering confusion left behind, with all its entailed suffering and death. Those who, when Boers, asserting their independence, successfully resisted us, were angry because British "honour" was not maintained by fighting to avenge a defeat, at the cost of more mortality and misery to our own soldiers and their antagonists, cannot have so much "enthusiasm of humanity" as protests like that indicated above would lead one to expect. Indeed, along with this sensitiveness which it seems will not let them look with patience on the pains of "the battle of life" as it quietly goes on around, they appear to have a callousness which not only tolerates but enjoys contemplating the pains of battles of the literal kind; as one sees in the demand for illustrated papers containing scenes of carnage, and in the greediness with which detailed accounts of bloody engagements are read. We may reasonably have our doubts about men whose feelings are such that they cannot bear the thought of hardships borne, mostly by the idle and the improvident, and who, nevertheless, have demanded thirty-one editions of *The Fifteen Decisive Battles of the World*, in which they may revel in accounts of slaughter. Nay, even still more remarkable is the contrast between the professed tender-heartedness and the actual hard-heartedness of those who would reverse the normal course of things that immediate miseries may be prevented, even at the cost of greater miseries hereafter produced. For on other occasions you may hear them, with utter disregard of bloodshed and death, contend that in the interests of humanity at large, it is well that the inferior races should be exterminated and their places occupied by the superior races. So that, marvellous to relate, though they cannot bear to think of the evils accompanying the struggle for existence as it is carried on without violence among individuals in their own society, they contemplate with equanimity such evils in their intense and wholesale forms, when inflicted by fire and sword on entire communities. Not worthy of much respect then, as it seems to me, is this generous consideration of the inferior at home which is accompanied by unscrupulous sacrifice of the inferior abroad.

Still less respectable appears this extreme concern for those of our own blood which goes along with utter unconcern for those of other blood, when we observe its methods. Did it prompt personal effort to relieve the suffering, it would rightly receive approving recognition. Were the many who express this cheap pity like the few who devote large parts of their time to aiding and encouraging, and occasionally amusing, those who, by ill-fortune or incapacity, are brought to lives of hardship, they would be worthy of unqualified admiration. The more there are of men and women who help the poor to help themselves—the more there are of those whose sympathy is exhibited directly and not by proxy, the more we may rejoice. But the immense majority of the persons who wish to mitigate by law the miseries of the unsuccessful and the reckless, propose to do this in small measure at their own cost and mainly at the cost of others—sometimes with their assent but mostly without. More than this is true; for those who are to be forced to do so much for the distressed, often equally or more require something doing for them. The deserving poor are among those who are taxed to support the undeserving poor. As, under the old Poor Law, the diligent and provident labourer had to pay that the good-for-nothings might not suffer, until frequently under this extra burden he broke down and himself took refuge in the workhouse—as, at present, the total rates levied in large towns for all public purposes, have reached such a height that they "cannot be exceeded without inflicting great hardship on the small shopkeepers and artisans, who already find it difficult enough to keep themselves free from the pauper taint"; so in all cases, the policy is one which intensifies the pains of those most deserving of pity, that the pains of those least deserving of pity may be mitigated. Men who are so sympathetic that they cannot let the struggle for existence bring on the unworthy the sufferings consequent on their incapacity or misconduct, are so unsympathetic that they can, deliberately, make the struggle for existence harder for the worthy, and inflict on them and their children artificial evils in addition to the natural evils they have to bear!

XVII

AUGUSTE COMTE

1798–1852

The parents of Comte were devout Roman Catholics—so much is indicated by the baptismal name which they imposed upon the infant: Isidore Auguste Marie François-Xavier. They were also royalists, but in the France of 1798 it was necessary to be more discreet on this point.

Isidore or Auguste Comte (he first used the name Auguste on becoming a collaborator of Saint-Simon) was born at Montpellier in southern France, where his father was employed in the revenue service. The elder Comte displayed a lack of vigor during elections, however, and was finally discharged. But he was a close-fisted business man: rigid economy, including abstention from cafés and theaters, had enabled him to amass 32,000 francs by the time he was seventy-four. Perhaps Auguste did not appreciate the middle-class virtues; at any rate the time came when he solemnly pronounced his father unworthy of such a son. Madame Comte on the other hand had more endearing qualities. Although inclined toward hypochondria, she was constantly solicitous for Auguste's well-being even in the most trivial matters; it was to her that he attributed his sentimental nature.

At school, first under the care of an old private teacher and then at the lycée of Montpellier, Auguste qualified as an infant prodigy, with a remarkable memory and a decided gift for mathematics, Latin, and rhetoric. His instructor in mathematics, a kind of universal genius, possessed the wide-ranging interests which were to distinguish his prize pupil, but he also stood for order and discipline and thought that democracy could be carried too far. Whatever impression these latter ideas made upon Comte as philosophical principles, they failed utterly to guide his action: he was an untamed pupil, rebellious against the powers in Church, State, and lycée.

The Polytechnic School at Paris to which Comte was nominated in 1814 further encouraged the factious spirit. It was a democratic oasis in an autocratic state, and Comte soon became a leader among students who despised the restored Bourbons and repeatedly challenged the authority of their professors. A row of the latter sort in 1816 ended his career at the Polytechnic—the entire student body was sent home. Comte however returned to Paris determined to be a journalist.

Unable to find an opening in this field, he supported himself by giving lessons in mathematics. He also studied the eighteenth-century philosophers. But the great discovery of Comte's life was Saint-Simonism. He attached himself to the head of the sect, becoming the secretary and collaborator of Saint-Simon; it became difficult to determine where the ideas of the master left off and those of the disciple began. For six or seven years Comte's contributions bulked large in the already bulky literature of Saint-Simonism. Certain of his works written during this period outline the system which he was to develop in much greater detail later on. Such was a *Prospectus* worked out in 1822.

The system itself was collected from a variety of sources. Aside from Saint-Simon, whose mere mouthpiece Comte is, in many respects, supposed to have been, philosophers from the ancient Greeks to his own contemporaries were drawn upon. Comte himself spoke of Condorcet as his "spiritual father," and from Condorcet his concept of progress and the "law" of three stages in intellectual development were at least in part derived. Montesquieu and Saint-Simon (as well as Condorcet) supplied him with the principle that sociology is basic to the art of politics. But the catalogue of influences is long and cannot be recited in full here; we must conclude that the substance though not the form and impact of Comte's philosophy was essentially borrowed.

About 1822 Comte's association with Saint-Simon drew to a close. Various reasons for the breach have been assigned: Comte was a rationalist, Saint-Simon a Christian pantheist; Comte had less confidence in the revolutionary ideas of the time; it was a difference of psychological make-up, said Comte. But a further reason existed: the younger man could now claim to be an intellectual leader in his own right. The transition to a distinctly Comtian point of view appeared in articles written between 1822 and 1825, and in 1826 he began a series of lectures on "Positive Philosophy," the name by which his system was henceforth to be known. These lectures were abruptly terminated by a mental breakdown.

Comte's condition, financial as well as emotional, had long been unstable. For a time it seemed likely that his circumstances might be eased by an appointment to the faculty of a projected engineering school in the United States. The prospect of residing in America, which teemed with liberty, honor,—and wealth, was stimulating. Comte read Benjamin Franklin on how to win success, and determined to correct his own faults by a methodical application of American principles. For three months, it is said, he kept away from women. The school in America failed to materialize; but the problem of his relations with women was not solved. It had appeared in his early youth and continued to plague him and to color his philosophical outlook almost until the end of his life. Marriage only complicated matters; his collapse was caused by a domestic difficulty. Even after the death of the unpredictable Madame Comte, the peace of middle age was finally shattered when he discovered the true but unattainable ideal in a woman much younger than himself.

After an interval of positive insanity (1826–27) during which he made an attempt to commit suicide, Comte resumed his writing and private teaching, continuing the lectures abandoned in 1826. His financial difficulties were removed by his appointment in 1832 as tutor in mathematics at the Polytechnic. He also helped to organize an institute for workingmen which provided free lectures along broadly cultural lines.

Much of Comte's time from 1830 to 1842 was given to publishing the six volumes of his lectures, the *Course of Positive Philosophy*. It was an attempt to systematize the physical, biological, and social sciences, leading up to (and including) what he called "social physics" or, later on, "sociology."

Comte's last and unsuccessful love affair strengthened a religious cast already noticeable in his philosophy. In 1850 he began to lecture on a Religion of Humanity and proposed a calendar of 558 great men of history to be venerated in place of the ordinary saints. The possibility of converting the Jesuit order occurred to him. One of his disciples (Comte by this time had a widespread and reverent though perhaps not numerous following) interviewed the General of the order. The emissary pointed out that in Comte's system the Mother and Child would be retained as symbols of Humanity, only God being abolished. The Jesuits, however, refused to abandon Christianity.

Comte's last great work was the *System of Positive Politics* (1851–54). This restated, with important additions, his synthetic view of society and propounded a method by which the ideal Positive State might be attained. Voluminous though it was, the work comprised only a fragment of his grand project of social transformation. He was planning further installments when death intervened in 1857. His last words were: "What an irreparable loss!"

Comte had few followers of great prominence. But his leading ideas profoundly affected subsequent thought. Although he raised sociology to the dignity of an independent branch of knowledge, his insistence on the unity of all social phenomena had repercussions in the fields of economics, political science, and history. His concept of society as an organism helped to undermine the prevailing doctrine of individualism and laissez-faire. As a recent commentator sees it, "The builders of the new state [guild socialists, syndicalists, communists, anarchists, etc.] are enormously indebted to Auguste Comte. . . . They may ignore his spiritual power, and avoid the pitfalls of his dictatorships, but in their aversion for metaphysical vaporizing, in their desire to relate political forms to underlying social and economic conditions, in the high value which they place upon science and technique, and above all in the supreme importance which they attach to economic production, they return again and again to the founder of modern social science, . . . the inspiration of all who would reduce social chaos to order, and impart to social forces the drive of progress."

REFERENCES

Most of Comte's works have been translated into English, but there are no very recent editions.

For estimates of Comte's work see H. E. Barnes, "The Political and Social Philosophy of August Comte" (*Open Court*, 1922, Vol. XXXVI, pp. 419–429, 497–512); Theodora Bosanquet, "Auguste Comte and the Positive Philosophers" [in F. J. C. Hearnshaw's (editor) *The Social and Political Ideas of Some Representative Thinkers of the Age of Reaction and Reconstruction*, 1932]. J. E. McGee's *A Crusade for Social Justice* (1932) treats of the religion of positivism in England.

A useful English biography is F. J. Gould's short study (1920). There is also a recent life (in French) by Henri Gouhier (1931).

READINGS FROM

EARLY ESSAYS ON SOCIAL PHILOSOPHY

AND

GENERAL VIEW OF POSITIVISM

Law of the Three Intellectual States.[1] In whatever way we study the general development of the human intellect, whether according to the rational method or empirically, we discover, despite all seeming irregularities, a fundamental Law to which its progress is necessarily and invariably subjected. This Law consists in the fact

[1] *Early Essays on Social Philosophy*, H. D. Hutton, trans. (1911), pp. 218–219, 220, 221, 229, 230, 232. Written in 1825.

that the intellectual system of man, and every portion of it, necessarily passes through three successive phases, the Theological, the Metaphysical, and the Positive or Scientific. Thus man began by considering phenomena of every kind as due to the direct and continuous influence of supernatural agents; he next regarded them as products of different abstract forces, residing in the bodies, but distinct and heterogeneous; while he ends by viewing them as subjected to a certain number of natural and invariable laws, which are merely the general expression of the relations observed in their development.

All who have adequately studied the state of the human mind at the various Epochs of Civilization will easily verify the correctness of this general statement. A very simple observation suffices to guide us to this verification now that the revolution has been effected in reference to the larger portion of our ideas. The education of the individual, so far as this is spontaneous, necessarily presents the same essential phases as that of the race and vice versa. Now, at the present day everyone who is on a level with his time can easily see, by his own experience, that he was during his infancy a theologian, in his youth a metaphysician, and has become a scientific thinker in his mature age. The history of the sciences proves directly that the same has taken place in reference to the whole human race. . . .

Man . . . necessarily begins by regarding all the bodies which attract his attention as so many living beings, animated with a life resembling his own, but generally superior, by reason of the greater power of most of them. Afterwards, continued observation leads man to convert this primitive hypothesis into another less enduring one, that, namely, of a dead nature guided by a larger or smaller number of invisible superhuman agents, distinct and independent of one another, corresponding in attributes and authority to the kind and extent of the phenomena attributed to their agency. . . .

The first effect of the progress of Observation was to dispose the human mind gradually to reduce the number of supernatural agents; attributing to one the functions which originally demanded several, according as the relations of phenomena acquired greater generality. This result, pushed as far as possible, finally simplified the Theological System so far as to reduce it to Unity.

From this period, the continuous action of the same principle which at first guided the human mind from Fetichism to Polytheism, and finally from Polytheism to Theism, led it to confine the direct intervention of the great supernatural cause within limits more and more narrow, always reserving its application for those phenomena whose laws remained unknown. . . .

Theological Philosophy, placing itself at the prime source of all phenomena, is essentially occupied in unfolding their efficient causes, while Positive Philosophy—laying aside all search after *causes*, as being inaccessible to the human mind—is exclusively occupied in discovering *laws*, that is to say, the constant relations of similitude and succession which subsist between facts. Between these two points of view is naturally interposed the Metaphysical, which regards each phenomenon as the product of an abstract force peculiar to itself. This method is valuable from the facility it gives for reasoning on phenomena without directly considering supernatural causes, which the human mind was thus enabled gradually to eliminate from its combinations. . . .

Now, seeing that for at least two centuries past, those Theological and Metaphysical methods which presided over our earliest intellectual efforts have become entirely sterile; seeing that the most extensive and important discoveries, those which do most honour to the human mind, have since this epoch, entirely resulted from the employment of the Positive Method, this fact alone clearly proves that to the latter must henceforward belong the exclusive direction of human thought. . . .

From the considerations, then, indicated above, results the demonstration, theoretical and experimental, of the general fact enunciated at first: the human intellect naturally passes successively, in every department of its activity, through three different theoretic phases—the Theological state, the Metaphysical state, and the Positive state. Of these the first is provisional, the second transitory, and the third final.

This fundamental law should henceforth be, in my opinion, the starting-point of all philosophical researches about man and society. . . .

Positivism Includes a Study of Social Phenomena.[1] All Positive speculations owe their first origin to the occupations of practical life; and consequently, they have always given some indication of their capacity for regulating our active powers, which had been omitted from every former synthesis. Their value in this respect has been and still is materially impaired by their want of breadth, and their isolated and incoherent character; but it has always been instinctively felt.

[1] *General View of Positivism*, in *System of Positive Polity*, J. H. Bridges, trans. (1875), Vol. I, pp. 8–9. The *General View* was first published in 1848.

The importance that we attach to theories which teach the laws of phenomena, and give us the power of prevision, is chiefly due to the fact that they alone can regulate our otherwise blind action upon the external world. Hence it is that while the Positive spirit has been growing more and more theoretical, and has gradually extended to every department of speculation, it has never lost the practical tendencies which it derived from its source; and this even in the case of researches useless in themselves, and only to be justified as logical exercises. From its first origin in mathematics and astronomy, it has always shown its tendency to systematise the whole of our conceptions in every new subject which has been brought within the scope of its fundamental principle. It exercised for a long time a modifying influence upon theological and metaphysical principles, which has gone on increasing; and since the time of Descartes and Bacon it has become evident that it is destined to supersede them altogether. Positivism has gradually taken possession of the preliminary sciences of Physics and Biology, and in these the old system no longer prevails. All that remained was to complete the range of its influence by including the study of social phenomena. For this study metaphysics had proved incompetent; by theological thinkers it had only been pursued indirectly and empirically as a condition of government. I believe that my work on Positive Philosophy has so far supplied what was wanting. I think it must now be clear to all that the Positive spirit can embrace the entire range of thought without lessening, or rather with the effect of strengthening its original tendency to regulate practical life. And it is a further guarantee for the stability of the new intellectual synthesis that Social science, which is the final result of our researches, gives them that systematic character in which they had hitherto been wanting, by supplying the only connecting link of which they all admit.

Positivism Also Emphasizes the Feelings.[1] This conception is already adopted by all true thinkers. All must now acknowledge that the Positive spirit tends necessarily towards the formation of a comprehensive and durable system, in which every practical as well as speculative subject shall be included. But such a system would still be far from realising that universal character without which Positivism would be incompetent to supersede Theology in the spiritual government of Humanity. For the element which really preponderates in every human being, that is to say, Affection, would still be left un-

[1] *Ibid.*, pp. 9–11, 11–12, 13.

touched. This element it is, and this only, which gives a stimulus and direction to the other two parts of our nature; without it the one would waste its force in ill-conceived, or, at least, useless studies, and the other in barren or even dangerous contention. With this immense deficiency the combination of our theoretical and active powers would be fruitless, because it would lack the only principle which could ensure its real and permanent stability. The failure would be even greater than the failure of Theology in dealing with practical questions; for the unity of human nature cannot really be made to depend either on the rational or the active faculties. In the life of the individual, and, still more, in the life of the race, the basis of unity, as I shall show . . . , must always be Feeling. It is to the fact that theology arose spontaneously from feeling that its influence is for the most part due. And although theology is now palpably on the decline, yet it will still retain in principle at least, some legitimate claims to the direction of society so long as the new philosophy fails to occupy this important vantage-ground. We come then to the final conditions with which the modern synthesis must comply. Without neglecting the spheres of Thought and Action it must also comprehend the moral sphere; and the very principle on which its claim to universality rests must be derived from Feeling. Then, and not till then, can the claims of theology be finally set aside. For then the new system will have surpassed the old in that which is the one essential purpose of all general doctrines. It will have shown itself able to effect what no other doctrine has done, that is, to bring the three primary elements of our nature into harmony. If Positivism were to prove incapable of satisfying this condition, we must give up all hope of systematisation of any kind. For while Positive principles are now sufficiently developed to neutralise those of Theology, yet, on the other hand, the influence of Theology would continue to be far greater. Hence it is that many conscientious thinkers in the present day are so inclined to despair for the future of society. They see that the old principles on which society has been governed must finally become powerless. What they do not see is that a new basis for morality is being gradually laid down. Their theories are too imperfect and incoherent to show them the direction towards which the present time is ultimately tending. It must be owned, too, that their view seems borne out by the present character of the Positive method. While all allow its utility in the treatment of practical, and even of speculative, problems, it seems to most men, and very naturally, quite unfit to deal with questions of morality.

But on closer examination they will see reason to rectify their judgment. They will see that the hardness with which Positive science has been justly reproached, is due to the speciality and want of purpose with which it has hitherto been pursued, and is not at all inherent in its nature. Originating as it did in the necessities of our material nature, which for a long time restricted it to the study of the inorganic world, it has not till now become sufficiently complete or systematic to harmonise well with our moral nature. But now that it is brought to bear upon social questions, which for the future will form its most important field, it loses all the defects peculiar to its long period of infancy. The very attribute of reality which is claimed by the new philosophy, leads it to treat all subjects from the moral still more than from the intellectual side. The necessity of assigning with exact truth the place occupied by the intellect and by the heart in the organisation of human nature and of society, leads to the decision that Affection must be the central point of the synthesis. In the treatment of social questions Positive science will be found utterly to discard those proud illusions of the supremacy of reason, to which it had been liable during its preliminary stages. Ratifying, in this respect, the common experience of men even more forcibly than Catholicism, it teaches us that individual happiness and public welfare are far more dependent upon the heart than upon the intellect. But, independently of this, the question of coördinating the faculties of our nature will convince us that the only basis on which they can be brought into harmonious union, is the preponderance of Affection over Reason, and even over Activity. . . .

Even with the individual, it is impossible to establish permanent harmony between our various impulses, except by giving complete supremacy to the feeling which prompts the sincere and habitual desire of doing good. This feeling is, no doubt, like the rest, in itself blind; it has to learn from reason the right means of obtaining satisfaction; and our active faculties are then called into requisition to apply those means. But common experience proves that after all the principal condition of right action is the benevolent impulse; with the ordinary amount of intellect and activity that is found in men this stimulus, if well sustained, is enough to direct our thoughts and energies to a good result. Without this habitual spring of action they would inevitably waste themselves in barren or incoherent efforts, and speedily relapse into their original torpor. Unity in our moral nature is, then, impossible, except so far as affection preponderates over intellect and activity. . . .

We have traced the Positive principle from its origin in the occupations of active life, and have seen it extending successively to every department of speculation. We now find it, in its maturity, and that as a simple result of its strict adherence to fact, embracing the sphere of affection, and making that sphere the central point of its synthesis. It is henceforth a fundamental doctrine of Positivism, a doctrine of as great political as philosophical importance, that the Heart preponderates over the Intellect.

It is true that this doctrine, which is the only basis for establishing harmony in our nature, had been, as I before remarked, instinctively accepted by theological systems. But it was one of the fatalities of society in its preliminary phase, that the doctrine was coupled with an error which, after a time, destroyed all its value. In acknowledging the superiority of the heart the intellect was reduced to abject submission. Its only chance of growth lay in resistance to the established system. This course it followed with increasing effect, till after twenty centuries of insurrection, the system collapsed. The natural result of the process was to stimulate metaphysical and scientific pride, and to promote views subversive of all social order. But Positivism, while systematically adopting the principle here spoken of as the foundation of individual and social discipline, interprets that principle in a different way. It teaches that while it is for the heart to suggest our problems, it is for the intellect to solve them. . . .

The Religion of Positivism.[1] The moral education of the Positivist is based both upon Reason and on Feeling, the latter having always the preponderance, in accordance with the primary principle of the system.

The result of the rational basis is to bring moral precepts to the test of rigorous demonstration, and to secure them against all danger from discussion, by showing that they rest upon the laws of our individual and social nature. By knowing these laws, we are enabled to form a judgment of the influence of each affection, thought, action, or habit, be that influence direct or indirect, special or general, privately or publicly exercised. Convictions based upon such knowledge will be as deep as any that are formed in the present day from the strictest scientific evidence, with that excess of intensity due to their higher importance and their close connection with our noblest feelings. . . .

No one knows so well as the Positivist that the principal source

[1] *Ibid.*, pp. 79, 80, 80–82.

of real morality lies in direct exercise of our social sympathies, whether systematic or spontaneous. He will spare no efforts to develope these sympathies from the earliest years by every method which sound philosophy can indicate. It is in this that moral education, whether private or public, principally consists; and to it mental education is always to be held subordinate. . . .

But however efficient the training received in youth, it will not be enough to regulate our conduct in after years, amidst all the distracting influences of practical life, unless the same spiritual power which provides the education prolong its influence over our maturity. Part of its task will be to recall individuals, classes, and even nations, when the case requires it, to principles which they have forgotten or misinterpreted, and to instruct them in the means of applying them wisely. And here, even more than in the work of education strictly so called, the appeal will be to Feeling rather than to pure Reason. Its force will be derived from Public Opinion strongly organised. If the spiritual power awards its praise and blame justly, public opinion, as I shall show . . ., will lend it the most irresistible support. This moral action of Humanity upon each of her members has always existed whenever there was any real community of principles and feelings. But its strength will be far greater under the Positive system. The reality of the doctrine and the social character of modern civilisation give advantages to the new spiritual power which were denied to Catholicism.

And these advantages are brought forward very prominently by the Positive system of commemoration. Commemoration, when regularly instituted, is a most valuable instrument in the hands of a spiritual power for continuing the work of moral education. It was the absolute character of Catholicism, even more than the defective state of mediæval society, that caused the failure of its noble aspirations to become the universal religion. In spite of all its efforts, its system of commemoration has always been restricted to very narrow limits, both in time and space. Outside these limits, Catholicism has always shown the same blindness and injustice that it now complains of receiving from its own opponents. Positivism, on the contrary, can yield the full measure of praise to all times and all countries, without either weakness or inconsistency. Possessing the true theory of human development, every mode and phase of that development will be celebrated. Thus every moral precept will be supported by the influence of posterity; and this in private life as well as in public, for the system of commemoration will be applied in the same spirit to the humblest services as well as to the highest.

While reserving special details for subsequent consideration in this treatise, I may yet give one illustration of this important aspect of Positivism; an illustration which probably will be the first step in the practical application of the system. I would propose to institute in Western Europe on any days that may be thought suitable, the yearly celebration of the three greatest of our predecessors, Cæsar, St. Paul, and Charlemagne, who are respectively the highest types of Greco-Roman civilisation, of Mediæval Feudalism, and of Catholicism which forms the link between the two periods. The services of these illustrious men have never yet been adequately recognised, for want of a sound historical theory enabling us to explain the prominent part which they played in the development of our race. This is true even in the case of St. Paul, notwithstanding the sanctity with which theology has invested him. Positivism gives him a still higher place; for it looks upon him as historically the founder of the religion which bears the inappropriate name of Christianity. In the other two cases the influence of Positive principles is even more necessary. For Cæsar has been almost equally misjudged by theological and by metaphysical writers; and Catholicism has done very little for the proper appreciation of Charlemagne. However, notwithstanding the absence of any systematic appreciation of these great men, yet from the reverence with which they are generally regarded, we can hardly doubt that the celebration here proposed would meet with ready acceptance throughout Western Europe.

To illustrate my meaning still further, I may observe that history presents cases where exactly the opposite course is called for, and which should be held up not for approbation but for infamy. Blame, it is true, should not be carried to the same extent as praise, because it stimulates the destructive instincts to a degree which is always painful and sometimes injurious. Yet strong condemnation is occasionally desirable. It strengthens social feelings and principles, if only by giving more significance to our approval. Thus, I would suggest that after doing honour to the three great men who have done so much to promote the development of our race, there should be a solemn reprobation of the two principal opponents of progress, Julian and Bonaparte; the latter being the more criminal of the two, the former the more insensate. Their influence has been sufficiently extensive to allow of all the Western nations joining in this damnatory verdict. . . .

Order and Progress.[1] It will not now be difficult to show that all the characteristics of Positivism are summed up in its motto, *Order and Progress*, a motto which has a philosophical as well as political bearing, and of which I shall always feel glad to have been the author.

Positivism is the only school which has given a definite significance to these two great conceptions, whether regarded from their scientific or their social aspect. With regard to Progress the assertion will hardly be disputed; no definition of it but the Positive ever having yet been given. In the case of Order it is less apparent; but . . . it is no less profoundly true. All previous philosophies had regarded Order as stationary, a conception which rendered it wholly inapplicable to modern politics. But Positivism, by rejecting the absolute and yet not introducing the arbitrary, represents Order in a totally new light, and adapts it to our progressive civilisation. It places it on the firmest possible foundation, that is, on the doctrine of the invariability of the laws of nature, which defends it against all danger from subjective chimeras. The Positivist regards artificial Order, in Social phenomena as in all others, as resting necessarily upon the Order of nature, in other words upon the whole series of natural laws.

But Order has to be reconciled with Progress: and here Positivism is still more obviously without a rival. Necessary as the reconciliation is, no other system has even attempted it. But the facility with which we are now enabled, by the encyclopædic scale, to pass from the simplest mathematical phenomena to the most complicated phenomena of political life, leads at once to a solution of the problem. Viewed scientifically, it is an instance of that necessary correlation of existence and movement which we find indicated in the inorganic world, and which becomes still more distinct in Biology. Finding it in all the lower sciences, we are prepared for its appearance in a still more definite shape in Sociology. Here its practical importance becomes more obvious, though it had been implicitly involved before. In Sociology the correlation assumes this form: Order is the condition of all Progress; Progress is always the object of Order. Or, to penetrate the question still more deeply, Progress may be regarded simply as the development of Order; for the order of nature necessarily contains within itself the germ of all possible progress. The rational view of human affairs is to look on all their changes, not as new Creations, but as new Evolutions. And we find this principle fully borne out in history. Every social innovation has its roots in the past; and the rudest

[1] *Ibid.*, pp. 83–84.

phases of savage life show the primitive trace of all subsequent improvement. . . .

Free Speech and Free Enquiry.[1] Positivism is now the only consistent advocate of free speech and free enquiry. Schools of opinion which do not rest on demonstration, and would consequently be shaken by any argumentative attacks, can never be sincere in their wish for Liberty, in the extended sense here given to it. Liberty of writing we have now had for a long time. But besides this we want liberty of speech; and also liberty of teaching; that is to say, the abandonment by the State of all its educational monopolies. Freedom of teaching, of which Positivists are the only genuine supporters, has become a condition of the first importance; and this not merely as a provisional measure, but as an indication of the normal state of things. In the first place, it is the only means by which any doctrine that has the power of fixing and harmonising men's convictions can become generally known. To legalise any system of education would imply that such a doctrine had been already found; it most assuredly is not the way to find it. . . .

Positivists would be the last to deny that education ought to be regularly organised. Only they assert, first, that as long as the spiritual interregnum lasts no organisation is possible; and secondly, that whenever the acceptance of a new synthesis makes it possible, it will be effected by the spiritual power to which that synthesis gives rise. In the meantime no general system of State education should be attempted; except so far as it may be wise to continue State assistance to those branches of instruction which are the most liable to be neglected by private enterprise, especially reading and writing. . . .

Government should no doubt exercise constant vigilance over all private educational institutions; but this should have nothing to do with their doctrines, but with their morality, a point scandalously neglected in the present state of the law. These should be the limits of State interference in education. With these exceptions it should be left to the unrestricted efforts of private associations, so as to give every opportunity for a definitive educational system to establish itself. For to pretend that any satisfactory system exists at present would only be a hypocritical subterfuge on the part of the authorities. The most important step towards freedom of education would be the suppression of all grants to theological or metaphysical societies,

[1] *Ibid.*, pp. 96, 96–97, 97.

leaving each man free to support the religion and the system of instruction which he prefers. . . .

Government and Popular Sovereignty.[1] But Positivism will have as beneficial an influence on public Order as on Liberty. It holds, in exact opposition to revolutionary prejudices, that the central power should preponderate over the local. The constitutionalist principle of separating the legislative from the executive is only an empirical imitation of the larger principle of separating temporal and spiritual power, which was adopted in the Middle Ages. There will always be a contest for political supremacy between the central and local authorities; and it is an error into which from various causes we have fallen recently, to attempt to balance them against each other. The whole tendency of French history has been to let the central power preponderate, until it degenerated and became retrograde towards the end of the seventeenth century. Our present preference for the local power is therefore an historical anomaly, which is sure to cease as soon as the fear of reaction has passed away. And as Republicanism secures us against any dangers of this kind, our political sympathies will soon resume their old course. The advantages of the central power are first that it is more directly responsible than the other; and secondly its increasingly practical character, which renders it more adapted to our essential needs and less disposed to set up any claims to spiritual influence. This last feature is of the highest importance, and is likely to become every day more marked. Whereas the local or legislative power, not having its functions clearly defined, is very apt to interfere in theoretical questions without being in any sense qualified for doing so. Its preponderance would then in most cases be injurious to intellectual freedom, which, as it feels instinctively, will ultimately result in the rise of a spiritual authority destined to supersede its own. . . .

Positivism whether looked at as a philosophical system or as an instrument of social renovation, cannot count upon much support from any of the classes, whether in Church or State, by whom the government of mankind has hitherto been conducted. There will be isolated exceptions of great value, and these will soon become more numerous; but the prejudices and passions of these classes will present serious obstacles to the work of moral and mental reorganisation which constitutes the second phase of the great Western revolution. Their

[1] *Ibid.*, pp. 98, 101–103, 106, 107–108.

faulty education and their repugnance to system prejudice them against a philosophy which subordinates specialties to general principles. Their aristocratic instincts make it very difficult for them to recognise the supremacy of Social Feeling; that doctrine which lies at the root of social regeneration, as conceived by Positivism. That no support can be expected from the classes who were in the ascendant before the Revolution, is of course obvious; and we shall probably meet with opposition, quite as real though more carefully concealed, from the middle classes, to whom that revolution transferred the authority and social influence which they had long been coveting. Their thoughts are entirely engrossed with the acquisition of power; and they concern themselves but little with the mode in which it is used, or the objects to which it is directed. They were quite convinced that the Revolution had found a satisfactory issue in the parliamentary system instituted during the recent period of political oscillation. They will long continue to regret that stationary period, because it was peculiarly favourable to their restless ambition. A movement tending to the complete regeneration of society is almost as much dreaded now by the middle classes as it was formerly by the higher. And both would at all events agree in prolonging, so far as republican institutions admitted, the system of theological hypocrisy, the only effective instrument of retrogression now left to them. This ignoble system offers the double attraction of securing respect and submission on the part of the masses, while imposing no unpleasant duties on their governors. All their critical and metaphysical prejudices indispose them to terminate the state of spiritual anarchy which is the greatest obstacle to social regeneration; while at the same time their ambition dreads the establishment of a new moral authority, the restrictive influence of which would of course press most heavily upon themselves. In the eighteenth century, men of rank, and even kings, accepted the purely negative philosophy that was then in vogue: it removed many obstacles, it was an easy path to reputation, and it imposed no great sacrifice. But we can hardly hope from this precedent that the wealthy and literary classes of our own time will be equally willing to accept Positive philosophy; the declared purpose of which is to discipline our intellectual powers, in order to reorganise our modes of life.

The avowal of such a purpose is quite sufficient to prevent Positivism from gaining the sympathies of any one of the governing classes. The classes to which it must appeal are those who have been left untrained in the present worthless methods of instruction by words and entities, who are animated with strong social instincts, and who consequently have the largest stock of good sense and good feeling. In a word it is among the working classes that the new philosophers will find their most energetic allies. The force necessary for social regeneration depends essentially on the combined action of those two extreme terms of the ultimate social order. Notwithstanding their difference of position, a difference which indeed is more apparent than real, there are strong affinities between them, both morally and intellectually. Both have the same sense of the real, the same preference for the useful, and the same tendency to subordinate special points to general principles. Morally they resemble each other in generosity of feeling, in wise unconcern for material prospects, and in indifference to worldly grandeur. This at least will be the case as soon as philosophers in the true sense of that word have mixed sufficiently with the nobler members of the working classes to raise their own character to its proper level. When the sympathies which unite them upon these essential points have had time to show themselves, it will be felt that the philosopher is, under certain aspects, a member of the working class fully trained; while the working man is in many respects a philosopher without the training. Both too will look with similar feelings upon the intermediate or capitalist class. As that class is necessarily the possessor of material power, the pecuniary existence of both will as a rule be dependent upon it. . . .

Positivism rejects the metaphysical doctrine of the Sovereignty of the people. But it appropriates all that is really sound in the doctrine, and this with reference not merely to exceptional cases but to the normal state; while at the same time it guards against the danger involved in its application as an absolute truth. In the hands of the revolutionary party the doctrine is generally used to justify the right of insurrection. Now in Positive Polity this right is looked upon as an ultimate resource with which no society should allow itself to dispense. . . .

The name of the whole body politic ought to be invoked in the announcement of any special measure of which the motives are sufficiently intelligible, and which directly concern the practical interests of the whole community. Under this head would be included decisions of law courts, declarations of war, etc. When society has reached the Positive state, and the sense of universal solidarity is more generally diffused, there will be even more significance and dignity in such expressions than there is now, because the name invoked will no longer be that of a special nation, but that of Humanity as a whole. It would be absurd however to extend this practice to those still more numerous cases where the people is incompetent to express any opinion, and has merely to adopt the opinion of superior officers who have obtained its confidence. This may be owing either to the difficulty of the question or to the fact of its application being indirect or limited. Such, for instance, would be enactments, very often of great importance, which deal with scientific principles; or again most questions relating to special professions or branches of industry. In all these cases popular good sense would under Positivist influence easily be kept clear from political illusions. It is only under the stimulus of metaphysical pride that such illusions become dangerous; and the untaught masses have but little experience of this feeling. . . .

Private Property and the Control of Industry.[1] The peculiar reality of Positivism, and its invariable tendency to concentrate our intellectual powers upon social questions, form a twofold reason for its presentation in a systematic form of the spontaneous principle of Communism; namely, that Property is in its nature social, and that it needs control. . . .

But the agreement here pointed out between sociological science and the spontaneous inspirations of popular judgment, goes no farther. Positivists accept, and indeed very much enlarge, the programme of Communism; but we reject its practical solution on the ground that it is at once inadequate and subversive. The chief difference between our own solution and theirs is that we substitute moral agencies for political. . . .

The ignorance of the true laws of social life under which Communists labour is evident in their dangerous tendency to suppress individuality. Not only do they ignore the inherent preponderance in our nature of the personal instincts; but they forget that, in the collective Organism, the separation of functions is a feature no less essential than the co-operation of functions. . . .

There is another point in which Communism is equally inconsistent with the laws of Sociology. Acting under false views of the constitution of our modern industrial system, it proposes to remove its directors, who form so essential a part of it. An army can no more exist without officers than without soldiers; and this elementary truth holds good of

[1] *Ibid.*, pp. 123, 125, 126, 127–128, 130, 130–131, 132, 133–134, 134, 135–136.

Industry as well as of War. The organisation of modern industry has not been found practicable as yet; but the germ of such organisation lies unquestionably in the division which has arisen spontaneously between Capitalist and Workman. No great works could be undertaken if each worker were also to be a director, or if the management, instead of being fixed, were entrusted to a passive and irresponsible body. It is evident that under the present system of industry there is a tendency to a constant enlargement of undertakings: each fresh step leads at once to still further extension. Now this tendency, so far from being opposed to the interests of the working classes, is a condition which will most seriously facilitate the real organisation of our material existence, as soon as we have a moral authority competent to control it. For it is only the larger employers that the spiritual power can hope to penetrate with a strong and habitual sense of duty to their subordinates. Without a sufficient concentration of material power, the means of satisfying the claims of morality would be found wanting, except at such exorbitant sacrifices, as would be soon found incompatible with all industrial progress. This is the weak point of every plan of reform which limits itself to the mode of acquiring power, whether public power or private, instead of aiming at controlling its use in whosever hands it may be placed. It leads to a waste of those forces which, when rightly used, form our principal resource in dealing with grave social difficulties.

The motives, therefore, from which modern Communism has arisen, however estimable, lead at present, in the want of proper scientific teaching, to a very wrong view both of the nature of the disease and of its remedy. A heavier reproach against it is that in one point it shows a manifest insufficiency of social instinct. Communists boast of their spirit of social union: but they limit it to the union of the present generation, stopping short of historical continuity, which yet is the principal characteristic of Humanity. When they have matured their moral growth, and have followed out in Time that connection which at present they only recognise in Space, they will at once see the necessity of these general conditions which at present they would reject. They will understand the importance of inheritance, as the natural means by which each generation transmits to its successor the result of its own labours and the means of improving them. The necessity of inheritance, as far as the community is concerned, is evident, and its extension to the individual is an obvious consequence. But whatever reproaches Communists may deserve in this respect are equally applicable to all the other progressive sects. They are all pervaded by an anti-historic spirit, which leads them to conceive of Society as though it had no ancestors; and this, although their own ideas for the most part can have no bearing except upon posterity. . . .

Were it not that Communism is provisionally useful in antagonising other doctrines equally erroneous, it would have then, no real importance, except that due to the motives which originated it; since its practical solution is far too chimerical and subversive ever to obtain acceptance. Yet, from the high morality of these motives, it will probably maintain and increase its influence until our working men find that their wants can be more effectually satisfied by gentler and surer means. . . .

The remedy we seek must be almost entirely of a moral kind. This truth, based as it is on real knowledge of human nature, the people will soon come to feel instinctively. And here Communists are, without knowing it, preparing the way for the ascendancy of Positivism. They are forcing upon men's notice in the strongest possible way a problem to which no peaceable and satisfactory solution can be given, except by the new philosophy.

That philosophy, disregarding all useless and irritating discussions as to the origin of wealth and the extent of its possession, proceeds at once to the moral rules which should regulate it as a social function. The distribution of power among men, of material power especially, lies so far beyond our means of intervention, that to set it before us as our main object to rectify the defects of the natural order in this respect, would be to waste our short life in barren and interminable disputes. The chief concern of the public is that power, in whosever hands it may be placed, should be exercised for their benefit; and this is a point to which we may direct our efforts with far greater effect. Besides, by regulating the employment of wealth, we do, indirectly, modify its tenure; for the mode in which wealth is held has some secondary influence over the right use of it.

The regulations required should be moral, not political, in their source; general, not special, in their application. Those who accept them will do so of their own free will, under the influence of their education. Thus their obedience, while steadily maintained, will have, as Aristotle long ago observed, the merit of voluntary action. By converting private property into a public function, we would subject it to no tyrannical interference; for this, by the destruction of free impulse and responsibility would prove most deeply degrading to man's character. Indeed, the comparison of proprietors with public functionaries will frequently be applied in the inverse sense; with the view, that is, of strengthening the latter rather than of weakening the former. . . .

Positivism being more pacific and more efficacious than Communism, because more true, is also broader and more complete in its solution of great social problems. The superficial view of property, springing too often from envious motives, which condemns Inheritance because it admits of possession without labour, is not subversive merely, but narrow. From the moral point of view we see at once the radical weakness of these empirical reproaches. They show blindness to the fact that this mode of transmitting wealth is really that which is most likely to call out the temper requisite for its right employment. It saves the mind and the heart from the mean and sordid habits which are so often engendered by slow accumulation of capital. The man who is born to wealth is more likely to feel the wish respected. And thus those whom we are inclined to condemn as idlers may very easily become the most useful of the rich classes, under a wise reorganisation of opinions and habits. Of course too, since with the advance of Civilisation the difficulty of living without industry increases, the class that we are speaking of becomes more and more exceptional. In every way, then, it is a most serious mistake to wish to upset society on account of abuses which are already in course of removal, and which admit of conversion to a most beneficial purpose. . . .

The method which is peculiar to Positivism of solving our great social problems by moral agencies, will be found applicable also to the settlement of industrial disputes, so far as the popular claims involved are well founded. These claims will thus become clear from all tendency to disorder, and will consequently gain immensely in force; especially when they are seen to be consistent with principles which are freely accepted by all, and when they are supported by a philosophic body of known impartiality and enlightenment. This spiritual power, while impressing on the people the duty of respecting their temporal leaders, will impose duties upon these latter, which they will find impossible to evade. As all classes will have received a common education, they will all alike be penetrated with the general principles on which these special obligations will rest. And these weapons, derived from no source but that of feeling and reason, and aided solely by public opinion, will wield an influence over practical life, of which nothing in the present day can give any conception. . . .

This is the only real solution of the disputes that are so constantly arising between workmen and their employers. Both parties will look to this philosophic authority as a supreme court of arbitration. . . .

True spiritual power confines itself to giving counsel: it never commands. But in such cases, unless the advice given by the philosophers has been wrong, the suspension of work is not likely to be sufficiently general to bring about any important result.

This theory of trade-unions is, in fact, in the industrial world, what the power of insurrection is with regard to the higher social functions; it is an ultimate resource which every collective organism must reserve. The principle is the same in the simpler and more ordinary cases as in the more unusual and important. In both the intervention of the philosophic body, whether solicited or not, whether its purpose be to organise legitimate but empirical efforts or to repress them, will largely influence the result.

We are now in a position to state with more precision the main practical difference between the policy of Positivism, and that of Communism or of Socialism. All progressive political schools agree in concentrating their attention upon the problem, How to give the people their proper place as a component element of modern Society, which ever since the Middle Ages has been tending more and more distinctly to its normal mode of existence. They also agree that the two great requirements of the working classes are, the organisation of Education, and the organisation of Labour. But here their agreement ends. When the means of effecting these two objects have to be considered, Positivists find themselves at issue with all other progressive schools. They maintain that the organisation of Industry must be based upon the organisation of Education, whereas it is commonly supposed that both may be begun simultaneously, or indeed that Labour may be organised irrespectively of Education. It may seem as if we are making too much of a mere question of arrangement; yet the difference is one which affects the whole character and method of social reconstruction. The plan usually followed is simply a repetition of the old attempt to reconstruct politically, without waiting for spiritual reconstruction: in other words, to raise the social edifice before its intellectual and moral foundations have been laid. Hence the attempts made to satisfy popular requirements by measures of a purely political kind, because they appear to meet the evil directly; a course as useless as it is destructive. Positivism, on the contrary, substitutes for such agencies an influence which is sure and peaceful, although it be gradual and indirect; the influence of a more enlightened morality, supported by a purer state of Public Opinion; such opinion being organised by competent minds, and diffused freely amongst the people. In fact, the whole question, whether the solution of the twofold problem before us is to be empirical, revolutionary, and therefore confined simply to France; or whether it is to be consistent, pacific, and applicable to the whole of Western Europe, depends upon the precedence or the postponement of the organisation of Labour to the organisation of Education. . . .

Education.[1] A system of education, if it deserve the name, presupposes the acceptance of a definite philosophical and social creed to determine its character and purpose. Children cannot be brought up in convictions contrary to those of their parents, or indeed without their parents' assistance. . . . Until some universal faith has been accepted on its own merits, all attempts made by Government to reform education must necessarily be reactionary; since they will always be based on some one of the retrogressive creeds which it is our object to supersede altogether.

It is with adults, then, that we must deal. We must endeavour to disseminate systematic convictions among them, and thus open the door to a real reform of education for the next generation. The press and the power of free speech offer many ways of bringing about this result, the most important being a more or less connected series of popular lectures on the various positive sciences, including history, which henceforth takes its place among them. Now for these lectures to produce their full effect, they must, even when treating of the most elementary point in mathematics, be thoroughly philosophic and consequently animated by a social spirit. They must be entirely independent of government, so as not to be hampered by any of the authorised views. Lastly, there is a condition in which all the rest are summed up. These lectures should be Occidental, not simply National. What we require is a free association of philosophers throughout Western Europe, formed by the voluntary coöperation of all who can contribute efficiently to this great preliminary work; their services being essentially gratuitous. It is a result which no system but Positivism is capable of effecting. By its agency that coalition between philosophers and the working classes, on which so much depends, will speedily be established.

[1] *Ibid.*, pp. 146, 147–148.

While the work of propagating Positivist convictions is going on in the free and unrestricted manner here described, the spiritual authority will at the same time be forming itself, and will be prepared to make use of these convictions as the basis for social regeneration. Thus the transitional state will be brought as nearly as possible into harmony with the normal state; and this the more in proportion as the natural affinity between philosophers and workmen is brought out more distinctly. The connection between Positivist lectures and Positivist clubs will illustrate my meaning. While the lectures prepare the way for the Future, the clubs work in the same direction by judging the Past, and advising for the Present; so that we have at once a beginning of the three essential functions of the new spiritual power. . . .

Moral Attitude of the Working Man.[1] The workman must learn to look upon himself, morally, as a public servant, with functions of a special and also of a general kind. Not that he is to receive his wages for the future from the State, instead of from a private hand. The present plan is perfectly well adapted to all services which are so direct and definite, that a common standard of value can be at once applied to them. Only let it be understood that the service is not sufficiently recompensed, without the social feeling of gratitude towards the agent that performs it, a feeling that is recognised already in the so-called liberal professions, where the client or patient is not dispensed from gratitude by payment of his fee. In this respect the republican instincts of the Convention have instinctively anticipated the teaching of philosophy. They valued the workman's labour at its true worth. Workmen have only to imagine labour suppressed or even suspended in the trade to which they may belong, to see its importance to the whole fabric of modern society. Their general functions as a class, the function of forming public opinion, and of supporting the action of the spiritual power, it is of course less easy for them to understand at present. But, as I have already shown, it follows so naturally from their character and position, and corresponds so perfectly with their requirements as a class, that they cannot fail to appreciate its importance when the course of events allows and indeed compels them to bring it into play. The only danger lies in their insisting on the possession of what metaphysicians call political rights, and in engaging in useless discussions about the

[1] *Ibid.*, pp. 153–154, 155, 155–156.

distribution of power, instead of fixing their attention on the manner in which it is used. . . .

For the people to rise to the true level of their position, they have only to develope and cultivate certain dispositions which already exist in them spontaneously. And the most important of these is absence of ambition for wealth or rank. Political metaphysicians would say that the sole object of the Great Revolution was to give the working classes easier access to political and civil power. But this, though it should always be open to them, is very far from meeting their true wants. Individuals among them may be benefited by it, but the mass is left unaffected, or rather is placed often in a worse position, by the desertion of the more energetic members. . . .

The monied classes, under the influence of blind routine, have lent their aid to this degrading policy, by continually preaching to the people the necessity of saving; a precept which is indeed incumbent on their own class, but not on others. Without saving, capital could not be accumulated and administered; it is therefore of the highest importance that the monied classes should be as economical as possible. But in other classes, and especially in those dependent on fixed wages, parsimonious habits are uncalled for and injurious; they lower the character of the labourer, while they do little or nothing to improve his physical condition; and neither the working classes nor their teachers should encourage them. Both the one and the other will find their truest happiness in keeping clear of all serious practical responsibility, and in allowing free play to their mental and moral faculties in public as well as private life. In spite of the Economists, savings-banks are regarded by the working classes with unmistakeable repugnance. And the repugnance is justifiable; they do harm morally, by checking the exercise of generous feelings. Again, it is the fashion to declaim against wine-shops; and yet, after all, they are at present the only places where the people can enjoy society. Social instincts are cultivated there which deserve our approval far more than the self-helping spirit which draws men to the savings-bank. No doubt this unconcern for money, wise as it is, involves real personal risk; but it is a danger which civilisation is constantly tending to diminish, without effacing qualities which do the workmen honour, and which are the source of its most cherished pleasures. The danger ceases when the mental and moral faculties are called into stronger exercise. The interest which Positivism will arouse among the people in public questions, will lead to the substitution of the club for the wine-shop.

In these questions, the generous inspirations of popular instinct hold out a model which philosophers will do well to follow themselves. Fondness for money is as much a disqualification for the spiritual government of Humanity, as political ambition. It is a clear proof of moral incompetence, which is generally connected in one way or other with intellectual feebleness. . . .

Transitional Dictatorship of the Proletariat.[1] All the views brought forward in this chapter bear out the statement with which it began, that the Proletariate forms the principal basis of the social system, not merely as finally constituted, but in its present state of transition; and admitting this, the present state will be seen to have no essential difference from the normal future to which it tends. The principal conditions of our transitional policy were described at the conclusion of the last chapter. The best security for them is to be found in the natural tendencies of the people of Western Europe and especially of France. Our governors will do well to follow these tendencies instead of attempting to lead them; for they are in perfect keeping with the two great requirements of the present time, Liberty and Public Order.

The freedom of thought and speech, which is enjoyed in France to an extent impossible in any other country, is due principally to the intellectual emancipation of French and especially of Parisian workmen. They have rid themselves of theology in all its forms, and yet have not accepted any metaphysical system. At the same time, though totally devoid at present of systematic convictions, there is in them a submissiveness of mind which predisposes them to receive convictions combining reality with utility. In all other classes there is a tendency to use forcible measures in support of doctrines that cannot hold their ground against discussion. It is only to the people that philosophers can look for the support and extension of Liberty, which is so essential to their objects; and from this they derive moral confidence far more reassuring than any legal security. However reactionary or stationary the views of particular leaders or sects may be, with such a population as that of Paris no real oppression is possible. Of all the claims which France has to the leadership of Europe, this is the strongest. The resistance which is still offered to freedom of association and freedom of education will soon be overcome by the force of its liberal sympathies. A population of such strong social feeling as

[1] *Ibid.*, pp. 158–161.

ours will certainly not allow itself to be permanently deprived of the power of meeting together freely in clubs; institutions most conducive both to its culture and to the protection of its interests. It will insist with equal force upon perfect liberty of teaching, feeling deeply the need of solid instruction, and the incapacity of metaphysicians and theologians to give it. Without popular pressure, the essential conditions of educational liberty will always be evaded.

And if Liberty depends upon popular support, Public Order, whether at home or abroad, depends upon it no less. The inclinations of the working classes are altogether on the side of peace. Their strong dislike of war is the principal reason of the present remarkable tranquillity of Europe. The foolish regret expressed by all the retrograde parties for the decline of the military spirit is a sufficient indication of what the popular feeling is; but even more significant is the necessity for compulsory enlistment, which began in France and has extended to other parts of Europe. There has been much factitious indignation on the subject, but at least it must be allowed, that in our armies, the officers are the only volunteers. Again, the working class is more free than any other from international prejudices, which still disunite the great family of Western nations, although they are very much weaker than formerly. They are strongest in the middle classes, a fact principally due to industrial competition. But working men feel how similar their wants and their conditions are in all countries, and this feeling checks their animosity. And the consciousness of union will become far stronger, now that the great social problem of their incorporation into modern society is being raised everywhere. No errors that statesmen can commit, whether in matters of war or peace, can prevent this from becoming the preponderating question in every European country; and thus it tends to preserve their mutual concord.

Popular sympathies of this sort are no doubt less conducive to internal tranquillity than to pacific foreign relations. But the alarm which is naturally aroused by the spiritual anarchy around us must not blind us to the real guarantees for Order which popular tendencies, rightly interpreted, hold out. It is to the people that we must look for the ascendancy of central over local power, which, as we have seen, is so indispensable to public order. The executive authority, provided only that it gives no cause to fear reaction, will always have their support when opposed by an assembly the prevalent tendencies of which will usually be adverse to their interests. They will always turn instinctively to the dictatorial rather than to the parliamentary branch of the administration; feeling that from its practical character and the directness of its action, it is more likely to meet their wants. Barren discussions on constitutional questions may suit ambitious members of the middle classes, by facilitating their arrival to power. But the people take very little interest in all this unmeaning agitation, and often treat it with merited contempt, knowing that it can be of no use to them, and that its only result is to evade their real wants by undermining the only authority that can do them justice. Consequently the people are certain to give their support to every government that deserves it; especially in France, where political passions have already yielded to the superior and more permanent interest of social questions. And while strengthening the central power, they may do much to elevate its character by confining it strictly to its practical function, and resisting any attempts that it may make to interfere with opinion. In all these respects the spontaneous influence of the working classes will be of material assistance in carrying out the systematic conceptions of social philosophy.

But a more striking proof of the political influence to be exercised by the people is this. The dictatorship which our transitional policy requires, as long as the spiritual interregnum lasts, must arise in the first instance from their ranks.

In the word *People*, especially in the French language, there is a fortunate ambiguity, which may serve to remind us that the proletariate class is not, properly speaking, a class at all, but constitutes the body of society. From it proceed the various special classes, which we may regard as organs necessary to that body. Since the abolition of royalty, the last remnant of caste, our political leaders have been recruited, for the most part, from the working class. In the normal state, however, it will be required as a preliminary condition, that the holder of dictatorial power shall have first received the political training which is given by the exercise of authority in his own business. In a settled state of society, Government, strictly so called, is a mere extension of civil influence. Ultimately, therefore, political power will fall into the hands of the great leaders of industry. Unworthy as they seem of it at present they will gradually become less so as spiritual reorganisation proceeds; and besides, the tenure of power will become less burdensome, because it will be confined to duties of a purely practical kind.

As yet, however, the case is very different; and therefore the wealthy, though ultimately they will be the administrators of power, are not those to whom it should as a rule be entrusted in our present condition. Special departments may be given to them with advantage, as we have seen proved recently, and that in cases where the functions to be performed had no relation whatever to industrial skill. But they are not competent as yet for dictatorial power, the power which has to supply the place of royalty. Individual exceptions of course there may be, though none have appeared hitherto, and at least they are not enough for our provisional system to rely on. As yet the wealthy classes have shown themselves too debased in thought and feeling for an office of such importance. Nor do we find greater aptitude for it outside the industrial class. Scientific men are most assuredly unfit for it, especially in France, where the system of Academies has narrowed the mind, withered the feelings, and enervated the character to such an extent, that most of them fail in the conduct of common life, and are utterly unworthy of the smallest post of authority, even in their own department.

All other classes failing us, we have to look to the working class, which has been left more free to form broad views, and in which the sense of duty has been better cultivated. On historical grounds I feel convinced that the workmen of France are more likely than any other class to supply men competent for supreme power, as long as the spiritual interregnum lasts; that is, for at least one generation. . . .

XVIII

JOHN STUART MILL

1806–1873

John Stuart Mill was born into the bosom of Utilitarianism [1] in 1806. His father, James Mill, the friend and propagandist of Jeremy Bentham, lost no time in preparing the child to carry on the doctrinal succession. Indeed, the most remarkable feature of John Stuart's career was, in his own opinion, his education. At the age of three he began the study of Greek—Latin was put off until he was eight—and at thirteen he could look back upon a record of performances in the classics, history, logic, and science that might have made him forever insufferable. But the provident James Mill had foreseen this possibility. "He wound up by saying that whatever I knew more than others, could not be ascribed to any merit in me but to the very unusual advantage which had fallen to my lot, of having a father who was able to teach me, and willing to give the necessary trouble and time." Conceit was permanently banished from John Stuart's make-up. But his independence of judgment was not impaired, and he lived to disagree with some of the most cherished dogmas of his elders. Nor was Mill blind to his father's personal defects; for example, James Mill reared a family out of all proportion to his income. That he later preached Malthusianism did not absolve him in the eyes of his son: John Stuart had to toil at the education of the younger children, a task he "greatly disliked." This experience may have tempered his natural optimism—at any rate he always felt that overpopulation might impede social progress. He himself had no children.

But the worst of James Mill's financial troubles ended when he obtained a responsible post in the London headquarters of the British East India Company. John Stuart had begun to study law, but at seventeen gave it up to take a clerkship in his father's office. His future was well provided for; he advanced steadily and when the company was dissolved in 1858 retired as head of the office on a pension of £1,500 a year. The occupation suited him more particularly because it left him ample time to pursue his own studies.

[1] The word was not used to designate the group until Mill so applied it in 1822.

At the beginning these made him a thoroughgoing Utilitarian. His first published writing was a letter defending one of his father's economic theories, and in 1825 he edited, filled out, and in part rewrote Bentham's *Treatise upon Evidence*, a remarkable effort for a boy not yet twenty. Very shortly, however, he began to question some of the Benthamite doctrines. A nervous disorder, probably brought on by overwork, induced a spiritual crisis which he compared to a religious conversion. He came to believe that the elder Utilitarians had too much neglected the realm of the feelings and the force of conscience as a motive for action. A reading of Marmontel, Wordsworth, Coleridge, and Goethe strengthened the conviction. About 1830 also he became acquainted with the Saint-Simonians and Auguste Comte. The effect was to broaden and humanize Mill's philosophy. A series of articles in 1831 led Carlyle to believe he had discovered a "new mystic." But this was reading too much into Mill's conversion; on personal acquaintance, Carlyle saw with regret that the core of Mill's Utilitarianism remained. Mill also gained in breadth of view from his friendship with Mrs. Taylor which began in 1831. Their relations were completely innocent, but as the lady happened to be married Mill's intimacy aroused a good deal of criticism. It seemed impossible to satisfy everyone, for when he married Mrs. Taylor in 1851, a year or two after the death of her husband, his mother and sisters refused to be reconciled to it. Mill's extraordinary interest in the "emancipation" of women dates from this friendship.

As early as 1822 Mill had formed a society to discuss and criticize the applications of Benthamism and during the 1830's he was a leading figure among the "Philosophical Radicals," a small but influential group most of whom were members of Parliament. Mill had charge of the party organ, the *London Review* (later merged with the *Westminster*) to which he contributed numerous articles and reviews.

His first book, the *Logic*, appeared in 1843. Its great success was matched in 1848 by that of the *Political Economy*. In the latter Mill combined the remains of his earlier individualism (and this perhaps predominated) with the enlarged social views of his maturer years. At least three short works of the later period have become classics: the essay on *Liberty* (1859), *Considerations on Representative Government* (1860), and *Utilitarianism* (1863). It has been said that these contain the essence of his political and social views.

Mill sat in Parliament for three years (1865–68). He was elected purely on his reputation, and made no effort to court his constituents either before or after election. This policy won and also lost him his seat. His supporters were indulgent at the beginning but by 1868 many of them had been alienated by his attacks on Governor Eyre for cruelties to the negroes in Jamaica, his advocacy of proportional representation, and his support of Bradlaugh, the atheistic working-class candidate. In Parliament his speeches though excellent in form were marred by poor delivery. Nevertheless he won universal respect in the House of Commons, and the leaders of the Liberal party, Gladstone and Bright, attached weight to his opinions. The last five years of his life were spent in writing. He died and was buried in France, at Avignon, in 1873.

Mill widened the scope of economic and political theory in England. In his hands it became at once more human and more humane—that is, cognizant of social forces that had been outside the range of earlier nineteenth-century doctrine. He remained, it is true, an individualist, and upheld private property on the ground of expediency. But to the conservative eye his individualism looked strangely like socialism. Certainly the existing state of affairs had, in his opinion, little to recommend it, and he did not hesitate to say that even communism was preferable.

REFERENCES

Mill's writings have been much reprinted. The most recent edition of his *Political Economy* is by Sir W. J. Ashley (1909).

For critical and expository accounts of Mill's work, see L. Stephen, *The English Utilitarians* (1900), Vol. III; E. Neff, *Carlyle and Mill* (1926); J. West, *John Stuart Mill* (Fabian Tract No. 168, 1913); W. L. Davidson, *Political Thought in England: the Utilitarians* (no date).

A complete text of the *Autobiography*, from the original manuscript, was published in 1924. Aside from this admirable book, the most important life is by A. Bain (1882). Mill's *Letters* (ed. H. S. R. Elliot, 1910) throw additional light on the development of his ideas.

READINGS FROM

PRINCIPLES OF POLITICAL ECONOMY

Distribution of Wealth Controllable by Society.[1] The principles which have been set forth in the first part of this treatise,[2] are, in certain respects, strongly distinguished from those on the considera-

[1] Pp. 199, 200. W. J. Ashley, editor, 1909. The text is that of the 7th ed. (1871), the last one revised by Mill.

[2] Part I deals with the Production of Wealth. (Editor.)

tion of which we are now about to enter. The laws and conditions of the Production of wealth partake of the character of physical truths. There is nothing optional or arbitrary in them. Whatever mankind produce, must be produced in the modes, and under the conditions, imposed by the constitution of external things, and by the inherent properties of their own bodily and mental structure. Whether they like it or not, their productions will be limited by the amount of their previous accumulation, and, that being given, it will be proportional to their energy, their skill, the perfection of their machinery, and their judicious use of the advantages of combined labour. Whether they like it or not, a double quantity of labour will not raise, on the same land, a double quantity of food, unless some improvement takes place in the processes of cultivation. Whether they like it or not, the unproductive expenditure of individuals will *pro tanto* tend to impoverish the community, and only their productive expenditure will enrich it. The opinions, or the wishes, which may exist on these different matters, do not control the things themselves. . . .

It is not so with the Distribution of wealth. That is a matter of human institution solely. The things once there, mankind, individually or collectively, can do with them as they like. They can place them at the disposal of whomsoever they please, and on whatever terms. Further, in the social state, in every state except total solitude, any disposal whatever of them can only take place by the consent of society, or rather of those who dispose of its active force. Even what a person has produced by his individual toil, unaided by any one, he cannot keep, unless by the permission of society. Not only can society take it from him, but individuals could and would take it from him, if society only remained passive; if it did not either interfere *en masse*, or employ and pay people for the purpose of preventing him from being disturbed in the possession. The distribution of wealth, therefore, depends on the laws and customs of society. The rules by which it is determined are what the opinions and feelings of the ruling portion of the community make them, and are very different in different ages and countries; and might be still more different, if mankind so chose. . . .

Private Property and Its Critics.[1] We proceed, then, to the consideration of the different modes of distributing the produce of land and labour, which have been adopted in practice, or may be

[1] *Ibid.*, pp. 201, 203–204, 208–211, 212, 213, 214, 215–217, 218–220.

conceived in theory. Among these, our attention is first claimed by that primary and fundamental institution, on which, unless in some exceptional and very limited cases, the economical arrangements of society have always rested, though in its secondary features it has varied, and is liable to vary. I mean, of course, the institution of individual property.

Private property, as an institution, did not owe its origin to any of those considerations of utility, which plead for the maintenance of it when established. Enough is known of rude ages, both from history and from analogous states of society in our own time, to show that tribunals (which always precede laws) were originally established, not to determine rights, but to repress violence and terminate quarrels. With this object chiefly in view, they naturally enough gave legal effect to first occupancy, by treating as the aggressor the person who first commenced violence, by turning, or attempting to turn, another out of possession. The preservation of the peace, which was the original object of civil government, was thus attained: while by confirming, to those who already possessed it, even what was not the fruit of personal exertion, a guarantee was incidentally given to them and others that they would be protected in what was so. . . .

The assailants of the principle of individual property may be divided into two classes: those whose scheme implies absolute equality in the distribution of the physical means of life and enjoyment, and those who admit inequality, but grounded on some principle, or supposed principle, of justice or general expediency, and not, like so many of the existing social inequalities, dependent on accident alone. At the head of the first class, as the earliest of those belonging to the present generation, must be placed Mr. Owen and his followers. M. Louis Blanc and M. Cabet have more recently become conspicuous as apostles of similar doctrines (though the former advocates equality of distribution only as a transition to a still higher standard of justice, that all should work according to their capacity, and receive according to their wants). The characteristic name for this economical system is Communism, a word of continental origin, only of late introduced into this country. The word Socialism, which originated among the English Communists, and was assumed by them as a name to designate their own doctrine, is now [1849], on the Continent, employed in a larger sense; not necessarily implying Communism, or the entire abolition of private property, but applied to any system which requires that the land and the instruments of production should be the property, not of individuals, but of communities or associations, or of the government. Among such systems, the two of highest intellectual pretension are those which, from the names of their real or reputed authors, have been called St. Simonism and Fourierism; the former defunct as a system, but which during the few years of its public promulgation sowed the seeds of nearly all the Socialist tendencies which have since spread so widely in France: the second, still [1865] flourishing in the number, talent, and zeal of its adherents.

Whatever may be the merits or defects of these various schemes, they cannot be truly said to be impracticable. No reasonable person can doubt that a village community, composed of a few thousand inhabitants, cultivating in joint ownership the same extent of land which at present feeds that number of people, and producing by combined labour and the most improved processes the manufactured articles which they required, could raise an amount of production sufficient to maintain them in comfort; and would find the means of obtaining, and if need be, exacting, the quantity of labour necessary for this purpose, from every member of the association who was capable of work. . . .

If, therefore, the choice were to be made between Communism with all its chances, and the present [1852] state of society with all its sufferings and injustices; if the institution of private property necessarily carried with it as a consequence, that the produce of labour should be apportioned as we now see it, almost in an inverse ratio to the labour —the largest portions to those who have never worked at all, the next largest to those whose work is almost nominal, and so in a descending scale, the remuneration dwindling as the work grows harder and more disagreeable, until the most fatiguing and exhausting bodily labour cannot count with certainty on being able to earn even the necessaries of life; if this or Communism were the alternative, all the difficulties, great or small, of Communism would be but as dust in the balance. But to make the comparison applicable, we must compare Communism at its best, with the régime of individual property, not as it is, but as it might be made. The principle of private property has never yet had a fair trial in any country; and less so, perhaps, in this country than in some others. The social arrangements of modern Europe commenced from a distribution of property which was the result, not of just partition, or acquisition by industry, but of conquest and violence: and notwithstanding what industry has been doing for many centuries to modify the work of force, the system still retains many and large traces of its origin. The laws of property have never yet conformed to the principles on which the justification of private property rests. They have made property of things which never ought to be property, and absolute property where only a qualified property ought to exist. They have not held the balance fairly between human beings, but have heaped impediments upon some, to give advantage to others; they have purposely fostered inequalities, and prevented all from starting fair in the race. That all should indeed start on perfectly equal terms is inconsistent with any law of private property: but if as much pains as has been taken to aggravate the inequality of chances arising from the natural working of the principle, had been taken to temper that inequality by every means not subversive of the principle itself; if the tendency of legislation had been to favour the diffusion, instead of the concentration of wealth—to encourage the subdivision of the large masses, instead of striving to keep them together; the principle of individual property would have been found to have no necessary connexion with the physical and social evils which almost all Socialist writers assume to be inseparable from it.

Private property, in every defence made of it, is supposed to mean the guarantee to individuals of the fruits of their own labour and abstinence. The guarantee to them of the fruits of the labour and abstinence of others, transmitted to them without any merit or exertion of their own, is not of the essence of the institution, but a mere incidental consequence which, when it reaches a certain height, does not promote, but conflicts with, the ends which render private property legitimate. To judge of the final destination of the institution of property, we must suppose everything rectified which causes the institution to work in a manner opposed to that equitable principle, of proportion between remuneration and exertion, on which in every vindication of it that will bear the light it is assumed to be grounded. We must also suppose two conditions realized, without which neither Communism nor any other laws or institutions could make the condition of the mass of mankind other than degraded and miserable. One of these conditions is universal education; the other, a due limitation of the numbers of the community. With these there could be no poverty, even under the present social institutions: and these being supposed, the question of Socialism is not, as generally stated by Socialists, a question of flying to the sole refuge against the evils which now bear down humanity; but a mere question of comparative advantages, which futurity must determine. We are too ignorant either of what individual agency in its best form, or Socialism in its best form, can accomplish, to be qualified to decide which of the two will be the ultimate form of human society.

If a conjecture may be hazarded, the decision will probably depend mainly on one consideration, viz. which of the two systems is consistent with the greatest amount of human liberty and spontaneity. After the means of subsistence are assured, the next in strength of the personal wants of human beings is liberty; and (unlike the physical wants, which as civilization advances become more moderate and more amenable to control) it increases instead of diminishing in intensity as the intelligence and the moral faculties are more developed. The perfection both of social arrangements and of practical morality would be, to secure to all persons complete independence and freedom of action, subject to no restriction but that of not doing injury to others: and the education which taught or the social institutions which required them to exchange the control of their own actions for any amount of comfort or affluence, or to renounce liberty for the sake of equality, would deprive them of one of the most elevated characteristics of human nature. It remains to be discovered how far the preservation of this characteristic would be found compatible with the Communistic organization of society. No doubt this, like all the other objections to the Socialist schemes, is vastly exaggerated. The members of the association need not be required to live together more than they do now, nor need they be controlled in the disposal of their individual share of the produce, and of the probably large amount of leisure which, if they limited their production to things really worth producing, they would possess. Individuals need not be chained to an occupation, or to a particular locality. The restraints of Communism would be freedom in comparison with the present condition of the majority of the human race. The generality of labourers in this and most other countries have as little choice of occupation or freedom of locomotion, are practically as dependent on fixed rules and on the will of others, as they could be on any system short of actual slavery; to say nothing of the entire domestic subjection of one half the species, to which it is the signal honour of Owenism and most other forms of Socialism that they assign equal rights, in all respects, with those of the hitherto dominant sex. But it is not by comparison with the present bad state of society that the claims of Communism can be estimated; nor is it sufficient that it should promise greater personal and mental freedom than is now enjoyed by those who have not enough of either to deserve the name. The question is, whether there would be any asylum left for individuality of character; whether public opinion would not be a tyrannical yoke; whether the absolute dependence of each on all, and surveillance of each by all, would not grind all down into a tame uniformity of thoughts, feelings, and actions. This is already one of the glaring evils of the existing state of society, notwithstanding a much greater diversity of education and pursuits, and a much less absolute dependence of the individual on the mass, than would exist in the Communistic régime. No society in which eccentricity is a matter of reproach can be in a wholesome state. It is yet to be ascertained whether the Communistic scheme would be consistent with that multiform development of human nature, those manifold unlikenesses, that diversity of tastes and talents, and variety of intellectual points of view, which not only form a great part of the interest of human life, but by bringing intellects into stimulating collision, and by presenting to each innumerable notions that he would not have conceived of himself, are the mainspring of mental and moral progression. . . .

The two elaborate forms of non-communistic Socialism known as St. Simonism and Fourierism are totally free from the objections usually urged against Communism; and though they are open to others of their own, yet by the great intellectual power which in many respects distinguishes them, and by their large and philosophic treatment of some of the fundamental problems of society and morality, they may justly be counted among the most remarkable productions of the past and present age. . . .

The most skilfully combined, and with the greatest foresight of objections, of all the forms of Socialism, is that commonly known as Fourierism. This system does not contemplate the abolition of private property, nor even of inheritance; on the contrary, it avowedly takes into consideration, as an element in the distribution of the produce, capital as well as labour. . . .

This system, unlike Communism, does not, in theory at least, withdraw any of the motives to exertion which exist in the present state of society. On the contrary, if the arrangement worked according to the intentions of its contrivers, it would even strengthen those motives; since each person would have much more certainty of reaping individually the fruits of increased skill or energy, bodily or mental, than under the present social arrangements can be felt by any but those who are in the most advantageous positions, or to whom the chapter of accidents is more than ordinarily favourable. The Fourierists, however, have still another resource. They believe that they have solved the great and fundamental problem of rendering labour attractive. That this is not impracticable, they contend by very strong arguments; in particular by one which they have in common with the Owenites, viz., that scarcely any labour, however severe, undergone by human beings for the sake of subsistence, exceeds in intensity that which other human beings, whose subsistence is already provided for, are found ready and even eager to undergo for pleasure. This certainly is a most significant fact, and one from which the student in social philosophy may draw important instructions. But the argument founded on it may easily be stretched too far. If occupations full of discomfort and fatigue are freely pursued by many persons as amusements, who does not see that they are amusements exactly because they are pursued freely, and may be discontinued at pleasure? The liberty of quitting a position often makes the whole difference between its being painful and pleasurable. Many a person remains in the same town, street, or house from January to December, without a wish or a thought tending towards removal, who, if confined to that same place by the mandate of authority, would find the imprisonment absolutely intolerable. . . .

Even from so brief an outline, it must be evident that this system does no violence to any of the general laws by which human action, even in the present imperfect state of moral and intellectual cultivation, is influenced: and that it would be extremely rash to pronounce it incapable of success, or unfitted to realize a great part of the hopes founded on it by its partisans. With regard to this, as to all other varieties of Socialism, the thing to be desired, and to which they have a just claim, is opportunity of trial. They are all capable of being tried on a moderate scale, and at no risk, either personal or pecuniary, to any except those who try them. It is for experience to determine how far or how soon any one or more of the possible systems of community of property will be fitted to substitute itself for the "organization of industry" based on private ownership of land and capital. In the meantime we may, without attempting to limit the ultimate capabilities of human nature, affirm, that the political economist, for a considerable time to come, will be chiefly concerned with the conditions of existence and progress belonging to a society founded on private property and individual competition; and that the object to be principally aimed at, in the present stage of human improvement, is not the subversion of the system of individual property, but the improvement of it, and the full participation of every member of the community in its benefits. . . .

The institution of property, when limited to its essential elements, consists in the recognition, in each person, of a right to the exclusive disposal of what he or she have produced by their own exertions, or received either by gift or by fair agreement, without force or fraud, from those who produced it. The foundation of the whole is the right of producers to what they themselves have produced. It may be objected, therefore, to the institution as it now exists, that it recognises rights of property in individuals over things which they have not produced. For example (it may be said) the operatives in a manufactory create, by their labour and skill, the whole produce; yet, instead of its belonging to them, the law gives them only their stipulated hire, and transfers the produce to some one who has merely supplied the funds, without perhaps contributing anything to the work itself, even in the form of superintendence. The answer to this is, that the labour of manufacture is only one of the conditions which must combine for the production of the commodity. The labour cannot be carried on without materials and machinery, nor without a stock of necessaries provided in advance to maintain the labourers during the production. All these things are the fruits of previous labour. If the labourers were possessed of them, they would not need to divide the produce with any one; but while they have them not, an equivalent must be given to those who have, both for the antecedent labour, and for the abstinence by which the produce of that labour, instead of being expended on indulgences, has been reserved for this use. The capital may not have been, and in most cases was not, created by the labour and abstinence of the present possessor; but it was created by the labour and abstinence of some former person, who may indeed have been wrongfully dispossessed of it, but who, in the present age of the world, much more probably transferred his claims to the present capitalist by gift or voluntary contract: and the abstinence at least must have been continued by each successive owner, down to the present. If it be said, as it may with truth, that those who have inherited the savings of others have an advantage which they may have in no way deserved, over the industrious whose predecessors have not left them anything; I not only admit, but strenuously contend, that this unearned advantage should be curtailed, as much as is consistent with justice to those who thought fit to dispose of their savings by giving them to their descendants. But while it is true that the labourers are at a disadvantage compared with those whose predecessors have saved, it is also true that the labourers are far better off than if those predecessors had not saved. They share in the advantage, though not to an equal extent with the inheritors. The terms of coöperation between present labour and the fruits of past labour and saving, are a subject for adjustment between the two parties. Each is necessary to the other. The capitalists can do nothing without labourers, nor the labourers without capital. If the labourers compete for employment, the capitalists on their part compete for labour to the full extent of the circulating capital of the country. Competition is often spoken of as if it were necessarily a cause of misery and degradation to the labouring class; as if high wages were not precisely as much a product of competition as low wages. The remuneration of labour is as much the result of the law of competition in the United States, as it is in Ireland, and much more completely so than in England.

The right of property includes then, the freedom of acquiring by contract. The right of each to what he has produced implies a right to what has been produced by others, if obtained by their free consent; since the producers must either have given it from good will, or exchanged it for what they esteemed an equivalent, and to prevent them from doing so would be to infringe their right of property in the product of their own industry. . . .

Prospects and Methods of Social Improvement.[1] It must always have been seen, more or less distinctly, by political economists, that the increase of wealth is not boundless: that at the end of what they term the progressive state lies the stationary state, that all progress in wealth is but a postponement of this, and that each step in advance is an approach to it. We have now been led to recognise that this ultimate goal is at all times near enough to be fully in view; that we are always on the verge of it, and that if we have not reached it long ago, it is because the goal itself flies before us. The richest and most prosperous countries would very soon attain the stationary state, if no further improvements were made in the productive arts, and if there were a suspension of the overflow of capital from those countries into the uncultivated or ill-cultivated regions of the earth.

This impossibility of ultimately avoiding the stationary state—this irresistible necessity that the stream of human industry should finally

[1] *Ibid.*, pp. 746, 747–748, 749–750, 752–754, 757, 759–760, 763–764, 772–774, 783–784, 791–793, 793–794.

spread itself out into an apparently stagnant sea—must have been, to the political economists of the last two generations, an unpleasing and discouraging prospect; for the tone and tendency of their speculations goes completely to identify all that is economically desirable with the progressive state, and with that alone. . . .

The doctrine that, to however distant a time incessant struggling may put off our doom, the progress of society must "end in shallows and in miseries," far from being, as many people still believe, a wicked invention of Mr. Malthus, was either expressly or tacitly affirmed by his most distinguished predecessors, and can only be successfully combated on his principles. Before attention had been directed to the principle of population as the active force in determining the remuneration of labour, the increase of mankind was virtually treated as a constant quantity; it was, at all events, assumed that in the natural and normal state of human affairs population must constantly increase, from which it followed that a constant increase of the means of support was essential to the physical comfort of the mass of mankind. The publication of Mr. Malthus' *Essay* is the era from which better views of this subject must be dated; and notwithstanding the acknowledged errors of his first edition, few writers have done more than himself, in the subsequent editions, to promote these juster and more hopeful anticipations.

Even in a progressive state of capital, in old countries, a conscientious or prudential restraint on population is indispensable, to prevent the increase of numbers from outstripping the increase of capital, and the condition of the classes who are at the bottom of society from being deteriorated. Where there is not, in the people, or in some very large proportion of them, a resolute resistance to this deterioration—a determination to preserve an established standard of comfort—the condition of the poorest class sinks, even in a progressive state, to the lowest point which they will consent to endure. The same determination would be equally effectual to keep up their condition in the stationary state, and would be quite as likely to exist. Indeed, even now, the countries in which the greatest prudence is manifested in the regulating of population are often those in which capital increases least rapidly. Where there is an indefinite prospect of employment for increased numbers, there is apt to appear less necessity for prudential restraint. If it were evident that a new hand could not obtain employment but by displacing, or succeeding to, one already employed, the combined influences of prudence and public opinion might in some measure be relied on for restricting the coming generation within the numbers necessary for replacing the present. . . .

Those who do not accept the present very early stage of human improvement as its ultimate type, may be excused for being comparatively indifferent to the kind of economical progress which excites the congratulations of ordinary politicians; the mere increase of production and accumulation. For the safety of national independence it is essential that a country should not fall much behind its neighbours in these things. But in themselves they are of little importance, so long as either the increase of population or anything else prevents the mass of the people from reaping any part of the benefit of them. I know not why it should be matter of congratulation that persons who are already richer than any one needs to be, should have doubled their means of consuming things which give little or no pleasure except as representative of wealth; or that numbers of individuals should pass over, every year, from the middle classes into a richer class, or from the class of the occupied rich to that of the unoccupied. It is only in the backward countries of the world that increased production is still an important object: in those most advanced, what is economically needed is a better distribution, of which one indispensable means is a stricter restraint on population. Levelling institutions, either of a just or of an unjust kind, cannot alone accomplish it; they may lower the heights of society, but they cannot, of themselves, permanently raise the depths.

On the other hand, we may suppose this better distribution of property attained, by the joint effect of the prudence and frugality of individuals, and of a system of legislation favouring equality of fortunes, so far as is consistent with the just claim of the individual to the fruits, whether great or small, of his or her own industry. We may suppose, for instance . . ., a limitation of the sum which any one person may acquire by gift or inheritance to the amount sufficient to constitute a moderate independence. Under this twofold influence society would exhibit these leading features: a well-paid and affluent body of labourers; no enormous fortunes, except what were earned and accumulated during a single lifetime; but a much larger body of persons than at present, not only exempt from the coarser toils, but with sufficient leisure, both physical and mental, from mechanical details, to cultivate freely the graces of life, and afford examples of them to the classes less favourably circumstanced for their growth. . . .

Whether the aggregate produce [of industry] increases absolutely or not, is a thing in which, after a certain amount has been obtained, neither the legislator nor the philanthropist need feel any strong interest: but, that it should increase relatively to the number of those who share in it, is of the utmost possible importance; and this (whether the wealth of mankind be stationary, or increasing at the most rapid rate ever known in an old country), must depend on the opinions and habits of the most numerous class, the class of manual labourers.

When I speak, either in this place or elsewhere, of "the labouring classes," or of labourers as a "class," I use those phrases in compliance with custom, and as descriptive of an existing, but by no means a necessary or permanent, state of social relations. I do not recognise as either just or salutary, a state of society in which there is any "class" which is not labouring; any human beings, exempt from bearing their share of the necessary labours of human life, except those unable to labour, or who have fairly earned rest by previous toil. So long, however, as the great social evil exists of a non-labouring class, labourers also constitute a class, and may be spoken of, though only provisionally, in that character.

Considered in its moral and social aspect, the state of the labouring people has latterly been a subject of much more speculation and discussion than formerly; and the opinion that it is not now what it ought to be, has become very general. The suggestions which have been promulgated, and the controversies which have been excited, on detached points rather than on the foundations of the subject, have put in evidence the existence of two conflicting theories, respecting the social position desirable for manual labourers. The one may be called the theory of dependence and protection, the other that of self-dependence.

According to the former theory, the lot of the poor, in all things which affect them collectively, should be regulated *for* them, not *by* them. They should not be required or encouraged to think for themselves, or give to their own reflection or forecast an influential voice in the determination of their destiny. It is supposed to be the duty of the higher classes to think for them, and to take the responsibility of their lot, as the commander and officers of an army take that of the soldiers composing it. This function, it is contended, the higher classes should prepare themselves to perform conscientiously, and their whole demeanour should impress the poor with a reliance on it, in order that, while yielding passive and active obedience to the rules prescribed for them, they may resign themselves in all other respects to a trustful *insouciance*, and repose under the shadow of their protectors. The relation between rich and poor, according to this theory (a theory also applied to the relation between men and women) should be only partly authoritative; it should be amiable, moral, and sentimental: affectionate tutelage on the one side, respectful and grateful deference on the other. The rich should be *in loco parentis* to the poor, guiding and restraining them like children. Of spontaneous action on their part there should be no need. They should be called on for nothing but to do their day's work, and to be moral and religious. Their morality and religion should be provided for them by their superiors, who should see them properly taught it, and should do all that is necessary to ensure their being, in return for labour and attachment, properly fed, clothed, housed, spiritually edified, and innocently amused.

This is the ideal of the future, in the minds of those whose dissatisfaction with the Present assumes the form of affection and regret towards the Past.[1] Like other ideals, it exercises an unconscious influence on the opinions and sentiments of numbers who never consciously guide themselves by any ideal. It has also this in common with other ideals, that it has never been historically realised. It makes its appeal to our imaginative sympathies in the character of a restoration of the good times of our forefathers. But no times can be pointed out in which the higher classes of this or any other country performed a part even distantly resembling the one assigned to them in this theory. It is an idealization, grounded on the conduct and character of here and there an individual. All privileged and powerful classes, as such, have used their power in the interest of their own selfishness, and have indulged their self-importance in despising, and not in lovingly caring for, those who were, in their estimation, degraded, by being under the necessity of working for their benefit. I do not affirm that what has always been must always be, or that human improvement has no tendency to correct the intensely selfish feelings engendered by power; but though the evil may be lessened, it cannot be eradicated, until the power itself is withdrawn. This, at least, seems to me undeniable, that long before the superior classes could be sufficiently improved to govern in the tutelary manner supposed, the inferior classes would be too much improved to be so governed. . . .

[1] Carlyle's *Past and Present* had appeared in 1843. (Editor.)

It is on a far other basis that the well-being and well-doing of the labouring people must henceforth rest. The poor have come out of leading-strings, and cannot any longer be governed or treated like children. To their own qualities must now be commended the care of their destiny. . . .

It appears to me impossible but that the increase of intelligence, of education, and of the love of independence among the working classes, must be attended with the corresponding growth of the good sense which manifests itself in provident habits of conduct, and that population, therefore, will bear a gradually diminishing ratio to capital and employment. This most desirable result would be much accelerated by another change, which lies in the direct line of the best tendencies of the time; the opening of industrial occupations freely to both sexes. The same reasons which make it no longer necessary that the poor should depend on the rich, make it equally unnecessary that women should depend on men; and the least which justice requires is that law and custom should not enforce dependence (when the correlative protection has become superfluous) by ordaining that a woman, who does not happen to have a provision by inheritance, shall have scarcely any means open to her of gaining a livelihood, except as a wife and mother. Let women who prefer that occupation, adopt it; but that there should be no option, no other *carrière* possible for the great majority of women, except in the humbler departments of life, is a flagrant social injustice. The ideas and institutions by which the accident of sex is made the groundwork of an inequality of legal rights, and a forced dissimilarity of social functions, must ere long be recognised as the greatest hindrance to moral, social, and even intellectual improvement. On the present occasion I shall only indicate, among the probable consequences of the industrial and social independence of women, a great diminution of the evil of over-population. It is by devoting one-half of the human species to that exclusive function, by making it fill the entire life of one sex, and interweave itself with almost all the objects of the other, that the animal instinct in question is nursed into the disproportionate preponderance which it has hitherto exercised in human life. . . .

Hitherto there has been no alternative for those who lived by their labour, but that of labouring either each for himself alone, or for a master. But the civilizing and improving influences of association, and the efficiency and economy of production on a large scale, may be obtained without dividing the producers into two parties with hostile interests and feelings, the many who do the work being mere servants under the command of the one who supplies the funds, and having no interests of their own in the enterprise except to earn their wages with as little labour as possible. The speculations and discussions of the last fifty years, and the events of the last thirty, are abundantly conclusive on this point. If the improvement which even triumphant military despotism has only retarded, not stopped, shall continue its course, there can be little doubt that the *status* of hired labourers will gradually tend to confine itself to the description of work-people whose low moral qualities render them unfit for anything more independent: and that the relation of masters and work-people will be gradually superseded by partnership, in one of two forms: in some cases, association of the labourers with the capitalist; in others, and perhaps finally in all, association of labourers among themselves.

The first of these forms of association has long been practised, not indeed as a rule, but as an exception. In several departments of industry there are already cases in which every one who contributes to the work, either by labour or by pecuniary resources, has a partner's interest in it, proportional to the value of his contribution. It is already a common practice to remunerate those in whom peculiar trust is reposed, by means of a percentage on the profits: and cases exist in which the principle is, with excellent success, carried down to the class of mere manual labourers. . . .

The form of association, however, which if mankind continue to improve, must be expected in the end to predominate, is not that which can exist between a capitalist as chief, and work-people without a voice in the management, but the association of the labourers themselves on terms of equality, collectively owning the capital with which they carry on their operations, and working under managers elected and removable by themselves. So long as this idea remained in a state of theory, in the writings of Owen or of Louis Blanc, it may have appeared, to the common modes of judgment, incapable of being realized, and not likely to be tried unless by seizing on the existing capital, and confiscating it for the benefit of the labourers; which is even now imagined by many persons, and pretended by more, both in England and on the Continent, to be the meaning and purpose of Socialism. But there is a capacity of exertion and self-denial in the masses of mankind, which is never known but on the rare occasions on which it is appealed to in the name of some great idea or elevated sentiment. Such an appeal was made by the French Revolution of

1848. For the first time it then seemed to the intelligent and generous of the working classes of a great nation that they had obtained a government who sincerely desired the freedom and dignity of the many, and who did not look upon it as their natural and legitimate state to be instruments of production, worked for the benefit of the possessors of capital. Under this encouragement, the ideas sown by Socialist writers, of an emancipation of labour to be effected by means of association, throve and fructified; and many working people came to the resolution, not only that they would work for one another, instead of working for a master tradesman or manufacturer, but that they would also free themselves, at whatever cost of labour or privation, from the necessity of paying, out of the produce of their industry, a heavy tribute for the use of capital; that they would extinguish this tax, not by robbing the capitalists of what they or their predecessors had acquired by labour and preserved by economy, but by honestly acquiring capital for themselves. If only a few operatives had attempted this arduous task, or if, while many attempted it, a few only had succeeded, their success might have been deemed to furnish no argument for their system as a permanent mode of industrial organization. But, excluding all the instances of failure, there exist, or existed a short time ago, upwards of a hundred successful, and many eminently prosperous, associations of operatives in Paris alone, besides a considerable number in the departments. . . .

It is not in France alone that these associations have commenced a career of prosperity. To say nothing at present of Germany, Piedmont, and Switzerland (where the Konsum-Verein of Zürich is one of the most prosperous coöperative associations in Europe), England can produce cases of success rivalling even those which I have cited from France. Under the impulse commenced by Mr. Owen, and more recently propagated by the writings and personal efforts of a band of friends, chiefly clergymen and barristers, to whose noble exertions too much praise can scarcely be given, the good seed was widely sown; the necessary alterations in the English law of partnership were obtained from Parliament, on the benevolent and public-spirited initiative of Mr. Slaney; many industrial associations, and a still greater number of coöperative stores for retail purchases, were founded. Among these are already many instances of remarkable prosperity, the most signal of which are the Leeds Flour Mill, and the Rochdale Society of Equitable Pioneers. Of this last association, the most successful of all, the history has been written in a very interesting manner by Mr. Holyoake; and the notoriety which by this and other means has been given to facts so encouraging, is causing a rapid extension of associations with similar objects in Lancashire, Yorkshire, London, and elsewhere. . . .

Associations like those which we have described, by the very process of their success, are a course of education in those moral and active qualities by which alone success can be either deserved or attained. As asociations multiplied, they would tend more and more to absorb all work-people, except those who have too little understanding, or too little virtue, to be capable of learning to act on any other system than that of narrow selfishness. As this change proceeded, owners of capital would gradually find it to their advantage, instead of maintaining the struggle of the old system with work-people of only the worst description, to lend their capital to the associations; to do this at a diminishing rate of interest, and at last, perhaps, even to exchange their capital for terminable annuities. In this or some such mode, the existing accumulations of capital might honestly, and by a kind of spontaneous process, become in the end the joint property of all who participate in their productive employment: a transformation which, thus effected, (and assuming of course that both sexes participate equally in the rights and in the government of the association,) would be the nearest approach to social justice, and the most beneficial ordering of industrial affairs for the universal good, which it is possible at present to foresee.

I agree, then, with the Socialist writers in their conception of the form which industrial operations tend to assume in the advance of improvement; and I entirely share their opinion that the time is ripe for commencing this transformation, and that it should by all just and effectual means be aided and encouraged. But while I agree and sympathize with Socialists in this practical portion of their aims, I utterly dissent from the most conspicuous and vehement part of their teaching, their declamations against competition. With moral conceptions in many respects far ahead of the existing arrangements of society, they have in general very confused and erroneous notions of its actual working; and one of their greatest errors, as I conceive, is to charge upon competition all the economical evils which at present exist. They forget that wherever competition is not, monopoly is; and that monopoly, in all its forms, is the taxation of the industrious for the support of indolence, if not of plunder. They forget, too, that with the exception of competition among labourers, all other competition is for the benefit of the labourers, by cheapening the articles they consume; that competition even in the labour market is a source not of low but of high wages, wherever the competition *for* labour exceeds the competition *of* labour, as in America, in the colonies, and in the skilled trades; and never could be a cause of low wages, save by the overstocking of the labour market through the too great numbers of the labourers' families; while, if the supply of labourers is excessive, not even Socialism can prevent their remuneration from being low. Besides, if association were universal, there would be no competition between labourer and labourer; and that between association and association would be for the benefit of the consumers, that is, of the associations; of the industrious classes generally.

I do not pretend that there are no inconveniences in competition, or that the moral objections urged against it by Socialist writers, as a source of jealousy and hostility among those engaged in the same occupation, are altogether groundless. But if competition has its evils, it prevents greater evils. . . . .

Instead of looking upon competition as the baneful and anti-social principle which it is held to be by the generality of Socialists, I conceive that, even in the present state of society and industry, every restriction of it is an evil, and every extension of it, even if for the time injuriously affecting some class of labourers, is always an ultimate good. To be protected against competition is to be protected in idleness, in mental dulness; to be saved the necessity of being as active and as intelligent as other people; and if it is also to be protected against being underbid for employment by a less highly paid class of labourers, this is only where old custom, or local and partial monopoly, has placed some particular class of artizans in a privileged position as compared with the rest; and the time has come when the interest of universal improvement is no longer promoted by prolonging the privileges of a few. If the slop-sellers and others of their class have lowered the wages of tailors, and some other artizans, by making them an affair of competition instead of custom, so much the better in the end. What is now required is not to bolster up old customs, whereby limited classes of labouring people obtain partial gains which interest them in keeping up the present organization of society, but to introduce new general practices beneficial to all; and there is reason to rejoice at whatever makes the privileged classes of skilled artizans feel that they have the same interests, and depend for their remuneration on the same general causes, and must resort for the improvement of their condition to the same remedies, as the less fortunately circumstanced and comparatively helpless multitude. . . .

The Sphere of Government.[1] We have now reached the last part of our undertaking; the discussion, so far as suited to this treatise (that is, so far as it is a question of principle, not detail), of the limits of the province of government: the question, to what objects governmental intervention in the affairs of society may or should extend, over and above those which necessarily appertain to it. No subject has been more keenly contested in the present age: the contest, however, has chiefly taken place round certain select points, with only flying excursions into the rest of the field. Those indeed who have discussed any particular question of government interference, such as state education (spiritual or secular), regulation of hours of labour, a public provision for the poor, &c., have often dealt largely in general arguments, far outstretching the special application made of them, and have shown a sufficiently strong bias either in favour of letting things alone, or in favour of meddling; but have seldom declared, or apparently decided in their own minds, how far they would carry either principle. The supporters of interference have been content with asserting a general right and duty on the part of government to intervene, wherever its intervention would be useful: and when those who have been called the *laisser-faire* school have attempted any definite limitation of the province of government, they have usually restricted it to the protection of person and property against force and fraud; a definition to which neither they nor any one else can deliberately adhere, since it excludes . . . some of the most indispensable and unanimously recognized of the duties of government. . . .

We must set out by distinguishing between two kinds of intervention by the government, which, though they may relate to the same subject, differ widely in their nature and effects, and require, for their justification, motives of a very different degree of urgency. The intervention may extend to controlling the free agency of individuals. Government may interdict all persons from doing certain things; or from doing them without its authorization; or may prescribe to them certain things to be done, or a certain manner of doing things which it is left optional with them to do or to abstain from. This is the *authoritative* interference of government. There is another kind of intervention which is not authoritative: when a government, instead of issuing a

[1] *Ibid.*, pp. 941, 942–944, 944–945, 947, 948–949, 950.

command and enforcing it by penalties, adopts the course so seldom resorted to by governments, and of which such important use might be made, that of giving advice, and promulgating information; or when, leaving individuals free to use their own means of pursuing any object of general interest, the government, not meddling with them, but not trusting the object solely to their care, establishes, side by side with their arrangements, an agency of its own for a like purpose. Thus, it is one thing to maintain a Church Establishment, and another to refuse toleration to other religions, or to persons professing no religion. It is one thing to provide schools or colleges, and another to require that no person shall act as an instructor of youth without a government licence. There might be a national bank, or a government manufactory, without any monopoly against private banks and manufactories. There might be a post-office, without penalties against the conveyance of letters by other means. There may be a corps of government engineers for civil purposes, while the profession of a civil engineer is free to be adopted by every one. There may be public hospitals, without any restriction upon private medical or surgical practice.

It is evident, even at first sight, that the authoritative form of government intervention has a much more limited sphere of legitimate action than the other. It requires a much stronger necessity to justify it in any case; while there are large departments of human life from which it must be unreservedly and imperiously excluded. Whatever theory we adopt respecting the foundation of the social union, and under whatever political institutions we live, there is a circle around every individual human being which no government, be it that of one, of a few, or of the many, ought to be permitted to overstep: there is a part of the life of every person who has come to years of discretion, within which the individuality of that person ought to reign uncontrolled either by any other individual or by the public collectively. That there is, or ought to be, some space in human existence thus entrenched around, and sacred from authoritative intrusion, no one who professes the smallest regard to human freedom or dignity will call in question: the point to be determined is, where the limit should be placed; how large a province of human life this reserved territory should include. I apprehend that it ought to include all that part which concerns only the life, whether inward or outward, of the individual, and does not affect the interests of others, or affects them only through the moral influence of example. With respect to the domain of the inward consciousness, the thoughts and feelings, and as much of external conduct as is personal only, involving no consequences, none at least of a painful or injurious kind, to other people; I hold that it is allowable in all, and in the more thoughtful and cultivated often a duty, to assert and promulgate, with all the force they are capable of, their opinion of what is good or bad, admirable or contemptible, but not to compel others to conform to that opinion; whether the force used is that of extra-legal coercion, or exerts itself by means of the law.

Even in those portions of conduct which do affect the interest of others, the onus of making out a case always lies on the defenders of legal prohibitions. It is not a merely constructive or presumptive injury to others which will justify the interference of law with individual freedom. To be prevented from doing what one is inclined to, or from acting according to one's own judgment of what is desirable, is not only always irksome, but always tends, *pro tanto*, to starve the development of some portion of the bodily or mental faculties, either sensitive or active; and unless the conscience of the individual goes freely with the legal restraint, it partakes, either in a great or in a small degree, of the degradation of slavery. Scarcely any degree of utility, short of absolute necessity, will justify a prohibitory regulation, unless it can also be made to recommend itself to the general conscience; unless persons of ordinary good intentions either believe already, or can be induced to believe, that the thing prohibited is a thing which they ought not to wish to do. . . .

A second general objection to government agency is that every increase of the functions devolving on the government is an increase of its power, both in the form of authority, and still more, in the indirect form of influence. The importance of this consideration, in respect to political freedom, has in general been quite sufficiently recognized, at least in England; but many, in latter times, have been prone to think that limitation of the powers of the government is only essential when the government itself is badly constituted; when it does not represent the people, but is the organ of a class, or coalition of classes: and that a government of sufficiently popular constitution might be trusted with any amount of power over the nation, since its power would be only that of the nation over itself. This might be true, if the nation, in such cases, did not practically mean a mere majority of the nation, and if minorities were only capable of oppressing, but not of being oppressed. Experience, however, proves that the depositaries of power who are mere delegates of the people, that is of a majority, are quite as ready (when they think they can count on popular support) as any organs of oligarchy to assume arbitrary power, and encroach unduly on the liberty of private life. The public collectively is abundantly ready to impose, not only its generally narrow views of its interests, but its abstract opinions, and even its tastes, as laws binding upon individuals. And the present civilization tends so strongly to make the power of persons acting in masses the only substantial power in society, that there never was more necessity for surrounding individual independence of thought, speech, and conduct, with the most powerful defences, in order to maintain that originality of mind and individuality of character, which are the only source of any real progress, and of most of the qualities which make the human race much superior to any herd of animals. Hence it is no less important in a democratic than in any other government, that all tendency on the part of public authorities to stretch their interference, and assume a power of any sort which can easily be dispensed with, should be regarded with unremitting jealousy. Perhaps this is even more important in a democracy than in any other form of political society; because, where public opinion is sovereign, an individual who is oppressed by the sovereign does not, as in most other states of things, find a rival power to which he can appeal for relief, or, at all events, for sympathy.

A third general objection to government agency rests on the principle of the division of labour. Every additional function undertaken by the government is a fresh occupation imposed upon a body already overcharged with duties. A natural consequence is that most things are ill done; much not done at all, because the government is not able to do it without delays which are fatal to its purpose; that the more troublesome, and less showy, of the functions undertaken, are postponed or neglected, and an excuse is always ready for the neglect; while the heads of the administration have their minds so fully taken up with official details, in however perfunctory a manner superintended, that they have no time or thought to spare for the great interests of the state, and the preparation of enlarged measures of social improvement. . . .

Though a better organization of governments would greatly diminish the force of the objection to the mere multiplication of their duties, it would still remain true that in all the more advanced communities the great majority of things are worse done by the intervention of government, than the individuals most interested in the matter would do them, or cause them to be done, if left to themselves. The grounds of this truth are expressed with tolerable exactness in the popular dictum, that people understand their own business and their own interests better, and care for them more, than the government does, or can be expected to do. This maxim holds true throughout the greatest part of the business of life, and wherever it is true we ought to condemn every kind of government intervention that conflicts with it. The inferiority of government agency, for example, in any of the common operations of industry or commerce, is proved by the fact, that it is hardly ever able to maintain itself in equal competition with individual agency, where the individuals possess the requisite degree of industrial enterprise, and can command the necessary assemblage of means. All the facilities which a government enjoys of access to information; all the means which it possesses of remunerating, and therefore of commanding, the best available talent in the market—are not an equivalent for the one great disadvantage of an inferior interest in the result.

It must be remembered, besides, that even if a government were superior in intelligence and knowledge to any single individual in the nation, it must be inferior to all the individuals of the nation taken together. It can neither possess in itself, nor enlist in its service, more than a portion of the acquirements and capacities which the country contains, applicable to any given purpose. . . .

I have reserved for the last place one of the strongest of the reasons against the extension of government agency. Even if the government could comprehend within itself, in each department, all the most eminent intellectual capacity and active talent of the nation, it would not be the less desirable that the conduct of a large portion of the affairs of the society should be left in the hands of the persons immediately interested in them. The business of life is an essential part of the practical education of a people; without which, book and school instruction, though most necessary and salutary, does not suffice to qualify them for conduct, and for the adaptation of means to ends. Instruction is only one of the desiderata of mental improvement; another, almost as indispensable, is a vigorous exercise of the active energies; labour, contrivance, judgment, self-control: and the natural stimulus to these is the difficuties of life. This doctrine is not to be confounded with the complacent optimism, which represents the evils of life as desirable things, because they call forth qualities adapted to combat with evils. It is only because the difficulties exist, that the qualities which combat with them are of any value. As practical beings it is our business to free human life from as many as possible of its difficulties, and not to keep up a stock of them as hunters preserve game for the exercise of pursuing it. But since the need of active talent and practical judgment in the affairs of life can only be diminished, and not, even on the most favourable supposition, done away with, it is important that those endowments should be cultivated not merely in a select few, but in all, and that the cultivation should be more varied and complete than most persons are able to find in the narrow sphere of their merely individual interests. A people among whom there is no habit of spontaneous action for a collective interest—who look habitually to their government to command or prompt them in all matters of joint concern—who expect to have everything done for them, except what can be made an affair of mere habit and routine—have their faculties only half developed; their education is defective in one of its most important branches. . . .

The preceding are the principal reasons, of a general character, in favour of restricting to the narrowest compass the intervention of a public authority in the business of the community: and few will dispute the more than sufficiency of these reasons, to throw, in every instance, the burthen of making out a strong case, not on those who resist, but on those who recommend, government interference. *Laisser-faire*, in short, should be the general practice: every departure from it, unless required by some great good, is a certain evil. . . .

PART V

"SCIENTIFIC" SOCIALISM

XIX

KARL MARX AND FRIEDRICH ENGELS

1818–1883 1820–1895

The social theories attributed to Karl Marx were the product of such a close collaboration with Friedrich Engels that the biographical background of Marx's work would be incomplete unless it dealt with both their lives. Marx was no doubt the indispensable partner, as Engels frankly admitted, and "scientific" socialism might have taken much the same shape if Engels had never appeared. But that does not destroy the practical value of the latter's contribution.

Marx and Engels first met at Cologne about 1842. Up to that time their careers, though alike in some respects, had for the most part been very different. Both were born in the Rhine province of Prussia: Marx in 1818, Engels in 1820. This district had been strongly revolutionary during the recent disturbances in France; it was also the most highly industrialized part of Germany. Manufacturing was particularly active in Barmen, Engels's native town. In the neighborhood of Trèves, Marx's birthplace, there existed a class of small peasant landowners, comfortably circumstanced, who "made wine and knew how to be happy." The remains of a system of communal landownership also survived. Marx visited the neighboring villages and interested himself in the condition of the country people.

Both Marx and Engels came of middle-class families, but there the similarity of their home surroundings ended. The father of Marx was a lawyer and a disciple of the eighteenth-century French philosophers. Although he had originally been a member of the Jewish faith, his sympathy with French thought had made Judaism unattractive to him, and in 1824 he became a convert to Christianity. The event was also due partly to a desire to escape the anti-Jewish reaction which followed the restoration of the Rhine province to Prussia, partly perhaps to the attractions of more cultivated Gentile society, and partly to the novel appeal of Christianity in the romantic and nationalist dress characteristic of the period. A close sympathy prevailed between father and son. Under his father's eye Karl absorbed the teachings of Locke, Diderot, and Voltaire and laid the first foundations of his materialist conception of history. As a friend of the Privy Councillor von Westphalen, patron of the young intellectuals of Trèves, he also learned to appreciate literature.

The early experiences of Engels were less agreeable than those of Marx but were perhaps equally calculated to produce a revolutionist. His father, a prosperous cotton manufacturer with establishments in Germany and England, appears to have combined the religious and money-making faculties in about equal proportions. His stern Protestantism and mercenary outlook led to frequent clashes with his son, but the latter in spite of rebellions was obliged, at seventeen, to enter a business office in Bremen. There he remained for three years, learning the technique of trade. But his spirit was not broken. Having fallen under the influence of Heine and Börne, and discovering some facility as a writer, he began at nineteen to write articles in praise of freedom and democracy. The first one, published under a pen name, attracted wide notice; in it he execrated the environment in which he had been reared. Some time later he entered the army as a volunteer artilleryman at Berlin, where he fell in with the more radical wing of the Hegelian group. By 1842 Engels already possessed a considerable reputation as a writer.

Marx had meanwhile been leading the quiet life of a scholar at the universities of Bonn and Berlin. Jena conferred the doctor's degree upon him in 1841. He studied jurisprudence as a "necessary evil," being more inclined toward history and philosophy. Like Engels he was attracted to the Young Hegelians at Berlin. His friendship for a member of this group who had attacked the official theology put a period to his hopes of obtaining a teaching post at Berlin. An opportunity to enter journalism then presented itself. Marx had contributed articles to the *Renische Zeitung*, a paper supported by middle-class radicals; he was now offered the post of editor, which he accepted. Once in control he gave the policy of the paper a new direction: instead of harping on the defects of religion he called attention to the evil condition of the peasantry and the urban working class. This line involved him in a controversy with the governor of the Rhine province, the upshot being that a censorship was imposed on the *Renische Zeitung*. Marx chose to resign rather than submit to official scrutiny. A short time before this he had married Jenny von Westphalen, the daughter of his old friend the Privy Councillor. The marriage turned out to be an extremely happy one and during the last thirty years of his life as an exile in London his family was one of the few sources of comfort to Marx.

Although Marx had been devoting more and more study to economic and social problems, he was not yet a communist. His conversion was completed shortly afterward by Moses Hess, a former editor of Marx's paper whom Marx defended against the attacks of a conservative journal. "I do not know communism," said Marx, "but a social philosophy that has as its aim the defense of the oppressed cannot be condemned so lightly."

Marx had familiarized himself with the doctrines of the French socialists, including Fourier, Cabet, and Saint-Simon. Finding the life of a propagandist in Germany too difficult he proceeded to Paris, the center of socialist agitation. There he associated with Heine, Proudhon, and Cabet and inaugurated the *Franco-German Yearbooks*, which began (and ended with the first number) in 1844. In the *Yearbooks* he completed the groundwork of his future philosophy.

Meanwhile Engels had been residing in Manchester, England, as his father's business agent. But he used the interval to continue his social education, participating in Chartism, the Owenite movement, and trade unionism. His business connections naturally gave him an inner knowledge of the capitalist system. These experiences he made use of in writing his *Condition of the Working Classes in England in 1844*, a severe indictment of capitalist society.

Engels's close friendship and association with Marx dates from Engels's return to France in 1844. He had contributed an article to Marx's *Yearbooks* and in the same year collaborated with him in writing *The Holy Family*. This work set forth in detail the idea that the proletariat must be the leaders of social change and that the basis of a program must be a scientific study of industry, production, and historic forces.

Marx's connection with *Vorwärts*, a Paris paper which attacked the Prussian government, led to his expulsion from France in 1845 on the protest of the Prussian authorities. From that time until 1848 he lived at Brussels, deep in the study of economics and in the composition of his *Poverty of Philosophy* (1847), a reply to Proudhon's *Philosophy of Poverty*. Formerly an admirer of Proudhon, Marx took sharp issue with Proudhon's proposal to turn wage-earners into property owners through the formation of corporate associations. He also elaborated his theory of communism and sketched the historical development of capitalist production. The book prepared the way for the *Communist Manifesto*.

The latter document was the outcome of the Communist League

which Marx and Engels were largely instrumental in forming during Marx's enforced residence in Brussels. The plan of federating various local groups of workers had occurred to Marx and Engels, and the latter was already at work in Paris on the project when Marx was visited by a representative group of working-class radicals. As a result of this meeting a congress was called together in London in 1847. The congress drafted a constitution for the new Communist League, and published a trial issue of a journal. It was this paper which originated the famous slogan, "Workers of all countries, unite!" The second convention of the League, which Marx attended, commissioned him to draw up a platform. His response, the celebrated *Communist Manifesto*, appeared in February, 1848. The document incorporated the ideas of both Marx and Engels, but its distinguishing features, the theory that the economic and social organization of an age determines its political and intellectual make-up, that history has been a series of class struggles, and that the proletariat has at last the opportunity of emancipating mankind from all oppression—these ideas Engels himself attributed exclusively to Marx.

The Communist League was comparatively short-lived. Almost immediately after its formation Marx and Engels became involved in the revolutionary events of 1848. The Belgian government, alarmed at the disturbances in France, swept out the group of Brussels radicals; Marx took refuge in Paris. But by this time Germany itself was rising and he and Engels returned to the Rhine province to help matters along. The absence of a communist organization in Germany and the belief that they could utilize the democratic movement as a step toward social revolution led them to found a journal at Cologne (the *Neue Renische Zeitung*) which depended on bourgeois financial support and devoted more of its attention to political than to social questions. When it became evident that middle-class revolution was a failure in Germany, Marx turned to the business of federating the local groups of communist workingmen in eastern Germany. But the work was interrupted by the Prussian reaction of 1849: the *Neue Renische Zeitung* was suppressed and Marx was expelled from Germany. He returned once more to Paris, only to be driven out a month later when the backwash of reaction reached France. England seemed to be the last refuge, and before the end of 1850 Marx and most of his colleagues of the *Zeitung* had assembled in London. The old Communist League was now reorganized, but dissensions among the leaders and the difficulty of organizing the German section in the face of

Prussian persecution caused the League to be disbanded in 1852 or 1853.

From the dissolution of the Communist League until the founding of the International Workingmen's Association in 1864 Marx and Engels were comparatively inactive politically. Their literary labors continued unabated, however, and they freely exchanged ideas and assistance. But the problem of making a living was a trying one especially for Marx. Engels unwillingly reëntered his father's business at Manchester, largely to aid his friend, whose only other regular source of income from 1851 to 1862 was a weekly article for the *New York Tribune*. Marx had become acquainted with the editor, Charles A. Dana, during the French Revolution of 1848.

The International Workingmen's Association, the famous "First International," grew out of conversations between French, English, and German workers who had been brought to London by the Exposition of 1862. In the beginning it was partly a protest against the suppression of the Poles then going on in Russia, partly an effort to protect wage standards and labor conditions. Marx was called upon to draft a program and deliver an inaugural address. In order to reconcile the mixed group of Polish and Italian patriots, communists, anarchists, and mere workingmen who formed the membership of the International the program was filled with compromises and ambiguities, and these eventually helped to destroy the International. The story of the disastrous conflict between Marx and Bakunin is related in another place.[1] For some years, however, the organization was the most influential international working-class movement, and Marxism dominated its councils from 1868 to 1870.

In the meanwhile Marx published the first volume of his massive work, *Capital* (1867), which presented, with a wealth of supporting data (the product of enormous erudition and research), the economic and social theories which he had been elaborating for the past twenty years.

Up to 1870 Engels had taken little part in the affairs of the International. In 1869, however, he was able to quit his father's business with a competence, and to put his organizing and linguistic talents at Marx's disposal in the business of the Association. Friends remarked that Engels could stammer in twelve languages; fortunately he wrote them much more fluently.

After 1873 Marx withdrew somewhat from public affairs. He continued to work on *Capital*, however, and with the aid of Engels acted

[1] Below, pp. 537, 538.

as the mentor of the international socialist movement. In the *Criticism of the Gotha Program* Marx upheld his principles against those of Lassalle in a movement toward compromise instigated by two German factions. He also contributed a chapter to Engels's *Anti-Dührung*, another counterblast against a German critic which became one of the standard textbooks of Marxism. By the early '80's, the two friends had the satisfaction of seeing their principles making rapid progress all over Europe. In 1878 failing health had compelled Marx to give up his work on *Capital*. Four years later the fatal decline set in; he died in 1883 and was buried in London.

For twelve years longer Engels carried on the work. Out of the manuscript left by Marx he edited and published two more volumes of *Capital* and continued to act as the international adviser and medium of communication between socialists all over the world. Engels's popularity among socialists was immense: he understood the value of advertising, and before his death in 1895 he saw a Second International revive the traditions of the First.

It is unnecessary to insist upon the influence of Marx and Engels when the evidence of it lies on every hand. "Like Rousseau," a recent critic has said of Marx, "it has been his fortune to preside after death over a revolution conceived in his name."

REFERENCES

There is a new translation of *Capital* (Vol. I) by E. and C. Paul (1927). Among the more recent editions of Marx's other works are *The Civil War in France* (1921, intro. by R. W. Postgate), and the *Critique of the Gotha Programme* (1933). Translations of some of Engels's works are: *The Conditions of the Working Class in England* (1892), *The Peasant War in Germany* (1926), *Socialism, Utopian and Scientific* (the English title of *Anti-Dührung* 1913). The *Communist Manifesto* has been edited with an elaborate introduction and notes by D. Ryazanov (1930).

Among the explanations and interpretations of Marxism may be mentioned L. B. Boudin's *The Theoretical System of Karl Marx* (1910), S. H. Chang's *The Marxian Theory of the State* (1931), and Sidney Hook's *Towards an Understanding of Karl Marx* (1933). See also Lenin's *State and Revolution*, extracts from which are printed below, pp. 567–588.

The standard biography of Marx is by F. Mehring (1923), that of Engels, by G. Mayer (1920), both in German. Useful lives in English are D. Ryazanov's *Karl Marx and Friedrich Engels* (1927) and *Karl Marx, Man, Thinker and Revolutionist* (1927), into both of which has gone much recent research; Max Beer's *Life and Teachings of Karl Marx* (1929); and Otto Ruhle's *Karl Marx, His Life and Work* (1929). *Karl Marx*, by H. J. Laski (1921), is a short biographical sketch and estimate of Marx's work.

MANIFESTO OF THE COMMUNIST PARTY [1]

A spectre is haunting Europe—the spectre of Communism. All the powers of old Europe have entered into a holy alliance to exorcise this spectre; Pope and Czar, Metternich and Guizot, French Radicals and German police-spies.

Where is the party in opposition that has not been decried as communistic by its opponents in power? Where the Opposition that has not hurled back the branding reproach of Communism, against the more advanced opposition parties, as well as against its reactionary adversaries?

Two things result from this fact.

I. Communism is already acknowledged by all European Powers to be itself a Power.

II. It is high time that Communists should openly, in the face of the whole world, publish their views, their aims, their tendencies, and meet this nursery tale of the Spectre of Communism with a Manifesto of the party itself.

To this end, Communists of various nationalities have assembled in London, and sketched the following Manifesto, to be published in the English, French, German, Italian, Flemish and Danish languages.

I
Bourgeois and Proletarians *

The history of all hitherto existing society † is the history of class struggles.

Freeman and slave, patrician and plebeian, lord and serf, guild-master ‡ and journeyman, in a word, oppressor and oppressed, stood

[1] Samuel Moore, trans. Footnotes marked with *, †, or ‡ are those of Engels added in 1888.

* By bourgeoisie is meant the class of modern Capitalists, owners of the means of social production and employers of wage-labor. By proletariat, the class of modern wage-laborers who, having no means of production of their own, are reduced to selling their labor-power in order to live.

† That is, all written history. In 1847, the pre-history of society, the social organization existing previous to recorded history, was all but unknown. Since then, Haxthausen discovered common ownership of land in Russia, Maurer proved it to be the social foundation from which all Teutonic races started in history, and by and by village communities were found to be, or to have been, the primitive form of society everywhere from India to Ireland. The inner organization of this primitive Communistic society was laid bare, in its typical form, by Morgan's crowning discovery of the true nature of the gens and its relation to the tribe. With the dissolution of these primeval communities society begins to be differentiated into separate and finally antagonistic classes. I have attempted to retrace this process of dissolution in "The Origin of the Family, Private Property and the State." (Chicago, Charles H. Kerr & Co.)

‡ Guild-master, that is a full member of a guild, a master within, not a head of, a guild.

in constant opposition to one another, carried on an uninterrupted, now hidden, now open fight, a fight that each time ended, either in a revolutionary re-constitution of society at large, or in the common ruin of the contending classes.

In the earlier epochs of history, we find almost everywhere a complicated arrangement of society into various orders, a manifold gradation of social rank. In ancient Rome we have patricians, knights, plebeians, slaves; in the middle ages, feudal lords, vassals, guild-masters, journeymen, apprentices, serfs; in almost all of these classes, again, subordinate gradations.

The modern bourgeois Society that has sprouted from the ruins of feudal society, has not done away with class antagonisms. It has but established new classes, new conditions of oppression, new forms of struggle in place of the old ones.

Our epoch, the epoch of the bourgeoisie, possesses, however, this distinctive feature; it has simplified the class antagonisms. Society as a whole is more and more splitting up into two great hostile camps, into two great classes directly facing each other: Bourgeoisie and Proletariat.

From the serfs of the middle ages sprang the chartered burghers of the earliest towns. From these burgesses the first elements of the bourgeoisie were developed.

The discovery of America, the rounding of the Cape, opened up fresh ground for the rising bourgeoisie. The East-Indian and Chinese markets, the colonization of America, trade with the colonies, the increase in the means of exchange and in commodities generally, gave to commerce, to navigation, to industry, an impulse never before known, and thereby, to the revolutionary element in the tottering feudal society, a rapid development.

The feudal system of industry, under which industrial production was monopolized by closed guilds, now no longer sufficed for the growing wants of the new markets. The manufacturing system took its place. The guild-masters were pushed on one side by the manufacturing middle class; division of labor between the different corporate guilds vanished in the face of division of labor in each single workshop.

Meantime the markets kept ever growing, the demand, ever rising. Even manufacture no longer sufficed. Thereupon, steam and machinery revolutionized industrial production. The place of manufacture was taken by the giant, Modern Industry, the place of the industrial middle class, by industrial millionaires, the leaders of whole industrial armies, the modern bourgeois.

Modern industry has established the world-market, for which the discovery of America paved the way. This market has given an immense development to commerce, to navigation, to communication by land. This development has, in its turn, reacted on the extension of industry; and in proportion as industry, commerce, navigation, railways extended, in the same proportion the bourgeoisie developed, increased its capital, and pushed into the background every class handed down from the Middle Ages.

We see, therefore, how the modern bourgeoisie is itself the product of a long course of development, of a series of revolutions in the modes of production and of exchange.

Each step in the development of the bourgeoisie was accompanied by a corresponding political advance of that class. An oppressed class under the sway of the feudal nobility, an armed and self-governing association in the mediaeval commune,* here independent urban republic (as in Italy and Germany), there taxable "third estate" of the monarchy (as in France), afterwards, in the period of manufacture proper, serving either the semi-feudal or the absolute monarchy as a counterpoise against the nobility, and, in fact, corner stone of the great monarchies in general, the bourgeoisie has at last, since the establishment of Modern Industry and of the world-market, conquered for itself, in the modern representative State, exclusive political sway. The executive of the modern State is but a committee for managing the common affairs of the whole bourgeoisie.

The bourgeoisie, historically, has played a most revolutionary part.

The bourgeoisie, wherever it has got the upper hand, has put an end to all feudal, patriarchal, idyllic relations. It has pitilessly torn asunder the motley feudal ties that bound man to his "natural superiors," and has left remaining no other nexus between man and man than naked self-interest, than callous "cash payment." It has drowned the most heavenly ecstacies of religious fervor, of chivalrous enthusiasm, of philistine sentimentalism, in the icy water of egotistical calculation. It has resolved personal worth into exchange value, and in place of the numberless indefeasible chartered freedoms, has set up

* "Commune" was the name taken, in France, by the nascent towns even before they had conquered from their feudal lords and masters, local self-government and political rights as "the Third Estate." Generally speaking, for the economical development of the bourgeoisie, England is here taken as the typical country; for its political development, France.

that single, unconscionable freedom—Free Trade. In one word, for exploitation, veiled by religious and political illusions, it has substituted naked, shameless, direct, brutal exploitation.

The bourgeoisie has stripped of its halo every occupation hitherto honored and looked up to with reverent awe. It has converted the physician, the lawyer, the priest, the poet, the man of science, into its paid wage-laborers.

The bourgeoisie has torn away from the family its sentimental veil, and has reduced the family relation to a mere money relation.

The bourgeoisie has disclosed how it came to pass that the brutal display of vigor in the Middle Ages, which Reactionists so much admire, found its fitting complement in the most slothful indolence. It has been the first to show what man's activity can bring about. It has accomplished wonders far surpassing Egyptian pyramids, Roman aqueducts, and Gothic cathedrals; it has conducted expeditions that put in the shade all former Exoduses of nations and crusades.

The bourgeoisie cannot exist without constantly revolutionizing the instruments of production, and thereby the relations of production, and with them the whole relations of society. Conservation of the old modes of production in unaltered form, was, on the contrary, the first condition of existence for all earlier industrial classes. Constant revolutionizing of production, uninterrupted disturbance of all social conditions, everlasting uncertainty and agitation distinguish the bourgeois epoch from all earlier ones. All fixed, fast-frozen relations, with their train of ancient and venerable prejudices and opinions, are swept away, all new-formed ones become antiquated before they can ossify. All that is solid melts into air, all that is holy is profaned, and man is at last compelled to face with sober senses, his real conditions of life, and his relations with his kind.

The need of a constantly expanding market for its products chases the bourgeoisie over the whole surface of the globe. It must nestle everywhere, settle everywhere, establish connections everywhere.

The bourgeoisie has through its exploitation of the world-market given a cosmopolitan character to production and consumption in every country. To the great chagrin of reactionists, it has drawn from under the feet of industry the national ground on which it stood. All old-established national industries have been destroyed or are daily being destroyed. They are dislodged by new industries, whose introduction becomes a life and death question for all civilized nations, by industries that no longer work up indigenous raw material, but raw material drawn from the remotest zones; industries whose products are consumed not only at home, but in every quarter of the globe. In place of the old wants, satisfied by the productions of the country, we find new wants, requiring for their satisfaction the products of distant lands and climes. In place of the old local and national seclusion and self-sufficiency, we have intercourse in every direction, universal inter-dependence of nations. And as in material, so also in intellectual production. The intellectual creations of individual nations become common property. National onesidedness and narrow-mindedness become more and more impossible, and from the numerous national and local literatures there arises a world-literature.

The bourgeoisie, by the rapid improvement of all instruments of production, by the immensely facilitated means of communication, draws all, even the most barbarian, nations into civilization. The cheap prices of its commodities are the heavy artillery with which it batters down all Chinese walls, with which it forces the barbarians' intensely obstinate hatred of foreigners to capitulate. It compels all nations, on pain of extinction, to adopt the bourgeois mode of production; it compels them to introduce what it calls civilization into their midst, *i.e.*, to become bourgeois themselves. In a word, it creates a world after its own image.

The bourgeoisie has subjected the country to the rule of the towns. It has created enormous cities, has greatly increased the urban population as compared with the rural, and has thus rescued a considerable part of the population from the idiocy of rural life. Just as it has made the country dependent on the towns, so it has made barbarian and semi-barbarian countries dependent on the civilized ones, nations of peasants on nations of bourgeois, the East on the West.

The bourgeoisie keeps more and more doing away with the scattered state of the population, of the means of production, and of property. It has agglomerated population, centralized means of production, and has concentrated property in a few hands. The necessary consequence of this was political centralization. Independent, or but loosely connected provinces, with separate interests, laws, governments, and systems of taxation, became lumped together in one nation, with one government, one code of laws, one national class-interest, one frontier and one customs-tariff.

The bourgeoisie, during its rule of scarce one hundred years, has created more massive and more colossal productive forces than have all preceding generations together. Subjection of Nature's forces to man, machinery, application of chemistry to industry and agriculture, steam-navigation, railways, electric telegraphs, clearing of whole continents for cultivation, canalization of rivers, whole populations conjured out of the ground—what earlier century had even a presentiment that such productive forces slumbered in the lap of social labor?

We see then: the means of production and of exchange on whose foundation the bourgeoisie built itself up, were generated in feudal society. At a certain stage in the development of these means of production and of exchange, the conditions under which feudal society produced and exchanged, the feudal organization of agriculture and manufacturing industry, in one word, the feudal relations of property became no longer compatible with the already developed productive forces; they became so many fetters. They had to burst asunder; they were burst asunder.

Into their places stepped free competition, accompanied by a social and political constitution adapted to it, and by the economical and political sway of the bourgeois class.

A similar movement is going on before our own eyes. Modern bourgeois society with its relations of production, of exchange and of property, a society that has conjured up such gigantic means of production and of exchange, is like the sorcerer, who is no longer able to control the powers of the nether world whom he has called up by his spells. For many a decade past the history of industry and commerce is but the history of the revolt of modern productive forces against modern conditions of production, against the property relations that are the conditions for the existence of the bourgeoisie and of its rule. It is enough to mention the commercial crises that by their periodical return put on its trial, each time more threateningly, the existence of the entire bourgeois society. In these crises a great part not only of the existing products, but also of the previously created productive forces, are periodically destroyed. In these crises there breaks out an epidemic that, in all earlier epochs, would have seemed an absurdity—the epidemic of over-production. Society suddenly finds itself put back into a state of momentary barbarism; it appears as if a famine, a universal war of devastation, had cut off the supply of every means of subsistence; industry and commerce seem to be destroyed; and why? Because there is too much civilization, too much means of subsistence, too much industry, too much commerce. The productive forces at the disposal of society no longer tend to further the development of the conditions of bourgeois property; on the contrary, they have become too powerful for these conditions, by which they are fettered, and so soon as they overcome these fetters, they bring disorder into the whole of bourgeois society, endanger the existence of bourgeois property. The conditions of bourgeois society are too narrow to comprise the wealth created by them. And how does the bourgeoisie get over these crises? On the one hand by enforced destruction of a mass of productive forces; on the other, by the conquest of new markets, and by the more thorough exploitation of the old ones. That is to say, by paving the way for more extensive and more destructive crises, and by diminishing the means whereby crises are prevented.

The weapons with which the bourgeoisie felled feudalism to the ground are now turned against the bourgeoisie itself.

But not only has the bourgeoisie forged the weapons that bring death to itself; it has also called into existence the men who are to wield those weapons—the modern working-class—the proletarians.

In proportion as the bourgeoisie, *i.e.*, capital, is developed, in the same proportion is the proletariat, the modern working-class, developed, a class of laborers, who live only so long as they find work, and who find work only so long as their labor increases capital. These laborers, who must sell themselves piecemeal, are a commodity, like every other article of commerce, and are consequently exposed to all the vicissitudes of competition, to all the fluctuations of the market.

Owing to the extensive use of machinery and to division of labor, the work of the proletarians has lost all individual character, and, consequently, all charm for the workman. He becomes an appendage of the machine, and it is only the most simple, most monotonous, and most easily acquired knack that is required of him. Hence, the cost of production of a workman is restricted, almost entirely, to the means of subsistence that he requires for his maintenance, and for the propagation of his race. But the price of a commodity, and also of labor, is equal to its cost of production. In proportion, therefore, as the repulsiveness of the work increases, the wage decreases. Nay more, in proportion as the use of machinery and division of labor increases, in the same proportion the burden of toil also increases, whether by prolongation of the working hours, by increase of the work exacted in a given time, or by increased speed of the machinery, etc.

Modern industry has converted the little workshop of the patriarchal master into the great factory of the industrial capitalist. Masses of laborers, crowded into the factories, are organized like soldiers. As privates of the industrial army they are placed under the command of a perfect hierarchy of officers and sergeants. Not only are they the slaves of the bourgeois class, and of the bourgeois State, they are daily and hourly enslaved by the machine, by the over-looker, and, above all, by the individual bourgeois manufacturer himself. The more openly this depotism proclaims gain to be its end and aim, the more petty, the more hateful and the more embittering it is.

The less the skill and exertion or strength implied in manual labor, in other words, the more modern industry becomes developed, the more is the labor of men superseded by that of women. Differences of age and sex have no longer any distinctive social validity for the working-class. All are instruments of labor, more or less expensive to use, according to their age and sex.

No sooner is the exploitation of the laborer by the manufacturer so far at an end, that he receives his wages in cash, than he is set upon by the other portions of the bourgeoisie, the landlord, the shopkeeper, the pawnbroker, etc.

The lower strata of the middle class—the small tradespeople, shopkeepers, and retired tradesmen generally, the handicraftsmen and peasants—all these sink gradually into the proletariat, partly because their diminutive capital does not suffice for the scale on which Modern Industry is carried on, and is swamped in the competition with the large capitalists, partly because their specialized skill is rendered worthless by new methods of production. Thus the proletariat is recruited from all classes of the population.

The proletariat goes through various stages of development. With its birth it begins to struggle with the bourgeoisie. At first the contest is carried on by individual laborers, then by the workpeople of a factory, then by the operatives of one trade, in one locality, against the individual bourgeois who directly exploits them. They direct their attacks not against the bourgeois conditions of production, but against the instruments of production themselves; they destroy imported wares that compete with their labor, they smash to pieces machinery, they set factories ablaze, they seek to restore by force the vanished status of the workman of the Middle Ages.

At this stage the laborers still form an incoherent mass scattered over the whole country, and broken up by their mutual competition. If anywhere they unite to form more compact bodies, this is not yet the consequence of their own active union, but of the union of the bourgeoisie, which class, in order to attain its own political ends, is compelled to set the whole proletariat in motion, and is moreover yet, for a time, able to do so. At this stage, therefore, the proletarians do not fight their enemies, but the enemies of their enemies, the remnants of absolute monarchy, the landowners, the non-industrial bourgeois, the petty bourgeoisie. Thus the whole historical movement is concentrated in the hands of the bourgeoisie; every victory so obtained is a victory for the bourgeoisie.

But with the development of industry the proletariat not only increases in number, it becomes concentrated in greater masses, its strength grows, and it feels that strength more. The various interests and conditions of life within the ranks of the proletariat are more and more equalized, in proportion as machinery obliterates all distinctions of labor, and nearly everywhere reduces wages to the same low level. The growing competition among the bourgeois, and the resulting commercial crises, make the wages of the workers ever more fluctuating. The unceasing improvement of machinery, ever more rapidly developing, makes their livelihood more and more precarious; the collisions between individual workmen and individual bourgeois take more and more the character of collisions between two classes. Thereupon the workers begin to form combinations (Trades' Unions) against the bourgeois; they club together in order to keep up the rate of wages; they found permanent associations in order to make provision beforehand for these occasional revolts. Here and there the contest breaks out into riots.

Now and then the workers are victorious, but only for a time. The real fruit of their battles lies, not in the immediate result, but in the ever expanding union of the workers. This union is helped on by the improved means of communication that are created by modern industry, and that place the workers of different localities in contact with one another. It was just this contact that was needed to centralize the numerous local struggles, all of the same character, into one national struggle between classes. But every class struggle is a political struggle. And that union, to attain which the burghers of the Middle Ages, with their miserable highways, required centuries, the modern proletarians, thanks to railways, achieve in a few years.

This organization of the proletarians into a class, and consequently into a political party, is continually being upset again by the competition between the workers themselves. But it ever rises up again, stronger, firmer, mightier. It compels legislative recognition of particular interests of the workers, by taking advantage of the divisions among the bourgeoisie itself. Thus the ten-hour bill in England was carried.

Altogether collisions between the classes of the old society further, in many ways, the course of development of the proletariat. The bourgeoisie finds itself involved in a constant battle. At first with the aristocracy; later on, with those portions of the bourgeoisie itself, whose interests have become antagonistic to the progress of industry; at all times, with the bourgeoisie of foreign countries. In all these battles it sees itself compelled to appeal to the proletariat, to ask for its help, and thus, to drag it into the political arena. The bourgeoisie itself, therefore, supplies the proletariat with its own elements of political and general education, in other words, it furnishes the proletariat with weapons for fighting the bourgeoisie.

Further, as we have already seen, entire sections of the ruling classes are, by the advance of industry, precipitated into the proletariat, are at least threatened in their conditions of existence. These also supply the proletariat with fresh elements of enlightenment and progress.

Finally, in times when the class-struggle nears the decisive hour, the process of dissolution going on within the ruling class, in fact, within the whole range of old society, assumes such a violent, glaring character, that a small section of the ruling class cuts itself adrift, and joins the revolutionary class, the class that holds the future in its hands. Just as, therefore, at an earlier period, a section of the nobility went over to the bourgeoisie, so now a portion of the bourgeoisie goes over to the proletariat, and in particular, a portion of the bourgeois ideologists, who have raised themselves to the level of comprehending theoretically the historical movement as a whole.

Of all the classes that stand face to face with the bourgeoisie today, the proletariat alone is a really revolutionary class. The other classes decay and finally disappear in the face of modern industry; the proletariat is its special and essential product.

The lower middle class, the small manufacturer, the shopkeeper, the artisan, the peasant, all these fight against the bourgeoisie, to save from extinction their existence as fractions of the middle class. They are, therefore, not revolutionary, but conservative. Nay more, they are reactionary, for they try to roll back the wheel of history.

If by chance they are revolutionary, they are so, only in view of their impending transfer into the proletariat; they thus defend not their present, but their future interests; they desert their own standpoint to place themselves at that of the proletariat.

The "dangerous class," the social scum, that passively rotting mass thrown off by the lowest layers of old society, may, here and there, be swept into the movement by a proletarian revolution; its conditions of life, however, prepare it far more for the part of a bribed tool of reactionary intrigue.

In the conditions of the proletariat, those of old society at large are already virtually swamped. The proletarian is without property; his relation to his wife and children has no longer anything in common with the bourgeois family-relations; modern industrial labor, modern subjection to capital, the same in England as in France, in America as in Germany, has stripped him of every trace of national character. Law, morality, religion, are to him so many bourgeois prejudices, behind which lurk in ambush just as many bourgeois interests.

All the preceding classes that got the upper hand, sought to fortify their already acquired status by subjecting society at large to their conditions of appropriation. The proletarians cannot become masters of the productive forces of society, except by abolishing their own previous mode of appropriation, and thereby also every other previous mode of appropriation. They have nothing of their own to secure and to fortify; their mission is to destroy all previous securities for, and insurances of, individual property.

All previous historical movements were movements of minorities, or in the interest of minorities. The proletarian movement is the self-conscious, independent movement of the immense majority, in the interest of the immense majority. The proletariat, the lowest stratum of our present society, cannot stir, cannot raise itself up, without the whole superincumbent strata of official society being sprung into the air.

Though not in substance, yet in form, the struggle of the proletariat with the bourgeoisie is at first a national struggle. The proletariat of each country must, of course, first of all settle matters with its own bourgeoisie.

In depicting the most general phases of the development of the proletariat, we traced the more or less veiled civil war, raging within existing society, up to the point where that war breaks out into open revolution, and where the violent overthrow of the bourgeoisie lays the foundation for the sway of the proletariat.

Hitherto, every form of society has been based, as we have already seen, on the antagonism of oppressing and oppressed classes. But in order to oppress a class, certain conditions must be assured to it under which it can, at least, continue its slavish existence. The serf, in the period of serfdom, raised himself to membership in the commune, just as the petty bourgeois, under the yoke of feudal absolutism, managed to develop into a bourgeois. The modern laborer, on the contrary, instead of rising with the progress of industry, sinks deeper and deeper below the conditions of existence of his own class. He becomes a pauper, and pauperism develops more rapidly than population and wealth. And here it becomes evident, that the bourgeoisie is unfit any longer to be the ruling class in society, and to impose its conditions of existence upon society as an over-riding law. It is unfit to rule, because it is incompetent to assure an existence to its slave within his slavery, because it cannot help letting him sink into such a state that it has to feed him, instead of being fed by him. Society can no longer live under this bourgeoisie, in other words, its existence is no longer compatible with society.

The essential condition for the existence, and for the sway of the bourgeois class, is the formation and augmentation of capital; the condition for capital is wage-labor. Wage-labor rests exclusively on competition between the laborers. The advance of industry, whose involuntary promoter is the bourgeoisie, replaces the isolation of the laborers, due to competition, by their involuntary combination, due to association. The development of Modern Industry, therefore, cuts from under its feet the very foundation on which the bourgeoisie produces and appropriates products. What the bourgeoisie therefore produces, above all, are its own grave-diggers. Its fall and the victory of the proletariat are equally inevitable.

II

Proletarians and Communists

In what relation do the Communists stand to the proletarians as a whole?

The Communists do not form a separate party opposed to other working-class parties.

They have no interests separate and apart from those of the proletariat as a whole.

They do not set up any sectarian principles of their own, by which to shape and mould the proletarian movement.

The Communists are distinguished from the other working-class parties by this only: (1) In the national struggles of the proletarians of the different countries, they point out and bring to the front the common interests of the entire proletariat independently of all nationality. (2) In the various stages of development which the struggle of the working-class against the bourgeoisie has to pass through, they always and everywhere represent the interests of the movement as a whole.

The Communists, therefore, are on the one hand, practically, the most advanced and resolute section of the working-class parties of every country, that section which pushes forward all others; on the other hand, theoretically, they have over the great mass of the proletariat the advantage of clearly understanding the line of march, the conditions, and the ultimate general results of the proletarian movement.

The immediate aim of the Communists is the same as that of all the other proletarian parties; formation of the proletariat into a class, overthrow of the bourgeois supremacy, a conquest of political power by the proletariat.

The theoretical conclusions of the Communists are in no way based on ideas or principles that have been invented, or discovered, by this or that would-be universal reformer.

They merely express, in general terms, actual relations springing from an existing class struggle, from a historical movement going on under our very eyes. The abolition of existing property relations is not at all a distinctive feature of Communism.

All property relations in the past have continually been subject to historical change consequent upon the change in historical conditions.

The French Revolution, for example, abolished feudal property in favor of bourgeois property.

The distinguishing feature of Communism is not the abolition of property generally, but the abolition of bourgeois property. But modern bourgeois private property is the final and most complete expression of the system of producing and appropriating products, that is based on class antagonism, on the exploitation of the many by the few.

In this sense, the theory of the Communists may be summed up in the single sentence: Abolition of private property.

We Communists have been reproached with the desire of abolishing the right of personally acquiring property as the fruit of a man's own labor, which property is alleged to be the ground work of all personal freedom, activity and independence.

Hard-won, self-acquired, self-earned property! Do you mean the property of the petty artisan and of the small peasant, a form of property that preceded the bourgeois form? There is no need to abolish that; the development of industry has to a great extent already destroyed it, and is still destroying it daily.

Or do you mean modern bourgeois private property?

But does wage-labor create any property for the laborer? Not a bit. It creates capital, *i.e.*, that kind of property which exploits wage-labor, and which cannot increase except upon condition of getting a new supply of wage-labor for fresh exploitation. Property, in its present form, is based on the antagonism of capital and wage-labor. Let us examine both sides of this antagonism.

To be a capitalist, is to have not only a purely personal, but a social status in production. Capital is a collective product, and only by the united action of many members, nay, in the last resort, only by the united action of all members of society, can it be set in motion.

Capital is therefore not a personal, it is a social power.

When, therefore, capital is converted into common property, into the property of all members of society, personal property is not thereby transformed into social property. It is only the social character of the property that is changed. It loses its class-character.

Let us now take wage-labor.

The average price of wage-labor is the minimum wage, *i.e.*, that quantum of the means of subsistence, which is absolutely requisite to keep the laborer in bare existence as a laborer. What, therefore, the wage-laborer appropriates by means of his labor, merely suffices to prolong and reproduce a bare existence. We by no means intend to abolish this personal appropriation of the products of labor, an appropriation that is made for the maintenance and reproduction of human life, and that leaves no surplus wherewith to command the labor of others. All that we want to do away with is the miserable character of this appropriation, under which the laborer lives merely to increase capital, and is allowed to live only in so far as the interest of the ruling class requires it.

In bourgeois society, living labor is but a means to increase accumulated labor. In Communist society, accumulated labor is but a means to widen, to enrich, to promote the existence of the laborer.

In bourgeois society, therefore, the past dominates the present; in Communist society, the present dominates the past. In bourgeois society capital is independent and has individuality, while the living person is dependent and has no individuality.

And the abolition of this state of things is called by the bourgeois, abolition of individuality and freedom! And rightly so. The abolition of bourgeois individuality, bourgeois independence, and bourgeois freedom is undoubtedly aimed at.

By freedom is meant, under the present bourgeois conditions of production, free trade, free selling and buying.

But if selling and buying disappears, free selling and buying disappear also. This talk about free selling and buying, and all the other "brave words" of our bourgeoisie about freedom in general, have a meaning, if any, only in contrast with restricted selling and buying, with the fettered traders of the Middle Ages, but have no meaning when opposed to the Communistic abolition of buying and selling, of the bourgeois conditions of production, and of the bourgeoisie itself.

You are horrified at our intending to do away with private property. But in your existing society, private property is already done away with for nine-tenths of the population; its existence for the few is solely due to its non-existence in the hands of those nine-tenths. You reproach us, therefore, with intending to do away with a form of property, the necessary condition for whose existence is, the non-existence of any property for the immense majority of society.

In one word, you reproach us with intending to do away with your property. Precisely so; that is just what we intend.

From the moment when labor can no longer be converted into capital, money, or rent, into a social power capable of being monopolized, *i.e.*, from the moment when individual property can no longer be transformed into bourgeois property, into capital, from that moment, you say, individuality vanishes.

You must, therefore, confess that by "individual" you mean no other person than the bourgeois, than the middle-class owner of property. This person must, indeed, be swept out of the way, and made impossible.

Communism deprives no man of the power to appropriate the products of society: all that it does is to deprive him of the power to subjugate the labor of others by means of such appropriation.

It has been objected, that upon the abolition of private property all work will cease, and universal laziness will overtake us.

According to this, bourgeois society ought long ago to have gone to the dogs through sheer idleness; for those of its members who work, acquire nothing, and those who acquire anything, do not work. The whole of this objection is but another expression of the tautology: that there can no longer be any wage-labor when there is no longer any capital.

All objections urged against the Communistic mode of producing and appropriating material products, have, in the same way, been urged against the Communistic modes of producing and appropriating intellectual products. Just as, to the bourgeois, the disappearance of class property is the disappearance of production itself, so the disappearance of class culture is to him identical with the disappearance of all culture.

That culture, the loss of which he laments, is, for the enormous majority, a mere training to act as a machine.

But don't wrangle with us so long as you apply, to our intended abolition of bourgeois property, the standard of your bourgeois notions of freedom, culture, law, etc. Your very ideas are but the outgrowth of the conditions of your bourgeois production and bourgeois property, just as your jurisprudence is but the will of your class made into a law for all, a will, whose essential character and direction are determined by the economic conditions of existence of your class.

The selfish misconception that induces you to transform into eternal laws of nature and of reason, the social forms springing from your present mode of production and form of property—historical relations that rise and disappear in the progress of production—this misconception you share with every ruling class that has preceded you. What you see clearly in the case of ancient property, what you admit in the case of feudal property, you are of course forbidden to admit in the case of your own bourgeois form of property.

Abolition of the family! Even the most radical flare up at this infamous proposal of the Communists.

On what foundation is the present family, the bourgeois family, based? On capital, on private gain. In its completely developed form this family exists only among the bourgeoisie. But this state of things finds its complement in the practical absence of the family among the proletarians, and in public prostitution.

The bourgeois family will vanish as a matter of course when its complement vanishes, and both will vanish with the vanishing of capital.

Do you charge us with wanting to stop the exploitation of children by their parents? To this crime we plead guilty.

But, you will say, we destroy the most hallowed of relations, when we replace home education by social.

And your education! Is not that also social, and determined by the social conditions under which you educate, by the intervention, direct or indirect, of society by means of schools, etc.? The Communists have not invented the intervention of society in education; they do but seek to alter the character of that intervention, and to rescue education from the influence of the ruling class.

The bourgeois clap-trap about the family and education, about the hallowed co-relation of parent and child, becomes all the more disgusting, the more, by the action of Modern Industry, all family ties among the proletarians are torn asunder, and their children transformed into simple articles of commerce and instruments of labor.

But you Communists would introduce community of women, screams the whole bourgeoisie in chorus.

The bourgeois sees in his wife a mere instrument of production. He hears that the instruments of production are to be exploited in common, and, naturally, can come to no other conclusion, than that the lot of being common to all will likewise fall to the women.

He has not even a suspicion that the real point aimed at is to do away with the status of women as mere instruments of production.

For the rest, nothing is more ridiculous than the virtuous indignation of our bourgeois at the community of women which, they pretend, is to be openly and officially established by the Communists. The Communists have no need to introduce community of women; it has existed almost from time immemorial.

Our bourgeois, not content with having the wives and daughters of their proletarians at their disposal, not to speak of common prostitutes, take the greatest pleasure in seducing each others' wives.

Bourgeois marriage is in reality a system of wives in common and thus, at the most, what the Communists might possibly be reproached with, is that they desire to introduce, in substitution for a hypocritically concealed, an openly legalized community of women. For the rest, it is self-evident, that the abolition of the present system of production must bring with it the abolition of the community of women springing from that system, *i.e.*, of prostitution both public and private.

The Communists are further reproached with desiring to abolish countries and nationalities.

The working men have no country. We cannot take from them what they have not got. Since the proletariat must first of all acquire political supremacy, must rise to be the leading class of the nation, must constitute itself the nation, it is, so far, itself national, though not in the bourgeois sense of the word.

National differences, and antagonisms between peoples, are daily more and more vanishing, owing to the development of the bourgeoisie, to freedom of commerce, to the world-market, to uniformity in the mode of production and in the conditions of life corresponding thereto.

The supremacy of the proletariat will cause them to vanish still faster. United action, of the leading civilized countries at least, is one of the first conditions for the emancipation of the proletariat.

In proportion as the exploitation of one individual by another is put an end to, the exploitation of one nation by another will also be put an end to. In proportion as the antagonism between classes within the nation vanishes, the hostility of one nation to another will come to an end.

The charges against Communism made from a religious, a philosophical, and generally, from an ideological standpoint, are not deserving of serious examination.

Does it require deep intuition to comprehend that man's ideas, views, and conceptions, in one word, man's consciousness, changes with every change in the conditions of his material existence, in his social relations and in his social life?

What else does the history of ideas prove, than that intellectual production changes in character in proportion as material production is changed? The ruling ideas of each age have ever been the ideas of its ruling class.

When people speak of ideas that revolutionize society, they do but express the fact, that within the old society, the elements of a new one have been created, and that the dissolution of the old ideas keeps even pace with the dissolution of the old conditions of existence.

When the ancient world was in its last throes, the ancient religions were overcome by Christianity. When Christian ideas succumbed in the 18th century to rationalist ideas, feudal society fought its death-battle with the then revolutionary bourgeoisie. The ideas of religious liberty and freedom of conscience, merely gave expression to the sway of free competition within the domain of knowledge.

"Undoubtedly," it will be said, "religious, moral, philosophical and juridical ideas have been modified in the course of historical development. But religion, morality, philosophy, political science, and law, constantly survived this change."

"There are besides, eternal truths, such as Freedom, Justice, etc., that are common to all states of society. But Communism abolishes eternal truths, it abolishes all religion, and all morality, instead of constituting them on a new basis; it therefore acts in contradiction to all past historical experience."

What does this accusation reduce itself to? The history of all past society has consisted in the development of class antagonisms, antagonisms that assumed different forms at different epochs.

But whatever form they may have taken, one fact is common to all past ages, viz., the exploitation of one part of society by the other. No wonder, then, that the social consciousness of past ages, despite all the multiplicity and variety it displays, moves within certain common forms, or general ideas, which cannot completely vanish except with the total disappearance of class antagonisms.

The Communist revolution is the most radical rupture with traditional property-relations; no wonder that its development involves the most radical rupture with traditional ideas.

But let us have done with the bourgeois objections to Communism.

We have seen above, that the first step in the revolution by the working-class, is to raise the proletariat to the position of ruling class, to win the battle of democracy.

The proletariat will use its political supremacy, to wrest, by degrees, all capital from the bourgeoisie, to centralize all instruments of production in the hands of the State, *i.e.*, of the proletariat organized as the ruling class; and to increase the total of productive forces as rapidly as possible.

Of course, in the beginning, this cannot be effected except by means of despotic inroads on the rights of property, and on the conditions of bourgeois production; by means of measures, therefore, which appear economically insufficient and untenable, but which, in the course of the movement, outstrip themselves, necessitate further inroads upon the old social order, and are unavoidable as a means of entirely revolutionizing the mode of production.

These measures will of course be different in different countries.

Nevertheless in the most advanced countries the following will be pretty generally applicable:

1. Abolition of property in land and application of all rents of land to public purposes.

2. A heavy progressive or graduated income tax.

3. Abolition of all right of inheritance.

4. Confiscation of the property of all emigrants and rebels.

5. Centralization of credit in the hands of the State, by means of a national bank with State capital and an exclusive monopoly.

6. Centralization of the means of communication and transport in the hands of the State.

7. Extension of factories and instruments of production owned by the State; the bringing into cultivation of waste lands, and the improvement of the soil generally in accordance with a common plan.

8. Equal liability of all to labor. Establishment of industrial armies, especially for agriculture.

9. Combination of agriculture with manufacturing industries; gradual abolition of the distinction between town and country, by a more equable distribution of population over the country.

10. Free education for all children in public schools. Abolition of children's factory labor in its present form. Combination of education with industrial production, etc., etc.

When, in the course of development, class distinctions have disappeared, and all production has been concentrated in the hands of a vast association of the whole nation, the public power will lose its political character. Political power, properly so called, is merely the organized power of one class for oppressing another. If the proletariat during its contest with the bourgeoisie is compelled, by the force of circumstances, to organize itself as a class, if, by means of a revolution, it makes itself the ruling class, and, as such, sweeps away by force the old conditions of production, then it will, along with these conditions, have swept away the conditions for the existence of class antagonisms, and of classes generally, and will thereby have abolished its own supremacy as a class.

In place of the old bourgeois society, with its classes and class antagonisms, we shall have an association, in which the free development of each is the condition for the free development of all.

III

Socialist and Communist Literature

1. *Reactionary Socialism*

(*a*) *Feudal Socialism.* Owing to their historical position, it became the vocation of the aristocracies of France and England to write pamphlets against modern bourgeois society. In the French revolution of July, 1830, and in the English reform agitation, these aristocracies again succumbed to the hateful upstart. Thenceforth, a serious political contest was altogether out of the question. A literary battle alone remained possible. But even in the domain of literature the old cries of the restoration period * had become impossible.

In order to arouse sympathy, the aristocracy were obliged to lose sight, apparently, of their own interests, and to formulate their indictment against the bourgeoisie in the interest of the exploited working-class alone. Thus the aristocracy took their revenge by singing lampoons on their new master, and whispering in his ears sinister prophecies of coming catastrophe.

In this way arose feudal socialism; half lamentation, half lampoon; half echo of the past, half menace of the future; at times, by its bitter, witty and incisive criticism, striking the bourgeoisie to the very hearts' core, but always ludicrous in its effect, through total incapacity to comprehend the march of modern history.

The aristocracy, in order to rally the people to them, waved the proletarian alms-bag in front for a banner. But the people, so often as it joined them, saw on their hindquarters the old feudal coats of arms, and deserted with loud and irreverent laughter.

One section of the French Legitimists, and "Young England," exhibited this spectacle.

In pointing out that their mode of exploitation was different to that of the bourgeoisie, the feudalists forget that they exploited under circumstances and conditions that were quite different, and that are now antiquated. In showing that, under their rule, the modern proletariat never existed, they forget that the modern bourgeoisie is the necessary offspring of their own form of society.

For the rest, so little do they conceal the reactionary character of their criticism, that their chief accusation against the bourgeoisie amounts to this, that under the bourgeois regime a class is being

* Not the English Restoration 1660 to 1689, but the French Restoration 1814 to 1830.

developed, which is destined to cut up root and branch the old order of society.

What they upbraid the bourgeoisie with is not so much that it creates a proletariat, as that it creates a revolutionary proletariat.

In political practice, therefore, they join in all coercive measures against the working-class; and in ordinary life, despite their high falutin phrases, they stoop to pick up the golden apples dropped from the tree of industry, and to barter truth, love, and honor for traffic in wool, beetroot-sugar and potato spirit.*

As the parson has ever gone hand in hand with the landlord, so has Clerical Socialism with Feudal Socialism.

Nothing is easier than to give Christain asceticism a Socialist tinge. Has not Christianity declaimed against private property, against marriage, against the State? Has it not preached in the place of these, charity and poverty, celibacy, and mortification of the flesh, monastic life and Mother Church? Christian Socialism is but the Holy Water with which the priest consecrates the heartburnings of the aristocrat.

(*b*) *Petty Bourgeois Socialism.* The feudal aristocracy was not the only class that was ruined by the bourgeoisie, not the only class whose conditions of existence pined and perished in the atmosphere of modern bourgeois society. The medieval burgesses and the small peasant bourgeoisie, were the precursors of the modern bourgeoisie. In those countries which are but little developed, industrially and commercially, these two classes still vegetate side by side with the rising bourgeoisie.

In countries where modern civilization has become fully developed, a new class of petty bourgeois has been formed, fluctuating between proletariat and bourgeoisie, and ever renewing itself as a supplementary part of bourgeois society. The individual members of this class, however, are being constantly hurled down into the proletariat by the action of competition, and, as modern industry develops, they even see the moment approaching when they will completely disappear as an independent section of modern society, to be replaced, in manufactures, agriculture and commerce, by overlookers, bailiffs and shopmen.

In countries like France, where the peasants constitute far more

* This applies chiefly to Germany where the landed aristocracy and squirearchy have large portions of their estates cultivated for their own account by stewards, and are, moreover, extensive beetroot-sugar manufacturers and distillers of potato spirits. The wealthier British aristocracy are, as yet, rather above that; but they, too, know how to make up for declining rents by lending their names to floaters of more or less shady joint-stock companies.

than half of the population, it was natural that writers who sided with the proletariat against the bourgeoisie, should use, in their criticism of the bourgeois regime, the standard of the peasant and petty bourgeois, and from the standpoint of these intermediate classes should take up the cudgels for the working-class. Thus arose petty bourgeois Socialism. Sismondi was the head of this school, not only in France, but also in England.

This school of Socialism dissected with great acuteness the contradictions in the conditions of modern production. It laid bare the hypocritical apologies of economists. It proved, incontrovertibly, the disastrous effects of machinery and division of labor; the concentration of capital and land in a few hands; overproduction and crises; it pointed out the inevitable ruin of the petty bourgeois and peasant, the misery of the proletariat, the anarchy in production, the crying inequalities in the distribution of wealth, the industrial war of extermination between nations, the dissolution of old moral bonds, of the old family relations, of the old nationalities.

In its positive aims, however, this form of Socialism aspires either to restoring the old means of production and of exchange, and with them the old property relations, and the old society, or to cramping the modern means of production and of exchange, within the framework of the old property relations that have been, and were bound to be, exploded by those means. In either case, it is both reactionary and Utopian.

Its last words are: corporate guilds for manufacture; patriarchal relations in agriculture.

Ultimately, when stubborn historical facts had dispersed all intoxicating effects of self-deception, this form of Socialism ended in a miserable fit of the blues.

(*c*) *German or "True" Socialism.* The Socialist and Communist literature of France, a literature that originated under the pressure of a bourgeoisie in power, and that was the expression of the struggle against this power, was introduced into Germany at a time when the bourgeoisie, in that country, had just begun its contest with feudal absolutism.

German philosophers, would-be philosophers, and beaux-esprits, eagerly seized on this literature, only forgetting, that when these writings immigrated from France into Germany, French social condition had not immigrated along with them. In contact with German social conditions, this French literature lost all its immediate practical significance, and assumed a purely literary aspect. Thus, to the German philosophers of the Eighteenth Century, the demands of the first French Revolution were nothing more than the demands of "Practical Reason" in general, and the utterance of the will of the revolutionary French bourgeoisie signified in their eyes the laws of pure Will, of Will as it was bound to be, of true human Will generally.

The work of the German literati consisted solely in bringing the new French ideas into harmony with their ancient philosophical conscience, or rather, in annexing the French ideas without deserting their own philosophic point of view.

This annexation took place in the same way in which a foreign language is appropriated, namely by translation.

It is well known how the monks wrote silly lives of Catholic Saints over the manuscripts on which the classical works of ancient heathendom had been written. The German literati reversed this process with the profane French literature. They wrote their philosophical nonsense beneath the French original. For instance, beneath the French criticism of the economic functions of money, they wrote "Alienation of Humanity," and beneath the French criticism of the bourgeois State they wrote, "Dethronement of the Category of the General," and so forth.

The introduction of these philosophical phrases at the back of the French historical criticisms they dubbed "Philosophy of Action," "True Socialism," "German Science of Socialism," " Philosophical Foundation of Socialism," and so on.

The French Socialist and Communist literature was thus completely emasculated. And, since it ceased in the hands of the German to express the struggle of one class with the other, he felt conscious of having overcome "French one-sidedness" and of representing, not true requirements, but the requirements of Truth, not the interests of the proletariat, but the interests of Human Nature, of Man in general, who belongs to no class, has no reality, who exists only in the misty realm of philosophical phantasy.

This German Socialism, which took its schoolboy task so seriously and solemnly, and extolled its poor stock-in-trade in such mountebank fashion, meanwhile gradually lost its pedantic innocence.

The fight of the German, and, especially, of the Prussian bourgeoisie, against feudal aristocracy and absolute monarchy, in other words, the liberal movement, became more earnest.

By this, the long-wished-for opportunity was offered to "True

Socialism" of confronting the political movement with the socialist demands, of hurling the traditional anathemas against liberalism, against representative government, against bourgeois competition, bourgeois freedom of the press, bourgeois legislation, bourgeois liberty and equality, and of preaching to the masses that they had nothing to gain, and everything to lose, by this bourgeois movement. German Socialism forgot, in the nick of time, that the French criticism, whose silly echo it was, presupposed the existence of modern bourgeois society, with its corresponding economic conditions of existence, and the political constitution adapted thereto, the very things whose attainment was the object of the pending struggle in Germany.

To the absolute governments, with their following of parsons, professors, country squires and officials, it served as a welcome scarecrow against the threatening bourgeoisie.

It was a sweet finish after the bitter pills of floggings and bullets, with which these same governments, just at that time, dosed the German working-class risings.

While this "True" Socialism thus served the governments as a weapon for fighting the German bourgeoisie, it, at the same time, directly represented a reactionary interest, the interest of the German Philistines. In Germany the petty bourgeois class, a relic of the 16th century, and since then constantly cropping up again under various forms, is the real social basis of the existing state of things.

To preserve this class, is to preserve the existing state of things in Germany. The industrial and political supremacy of the bourgeoisie threatens it with certain destruction; on the one hand, from the concentration of capital; on the other, from the rise of a revolutionary proletariat. "True" Socialism appeared to kill these two birds with one stone. It spread like an epidemic.

The robe of speculative cobwebs, embroidered with flowers of rhetoric, steeped in the dew of sickly sentiment, this transcendental robe in which the German Socialists wrapped their sorry "eternal truths," all skin and bone, served to wonderfully increase the sale of their goods amongst such a public.

And on its part, German Socialism recognized, more and more, its own calling as the bombastic representative of the petty bourgeois Philistine.

It proclaimed the German nation to be the model nation, and the German petty Philistine to be the typical man. To every villainous meanness of this model man it gave a hidden, higher, socialistic interpretation, the exact contrary of its true character. It went to the extreme length of directly opposing the "brutally destructive" tendency of Communism, and of proclaiming its supreme and impartial contempt of all class struggles. With very few exceptions, all the so-called Socialist and Communist publications that now (1847) circulate in Germany belong to the domain of this foul and enervating literature.

2. *Conservative or Bourgeois Socialism*

A part of the bourgeoisie is desirous of redressing social grievances, in order to secure the continued existence of bourgeois society.

To this section belong economists, philanthropists, humanitarians, improvers of the condition of the working-class, organizers of charity, members of societies for the prevention of cruelty to animals, temperance fanatics, hole and corner reformers of every imaginable kind. This form of Socialism has, moreover, been worked out into complete systems.

We may cite Proudhon's "Philosophie de la Misère" as an example of this form.

The socialistic bourgeois want all the advantages of modern social conditions without the struggles and dangers necessarily resulting therefrom. They desire the existing state of society minus its revolutionary and disintegrating elements. They wish for a bourgeoisie without a proletariat. The bourgeoisie naturally conceives the world in which it is supreme to be the best; and bourgeois socialism develops this comfortable conception into various more or less complete systems. In requiring the proletariat to carry out such a system, and thereby to march straightway into the social New Jerusalem, it but requires in reality, that the proletariat should remain within the bounds of existing society, but should cast away all its hateful ideas concerning the bourgeoisie.

A second and more practical, but less systematic, form of this socialism sought to depreciate every revolutionary movement in the eyes of the working-class, by showing that no mere political reform, but only a change in the material conditions of existence, in economical relations, could be of any advantage to them. By changes in the material conditions of existence, this form of Socialism, however, by no means understands abolition of the bourgeois relations of production, an abolition that can be effected only by a revolution, but administrative reforms, based on the continued existence of these relations; reforms, therefore, that in no respect affect the relations between capital and labor, but, at the best, lessen the cost, and simplify the administrative work, of bourgeois government.

Bourgeois Socialism attains adequate expression, when, and only when, it becomes a mere figure of speech.

Free trade: for the benefit of the working-class. Protective duties: for the benefit of the working-class. Prison Reform: for the benefit of the working-class. This is the last word and the only seriously meant word of bourgeois Socialism.

It is summed up in the phrase: the bourgeois is a bourgeois—for the benefit of the working-class.

3. *Critical-Utopian Socialism and Communism*

We do not here refer to that literature which, in every great modern revolution, has always given voice to the demands of the proletariat: such as the writings of Babeuf and others.

The first direct attempts of the proletariat to attain its own ends were made in times of universal excitement, when feudal society was being overthrown. These attempts necessarily failed, owing to the then undeveloped state of the proletariat, as well as to the absence of the economic conditions for its emancipation, conditions that had yet to be produced, and could be produced by the impending bourgeois epoch alone. The revolutionary literature that accompanied these first movements of the proletariat had necessarily a reactionary character. It inculcated universal asceticism and social leveling in its crudest form.

The Socialist and Communist systems properly so-called, those of St. Simon, Fourier, Owen and others, spring into existence in the early undeveloped period, described above, of the struggle between proletariat and bourgeoisie (see Section I. Bourgeois and Proletarians).

The founders of these systems see, indeed, the class antagonisms, as well as the action of the decomposing elements in the prevailing form of society. But the proletariat, as yet in its infancy, offers to them the spectacle of a class without any historical initiative or any independent political movement.

Since the development of class antagonism keeps even pace with the development of industry, the economic situation, as they find it, does not as yet offer to them the material conditions for the emancipation of the proletariat. They therefore search after a new social science, after new social laws, that are to create these conditions.

Historical action is to yield to their personal inventive action, historically created conditions of emancipation to fantastic ones, and the gradual, spontaneous class-organization of the proletariat to an organization of society specially contrived by these inventors. Future history resolves itself, in their eyes, into the propaganda and the practical carrying out of their social plans.

In the formation of their plans they are conscious of caring chiefly for the interests of the working-class, as being the most suffering class. Only from the point of view of being the most suffering class does the proletariat exist for them.

The undeveloped state of the class struggle, as well as their own surroundings, cause Socialists of this kind to consider themselves far superior to all class antagonisms. They want to improve the condition of every member of society, even that of the most favored. Hence, they habitually appeal to society at large, without distinction of class; nay, by preference, to the ruling class. For how can people, when once they understand their system, fail to see in it the best possible plan of the best possible state of society?

Hence, they reject all political, and especially all revolutionary action; they wish to attain their ends by peaceful means, and endeavor, by small experiments, necessarily doomed to failure, and by the force of example, to pave the way for the new social Gospel.

Such fantastic pictures of future society, painted at a time when the proletariat is still in a very undeveloped state, and has but a fantastic conception of its own position, correspond with the first instinctive yearnings of that class for a general reconstruction of society.

But these Socialist and Communist publications contain also a critical element. They attack every principle of existing society. Hence they are full of the most valuable materials for the enlightenment of the working-class. The practical measures proposed in them, such as the abolition of the distinction between town and country, of the family, of the carrying on of industries for the account of private individuals, and of the wage system, the proclamation of social harmony, the conversion of the functions of the State into a mere superintendence of production, all these proposals point solely to the disappearance of class antagonisms which were, at that time, only just cropping up, and which, in these publications, are recognized under their earliest, indistinct and undefined forms only. These proposals, therefore, are of a purely Utopian character.

The significance of Critical-Utopian Socialism and Communism bears an inverse relation to historical development. In proportion as the modern class struggle develops and takes definite shape, this fantastic standing apart from the contest, these fantastic attacks on it lose all practical value and all theoretical justification. Therefore, although the originators of these systems were, in many respects, revolutionary, their disciples have, in every case, formed mere reactionary sects. They hold fast by the original views of their masters, in opposition to the progressive historical development of the proletariat. They, therefore, endeavor and that consistently, to deaden the class struggle and to reconcile the class antagonisms. They still dream of experimental realization of their social Utopias, of founding isolated "phalanstères," of establishing "Home Colonies," of setting up a "Little Icaria"*—duodecimo editions of the New Jerusalem, and to realize all these castles in the air, they are compelled to appeal to the feelings and purses of the bourgeois. By degrees they sink into the category of the reactionary conservative Socialists depicted above, differing from these only by more systematic pedantry, and by their fanatical and superstitious belief in the miraculous effects of their social science.

They, therefore, violently oppose all political action on the part of the working-class; such action, according to them, can only result from blind unbelief in the new Gospel.

The Owenites in England, and the Fourierists in France, respectively, oppose the Chartists and the "Réformistes."

IV

Position of the Communists in Relation to the Various Existing Opposition Parties

Section II has made clear the relations of the Communists to the existing working-class parties, such as the Chartists in England and the Agrarian Reformers in America.

The Communists fight for the attainment of the immediate aims, for the enforcement of the momentary interests of the working-class; but in the movement of the present, they also represent and take care of the future of that movement. In France the Communists ally themselves with the Social-Democrats,† against the conservative and

* Phalanstères were socialist colonies on the plan of Charles Fourier. Icaria was the name given by Cabet to his Utopia and, later on, to his American Communist colony.

† The party then represented in parliament by Ledru-Rollin, in literature by Louis Blanc, in the daily press by the Réforme. The name of Social Democracy signified, with these its inventors, a section of the Democratic or Republican party more or less tinged with Socialism.

radical bourgeoisie, reserving, however, the right to take up a critical position in regard to phrases and illusions traditionally handed down from the great Revolution.

In Switzerland they support the Radicals, without losing sight of the fact that this party consists of antagonistic elements, partly of Democratic Socialists, in the French sense, partly of radical bourgeois.

In Poland they support the party that insists on an agrarian revolution, as the prime condition for national emancipation, that party which fomented the insurrection of Cracow in 1846.

In Germany they fight with the bourgeoisie whenever it acts in a revolutionary way, against the absolute monarchy, the feudal squirearchy, and the petty bourgeoisie.

But they never cease, for a single instant, to instill into the working-class the clearest possible recognition of the hostile antagonism between bourgeoisie and proletariat, in order that the German workers may straightway use, as so many weapons against the bourgeoisie, the social and political conditions that the bourgeoisie must necessarily introduce along with its supremacy, and in order that, after the fall of the reactionary classes in Germany, the fight against the bourgeoisie itself may immediately begin.

The Communists turn their attention chiefly to Germany, because that country is on the eve of a bourgeois revolution, that is bound to be carried out under more advanced conditions of European civilization, and with a more developed proletariat, than that of England was in the seventeenth, and of France in the eighteenth century, and because the bourgeois revolution in Germany will be but the prelude to an immediately following proletarian revolution.

In short, the Communists everywhere support every revolutionary movement against the existing social and political order of things.

In all these movements they bring to the front, as the leading question in each, the property question, no matter what its degree of development at the time.

Finally, they labor everywhere for the union and agreement of the democratic parties of all countries.

The Communists disdain to conceal their views and aims. They openly declare that their ends can be attained only by the forcible overthrow of all existing social conditions. Let the ruling classes tremble at a Communistic revolution. The proletarians have nothing to lose but their chains. They have a world to win.

Working men of all countries, unite!

Twenty-five Years Later.[1] However much the state of things may have altered during the last 25 years, the general principles laid down in this Manifesto, are, on the whole, as correct today as ever. Here and there some detail might be improved. The practical application of the principles will depend, as the manifesto itself states, everywhere and at all times, on the historical conditions for the time being existing, and, for that reason, no special stress is laid on the revolutionary measures proposed at the end of Section II. That passage would, in many respects, be very differently worded today. In view of the gigantic strides of Modern Industry since 1848, and of the accompanying improved and extended organization of the working-class, in view of the practical experience gained, first in the February revolution, and then, still more, in the Paris Commune, where the proletariat for the first time held political power for two whole months, this program has in some details become antiquated. One thing especially was proved by the Commune, viz., that "the working-class cannot simply lay hold of the ready-made State machinery, and wield it for its own purposes." (See "The Civil War in France; Address of the General Council of the International Working-men's Association," London, Truelove, 1871, p. 15; and Chicago, Charles K. Kerr & Co., where this point is further developed.) Further, it is self-evident, that the criticism of socialist literature is deficient in relation to the present time, because it comes down only to 1847; also, that the remarks on the relation of the Communists to the various opposition-parties (Section IV), although in principle still correct, yet in practice are antiquated, because the political situation has been entirely changed, and the progress of history has swept from off the earth the greater portion of the political parties there enumerated.

But then, the Manifesto has become a historical document which we have no longer any right to alter.

[1] From Marx and Engels's preface to the 1872 edition of the Manifesto.

XX

EDUARD BERNSTEIN

1850–1932

The family of Eduard Bernstein was Jewish, and came originally from Poland. He himself was born in Berlin, in 1850, the son of a locomotive engineer. After completing his education in the gymnasium (higher secondary school) he entered business at sixteen as a bank clerk. Seemingly headed for respectable oblivion, he fell under the influence of an uncle, editor of the Berlin *Volkszeitung*, who interested him in Marxism, and in 1872 he joined the Social Democratic party. Six years later he began a journalistic career as secretary to Karl Höchberg, wealthy founder of the socialist *Zukunft*.

But the engagement was cut short. Bismarck's anti-socialist law of 1878 compelled Bernstein to leave Germany: he did not return until twenty years afterward. During the first ten years of exile he resided in Zurich, Switzerland, editing the *Socialdemocrat*, the official party organ, which was also in exile. In 1888, at the instigation of Bismarck, the Swiss authorities ejected him. In the meanwhile he had several times visited London, becoming personally acquainted with Marx and Engels, and he now took refuge there permanently.

In England Bernstein continued his work as a journalist, acting as correspondent for the Berlin *Vorwärts*. He also wrote extensively on the history and theory of socialism and was on intimate terms with the leaders of the British movement. Although for a long time prejudiced against the tone and methods of the Fabians, he is said to have been markedly influenced by their belief in gradual evolution as a means of attaining the socialistic ideal. His reading of Lassalle, whose writings he later edited, perhaps worked to the same end. In any event he published a series of articles in 1897–98 on the problems of socialism, in which he attempted to prove that the classic Marxian doctrine needed revision. These were summed up in *Evolutionary Socialism* (1899), the book by which he is perhaps best known to readers outside of Germany.

These views aroused a controversy which went on in Germany for years, Karl Kautsky as the champion of "orthodox" Marxism being his chief opponent. Bernstein's revisionism was voted down by a large majority at the Hanover congress of the Social Democratic party in 1899, but on his return to Germany in 1901 he gained a numerous following among the younger members of the party. Indeed, it is said that von Bülow, the German chancellor, lifted the ban against Bernstein in order to promote discord in the ranks of the socialists.

In 1902 Bernstein was elected to the Reichstag. Although a reputed pacifist, he joined the majority of his party in voting the war credits in 1914 and for a time acted as counsellor to the treasury. But his old convictions finally reasserted themselves: he forswore all coöperation with the government, patched up a reconciliation with Kautsky, and in 1915 joined in a manifesto declaring that the Social Democrats, although they had voted for the budget, ought to renounce their responsibility for the war policy of the empire. In spite of the fact that he was a right-wing socialist, the same convictions caused him to join the group which early in 1916 broke away from the party to form the Independent Social Democratic party. In 1919, however, he rejoined the majority socialists. During the war Bernstein worked for peace, especially with England where he had many friends. An opponent of revolution, he tried to prevent the infiltration of Bolshevism into Germany.

After the war Bernstein was one of the first Germans to admit the war responsibility of the Central Powers and to recognize the justice of reparations. In 1928 he withdrew from parliamentary activities on account of age. He died in Berlin in 1932. Bernstein, it has been asserted, was "throughout his life more an adherent of radical democracy than of one-sided socialism."

REFERENCES

Aside from *Evolutionary Socialism* the following works of Bernstein have been translated into English: *Cromwell and Communism* (1930), *My Years of Exile* (1921), and *Ferdinand Lassalle as a Social Reformer* (1893).

The only extended account of his life is his own reminiscences, *My Years of Exile* (1921), which cover only a part of his career.

READINGS FROM

EVOLUTIONARY SOCIALISM

Economic Catastrophe Unlikely.[1] It has been maintained in a certain quarter that the practical deductions from my treatises would be the abandonment of the conquest of political power by

[1] Published by the Viking Press, Inc., New York. Edith C. Harvey, translator (1909, German edition, 1899); preface, pp. x–xi.

the proletariat organised politically and economically. That is quite an arbitrary deduction, the accuracy of which I altogether deny.

I set myself against the notion that we have to expect shortly a collapse of the bourgeois economy, and that social democracy should be induced by the prospect of such an imminent, great, social catastrophe to adapt its tactics to that assumption. That I maintain most emphatically.

The adherents of this theory of a catastrophe, base it especially on the conclusions of the *Communist Manifesto*. This is a mistake in every respect.

The theory which the *Communist Manifesto* sets forth of the evolution of modern society was correct as far as it characterised the general tendencies of that evolution. But it was mistaken in several special deductions, above all in the estimate of the *time* the evolution would take. The last has been unreservedly acknowledged by Friedrich Engels, the joint author with Marx of the *Manifesto*, in his preface to the *Class War in France*. But it is evident that if social evolution takes a much greater period of time than was assumed, it must also take upon itself *forms* and lead to forms that were not foreseen and could not be foreseen then.

Social conditions have not developed to such an acute opposition of things and classes as is depicted in the *Manifesto*. It is not only useless, it is the greatest folly to attempt to conceal this from ourselves. The number of members of the possessing classes is to-day not smaller but larger. The enormous increase of social wealth is not accompanied by a decreasing number of large capitalists but by an increasing number of capitalists of all degrees. The middle classes change their character but they do not disappear from the social scale.

The concentration in productive industry is not being accomplished even to-day in all its departments with equal thoroughness and at an equal rate. In a great many branches of production it certainly justifies the forecasts of the socialist critic of society; but in other branches it lags even to-day behind them. The process of concentration in agriculture proceeds still more slowly. Trade statistics show an extraordinarily elaborated graduation of enterprises in regard to size. No rung of the ladder is disappearing from it. The significant changes in the inner structure of these enterprises and their interrelationship cannot do away with this fact. . . .

Evolutionary Socialism Justified.[1] In all advanced countries we see the privileges of the capitalist bourgeoisie yielding step by step to democratic organisations. Under the influence of this, and driven by the movement of the working classes which is daily becoming stronger, a social reaction has set in against the exploiting tendencies of capital, a counteraction which, although it still proceeds timidly and feebly, yet does exist, and is always drawing more departments of economic life under its influence. Factory legislation, the democratising of local government, and the extension of its area of work, the freeing of trade unions and systems of coöperative trading from legal restrictions, the consideration of standard conditions of labour in the work undertaken by public authorities—all these characterise this phase of the evolution.

But the more the political organisations of modern nations are democratised the more the needs and opportunities of great political catastrophes are diminished. He who holds firmly to the catastrophic theory of evolution must, with all his power, withstand and hinder the evolution described above, which, indeed, the logical defenders of that theory formerly did. But is the conquest of political power by the proletariat simply to be by a political catastrophe? Is it to be the appropriation and utilisation of the power of the State by the proletariat exclusively against the whole non-proletarian world?

He who replies in the affirmative must be reminded of two things. In 1872 Marx and Engels announced in the preface to the new edition of the *Communist Manifesto* that the Paris Commune had exhibited a proof that "the working classes cannot simply take possession of the ready-made State machine and set it in motion for their own aims." And in 1895 Friedrich Engels stated in detail in the preface to *War of the Classes* that the time of political surprises, of the "revolutions of small conscious minorities at the head of unconscious masses" was to-day at an end, that a collision on a large scale with the military would be the means of checking the steady growth of social democracy and of even throwing it back for a time—in short, that social democracy would flourish far better by lawful than by unlawful means and by violent revolution. And he points out in conformity with this opinion that the next task of the party should be "to work for an uninterrupted increase of its votes" or to carry on a slow *propaganda of parliamentary activity*.

[1] Preface, pp. xi–xvi.

Thus Engels, who, nevertheless, as his numerical examples show, still somewhat overestimated the rate of process of the evolution! Shall we be told that he abandoned the conquest of political power by the working classes, because he wished to avoid the steady growth of social democracy secured by lawful means being interrupted by a political revolution?

If not, and if one subscribes to his conclusions, one cannot reasonably take any offence if it is declared that for a long time yet the task of social democracy is, instead of speculating on a great economic crash, "to organise the working classes politically and develop them as a democracy and to fight for all reforms in the State which are adapted to raise the working classes and transform the State in the direction of democracy."

That is what I have said in my impugned article and what I still maintain in its full import. As far as concerns the question propounded above it is equivalent to Engels's dictum, for democracy is, at any given time, as much government by the working classes as these are capable of practising according to their intellectual ripeness and the degree of social development they have attained. Engels, indeed, refers at the place just mentioned to the fact that the *Communist Manifesto* has "proclaimed the conquest of the democracy as one of the first and important tasks of the fighting proletariat."

In short, Engels is so thoroughly convinced that the tactics based on the presumption of a catastrophe have had their day, that he even considers a revision of them necessary in the Latin countries where tradition is much more favourable to them than in Germany. "If the conditions of war between nations have altered," he writes, "no less have those for the war between classes." Has this already been forgotten?

No one has questioned the necessity for the working classes to gain the control of government. The point at issue is between the theory of a social cataclysm and the question whether with the given social development in Germany and the present advanced state of its working classes in the towns and the country, a sudden catastrophe would be desirable in the interest of the social democracy. I have denied it and deny it again, because in my judgment a greater security for lasting success lies in a steady advance than in the possibilities offered by a catastrophic crash.

And as I am firmly convinced that important periods in the development of nations cannot be leapt over I lay the greatest value on the next tasks of social democracy, on the struggle for the political rights of the working man, on the political activity of working men in town and country for the interests of their class, as well as on the work of the industrial organisation of the workers.

In this sense I wrote the sentence that the movement means everything for me and that what is *usually* called "the final aim of socialism" is nothing; and in this sense I write it down again to-day. Even if the word "usually" had not shown that the proposition was only to be understood conditionally, it was obvious that it *could* not express indifference concerning the final carrying out of socialist principles, but only indifference—or, as it would be better expressed, carelessness—as to the form of the final arrangement of things. I have at no time had an excessive interest in the future, beyond general principles; I have not been able to read to the end any picture of the future. My thoughts and efforts are concerned with the duties of the present and the nearest future, and I only busy myself with the perspectives beyond so far as they give me a line of conduct for suitable action now.

The conquest of political power by the working classes, the expropriation of capitalists, are no ends in themselves but only means for the accomplishment of certain aims and endeavours. As such they are demands in the programme of social democracy and are not attacked by me. Nothing can be said beforehand as to the circumstances of their accomplishment; we can only fight for their realisation. But the conquest of political power necessitates the possession of political *rights;* and the most important problem of tactics which German social democracy has at the present time to solve, appears to me to be to devise the best ways for the extension of the political and economic rights of the German working classes. . . .

On the Socialist Program.[1] It does not lie in the plan of this work to undertake an estimation of individual points of the socialist programme of action. As far as concerns the immediate demands of the Erfurt programme of the German social democracy, I do not feel in any way tempted to propose changes with respect to them. Probably, like every social democrat, I do not hold all points equally important or equally expedient. . . .

Let me here quote two sentences from [an article of mine] which indicate the point of view which I upheld at that time with regard to

[1] Pp. 167, 168–172, 174, 179–180.

the action of social democracy, and which will show how much or how little my opinions have changed since then:—

"To demand simply the maintenance of all those without employment out of the state money means to commit to the trough of the state not only everyone who cannot find work but everyone that will not find work. . . . One need really be no anarchist in order to find the eternal heaping of duties on the state too much of a good thing. We will hold fast to the principle that the modern proletarian is indeed poor but that he is no pauper. In this distinction lies a whole world, the nature of our fight, the hope of our victory."

"We propose the formula: 'Conversion of the standing armies to citizen armies' because it maintains the aim and yet leaves the party a free hand to-day (when the disbanding of standing armies is utterly impossible) to demand a series of measures which narrow as much as possible the antagonism between army and people as, for example, the abolition of special military courts of justice, lessening of time of service, etc."

But has social democracy, as the party of the working classes and of peace, an interest in the maintenance of the fighting power? From many points of view it is very tempting to answer the question in the negative, especially if one starts from the sentence in the *Communist Manifesto:* "The proletarian has no fatherland." This sentence might, in a degree, perhaps, apply to the worker of the 'forties without political rights, shut out of public life. To-day in spite of the enormous increase in the intercourse between nations it has already forfeited a great part of its truth and will always forfeit more, the more the worker, by the influence of socialism, moves from being a proletarian to a citizen. The workman who has equal rights as a voter for state and local councils, and who thereby is a fellow owner of the common property of the nation, whose children the community educates, whose health it protects, whom it secures against injury, has a fatherland without ceasing on that account to be a citizen of the world, just as the nations draw nearer one another, without, therefore, ceasing to lead a life of their own.

The complete breaking up of nations is no beautiful dream, and in any case is not to be expected in the near future. But just as little as it is to be wished that any other of the great civilised nations should lose its independence, just as little can it be a matter of indifference to German social democracy whether the German nation, which has indeed carried out, and is carrying out, its honourable share in the civilising work of the world, should be repressed in the council of the nations.

In the foregoing is shown in principle the point of view from which the social democracy has to take its position under present conditions with regard to questions of foreign politics. If the worker is still no full citizen, he is not without rights in the sense that national interests can be indifferent to him. And if also social democracy is not yet in power, it already takes a position of influence which lays certain obligations upon it. Its words fall with great weight in the scale. With the present composition of the army and the complete uncertainty as to the change in methods of war, etc., brought about by the use of guns of small bore, the Imperial Government will think ten times before venturing on a war which has social democracy as its determined opponent. Even without the celebrated general strike social democracy can speak a very important, if not decisive, word for peace and will do this according to the device of the International as often and as energetically as it is necessary and possible. It will also, according to its programme, in the cases when conflicts arise with other nations and direct agreement is not possible, stand up for settling the difference by means of arbitration. But it is not called upon to speak in favour of renunciation of the preservation of German interests, present or future, if or because English, French, or Russian Chauvinists take umbrage at the measures adopted. Where, on the German side, it is not a question merely of fancies or of the particular interests of separate groups which are indifferent or even detrimental to the welfare of the nation, where really important national interests are at stake, internationalism can be no reason for a weak yielding to the pretensions of foreign interested parties.

This is no new idea, but simply the putting together of the lines of thought which lie at the bottom of all the declarations of Marx, Engels, and Lassalle on the questions of foreign politics. It is also no attitude endangering peace which is here recommended. Nations to-day no longer lightly go to war, and a firm stand can under some circumstances be more serviceable to peace than continuous yielding.

The doctrine of the European balance of power seems to many to be out of date to-day, and so it is in its old form. But in a changed form the balance of power still plays a great part in the decision of vexed international questions. It still comes occasionally to the question of how strong a combination of powers supports any given measure in order that it may be carried through or hindered. I consider it a legitimate task of German Imperial politics to secure a right to have a voice in the discussion of such cases; and to oppose, on principle, proper steps to that end, I consider, falls outside the domain of the tasks of social democracy. . . .

Meanwhile, owing to the want of responsibility in the management of the foreign policy of Germany, there can be no question of positive support from the social democracy, but only of the right foundation of its negative attitude. Without a guarantee that such undertakings should not be turned to account over the heads of the people's representative House for other aims than those announced, say as a means to achieve some temporary success which might surrender the greater interests of the future, without some such pledge social democracy can take upon itself no share in the measures of foreign policy. . . .

There are socialists to whom every admission of national interests appears as Chauvinism or as an injury to the internationalism and class policy of the proletariat. As in his time Domela Nieuwenhuis declared Bebel's well-known assertion—that in case of an attack on the part of Russia the social democracy would set up their men for the defence of Germany—to be Chauvinism, so lately, Mr. Belfort Bax also found reprehensible jingoism in a similar assertion by Mr. Hyndman.

It must be admitted that it is not always easy to fix the boundary where the advocacy of the interests of one's nation ceases to be just and to pass into pseudo-patriotism; but the remedy for exaggeration on this side certainly does not lie in greater exaggeration on the other. It is much more to be sought in a movement for the exchange of thought between the democracies of the civilised countries and in the support of all factors and institutes working for peace. . . .

PART VI

STATE SOCIALISM, LIMITED AND UNLIMITED

XXI

HENRY GEORGE

1839–1897

The mercantile yet thoroughly religious and ethical tone of Henry George's philosophy no doubt reflects his early home life. His father, a publisher of religious books in Philadelphia, where George was born in 1839, had previously been a dry-goods merchant and a custom-house clerk. The boy was the second of ten children. Both parents—his mother in particular—were devoted to religion, and although Henry slipped away later on, he speedily found his way back into the fold.

Young George left school at thirteen. Wide reading and attendance at popular lectures served to fill out his education. A marked taste for poetry exhibited itself afterward in the lyrical quality of his own writing. His first business experience was gained as an errand boy and then an insurance-office clerk. But the greatest event of his boyhood was a voyage to Australia and India; he travelled as a paid hand. Returning to America he cast about for a job, finally entering a printing office. Printing and newspaper work were to be his main reliance from then on, but for some time he interspersed them with mining projects, store clerking, and further experience at sea.

In the course of these activities George went to the Pacific coast, finally settling in San Francisco where he obtained work on a newspaper. In 1861, after losing his position, he married and for some time lived in the direst poverty, painfully supporting his family with printing and newspaper work and occasional excursions into selling clothes-wringers and carriage brakes. This experience magnified the problem of poverty. It was driven home by a trip to New York, where he saw the extremes of luxury and want flourishing side by side.

Meanwhile he had obtained regular and remunerative employment on the San Francisco *Times*, had risen rapidly from printer to managing editor, but had resigned in 1868 because his salary showed no prospect of approaching what he considered his deserts. This, however, was followed by further newspaper work and several ventures into politics. As a candidate for the California state assembly he was defeated through the influence of the Central Pacific Railroad, subsidies to which he had opposed. The land speculation consequent upon the completion of the railroad to Sacramento and Oakland furnished him with further object lessons for his slowly maturing economic theories.

These had been foreshadowed in a magazine article in 1868. Three years later he sketched the main outlines of his system in a pamphlet on *Our Land and Land Policy*, and during the depression year of 1877 sat down to elaborate his thesis. The work was completed in 1879. After some difficulty in securing a publisher *Progress and Poverty* appeared.

The solution of his problem, said George, had come through a flash of insight, "an ecstatic vision." A thorough study of the economists, however, which he undertook in preparation for *Progress and Poverty*, showed him that he had been forestalled on many points. The discovery gratified him as confirming his own views, and he made much of Ricardo's theory of rent. In fact, some of the theory of many eighteenth- and nineteenth-century writers could be fitted into his system. Such were the Physiocrats (with their *impôt unique*), Spence, Ogilvie, Paine, Malthus, James and John Stuart Mill, Karl Marx, and Herbert Spencer. One Patrick Dove, writing on the *Theory of Human Progression* in 1850 had even "advanced the identical solution that was proposed by George."

The remainder of George's life was spent in propagating his new ideas. He moved to New York and while waiting for his book to take hold made a living by writing and lecturing. The land question was then at fever heat in Ireland; in 1881 he published a book on the subject. Engaged by the New York *Irish World* as its correspondent, he travelled to Ireland and England, meeting the leaders of the land movement and speaking and writing on his specialty. The expedition made him an international figure. When he returned to New York he was given a public reception in which representatives of labor joined. Trips to Great Britain in 1883 and 1884 increased his reputation abroad and left a lasting impression on the British socialist and labor movement.

In 1886 George published *Protection and Free Trade*. The same year he ran for mayor of New York, and although defeated after a hot campaign he polled a large minority. But he had lacked watchers at the polls, and therefore declared that if the votes had been properly counted he would have been victorious. The following years were spent in organizing Land and Labor Clubs throughout the country and in writing and lecturing. In 1887 he published *The Science of Political*

Economy and in 1891 a reply to Pope Leo XIII's encyclical on the labor question. He again visited England and Australia.

George supported Bryan and the silver platform in 1896. The next year he campaigned a second time for the mayoralty of New York. But the strain of constant speaking was too great and on the eve of the election he died following a stroke of apoplexy.

Estimates of Henry George's influence vary. Professor Dewey suggests that it was circumscribed by the fact that George was an American and moreover not an academic economist. It is true that few professional economists adopted his principles. But a number of wealthy and influential laymen supported him, "attracted perhaps," says Professor Tugwell, "by the fact that his scheme seemed to offer no threat to the business system." The Fabian Society also, and British reformers generally, gratefully acknowledged their debt to Henry George. Tolstoy became his reverent disciple. Some attempts, more or less successful, have been made in Australia and elsewhere to put his theories into practice. On the whole, however much the enthusiastic claims of his followers are discounted, there can be little doubt that Henry George was a great liberalizing force, particularly in England.

REFERENCES

George's *Complete Works* have been published in ten volumes (1906–11). F. Brown has assembled *Significant Paragraphs from Progress and Poverty* (1928).

The fullest commentary on George's work is G. R. Geiger's *The Philosophy of Henry George* (1933).

The standard biography is that of George's son, Henry George (1911). L. F. Post's *The Prophet of San Francisco* (1930) adds the reminiscences of a disciple. Excellent biographical and critical articles are to be found in the *Dictionary of American Biography* and the *Encyclopedia of the Social Sciences*.

READINGS FROM

PROGRESS AND POVERTY

The Synthesis of Opposites.[1] In certain respects this book will be best appreciated by those who have some knowledge of economic literature; but no previous reading is necessary to the understanding of the argument or the passing of judgment upon its conclusions. The

[1] *Progress and Poverty* (1926, first published 1879. Copyright by Doubleday, Doran and Co., New York), preface, pp. xi, xv

facts upon which I have relied are not facts which can be verified only by a search through libraries. They are facts of common observation and common knowledge, which every reader can verify for himself, just as he can decide whether the reasoning from them is or is not valid. . . .

What I have done in this book, if I have correctly solved the great problem I have sought to investigate, is, to unite the truth perceived by the school of Smith and Ricardo to the truth perceived by the schools of Proudhon and Lassalle; to show that *laissez faire* (in its full true meaning) opens the way to a realization of the noble dreams of socialism; to identify social law with moral law, and to disprove ideas which in the minds of many cloud grand and elevating perceptions. . . .

Progress and Poverty.[1] Unpleasant as it may be to admit it, it is at last becoming evident that the enormous increase in productive power which has marked the present century and is still going on with accelerating ratio, has no tendency to extirpate poverty or to lighten the burdens of those compelled to toil. It simply widens the gulf between Dives and Lazarus, and makes the struggle for existence more intense. The march of invention has clothed mankind with powers of which a century ago the boldest imagination could not have dreamed. But in factories where labor-saving machinery has reached its most wonderful development, little children are at work; wherever the new forces are anything like fully utilized, large classes are maintained by charity or live on the verge of recourse to it; amid the greatest accumulations of wealth, men die of starvation, and puny infants suckle dry breasts; while everywhere the greed of gain, the worship of wealth, shows the force of the fear of want. The promised land flies before us like the mirage. The fruits of the tree of knowledge turn as we grasp them to apples of Sodom that crumble at the touch.

It is true that wealth has been greatly increased, and that the average of comfort, leisure, and refinement has been raised; but these gains are not general. In them the lowest class do not share. I do not mean that the condition of the lowest class has nowhere nor in anything been improved; but that there is nowhere any improvement which can be credited to increased productive power. I mean that the tendency of what we call material progress is in nowise to improve the

[1] *Ibid.*, pp. 8–10.

condition of the lowest class in the essentials of healthy, happy human life. Nay, more, that it is still further to depress the condition of the lowest class. The new forces, elevating in their nature though they be, do not act upon the social fabric from underneath, as was for a long time hoped and believed, but strike it at a point intermediate between top and bottom. It is as though an immense wedge were being forced, not underneath society, but through society. Those who are above the point of separation are elevated, but those who are below are crushed down.

This depressing effect is not generally realized, for it is not apparent where there has long existed a class just able to live. Where the lowest class barely lives, as has been the case for a long time in many parts of Europe, it is impossible for it to get any lower, for the next lowest step is out of existence, and no tendency to further depression can readily show itself. But in the progress of new settlements to the conditions of older communities it may clearly be seen that material progress does not merely fail to relieve poverty—it actually produces it. In the United States it is clear that squalor and misery, and the vices and crimes that spring from them, everywhere increase as the village grows to the city, and the march of development brings the advantages of the improved methods of production and exchange. It is in the older and richer sections of the Union that pauperism and distress among the working classes are becoming most painfully apparent. If there is less deep poverty in San Francisco than in New York, is it not because San Francisco is yet behind New York in all that both cities are striving for? When San Francisco reaches the point where New York now is, who can doubt that there will also be ragged and barefooted children on her streets?

This association of poverty with progress is the great enigma of our times. It is the central fact from which spring industrial, social, and political difficulties that perplex the world, and with which statesmanship and philanthropy and education grapple in vain. From it come the clouds that overhang the future of the most progressive and self-reliant nations. It is the riddle which the Sphinx of Fate puts to our civilization, and which not to answer is to be destroyed. So long as all the increased wealth which modern progress brings goes but to build up great fortunes, to increase luxury and make sharper the contrast between the House of Have and the House of Want, progress is not real and cannot be permanent. The reaction must come. The tower leans from its foundations, and every new story but hastens the final catastrophe. To educate men who must be condemned to poverty, is but to make them restive; to base on a state of most glaring social inequality political institutions under which men are theoretically equal, is to stand a pyramid on its apex.

Wrong Explanations and Remedies.[1] All-important as this question is, pressing itself from every quarter painfully upon attention, it has not yet received a solution which accounts for all the facts and points to any clear and simple remedy. This is shown by the widely varying attempts to account for the prevailing depression. They exhibit not merely a divergence between vulgar notions and scientific theories, but also show that the concurrence which should exist between those who avow the same general theories breaks up upon practical questions into an anarchy of opinion. Upon high economic authority we have been told that the prevailing depression is due to over-consumption; upon equally high authority, that it is due to over-production; while the wastes of war, the extension of railroads, the attempts of workmen to keep up wages, the demonetization of silver, the issues of paper money, the increase of labor-saving machinery, the opening of shorter avenues to trade, etc., are separately pointed out as the cause, by writers of reputation.

And while professors thus disagree, the ideas that there is a necessary conflict between capital and labor, that machinery is an evil, that competition must be restrained and interest abolished, that wealth may be created by the issue of money, that it is the duty of government to furnish capital or to furnish work, are rapidly making way among the great body of the people, who keenly feel a hurt and are sharply conscious of a wrong. Such ideas, which bring great masses of men, the repositories of ultimate political power, under the leadership of charlatans and demagogues, are fraught with danger; but they cannot be successfully combated until political economy shall give some answer to the great question which shall be consistent with all her teachings, and which shall commend itself to the perceptions of the great masses of men. . . .

I propose in the following pages to attempt to solve by the methods of political economy the great problem I have outlined. I propose to seek the law which associates poverty with progress, and increases want with advancing wealth. . . .

[1] *Ibid.*, pp. 10–11, 12.

The Justification of Interest.[1] That interest does not depend on the productiveness of labor and capital is proved by the general fact that where labor and capital are most productive interest is lowest. That it does not depend reversely upon wages (or the cost of labor), lowering as wages rise, and increasing as wages fall, is proved by the general fact that interest is high when and where wages are high, and low when and where wages are low. . . .

What is the reason and justification of interest? Why should the borrower pay back to the lender more than he received? These questions are worth answering, not merely from their speculative, but from their practical importance. The feeling that interest is the robbery of industry is widespread and growing, and on both sides of the Atlantic shows itself more and more in popular literature and in popular movements. . . .

I am inclined to think that if all wealth consisted of such things as planes, and all production was such as that of carpenters—that is to say, if wealth consisted but of the inert matter of the universe, and production of working up this inert matter into different shapes, that interest would be but the robbery of industry, and could not long exist. . . .

But all wealth is not of the nature of planes, or planks, or money, which has no reproductive power; nor is all production merely the turning into other forms of this inert matter of the universe. It is true that if I put away money, it will not increase. But suppose, instead, I put away wine. At the end of a year I will have an increased value, for the wine will have improved in quality. Or supposing that in a country adapted to them, I set out bees; at the end of a year I will have more swarms of bees, and the honey which they have made. Or, supposing, where there is a range, I turn out sheep, or hogs, or cattle; at the end of the year I will, upon the average, also have an increase. . . .

Now the interchangeability of wealth necessarily involves an average between all the species of wealth of any special advantage which accrues from the possession of any particular species, for no one would keep capital in one form when it could be changed into a more advantageous form. No one, for instance, would grind wheat into flour and keep it on hand for the convenience of those who desire from time to time to exchange wheat or its equivalent for flour, unless he could by such exchange secure an increase equal to that which, all things con-

[1] *Ibid.*, pp. 174, 175, 180, 181–183, 185–186, 187.

sidered, he could secure by planting his wheat. No one, if he could keep them, would exchange a flock of sheep now for their net weight in mutton to be returned next year; for by keeping the sheep he would not only have the same amount of mutton next year, but also the lambs and the fleeces. No one would dig an irrigating ditch, unless those who by its aid are enabled to utilize the reproductive forces of nature would give him such a portion of the increase they receive as to make his capital yield him as much as theirs. And so, in any circle of exchange, the power of increase which the reproductive or vital force of nature gives to some species of capital must average with all; and he who lends, or uses in exchange, money, or planes, or bricks, or clothing, is not deprived of the power to obtain an increase, any more than if he had lent or put to a reproductive use so much capital in a form capable of increase.

There is also in the utilization of the variations in the powers of nature and of man which is effected by exchange, an increase which somewhat resembles that produced by the vital forces of nature. In one place, for instance, a given amount of labor will secure 200 in vegetable food or 100 in animal food. In another place, these conditions are reversed, and the same amount of labor will produce 100 in vegetable food or 200 in animal. In the one place, the relative value of vegetable to animal food will be as two to one, and in the other as one to two; and, supposing equal amounts of each to be required, the same amount of labor will in either place secure 150 of both. But by devoting labor in the one place to the procurement of vegetable food, and in the other, to the procurement of animal food, and exchanging to the quantity required, the people of each place will be enabled by the given amount of labor to procure 200 of both, less the losses and expenses of exchange; so that in each place the produce which is taken from use and devoted to exchange brings back an increase. Thus Whittington's cat, sent to a far country where cats are scarce and rats are plenty, returns in bales of goods and bags of gold. . . .

Were the quality and capacity of matter everywhere uniform, and all productive power in man, there would be no interest. The advantage of superior tools might at times be transferred on terms resembling the payment of interest, but such transactions would be irregular and intermittent—the exception, not the rule. For the power of obtaining such returns would not, as now, inhere in the possession of capital, and the advantage of time would operate only in peculiar circumstances. That I, having a thousand dollars, can certainly let it out at interest, does not arise from the fact that there are others, not having a thousand dollars, who will gladly pay me for the use of it, if they can get it no other way; but from the fact that the capital which my thousand dollars represents has the power of yielding an increase to whomsoever has it, even though he be a millionaire. For the price which anything will bring does not depend upon what the buyer would be willing to give rather than go without it, so much as upon what the seller can otherwise get. For instance, a manufacturer who wishes to retire from business has machinery to the value of $100,000. If he cannot, should he sell, take this $100,000 and invest it so that it will yield him interest, it will be immaterial to him, risk being eliminated, whether he obtains the whole price at once or in installments, and if the purchaser has the requisite capital, which we must suppose in order that the transaction may rest on its own merits, it will be immaterial whether he pay at once or after a time. If the purchaser has not the required capital, it may be to his convenience that payments should be delayed, but it would be only in exceptional circumstances that the seller would ask, or the buyer would consent, to pay any premium on this account; nor in such cases would this premium be properly interest. For interest is not properly a payment made for the use of capital, but a return accruing from the increase of capital. If the capital did not yield an increase, the cases would be few and exceptional in which the owner would get a premium. . . .

Primarily, the benefits which arise from use go to labor, and the benefits which arise from increase, to capital. But, inasmuch as the division of labor and the interchangeability of wealth necessitate and imply an averaging of benefits, in so far as these different modes of production correlate with each other, the benefits that arise from one will average with the benefits that arise from the others, for neither labor nor capital will be devoted to any mode of production while any other mode which is open to them will yield a greater return. That is to say, labor expended in the first mode of production will get, not the whole return, but the return minus such part as is necessary to give to capital such an increase as it could have secured in the other modes of production, and capital engaged in the second and third modes will obtain, not the whole increase, but the increase minus what is sufficient to give to labor such reward as it could have secured if expended in the first mode.

Thus interest springs from the power of increase which the reproductive forces of nature, and the in effect analogous capacity for exchange, give to capital. It is not an arbitrary, but a natural thing; it is not the result of a particular social organization, but of laws of the universe which underlie society. It is, therefore, just. . . .

False Capital and Interest.[1] The belief that interest is the robbery of industry is, I am persuaded, in large part due to a failure to discriminate between what is really capital and what is not, and between profits which are properly interest and profits which arise from other sources than the use of capital. In the speech and literature of the day every one is styled a capitalist who possesses what, independent of his labor, will yield him a return, while whatever is thus received is spoken of as the earnings or takings of capital, and we everywhere hear of the conflict of labor and capital. Whether there is, in reality, any conflict between labor and capital, I do not yet ask the reader to make up his mind; but it will be well here to clear away some misapprehensions which confuse the judgment. . . .

Land values, which constitute such an enormous part of what is commonly called capital, are not capital at all; and . . . rent, which is as commonly included in the receipts of capital, and which takes an ever-increasing portion of the produce of an advancing community, is not the earnings of capital, and must be carefully separated from interest. It is not necessary now to dwell further upon this point. Attention has likewise been called to the fact that the stocks, bonds, etc., which constitute another great part of what is commonly called capital, are not capital at all; but, in some of their shapes, these evidences of indebtedness so closely resemble capital and in some cases actually perform, or seem to perform, the functions of capital, while they yield a return to their owners which is not only spoken of as interest, but has every semblance of interest, that it is worth while, before attempting to clear the idea of interest from some other ambiguities that beset it, to speak again of these at greater length.

Nothing can be capital, let it always be remembered, that is not wealth—that is to say, nothing can be capital that does not consist of actual, tangible things, not the spontaneous offerings of nature, which have in themselves, and not by proxy, the power of directly or indirectly ministering to human desire.

Thus, a government bond is not capital, nor yet is it the representative of capital. The capital that was once received for it by the gov-

[1] *Ibid.*, pp. 189–194.

ernment has been consumed unproductively—blown away from the mouths of cannon, used up in war ships, expended in keeping men marching and drilling, killing and destroying. The bond cannot represent capital that has been destroyed. It does not represent capital at all. It is simply a solemn declaration that the government will, some time or other, take by taxation from the then existing stock of the people, so much wealth, which it will turn over to the holder of the bond; and that, in the meanwhile, it will, from time to time, take, in the same way, enough to make up to the holder the increase which so much capital as it some day promises to give him would yield him were it actually in his possession. The immense sums which are thus taken from the produce of every modern country to pay interest on public debts are not the earnings or increase of capital—are not really interest in the strict sense of the term, but are taxes levied on the produce of labor and capital, leaving so much less for wages and so much less for real interest.

But, supposing the bonds have been issued for the deepening of a river bed, the construction of lighthouses, or the erection of a public market; or supposing, to embody the same idea while changing the illustration, they have been issued by a railroad company. Here they do represent capital, existing and applied to productive uses, and like stock in a dividend paying company may be considered as evidences of the ownership of capital. But they can be so considered only in so far as they actually represent capital, and not as they have been issued in excess of the capital used. Nearly all our railroad companies and other incorporations are loaded down in this way. Where one dollar's worth of capital has been really used, certificates for two, three, four, five, or even ten, have been issued, and upon this fictitious amount interest or dividends are paid with more or less regularity. Now, what, in excess of the amount due as interest to the real capital invested, is thus earned by these companies and thus paid out, as well as the large sums absorbed by managing rings and never accounted for, is evidently not taken from the aggregate produce of the community on account of the services rendered by capital—it is not interest. If we are restricted to the terminology of economic writers who decompose profits into interest, insurance, and wages of superintendence, it must fall into the category of wages of superintendence.

But while wages of superintendence clearly enough include the income derived from such personal qualities as skill, tact, enterprise, organizing ability, inventive power, character, etc., to the profits we are speaking of there is another contributing element, which can only arbitrarily be classed with these—the element of monopoly.

When James I granted to his minion the exclusive privilege of making gold and silver thread, and prohibited, under severe penalties, every one else from making such thread, the income which Buckingham enjoyed in consequence did not arise from the interest upon the capital invested in the manufacture, nor from the skill, etc., of those who really conducted the operations, but from what he got from the king—viz., the exclusive privilege—in reality the power to levy a tax for his own purposes upon all the users of such thread. From a similar source comes a large part of the profits which are commonly confounded with the earnings of capital. Receipts from the patents granted for a limited term of years for the purpose of encouraging invention are clearly attributable to this source, as are the returns derived from monopolies created by protective tariffs under the pretense of encouraging home industry. But there is another far more insidious and far more general form of monopoly. In the aggregation of large masses of capital under a common control there is developed a new and essentially different power from that power of increase which is a general characteristic of capital and which gives rise to interest. While the latter is, so to speak, constructive in its nature, the power which, as aggregation proceeds, rises upon it is destructive. It is a power of the same kind as that which James granted to Buckingham, and it is often exercised with as reckless a disregard, not only of the industrial, but of the personal rights of individuals. A railroad company approaches a small town as a highwayman approaches his victim. The threat, "If you do not accede to our terms we will leave your town two or three miles to one side!" is as efficacious as the "Stand and deliver," when backed by a cocked pistol. For the threat of the railroad company is not merely to deprive the town of the benefits which the railroad might give; it is to put it in a far worse position than if no railroad had been built. Or if, where there is water communication, an opposition boat is put on; rates are reduced until she is forced off, and then the public are compelled to pay the cost of the operation, just as the Rohillas were obliged to pay the forty lacs with which Surajah Dowlah hired a Warren Hastings and an English force to assist him in desolating their country and decimating their people. And just as robbers unite to plunder in concert and divide the spoil, so do the trunk lines of railroads unite to raise rates and pool their earnings, or the Pacific roads form a combination with the Pacific

Mail Steamship Company by which toll gates are virtually established on land and ocean. And just as Buckingham's creatures, under authority of the gold threat patent, searched private houses, and seized papers and persons for purposes of lust and extortion, so does the great telegraph company which, by the power of associated capital deprives the people of the United States of the full benefits of a beneficent invention, tamper with correspondence and crush out newspapers which offend it.

It is necessary only to allude to these things, not to dwell on them. Every one knows the tyranny and rapacity with which capital when concentrated in large amounts is frequently wielded to corrupt, to rob, and to destroy. What I wish to call the reader's attention to is that profits thus derived are not to be confounded with the legitimate returns of capital as an agent of production. They are for the most part to be attributed to a maladjustment of forces in the legislative department of government, and to a blind adherence to ancient barbarisms and the superstitious reverence for the technicalities of a narrow profession in the administration of law; while the general cause which in advancing communities tends, with the concentration of wealth, to the concentration of power, is the solution of the great problem we are seeking for, but have not yet found.

Any analysis will show that much of the profits which are, in common thought, confounded with interest are in reality due, not to the power of capital, but to the power of concentrated capital, or of concentrated capital acting upon bad social adjustments. And it will also show that what are clearly and properly wages of superintendence are very frequently confounded with the earnings of capital.

And, so, profits properly due to the elements of risk are frequently confounded with interest. Some people acquire wealth by taking chances which to the majority of people must necessarily bring loss. Such are many forms of speculation, and especially that mode of gambling known as stock dealing. Nerve, judgment, the possession of capital, skill in what in lower forms of gambling are known as the arts of the confidence man and blackleg, give advantage to the individual; but, just as at a gaming table, whatever one gains some one else must lose.

Now, taking the great fortunes that are so often referred to as exemplifying the accumulative power of capital—the Dukes of Westminster and Marquises of Bute, the Rothschilds, Astors, Stewarts, Vanderbilts, Goulds, Stanfords, and Floods—it is upon examination readily seen that they have been built up, in greater or less part, not by interest, but by elements such as we have been reviewing.

How necessary it is to note the distinctions to which I have been calling attention is shown in current discussions, where the shield seems alternately white or black as the standpoint is shifted from one side to the other. On the one hand we are called upon to see, in the existence of deep poverty side by side with vast accumulations of wealth, the aggressions of capital on labor, and in reply it is pointed out that capital aids labor, and hence we are asked to conclude that there is nothing unjust or unnatural in the wide gulf between rich and poor; that wealth is but the reward of industry, intelligence, and thrift; and poverty but the punishment of indolence, ignorance, and imprudence. . . .

Rent Impoverishes Labor.[1] Nothing can be clearer than the proposition that the failure of wages to increase with increasing productive power is due to the increase of rent.

Three things unite to production—labor, capital, and land.

Three parties divide the produce—the laborer, the capitalist, and the land owner.

If, with an increase of production the laborer gets no more and the capitalist no more it is a necessary inference that the land owner reaps the whole gain.

And the facts agree with the inference. Though neither wages nor interest anywhere increase as material progress goes on, yet the invariable accompaniment and mark of material progress is the increase of rent—the rise of land values.

The increase of rent explains why wages and interest do not increase. The cause which gives to the land holder is the cause which denies to the laborer and capitalist. That wages and interest are higher in new than in old countries is not, as the standard economists say, because nature makes a greater return to the application of labor and capital, but because land is cheaper, and, therefore, as a smaller proportion of the return is taken by rent, labor and capital can keep for their share a larger proportion of what nature does return. It is not the total produce, but the net produce, after rent has been taken from it, that determines what can be divided as wages and interest. Hence, the rate of wages and interest is everywhere fixed, not so much by the productiveness of labor as by the value of land. Wherever the value

[1] *Ibid.*, pp. 220–222.

of land is relatively low, wages and interest are relatively high; wherever land is relatively high, wages and interest are relatively low.

If production had not passed the simple stage in which all labor is directly applied to the land and all wages are paid in its produce, the fact that when the land owner takes a larger portion the laborer must put up with a smaller portion could not be lost sight of.

But the complexities of production in the civilized state, in which so great a part is borne by exchange, and so much labor is bestowed upon materials after they have been separated from the land, though they may to the unthinking disguise, do not alter the fact that all production is still the union of the two factors, land and labor, and that rent (the share of the land holder) cannot be increased except at the expense of wages (the share of the laborer) and interest (the share of capital). Just as the portion of the crop, which in the simpler forms of industrial organization the owner of agricultural land receives at the end of the harvest as his rent, lessens the amount left to the cultivator as wages and interest, so does the rental of land on which a manufacturing or commercial city is built lessen the amount which can be divided as wages and interest between the laborer and capital there engaged in the production and exchange of wealth.

In short, the value of land depending wholly upon the power which its ownership gives of appropriating wealth created by labor, the increase of land values is always at the expense of the value of labor. And, hence, that the increase of productive power does not increase wages, is because it does increase the value of land. Rent swallows up the whole gain and pauperism accompanies progress. . . .

The Remedy.[1] There is but one way to remove an evil—and that is, to remove its cause. Poverty deepens as wealth increases, and wages are forced down while productive power grows, because land, which is the source of all wealth and the field of all labor, is monopolized. To extirpate poverty, to make wages what justice commands they should be, the full earnings of the laborer, we must therefore substitute for the individual ownership of land a common ownership. Nothing else will go to the cause of the evil—in nothing else is there the slightest hope.

This, then, is the remedy for the unjust and unequal distribution of wealth apparent in modern civilization, and for all the evils which flow from it:

We must make land common property. . . .

[1] *Ibid.*, pp. 326, 331. 332, 333–334, 401, 402, 403–405.

When it is proposed to abolish private property in land the first question that will arise is that of justice. Though often warped by habit, superstition, and selfishness into the most distorted forms, the sentiment of justice is yet fundamental to the human mind, and whatever dispute arouses the passions of men, the conflict is sure to rage, not so much as to the question "Is it wise?" as to the question "Is it right?" . . .

What constitutes the rightful basis of property? What is it that enables a man justly to say of a thing, "It is mine"? From what springs the sentiment which acknowledges his exclusive right as against all the world? Is it not, primarily, the right of a man himself to the use of his own powers, to the enjoyment of the fruits of his own exertions? Is it not this individual right, which springs from and is testified to by the natural facts of individual organization—the fact that each particular pair of hands obey a particular brain and are related to a particular stomach; the fact that each man is a definite, coherent, independent whole—which alone justifies individual ownership? As a man belongs to himself, so his labor when put in concrete form belongs to him.

And for this reason, that which a man makes or produces is his own, as against all the world—to enjoy or to destroy, to use, to exchange, or to give. No one else can rightfully claim it, and his exclusive right to it involves no wrong to any one else. Thus there is to everything produced by human exertion a clear and indisputable title to exclusive possession and enjoyment, which is perfectly consistent with justice, as it descends from the original producer, in whom it vested by natural law. The pen with which I am writing is justly mine. No other human being can rightfully lay claim to it, for in me is the title of the producers who made it. It has become mine, because transferred to me by the stationer, to whom it was transferred by the importer, who obtained the exclusive right to it by transfer from the manufacturer, in whom, by the same process of purchase, vested the rights of those who dug the material from the ground and shaped it into a pen. Thus, my exclusive right of ownership in the pen springs from the natural right of the individual to the use of his own faculties. . . .

Nature acknowledges no ownership or control in man save as the result of exertion. In no other way can her treasures be drawn forth, her powers directed, or her forces utilized or controlled. She makes no discriminations among men, but is to all absolutely impartial. She knows no distinction between master and slave, king and subject, saint and sinner. All men to her stand upon an equal footing and have equal rights. She recognizes no claim but that of labor, and recognizes that without respect to the claimant. If a pirate spread his sails, the wind will fill them as well as it will fill those of a peaceful merchantman or missionary bark; if a king and a common man be thrown overboard, neither can keep his head above water except by swimming; birds will not come to be shot by the proprietor of the soil any quicker than they will come to be shot by the poacher; fish will bite or will not bite at a hook in utter disregard as to whether it is offered them by a good little boy who goes to Sunday-school, or a bad little boy who plays truant; grain will grow only as the ground is prepared and the seed is sown; it is only at the call of labor that ore can be raised from the mine; the sun shines and the rain falls, alike upon just and unjust. The laws of nature are the decrees of the Creator. There is written in them no recognition of any right save that of labor; and in them is written broadly and clearly the equal right of all men to the use and enjoyment of nature; to apply to her by their exertions, and to receive and possess her reward. Hence, as nature gives only to labor, the exertion of labor in production is the only title to exclusive possession.

This right of ownership that springs from labor excludes the possibility of any other right of ownership. If a man be rightfully entitled to the produce of his labor, then no one can be rightfully entitled to the ownership of anything which is not the produce of his labor, or the labor of some one else from whom the right has passed to him. If production give to the producer the right to exclusive possession and enjoyment, there can rightfully be no exclusive possession and enjoyment of anything not the production of labor, and the recognition of private property in land is a wrong. For the right to the produce of labor cannot be enjoyed without the right to the free use of the opportunities offered by nature, and to admit the right of property in these is to deny the right of property in the produce of labor. When non-producers can claim as rent a portion of the wealth created by producers, the right of the producers to the fruits of their labor is to that extent denied. . . .

We should satisfy the law of justice, we should meet all economic requirements, by at one stroke abolishing all private titles, declaring all land public property, and letting it out to the highest bidders in lots to suit, under such conditions as would sacredly guard the private right to improvements. . . .

But such a plan, though perfectly feasible, does not seem to me the best. Or rather I propose to accomplish the same thing in a simpler, easier, and quieter way, than that of formally confiscating all the land and formally letting it out to the highest bidders.

To do that would involve a needless shock to present customs and habits of thought—which is to be avoided.

To do that would involve a needless extension of governmental machinery—which is to be avoided. . . .

I do not propose either to purchase or to confiscate private property in land. The first would be unjust; the second needless. Let the individuals who now hold it still retain, if they want to, possession of what they are pleased to call *their* land. Let them continue to call it *their* land. Let them buy and sell, and bequeath and devise it. We may safely leave them the shell, if we take the kernel. *It is not necessary to confiscate land; it is only necessary to confiscate rent.* . . .

We already take some rent in taxation. We have only to make some changes in our modes of taxation to take it all.

What I, therefore, propose, as the simple yet sovereign remedy, which will raise wages, increase the earnings of capital, extirpate pauperism, abolish poverty, give remunerative employment to whoever wishes it, afford free scope to human powers, lessen crime, elevate morals, and taste, and intelligence, purify government and carry civilization to yet nobler heights, is—*to appropriate rent by taxation.*

In this way the State may become the universal landlord without calling herself so, and without assuming a single new function. In form, the ownership of land would remain just as now. No owner of land need be dispossessed, and no restriction need be placed upon the amount of land any one could hold. For, rent being taken by the State in taxes, land, no matter in whose name it stood, or in what parcels it was held, would be really common property, and every member of the community would participate in the advantages of its ownership.

Now, insomuch as the taxation of rent, or land values, must necessarily be increased just as we abolish other taxes, we may put the proposition into practical form by proposing—

To abolish all taxation save that upon land values.

As we have seen, the value of land is at the beginning of society nothing, but as society develops by the increase of population and the advance of the arts, it becomes greater and greater. In every civilized country, even the newest, the value of the land taken as a whole is sufficient to bear the entire expenses of government. In the better developed countries it is much more than sufficient. Hence it will not be enough merely to place all taxes upon the value of land. It will be necessary, where rent exceeds the present governmental revenues, commensurately to increase the amount demanded in taxation, and to continue this increase as society progresses and rent advances. But this is so natural and easy a matter, that it may be considered as involved, or at least understood, in the proposition to put all taxes on the value of land. That is the first step, upon which the practical struggle must be made. When the hare is once caught and killed, cooking him will follow as a matter of course. When the common right to land is so far appreciated that all taxes are abolished save those which fall upon rent, there is no danger of much more than is necessary to induce them to collect the public revenues being left to individual land holders.

Experience has taught me (for I have been for some years endeavoring to popularize this proposition) that wherever the idea of concentrating all taxation upon land values finds lodgment sufficient to induce consideration, it invariably makes way, but that there are few of the classes most to be benefited by it, who at first, or even for a long time afterward, see its full significance and power. It is difficult for workingmen to get over the idea that there is a real antagonism between capital and labor. It is difficult for small farmers and homestead owners to get over the idea that to put all taxes on the value of land would be unduly to tax them. It is difficult for both classes to get over the idea that to exempt capital from taxation would be to make the rich richer, and the poor poorer. These ideas spring from confused thought. But behind ignorance and prejudice there is a powerful interest, which has hitherto dominated literature, education, and opinion. A great wrong always dies hard, and the great wrong which in every civilized country condemns the masses of men to poverty and want, will not die without a bitter struggle. . . .

Effects on Production and Distribution.[1] To abolish the taxation which, acting and reacting, now hampers every wheel of exchange and presses upon every form of industry, would be like removing an immense weight from a powerful spring. Imbued with fresh energy, production would start into new life, and trade would receive a stimulus which would be felt to the remotest arteries. The present method of taxation operates upon exchange like artificial deserts and mountains; it costs more to get goods through a custom house than

[1] *Ibid.*, pp. 431–433, 434–439.

it does to carry them around the world. It operates upon energy, and industry, and skill, and thrift, like a fine upon those qualities. If I have worked harder and built myself a good house while you have been contented to live in a hovel, the tax-gatherer now comes annually to make me pay a penalty for my energy and industry, by taxing me more than you. If I have saved while you wasted, I am mulct, while you are exempt. If a man build a ship we make him pay for his temerity, as though he had done an injury to the state; if a railroad be opened, down comes the tax-collector upon it, as though it were a public nuisance; if a manufactory be erected we levy upon it an annual sum which would go far toward making a handsome profit. We say we want capital, but if any one accumulate it, or bring it among us, we charge him for it as though we were giving him a privilege. We punish with a tax the man who covers barren fields with ripening grain, we fine him who puts up machinery, and him who drains a swamp. How heavily these taxes burden production only those realize who have attempted to follow our system of taxation through its ramifications, for, as I have before said, the heaviest part of taxation is that which falls in increased prices. But manifestly these taxes are in their nature akin to the Egyptian Pasha's tax upon date-trees. If they do not cause the trees to be cut down, they at least discourage the planting.

To abolish these taxes would be to lift the whole enormous weight of taxation from productive industry. The needle of the seamstress and the great manufactory; the cart-horse and the locomotive; the fishing boat and the steamship; the farmer's plow and the merchant's stock, would be alike untaxed. All would be free to make or to save, to buy or to sell, unfined by taxes, unannoyed by the tax-gatherer. Instead of saying to the producer, as it does now, "The more you add to the general wealth the more shall you be taxed!" the state would say to the producer, "Be as industrious, as thrifty, as enterprising as you choose, you shall have your full reward! You shall not be fined for making two blades of grass grow where one grew before; you shall not be taxed for adding to the aggregate wealth." . . .

And to shift the burden of taxation from production and exchange to the value or rent of land would not merely be to give new stimulus to the production of wealth; it would be to open new opportunities. For under this system no one would care to hold land unless to use it, and land now withheld from use would everywhere be thrown open to improvement.

The selling price of land would fall; land speculation would receive its death blow; land monopolization would no longer pay. Millions and millions of acres from which settlers are now shut out by high prices would be abandoned by their present owners or sold to settlers upon nominal terms. And this not merely on the frontiers, but within what are now considered well settled districts. Within a hundred miles of San Francisco would be thus thrown open land enough to support, even with present modes of cultivation, an agricultural population equal to that now scattered from the Oregon boundary to the Mexican line—a distance of 800 miles. In the same degree would this be true of most of the Western States, and in a great degree of the older Eastern States, for even in New York and Pennsylvania is population yet sparse as compared with the capacity of the land. And even in densely populated England would such a policy throw open to cultivation many hundreds of thousands of acres now held as private parks, deer preserves, and shooting grounds.

For this simple device of placing all taxes on the value of land would be in effect putting up the land at auction to whomsoever would pay the highest rent to the state. The demand for land fixes its value, and hence, if taxes were placed so as very nearly to consume that value, the man who wished to hold land without using it would have to pay very nearly what it would be worth to any one who wanted to use it.

And it must be remembered that this would apply, not merely to agricultural land, but to all land. Mineral land would be thrown open to use, just as agricultural land; and in the heart of a city no one could afford to keep land from its most profitable use, or on the outskirts to demand more for it than the use to which it could at the time be put would warrant. Everywhere that land had attained a value, taxation, instead of operating, as now, as a fine upon improvement, would operate to force improvement. Whoever planted an orchard, or sowed a field, or built a house, or erected a manufactory, no matter how costly, would have no more to pay in taxes than if he kept so much land idle. The monopolist of agricultural land would be taxed as much as though his land were covered with houses and barns, with crops and with stock. The owner of a vacant city lot would have to pay as much for the privilege of keeping other people off of it until he wanted to use it, as his neighbor who has a fine house upon his lot. It would cost as much to keep a row of tumble-down shanties upon valuable land as though it were covered with a grand hotel or a pile of great warehouses filled with costly goods.

Thus, the bonus that wherever labor is most productive must now be paid before labor can be exerted would disappear. The farmer would not have to pay out half his means, or mortgage his labor for years, in order to obtain land to cultivate; the builder of a city homestead would not have to lay out as much for a small lot as for the house he puts upon it; the company that proposed to erect a manufactory would not have to expend a great part of their capital for a site. And what would be paid from year to year to the state would be in lieu of all the taxes now levied upon improvements, machinery, and stock.

Consider the effect of such a change upon the labor market. Competition would no longer be one-sided, as now. Instead of laborers competing with each other for employment, and in their competition cutting down wages to the point of bare subsistence, employers would everywhere be competing for laborers, and wages would rise to the fair earnings of labor. For into the labor market would have entered the greatest of all competitors for the employment of labor, a competitor whose demand cannot be satisfied until want is satisfied—the demand of labor itself. The employers of labor would not have merely to bid against other employers, all feeling the stimulus of greater trade and increased profits, but against the ability of laborers to become their own employers upon the natural opportunities freely opened to them by the tax which prevented monopolization.

With natural opportunities thus free to labor; with capital and improvements exempt from tax, and exchange released from restrictions, the spectacle of willing men unable to turn their labor into the things they are suffering for would become impossible; the recurring paroxysms which paralyze industry would cease; every wheel of production would be set in motion; demand would keep pace with supply, and supply with demand; trade would increase in every direction, and wealth augment on every hand.

But great as they thus appear, the advantages of a transference of all public burdens to a tax upon the value of land cannot be fully appreciated until we consider the effect upon the distribution of wealth.

Tracing out the cause of the unequal distribution of wealth which appears in all civilized countries, with a constant tendency to greater and greater inequality as material progress goes on, we have found it in the fact that, as civilization advances, the ownership of land, now in private hands, gives a greater and greater power of appropriating the wealth produced by labor and capital.

Thus, to relieve labor and capital from all taxation, direct and indirect, and to throw the burden upon rent, would be, as far as it went, to counteract this tendency to inequality, and, if it went so far as to take in taxation the whole of rent, the cause of inequality would be totally destroyed. Rent, instead of causing inequality, as now, would then promote equality. Labor and capital would then receive the whole produce, minus that portion taken by the state in the taxation of land values, which, being applied to public purposes, would be equally distributed in public benefits.

That is to say, the wealth produced in every community would be divided into two portions. One part would be distributed in wages and interest between individual producers, according to the part each had taken in the work of production; the other part would go to the community as a whole, to be distributed in public benefits to all its members. In this all would share equally—the weak with the strong, young children and decrepit old men, the maimed, the halt, and the blind, as well as the vigorous. And justly so—for while one part represents the result of individual effort in production, the other represents the increased power with which the community as a whole aids the individual.

Thus, as material progress tends to increase rent, were rent taken by the community for common purposes the very cause which now tends to produce inequality as material progress goes on would then tend to produce greater and greater equality. . . .

XXII

ADOLPH WAGNER

1835–1917

Adolph Wagner was born at Erlangen, Bavaria, in 1835. Most of his life was spent in universities; his father was a physiologist and a professor at Göttingen and he himself taught for almost sixty years. Perhaps it counted for something in his son's intellectual history that the elder Wagner was a strong opponent of the prevailing materialism.

Between 1853 and 1857 Adolph studied at the universities of Göttingen and Heidelberg, a period during which nationalistic feeling in Germany ran high. But the failure of the Frankfort parliament had brought disillusionment to many, and Wagner himself was somewhat affected by the reaction. He had at first been drawn toward the study of law; the spirit of the times however diverted him to economics.

As a student of economics Wagner fell under diverse influences—the historical viewpoint of Roscher, Knies, etc., but particularly the nationalistic yet classical and deductive approach of K. H. Rau, who introduced him to the theories of the English defenders of free competition. Wagner's doctoral thesis was a study of banking and his interest and writings for some time related chiefly to monetary problems.

As a student and later on as a teacher, Wagner was also affected by other and less conventional doctrines. One of his professors had been Robert von Mohl, a strong advocate of German unification and actually the first of the "Socialists of the Chair," although the term itself was invented later on. Von Mohl pointed out the ill-effects of machine production on the status of the workers and the middle class and denied the all-sufficiency of self-help; he believed that a drastic change in the social structure was necessary and recommended factory legislation, profit-sharing, and the education of workingmen.

During the early part of his professional career Wagner's views took on a decidedly nationalistic and social complexion. While he was teaching at the commercial academy of Vienna (1858–63), a study of Sir Robert Peel's Bank Act and the crisis of 1857 prompted him to question certain points of the accepted classical economy. But his real spiritual conversion is said to have come in the midst of an economic congress at Hanover in 1864. The subject under discussion was the evils of a paper-money régime—a policy which Wagner himself strongly opposed. But when one enthusiast exclaimed, "Let the state itself perish rather than adopt paper money!" Wagner's patriotism revolted against "Manchesterism" and all its works.

In 1864 Wagner accepted a post at the University of Dorpat, Russia, where he remained (in "banishment" as he considered it) until 1868. The aspect of Dorpat with its ruined cathedral and "most German of all universities" roused his patriotic sensibilities, and after the conquest of Alsace-Lorraine (which he yearned for and later rejoiced in) he talked of the restoration to Germany of Dorpat itself. His Russian sojourn had other results: the recent emancipation of the serfs (1861) and the agrarian communism of Russia called his attention forcibly to the problem of property. In 1870 he was appointed to the faculty of the University of Berlin where he remained until his retirement in 1916.

Perhaps the most important contributor to Wagner's revised social and economic theories was Karl Rodbertus, with whose works Wagner first became acquainted in 1868. Rodbertus was a nationalist and a monarchist as well as a socialist. The emphasis he placed on state control was designed in part to preserve the state. Wagner dubbed him the Ricardo of socialism. The influence of Rodbertus, however, was somewhat offset in Wagner's case by that of Albert Schäffle, who undertook to reconcile capitalism with the claims of labor.

Wagner first stated his own position in *The Abolition of Private Property in Land* (1870). A fuller and more systematic treatment appeared in 1876 as the *Foundations of Political Economy*. His method was partly historical and partly deductive. Accepting self-interest as the only *constant* motive, he criticized the classical school of economists for false applications of sound principles. On the other hand, while he paid homage to the historical economists by employing the historical method, he opposed their total repudiation of deductive and abstract reasoning.

Wagner's general point of view in social matters was shared by a group of his academic colleagues, including Gustav Schmoller, Lujo Brentano, Adolph Held, and Albert Schäffle. In 1871 a commentator referred to them as "Socialists of the Chair" (that is, of the professorial chair). The name stuck; in 1872 a conference was held at Eisenach, and Schmoller in his opening address spoke of the party as "Kathedersozialisten." At this meeting a Union for Social Politics was formed; Socialism of the Chair became an organized movement. In the same year Wagner's celebrated "Speech on the Social Question" greatly strengthened his own influence.

Rodbertus was disposed to scoff at the Socialists of the Chair as illogical "sweetened-water thinkers" but he remained on friendly terms with Wagner. The latter represented, indeed, the more socialistic wing of the group, and he is described as a state socialist to distinguish him from the less radical members.

Socialists of the Chair regarded economics as primarily an ethical science; to Wagner it was certainly as much an affair of the heart as of the head. He therefore supported the effort to create a social movement in German Protestantism similar to that which, largely through the influence of Bishop von Ketteler, had made its appearance among the Catholics of Germany. He took part enthusiastically in an Evangelical Social Congress and in 1881 joined the Christian Social party, becoming its first president. The party had been founded by Adolph Stöcker, court preacher to the Hohenzollerns; highly monarchist, it is said to have been more anti-Semite than either Christian or Social.

In 1882 Wagner entered the lower house of the Prussian legislature. He affiliated with the Conservative party in order, says his biographer, to aid in socializing the traditionally Christian side of the house. But he was something of a hot-head politically and too honest to make a good party man. He retired in 1885. The rest of his life was principally devoted to writing and academic duties at the university. In 1910 he was made a life member of the Prussian house of lords. Six years later he gave up his professorship. He died in 1917, a year before the downfall of the monarchy he had so loyally served.

The influence of Wagner in social matters is somewhat hard to estimate. His scientific method in economics did not become popular and he left no school to keep it alive. One immediately connects his social program with the policy of Bismarck during the 1880's—and indeed the latter consulted him more than once. But whatever Bismarck owed to Wagner and his group (and it may have been considerable) it was only one element in the rather complex set of forces that determined the chancellor's policy. At the time, however, Wagner was "regarded as the foremost scientific exponent of State Socialism in Germany." His works therefore had at least a propaganda value: they provided an intellectual basis for the social measures which the government was bent upon carrying through. For us they are an excellent résumé of the social policies of the empire.

REFERENCES

So far as is known, none of Wagner's writings have been translated into English. There is, however, a French translation of his *Foundations of Political Economy* (1904). An extensive bibliography of his works is given in the *Handwörterbuch der Staatswissenschaft*, Vol. VIII (1928).

There is very little in English on Wagner's views and influence. A few references are in A. Ashley's *The Social Policy of Bismarck* [*Birmingham Studies in Social Economics*, Vol. III (1912)], R. T. Ely's *French and German Socialism* (1883), and W. H. Dawson's *Bismarck and State Socialism* (1891). See also Gide and Rist's *History of Economic Doctrines*. A list of descriptive and critical works in German is given in the *Deutsches biographisches Jahrbuch* (1928), p. 193.

No extended biography of Wagner has yet appeared. Useful sketches are H. Schumacher's "Adolph Wagner" [*Deutsches biographisches Jahrbuch* (1928), pp. 173–193] and Hugo Tillmann's "Adolph Wagner" [*Westermanns Monatshefte* (1918), Vol. 123, pp. 677–681].

READINGS FROM

SPEECH ON THE SOCIAL QUESTION[1]

The Ethical Viewpoint in Economics. My idea, briefly stated, proceeds from the notion that political economy must again partake rather of the character of an ethical science in order to be able properly to handle the social question. . . . I wish to stress the moral and therefore Christian obligations which wealth, education, and social position impose, even in dealing with the social question from the economic standpoint. . . .

The Conflict of Socialism and Laissez-faire. The science of political economy is engaged, at present, in a great crisis. . . . That this crisis arises specifically in Germany may be regarded as a happy sign of national freshness and strength. Much has contributed to it. History and statistics have shown that many theses, though true relatively speaking, are unreliable generalizations—theses which the older political economy had elevated to absolutely valid axioms, and the newer journalism, to absolutely incontrovertible laws of nature. The mighty political events of our day which have so often taken place in contradiction to current economic teachings and to political doctrines . . . have likewise had their effect in this crisis. But much as one may regret that political economy ever needed such admonition,

[1] Delivered at the Evangelical Free Churchmen's Assembly in the royal garrison church, Berlin, October 12, 1871. Translated for the present volume.

the emergence of the social or labor question has undeniably had a more powerful influence than anything else. In the first place, the admittedly one-sided, often malicious and hateful, criticism which the theorists and practical agitators of socialism unsparingly heaped upon the deep-seated economic, cultural, and moral wrongs of our modern society, has completely torn the cloud of rosy-colored optimism with which the new British school of political economy—so long exclusively dominant—veiled all evil conditions.

The program of most socialists may be mocked at as utopian; the agitation which certain unscrupulous and often insincere leaders carry on amongst the ignorant and passionate working masses for the overthrow of the existing systems of economics and private wealth and the erection of a social, producing and labor organization which is opposed to human nature; the senseless decisions of a Basel International Workingmen's congress regarding the abolition, at one stroke, of inheritance rights and private ownership of land, and so on—these things one may rightfully condemn as criminal and prove them to be tendencies destructive of political economy. Nevertheless on many points one may and one must agree with socialist criticism of the present economic system. Of course it will be objected by the other side (the side, that is, which unjustly and vainly calls itself "politico-economic") that the socialists lay the blame for admittedly evil economic and social conditions entirely upon the present economic system instead of tracing them back to the inherent weakness of all human institutions. It is true that socialist criticism rejects the good with the bad. But that objection does not meet the main point. The criticisms of a Marx and a Lassalle, for example, to say nothing of earlier ones, showed a masterful grasp of at least this fact, that certain tendencies toward the pronounced increase of such unhealthy conditions were due to the present economic system.

The facts which this criticism exposed in the most glaring light stand in too sharp contrast to that alleged harmony of interests and security for the whole economic system which ought presumably to result from the free play of individual economic self-interest and from recognition of the principle of *laisser faire et passer* as the economic policy of the state. The countless and undeniably favorable results of free competition, the unleashing of which has been the chief object of economic legislation in recent generations, are indeed recognized. But upon deeper consideration political economy recognized (and in fact socialist criticism pointed the way to it) that the mere release of free competition is too exclusively a negative principle in the political economy of a state. . . .

Two great principles of right had however continued to stand and had been worked out with increasing clarity: the elemental thesis of man's personal liberty and his complete freedom to earn a living, and the thesis of unlimited and constantly more absolute private ownership of movable goods and real property, including the recognition of existing private wealth, especially inherited rights. Actually, these two principles operate as limitations on free competition: as natural, indisputable limitations (according to the teachings of political economy), but also as the sole and very drastic ones. . . . Yet socialist criticism has rightly shown that, for example, it is first necessary to prove the postulate that present-day private possession of wealth (so decisive in the distribution of economic wealth) must be considered as the natural, immutable basis of the economic system; for this right . . . . is in part a product of accidental historical development.

In consequence of this conception, therefore, the so-called "natural state" became an unqualified "must-be" of political economy. The ethical "should-be" remained quite disregarded. The notion of the moral responsibility of the individual, of society, and of the state for the shaping of economic relationships disappeared. Thus the fact that economic processes are always simultaneously the product of human actions was completely overlooked. But moral responsibility for human actions is not dispensed with even if they are permitted and even if they proceed from the strong but not invincible force of economic individualism within us. The dangerous moral consequences of this attitude have shown themselves all too abundantly in the theory and still more in the practice of political economy. . . .

In the interest of a just solution of the labor question important demands of an ethical nature are to be made not only upon business men but also upon the upper, wealthier classes as a whole. Here too the opinion has become too widespread that wealth imposes no obligations other than a few legal duties, besides (at the most) a few duties in the way of private charity, etc. It was felt that the legal duties were discharged if goods and labor itself were purchased at the market price and if the state and community taxes were conscientiously paid. It was thought that the moral duties incumbent upon the wealthy from a religious, ecclesiastical, humanitarian, and ethical standpoint were fulfilled by voluntary contributions to charitable, religious, and cultural organizations for the lower and poorer classes—a private support of the poor which often has harmful effects. Every one may do with his wealth what seems good to him—that is the attitude of the higher classes and indeed of the better element of them, generally speaking. The teaching of political economy has at most called attention to the baneful effects of luxury. Up to the present the positive law of our modern states, with its one-sided and increasingly absolute notion of property, has done no more.

In opposition to that idea, the political economist may stress the fact that wealth is justly to be regarded as a talent given in trust according to the beautiful Christian conception—a talent which is also an aristocratic one in the best sense of the word. We must employ our wealth not only in our own interest but in that of our fellow men, and we are responsible to God and our conscience for so employing it. . . .

The usual justification of the luxury of courts from Louis XIV to Napoleon III and Eugénie, the idea that rank squandering and adornment gives work to the lower classes, is economically quite unsound. Rather does a limitation of the luxury of the rich, working through intermediate agencies, regularly result in a betterment of working-class conditions. . . .

Many other uses of wealth involve not only morality but also serious questions of justice, and even if they are permitted by actual law it only proves that the latter is unjust and that the concept of ownership is understood in too absolute a fashion. Here again socialist complaints are largely well-founded. I wish to refer here merely to abuse of the authority vested by positive law in real property. The history of law shows, and analysis establishes, that the ownership of land was always a more limited ownership than that of movable goods. . . .

Here I touch upon that very disputable point, the duty of the state with regard to the social question. I should like to express a general warning. In the social question generally, and particularly in this matter, catch-words and party and academic doctrines have heretofore exercised almost unlimited power. However, I venture boldly to assert that they wield a greater influence among practical men than the rider of principles and doctrines exerts over professors in my much-condemned profession. Above all things let us guard against this unfortunate power of catch-words. In the mutually exclusive dogmas of "self-help" and "state-help," and the way in which they are made to confront one another, I can see only one slogan—war.

The severest partisans of self-help in social matters condemn the state to the utmost passivity. Here also they proclaim *laissez-faire et passer* to be the sole healing dogma, and demand that the immediately interested parties (especially the workers) should do and provide everything for themselves. According to this view the state has only to give the workers and their unions a sort of necessary public position . . . and create the civil form necessary for the institutions which serve the interests of the workers and small people. That such a scheme is not sufficient a cursory glance into the history of factory legislation certainly ought to show. On the other hand, most brands of socialism, going to the other extreme, reject self-help almost entirely and usually demand the most extensive state-help as the way to salvation.

The Moderate Viewpoint. Certainly more true and confirmed by historical experience is the intermediate standpoint, which does not recognize an absolute antithesis between self-help and state-help as do the extremists in both parties. Here as in other socio-political and economic questions neither the principle of passivity nor that of intervention can unreservedly be the standard. A simple rule cannot be given; it must rather be decided, case by case according to the concrete situation, whether or not the state should intervene. . . .

In my opinion the place where even very extensive demands on the part of the lower classes, the workers' parties, and the socialists are for the most part justified is in the realm of taxation—the better division of the tax burden. . . .

Although I run the risk (along with many of my colleagues) of being thrown to the "shameless socialists" by one-sided Manchesterites I am not afraid to pronounce it to be an unavoidable task and duty of the upper classes and of the state to examine socialist criticism impartially and recognize the kernel of justice in socialist demands.

If we strip socialist criticism of all excesses . . . there is left at the core something like the following: The present economic system, based on free competition and valid rights to private wealth, embodies within itself not only undeniably great advantages for increasing the production of goods but at least the tendency to enlarge still further the existing inequalities in wealth and income. The labor burden and the enjoyment of production—not the products of labor alone, as the socialists too extensively claim, but the products resulting from the coöperation of labor—these are too unevenly divided amongst the people taking part in production. The advantages of technical improvements in production redound, at least in greater part, to the benefit of the capitalists and proprietors rather than to the workers—especially in industry in the narrow sense. Thus the situation of the workers as a class becomes relatively worse even if their condition, in an absolute sense, improves (which cannot generally speaking be denied). The rift between the workers and the upper classes gets larger; in consequence of the decisive importance of the machine age, the division of labor, and the combined influence of both (these being the advantages of large-scale production) the workers in industry become increasingly dependent upon capitalists: those who have not, upon those who have. Thus it becomes more and more difficult—in most cases practically impossible—to rise from the working class into a higher one. Theoretically, of course, the worker still has that opportunity—according to the principles of freedom of trade and free choice of occupation. But he is no longer like the private in the French army who, they say, carries a marshal's baton in his knapsack: the immense majority leave the baton peacefully in the knapsack and lose the knapsack to boot. . . .

Socialist criticism on the above points does not contradict the teachings of political economy as it is said to do; it is true that inequalities of wealth and class contrasts have a tendency to grow more pronounced in our present economic system.

Conservative and Radical Reform Measures Considered. This fact is of course obnoxious from the socio-political, economic, moral viewpoint. The question therefore arises of putting a stop to this tendency or employing means against it. As far as possible this must be done without weakening the favorable effect which the existing system of free competition has upon production.

Various proposals have been advanced by the socialists and others, in which evils are not optimistically overlooked. We can trace these proposals back to a few basic principles, arranging them in three groups which I shall designate as reactionary, radical, and reform.

I. One party sees the remedy in a return to earlier essential limitations of free competition, certain restrictive measures being envisaged such as the old craft guilds. I call these proposals reactionary—in the literal sense, because they wish to restore the old—but also in the recognized secondary meaning of the word, for they derive from a false conservatism, at least frequently and in general. . . .

Proposals of this sort for the most part abandon the advantages of free competition: large volume trade, machine technique, better division of labor, and consequently cheap mass-production. Even if one were not inclined to reject them on that ground alone, it is certainly impossible to understand how the immensely increased population of today could satisfactorily utilize the business forms of an earlier time. . . .

Nevertheless here again deliberation is seriously required. Let us beware of entirely rejecting the proof from experience and forming a system of free competition ever wider and more fraught with consequences—forming it, that is, out of merely *a priori*, presumably absolute and valid principles and deductions. . . .

II. The second group of proposals embraces those radical projects of the thoroughgoing socialists—that is, of part of the so-called social democrats; for example, those who advocate the International Workingmen's Association. Here, in the most one-sided fashion, the existing social and economic system and the right to private wealth is made the sole cause of the downtrodden condition of the lower classes, the workers. This system (they say) is incapable of basic improvement; help therefore is to be found only in its complete reorganization. Hence the well-known demands of the party: the complete abolition of the position of laborer or servant in the business of a particular proprietor and capitalist; next, the doing away with the right of private ownership of property and inheritance right; the workers' claim to capital simply as the result of their unjustly withheld reward; delivery of the entire product of industry to the workers because it is produced exclusively by labor; and so on. For the execution of these projects appeal is more often made to force, "the midwife of every great social and political advance."

But even if violence were to succeed, which for the present is still very improbable, there is lacking any clear idea as to how the new economic system should be introduced and then carried through and maintained. Even the leaders express themselves very vaguely on this point. Most of them hope that further means of development "will soon be discovered" when once the existing order is overthrown—the usual argument of crackbrained revolutionary fanatics. This is a renunciation of even the vaguest idea. It naturally follows that without a strong sense of individual responsibility there would be no private interest in sound work or in the accumulation of capital. In place of the present motive and of the unendurable power (as it is held) of the capitalist and proprietor there would have to be introduced the much more despotic power of the indispensable directors of the socialist community (or whatever the particular social creation might be called). Otherwise all production would be impossible. We may well deny ourselves a closer approach to such brain specters. Every honest man, whatever party he may belong to, will scorn to beguile ignorant and passionate masses of workingmen with such nonsense.

Moderate Types of Reform Considered. III. In opposition to reactionary schemes and radical upheavals there is a third group of proposals—the plans of reformers. Here the ground of reality, present-day social, economic and private rights, is recognized and help against existing abuses is sought along the path of reform—that is, in the appropriate further development of the existing order together with such modifications of it as are necessary. Indeed, reform means neither revolution nor standing still nor going backwards.

The plans of reformers differ, first, according to the number of improvements they envisage. One group foresees only absolute improvement; the other, relative betterment as well, so that the class condition of the workers is raised in relation to that of the higher classes. The latter I consider right and practicable in view of the above-mentioned tendency towards increasing differences in wealth in the present economic system.

Reform efforts still further diverge in that according to the one plan the workers strive to better their condition themselves. This is the principle of pure self-help. According to the other plan the workers are to be supported in this endeavor by the upper classes and eventually by the state. This is the principle of state-help in various degrees. From what I have already said, the coöperation of the upper classes and of the state seems to me essential and the duty of both. Of course there is no universally valid, extremely simple recipe for the application of the state aid for which political and economic dilletantism so eagerly strives. A decision can only be reached by taking into account the concrete situation in individual countries, especially with reference to the political points involved.

Finally the reform efforts differ according to the various methods of attaining their ends. On one hand, the workers are to be armed for social and economic war. Here the important thing is to strengthen the workers as combatants in the competitive battle so that the prospect of victory draws ever closer. The other path to the goal is by peacefully adjusting the opposed interests of workers and capitalistic proprietors through mutual agreement on equitable bases and through a mutual willingness to get together. These two methods are to be considered especially in settling matters of wages and hours, the most important difficulty involved in the "labor question."

In the first case, the workers unite in order to organize themselves for social war under the system of free competition, in particular for that battle in which the wage-scale will be decided by the much-discussed law of supply and demand. Here the workers try to win their demands by victory in competition. They unite in temporary or permanent unions for one special purpose or as a means of constantly guarding their manifold interests. The unions collect money for a "war chest" even in "peace-time"; thus they can threaten to suspend work on a great scale—to "strike," as it is called—or, in case of prolonged refusal to meet their demands, they can actually take the lead and support those who have stopped working. The unions of a trade fraternize more or less with those of other places, and with those of other trades in a province, a country, or even throughout the modern state system, in order to support each other financially by common action during strikes. A marvellous and energetic realization of *viribus unitis*, of *l'union fait la force*.

The workers in the factories, mines, and trades have recently advanced eagerly in this direction. Earlier legal restraints on the right of workers to combine have now mostly been abandoned following the example of England, and rightly so. This is merely equitable treatment, for similar agreements between proprietors could not be prevented. On the basis of the competitive system one could not possibly withhold from the worker the organization of his own forces—the most workable, yes, often the sole, weapon with which he could wage the competitive battle in which he was placed, with any hope of success.

Nor can it be denied that with this weapon the workers have put through a large part of their justifiable demands—not always directly by strikes, which they have frequently lost, but by the threat of them, which naturally only their organization made possible. But, on the other hand, strikes, etc., are decidedly two-edged methods. Great sacrifices are regularly made by both sides and by the whole economic system whose production stagnates. Personal relationships are embittered for a long time and property damage is not always avoided. Such a sharpening of strife as a prelude to the solution of the social question is naturally opposed to a humane, ethical, Christian conception. But to complain of the freedom to unionize, or of trade unions, the international labor union, and strikes, is useless for those who on their side have steadily upheld free competition to the uttermost and have seen in it the universal means of salvation for all the economic ills of society—and have used it for their own advantage. Among the adherents of the prevailing system a moral indignation over the movement in the working world is comical and at the same time repugnant. You always wanted fighting, for what is competition but fighting? From your own standpoint the workers are thoroughly right in their utmost efforts toward organization which strengthens them in battle. Their action is a necessary consequence of the prevailing system.

The state has no right or interest in being hostile to the trade-union system so long as it is limited to economic aims. The union may rather expect relief from the state through good laws regarding the legal situation [of trade unions]. Only excesses are to be guarded against and punished, especially deeds of violence and threats against those who labor and are outside the union, workers not taking part in the strike.

Trade-union life, particularly as we see it in the great English trade unions and as it has also been spreading recently on the continent, at present aims preferably though not of course exclusively at strengthening the worker for the battle of competition. In addition it builds up a tremendous organization of workers' insurance, cultural activities, etc., and this earns still more the support of public opinion and legislation. . . .

Combinations, labor unions, strikes, international union—these are the weapons of the worker in combat. So long as no better means are found to raise the condition of the workers it seems to me that we cannot seriously advise against using them. But again it is particularly the fault of the higher classes, the proprietor and capitalist group, and the entire wealthy class that matters have taken the course described. Again and again the reproach must be made against these classes that they have been lacking in a sense of moral duty, in a frank, unselfish attitude toward the working classes. Otherwise much would have been freely conceded which only fear of the organized power of the workers has secured. Unfortunately this is true of those institutions for reconciling interests, such as the courts and boards on the Mundella [1] pattern, upon which may be built hopes for a better future, in spite of the few experiments thus far. These institutions are supposed, where possible, to nip in the bud disputes arising between employer and employe. They have been mostly supported by the "masters" as the lesser of two evils in order to avoid eternal squabbling. As long as this is the case they will scarcely spread the blessings they are capable of, for the worker will see very plainly that it is only fear that impels the masters to lower themselves to treat with him on equal terms. On the other hand, if such boards of conciliation are voluntarily created by the employers in conjunction with the employes and if these boards are summoned to meet under laws which enlarge their sphere of influence until they become true chambers of labor, then, indeed, much may be expected of them. Both parties would have to elect an equal number of representatives to these chambers, and a majority should decide all questions in dispute regarding trade regulations, contracts of labor, factory laws, the employment of women and children, sanitary police, and insurance funds. Perhaps for a certain length of time such bodies might gradually take over the fixing of wage scales and daily hours of labor. Here, too, the chief thing is free personal intercourse, the meeting of both parties as equals at least in the sessions of the chamber, and self-expression regarding complaints and criticisms of the opposite group. . . .

Finally I turn to the specific proposals of the social reform parties. . . .

I divide these proposals into two groups. One set, while holding fast to the existing economic system with its rights of private ownership and free competition, desire to do away completely with the wage system—the employment of workers by private proprietors—or at least to modify it extensively. In the proposals of the other group there is no pretense of such a far-reaching effort. Instead they aim only at improving the position of the wage earner.

Proposals of the former sort therefore envisage in certain respects the same goal as that of many of the socialist parties, only they wish to attain their end by entirely different means. . . .

In this group of plans belongs particularly the proposal that the workers shall form independent producers' associations for themselves—that is, societies which carry on the business on their own

[1] A. J. Mundella, an Englishman and proprietor of a hosiery mill, advocated boards of conciliation and used them in his own business. (Editor.)

account. To the extent that workers become proprietors themselves they cease to be merely workers in the economic sense of the word and receive the profits of the undertaking as wages. However desirable this may be, there is little reason to believe that for the present and in view of the small number of experiments such associations would take the place of private ventures to any appreciable extent. The advantages of the producers' association as a form of business enterprise are of course easily demonstrable: the productivity of labor in the association will rise, for the interests of worker and proprietor coincide. The favorable moral results of mutual control must be admitted. But the difficulties arising elsewhere are still very important. Securing capital and credit is perhaps not even the greatest. Even if one regards assistance by the state (demanded by Lassalle and others) as extremely difficult of execution, perhaps right here the upper classes, the self-governing bodies of the community, etc., can help by offering credit and by favoring the conversion of existing private businesses into associations—somewhat in the same way that savings banks were first enfranchised. . . . Moreover the usual argument against state credit-assistance, namely, that such a principle is inadmissible especially in the interests of a single class, cannot be regarded as pertinent; for the principle is arbitrary and there have been frequent exceptions. Of greater weight is the consideration that the state would have to exercise a scarcely practicable control and regulate the various undertakings with state funds. How this is to take place one asks in vain of Lassalle and his followers. . . .

More difficult than getting capital, it seems to me, is the organization of a uniform, capable management—a sound control—and the assumption of risk of loss as well as of gain by the worker.

The state alone will be able to help, of course, through beneficent legislation in regard to the private rights and functions of the producers' associations. Meanwhile perhaps the opportunity may arise of trying out such undertakings in state institutions (mines and foundries) and on the state domains.

In view of these difficulties it is comprehensible why advocates of this scheme have had chiefly in mind a nearer if similar goal: namely, while maintaining the wage system, to secure for the workers a share in the profits and capital of private undertakings. The division of capital can take place in this way: the workers invest their savings in the business employing them by securing small scripts or shares in it; they may receive a share of the current pay bonus; or better still, the portion of earnings allotted to them at the end of the work period, which need be underwritten only at that time (this is the industrial sharing or bonus system). Several successful examples in mining, manufacturing, and even in agriculture are at hand in England and Germany. Benevolent proprietors, and also those who are more foresighted with regard to their own interests and are tired of endless bickerings, have taken the initiative. . . .

A Program of Moderate Reform. For the present at any rate, the proposals of the second group, which seek to improve the position of those who work in a business owned by someone else, deserve more consideration than those just discussed. Even the present practical agitation amongst workingmen has this object in view and, as it seems to me, rightly so. For that is surely more attainable than the establishment of producers' associations and industrial sharing. It is quite as attainable as the socialist plans for a revolution, even if this really improved the situation.

The individual measures to be considered form a compact system. One which concerns a very special point, for example housing reform, also has a favorable effect in other directions. As a survey the following arrangement in six divisions may be useful.

1. In the foreground stands increased wages, in recent days touching upon, and indeed on the whole properly enough connected more and more closely with, shortening the working day and abolishing all Sunday labor. Higher wages is the preliminary to a better, sounder material way of life, and at the same time to the uplift of culture and morality. . . .

The previous efforts to shorten the hours of labor of adult male workers have differed greatly from one country to another according to the situation. In one place a maximum of twelve hours is called a "normal working day," in another place it is ten hours, in still another even nine or eight hours. These have hardly ever been exaggerated demands in countries where they have been made. Experience has already proven that a moderate decrease of working hours does not diminish but occasionally increases the capacity to labor. . . .

Recently a part of the Social Democratic party vigorously demanded legal regulation of the working day so that it would not be abnormally long. This may be a matter that can be more easily regulated by the boards of conciliation and labor chambers mentioned above than by the state. However, I cannot accept as conclusive the usual arguments of the Manchester school against the "enormity" of a legally-ordained normal working day. Some of them are the same people who recently attacked the limitation of hours of children's labor, the boundless blessings of which no sensible, decent man longer disputes. . . .

Again, it is important that industrial countries, while leaving a certain amount of room for free action, should proceed to fix the hours of labor in individual countries and businesses with measurable uniformity. Otherwise the protective policy of one state would be easily rendered nugatory by the passive policy of another through competition in the world market.

The establishment of wage-scales by the state is much more doubtful. . . . But here, certainly, a field of successful endeavor for labor-councils presents itself. . . .

2. A second group of efforts and regulations has to do with the security of workers in cases of sickness, invalidism, incapacity, old age, the care of widows and orphans, etc. . . .

The most complex problem of workingmen's insurance is whether insurance shall be made legally compulsory by the state. Certainly it is also true here that freedom is better than compulsion. But if the goal is to be attained by free action, knowledge of the idea and a sense of duty must already be widespread. It is a matter of history that in such cases compulsion often properly makes a beginning but may later be dropped when insight satisfactorily replaces it. Such was the case in the related matter of domestic fire-insurance. . . .

3. A third field is that of factory legislation, so-called. Under this heading it is now customary to include a long list of important, closely-related measures for the protection of factory workers. Here, namely, belong laws regarding the employment of women and children in factories and mines; bodily and spiritual hazards in the factories; liability of employers for injuries received through the negligence of employers; the payment of wages (prohibition of the "truck system" or the payment of wages in goods); the attendance at school of children employed in factories; the abolition of Sunday labor; and so on.

Fortunately a good deal has happened here to meet the highly justifiable demands of the working-class interest. Unfortunately, however, inertia, egoism, and the lack of a sense of moral duty, not to mention the simplest obligations of humanity, religion, and Christianity, have nowhere occasioned worse results. . . .

Public opinion and the sense of honor of the upper classes did not prevent abuses in the factories. The church neglected her most sacred duties, in religious England of all places. Never has the theory of a laissez-faire state policy and mere self-help for the workers been a more disgraceful fiasco. On that point I should like to refer you to works like those of Marx. Even if you subtract a great deal from the gloomy picture, there still remains enough to make anyone shudder. After such experiences it is incomprehensible to me how a sensible and honorable man can still believe in the sole saving grace of the dogma of laissez-faire. A beautiful "economic harmony" indeed!

No, let us not hide it from ourselves: in this case the far-reaching intervention of the state and the principle of state compulsion have been the first to render available the simplest duties of humanity and Christianity. And not only the workers but the better proprietors have very properly asked for it. The public conscience has at last been reawakened. . . .

We in Germany have made laudable progress through trade regulations and the new employers' liability act. Much good has already been accomplished. But the last word is still to be spoken. For example, we have unfortunately as yet omitted—for unsatisfactory reasons—to establish the excellent English system of factory inspection. We are assured, however, that the legal regulations will not be merely paper ones.

The whole question of factory legislation seems to me to have a fundamental significance for the position of the state in relation to the labor question. It has been proved that in countless cases individual workers and even workers organized in unions cannot help themselves—against the truck system, not at all. It has further been shown that the intervention of the state has been quite successful here, even in matters where it was at first regarded as quite impossible. Hence it may be inferred that excessive anxiety regarding the extension of the influence of the state in the labor question may be unfounded in many other cases. I am thinking of the establishment of the normal working day and such matters.

4. A fourth group of reforms has to do with procuring better quality, and if possible cheaper, foodstuffs and commodities. Here

the coöperative stores are of great significance and the advantage which the individual worker derives from them is also properly recognized. . . .

Further housing reform! . . . May there be no necessity for the intervention of the communities, of the state, to improve the living conditions of the workers. To me it seems desirable that communities and states should not become builders and renters of homes. But such assistance is not to be refused on the customary pretexts. It is to be actually rendered—but voluntarily, on the initiative of the well-to-do, the property owners. Only under those circumstances can the state limit itself to promoting building companies through beneficial legislation, the issuance of an appropriate building ordinance for workers' dwellings, the improvement of street railways in large cities, and so on. . . .

5. A fifth group of reform measures concerns especially now the spiritual, moral, and religious improvement of the lower classes. . . . In my opinion a good school system comes first of all—not necessarily free, but cheap, with compulsory attendance and an appropriate curriculum. Of course not only the demand for the utmost cheapness, but for the increased efficiency, of the primary school will only be met when a more generous grant to the schools and better pay for teachers are finally achieved. . . .

Concerning the important question of popular literature as a means of cultural training and moral improvement for the lower classes, permit me to observe that it is precisely the publications emanating from the church and from the politically conservative side which often most easily miss their mark on account of their one-sided and tasteless tendency. . . . You cannot persuade our working circles with tracts. Do not forget either that you are dealing with adults, not with children.

Among the tasks in the spreading of culture is another which I should not like to overlook in this place. . . . In all classes the moral sense of individuals and a sound public opinion should react against premature and too large families instead of beautifying them with hollow sophisms. Among the lower and even more so among the middle classes this is connected with the lowering of the general standard of living. Here the clergy through their contacts have many opportunities to warn, for example, against early marriage. Even tolerable economic wealth is not reconcilable with a rapid increase of the proletariat. . . .

6. I arrive finally at my sixth and last point. This, however, as I have already said, seems to me one of the most important. It is the question of tax reform. Indeed, I am convinced that on this point the demands of the workers' parties are in the main well-founded. Here the clash of interest between high and low is specially pronounced. In all circles of the upper and more wealthy classes it is unpopular to mention a tax increase which would fall upon these classes. The interested groups among them cannot individually reproach each other. Representatives of the "landed interest" and of "movable" capital have consistently shown themselves to be equally selfish and short-sighted. . . .

Naturally it is impossible here either to lay down the main features of a good system of tax reform or to develop it in detail. I shall limit myself to a few references, although they are ones which are most likely to be misinterpreted.

The indirect taxes in this country amount as a rule to from two-thirds to four-fifths of the total tax income, including the so-called duties. The baneful influence of all these indirect taxes is already far too greatly extended. But argument is worth while concerning the excessive importance of these taxes in our tax system and concerning the selection of objects of taxation, especially the high taxes on important articles of consumption of the lower classes: salt, bread, meat, beer, sugar, coffee, etc. Indeed, if the laborer who among us pays easily ten per cent of his income in salt tax alone (often 1 ⅔ thalers per family) complains about unjust tax-distribution, I must in all honesty keep silent. . . .

Differential tax rates should be established in the case of direct taxes. Funded income from land and capital should be much more highly taxed than unfunded income proceeding from personal labor. . . . The much-discussed principle of progressive taxation of higher incomes should be introduced in moderation. It is a sure, just, and very practical means (among other things) of offsetting the tendency toward greater differences of wealth which prevails in our present-day economic system. . . .

The right of inheritance and private ownership of property should be retained as economically and morally necessary for the family bond and absolutely essential to state economy. But they should be retained to the extent that they fulfill these conditions. Without any harm, then, the inheritance-rights of the more remote degrees of relationship may be abolished in favor of the state, and a rational, productive, beneficial system introduced which would not curtail but even assist the creation of an estate—a system of progressive inheritance taxes for all degrees of relationship in the case of intestate as well as of testamentary succession. . . .

In a general way this seems to me to be the social reform policy which is dictated as much by wisdom and self-interest as by humanity and the moral and Christian sense of duty of the upper classes. . . .

Of course it is a long step from approval of the program to its practical execution. May there be granted to us Germans also the great statesman who will undertake to carry it out. . . .

I have not presented . . . a solution of the social question. A solution is really impossible. Misery and woe, want and starvation, wealth and riches, will always exist side by side in this world; there will always be differences in wealth which cannot be traced to actual merit or to personal guilt. But it is for us to diminish, so far as we can, the resulting evils and the existing inequalities. This is always possible to an appreciable degree. If we have done this we have done our duty. And that can be demanded of us—no more than that, but also no less.

XXIII

SIDNEY WEBB

1859–

Sidney James Webb (since 1929 Lord Passfield) was born in London in 1859. His mother, a woman of practical and even advanced views where the family régime was concerned, was the proprietor of a hairdressing shop when she married Sidney Webb's father. The latter, an accountant by profession, had a more intellectual turn. He was an admirer of John Stuart Mill and a confirmed Radical, with enough public spirit to drudge willingly though unpaid on petty local-government boards.

Sidney Webb's early education (such of it as he did not obtain unguided, and this was considerable) was gained in private schools, the City of London College, and Birkbeck Institute. As a child he had been sent to Switzerland and Germany to acquire French and German. When family reverses occurred, therefore, and he was obliged to leave off regular schooling, the knowledge of languages obtained him a clerkship in the London office of a colonial broker. The University of London's evening classes were a means of continuing his education. He finally received a degree in law and was admitted to the bar. But before this occurred he had deserted a business career for the civil service, and at nineteen entered the War Office as a result of his success in competitive examination. By similar means he became surveyor of taxes and finally a member of the Colonial Office staff.

Meanwhile he had embarked on the study of economics, adopting many of the views of John Stuart Mill. For a time he lectured (unpaid) on that subject at the Christian Socialist Working Men's College. More important, however, was his entrance into the Fabian Society in 1885. This group, one of the earliest British socialist organizations, had been founded in 1884, the offspring of an ethical society. Its discussions had been abstract and utopian. But Sidney Webb "brought them down to earth": he was a stickler for facts. Bernard Shaw, one of the original Fabians, describes Webb as he first saw him at a debating club: "He knew all about the subject of the debate, knew more than the lecturer; knew more than anybody present; had read everything that had been written on the subject; and remembered all the facts that bore on it." Omniscience where social matters are concerned has continued to be Sidney Webb's leading characteristic. In 1889 he contributed one of the most important essays to "the most important single publication in British Socialism," *Fabian Essays*, the manifesto of the society.

In 1890 Beatrice Potter, the daughter of a financier and railroad magnate, met "the little figure with the big head" as she has described him. Two years later they were married. Miss Potter had already proved her mettle as an economic historian and an advocate of the labor movement, having served on Charles Booth's survey of London and written *The Coöperative Movement in Great Britain* (1891). Her marriage was the beginning of an intellectual and literary partnership which has become proverbial. It was more perfect because the Webbs were financially independent. Sidney Webb had retired from the Colonial Office in 1891, and the couple could now devote their entire energy to the promotion of social reform.

The collaboration of the Webbs, exhibited in many books on economic history and social theory, has been so close that it is almost impossible to separate their views on any given subject. The sources of their philosophy were also much the same. Both had been strongly influenced by the evolutionary point of view of Herbert Spencer; Mrs. Webb, in fact, was the intimate friend of Spencer until his death—although he thought it necessary to supplant her as his prospective literary executor when she married a socialist. The evolutionary thesis as well as a belief that exact knowledge of the past supplies a guide to action in the future is at the back of the Webbs' historical studies. The more notable of these include *The History of Trade Unionism* (1894), *English Local Government* (1906–22), and *English Poor Law History* (1927–29). It may be remarked that their enormous literary production has been made possible by the employment, especially in later times, of a number of research assistants.

Although the Webbs have not hesitated to lay down the specifications of a complete socialist society in, for example, *A Constitution for the Socialist Commonwealth* (1920), they have become identified with the policy of piecemeal reform. It was Sidney Webb who struck off the phrase, "the inevitability of gradualness." Not only the influence of Herbert Spencer but the conditions of English society at the end of the nineteenth century contributed to this point of view.

The absence of strong class conflict and the attainment of political democracy seemed to make revolution impossible and unnecessary.

The intellectual contribution of the Webbs to almost every phase of the British labor movement has been noteworthy. They have encouraged and criticized the consumers' coöperative movement and have sat on numerous governmental commissions investigating social questions. Their Minority Report on the poor laws (1909) has become a classic. On retiring from government service in 1891 Sidney Webb was elected to the London County Council on which as chairman of the Technical Education Board he devoted most of his time to promoting that subject. He was also one of the founders of the London School of Economics, acting as (unpaid) professor of public administration from 1912 to 1927.

Sidney Webb's connection with the British Labor party, however, was destined to bring him much wider fame. In 1893 he was one of those who advocated the abandonment of labor's political alliance with the Liberals and the formation of a separate Labor party. The step was taken in 1900. After the war he drafted the new and more radical program of the party, "Labor and the New Social Order." In 1922 a mining district urged him to run for Parliament. It was characteristic that he wrote *A History of the Durham Miners* for the instruction of his future constituents. He took office in the first Labor cabinet as president of the Board of Trade. In the second Labor government he was Secretary of State for Dominion Affairs (1929–30) and for the Colonies (1929–31). (These departments, formerly under a single minister, were divided in 1930.) In 1929 he accepted a barony in order to strengthen the small Labor group in the House of Lords.

The theory and policy of the Webbs, while powerful (perhaps dominant) in Labor circles, have encountered considerable opposition within the movement. Syndicalists and guild socialists have raised objections to their emphasis on state action; the policy of "gradualism" has been a particular object of attack. The Webbs, however. have always been willing to alter their viewpoint if changed conditions seemed to warrant it. So when two Labor governments (1924 and 1929–31) displayed an impotence that could not be entirely argued away, even the Webbs began to feel that something was wrong. Perhaps out of disappointment and "temporary exasperation" Mrs. Webb, at a Fabian meeting early in 1932, "threw gradualism overboard." But there are other forces at work which may make the feeling more permanent. Long advocates of systematic and detailed state control in social and economic matters, the Webbs are profoundly impressed with Russia's program of social planning. A visit to Russia undertaken in 1932 has perhaps driven the lesson home.

REFERENCES

Besides the works mentioned above, some of the Webbs' more important books are *Industrial Democracy* (1897), *The Consumers' Coöperative Movement* (1921), and *The Decay of Capitalist Civilization* (1923).

Criticism of the Webbs' theories and a sketch of their recent activities are given in G. D. H. Cole's "The Webbs: Prophets of a New Order" (*Current History*, November, 1932).

Mrs. Webb's autobiography, *My Apprenticeship* (1926), deals with her earlier career and contains some references to Sidney Webb; a second volume is in prospect. The only other biography is Mary Agnes Hamilton's *Sidney and Beatrice Webb* (1933).

READINGS FROM

FABIAN ESSAYS IN SOCIALISM

The Development of the Democratic Ideal.[1] In discussing the historic groundwork of Socialism, it is worth remembering that no special claim is made for Socialism in the assertion that it possesses a basis in history. Just as every human being has an ancestry, unknown to him though it may be; so every idea, every incident, every movement has in the past its own long chain of causes, without which it could not have been. Formerly we were glad to let the dead bury their dead: nowadays we turn lovingly to the records, whether of persons or things; and we busy ourselves willingly among origins, even without conscious utilitarian end. We are no longer proud of having ancestors, since everyone has them; but we are more than ever interested in our ancestors, now that we find in them the fragments which compose our very selves. The historic ancestry of the English social organization during the present century stands witness to the irresistible momentum of the ideas which Socialism denotes. The record of the century in English social history begins with the trial and hopless failure of an almost complete industrial individualism, in which, however, unrestrained private ownership of land and capital was accompanied by subjection to a political oligarchy. So little element of permanence was there in this individualistic order that,

[1] From Sidney Webb's essay on the historical basis of socialism (1889), pp. 30–32, 33–35.

with the progress of political emancipation, private ownership of the means of production has been, in one direction or another, successively regulated, limited and superseded, until it may now fairly be claimed that the Socialist philosophy of to-day is but the conscious and explicit assertion of principles of social organization which have been already in great part unconsciously adopted. The economic history of the century is an almost continuous record of the progress of Socialism.

Socialism too, has in the record of its internal development a history of its own. Down to the present generation, the aspirant after social regeneration naturally vindicated the practicability of his ideas by offering an elaborate plan with specifications of a new social order from which all contemporary evils were eliminated. Just as Plato had his Republic and Sir Thomas More his Utopia, so Babœuf had his Charter of Equality, Cabet his Icaria, St. Simon his Industrial System, and Fourier his ideal Phalanstery. Robert Owen spent a fortune in pressing upon an unbelieving generation his New Moral World; and even Auguste Comte, superior as he was to many of the weaknesses of his time, must needs add a detailed Polity to his Philosophy of Positivism.

The leading feature of all these proposals was what may be called their statical character. The ideal society was represented as in perfectly balanced equilibrium, without need or possibility of future organic alteration. Since their day we have learned that social reconstruction must not be gone at in this fashion. Owing mainly to the efforts of Comte, Darwin, and Herbert Spencer, we can no longer think of the ideal society as an unchanging State. The social ideal from being static has become dynamic. The necessity of the constant growth and development of the social organism has become axiomatic. No philosopher now looks for anything but the gradual evolution of the new order from the old, without breach of continuity or abrupt change of the entire social tissue at any point during the process. The new becomes itself old, often before it is consciously recognized as new; and history shews us no example of the sudden substitutions of Utopian and revolutionary romance.

Though Socialists have learnt this lesson better than most of their opponents, the common criticism of Socialism has not yet noted the change, and still deals mainly with the obsolete Utopias of the pre-evolutionary age. Parodies of the domestic details of an imaginary Phalanstery, and homilies on the failure of Brook Farm or Icaria, may be passed over as belated and irrelevant now that Socialists are only advocating the conscious adoption of a principle of social organization which the world has already found to be the inevitable outcome of Democracy and the Industrial Revolution. For Socialism is by this time a wave surging throughout all Europe; and for want of a grasp of the series of apparently unconnected events by which and with which it has been for two generations rapidly coming upon us—for want, in short, of knowledge of its intellectual history, we in England to-day see our political leaders in a general attitude of astonishment at the changing face of current politics; both great parties drifting vaguely before a nameless undercurrent which they fail utterly to recognize or understand. With some dim impression that Socialism is one of the Utopian dreams they remember to have heard comfortably disposed of in their academic youth as the impossible ideal of Humanity-intoxicated Frenchmen, they go their ways through the nineteenth century as a countryman blunders through Cheapside. One or two are history fanciers, learned in curious details of the past: the present eludes these no less than the others. They are so near to the individual events that they are blind to the onward sweep of the column. They cannot see the forest for the trees. . . .

The main stream which has borne European society towards Socialism during the past 100 years is the irresistible progress of Democracy. De Tocqueville drove and hammered this truth into the reluctant ears of the Old World two generations ago; and we have all pretended to carry it about as part of our mental furniture ever since. But like most epigrammatic commonplaces, it is not generally realized; and De Tocqueville's book has, in due course, become a classic which everyone quotes and nobody reads. The progress of Democracy is, in fact, often imagined, as by Sir Henry Maine, to be merely the substitution of one kind of political machinery for another; and there are many political Democrats to-day who cannot understand why social or economic matters should be mixed up with politics at all. It was not for this that they broke the power of the aristocracy: they were touched not so much with love of the many as with hatred of the few; and, as has been acutely said—though usually by foolish persons—they are Radicals merely because they are not themselves lords. But it will not long be possible for any man to persist in believing that the political organization of society can be completely altered without corresponding changes in economic and social relations. De Tocqueville expressly pointed out that the progress of Democracy meant nothing less than a complete dissolution of the nexus by which society was held together under the old *régime*. This dissolution is followed by a period of anarchic spiritual isolation of the individual from his fellows, and to that extent by a general denial of the very idea of society. But man is a social animal; and after more or less interval there necessarily comes into existence a new nexus, differing so entirely from the old-fashioned organization that the historic fossil goes about denying that it is a nexus at all, or that any new nexus is possible or desirable. To him, mostly through lack of economics, the progress of Democracy is nothing more than the destruction of old political privileges; and, naturally enough, few can see any beauty in mere dissolution and destruction. Those few are the purely political Radicals abhorred of Comte and Carlyle: they are in social matters the empiricist survivals from a pre-scientific age.

The mere Utopians, on the other hand, who wove the baseless fabric of their visions of reconstructed society on their own private looms, equally failed, as a rule, to comprehend the problem of the age. They were, in imagination, resuscitated Joseph the Seconds, benevolent despots who would have poured the old world, had it only been fluid, into their new moulds. Against their crude plans the Statesman, the Radical, and the Political Economist were united; for they took no account of the blind social forces which they could not control, and which went on inexorably working out social salvation in ways unsuspected by the Utopian.

In the present Socialist movement these two streams are united: advocates of social reconstruction have learnt the lesson of Democracy, and know that it is through the slow and gradual turning of the popular mind to new principles that social reorganization bit by bit comes. All students of society who are abreast of their time, Socialists as well as Individualists, realize that important organic changes can only be (1) democratic, and thus acceptable to a majority of the people, and prepared for in the minds of all; (2) gradual, and thus causing no dislocation, however rapid may be the rate of progress; (3) not regarded as immoral by the mass of the people, and thus not subjectively demoralizing to them; and (4) in this country at any rate, constitutional and peaceful. Socialists may therefore be quite at one with Radicals in their political methods. Radicals, on the other hand, are perforce realizing that mere political levelling is insufficient to save a State from anarchy and despair. Both sections have been driven to recognize that the root of the difficulty is economic; and there is every day a wider consensus that the inevitable outcome of Democracy is the control by the people themselves, not only of their own political organization, but, through that, also of the main instruments of wealth production; the gradual substitution of organized coöperation for the anarchy of the competitive struggle; and the consequent recovery, in the only possible way, of what John Stuart Mill calls "the enormous share which the possessors of the instruments of industry are able to take from the produce." The economic side of the democratic ideal is, in fact, Socialism itself. . . .

The Period of Anarchy.[1] The result of the industrial revolution, with its dissolution of mediævalism amid an impetuous reaction against the bureaucratic tyranny of the past, was to leave all the new elements of society in a state of unrestrained license. Individual liberty, in the sense of freedom to privately appropriate the means of production, reached its maximum at the commencement of the century. No sentimental regulations hindered the free employment of land and capital to the greatest possible pecuniary gain of the proprietors, however many lives of men, women and children were used up in the process. Ignorant or unreflecting capitalists still speak of that terrible time with exultation. "It was not five per cent or ten per cent," says one, "but thousands per cent that made the fortunes of Lancashire."

Mr. Herbert Spencer and those who agree in his worship of Individualism,[2] apparently desire to bring back the legal position which made possible the "white slavery" of which the "sins of legislators" have deprived us; but no serious attempt has ever been made to get repealed any one of the Factory Acts. Women working half naked in the coal mines; young children dragging trucks all day in the foul atmosphere of the underground galleries; infants bound to the loom for fifteen hours in the heated air of the cotton mill, and kept awake only by the overlooker's lash; hours of labor for all, young and old, limited only by the utmost capabilities of physical endurance; complete absence of the sanitary provisions necessary to a rapidly growing population: these and other nameless iniquities will be found recorded as the results of freedom of contract and complete *laisser faire* in the impartial pages of successive blue-book reports. But the Liberal mill-owners of the day, aided by some of the political economists, stubbornly resisted every attempt to interfere with their freedom to

[1] *Ibid.*, pp. 40–43.

[2] Few, however, of Mr. Spencer's followers appear to realize that he presupposes Land Nationalization as the necessary condition of an Individualist community (see "Social Statics," *passim*). [Author's note.]

use "their" capital and "their" hands as they found most profitable, and (like their successors to-day) predicted of each restriction as it arrived that it must inevitably destroy the export trade and deprive them of all profit whatsoever.

But this "acute outbreak of individualism, unchecked by the old restraints, and invested with almost a religious sanction by a certain soulless school of writers," was inevitable, after the economic blundering of governments in the eighteenth century. Prior to the scientific investigation of economic laws, men had naturally interfered in social arrangements with very unsatisfactory results. A specially extravagant or a specially thrifty king debased the currency, and then was surprised to find that in spite of stringent prohibitions prices went up and all good money fled the country. Wise statesmen, to keep up wages, encouraged the woollen manufactures of England by ruining those of Ireland, and were then astonished to find English wages cut by Irish pauper immigration. Benevolent parliaments attempted to raise the worker's income by poor law allowances, and then found that they had lowered it. Christian kings eliminated half the skilled artisans from their kingdoms, and then found that they had ruined the rest by disabling industry. Government inspectors ordered how the cloth should be woven, what patterns should be made, and how broad the piece should be, until the manufacturers in despair cried out merely to be let alone.

When the early economists realized how radically wrong had been even the well-meant attempts to regulate economic relations by legislation, and how generally these attempts multiplied private monopolies, they leaned in their deductions heavily towards complete individual liberty. The administration of a populous state is such a very difficult matter, and when done on false principles is so certain to be badly done, that it was natural to advocate rather no administration at all than the interference of ignorant and interested bunglers. Nature, glorified by the worship of a famous school of French philosophers and English poets, and as yet unsuspected of countless crimes of "the struggle for existence," appeared at least more trustworthy than Castlereagh. Real democratic administration seemed, in the time of the "White Terror," and even under the milder Whig hypocrisy which succeeded it, hopelessly remote. The best thing to work and fight for was, apparently, the reduction to impotence and neutrality of all the "Powers that Be." Their influence being for the moment hostile to the people, it behoved the people to destroy their influence altogether. And so grew up the doctrine of what Professor Huxley has since called "Administrative Nihilism." It was the apotheosis of *Laisser Faire, Laisser Aller*. . . .

The Intellectual and Moral Revolt.[1] The new creed of "Philosophic Radicalism" did not have matters all its own way. Its doctrines might suit mill owners and merchant princes, and all who were able to enjoy the delight of their own strength in the battle of life. But it was essentially a creed of Murdstones and Gradgrinds; and the first revolt came from the artistic side. The "nest of singing birds" at the Lakes would have none of it, though De Quincey worked out its abstract economics in a manner still unsurpassed. Coleridge did his best to drown it in German Transcendentalism. Robert Owen and his following of enthusiastic communistic coöperators steadfastly held up a loftier ideal. The great mass of the wage earners never bowed the knee to the principles upon which the current "White Slavery" was maintained. But the first man who really made a dint in the individualist shield was Carlyle, who knew how to compel men to listen to him. Oftener wrong than right in his particular proposals, he managed to keep alive the faith in nobler ends than making a fortune in this world and saving one's soul in the next. Then came Maurice, Kingsley, Ruskin, and others who dared to impeach the current middle-class cult; until finally, through Comte and John Stuart Mill, Darwin and Herbert Spencer, the conception of the Social Organism has at last penetrated to the minds, though not yet to the books, even of our professors of Political Economy.

Meanwhile, caring for none of these things, the practical man had been irresistibly driven in the same direction. In the teeth of the current Political Economy, and in spite of all the efforts of the mill-owning Liberals, England was compelled to put forth her hand to succor and protect her weaker members. Any number of Local Improvement Acts, Drainage Acts, Truck Acts, Mines Regulation Acts, Factory Acts, Public Health Acts, Adulteration Acts, were passing into law. The liberty of the property owner to oppress the propertyless by the levy of the economic tribute of rent and interest began to be circumscribed, pared away, obstructed and forbidden in various directions. Slice after slice has gradually been cut from the profits of capital, and therefore from its selling value, by socially beneficial restrictions on its user's liberty to do as he liked with it. Slice after

[1] *Ibid.*, pp. 45–48, 49–53, 53–56.

slice has been cut off the incomes from rent and interest by the gradual shifting of taxation from consumers to persons enjoying incomes above the average of the kingdom. Step by step the political power and political organization of the country have been used for industrial ends, until to-day the largest employer of labor is one of the ministers of the Crown (the Postmaster-General); and almost every conceivable trade is, somewhere or other, carried on by parish, municipality, or the National Government itself without the intervention of any middleman or capitalist. The theorists who denounce the taking by the community into its own hands of the organization of its own labor as a thing economically unclean, repugnant to the sturdy individual independence of Englishmen, and as yet outside the sphere of practical politics, seldom have the least suspicion of the extent to which it has already been carried. Besides our international relations and the army, navy, police and the courts of justice, the community now carries on for itself, in some part or another of these islands, the post office, telegraphs, carriage of small commodities, coinage, surveys, the regulation of the currency and note issue, the provision of weights and measures, the making, sweeping, lighting, and repairing of streets, roads, and bridges, life insurance, the grant of annuities, shipbuilding, stockbroking, banking, farming, and money-lending. It provides for many thousands of us from birth to burial—midwifery, nursery, education, board and lodging, vaccination, medical attendance, medicine, public worship, amusements, and interment. It furnishes and maintains its own museums, parks, art galleries, libraries, concert-halls, roads, streets, bridges, markets, slaughter-houses, fire-engines, lighthouses, pilots, ferries, surfboats, steamtugs, life-boats, cemeteries, public baths, washhouses, pounds, harbours, piers, wharves, hospitals, dispensaries, gasworks, waterworks, tramways, telegraph cables, allotments, cow meadows, artizans' dwellings, schools, churches, and reading-rooms. It carries on and publishes its own researches in geology, meteorology, statistics, zoölogy, geography, and even theology. In our Colonies the English Government further allows and encourages the communities to provide for themselves railways, canals, pawnbroking, theatres, forestry, cinchona farms, irrigation, leper villages, casinos, bathing establishments, and immigration, and to deal in ballast, guano, quinine, opium, salt, and what not. Every one of these functions, with those of the army, navy, police, and courts of justice, were at one time left to private enterprise, and were a source of legitimate individual investment of capital. Step by step the community has absorbed them, wholly or partially; and the area of private exploitation has been lessened. Parallel with this progressive nationalization or municipalization of industry, there has gone on the elimination of the purely personal element in business management. The older economists doubted whether anything but banking and insurance could be carried on by joint stock enterprise: now every conceivable industry, down to baking and milk-selling, is successfully managed by the salaried officers of large corporations of idle shareholders. More than one-third of the whole business of England, measured by the capital employed, is now done by joint stock companies, whose shareholders could be expropriated by the community with no more dislocation of the industries carried on by them than is caused by the daily purchase of shares on the Stock Exchange. . . .

Even in the fields still abandoned to private enterprise, its operations are . . . every day more closely limited, in order that the anarchic competition of private greed, which at the beginning of the century was set up as the only infallibly beneficent principle of social action, may not utterly destroy the State. All this has been done by "practical" men, ignorant, that is to say, of any scientific sociology, believing Socialism to be the most foolish of dreams, and absolutely ignoring, as they thought, all grandiloquent claims for social reconstruction. Such is the irresistible sweep of social tendencies, that in their every act they worked to bring about the very Socialism they despised; and to destroy the Individualist faith which they still professed. They builded better than they knew.

It must by no means be supposed that these beginnings of social reorganization have been effected, or the proposals for their extension brought to the front, without the conscious efforts of individual reformers. The "Zeitgeist" is potent; but it does not pass Acts of Parliament without legislators, or erect municipal libraries without town councillors. Though our decisions are moulded by the circumstances of the time, and the environment at least roughhews our ends, shape them as we will; yet each generation decides for itself. It still rests with the individual to resist or promote the social evolution, consciously or unconsciously, according to his character and information. The importance of complete consciousness of the social tendencies of the age lies in the fact that its existence and comprehensiveness often determine the expediency of our particular action: we move with less resistance with the stream than against it.

The general failure to realize the extent to which our unconscious

Socialism has already proceeded—a failure which causes much time and labor to be wasted in uttering and elaborating on paper the most ludicrously unpractical anti-socialist demonstrations of the impossibility of matters of daily occurrence—is due to the fact that few know anything of local administration outside their own town. It is the municipalities which have done most to "socialize" our industrial life; and the municipal history of the century is yet unwritten. A few particulars may here be given as to this progesssive "municipalization" of industry. Most of us know that the local governments have assumed the care of the roads, streets and bridges, once entirely abandoned to individual enterprise, as well as the lighting and cleansing of all public thoroughfares, and the provision of sewers, drains and "storm-water courses." It is, perhaps, not so generally known that no less than £7,500,000 is annually expended on these services in England and Wales alone, being about 5 per cent of the rent of the country. The provision of markets, fairs, harbors, piers, docks, hospitals, cemeteries and burial grounds, is still shared with private capitalists; but those in public hands absorb nearly £2,000,000 annually. Parks, pleasure grounds, libraries, museums, baths, and washhouses cost the public funds over half a million sterling. All these are, however, comparatively unimportant services. It is in the provision of gas, water, and tramways that local authorities organize labor on a large scale. Practically half the gas consumers in the kingdom are supplied by public gas works, which exist in 168 separate localities, with an annual expenditure of over three millions. It need hardly be added that the advantage to the public is immense, in spite of the enormous price paid for the works in many instances; and that the further municipalization of the gas industry is proceeding with great rapidity, no fewer than twelve local authorities having obtained loans for the purpose (and one for electric lighting) in a single year (Local Government Board Report, 1887–88, c—5526, pp. 319–367). With equal rapidity is the water supply becoming a matter of commercial organization, the public expenditure already reaching nearly a million sterling annually. Sixty-five local authorities borrowed money for water supply in 1887–88, rural and urban districts being equally represented (c—5550, pp. 319–367). Tramways and ferries are undergoing the same development. About thirty-one towns, including nearly all the larger provincial centres, own some or all of their own tramways. Manchester, Bradford, Birmingham, Oldham, Sunderland, and Greenock lease their undertakings; but among the municipalities

Huddersfield has the good sense to work its lines without any "middleman" intervention, with excellent public results. The tramway mileage belonging to local authorities has increased five-fold since 1878, and comprises more than a quarter of the whole (House of Commons Return, 1887–88, No. 347). The last important work completed by the Metropolitan Board of Works was the establishment of a "free steam ferry" on the Thames, charged upon the rates. This is, in some respects, the most significant development of all. The difference between a free steam ferry and a free railway is obviously only one of degree.

A few more cases are worth mentioning. Glasgow builds and maintains seven public "common lodging houses"; Liverpool provides science lectures; Manchester builds and stocks an art gallery; Birmingham runs schools of design; Leeds creates extensive cattle markets and Bradford supplies water below cost price. There are nearly one hundred free libraries and reading rooms. The minor services now performed by public bodies are innumerable. This "Municipal Socialism" has been rendered possible by the creation of a local debt now reaching over £181,000,000. Nearly £10,000,000 is annually paid as interest and sinking fund on the debt; and to this extent the pecuniary benefit of municipalization is diminished. The full advantages of the public organization of labor remain, besides a considerable pecuniary profit; whilst the objective differentiation of the economic classes (by the separation of the idle *rentier* from the manager or *entrepreneur*) enormously facilitates popular comprehension of the nature of the economic tribute known as interest. To the extent, moreover, that additional charges are thrown upon the rates, the interest paid to the capitalist is levied mainly at the cost of the landlord, and we have a corresponding "nationalization" of so much of the economic rent. The increase in the local rates has been 36 per cent, or nearly £7,000,000, in eleven years, and is still growing. They now amount to over twenty-six millions sterling in England and Wales alone, or about 17 per cent of the rental of the country. . . .

Nor is there any apparent prospect of a slackening of the pace of this unconscious abandonment of individualism. No member of Parliament has so much as introduced a Bill to give effect to the anarchist principles of Mr. Herbert Spencer's "Man *versus* the State." The not disinterested efforts of the Liberty and Property Defence League fail to hinder even Conservative Parliaments from further

Socialist legislation. Mr. Gladstone remarked to a friend in 1886 that the Home Rule question would turn the Liberal party into a Radical party. He might have said that it would make both parties Socialist. Free elementary and public technical education is now practically accepted on both sides of the House, provided that the so-called "voluntary schools," themselves half maintained from public funds, are not extinguished. Mr. Chamberlain and the younger Conservatives openly advocate far-reaching projects of social reform through State and municipal agency, as a means of obtaining popular support. The National Liberal Federation adopts the special taxation of urban ground values as the main feature in its domestic programme, notwithstanding that this proposal is characterized by old-fashioned Liberals as sheer confiscation of so much of the landlords' property. The London Liberal and Radical Union, which has Mr. John Morley for its president, even proposes that the County Council shall have power to rebuild the London slums at the sole charge of the ground landlord. It is, therefore, not surprising that the Trades Union Congress should now twice have declared in favor of "Land Nationalization" by large majorities, or that the bulk of the London County Council should be returned on an essentially Socialist platform. The whole of the immediately practicable demands of the most exacting Socialist are, indeed, now often embodied in the current Radical programme; and the following exposition of it, from the pages of the *Star* newspaper, 8th August, 1888, may serve as a statement of the current Socialist demands for further legislation.[1]

Revision of Taxation

Object.—Complete shifting of burden from the workers, of whatever grade, to the recipients of rent and interest, with a view to the ultimate and gradual extinction of the latter class.

Means.—1. Abolition of all customs and excise duties, except those on spirits. 2. Increase of income tax, differentiating in favor of earned as against unearned incomes, and graduating cumulatively by system of successive levels of abatement. 3. Equalization and increase of death duties and the use of the proceeds as capital, not income. 4. Shifting of local rates and house duty from occupier to owner, any contract to the contrary notwithstanding. 5. Compulsory redemption of existing land tax and reimposition on all ground rents and increased values. 6. Abolition of fees on licenses for employment. 7. Abolition of police-court fees.

[1] It is interesting to compare this programme, with its primary insistence on economic and social reform, with the bare political character of the "Five Points" of the Chartists, viz., Manhood Suffrage, Vote by Ballot, Annual Parliaments, Payment of Members relieved from the property qualification, and Equal Electoral Districts. [Author's note.]

Extension of Factory Acts

Object.—To raise, universally, the standard of comfort by obtaining the general recognition of a minimum wage and a maximum working day.

Means.—1. Extension of the general provisions of the Factory and Workshops Acts (or the Mines Regulation Acts, as the case may be) to all employers of labor. 2. Compulsory registration of all employers of more than three (?) workers. 3. Largely increased number of inspectors, and these to include women, and to be mainly chosen from the wage-earning class. 4. Immediate reduction of maximum hours to eight per day in all Government and municipal employment, in all mines, and in all licensed monopolies such as railways, tramways, gasworks, water-works, docks, harbors, etc.; and in any trade in which a majority of the workers desire it. 5. The compulsory insertion of clauses in all contracts for Government or municipal supplies, providing that (*a*) there shall be no sub-contracting, (*b*) that no worker shall be employed more than eight hours per day, and (*c*) that no wages less than a prescribed minimum shall be paid.

Educational Reform

Object.—To enable all, even the poorest, children to obtain not merely some, but the best education they are capable of.

Means.—1. The immediate abolition of all fees in public elementary schools, Board or voluntary, with a corresponding increase in the Government grant. 2. Creation of a Minister for Education, with control over the whole educational system, from the elementary school to the University, and over all educational endowments. 3. Provision of public technical and secondary schools wherever needed, and creation of abundant public secondary scholarships. 4. Continuation, in all cases of elementary education at evening schools. 5. Registration and inspection of all private educational establishments.

Re-organization of Poor Law Administration

Object.—To provide generously, and without stigma, for the aged, the sick, and those destitute through temporary want of employment, without relaxing the "tests" against the endowment of able-bodied idleness.

Means.—1. The separation of the relief of the aged and the sick from the workhouse system, by a universal system of aged pensions, and public infirmaries. 2. The industrial organization and technical education of all able-bodied paupers. 3. The provision of temporary relief works for the unemployed. 4. The supersession of the Boards of Guardians by the local municipal authorities.

Extension of Municipal Activity

Object.—The gradual public organization of labor for all public purposes, and the elimination of the private capitalist and middleman.

Means.—1. The provision of increased facilities for the acquisition of land, the destruction without compensation of all dwellings found unfit for habitation, and the provision of artisan dwellings by the municipality. 2. The facilitation of every extension of municipal administration, in London and all other towns, of gas, water, markets, tramways, hospitals, cemeteries, parks, museums, art galleries, libraries, reading-rooms, schools, docks, harbors, rivers, etc. 3. The provision of abundant facilities for the acquisition of land by local rural authorities, for allotments, common pastures, public halls, reading rooms, etc.

Amendment of Political Machinery

Object.—To obtain the most accurate representation and expression of the desires of the majority of the people at every moment.

Means.—1. Reform of registration so as to give a vote, both Parliamentary and municipal, to every adult. 2. Abolition of any period of residence as a qualification for registration. 3. Bi-annual registration by special public officer. 4. Annual Parliaments. 5. Payment of election expenses, including postage of election addresses and polling cards. 6. Payment of all public representatives, parliamentary, county, or municipal. 7. Second ballot. 8. Abolition or painless extinction of the House of Lords.

This is the programme to which a century of industrial revolution has brought the Radical working man. Like John Stuart Mill, though less explicitly, he has turned from mere political Democracy to a complete, though unconscious, Socialism. . . .

The New Synthesis.[1] It need hardly be said that the social philosophy of the time did not remain unaffected by the political evolution and the industrial development. Slowly sinking into men's minds all this while was the conception of a new social nexus, and a new end of social life. It was discovered (or rediscovered) that a society is something more than an aggregate of so many individual units—that it possesses existence distinguishable from those of any of its components. A perfect city became recognized as something more than any number of good citizens—something to be tried by other tests, and weighed in other balances than the individual man. The community must necessarily aim, consciously or not, at its continuance as a community: its life transcends that of any of its members; and the interests of the individual unit must often clash with those of the whole. Though the social organism has itself evolved from the union of individual men, the individual is now created by the social organism of which he forms a part: his life is born of the larger life;

[1] *Ibid.*, pp. 56–61.

his attributes are moulded by the social pressure; his activities, inextricably interwoven with others, belong to the activity of the whole. Without the continuance and sound health of the social organism, no man can now live or thrive; and its persistence is accordingly his paramount end. His conscious motive for action may be, nay always must be, individual to himself; but where such action proves inimical to the social welfare, it must sooner or later be checked by the whole, lest the whole perish through the error of its member. The conditions of social health are accordingly a matter for scientific investigation. There is, at any moment, one particular arrangement of social relations which involves the minimum of human misery then and there possible amid the "niggardliness of nature." Fifty years ago it would have been assumed that absolute freedom in the sense of individual or "manly" independence, plus a criminal code, would spontaneously result in such an arrangement for each particular nation; and the effect was the philosophic apotheosis of *Laisser Faire*. To-day every student is aware that no such optimistic assumption is warranted by the facts of life. We know now that in natural selection at the stage of development where the existence of civilized mankind is at stake, the units selected from are not individuals, but societies. Its action at earlier stages, though analogous, is quite dissimilar. Among the lower animals physical strength or agility is the favored quality: if some heaven-sent genius among the cuttle-fish developed a delicate poetic faculty, this high excellence would not delay his succumbing to his hulking neighbor. When, higher up in the scale, mental cunning became the favored attribute, an extra brain convolution, leading primitive man to the invention of fire or tools, enabled a comparatively puny savage to become the conqueror and survivor of his fellows.

Brain culture accordingly developed apace; but we do not yet thoroughly realize that this has itself been superseded as the "selected" attribute, by social organization. The cultivated Athenians, Saracens, and Provençals, went down in the struggle for existence before their respective competitors, who, individually inferior, were in possession of a, at that time, more valuable social organization. The French nation was beaten in the last war, not because the average German was an inch and a half taller than the average Frenchman, or because he had read five more books, but because the German social organism was, for the purposes of the time, superior in efficiency to the French. If we desire to hand on to the afterworld our direct influence, and not merely the memory of our excellence, we must take even more care to improve the social organism of which we form part, than to perfect our own individual developments. Or rather, the perfect and fitting development of each individual is not necessarily the utmost and highest cultivation of his own personality, but the filling, in the best possible way, of his humble function in the great social machine. We must abandon the self-conceit of imagining that we are independent units, and bend our jealous minds, absorbed in their own cultivation, to this subjection to the higher end, the Common Weal. Accordingly, conscious "direct adaptation" steadily supplants the unconscious and wasteful "indirect adaptation" of the earlier form of the struggle for existence; and with every advance in sociological knowledge, Man is seen to assume more and more, not only the mastery of "things," but also a conscious control over social destiny itself.

This new scientific conception of the Social Organism has put completely out of countenance the cherished principles of the Political Economist and the Philosophic Radical. We left them sailing gaily into Anarchy on the stream of *Laisser Faire.* Since then the tide has turned. The publication of John Stuart Mill's *Political Economy* in 1848 marks conveniently the boundary of the old individualist Economics. Every edition of Mill's book became more and more socialistic. After his death the world learnt the personal history, penned by his own hand, of his development from a mere political democrat to a convinced Socialist.

The change in tone since then has been such that one competent economist, professedly anti-socialist, publishes regretfully to the world that all the younger men are now Socialists, as well as many of the older Professors. It is, indeed, mainly from these that the world has learnt how faulty were the earlier economic generalizations, and above all, how incomplete as guides for social or political action. These generalizations are accordingly now to be met with only in leading articles, sermons, or the speeches of Ministers or Bishops. The Economist himself knows them no more.

The result of this development of Sociology is to compel a revision of the relative importance of liberty and equality as principles to be kept in view in social administration. In Bentham's celebrated "ends" to be aimed at in a civil code, liberty stands predominant over equality, on the ground that full equality can be maintained only by the loss of security for the fruits of labor. That exposition remains as true as ever; but the question for decision remains, how much liberty?

Economic analysis has destroyed the value of the old criterion of respect for the equal liberty of others. Bentham, whose economics were weak, paid no attention to the perpetual tribute on the fruits of others' labor which full private property in land inevitably creates. In his view liberty and security to property meant that every worker should be free to obtain the full result of his own labor; and there appeared no inconsistency between them. The political economist now knows that with free competition and private property in land and capital, no individual can possibly obtain the full result of his own labor. The student of industrial development, moreover, finds it steadily more and more impossible to trace what is precisely the result of each separate man's toil. Complete rights of liberty and property necessarily involve, for example, the spoliation of the Irish cottier tenant for the benefit of Lord Clanricarde. What then becomes of the Benthamic principle of the greatest happiness of the greatest number? When the Benthamite comes to understand the Law of Rent, which of the two will he abandon? For he cannot escape the lesson of the century, taught alike by the economists, the statesmen, and the "practical men," that complete individual liberty, with unrestrained private ownership of the instruments of wealth production, is irreconcileable with the common weal. The free struggle for existence among ourselves menaces our survival as a healthy and permanent social organism. Evolution, Professor Huxley declares, is the substitution of consciously regulated coördination among the units of each organism, for blind anarchic competition. Thirty years ago Herbert Spencer demonstrated the incompatibility of full private property in land with the modern democratic State; and almost every economist now preaches the same doctrine. The Radical is rapidly arriving, from practical experience, at similar conclusions; and the steady increase of the government regulation of private enterprise, the growth of municipal administration, and the rapid shifting of the burden of taxation directly to rent and interest, mark in treble lines the statesman's unconscious abandonment of the old Individualism, and our irresistible glide into collectivist Socialism.

It was inevitable that the Democracy should learn this lesson. With the masses painfully conscious of the failure of Individualism to create a decent social life for four-fifths of the people, it might have been foreseen that Individualism could not survive their advent to political power. If private property in land and capital necessarily keeps the many workers permanently poor (through no fault of their own) in order to make the few idlers rich (from no merit of their own), private property in land and capital will inevitably go the way of the feudalism which it superseded. The economic analysis confirms the rough generalization of the suffering people. The history of industrial evolution points to the same result; and for two generations the world's chief ethical teachers have been urging the same lesson. No wonder the heavens of Individualism are rolling up before our eyes like a scroll; and even the Bishops believe and tremble.

It is, of course, possible, as Sir Henry Maine and others have suggested, that the whole experience of the century is a mistake, and that political power will once more swing back into the hands of a monarch or an aristocratic oligarchy. It is, indeed, want of faith in democracy which holds back most educated sympathisers with Socialism from frankly accepting its principles. What the economic side of such political atavism would be it is not easy to forecast. The machine industry and steam power could hardly be dismissed with the caucus and the ballot-box. So long, however, as Democracy in political administration continues to be the dominant principle, Socialism may be quite safely predicted as its economic obverse, in spite of those freaks or aberrations of Democracy which have already here and there thrown up a short-lived monarchy or a romantic dictatorship. Every increase in the political power of the proletariat will most surely be used by them for their economic and social protection. In England, at any rate, the history of the century serves at once as their guide and their justification.

Thirty Years After.[1] What is most interesting to one, at least, of the contributors, is to mark, in the light of thirty years of subsequent experience and thirty years' advance of Political Science, where we went wrong and what we omitted. . . .

It is perhaps significant that the part of the book that comes most triumphantly through the ordeal of such an examination is, throughout, the economic analysis. . . .

Our history, though I believe, essentially accurate, was plainly based on less solid a ground of knowledge. . . .

Moreover, our knowledge of the social and industrial forces of our country was far from complete. We evidently attached quite insufficient importance to Trade Unionism, which the book never mentions as a political force, or as constituting any essential part of the

[1] From Sidney Webb's introduction to the 1920 edition of *Fabian Essays*, pp. iv–vii, ix–xv.

social structure. It is clear that we had little notion, in 1889, of the enduring value and indispensable social function of Vocational Organisation of any sort; and we had no anticipation that it was to be, as is nowadays commonly accepted, a permanent part of social organisation, destined in the State of To-morrow, for important public functions. We very soon set about remedying this particular gap in our knowledge; and the publication, in 1894, of the *History of Trade Unionism*, and at the end of 1897, of the comprehensive analysis of the whole structure and function of the workmen's organisations entitled *Industrial Democracy*, effectively brought the Trade Union Movement into our common consciousness. We may perhaps say that it did more than this. It laid the foundation for, and possibly contributed to promote, in a younger generation, the whole series of studies of different aspects of Vocational Organisation, and its place in the society of the future, which, whatever we may think of their elaboration into what is called "Guild Socialism," constitute, perhaps, the most important addition that this century has yet made to Socialist thought.

We were similarly unappreciative of the Coöperative Movement. . . . Our omission was made good by the publication, in 1890, of *The Coöperative Movement in Great Britain*, by one [1] who presently joined the group. . . .

We concerned ourselves more about Local Government than about Trade Unionism or Coöperation; but in 1889, in common with most Socialists (and, for that matter, also most Individualists), we were still groping for the illuminating idea that would assign to our Local Authorities their proper place and function in the Social Organism. In these Essays we slipped into thinking of them as organising production for the sake of the unemployed and as ultimately developing, side by side with capitalist enterprise, alternative factories and shops, which would, under the management of Town and County Councils, beat the profit-maker with his own weapons, at his own game. It did not occur to us in 1889 that the Parish Vestry, the Municipality, and the County Council were, like the Coöperative Societies, essentially Associations of Consumers, not Associations of Producers; Associations in which membership was obligatory on all local residents, instead of being voluntary, but the function of which was equally the collective provision for the citizens, as consumers, of whatever they required. When we tumbled to this idea—an impor-

[1] Beatrice Potter, later Mrs. Sidney Webb.

tant addition to Socialist theory—we saw at once the extensive sphere that must necessarily be assigned, in any highly organised and densely populated community, to "Municipal Socialism," as contrasted with the "State Socialism," which is what had commonly been thought of prior to that date; and the important part to be played in the Socialist State by its various democratically organised and practically autonomous Local Governing Bodies. We came very vividly to appreciate the significance of their manifold functions in ridding us from the hypothetical tyranny of a single national employer, inevitably bureaucratic in character, no less than from the incubus of an all-pervading uniformity of social life. . . .

It is plain to-day that we went far astray in what was said about Unemployment and the Unemployed. . . . Through lack of adequate investigation of the phenomena, we erred, in common not only with other Socialists, but also with the ordinary Economists and Politicians, in assuming that recurrent periods of widespread unemployment could not in practice be prevented under any system short of a completely organised Collectivism. . . . But our failure to devise any practicable method of dealing with the "non-effectives" was not confined to the problems presented by the able-bodied adults who might find themselves involuntarily unemployed. There was, in 1889, on the side of the Socialists, no study of, and no scheme for the social provision for any of the non-effectives of society, whether orphan children, the sick or the infirm, the involuntarily unemployed or the aged. . . . This gap in our knowledge we did not fill until the appointment in 1905, of Mr. George Lansbury and Mrs. Sidney Webb to the Royal Commission on the Poor Law and the Relief of Distress from Unemployment; which resulted, after four years of strenuous investigation, in which a good many other members of the Society took part, in the working out of an elaborate scheme—constituting the Minority Report of the Commission—first, for the actual prevention of any widespread or continuous Unemployment, even in our present social order, by the maintenance at an approximately even level, of the aggregate weekly demand for wage-labour, season by season, and year by year, to be effected by nothing more impracticable than a rearrangement of the present public orders for works and services—a course which has been demonstrated to be both statistically adequate and easily within the capacity of the first Government that chooses to undertake it; and secondly, for the wisely designed full and ample provision, under Democratic control, of whatever is required for the efficient nurture and maintenance of every section of the "non-effectives," from the orphan infant to the friendless aged. . . .

A more general shortcoming, affecting both structure and function, was our failure to "think internationally." With the partial exception of William Clarke, we had none of us given attention either to the continental Socialist Movements, or to international relations. We had not attended the first congress, at Paris in 1889, of the revived "Internatonal," and, except for our studies of Proudhon, Lassalle and Karl Marx, and for some slight personal acquaintance with Socialist exiles in London, we knew practically nothing of what was happening in the Socialist world outside our own country. But here, too, we quickly improved our qualifications. The Fabian Society was represented in the next International Socialist Congress at Brussels in 1891, and has ever since taken its share in international relations. But we had our own view of internationalism. We had little sympathy with the ideal of a universal cosmopolitanism which some Socialists and many Liberals more or less consciously cherished, as an exaggeration, if not a perversion, of the teachings of Mazzini on the one hand, and Cobden on the other. What we aimed at was, literally, an organised "internationalism," in which national characteristics among the manual-working wage-earners no less than among governments, far from becoming obliterated or straightened out into a mechanical uniformity, would be not only separately developed, but also differentiated even further than at present. We counted on each racial group or Nation-State pursuing its own evolution, and shaping its own destiny, uninterruptedly in its own way, intensifying thereby its characteristic faculties, and thus increasing the special services that it could render to the world. . . . This, at any rate, was the synthesis between patriotism and internationalism that we evolved for ourselves; and to this we tenaciously held; yielding neither to "Imperialism" on the one hand, nor to "Little Englandism" on the other. . . .

Generally, it may be said, I think, that we concentrated our thought too much on the actual conditions that would in an effective Democracy enable the great mass of the people to secure for themselves material prosperity, social freedom and a progressive advance in civilisation, with all the development of individual personality that these conditions alone can make possible. We did not sufficiently remember that it is equally indispensable that the whole people should feel themselves to be prosperous; that they should have an acute consciousness of their freedom; that they should, as a completely Democratic community, not merely govern but also be continuously aware of the government they are exercising. It was not—as is always ignorantly alleged of Socialists—that we put our faith too exclusively in "machinery," even social machinery; or that we "ignored human nature" in the ordinary sense. . . . But we did not sufficiently allow for the psychological fact that no man is free who does not think himself free; and that no one is benefiting by the responsibilities of governing, unless he is aware he is governing. . . . We presently acquired something of what we lacked from our nearer acquaintance with Coöperation, Municipal Government, and, above all, Trade Unionism; but much had to be learned from the studies some of us subsequently made in what may be called Social Psychology, to which some of us contributed.[1] . . .

One final word may be allowed upon an error that we did not make, although the Fabian Society has been persistently accused of it. Though we put no faith in a "physical force" revolution, achieved by a "class-conscious minority," we did not expect that Socialism could ever be realised, or, indeed, that much progress could be made toward it, without the formation, and the entry into British politics, of a definitely Socialist Party, putting itself in opposition to both the Liberal and the Conservative Parties. This is the doctrine very distinctly emphasised in these essays, notably the last two. . . . We believed, with all our might, in what was called "permeation"—that is to say, the inculcation of Socialist thought and Socialist projects into the minds not merely of complete converts, but of those whom we found in disagreement with us—and we spared no pains in these propagandist efforts, not among political Liberals or Radicals only, but also among political Conservatives; not only among Trade Unionists and Coöperators, but also among Employers and Financiers. . . . But we were at the same time striving persistently to get on foot an independent political party, which would hold Socialist views and adopt a definitely Socialist programme. We recognised—as events proved, accurately—that for such a party, in this country and gen-

[1] Mention may be made of *The Quintessence of Ibsenism* by G. Bernard Shaw, 1891; and, indeed, all his subsequent works; together with the books and plays of H. Granville Barker; and, in another field, Fabian Tract No. 180, *The Philosophy of Socialism*, and other works by A. Clutton Brock. Specially significant are *Human Nature in Politics*, 1908, and *The Great Society*, 1914, both by Graham Wallas; see also his *Life of Francis Place*, 1898, revised edition, 1918. [Author's note.]

eration, the only practicable basis was the wage-earning class, and the only available machinery was the Trade Union organisation. We had, in 1889, already been at it for a couple of years, taking every opportunity, by lecture and pamphlet, and by personal intercourse, to persuade the Trade Unions and Trade Councils to constitute such a Party of Labour, to which we promised whatever personal assistance we could give. For seven years these efforts produced next to no apparent result. Not until 1893 came the formation—in which the Fabian Society gladly took part—of the Independent Labour Party. In 1900, when at last the Trades Union Congress was induced to set up the "Labour Representation Committee," which became, in 1906, the present Labour Party, the Fabian Society participated in the very first meeting; and it has ever since formed a constituent part of the organisation, sending one or more of its members to the Executive Committee. Those who read *Labour and the New Social Order*—the detailed constructive programme which the Labour Party adopted for the General Election of 1918—will see how completely and definitely "Socialist" this party has become; and how exactly it corresponds with what the last two essays of the present volume had, in 1889, in contemplation. It is also instructive to contrast this programme with that printed in the second of these Essays, as representing all that we had managed, even nominally, to impose on the most advanced "Radicalism" of 1888.[1] What the Labour Party will make of British social politics during the next thirty years, by which time some one else may write a new Introduction for another edition of *Fabian Essays*, offers material for an interesting forecast, from which I prudently refrain.

[1] See above, pp. 521–523. (Editor.)

PART VII

WORKERS' CONTROL: FUNCTIONAL THEORIES REVOLUTIONARY AND EVOLUTIONARY

XXIV

MICHAEL BAKUNIN

1814–1876

Michael Alexandrovitch Bakunin was not the first member of his family to engage in revolutionary activities. Relatives of his mother had taken part in the disturbances of 1825 after the death of Alexander I and some suspicion had even rested upon his father. The latter had indeed in early life felt the attraction of Voltaire and Rousseau but the taking of the Bastille (which he witnessed) seemed to cure him of radical ideas. A deposit of humanitarian remained, however, and after a period of service in the Russian diplomatic corps he settled down to preside over his 1,200 serfs with more than ordinary solicitude. His wife did not share the intellectual interests of her husband. She is described as cold and reserved, with a haughtiness that bore heavily upon her son.

Michael, one of eleven children, was born in 1814 at Preamouchino, a village located midway between Moscow and St. Petersburg (now Leningrad). The children were educated at home under the guidance of their parents and numerous private tutors. The principles of Rousseau again appeared; the father, himself an amateur naturalist, inspired his children with a love of nature. They were also instructed in foreign languages. From stories of his father's travels and the reading of tales of exploration Michael acquired a taste for adventure. Perhaps he chose a military career as the shortest cut to it: at any rate he entered the military academy at sixteen and studied assiduously for three years. But a love affair interrupted his studies; he failed the examinations and was transferred to garrison duty. Homesick, disgusted with army life yet unable to resign, he turned to the study of geography, physics, grammar, and history. At last he defied the authorities and returned home.

In 1835 his father was able to obtain his legal release from the army. At this time Michael formed the acquaintance of a group of young philosophical idealists at Moscow. When a family quarrel, the result of Michael's attempts to regulate the love affairs of his sisters, caused him to leave home he went to Moscow and joined this circle. The members were students of Schelling, Fichte, and Hegel: Bakunin adopted a philosophy which reconciled spiritual liberty with submission to absolutism in government. But this transcendental belief was somewhat shaken when Alexander Herzen and Nicolai Ogareff, who had been deported from Russia for revolutionary activities, returned to Moscow and entered the group.

In 1840 Bakunin went to Berlin to study Hegelianism at closer range. There he mingled with the younger followers of Hegel who were using the master's doctrine to criticize political absolutism and religious idealism. Bakunin's ideas underwent a drastic change. Abandoning his concept of liberty as a purely spiritual ideal he came to believe that liberty meant emancipation from authority of every kind. This, he felt, made it his duty actively to support revolutionary doctrines, and in 1842 he published an article (under a pen name) announcing his new beliefs and predicting a complete social revolution in Germany. "The will to destroy," he wrote, "is also a will to create."

Bakunin now began a roving, vagabond life, visiting various revolutionary centers in Europe, and living on loans (which turned out to be gifts) from his relatives. His fine athletic figure, his childishly frank and simple nature attracted almost everyone. In 1843 and 1847 he was in Switzerland where he mingled with the communist followers of Weitling and made the acquaintance of Adolf Vogt. But it was at Paris, where he arrived in 1845, that his most significant contacts were made. His meeting with Proudhon, the man who, in Bakunin's words, "adored Satan and proclaimed anarchy," led to decisive results. Bakunin was immediately sympathetic toward most of Proudhon's ideas (although he objected to his traditionary idealism) and adopted them as fundamental parts of his own system. His reaction to Karl Marx was much less favorable, and this foreshadowed their later rivalry. Long conversations, profitable at least to Bakunin, took place, but there could be little sympathy between one who regarded the alliance with Russia as the cause of reaction in Germany and one who expected the Slavic peoples to become the leaders of human emancipation. With Bakunin's Slavism went a detestation of the Jewish people, whom he characterized as "restless, intriguing, exploiting, and bourgeois, by tradition and instinct." Marx was a Jew.

The revolutions which swept Europe in 1848 called Bakunin into action at several points along the battle line. Expelled from France in 1847 for a speech at a banquet celebrating the Polish insurrection of 1830, he had taken refuge in Belgium; after the February revolution in France he returned to Paris and from there went on to Germany where he took part in the risings at Prague and Dresden. The Dresden affair proved his undoing; he was arrested and condemned to death by the government of Saxony. Instead of carrying out the sentence, however, Saxony handed him over to Austria which repeated the process of condemnation and delivered him to Russia. Justice (or what passed for it) was at last done: in 1851 he was imprisoned and six years later sent into what was meant to be perpetual exile in Siberia. A curious incident of his imprisonment is his correspondence with the Czar. Nicholas I wrote to Bakunin suggesting that he unburden himself to his paternal sovereign. The invitation was accepted and Bakunin transmitted his "Confessions," in which he set forth his political philosophy, admitted his sins, and begged for death rather than imprisonment. The motives of neither correspondent were perhaps quite so simple as they appeared to be on the surface.

In 1861 Bakunin escaped from Siberia and proceeded by way of Japan and America to London where a group of his friends, fugitives from the continent, resided. For a time he joined with two of them in conducting a political paper, but finding their ideas on the subject of a Russian revolution too mild, went to Italy and established a journal of his own. There he combated the principles of Mazzini—his deism, his idealistic outlook, and his theories of centralized government. Bakunin even formed a secret society against the Mazzinians which spread to France, Spain, and Poland.

The formation of the League of Peace and Liberty, an international pacifist organization, determined Bakunin, in 1867, to capture it as a medium for his own propaganda by boring from within. The attempt was a failure and he turned to Karl Marx's recently formed International Workingmen's Association. Some time previously he had organized a Social Democratic Alliance; having joined the International he continued to surround himself with this group whose object was a kind of disguised dictatorship of the association. Bakunin now travelled extensively in southwestern France spreading his doctrines among the more radical sections of the International. In a series of brilliant articles in *L'Egalité*, of which he had become editor-in-chief, he explained his program and attacked those who sought to divert the International from its revolutionary object.

The Franco-Prussian War and its aftermath seemed to present the opportunity for a social upheaval. During the siege of Paris Bakunin appeared in Lyon and set up a central committee of safety for what it was hoped would be all of France. Taking advantage of a local wage dispute his followers got possession of the city hall. But Bakunin was unable to incite a conflict between the workers and the national guard, and the authorities soon recovered control. He then looked into the situation at Marseilles; the disorganized condition of the International in that place, however, made a similar attempt impossible. Bakunin welcomed the rising of the Paris Commune in 1871 as a real working-class movement and therefore a valuable precedent, but he regarded it as premature and too much imbued with old-fashioned revolutionary ideas.

Even before the war a conflict had broken out between Marx and Bakunin which was to wreck the International. Partisan biographers of the chief actors have succeeded in making this conflict obscure, but the following is one version of it. Goaded by a series of articles in *L'Egalité* which criticized the General Council of the International and which he believed to be inspired by Bakunin, Marx began a violent and more or less secret campaign against the latter, accusing him of trying to dominate the movement and of acting as an agent of the Russian government. Bakunin for his part professed to believe that Marx was a tool of Bismarck. But it was a conflict of principles as well as of personalities. At the congress of Basel (1869) the collectivist partisans of Bakunin—who advocated economic struggle as opposed to political action and rejected democracy and the coercive state—won substantial advantages over the authoritarian communists allied with Marx. The situation was soon reversed, and ultimately the Hague congress of 1872 professed to discover that a secret society headed by Bakunin had existed in the International: it therefore expelled him. The action did not weaken Bakunin's influence with his own sympathizers. But the International, after moving its headquarters to the United States, expired in 1876.

In the same year Bakunin himself died. He had retired from active leadership in 1873, warning his followers that reaction centered in Germany and was represented "as much by the socialism of Marx as by the diplomacy of Bismarck," both of whom were working for the "pan-Germanization of Europe."

Writing absorbed a minor part of Bakunin's energy. He was a man of action and laid no claim to being the head of a philosophical school. Yet his literary output was very large. It took the form of articles and tracts, however, the longer works which he commenced never getting finished. The sources of some of Bakunin's doctrines have already been indicated. Proudhon and Marx, particularly the former, permeated his thought, but Feuerbach, Comte, Darwin, and Büchner also left their impress. From Proudhon he derived his federalism, his criticism of the state, and his opposition to authoritarian communism; from Marx, his idea of the class struggle and his materialist theory of history—from both, his distinction between political and economic society. His work no doubt lay in the field of synthesis and perhaps embodied few original ideas, but according to his leading commentator, "recent investigation shows that Bakunin was a thinker of wide range and lasting influence."

On his deathbed Bakunin confessed to a friend that "all his philosophy had been built upon a false foundation: all was vitiated because he had begun by taking man as an individual, whereas he is really a member of a collective whole." But everyone did not perceive this fallacy (if it is a fallacy), for later reformers continued to propagate his ideas. Prince Kropotkin considered himself Bakunin's direct doctrinal heir, while the syndicalism of the French General Confederation of Labor sprang in part from the collectivism of Bakunin and his adherents.

REFERENCES

Selected editions of Bakunin's works have been published in French, German, and Spanish. Little or nothing is available in English except *God and the State* (1882).

The leading biographer of Bakunin is Max Nettlau; unfortunately his work exists only in duplicated manuscript copies (in German). One of these is possessed by Columbia University. Another scholarly work (biographical and critical) is Marc de Préaudeau's *Michel Bakounine, le collectivisme dans l'International* . . . (1911). A recent biography treating the more intimate phases of Bakunin's career is Hélène Iswolsky's *La Vie de Bakounine* (1930). There is no biography in English.

READINGS FROM

VARIOUS WORKS [1]

Economic Emancipation before Political Emancipation.[2] The International Workingmen's Association, in order to remain faithful to its principle and not to deviate from the only path which can lead

[1] Translation by the present editor.

[2] From *Egalité*, 28 Aug. 1869 (*Œuvres*, Vol. 5, pp. 190–195, 196, 197–199).

it into a safe haven, must above all guard against the influence of two kinds of bourgeois socialists: the partisans of *bourgeois policy, including even bourgeois revolutionists,* and those of *bourgeois coöperation,* the so-called *practical* men.

Let us consider the first ones first.

Economic emancipation . . . is the basis of every other kind of emancipation. In these words we have epitomized the entire policy of the International.

In fact we read in the preamble of our general statutes the following declaration:

"*That the subjection of labor to capital is the source of all servitude—political, moral and material*—and that for this reason the emancipation of the workers is the grand object to which every political movement must be subordinated."

It is well understood that every political movement which does not have for its *immediate and direct* object the *definitive and complete* economic emancipation of the workers, and which does not have inscribed upon its banner in a very decided and clear manner the principle of *economic equality—i.e.*, the *complete restitution* of capital to labor or indeed *social liquidation*—that every such political movement is bourgeois, and, as such, must be excluded from the International.

Consequently the policy of bourgeois democrats or bourgeois socialists must be pitilessly excluded, for these, by declaring that "political liberty necessarily *precedes* economic emancipation," can mean nothing but this: "Political reforms or political revolution should *precede* economic reforms or economic revolution; consequently the workers should ally themselves with the more or less radical members of the bourgeoisie in order to bring about with them the first reforms, and then effect the second ones in opposition to them."

We strongly protest against this fatal theory which could end, for the workers, only in making them serve once more as an instrument against themselves, and in delivering them again to bourgeois exploitation.

Gaining political liberty *first* can only mean gaining *nothing but* political liberty at first, meanwhile leaving—at least for some days—economic and social relations in their present state, that is, leaving proprietors and capitalists insolently rich and workers poor.

But once liberty is won, it is said, it will give the workers an instrument for gaining *equality* and *economic justice* later on.

Liberty is in fact a magnificent and powerful instrument. The only thing is to know whether the workers can really make use of it, whether it will really be in their possession, or whether, as has always been the case up to now, their political liberty will be only a deceitful outward show, a fiction.

Might not a worker, in his present economic situation, to whom one spoke of political liberty—might he not answer with the refrain of a well-known song:

> Speak not of liberty
> Poverty—that is the slavery!

And in fact one must be in love with illusions to imagine that a worker, in his present economic and social condition, could fully profit from, or really and seriously utilize, his political liberty. In order to do it he lacks two little things, leisure and material means.

Moreover, did we not see this in France on the morrow of the revolution of 1848, the most radical revolution one could wish for from the political point of view?

The French workers were certainly neither indifferent nor unintelligent, and yet in spite of universal suffrage they had to let the bourgeoisie alone. Why? Because they lacked the material means necessary to make political liberty a reality, because they remained enslaved to labor which was forced upon them by hunger, while the bourgeois radicals, liberals, and even conservatives, some previously republicans, others converted afterwards, came and went, agitated, spoke and conspired freely, some because they possessed an income from securities, others thanks to the State budget which had naturally been maintained and even reinforced more than ever. . . .

But, it is said, the workers having become wiser through this very experience, will never again send members of the bourgeoisie to constituent or legislative assemblies—they will send simple workers. Poor as they are, the workers can well afford to maintain their deputies. Do you know what the result will be? The worker deputies, transported into bourgeois conditions of living and into an atmosphere of political ideas entirely bourgeois, ceasing to be workers in fact in order to become statesmen, will become bourgeois—will perhaps be even more bourgeois than the bourgeoisie themselves. For men do not make positions; on the contrary, positions make men. . . .

Since the bourgeois socialists are striving to-day to organize, *with the bait of socialism*, a formidable working-class agitation in order to win political liberty, a liberty which as we have just seen would profit only the bourgeoisie, and since the working masses, having come to appreciate their position, and, enlightened and directed by the principle of the International, are in fact organizing and beginning to form a veritable power, not national but international, not to protect the interests of the bourgeoisie but to protect their own, and since even to realize this bourgeois ideal of complete political liberty and republican institutions a revolution is necessary and no revolution can be victorious except through the power of the people—since all this is so, this power must cease to pull bourgeois chestnuts out of the fire, and must henceforth work only for the triumph of the people's cause, the cause of all who labor as opposed to all who exploit labor. . . .

But revolutions are not improvised. They are not made arbitrarily either by individuals or even by the most powerful associations. Independent of every will and every conspiracy, they are brought on by the force of things. They can be foreseen, sometimes their approach can be felt, but the explosion can never be accelerated.

Convinced of this truth, we ask ourselves this question: What policy should the International follow during this more or less long period separating us from this terrible social revolution of which everyone to-day has a presentiment?

Laying aside, as the statutes command, all national and local politics, it [the International] will give to working-class agitation in all countries an *essentially economic* character, setting up as its goal the shortening of the hours of labor and the increase of wages; as a means, *the association of the working masses* and the formation of *funds for resistance*. . . .

Finally, it will spread out and organize across the frontiers of all countries, so that when the revolution, brought on by the force of circumstances, breaks out it [the International] will be a real force, knowing what must be done and so being capable of controlling the revolution and of directing it really advantageously for the people—a substantial, international organization of workers' associations of all countries, capable of replacing the present political world of States and bourgeoisie which is dying out. . . .

Federalism.[1] In conformity with the unanimous sentiment of the Congress of Geneva[2] we ought to proclaim:

1st. That in order to secure the triumph of liberty, justice, and

[1] From "Federalism, Socialism, and Anti-theologism," written *c.* 1867–68 (*Œuvres*, Vol. I, pp. 15–21).

[2] *I.e.*, the congress of the League of Peace and Liberty, Sept., 1867, of which Bakunin was then a member.

peace in the international relations of Europe, so as to make civil war impossible among the different peoples who compose the European family, there is only one means: that is, to constitute *a United States of Europe.*

2d. That the States of Europe can never be formed with States as they are to-day constituted, in view of their monstrous inequality of power.

3d. That the example of the defunct Germanic Confederation has proved in peremptory fashion that a confederation of monarchies is ridiculous, and that it is powerless to guarantee either peace or the liberty of populations.

4th. That no centralized, bureaucratic, and hence military State, even though it is called a republic, can seriously and sincerely enter an international confederation. By its constitution, which will always be an open or disguised negation of internal liberty, it would necessarily be a declaration of permanent war, a menace to the existence of neighboring countries. Founded essentially on a former act of violence, conquest, or what in private life is called burglary—an act blessed by the Church (whatever the religion happens to be), consecrated by time and so transformed into a historic right—and supported by that divine consecration of triumphant violence as by an exclusive and supreme right, each centralized State thus takes a position absolutely opposed to the right of other States, never recognizing them in the treaties it concludes with them except from motives of political interest or on account of weakness.

5th. That all the adherents of the League ought consequently to bend every effort toward reconstituting their respective countries, so as to replace the old organization, founded from top to bottom on violence and the principle of authority, by a new organization having as its basis only the interests, needs and natural attractions of the populations, and having no other principle but that of the free federation of individuals in communes, communes in provinces, provinces in nations, and finally, nations in the United States—first of Europe and then of the entire world.

6th. Consequently the absolute abandonment of everything called the historic right of States; all questions relating to natural, political, strategic, commercial frontiers should be considered as belonging to ancient history and energetically rejected by all adherents of the League.

7th. Recognition of the absolute right of each nation, large or small, of each people, weak or strong, of each province, each commune, to complete autonomy, provided that its internal constitution is not a menace and a danger to the autonomy and liberty of neighboring countries.

8th. That even if a country is part of another State and has joined it freely, it is not therefore obliged to remain attached to it forever. No perpetual obligation can be admitted by human justice, which is the only power that can have authority among us; and we shall never recognize any other rights or duties but those founded on liberty. The right to unite freely and to secede with equal freedom is the first, the most important of all political rights, the one without which confederation would never be anything but disguised centralization. . . .

10th. . . The League, precisely because it is the League of Peace, and because it is convinced that peace can be gained and founded only on the most intimate and complete solidarity of peoples in justice and liberty, should boldly proclaim its sympathy for every national insurrection against every kind of oppression either abroad or at home, provided that the insurrection is carried on in the name of our principles and as much in the political as in the economic interest of the masses, but not with the intention of founding a powerful state.

11th. The League will wage war to the bitter end against everything called the glory, grandeur, and power of States. To all those false and malevolent idols to whom millions of human victims have been offered up we shall oppose the glories of human intelligence as they manifest themselves in science and in universal prosperity founded upon labor, justice, and liberty.

12th. The League will recognize *nationality* as a natural fact, having an incontestible right to existence and free development, but not as a principle—for every principle should have the character of universality, and nationality on the contrary is only an exclusive, separate fact. This so-called *principle of nationality* as laid down in our day by the governments of France, Russia, and Prussia and even by many German, Polish, Italian, and Hungarian patriots, is only a derivative which reaction has opposed to the spirit of revolution: highly aristocratic at bottom, causing scorn to be cast on the dialects of illiterate populations, implicitly denying the liberty of provinces and the real autonomy of communes, and upheld in all countries not by the masses whose real interests it systematically sacrifices to the so-called public welfare (that is, the welfare of the privileged classes)—this principle expresses nothing but the pretended historical rights and ambitions of States. The right of nationality therefore can never be considered by the

League except as a consequence of the supreme principle of liberty, ceasing to be a right the moment it sets itself up against or even independent of liberty.

13th. Unity is the goal toward which humanity irresistibly tends. But it becomes fatal, destructive of the intelligence, dignity and prosperity of individuals and peoples whenever it is achieved without liberty, whether through violence or through the authority of a theological, metaphysical, political, or even an economic, idea. Patriotism which leads to unity without liberty is a bad kind of patriotism, always baneful to the popular and real interests of the country which it pretends to exalt and serve; a friend—often without wishing it—of reaction; an enemy of revolution: that is, of the emancipation of nations and men. The League can recognize only one kind of unity: that which is constituted freely by the federation of autonomous parts in a whole, so that the latter, ceasing to be the negation of particular rights and interests, ceasing to be the cemetery in which the prosperity of localities is forcibly interred, will become on the contrary the source of all autonomy and prosperity. The League will therefore vigorously attack all religious, political, economic, and social organization that is not penetrated by this great principle of liberty: without it there is no justice, no intelligence, no prosperity, no humanity. . . .

Religion and Liberty.[1] We are convinced that no great political and social transformation has been accomplished in the world unless accompanied and often preceded by an analogous movement of philosophic and religious ideas which guide the conscience of individuals as much as they do that of society.

As all religions with their gods have never been anything but the creation of the believing and credulous fancy of man who has not yet attained the height of pure reflection and free thought resting on science, the religious heaven has been only a mirage in which man, exalted by faith, has for so long rediscovered his own image enlarged and reversed, that is, deified.

The history of religions, of the grandeur and decadence of gods who have succeeded one another, is therefore nothing but the history of the development of the intelligence and collective conscience of mankind. In proportion as [men] discovered either in themselves or outside of themselves a power, a capacity, any quality whatever, they attributed it to their gods, after having magnified and enlarged it immeasur-

[1] *Ibid.*, pp. 61–65.

ably, as children ordinarily do, by an act of religious fancy. Thus, thanks to this modesty and generosity of mankind, heaven was enriched with the spoils of earth, and as a natural consequence the richer heaven grew, the poorer did humanity become. Once a goddess was installed she was naturally proclaimed the mistress, source, and dispenser of all things: the real world no longer existed except through her, and man after having unconsciously created her, knelt before her and declared himself her creature, her slave.

Christianity is the religion par excellence precisely because it exhibits and manifests the very essence of all religion, namely, the systematic, absolute impoverishment, annihilation and subjection of humanity for the profit of divinity—a ruling principle not only in all religion, but in every metaphysic also, whether it is theistic or pantheistic. God being everything, the real world and man are nothing. God being truth, justice, and everlasting life, man is falsehood, injustice, and death. God being the master, man is the slave. Incapable of finding for himself the path of justice and truth, he must receive them as a revelation from on high through the medium of envoys and those chosen by divine grace. Whoever speaks of revelation speaks of revealers, of prophets, of priests, and the latter once recognized as the earthly representatives of divinity, as the teachers and initiators of humanity into eternal life, receive by that very fact the mission of directing, governing, and commanding here below. All men owe them faith and absolute obedience; slaves of God, they must also be slaves of the Church and of the State in so far as the latter is blessed by the Church. This is what Christianity alone of all religions which exist or have existed has perfectly understood; it is what Roman Catholicism alone of all Christian sects has proclaimed and realized with rigorous logic. That is why Christianity is the absolute religion, the final religion, and why the apostolic and Roman Church is the sole legitimate and divine heir.

With all due respect, therefore, for the semi-philosophers and all the so-called religious thinkers, *the existence of God implies the abdication of human reason and justice, it is the negation of human liberty and ends not only in theoretical but in practical slavery.*

Unless we wish to be slaves therefore, we cannot, we must not, make the least concession to theology, for in that mystical and rigorously logical alphabet whoever begins at A is fated to arrive at Z, and whoever wishes to adore God must renounce his liberty and his dignity as a man.

God exists, therefore man is a slave.

Man is intelligent, just, free—therefore God does not exist.

We defy anyone to break this circle—let him now take his choice.

Moreover history demonstrates to us that the priests of all religions, except those of persecuted Churches, have been the allies of tyranny. And even these last, at the same time that they fought and cursed the powers which oppressed them, have they not disciplined their own believers, and by so doing have they not always prepared the elements of a new tyranny? Intellectual slavery of any kind whatever will always have as a natural consequence political and social slavery. To-day Christianity, in all its varied forms, and along with it, doctrinaire and deistic metaphysics which is its offspring and which is at bottom only disguised theology, constitute without a doubt the most formidable obstacle to the emancipation of society; the proof is that governments and all the statesmen of Europe who are themselves neither metaphysicians, theologians, nor deists and who deep in their hearts do not believe either in God or Devil, passionately and stubbornly protect metaphysics as well as religion (whatever the religion may be), if it teaches—as all of them do however—patience, resignation, submission.

XXV

GEORGES SOREL

1847–1922

Georges Sorel was born at Cherbourg in 1847 and all of his youth was spent in Normandy. Reared by an extremely pious mother, he remained throughout life deeply concerned with the moral aspect of things, and although he afterwards wrote in an anti-clerical vein he generally spoke of the Church with respect.

From 1863 to 1867 Sorel attended the Polytechnic School. He then entered the civil service as an engineer in the Department of Highways and Bridges where, in the course of twenty-five years, he rose to chief engineer and was awarded the cross of the Legion of Honor. This experience affected his modes of thought in two ways: he was led to interpret the existing economic system from the viewpoint of an engineer and came to entertain a supreme contempt for the bourgeois with whom he associated. Their ignorance, he said, was only equalled by their cowardice.

These sentiments drew him into socialism. As his ideas seemed to be too much out of harmony with the existing régime, he retired from government service in 1892 with a modest pension in order to devote himself to a study of social problems. For several years he contributed to Marxist periodicals. Gradually, however, he found himself out of sympathy with both the revisionist school and the so-called orthodox school of Marxism. In contrast with socialists generally, who remained aloof from the Dreyfus controversy as having nothing to do with the class struggle, Sorel became a partisan of the persecuted Jewish army officer. The attitude is interesting in view of his later anti-Semitism.

At this time he also professed to see nothing contradictory between the spiritual objects of democracy and those of socialism.

Sorel's ideas changed shortly without, however, bringing him closer to the majority of socialists. A study of economic history and of the British labor movement convinced him that "the whole future of socialism resides in the autonomous development of trade unions."

Observation of the French unions (syndicates) and the influence of Ferdinand Pelloutier confirmed this belief. Pelloutier, like Sorel, held that the moral education of the proletariat was indispensable, and had therefore become the apostle of revolutionary syndicalism. Sorel put forward his new views in 1898; he elaborated them in a series of articles in the *Socialist Movement* which he helped to found in 1899. These articles formed the substance of *Reflections on Violence* (1908).

Sorel's philosophy thus evolved from diverse sources. Besides those already mentioned, the strong influence of Henri Bergson must be noted. Sorel's "myth" of the general strike, perhaps his most original conception, was, he asserted, an application of Bergson's theory of intuition. He also drew something from the pragmatism and anti-rationalism of William James. There were also, of course, elements of Marxism in Sorel's thought, but it is said that he borrowed more from Proudhon, Bergson, Nietzsche, and Renan than he did from Marx. He undoubtedly lays more emphasis on the "mystical and subconscious factors in social development" than on the economic factors which Marx considered primary.

Scarcely had Sorel aligned himself with the syndicalists before rifts began to appear. The moral culture of the working class which was uppermost in Sorel's mind had a decidedly minor place in the imagination of rank-and-file syndicalists, who looked forward to more material rewards as the goal of the revolution. A tendency toward opportunist alliances, neo-Malthusianism, and sabotage were additional grievances to Sorel. These were simply manifestations of the decline of the militant spirit of the movement, which in his eyes was its most valuable possession. As a propagandist of violence (it should be emphasized that Sorel always opposed indiscriminate brutality) he felt moved to protest, and in 1910 announced that syndicalism had failed to come up to his expectations.

The moral regeneration of society still being one of Sorel's main objectives, he was ready to welcome it even if it made its appearance among the despised bourgeoisie. So when Paul Bourget, the psychological novelist, endeavored to translate Sorel's philosophy into bourgeois terms, Sorel was distinctly sympathetic. Having put off his democratic sentiments when he embraced syndicalism, he now coöperated in an attempt to unite the radical and the reactionary anti-democrats. A nationalistic and traditionalist bias appeared in his work; he was on friendly terms with Charles Maurras and the group who sought to reëstablish the hereditary monarchy in France. But this alliance was also short-lived. The bourgeoisie seemed to offer even less than the working class. By 1914 therefore his sympathies were again gravitating toward the proletariat.

The war added to Sorel's disgust for the governing classes. He regarded the democratic professions of the Allies as merely a cloak for "repulsive plutocratic realities." But the advent of the Bolsheviks to power in Russia filled him with new hope—in spite of their Jewish partisans. "He elegantly reconciles Bolshevism with anti-Semitism by charging to the Jews whatever is excessive or worthy of condemnation in Russian developments." Sorel died in 1922, however, before the Soviet régime had consolidated itself. Being ordinarily a pessimist, he doubted whether it could survive.

The direct influence of Sorel on the workers' movement was probably small. It was said that not half a dozen members of the General Confederation of Labor (the French syndicalist organization) had read his *Reflections on Violence*. The pessimistic tone of his writings and their diffuseness and obscurity no doubt repelled the ordinary reader. But if Sorel was obscure it was because he wished to stimulate people to think for themselves; on the other hand his witty, epigrammatic style might seem to atone at least partially for any failure to be clear. At all events Sorel's work became widely known among intellectuals, and many writers adopted his ideas. The fascist movement in Italy was partly inspired by them. Mussolini has said that he owes to Sorel his philosophy of action, which, after all, seems to be the most important part of fascist philosophy.

REFERENCES

Sorel wrote on literature and ethics as well as on socialism, but so far as is known the only work translated into English is his *Reflections on Violence*.

There is no full-length biography of Sorel. The most complete exposition of his theories is given in Gaétan Pirou's sketch, *Georges Sorel* (French, 1927), which also contains an outline of his career. See also Louis Levine, *Syndicalism in France* (1914), and Georges Guy-Grand, "Georges Sorel et les problèmes contemporaines" (*La Grande Revue*, December, 1922, pp. 293–324).

READINGS FROM

REFLECTIONS ON VIOLENCE

Why Reflect on Violence?[1] The reflections that I submit to the readers of the *Mouvement Socialiste* [2] on the subject of violence

[1] Published by The Viking Press, Inc., New York. T. E. Hulme, translator (1914), pp. 43–44, 47–48.

[2] In which most of the *Reflections* was first published in 1906.

have been inspired by some simple observations about very evident facts, which play an increasingly marked rôle in the history of contemporary classes.

For a long time I had been struck by the fact that the *normal development* of strikes is accompanied by an important series of acts of violence; but certain learned sociologists seek to disguise a phenomenon that every one who cares to use his eyes must have noticed. Revolutionary syndicalism keeps alive in the minds of the masses the desire to strike, and only prospers when important strikes, accompanied by violence, take place. Socialism tends to appear more and more as a theory of revolutionary syndicalism—or rather as a philosophy of modern history, in as far as it is under the influence of this syndicalism. It follows from these incontestable data, that if we desire to discuss Socialism with any benefit, we must first of all investigate the functions of violence in actual social conditions.

I do not believe that this question has yet been approached with the care it admits of; I hope that these reflections will lead a few thinkers to examine the problems of proletarian violence more closely. I cannot too strongly recommend this investigation to the *new school* which, inspired by the principles of Marx rather than by the formulas taught by the official proprietors of Marxism, is about to give to Socialist doctrines a sense of reality and a gravity which it certainly has lacked for several years. Since the *new school* calls itself Marxist, syndicalist, revolutionary, it should have nothing so much at heart as the investigation of the exact historical significance of the spontaneous movements which are being produced in the working classes, movements which may possibly ensure that the future direction of social development will conform to Marx's ideas.

Socialism is a philosophy of the history of contemporary institutions, and Marx has always argued as a philosopher of history when he was not led away by personal polemics to write about matters outside the proper scope of his own system. . . .

To examine the effects of violence it is necessary to start from its distant consequences and not from its immediate results. We should not ask whether it is more or less directly advantageous for contemporary workmen than adroit diplomacy would be, but we should inquire what will result from the introduction of violence into the relations of the proletariat with society. We are not comparing two kinds of reformism, but we are endeavouring to find out what contemporary violence is in relation to the future social revolution.

Many will reproach me for not having given any information which might be useful for tactical purposes; no formulas, no recipes. What then was the use of writing at all? Clear-headed people will say that these studies are addressed to men who live outside the realities of everyday life and outside the true movement—that is, outside editors' offices, parliamentary lobbies, and the antechambers of the Socialist financiers. Those who have become scientists merely by coming into contact with Belgian sociology will accuse me of having a metaphysical rather than a scientific mind. These are opinions which will scarcely touch me, since I have never paid any attention to the views of people who think vulgar stupidity the height of wisdom, and who admire above all men who speak and write without thinking. . . .

Perversion of the Concept of Class War.[1] Everybody complains that discussions about Socialism are generally exceedingly obscure. This obscurity is due, for the most part, to the fact that contemporary Socialists use a terminology which no longer corresponds to their ideas. The best known among the people who call themselves *revisionists* do not wish to appear to be abandoning certain phrases, which have served for a very long time as a label to characterise Socialist literature. When Bernstein, perceiving the enormous contradiction between the language of social democracy and the true nature of its activity, urged his German comrades to have the courage to appear what they were in reality, and to revise a doctrine that had become mendacious, there was a universal outburst of indignation at his audacity; and the reformists themselves were not the least eager of the defenders of the ancient formula. . . .

This idolatry of words plays a large part in the history of all ideologies; the preservation of a Marxist vocabulary by people who have become completely estranged from the thought of Marx constitutes a great misfortune for Socialism. The expression "class war," for example, is employed in the most improper manner; and until a precise meaning can be given to this term, we must give up all hope of a reasonable exposition of Socialism.

To most people the class war is the *principle of Socialist tactics*. That means that the Socialist party founds its electoral successes on the clashing of interests which exists in an acute state between certain groups, and that, if need be, it would undertake to make this hostility still more acute; their candidates ask the poorest and most

[1] Pp. 52–53. 54–55.

numerous class to look upon themselves as forming a corporation, and they offer to become the advocates of this corporation; they promise to use their influence as representatives to improve the lot of the disinherited. Thus we are not very far from what happened in the Greek states; Parliamentary Socialists are very much akin to the demagogues who clamoured constantly for the abolition of debts, and the division of landed property, who put all public charges upon the rich, and invented plots in order to get large fortunes confiscated. . . . Here, certainly, is a war between two classes as clearly defined as it can be; but it seems to me absurd to assert that it was in this way that Marx understood the class war, which, according to him, was the essence of Socialism. . . .

Nowadays Parliamentary Socialists no longer entertain the idea of insurrection; if they still occasionally speak of it, it is merely to give themselves airs of importance; they teach that the ballot-box has replaced the gun; but the means of acquiring power may have changed without there being any change of mental attitude. Electoral literature seems inspired by the purest demagogic doctrines; Socialism makes its appeal to the discontented without troubling about the place they occupy in the world of production; in a society as complex as ours, and as subject to economic upheavals, there is an enormous number of discontented people in all classes—that is why Socialists are often found in places where one would least expect to meet them. Parliamentary Socialism speaks as many languages as it has types of clients. It makes its appeal to workmen, to small employers of labour, to peasants; and in spite of Engels, it aims at reaching the farmers; it is at times patriotic; at other times it declares against the Army. It is stopped by no contradiction, experience having shown that it is possible, in the course of an electoral campaign, to group together forces which, according to Marxian conceptions, should normally be antagonistic. Besides, cannot a Member of Parliament be of service to electors of every economic situation? . . .

Restoring the Ideal of Class War.[1] According to Marx, capitalism, by reason of the innate laws of its own nature, is hurrying along a path which will lead the world of to-day, with the inevitability of the evolution of organic life, to the doors of the world of to-morrow. This movement comprises a long period of capitalistic construction, and it ends by a rapid destruction, which is the work of the prole-

[1] Pp. 84–86.

tariat. Capitalism creates the heritage which Socialism will receive, the men who will suppress the present régime, and the means of bringing about this destruction, at the same time that it preserves the results obtained in production. Capitalism begets new ways of working; it throws the working class into revolutionary organisations by the pressure it exercises on wages; it restricts its own political basis by competition, which is constantly eliminating industrial leaders. Thus, after having solved the great problem of the organisation of labour, to effect which Utopians have brought forward so many naïve or stupid hypotheses, capitalism provokes the birth of the cause which will overthrow it, and thus renders useless everything that Utopians have written to induce enlightened people to make reforms; and it gradually ruins the traditional order, against which the critics of the idealists had proved themselves to be so deplorably incompetent. It might therefore be said that capitalism plays a part analogous to that attributed by Hartmann to The Unconscious in nature, since it prepares the coming of social reforms which it did not intend to produce. Without any coördinated plan, without any directive ideas, without any ideal of a future world, it is the cause of an inevitable evolution; it draws from the present all that the present can give towards historical development; it performs in an almost mechanical manner all that is necessary, in order that a new era may appear, and that this new era may break every link with the idealism of the present times, while preserving the acquisitions of the capitalistic economic system.

Socialists should therefore abandon the attempt (initiated by the Utopians) to find a means of inducing the enlightened middle class to prepare the *transition to a more perfect system of legislation;* their sole function is that of explaining to the proletariat the greatness of the revolutionary part they are called upon to play. By ceaseless criticism the proletariat must be brought to perfect their organisations; they must be shown how the embryonic forms which appear in their unions may be developed, so that, finally, they may build up institutions without any parallel in the history of the middle class; that they may form ideas which depend solely on their position as producers in large industries, and which owe nothing to middle-class thought; and that they may acquire *habits of liberty* with which the middle class nowadays are no longer acquainted.

This doctrine will evidently be inapplicable if the middle class and the proletariat do not oppose each other implacably, with all the forces at their disposal; the more ardently capitalist the middle class is, the more the proletariat is full of a warlike spirit and confident of its revolutionary strength, the more certain will be the success of the proletarian movement. . . .

Syndicalist Attitude toward the State.[1] Syndicalism in France is engaged on an antimilitarist propaganda, which shows clearly the immense distance which separates it from Parliamentary Socialism in its conception of the nature of the State. Many newspapers believe that all this is merely an exaggerated humanitarian movement . . .; this is a great error. We should be misconceiving the nature of the movement if we supposed that it was merely a protest against harshness of discipline, against the length of military service, or against the presence, in the higher ranks, of officers hostile to the existing institutions of the country; these are the reasons which led many middle-class people to applaud declamations against the army at the time of the Dreyfus case, but they are not the Syndicalists' reasons.

The army is the clearest and the most tangible of all possible manifestations of the State, and the one which is most firmly connected with its origins and traditions. Syndicalists do not propose to reform the State, as the men of the eighteenth century did; they want to destroy it, because they wish to realise this idea of Marx's that the Socialist revolution ought not to culminate in the replacement of one governing minority by another minority. The Syndicalists outline their doctrine still more clearly when they give it a more ideological aspect, and declare themselves antipatriotic—following the example of the *Communist Manifesto*.

It is impossible that there should be the slightest understanding between Syndicalists and official Socialists on this question; the latter, of course, speak of breaking up everything, but they attack men in power rather than power itself; they hope to possess the State forces, and they are aware that on the day when they control the Government they will have need of an army; they will carry on foreign politics, and consequently they in their turn will have to praise the feeling of devotion to the fatherland. . . .

The General Strike an Ideal Form of Violence.[2] Every time that we attempt to obtain an exact conception of the ideas behind proletarian violence we are forced to go back to the notion of the

[1] Pp. 122–124.
[2] Pp. 126, 131–137.

general strike; and this same conception may render many other services, and throw an unexpected light on all the obscure parts of Socialism. . . .

The possibility of the actual realisation of the general strike has been much discussed; it has been stated that the Socialist war could not be decided in one single battle. To the people who think themselves cautious, practical, and scientific the difficulty of setting great masses of the proletariat in motion at the same moment seems prodigious; they have analysed the difficulties of detail which such an enormous struggle would present. It is the opinion of the Socialist-sociologists, as also of the politicians, that the general strike is a popular dream, characteristic of the beginnings of a working-class movement; we have had quoted against us the authority of Sidney Webb, who has decreed that the general strike is an illusion of youth, of which the English workers—whom the monopolists of sociology have so often presented to us as the depositaries of the true conception of the working-class movement—soon rid themselves.

That the general strike is not popular in contemporary England, is a poor argument to bring against the historical significance of the idea, for the English are distinguished by an extraordinary lack of understanding of the class war; their ideas have remained very much dominated by medieval influences: the guild, privileged, or at least protected by laws, still seems to them the ideal of working-class organisation; it is for England that the term *working-class aristocracy*, as a name for the trades unionists, was invented, and, as a matter of fact, trades unionism does pursue the acquisition of legal privileges. We might therefore say that the aversion felt by England for the general strike should be looked upon as strong presumptive evidence in favour of the latter by all those who look upon the class war as the essence of Socialism.

Moreover, Sidney Webb enjoys a reputation for competence which is very much exaggerated; all that can be put to his credit is that he has waded through uninteresting blue-books, and has had the patience to compose an extremely indigestible compilation on the history of trades unionism; he has a mind of the narrowest description, which could only impress people unaccustomed to reflection. Those who introduced his fame into France knew nothing at all about Socialism; and if he is really in the first rank of contemporary authors of economic history, as his translator affirms, it is because the intellectual level of these historians is rather low; moreover, many examples show us that it is possible to be a most illustrious professional historian and yet possess a mind something less than mediocre.

Neither do I attach any importance to the objections made to the general strike based on considerations of a practical order. The attempt to construct hypotheses about the nature of the struggles of the future and the means of suppressing capitalism, on the model furnished by history, is a return to the old methods of the Utopists. There is no process by which the future can be predicted scientifically, nor even one which enables us to discuss whether one hypothesis about it is better than another; it has been proved by too many memorable examples that the greatest men have committed prodigious errors in thus desiring to make prediction about even the least distant future.

And yet without leaving the present, without reasoning about this future, which seems for ever condemned to escape our reason, we should be unable to act at all. Experience shows that the *framing of a future, in some indeterminate time*, may, when it is done in a certain way, be very effective, and have very few inconveniences; this happens when the anticipations of the future take the form of those myths, which enclose within them all the strongest inclinations of a people, of a party or of a class, inclinations which recur to the mind with the insistence of instincts in all the circumstances of life; and which give an aspect of complete reality to the hopes of immediate action by which, more easily than by any other method, men can reform their desires, passions, and mental activity. We know, moreover, that these social myths in no way prevent a man profiting by the observations which he makes in the course of his life, and form no obstacle to the pursuit of his normal occupations.

The truth of this may be shown by numerous examples.

The first Christians expected the return of Christ and the total ruin of the pagan world, with the inauguration of the kingdom of the saints, at the end of the first generation. The catastrophe did not come to pass, but Christian thought profited so greatly from the apocalyptic myth that certain contemporary scholars maintain that the whole preaching of Christ referred solely to this one point. The hopes which Luther and Calvin had formed of the religious exaltation of Europe were by no means realised; these fathers of the Reformation very soon seemed men of a past era; for present-day Protestants they belong rather to the Middle Ages than to modern times, and the problems which troubled them most occupy very little place in contemporary Protestantism. Must we for that reason deny the immense result which came from their dreams of Christian renovation? It must be admitted that the real developments of the Revolution did not in any way resemble the enchanting pictures which created the enthusiasm of its first adepts; but without those pictures would the Revolution have been victorious? Many Utopias were mixed up with the Revolutionary myth, because it had been formed by a society passionately fond of imaginative literature, full of confidence in "science," and very little acquainted with the economic history of the past. These Utopias came to nothing; but it may be asked whether the Revolution was not a much more profound transformation than those dreamed of by the people who in the eighteenth century had invented social Utopias. In our own times Mazzini pursued what the wiseacres of his time called a mad chimera; but it can no longer be denied that, without Mazzini, Italy would never have become a great power, and that he did more for Italian unity than Cavour and all the politicians of his school.

A knowledge of what the myths contain in the way of details which will actually form part of the history of the future is then of small importance; they are not astrological almanacs; it is even possible that nothing which they contain will ever come to pass,—as was the case with the catastrophe expected by the first Christians. In our own daily life, are we not familiar with the fact that what actually happens is very different from our preconceived notion of it? And that does not prevent us from continuing to make resolutions. Psychologists say that there is heterogeneity between the ends in view and the ends actually realised: the slightest experience of life reveals this law to us, which Spencer transferred into nature, to extract therefrom his theory of the multiplication of effects.

The myth must be judged as a means of acting on the present; any attempt to discuss how far it can be taken literally as future history is devoid of sense. *It is the myth in its entirety which is alone important:* its parts are only of interest in so far as they bring out the main idea. No useful purpose is served, therefore, in arguing about the incidents which may occur in the course of a social war, and about the decisive conflicts which may give victory to the proletariat; even supposing the revolutionaries to have been wholly and entirely deluded in setting up this imaginary picture of the general strike, this picture may yet have been, in the course of the preparation for the Revolution, a great element of strength, if it has embraced all the aspirations of

Socialism, and if it has given to the whole body of Revolutionary thought a precision and a rigidity which no other method of thought could have given.

To estimate, then, the significance of the idea of the general strike, all the methods of discussion which are current among politicians, sociologists, or people with pretensions to political science, must be abandoned. Everything which its opponents endeavour to establish may be conceded to them, without reducing in any way the value of the theory which they think they have refuted. The question whether the general strike is a partial reality, or only a product of popular imagination, is of little importance. All that it is necessary to know is, whether the general strike contains everything that the Socialist doctrine expects of the revolutionary proletariat.

To solve this question we are no longer compelled to argue learnedly about the future; we are not obliged to indulge in lofty reflections about philosophy, history, or economics; we are not on the plane of theories, and we can remain on the level of observable facts. We have to question men who take a very active part in the real revolutionary movement amidst the proletariat, men who do not aspire to climb into the middle class and whose mind is not dominated by corporative prejudices. These men may be deceived about an infinite number of political, economical, or moral questions; but their testimony is decisive, sovereign, and irrefutable when it is a question of knowing what are the ideas which most powerfully move them and their comrades, which most appeal to them as being identical with their socialistic conceptions, and thanks to which their reason, their hopes, and their way of looking at particular facts seem to make but one indivisible unity.

Thanks to these men, we know that the general strike is indeed what I have said: the *myth* in which Socialism is wholly comprised, *i.e.*, a body of images capable of evoking instinctively all the sentiments which correspond to the different manifestations of the war undertaken by Socialism against modern society. Strikes have engendered in the proletariat the noblest, deepest, and most moving sentiments that they possess; the general strike groups them all in a coordinated picture, and, by bringing them together, gives to each one of them its maximum of intensity; appealing to their painful memories of particular conflicts, it colours with an intense life all the details of the composition presented to consciousness. We thus obtain that intuition of Socialism which language cannot give us with perfect clearness—and we obtain it as a whole, perceived instantaneously. . . .

Apology for Violence.[1] It would serve no purpose to explain to the poor that they ought not to feel sentiments of jealousy and vengeance against their masters; these feelings are too powerful to be suppressed by exhortations; it is on the widespread prevalence of these feelings that democracy chiefly founds its strength. Social war, by making an appeal to the honour which develops so naturally in all organised armies, can eliminate those evil feelings against which morality would remain powerless. If this were the only reason we had for attributing a high civilising value to revolutionary Syndicalism, this reason alone would, it seems to me, be decisive in favour of the apologists for violence.

The conception of the general strike, engendered by the practice of violent strikes, admits the conception of an irrevocable overthrow. There is something terrifying in this which will appear more and more terrifying as violence takes a greater place in the mind of the proletariat. But, in undertaking a serious, formidable, and sublime work, Socialists raise themselves above our frivolous society and make themselves worthy of pointing out new roads to the world. . . .

[1] Pp. 298–299.

XXVI

NICOLAI LENIN

1870–1924

Vladimir Ilich Ulianov, known later on as Nicolai Lenin, was born in 1870 at Simbirsk in eastern Russia. His father came of a mercantile family, but having attained the post of inspector of public schools in Simbirsk and the grade of active state counsellor he was enrolled in the ranks of the nobility. His mother was of middle-class German parentage, her father having been a surgeon in the Russian army. Vladimir prepared for the university at the local gymnasium or high school and in 1887 went on to the University of Kazan intending to study law. His stay was brief. In defiance of the authorities he attended a meeting in protest against student living conditions, was arrested along with forty others and subsequently expelled.

Ulianov's family background as well as his own views were already suspect in the eyes of a constitutionally suspicious government. It is assumed that his parents had set him on the road toward radicalism, for although nothing very definite is known concerning the elder Ulianovs' political ideas, it is considered significant that all their children (three sons and three daughters) became revolutionaries. But it was the brief career of Vladimir's elder brother that focussed the unwelcome attention of the government upon the entire family. Alexander Ulianov had joined a group of terrorists and participated in an unsuccessful plot to assassinate the Czar. Caught red-handed he had been tried and executed (along with the other conspirators) in the very year his brother entered the university. As a result the Ulianovs were placed under surveillance. But their state pension was not withdrawn, and it is interesting to note that the future Lenin was supported for a time by the government which he helped at last to overthrow. Alexander's death deeply impressed his brother but it would be wrong to assume that Vladimir's subsequent opposition to the czarist régime was inspired mainly by revenge. He would probably have been a revolutionist in any event, although he did draw the rather dry lesson from Alexander's taking-off that terrorism is extremely inefficient.

Ejection from the university left Ulianov free to continue his education in less formal ways. Through acquaintance with the members of a Marxist study circle he was led to investigate their master's doctrines and soon became an active propagandist among the young people of the neighborhood. His family were now living at Samara. Meanwhile, after several vain attempts to reënter the university he continued to study law independently. In 1891 he passed the bar examinations at St. Petersburg (now Leningrad) with high honors and returned to Samara, entering the office of an attorney of liberal views. But his chief interest continued to be the study and propagation of Marx's philosophy. In 1893 he wrote *New Economic Developments in the Life of the Peasants*, which was the basis for part of his later work, *The Development of Capitalism in Russia*. The same year he removed to St. Petersburg, again becoming an assistant to a radical lawyer. His real purpose in going to the capital, however, was to be at the center of the Russian socialist movement.

Ulianov remained in St. Petersburg from 1893 to 1895 and immediately became a prominent member of the socialist group. He familiarized himself with the labor laws and factory regulations and conducted study circles among the workmen, gaining a detailed knowledge of their existence. As his own interpretation of Marxism became more and more revolutionary and communistic, he found himself out of sympathy with the more moderate elements of the Social Democratic party.

To recuperate from an illness and at the same time strengthen the foreign connections of the local Marxist group Ulianov went abroad in 1895. He visited the Russian socialist émigrés in Switzerland, becoming acquainted with Plekhanov, the Marxist scholar whom at this time Ulianov recognized as his intellectual leader. He also travelled in Germany and France, meeting local leaders of socialism as well as Russian sympathizers. Later on in 1895 he returned to Russia and prepared to publish a socialist newspaper, *The Workmen's Cause*.

Before the project could be put in operation however the Russian police intervened and the entire staff were imprisoned. Ulianov was placed in solitary confinement. This lasted for a year; he was then exiled to Siberia. Krupskaya, his socialist comrade and future wife, although banished to a different place, followed him to the town near the Mongolian border where he lived for the next three years. Ulianov spent his enforced leisure in writing and study, with hunting (to which he was much attached) and skating as diversions. He finished *The Development of Socialism in Russia* and composed *The Tasks of the Russian Social Democrats.* With Krupskaya he also translated the Webbs' *History of Trade Unionism.*

Released in 1900, Ulianov returned to Russia, assuming the name of "Nicolai Lenin." Krupskaya followed him somewhat later as his wife. The next five years were spent abroad. With two companions he was delegated by the revolutionary wing of the party to reëstablish the connection with Plekhanov and his group and to revive the newspaper project which had brought about Lenin's imprisonment four years before. At Munich two newspapers were established: *Iskra* (*The Spark*) and *Zarya* (*The Dawn*). The object of the venture was to unite the two factions of the party, provide them with information, and work out a program. Plekhanov had a voice in these transactions, and his cautious spirit failed to harmonize with the more adventurous ideas of Lenin. A party program was agreed upon which was drafted by Lenin but which embodied liberalism and moderation rather than Lenin's own views. Party faction was rife. At the congress of 1903 the Bolshevist group with which Lenin identified himself and the Menshevist group defined themselves as antagonistic elements. The party newspapers in the meanwhile had been moved from Munich to London and then to Geneva. It was during Lenin's brief residence in London that he first met Leon Trotsky, recently escaped from exile in Siberia. They collaborated on *Iskra* but until their alliance in 1917 were usually in opposite camps so far as party policies were concerned.

After the congress of 1903 the party split became still more marked. Lenin resigned from the editorial board of *Iskra* and from the central committee of the party. With the support of his friends he founded another paper as the medium of the Bolshevists, who were now becoming a separately organized group.

The Russian revolution of 1905 precipitated the Social Democrats into "practical" politics. Following the notorious massacre before the Winter Palace in St. Petersburg the Bolshevists began to urge the people to revolt, and when a general strike had compelled the government to assume an attitude of conciliation Lenin judged it safe to return to Russia. First at St. Petersburg and then at Moscow he carried on vigorous propaganda for an armed rising. How to rouse the peasants was one of his main problems. Councils of workingmen's deputies, or soviets, now appeared for the first time in Russian history and Lenin quickly grasped their significance as a revolutionary force. The Moscow soviet, indeed, ordered an armed uprising. But the military power of the government prevailed and the rebels were punished with great severity.

The rulers of Russia, however, thought it necessary to set up a Duma, or parliament, as a gesture toward liberalism. The Social Democrats at a party congress decided to participate in it, and Lenin, convinced that a revolutionary movement was impossible for some time to come, also urged his followers to abandon their boycott of the rather anemic Duma. For his own part, after twice withdrawing to Finland to avoid the attentions of the police, he was compelled to leave Russia for good.

From 1906 to the outbreak of the World War Lenin was occupied chiefly in attempting to hold his party to strict Marxist doctrines (as he conceived them) and in fanning every spark of unrest that appeared in Russia. With the first object in view he wrote *Materialism and Empirio-Criticism*, having detected in the latter school of thought an attempt to unite religion with socialism. When labor strife broke out in the Siberian gold fields he removed to Cracow, Austria, a town on the Russian border, and established *Pravda* (*Truth*) which was circulated from St. Petersburg. Meanwhile, contact with the Second International, the international socialist organization, had convinced him that little was to be expected from that body. Its failure to oppose the war in 1914 discredited it completely in his eyes.

When the war broke out Lenin was still in Cracow. The patriotic fervor of most of the national socialist parties at that crisis filled him with disgust. In his opinion the war was merely an imperialistic conflict which might, however, be used to further the revolution in Russia. He advised his own partisans in the Duma to regulate their conduct accordingly. They did so, with the result that they were speedily condemned to penal servitude in Siberia. Meanwhile Lenin himself had been imprisoned as a spy by the Austrian authorities, but when a leader of the Austrian socialists pointed out that he was an enemy of the Czar he was released and permitted to travel to Switzerland.

When the Czar's government was overthrown in March, 1917, and a Liberal régime took its place, Lenin found it possible to return to Russia. He travelled on a safe-conduct through Germany with the understanding that he would try to secure the exchange of an equal number of German war prisoners for all socialists allowed to follow him. Once in Russia he attacked the government for continuing the "imperialistic" war and demanded radical measures of socialism. The propaganda began to take effect—it spread to the army and navy and made headway among the soviets. These had again sprung up to represent the workers and soldiers, and Lenin now looked upon them as the nucleus for a future socialist state.

But the Bolshevists were unrepresented in the provisional government and for several months had no great influence in the powerful Petrograd soviet. Various efforts were made to suppress them and an abortive rising in July was laid at their door. It was after the latter event that Lenin withdrew to Finland to escape prosecution. The provisional government in the meanwhile met with one setback after another. The peasants were clamoring for land, an offensive against Austria failed, the armies disintegrated, and continual postponement of the meeting of a constituent assembly caused dissatisfaction. The efforts of Alexander Kerensky, a former leader of the Petrograd soviet who had become virtual dictator, to secure bourgeois support for the provisional government came to nothing. The Bolshevists continued their attacks on the administration and became more powerful as the government grew weaker. But Lenin had perhaps as much difficulty in inducing his followers to take the next step as he had in outwitting the government. They had come to believe that an armed uprising was unnecessary—that power would inevitably fall into their hands. But from his retreat in Finland Lenin urged the immediate use of force and found time to compose his famous commentary on it, *State and Revolution*.

Ever since Lenin's return to Russia Trotsky had given him valuable aid, although up to that time Trotsky had been generally a partisan of the Menshevists. He had become president of the Petrograd soviet and now mediated between those who favored and those who hung back from the use of force. At last the Bolshevists were won over to Lenin's point of view. A rising was fixed for 7 November when the All-Russian Congress of Soviets was to assemble. On that day the government shut down the Bolshevist newspapers.

The response was immediate and decisive. Armed partisans of the soviets reopened the newspapers, extinguished the government press, and with very little bloodshed seized control of Petrograd. The provisional government disappeared.

The first stage of the revolution came to an end when the Bolshevists assumed control, with Lenin as president and Trotsky as foreign minister in the new government. The ruling group, however, decided to admit, conditionally, non-Bolshevists to the administration.

From that time until his death it was perhaps as true of Lenin as it ever has been of any individual that his history was the history of Russia. The last stage of his career can therefore only be indicated here. He dealt ruthlessly with counter-revolutionaries, dissenters in the civil service, and all opponents of the new communist régime. He postponed democracy to a day when the communist order should be fully accepted by the masses and a dictatorship no longer necessary. He made an unfavorable peace with Germany rather than carry on a disastrous war, and fought off the attacks of Poland and the intervention of the Allies. In the process of communization the strong hand of government became so burdensome even to the classes (particularly the peasants) whom it was supposed to benefit that Lenin found it necessary to make concessions. In 1921, therefore, the "New Economic Policy" was introduced which permitted the resumption of a certain amount of private trading for profit. This, in fact, was only another example of Lenin's ability to compromise without relinquishing his driving idea. The final stages of the revolution had not been negotiated, however, before Lenin's physical endurance gave out. He laid down his work temporarily in 1922 in order to recuperate but after a brief attempt to resume found it necessary to give up active participation in the government. For a time his health seemed to improve, but the hope of recovery was illusory and he died at the beginning of 1924.

REFERENCES

Lenin's *Collected Works* are now in process of publication by the Marx-Engels-Lenin Institute of Moscow. The English translation (ed. Moissaye J. Olgin) is issued in America by International Publishers. Two volumes of *Selections from Lenin* covering the period 1893–1914 have been edited by Pierre Pascal.

There are numerous estimates of Lenin's life and work. Among the more recent biographies in English are James Maxton's *Lenin, Red Dictator* (1931), D. S. Mirsky's *Lenin* (1931), and F. J. P. Veale's *The Man from the Volga* (1932).

READINGS FROM

STATE AND REVOLUTION

The Bourgeois State and Opportunist Socialism.[1] The question of the state is acquiring at present a particular importance, both as theory, and from the point of view of practical politics. The imperialist war has greatly accelerated and intensified the transformation of monopoly capitalism into state-monopoly capitalism. The monstrous oppression of the labouring masses by the state—which connects itself more and more intimately with the all-powerful capitalist combines—is becoming ever more monstrous. The foremost countries are being converted—we speak here of their "rear"—into military convict labour prisons for the workers.

The unheard-of horrors and miseries of the protracted war are making the position of the masses unbearable and increasing their indignation. An international proletarian revolution is clearly rising. The question of its relation to the state is acquiring a practical importance.

The elements of opportunism accumulated during the decades of comparatively peaceful development have created a predominance of social-chauvinism in the official Socialist parties of the whole world (Plekhanov, Potresov, Breshkovskaya, Rubanovich, and, in a slightly concealed form, Messrs. Tsereteli, Chernov and Co., in Russia; Scheidemann, Legien, David and others in Germany; Renaudel, Guesde, Vandervelde in France and Belgium; Hyndman and the Fabians in England, etc., etc.). Socialism in words, chauvinism in deeds is characterised by a base, servile adaptation of the "leaders of Socialism" to the interests not only of "their" national bourgeoisie, but also of "their" state—for a whole series of smaller, weaker nationalities have long since been exploited and enslaved by most of the so-called great powers. The imperialist war is just a war for division and re-division of this kind of booty. The struggle for the emancipation of the labouring masses from the influence of the bourgeoisie in general, and the imperialist bourgeoisie in particular, is impossible without a struggle against the opportunist superstitions concerning the "state." . . .

[1] *Collected Works*, edited by the Marx-Engels-Lenin Institute, Moscow. English translation by Moissaye J. Olgin, copyright by the International Publishing Co., New York (1932), Vol. XXI, Bk. ii, p. 149. *State and Revolution* was written in August and September. 1917, and first published in 1918.

The State as the Product of Class Antagonism.[1] What is now happening to Marx's doctrine has, in the course of history, often happened to the doctrines of other revolutionary thinkers and leaders of oppressed classes struggling for emancipation. During the lifetime of great revolutionaries, the oppressing classes have visited relentless persecution on them and received their teaching with the most savage hostility, the most furious hatred, the most ruthless campaign of lies and slanders. After their death, attempts are made to turn them into harmless icons, canonise them, and surround their *names* with a certain halo for the "consolation" of the oppressed classes and with the object of duping them, while at the same time emasculating and vulgarising the *real essence* of their revolutionary theories and blunting their revolutionary edge. At the present time, the bourgeoisie and the opportunists within the labour movement are coöperating in this work of adulterating Marxism. They omit, obliterate, and distort the revolutionary side of its teaching, its revolutionary soul. They push to the foreground and extol what is, or seems, acceptable to the bourgeoisie. All the social-chauvinists are now "Marxists"—joking aside! And more and more do German bourgeois professors, erstwhile specialists in the demolition of Marx, speak now of the "national-German" Marx, who, they aver, has educated the labour unions which are so splendidly organised for conducting the present predatory war!

In such circumstances, the distortion of Marxism being so widespread, it is our first task to *resuscitate* the real teachings of Marx on the state. For this purpose it will be necessary to quote at length from the works of Marx and Engels themselves. . . .

Let us begin with the most popular of Engels' works, *Der Ursprung der Familie, des Privateigentums und des Staats*, the sixth edition of which was published in Stuttgart as far back as 1894. . . .

Summarising his historical analysis Engels says:

> The state is therefore by no means a power imposed on society from the outside; just as little is it "the reality of the moral idea," "the image and reality of reason," as Hegel asserted. Rather, it is a product of society at a certain stage of development; it is the admission that this society has become entangled in an insoluble contradiction with itself, that it is cleft into irreconcilable antagonisms which it is powerless to dispel. But in order that these antagonisms, classes with conflicting economic interests, may not consume themselves and society in sterile struggle, a power apparently standing above society becomes necessary,

[1] *Ibid.*, pp. 153, 154, 154–156.

whose purpose is to moderate the conflict and keep it within the bounds of "order"; and this power arising out of society, but placing itself above it, and increasingly separating itself from it, is the state.

Here we have, expressed in all its clearness, the basic idea of Marxism on the question of the historical rôle and meaning of the state. The state is the product and the manifestation of the *irreconcilability* of class antagonisms. The state arises when, where, and to the extent that the class antagonisms *cannot* be objectively reconciled. And, conversely, the existence of the state proves that the class antagonisms *are* irreconcilable.

It is precisely on this most important and fundamental point that distortions of Marxism arise along two main lines.

On the one hand, the bourgeois, and particularly the petty-bourgeois, ideologists, compelled under the pressure of indisputable historical facts to admit that the state only exists where there are class antagonisms and the class struggle, "correct" Marx in such a way as to make it appear that the state is an organ for *reconciling* the classes. According to Marx, the state could neither arise nor maintain itself if a reconciliation of classes were possible. But with the petty-bourgeois and philistine professors and publicists, the state—and this frequently on the strength of benevolent references to Marx!—becomes a conciliator of the classes. According to Marx, the state is an organ of class *domination*, an organ of *oppression* of one class by another; its aim is the creation of "order" which legalises and perpetuates this oppression by moderating the collisions between the classes. But in the opinion of the petty-bourgeois politicians, order means reconciliation of the classes, and not oppression of one class by another; to moderate collisions does not mean, they say, to deprive the oppressed classes of certain definite means and methods of struggle for overthrowing the oppressors, but to practice reconciliation.

For instance, when, in the Revolution of 1917,[1] the question of the real meaning and rôle of the state arose in all its vastness as a practical question demanding immediate action on a wide mass scale, all the Socialist-Revolutionaries and Mensheviks suddenly and completely sank to the petty-bourgeois theory of "reconciliation" of the classes by the "state." Innumerable resolutions and articles by politicians of both these parties are saturated through and through with this purely petty-bourgeois and philistine theory of "reconciliation."

[1] *I.e.*, the March Revolution which ended in the establishment of the republic overthrown by the Bolsheviki in November, 1917.

That the state is an organ of domination of a definite class which *cannot* be reconciled with its antipode (the class opposed to it)—this petty-bourgeois democracy is never able to understand. Its attitude towards the state is one of the most telling proofs that our Socialist-Revolutionaries and Mensheviks are not Socialists at all (which we Bolsheviks have always maintained), but petty-bourgeois democrats with a near-Socialist phraseology.

On the other hand, the "Kautskyist" distortion of Marx is far more subtle. "Theoretically," there is no denying that the state is the organ of class domination, or that class antagonisms are irreconcilable. But what is forgotten or glossed over is this: if the state is the product of the irreconcilable character of class antagonisms, if it is a force standing *above* society and "increasingly separating itself from it," then it is clear that the liberation of the oppressed class is impossible not only without a violent revolution, *but also without the destruction* of the apparatus of state power, which was created by the ruling class and in which this "separation" is embodied. As we shall see later, Marx drew this theoretically self-evident conclusion from a concrete historical analysis of the problems of revolution. And it is exactly this conclusion which Kautsky—as we shall show fully in our subsequent remarks—has "forgotten" and distorted. . . .

Violent Revolution and the Dictatorship of the Proletariat.[1] Engels' words regarding the "withering away" of the state enjoy such popularity, they are so often quoted, and they show so clearly the essence of the usual adulteration by means of which Marxism is made to look like opportunism, that we must dwell on them in detail. Let us quote the whole passage from which they are taken.

> The proletariat seizes state power, and then transforms the means of production into state property. But in doing this, it puts an end to itself as the proletariat, it puts an end to all class differences and class antagonisms, it puts an end also to the state as the state. Former society, moving in class antagonisms, had need of the state, that is, an organisation of the exploiting class at each period for the maintenance of its external conditions of production; therefore, in particular, for the forcible holding down of the exploited class in the conditions of oppression (slavery, bondage or serfdom, wage-labour) determined by the existing mode of production. The state was the official representative of society as a whole, its embodiment in a visible corporate body; but it was this only in so far as it was the state of that class which itself, in its epoch, rep-

[1] *Ibid.*, pp. 161–163, 164–165, 166, 167–168, 168–169, 169–170, 171, 172–173, 178–179, 179–180.

> resented society as a whole: in ancient times, the state of the slave-owning citizens; in the Middle Ages, of the feudal nobility; in our epoch, of the bourgeoisie. When ultimately it becomes really representative of society as a whole, it makes itself superfluous. As soon as there is no longer any class of society to be held in subjection; as soon as, along with class domination and the struggle for individual existence based on the former anarchy of production, the collisions and excesses arising from these have also been abolished, there is nothing more to be repressed, and a special repressive force, a state, is no longer necessary. The first act in which the state really comes forward as the representative of society as a whole—the seizure of the means of production in the name of society—is at the same time its last independent act as a state. The interference of a state power in social relations becomes superfluous in one sphere after another, and then becomes dormant of itself. Government over persons is replaced by the administration of things and the direction of the processes of production. The state is not "abolished," *it withers away.* It is from this standpoint that we must appraise the phrase "people's free state"—both its justification at times for agitational purposes, and its ultimate scientific inadequacy—and also the demand of the so-called Anarchists that the state should be abolished overnight.

Without fear of committing an error, it may be said that of this argument by Engels so singularly rich in ideas, only one point has become an integral part of Socialist thought among modern Socialist parties, namely, that, unlike the Anarchist doctrine of the "abolition" of the state, according to Marx the state "withers away." To emasculate Marxism in such a manner is to reduce it to opportunism, for such an "interpretation" only leaves the hazy conception of a slow, even, gradual change, free from leaps and storms, free from revolution. The current popular conception, if one may say so, of the "withering away" of the state undoubtedly means a slurring over, if not a negation, of revolution.

Yet, such an "interpretation" is the crudest distortion of Marxism, which is advantageous only to the bourgeoisie; in point of theory, it is based on a disregard for the most important circumstances and considerations pointed out in the very passage summarising Engels' ideas, which we have just quoted in full.

In the first place, Engels at the very outset of his argument says that, in assuming state power, the proletariat by that very act "puts an end to the state as the state." One is "not accustomed" to reflect on what this really means. Generally, it is either ignored altogether, or it is considered as a piece of "Hegelian weakness" on Engels' part. As a matter of fact, however, these words express succinctly the experience of one of the greatest proletarian revolutions—the Paris Commune of 1871, of which we shall speak in greater detail in its proper place. As a matter of fact, Engels speaks here of the destruction of the bourgeois state by the proletarian revolution, while the words about its withering away refer to the remains of *proletarian* statehood *after* the Socialist revolution. The bourgeois state does not "wither away," according to Engels, but is "put an end to" by the proletariat in the course of the revolution. What withers away after the revolution is the proletarian state or semi-state.

Secondly, the state is a "special repressive force." This splendid and extremely profound definition of Engels' is given by him here with complete lucidity. It follows from this that the "special repressive force" of the bourgeoisie for the suppression of the proletariat, of the millions of workers by a handful of the rich, must be replaced by a "special repressive force" of the proletariat for the suppression of the bourgeoisie (the dictatorship of the proletariat). It is just this that constitutes the destruction of "the state as the state." It is just this that constitutes the "act" of "the seizure of the means of production in the name of society." And it is obvious that such a substitution of one (proletarian) "special repressive force" for another (bourgeois) "special repressive force" can in no way take place in the form of a "withering away." . . .

The "people's free state" was a demand in the programme of the German Social-Democrats and their current slogan in the 'seventies. There is no political substance in this slogan other than a pompous middle-class circumlocution of the idea of democracy. In so far as it referred in a lawful manner to a democratic republic, Engels was prepared to "justify" its use "at times" from a propaganda point of view. But this slogan was opportunist, for it not only expressed an exaggerated view of the attractiveness of bourgeois democracy, but also a lack of understanding of the Socialist criticism of every state in general. We are in favour of a democratic republic as the best form of the state for the proletariat under capitalism, but we have no right to forget that wage slavery is the lot of the people even in the most democratic bourgeois republic. Furthermore, every state is a "special repressive force" for the suppression of the oppressed class. Consequently, *no* state is either "free" or a "people's state." Marx and Engels explained this repeatedly to their party comrades in the 'seventies. . . .

In the same work of Engels, from which every one remembers his argument on the "withering away" of the state, there is also a disquisition on the significance of a violent revolution. The historical analysis of its rôle becomes, with Engels, a veritable panegyric on violent revolution. This, of course, "no one remembers"; to talk or even to think of the importance of this idea is not considered good form by contemporary Socialist parties, and in the daily propaganda and agitation among the masses it plays no part whatever. Yet it is indissolubly bound up with the "withering away" of the state in one harmonious whole. . . .

The replacement of the bourgeois by the proletarian state is impossible without a violent revolution. The abolition of the proletarian state, *i.e.*, of all states, is only possible through "withering away." . . .

> In the course of its development,—wrote Marx in the *Poverty of Philosophy*—the working class will replace the old bourgeois society by an association which excludes classes and their antagonism, and there will no longer be any real political power, for political power is precisely the official expression of the class antagonism within bourgeois society.

It is instructive to compare with this general statement of the idea of the state disappearing after classes have disappeared, the statement contained in the *Communist Manifesto*, written by Marx and Engels a few months later—to be exact, in November, 1847:

> In depicting the most general phases of the development of the proletariat, we traced the more or less veiled civil war, raging within existing society, up to the point where that war breaks out into open revolution, and where the violent overthrow of the bourgeoisie lays the foundation for the sway of the proletariat. . . .
>
> We have seen above that the first step in the revolution by the working class is to raise [literally "promote"] the proletariat to the position of ruling class, to establish democracy.
>
> The proletariat will use its political supremacy to wrest by degrees all capital from the bourgeoisie, to centralise all instruments of production in the hands of the state, *i.e.*, of the proletariat organised as the ruling class; and to increase the total of productive forces as rapidly as possible.

Here we have a formulation of one of the most remarkable and most important ideas of Marxism on the subject of the state, namely, the idea of the "dictatorship of the proletariat" (as Marx and Engels began to term it after the Paris Commune); and also a definition of the state, in the highest degree interesting, but nevertheless also belonging to the category of "forgotten words" of Marxism: "*the state*, i.e., *the proletariat organised as the ruling class.*" . . .

The state is a special organisation of force; it is the organisation of violence for the suppression of some class. What class must the proletariat suppress? Naturally, the exploiting class only, *i.e.*, the bourgeoisie. The toilers need the state only to overcome the resistance of the exploiters, and only the proletariat can direct this suppression and bring it to fulfilment, for the proletariat is the only class that is thoroughly revolutionary, the only class that can unite all the toilers and the exploited in the struggle against the bourgeoisie, in completely displacing it. . . .

The petty-bourgeois democrats, these sham Socialists who have substituted for the class struggle dreams of harmony between classes, imagined even the transition to Socialism in a dreamy fashion—not in the form of the overthrow of the rule of the exploiting class, but in the form of the peaceful submission of the minority to a majority conscious of its aims. This petty-bourgeois Utopia, indissolubly connected with the idea of the state's being above classes, in practice led to the betrayal of the interests of the toiling classes, as was shown, for example, in the history of the French revolutions of 1848 and 1871, and in the participation of "Socialists" in bourgeois cabinets in England, France, Italy and other countries at the end of the nineteenth and the beginning of the twentieth centuries. . . .

The overthrow of bourgeois rule can be accomplished only by the proletariat, as the particular class, which, by the economic conditions of its existence, is being prepared for this work and is provided both with the opportunity and the power to perform it. While the capitalist class breaks up and atomises the peasantry and all the petty-bourgeois strata, it welds together, unites and organises the town proletariat. Only the proletariat—by virtue of its economic rôle in large-scale production—is capable of leading *all* the toiling and exploited masses, who are exploited, oppressed, crushed by the bourgeoisie not less, and often more, than the proletariat, but who are incapable of carrying on the struggle for their freedom *independently*. . . .

The proletariat needs state power, the centralised organisation of force, the organisation of violence, both for the purpose of crushing the resistance of the exploiters and for the purpose of *guiding* the great mass of the population—the peasantry, the petty-bourgeoisie, the semi-proletarians—in the work of organising Socialist economy.

By educating a workers' party, Marxism educates the vanguard of the proletariat, capable of assuming power and of *leading the whole people* to Socialism, of directing and organising the new order, of being the teacher, guide and leader of all the toiling and exploited in the task of building up their social life without the bourgeoisie and against the bourgeoisie. As against this, the opportunism predominant at present breeds in the workers' party representatives of the better-paid workers, who lose touch with the rank and file, "get along" fairly well under capitalism, and sell their birthright for a mess of pottage, *i.e.*, renounce their rôle of revolutionary leaders of the people against the bourgeoisie.

"The state, *i.e.*, the proletariat organised as the ruling class"—this theory of Marx's is indissolubly connected with all his teaching concerning the revolutionary rôle of the proletariat in history. The culmination of this rôle is proletarian dictatorship, the political rule of the proletariat.

But, if the proletariat needs the state, as a *special* form of organisation of violence *against* the capitalist class, the following question arises almost automatically: is it thinkable that such an organisation can be created without a preliminary break-up and destruction of the state machinery created for *its own* use by the bourgeoisie? The *Communist Manifesto* leads straight to this conclusion, and it is of this conclusion that Marx speaks when summing up the experience of the revolution of 1848–1851.

On the question of the state which we are concerned with, Marx sums up his conclusions from the revolution of 1848–1851 in the following observations contained in his work, *The Eighteenth Brumaire of Louis Bonaparte*. . . .

The first French Revolution developed centralisation, "but at the same time it developed the scope, the attributes and the servants of the government power. Napoleon perfected this state machinery. The legitimate monarchy and the July monarchy added nothing to it but a greater division of labour. . . .

"Finally, in its struggle against the revolution, the parliamentary Republic found itself compelled to strengthen with its repressive measures, the resources and the centralisation of the government power. *All revolutions brought this machine to greater perfection, instead of breaking it up* [the italics are ours]. The parties which alternately contended for supremacy looked on the capture of this vast state edifice as the chief spoils of the victor."

In this remarkable passage Marxism makes a tremendous step forward in comparison with the position of the *Communist Manifesto*. There the question of the state still is treated extremely in the abstract, in the most general terms and expressions. Here the question is treated in a concrete manner, and the conclusion is most precise, definite, practical and palpable: all revolutions which have taken place up to the present have helped to perfect the state machinery, whereas it must be shattered, broken to pieces.

This conclusion is the chief and fundamental thesis in the Marxist theory of the state. Yet it is this fundamental thesis which has been not only completely *forgotten* by the dominant official Social-Democratic parties, but directly *distorted* (as we shall see later) by the foremost theoretician of the Second International, K. Kautsky. . . .

The problem of the state is put concretely: how did the bourgeois state, the state machinery necessary for the rule of the bourgeoisie, come into being? What were its changes, what its evolution in the course of the bourgeois revolutions and in the face of the independent actions of the oppressed classes? What are the tasks of the proletariat relative to this state machinery?

The centralised state power peculiar to bourgeois society came into being in the period of the fall of absolutism. Two institutions are especially characteristic of this state machinery: bureaucracy and the standing army. In their works, Marx and Engels mention repeatedly the thousand threads which connect these institutions with the bourgeoisie. The experience of every worker illustrates this connection in the clearest and most impressive manner. From its own bitter experience, the working class learns to recognise this connection; that is why it so easily acquires, so completely absorbs the doctrine revealing this inevitable connection, a doctrine which the petty-bourgeois democrats either ignorantly and light-heartedly deny, or, still more light-heartedly, admit "in general," forgetting to draw adequate practical conclusions.

Bureaucracy and the standing army constitute a "parasite" on the body of bourgeois society—a parasite born of the internal antagonisms which tear that society asunder, but essentially a parasite, "clogging every pore" of existence. The Kautskyist opportunism prevalent at present within official Social-Democracy considers this view of the state as a *parasitic organism* to be the peculiar and exclusive property of Anarchism. Naturally, this distortion of Marxism is extremely useful to those philistines who have brought Socialism to the unheard-of disgrace of justifying and embellishing the imperialist war by applying to it the term of "national defence"; but none the less it is an absolute distortion.

The development, perfecting and strengthening of the bureaucratic and military apparatus has been going on through all the bourgeois revolutions of which Europe has seen so many since the fall of feudalism. It is particularly the petty bourgeoisie that is attracted to the side of the big bourgeoisie and to its allegiance, largely by means of this apparatus, which provides the upper strata of the peasantry, small artisans and tradesmen with a number of comparatively comfortable, quiet and respectable berths raising their holders *above* the people. Consider what happened in Russia during the six months following March 12, 1917. The government posts which hitherto had been given by preference to members of the Black Hundreds now became the booty of Cadets, Mensheviks and S.-R.'s.[1] Nobody really thought of any serious reform. They were to be put off "until the Constituent Assembly," which, in its turn, was eventually to be put off until the end of the war! But there was no delay, no waiting for a Constituent Assembly in the matter of dividing the spoils, of getting hold of the berths of ministers, assistant-ministers, governor-generals, etc., etc.! The game that went on of changing the combination of persons forming the Provisional Government was, in essence, only the expression of this division and re-division of the "spoils," which was going on high and low, throughout the country, throughout the central and local government. The practical results of the six months between March 12 and September 9, 1917, beyond all dispute, are: reforms shelved, distribution of officials' berths accomplished, and "mistakes" in the distribution corrected by a few re-distributions.

But the longer the process of "re-apportioning" the bureaucratic apparatus among the various bourgeois and petty-bourgeois parties (among the Cadets, S.-R.'s and Mensheviks, if we take the case of Russia) goes on, the more clearly the oppressed classes, with the proletariat at their head, realise that they are irreconcilably hostile to the *whole* of bourgeois society. Hence the necessity for all bourgeois parties, even for the most democratic and "revolutionary-democratic" among them, to increase their repressive measures against the revolutionary proletariat, to strengthen the apparatus of repression, *i.e.*, the same state machinery. Such a course of events compels the revolution "*to concentrate all its forces of destruction*" against the state power, and

[1] Socialist-Revolutionaries.

to regard the problem as one, not of perfecting the machinery of the state, but of *breaking up and annihilating it*. . . .

The last preface to a new German edition of the *Communist Manifesto* signed by both its authors is dated June 24, 1872. In this preface the authors, Karl Marx and Friedrich Engels, say that the programme of the *Communist Manifesto* is now "in places out of date."

> One thing especially—they continue—was proved by the Commune, *viz.*, *that the "working class cannot simply lay hold of the ready-made state machinery and wield it for its own purposes.*" . . .

It is most characteristic that it is precisely this vital correction which has been distorted by the opportunists, and its meaning, probably, is not known to nine-tenths, if not ninety-nine-hundredths, of the readers of the *Communist Manifesto*. We shall deal with this distortion more fully further on, in a chapter devoted specially to distortions. It will be sufficient here to note that the current vulgar "interpretation" of Marx's famous utterance quoted above consists in asserting that Marx is here emphasising the idea of gradual development, in contradistinction to a seizure of power, and so on.

As a matter of fact, *exactly the opposite is the case*. Marx's idea is that the working class must *break up*, *shatter* the "ready-made state machinery," and not confine itself merely to taking possession of it.

On April 12, 1871, *i.e.*, just at the time of the Commune, Marx wrote to Kugelmann:

> If you look at the last chapter of my *Eighteenth Brumaire*, you will see that I declare that the next attempt of the French Revolution must be: not, as in the past, to transfer the bureaucratic and military machinery from one hand to the other, but to *break it up* [Marx's italics—the original is *Zerbrechen*]; and this is the precondition of any real people's revolution on the Continent. And this is what our heroic party comrades in Paris have attempted.

In these words, "to break up the bureaucratic and military machinery," is contained, briefly formulated, the principal lesson of Marxism on the tasks of the proletariat in relation to the state during a revolution. And it is just this lesson which has not only been forgotten, but downright distorted, by the prevailing Kautskyist "interpretation" of Marxism. . . .

It is interesting to note two particular points in the passage of

Marx quoted. First, he confines his conclusions to the Continent. This was natural in 1871, when England was still the model of a purely capitalist country, but without a military machine and, in large measure, without a bureaucracy. Hence Marx excluded England, where a revolution, even a people's revolution, could be imagined, and was then possible, *without* the preliminary condition of destroying the "ready-made state machinery."

Today, in 1917, in the epoch of the first great imperialist war, this exception made by Marx is no longer valid. Both England and America, the greatest and last representatives of Anglo-Saxon "liberty" in the sense of the absence of militarism and bureaucracy, have today plunged headlong into the all-European dirty, bloody morass of military bureaucratic institutions to which everything is subordinated and which trample everything under foot. Today, both in England and in America, the "precondition of any real people's revolution" is the *break-up*, the *shattering* of the "ready-made state machinery" (brought in those countries, between 1914 and 1917, to general "European" imperialist perfection). . . .

Proletarian Machinery of Government.[1] [Marx] stated that the "breaking up" of the state machinery is demanded by the interests both of the workers and of the peasants, that it unites them, that it places before them the common task of removing the "parasite" and replacing it by something new.

By what exactly?

In 1847, in the *Communist Manifesto*, Marx answered this question still in a purely abstract manner, stating the problems rather than the methods of solving them. To replace this machinery by "the proletariat organised as the ruling class," by "establishing democracy"—such was the answer of the *Communist Manifesto*.

Without resorting to Utopias, Marx waited for the *experience* of a mass movement to produce the answer to the problem as to the exact forms which this organisation of the proletariat as the ruling class will assume and as to the exact manner in which this organisation will be combined with the most complete, most consistent "establishment of democracy."

The experiment of the Commune, meagre as it was, was subjected by Marx to the most careful analysis in his *The Civil War in France*. Let us quote the most important passages of this work. . . .

[1] *Ibid.*, pp. 181–182, 182–183, 183–184, 185, 186, 187–188, 188–189.

> The Commune was formed of municipal councillors, chosen by universal suffrage in various wards of the town, responsible and revocable at short terms. The majority of its members were naturally working men, or acknowledged representatives of the working class. . . . Instead of continuing to be the agent of the Central Government, the police was at once stripped of its political attributes, and turned into the responsible and at all times revocable agent of the Commune. So were the officials of all other branches of the administration. From the members of the Commune downwards, the public service had to be done at *workmen's wages*. The vested interests and the representation allowances of the high dignitaries of state disappeared along with the high dignitaries themselves. . . .
>
> Having once got rid of the standing army and the police, the physical force elements of the old government, the Commune was anxious to break the spiritual force of repression, the "parson power." . . .
>
> The judicial functionaries were to be divested of [their] sham independence.
>
> . . . Like the rest of public servants, magistrates and judges were to be elective, responsible and revocable.

Thus the Commune would appear to have replaced the shattered state machinery "only" by fuller democracy: abolition of the standing army; all officials to be fully elective and subject to recall. But, as a matter of fact this "only" signifies as a gigantic replacement of one type of institution by others of a fundamentally different order. Here we observe a case of "transformation of quantity into quality": democracy, introduced as fully and consistently as is generally thinkable, is transformed from capitalist democracy into proletarian democracy; from the state (*i.e.*, a special force for the suppression of a particular class) into something which is no longer really the state in the accepted sense of the word.

It is still necessary to suppress the bourgeoisie and crush its resistance. This was particularly necessary for the Commune; and one of the reasons of its defeat was that it did not do this with sufficient determination. But the organ of suppression is now the majority of the population, and not a minority, as was always the case under slavery, serfdom, and wage labour. . . .

The Commune's measure emphasised by Marx, particularly worthy of note, is: the abolition of all representation allowances, and of all money privileges in the case of officials, the reduction of the remuneration of *all* servants of the state to "*workingmen's wages*." Here is shown, more clearly than anywhere else, the *break* from a bourgeois democracy to a proletarian democracy, from the democracy of the oppressors to the democracy of the oppressed classes, from the state as a "special force for suppression" of a given class to the suppression of the oppressors by the *whole force* of the majority of the people—the workers and the peasants. . . .

> The Commune—says Marx—was to be a working, not a parliamentary body, executive and legislative at the same time. . . .
>
> Instead of deciding once in three or six years which member of the ruling class was to represent the people in Parliament, universal suffrage was to serve the people, constituted in Communes, as individual suffrage serves every other employer in the search for the workmen and managers in his business. . . .

To decide once every few years which member of the ruling class is to repress and oppress the people through parliament—this is the real essence of bourgeois parliamentarism, not only in parliamentary-constitutional monarchies, but also in the most democratic republics. . . .

The venal and rotten parliamentarism of bourgeois society is replaced in the Commune by institutions in which freedom of opinion and discussion does not degenerate into deception, for the parliamentarians must themselves work, must themselves execute their own laws, must themselves verify their results in actual life, must themselves be directly responsible to their electorate. Representative institutions remain, but parliamentarism as a special system, as a division of labour between the legislative and the executive functions, as a privileged position for the deputies, *no longer exists*. Without representative institutions we cannot imagine democracy, not even proletarian democracy; but we can and *must* think of democracy without parliamentarism, if criticism of bourgeois society is not mere empty words for us, if the desire to overthrow the rule of the bourgeoisie is our serious and sincere desire, and not a mere "election cry" for catching workingmen's votes. . . .

We are not Utopians, we do not indulge in "dreams" of how best to do away *immediately* with all administration, with all subordination; these Anarchist dreams, based upon a lack of understanding of the task of proletarian dictatorship, are basically foreign to Marxism, and, as a matter of fact, they serve but to put off the Socialist revolution until human nature is different. No, we want the Socialist revolution with human nature as it is now, with human nature that cannot do without subordination, control and "managers."

But if there be subordination, it must be to the armed vanguard of all the exploited and the labouring—to the proletariat. The specific "commanding" methods of the state officials can and must begin to be replaced—immediately, within twenty-four hours—by the simple functions of "managers" and bookkeepers, functions which are now already within the capacity of the average city dweller and can well be performed for "workingmen's wages."

We organise large-scale production, starting from what capitalism has already created; we workers *ourselves*, relying on our own experience as workers, establishing a strict, an iron discipline, supported by the state power of the armed workers, shall reduce the rôle of the state officials to that of simply carrying out our instructions as responsible, moderately paid "managers" (of course, with technical knowledge of all sorts, types and degrees). This is *our* proletarian task, with this we can and must *begin* when carrying through a proletarian revolution. Such a beginning, on the basis of large-scale production, of itself leads to the gradual "withering away" of all bureaucracy, to the gradual creation of a new order, an order without quotation marks, an order which has nothing to do with wage slavery, an order in which the more and more simplified functions of control and accounting will be performed by each in turn, will then become a habit, and will finally die out as *special* functions of a special stratum of the population. . . .

The Lower and Higher Phases of Communism.[1] In the *Critique of the Gotha Programme*, Marx goes into some detail to disprove the Lassallean idea of the workers' receiving under socialism the "undiminished" or "full product of their labour." Marx shows that out of the whole of the social labour of society, it is necessary to deduct a reserve fund, a fund for the expansion of production, for the replacement of worn-out machinery, and so on; then, also, out of the means of consumption must be deducted a fund for the expenses of management, for schools, hospitals, homes for the aged, and so on.

Instead of the hazy, obscure, general phrase of Lassalle's—"the full product of his labour for the worker"—Marx gives a sober estimate of exactly how a Socialist society will have to manage its affairs, Marx undertakes a *concrete* analysis of the conditions of life of a society in which there is no capitalism, and says:

> What we are dealing with here [analysing the programme of the party] is not a Communist society which has *developed* on its own foundations, but, on the contrary, one which is just *emerging* from capitalist society, and which therefore in all respects—economic, moral and intellectual—still bears the birthmarks of the old society from whose womb it sprung.

[1] *Ibid.*, pp. 221–223, 223–226, 229–231.

And it is this Communist society—a society which has just come into the world out of the womb of capitalism, and which, in all respects, bears the stamp of the old society—that Marx terms the "first," or lower, phase of Communist society.

The means of production are no longer the private property of individuals. The means of production belong to the whole of society. Every member of society, performing a certain part of socially-necessary work, receives a certificate from society to the effect that he has done such and such a quantity of work. According to this certificate, he receives from the public warehouses, where articles of consumption are stored, a corresponding quantity of products. Deducting that proportion of labour which goes to the public fund, every worker, therefore, receives from society as much as he has given it.

"Equality" seems to reign supreme.

But when Lassalle, having in view such a social order (generally called Socialism, but termed by Marx the first phase of Communism), speaks of this as "just distribution," and says that this is "the equal right of each to an equal product of labour," Lassalle is mistaken, and Marx exposes his error.

"Equal right," says Marx, we indeed have here; but it is *still* a "bourgeois right," which, like every right, *presupposes inequality*. Every right is an application of the *same* measure to *different* people who, in fact, are not the same and are not equal to one another; this is why "equal right" is really a violation of equality, and an injustice. In effect, every man having done as much social labour as every other, receives an equal share of the social products (with the above-mentioned deductions).

But different people are not alike: one is strong, another is weak; one is married, the other is not; one has more children, another has less, and so on.

> . . . With equal labour—Marx concludes—and therefore an equal share in the social consumption fund, one man in fact receives more than the other, one is richer than the other, and so forth. In order to avoid all these defects, rights, instead of being equal, must be unequal.

The first phase of Communism, therefore, still cannot produce justice and equality; differences, and unjust differences, in wealth will still exist, but the *exploitation* of man by man will have become impossible, because it will be impossible to seize as private property the *means of production*, the factories, machines, land, and so on.

In tearing down Lassalle's petty-bourgeois, confused phrase about "equality" and "justice" *in general*, Marx shows the *course of development* of Communist society, which is forced at first to destroy *only* the "injustice" that consists in the means of production having been seized by private individuals, and which *is not capable* of destroying at once the further injustice consisting in the distribution of the articles of consumption "according to work performed" (and not according to need). . . .

Marx not only takes into account with the greatest accuracy the inevitable inequality of men; he also takes into account the fact that the mere conversion of the means of production into the common property of the whole of society ("Socialism" in the generally accepted sense of the word) *does not remove* the defects of distribution and the inequality of "bourgeois right" which *continue to rule* as long as the products are divided "according to work performed."

> But these defects—Marx continues—are unavoidable in the first phase of Communist society, when, after long travail, it first emerges from capitalist society. Justice can never rise superior to the economic conditions of society and the cultural development conditioned by them.

And so, in the first phase of Communist society (generally called Socialism) "bourgeois right" is *not* abolished in its entirety, but only in part, only in proportion to the economic transformation so far attained, *i.e.*, only in respect of the means of production. "Bourgeois right" recognises them as the private property of separate individuals. Socialism converts them into common property. *To that extent*, and to that extent alone, does "bourgeois right" disappear.

However, it continues to exist as far as its other part is concerned; it remains in the capacity of regulator (determining factor) distributing the products and alloting labour among the members of society. "He who does not work, shall not eat"—this Socialist principle is *already* realised; "for an equal quantity of labour, an equal quantity of products"—this Socialist principle is also *already* realised. However, this is not yet Communism, and this does not abolish "bourgeois right," which gives to unequal individuals, in return for an unequal (in reality unequal) amount of work, an equal quantity of products.

This is a "defect," says Marx, but it is unavoidable during the first phase of Communism; for, if we are not to fall into Utopianism, we cannot imagine that, having overthrown capitalism, people will at once learn to work for society *without any standards of right;* indeed, the abolition of capitalism *does not immediately lay* the economic foundations for *such* a change.

And there is no other standard yet than that of "bourgeois right." To this extent, therefore, a form of state is still necessary, which, while maintaining public ownership of the means of production, would preserve the equality of labour and equality in the distribution of products.

The state is withering away in so far as there are no longer any capitalists, any classes, and, consequently, no *class* can be suppressed.

But the state has not yet altogether withered away, since there still remains the protection of "bourgeois right" which sanctifies actual inequality. For the complete extinction of the state, complete Communism is necessary.

Marx continues:

> In a higher phase of Communist society, when the enslaving subordination of individuals in the division of labour has disappeared, and with it also the antagonism between mental and physical labour; when labour has become not only a means of living, but itself the first necessity of life; when, along with the all-round development of individuals, the productive forces too have grown, and all the springs of social wealth are flowing more freely—it is only at that stage that it will be possible to pass completely beyond the narrow horizon of bourgeois rights, and for society to inscribe on its banners: from each according to his ability: to each according to his needs!

Only now can we appreciate the full correctness of Engels' remarks in which he mercilessly ridiculed all the absurdity of combining the words "freedom" and "state." While the state exists there is no freedom. When there is freedom, there will be no state.

The economic basis for the complete withering away of the state is that high stage of development of Communism when the antagonism between mental and physical labour disappears, that is to say, when one of the principal sources of modern *social* inequality disappears—a source, moreover, which it is impossible to remove immediately by the mere conversion of the means of production into public property, by the mere expropriation of the capitalists.

This expropriation will make a gigantic development of the productive forces *possible*. And seeing how incredibly, even now, capitalism *retards* this development, how much progress could be made even on the basis of modern technique at the level it has reached, we have a right to say, with the fullest confidence, that the expropriation of the capitalists will inevitably result in a gigantic development of the productive forces of human society. But how rapidly this development will go forward, how soon it will reach the point of breaking away from the diversion of labour, of removing the antagonism between mental and physical labour, of transforming work into the "first necessity of life"—this we do not and *cannot* know.

Consequently, we have a right to speak solely of the inevitable withering away of the state, emphasising the protracted nature of this process and its dependence upon the rapidity of development of the *higher phase* of Communism; leaving quite open the question of lengths of time, or the concrete forms of withering away, since material for the solution of such questions is *not available.*

The state will be able to wither away completely when society has realised the rule: "From each according to his ability; to each according to his needs," *i.e.*, when people have become accustomed to observe the fundamental rules of social life, and their labour is so productive, that they voluntarily work *according to their ability.* "The narrow horizon of bourgeois rights," which compels one to calculate, with the hard-heartedness of a Shylock, whether he has not worked half an hour more than another, whether he is not getting less pay than another—this narrow horizon will then be left behind. There will then be no need for any exact calculation by society of the quantity of products to be distributed to each of its members; each will take freely "according to his needs." . . .

Until the "higher" phase of Communism arrives, the Socialists demand the *strictest* control, *by society and by the state*, of the quantity of labour and the quantity of consumption; only this control must *start* with the expropriation of the capitalists, with the control of the workers over the capitalists, and must be carried out, not by a state of bureaucrats, but by a state of *armed workers.*

Self-seeking defence of capitalism by the bourgeois ideologists . . . consists in that they *substitute* disputes and discussions about the distant future for the essential imperative questions of present-day policy: the expropriation of the capitalists, the conversion of *all* citizens into workers and employees of *one* huge "syndicate"—the whole state—and the complete subordination of the whole of the work of this syndicate to the really democratic state of the *Soviets of Workers' and Soldiers' Deputies.* . . .

Capitalism, as it develops, itself creates *prerequisites* for "every one" *to be able* really to take part in the administration of the state.

Among such prerequisites are: universal literacy, already realised in most of the advanced capitalist countries, then the "training and disciplining" of millions of workers by the huge, complex, and socialised apparatus of the post-office, the railways, the big factories, large-scale commerce, banking, etc., etc.

With such *economic* prerequisites it is perfectly possible, immediately, within twenty-four hours after the overthrow of the capitalists and bureaucrats, to replace them, in the control of production and distribution, in the business of *control* of labour and products, by the armed workers, by the whole people in arms. (The question of control and accounting must not be confused with the question of the scientifically educated staff of engineers, agronomists and so on. These gentlemen work today, obeying the capitalists; they will work even better tomorrow, obeying the armed workers.)

Accounting and control—those are the *chief* things necessary for the organising and correct functioning of the *first phase* of Communist society. *All* citizens are here transformed into hired employees of the state, which is made up of the armed workers. *All* citizens become employees and workers of *one* national state "syndicate." All that is required is that they should work equally, should regularly do their share of work, and should receive equal pay. The accounting and control necessary for this have been *simplified* by capitalism to the utmost, till they have become the extraordinarily simple operations of watching, recording and issuing receipts, within the reach of anybody who can read and write and knows the first four rules of arithmetic.

When the *majority* of the people begin everywhere to keep such accounts and maintain such control over the capitalists (now converted into employees) and over the intellectual gentry, who still retain capitalist habits, this control will really become universal, general, national; and there will be no way of getting away from it, there will be "nowhere to go."

The whole of society will have become one office and one factory, with equal work and equal pay.

But this "factory" discipline, which the proletariat will extend to the whole of society after the defeat of the capitalists and the overthrow of the exploiters, is by no means our ideal, or our final aim. It is but a *foothold* necessary for the radical cleansing of society of all the hideousness and foulness of capitalist exploitation, *in order to advance further.*

From the moment when all members of society, or even only the overwhelming majority, have learned how to govern the state *themselves*, have taken this business into their own hands, have "established" control over the insignificant minority of capitalists, over the gentry with capitalist leanings, and the workers thoroughly demoralised by capitalism—from this moment the need for any government begins to disappear. The more complete the democracy, the nearer the moment when it begins to be unnecessary. The more democratic the "state" consisting of armed workers, which is "no longer a state in the proper sense of the word," the more rapidly does *every* state begin to wither away.

For when *all* have learned to manage, and independently are actually managing by themselves social production, keeping accounts, controlling the idlers, the gentlefolk, the swindlers and similar "guardians of capitalist traditions," then the escape from this national accounting and control will inevitably become so increasingly difficult, such a rare exception, and will probably be accompanied by such swift and severe punishment (for the armed workers are men of practical life, not sentimental intellectuals, and they will scarcely allow any one to trifle with them), that very soon the *necessity* of observing the simple, fundamental rules of every-day social life in common will have become a *habit*.

The door will then be wide open for the transition from the first phase of Communist society to its higher phase, and along with it to the complete withering away of the state. . . .

Postscript.[1] This pamphlet was written in August and September, 1917. I had already drawn up the plan for the next, the seventh chapter, on the "Experience of the Russian Revolutions of 1905 and 1917." But, outside of the title, I did not succeed in writing a single line of the chapter; what "interfered" was the political crisis—the eve of the October[2] Revolution of 1917. Such "interference" can only be welcomed. However, the second part of the pamphlet (devoted to the "Experience of the Russian Revolutions of 1905 and 1917") will probably have to be put off for a long time. It is more pleasant and useful to go through the "experience of the revolution" than to write about it.

THE AUTHOR.

Petrograd, December 13, 1917.

[1] *Ibid.*, p. 247.

[2] Or November, according to the Gregorian calendar. (Editor.)

XXVII

S. G. HOBSON

c. 1865(?)-

S. G. Hobson was born at Besbrook in the county of Armagh, Ireland, and educated at Quaker schools in Somersetshire, England. One of his schoolmasters gave him the works of Carlyle and Ruskin to read and it is said that he was thus converted to socialism. A journalist by profession, he has also lectured extensively in England and from time to time in America to which his business has frequently called him.

But for many years Hobson's main interest has been the promotion of socialism. He joined the Fabian Society in 1887, a few years after its formation, serving as a member of the executive committee from 1900 to 1909. In 1893 he helped to found the Independent Labor party and established its organization in south Wales. An unsuccessful labor candidate for Parliament at East Bristol in 1895 (before the advent of the Labor party), he campaigned as a socialist at Rochdale in 1905 but was again defeated. When the Labor Representation Committee (the parent of the Labor party) was formed, Hobson for a time opposed support of it by the socialists. Ultimately, however, he accepted the Labor party as a "political expression of the class struggle." But within a few years his earlier hesitation was vindicated. The tactics of the Labor party seemed to demonstrate that it had more in common with liberalism than with socialism and that there was no present prospect of a radical change of heart. Accordingly Hobson and others of similar views began an attempt to weld the various socialist groups into a united and thoroughly socialist party.

Matters came to a head with the so-called "Grayson incident." Elected to Parliament in 1907 as an independent socialist, Victor Grayson irritated his older and more steady-going labor colleagues by flouting the authority of the Speaker in the House of Commons and attempting to speak out of turn on unemployment and relations with Russia. He was suspended by the House. The significant point was that the majority of the Labor party seemed virtually to repudiate him. Hobson therefore proposed to the Fabian Society that it should withdraw from affiliation with the Labor party and help to organize "a definite and avowed Socialist Party." The motion was defeated and Hobson resigned. He thereupon carried the appeal to the country, touring England in behalf of the proposed movement. The outcome of the dissenters' efforts was the British Socialist party, a union of various socialist elements including the old Social Democratic Federation and certain branches of the Independent Labor party. After the first batch of adherents, however, the new movement attracted few recruits. Some years afterward, in 1916, it even affiliated with the hitherto despised Labor party. By this time, however, Hobson was off on a more promising tack, the enterprise by which he is best known—guild socialism.

In the first years of this century a number of Englishmen had begun to discuss the revival of the medieval guild as a means of restoring the integrity and independence of labor. At this stage the guild movement was largely a craftsman's protest against the shoddy products of modern industry—A. J. Penty, its chief exponent, was himself an architect. The virtues of medievalism were not lost on Hobson. He had not only read Carlyle and Ruskin as a youth but had been personally acquainted with William Morris. But he had also preached orthodox socialism for many years, and it was to be expected that on adopting guildism he would endeavor to assimilate the old to the new.

Between 1912 and 1915, therefore, Hobson reformulated guild doctrine in collaboration with A. R. Orage, editor of the *New Age*, the latter journal becoming an organ of the movement. A series of articles written by Hobson and expanded under the editorship of Orage were republished in 1914 as *National Guilds*. The book became the most widely read of all guild documents. It marked the end of the predominantly medievalist phase of guildism—the object now was not to supplant but to reorganize large-scale industry, and the appeal was increasingly directed toward the trade unions as the agency by which workers' control in industry might be achieved. Largely owing to Hobson the doctrine received a strong infusion of Marxist ideology. It also borrowed something from syndicalism.

With the formation of a National Guilds League in 1915, guild socialism became an organized movement. It had attracted a group of very effective writers and speakers, including G. D. H. Cole, R. H. Tawney, Bertrand Russell, C. H. Douglas, and J. L. Hammond. Most of these had very decided and provocative ideas of their own as to what guild policy should be; the result was that guild socialism resembled one long series of arguments. The chief controversy in which Hobson engaged turned on the position of the state in a guild society. A faction headed by G. D. H. Cole wished to destroy the state and replace it by a "national commune" which would take over some of its sovereign prerogatives. Hobson on the other hand believed that the traditional state ought to be retained, among other things as a focus of nationalism. He clarified his position in *National Guilds and the State* (1920).

Hobson was a prime mover in putting guild theories into actual practice. In 1920 he induced the builders' unions of Manchester to inaugurate a building guild and a similar enterprise was launched in London. The venture was at first a success: the government, then in the midst of a housing program, allotted a number of contracts to the guilds, which executed them with marked efficiency and economy. A number of guilds were established in other lines of industry, and as the movement gathered headway a National Building Guild sprang up which absorbed most of the local bodies. In 1922 a National Guild Council was formed to federate a large number of trade unions which had associated themselves with the movement.

But the fate of guildism seemed to depend upon the prosperity of the building guilds, and this in turn depended upon the special conditions of government contracts. At the beginning the government had virtually advanced capital and credit to the guilds; in 1921 and 1922 it withdrew them, and when the guilds, being unable to secure adequate private financing, attempted rashly to go on without it almost the whole structure collapsed. A few small guilds managed to survive, but the National Building Guild went bankrupt, the Council disappeared, and finally, in 1925, even the parent body, the National Guilds League, was dissolved.

The downfall of guildism as an organized movement did not mean that the efforts of Hobson and his colleagues had gone for nothing; a number of their doctrines are now generally accepted by other schools of British socialism. A greater measure of workers' control in industry, more responsibility for the separate industry in matters of social policy and action, and less emphasis on state control—these are some of the legacies of guild socialism to modern reformist thought.

REFERENCES

Besides the works mentioned, Hobson is also the author of *Guild Principles in War and Peace* (1917), *Irish Home Rule* (1912), and *The House of Industry* (1931).

Biographical details are very meager: Hobson has managed to evade even *Who's Who*. Books dealing with the guild movement provide some account of his career. Of these the most important (in English) is Niles Carpenter's *Guild Socialism* (1922). G. D. H. Cole's article "Guild Socialism" in the *Encyclopedia of the Social Sciences* brings the account up to date. See also André Philip, *Guild-socialisme et trade-unionisme* (1923).

READINGS FROM

NATIONAL GUILDS [1]

Emancipation and the Wage System.[2] For over eighty years Great Britain, by parliamentary stitching and patching, has contrived to maintain social order. The worker has been docile because he believed in gradual reform, and because it was promised him and in part secured to him. Had he not believed in gradual reform—the broadening down from precedent to precedent—all the promises in the world would not have kept him in bondage. It is certain, however, that he will continue docile, until he grasps the true meaning of emancipation. . . .

What, then, is the essence of emancipation? The answer is simple: the rescue from oppressed or evil living and the inauguration of a healthy method of life. The application of this broad definition depends upon our understanding and appreciation of the fundamentals upon which the existing social structure is based. It will hardly be denied that the foundation of society is labour. It follows, if the conditions that govern labour are evil and oppressive, that real emancipation consists in replacing those conditions by a new scheme of life. It is an appalling thought, yet not without justification, that the primary condition of labour—life for a subsistence wage—marks no advance upon previous epochs. Apart from purely superficial effects, it may with truth be contended that, fundamentally, wage serfdom (seldom if ever more than a month from starvation) is in no way an advance upon chattel slavery. Changes there have been, bringing in their train social and spiritual modifications, but in essence our

[1] The full title is *National Guilds; an Inquiry into the Wage System and the Way Out*, A. R. Orage, ed. (1914). This edition, the first, does not bear Hobson's name.

[2] Pp. 1, 2–3, 4–5, 13–14, 17–18.

wage-paid population is but helotry clipped of some of its more savage features. . . .

The conclusion is obvious—there can be no emancipation save only from the wage system. The way out is to smash wages. It is a curious commentary upon Socialist propaganda in Great Britain that we seldom hear a word against the wage system *as a system of wages*. The plea is for higher wages, shorter hours, or what not, but never for the complete abolition of wages as such. The result is that the younger generation of Socialists never learn that this was once a salient feature of the Socialist crusade: they do not learn it because the older Socialists have forgotten it. It is to the credit of the old Social Democratic Federation that they always thoroughly understood that the real enemy was the wage system. They realised that wages were the mark of a class, and that the class struggle (*lutte de classe*, not *guerre de classe*) meant first and last the complete destruction of the economic bondage implied in the wage system. Yet never was the need greater than to-day to press forward a conscious attack upon it. Parliamentary legislation is based upon the continuance of the wage system. The Insurance Act, the Eight Hours' Day, the Shops Act—all that body of factory rules and regulations—they all postulate wages as the basis of industrial life. Not only so, but the cost and burden of this mass of legislation fall upon labour, whilst the economic benefits steadily filter into the pockets of the exploiters. It is the queerest topsy-turvy imaginable. . . . Nominally imposed in the interests of the workman, to dignify and sweeten his life, in reality they are a concession to the queasy stomach of a more fastidious generation that hates to witness brutality but greedily battens upon its profits. It does not like either to kill the animal or see it killed, nor will it do the cooking; it is content to see the meat upon the table in sumptuous surroundings. And it has discovered that the more it regulates every process from the killing to the eating, the better is the flavour of the viands.

How, then, is this evil and oppressive wage system to be destroyed? Assuredly the first step is for labour to realise it as the enemy, and to determine never to deviate from the work of its destruction. It is pathetic and tragical how easily labour does deviate on the slightest pretext. Labour's adventure into politics during the last decade has been an exhausting deviation and an appalling waste of time and nervous energy. The second step is to realise that an economic struggle must necessarily be waged in the industrial sphere. Next, labour must realise that its emancipation can only become possible when it has absorbed every shilling of surplus value. The way to do this is by tireless and unrelenting inroads upon rent and interest. The daily and weekly Socialist bulletins should tell, not of some trivial success at a municipal election, or of some unusually flowery flow of poppycock in Parliament, but of wages so raised that rent-mongers and profiteers find their incomes *pro tanto* reduced. And there is no other way. Profits are in substance nothing but rent. Rent, whatever its form, reduced to its elements, is nothing more and nothing less than the economic power which one man exercises more or less oppressively over another man or body of men. Destroy the power to exact rent and *ipso facto* rent is destroyed. This is the only way of salvation, of emancipation—the only possible release from bondage. . . .

From the death of villeinage, down through the later feudal period, wages obtained, but were profoundly modified by other factors, which disappeared with the advent of the great industry. The workman was then largely, if not completely, master of any process of the manufacture in which he was engaged. Traditionally he was a journeyman for only a period of his life, and had reasonable expectation of dying a master-workman. If his hours were long and his work laborious, at least he enjoyed many social amenities. If his house was darksome or insanitary, at least he was not the victim of slum or quasi-slum life, and his children lived in the sun. They sang and danced, inheriting and transmitting a good physique. We are the last to idealise the conditions of the feudal period; it had its horrors even as to-day. Our point is that the wage system never crystallised under feudalism into a hard-and-fast social régime, binding down the workman to a monotonous round of bare subsistence, varied by periods of unemployment, and ending prematurely in the grave or the workhouse. Economists of every school agree that labour is only a commodity to be bought and sold according to the supply and the demand. And under modern conditions so it is, neither less nor more. The feudal system, unconscious of Adam Smith and his brood, believed that it was something more than a mere commodity; it at least acted as though labour were a human activity of social as well as of economic value and significance. *The influence of the mediæval guilds remained, humanising feudal conceptions of work, which under the large industry became always non-human and often inhuman. . . .*

We expect that some misapprehension exists as to the meaning we attach to wages. "Surely," says one, "wages must always exist in one form or another. What the workman receives, whatever its name, is in substance nothing but wages." It seems necessary, therefore, to make clear precisely the meaning we attach to the wage system. An employer, as he pockets his profits, does not regard them, except jocularly, as wages. He gets his profits out of the wages of his employees. No wages, no profits. In other words, the wage system is the arrangement whereby the capitalist produces his wares and is enabled to sell them at a profit. This means that he must absolutely treat labour as a commodity that enters into the cost of production, buying it precisely as he buys the other requisite ingredients. In Lancashire and Yorkshire it is not uncommon to see a notice: "Power for Sale." Just as the weaver buys this power at the lowest market price, consistent with efficient service, so he buys labour. And just as the production and transmission of power must be efficiently maintained, including all the latest mechanical improvements, so also must human power be maintained, the distance above the subsistence line being the exact analogue to the mechanical improvements in the power supply. Subject, however, to the economy of this margin above subsistence, the essence of the wage system is that labour must be mere material for exploitation, to be purchased in the neighbourhood of bare subsistence just as ore is bought in Spain or cotton in Alabama. Wages is the name given to the price paid for the commodity called Labour. But the political economists are agreed that Labour is a commodity. What of it? We don't care a pinch of snuff. Like Gladstone, we banish political economy to Saturn. We must cease to regard labour as something for which a price must be paid as a mere commodity. The new conception must regard labour as something sanctified by human effort, into which that sacred thing personality has entered. We decline with indignation to count labour as subsidiary to profits, as something on the level with the inanimate. Workmen are not "finished and finite clods untroubled by a spark." Yet so long as they accept the wage system, they bind themselves to the devilish principle that their lives are of less account than dividends, that they are but a part of production for purposes beyond their control and benefit. No wages, no profits. The Socialist line of attack is to kill profiteering by transforming the conception of labour as a commodity into labour as the essence of our industrial life. . . .

Transition from the Wage System.[1] How, then, are we to escape from the slavery of wagedom?

We have had to consider another aspect of this problem in the course of our inquiry. We have found that economic power is the dominant factor in the political sphere; as we have shown, time and time again, economic power precedes political power. Therefore it would be futile to look to the surface play of politics for release. We must resolutely face the necessities of the situation: the battle must be fought in the economic sphere, for where wealth is produced, there and only there are the wage slaves in their true element; there and only there must the great change be effected. If, then, the revolution is to be economic (the political moon subsequently reflecting the light of the economic sun), what material has the wage slave wherewith to fight? He can only control two factors: (*a*) labour power; (*b*) labour organization. He is the absolute possessor of labour power until he sells it for wages; the wages he gets are modified by his capacity for trade organisation. Therefore the struggle must proceed on two parallels: first, the determination, final and considered, never again to sell labour for wages (this determination involves proprietorship of the ultimate products of labour); secondly, the complete organisation of labour upon a footing of industrial war. And anything less than complete organisation spells failure. . . .

Let us confess that the difficulties are stupendous. Let us further confess that these difficulties are mainly in our own ranks. For example, it is apparent that the political Socialists and Labourists are prompt to congratulate themselves every time a strike fails. "Just what we told you," they say, smiling; "the day of the strike is over; you must entrust your affairs to us politicians." Of course strikes are failures. They fail because as yet there is barely a vestige of effective organisation; they fail for want of a true objective. . . .

General Features of the Modern Guild.[2] As its name implies, Guild Socialism is necessarily a work of democratic social reconstruction. It is democracy applied to industry. Herein it differs fundamentally from State Socialism, which leaves to the bureaucrat the task of organising the industrial army without regard to the democratic principle. The term "Guild" implies voluntary organisation and democratic management. Historically considered, this is its true

[1] Pp. 99–100.
[2] Pp. 122–123, 132–137.

connotation. It is because of this tradition that we apply the word "Guild" to that democratic industrial organisation which our inquiry into the wage system has persuaded us is necessary if the future of the British national as well as working community is to be ensured. We have seen how certain it is that if the mass of the population consciously accepts the labour commodity theory and accordingly sells itself for wages, the servile state becomes inevitable. That way lie despair and the denial of every ideal, every hope and every democratic expectation for the future. The future welfare of Great Britain is bound up in its present will-power and capacity so to reorganise itself that it can produce and distribute wealth relieved from the incubus of competitive wages, rent, interest and profits. As we have already proved, the first step is the abolition of the wage system, for it is by means of wages that rent, interest and profits are exacted. But a mere declaration that wages are abolished is obviously absurd, unless an effective and superior substitute for the wage system is forthcoming. That substitute, in its turn, depends upon the coherence of the new organisation. . . .

There is no mystery attaching to the organisation of the Guild. It means the regimentation into a single fellowship of all those who are employed in any given industry. This does not preclude whatever subdivisions may be convenient in the special trades belonging to the main industry. Thus the iron and steel industry may comprise fourteen or fifteen subdivisions, but all living integral parts of the parent Guild. The active principle of the Guild is industrial democracy. Herein it differs from State Socialism or Collectivism. In the one case control comes from without and is essentially bureaucratic; in the other, the Guild manages its own affairs, appoints its own officers from the general manager to the office boy, and deals with the other Guilds and with the State as a self-contained unit. It rejects State bureaucracy; but, on the other hand, it rejects Syndicalism, because it accepts co-management with the State, always, however, subject to the principle of industrial democracy. Co-management must not be held to imply the right of any outside body to interfere in the detailed administration of the Guild; but it rightly implies formal and effective coöperation with the State in regard to large policy, for the simple reason that the policy of a Guild is a public matter, about which the public, as represented by the State, has an indefeasible right to be consulted and considered. It is not easy to understand precisely how far the Syndicalist disregards the State, as such; nor is it necessary to our task that we should make any such inquiry. For ourselves we are clear that the Guilds ought not and must not be the absolute possessors of their land, houses, and machinery. We remain Socialists because we believe that in the final analysis the State, as representing the community at large, must be the final arbiter. We can perhaps make our meaning clear by an analogy. Suppose Ireland, Scotland, and Wales to be self-governing bodies, but all subject to the Imperial Parliament, in which by that time we would expect all the self-governing Colonies to be represented. Assume it to be necessary for the Imperial Parliament to levy contributions upon its constituent units. So many millions would have to be collected from England, so much from Ireland, Scotland, Wales, Canada, South Africa and Australia. The amounts would be agreed upon by a representative Imperial Parliament, but the methods of levying the tax would rest with each self-governing group, who would not tolerate any external interference. In this sense the Guilds would have large communal responsibilities, upon which they must agree with and often defer to the public; but those responsibilities once defined, the industrial democratic Guild, by its own methods and machinery, will do the rest.

We thus are partly in agreement with the State Socialist or Collectivist, who believes in conserving the State organisation and reserving to it certain functions, which we shall hereafter endeavour to define; but we are also in substantial agreement with the Syndicalist, whose real contention, after all, is that the work men do they shall themselves control, being, through their unions, their own economic masters. Nor can we see that Syndicalism reasonably interpreted excludes the possibility of a purified political system concerning itself with the national soul.

But the recognition of State organisation and State functions does not invalidate our main contention that economics must precede politics. On the contrary, it strengthens it. The difficulty with modern statesmanship is that it has to spend its strength on ways and means when it ought to be doing far greater work. It is like a scientist or an artist who is perpetually distracted from his real work by domestic worries. Remove from statesmanship the incubus of financial puzzledom and it may achieve glory in the things that matter. And in all human probability a finer type of politician will be called into activity. Financial considerations corrode politics as effectually as they do the individual worker. Now, if the Guilds are in economic command, if, further, their labours exceed in results the present wage system, it follows that they will not be miserly in devoting all the money that is required for the cultural development of the community. The Syndicalists tell us that the unions can do this better than the State. We are emphatically of opinion that a totally different type of administrator from the industrialist is required for statesmanship. The one type is rightly a master of industrial methods, the other is of disciplined imagination and spiritual perceptions. The fine arts, education (including university control), international relations, justice, public conduct—these and many other problems will call and do call (in vain nowadays) for a special order of intellect, and must be susceptible, not to the particular influence of the Guilds as such, but to the influence of what Arnold called the best mind of the community.

At the outset, the most important task of the Guilds will be the industrial reorganisation of society upon the basis of mutuality: in other words, the abolition of the wage system. This will carry them far. It involves the final solution of unemployment. Every member of the Guild will possess equal rights with all the others, and accordingly will be entitled to maintenance whether working or idle, whether sick or well. Further, it will be for the Guilds to decide, by democratic suffrage, what hours shall be worked and generally the conditions of employment. All that mass of existing legislation imposing factory regulations, or relating to mining conditions, to the limitation of the hours of work (legislation which we have previously described as sumptuary), will go by the board. The Guilds will rightly consider their own convenience and necessities. It may be discovered, for example, that times and conditions suitable to the Engineering Guild will not suit the Agricultural Guild. Legislation attempted from the outside would in such an organisation be regarded as impertinent. Even the existing old age pensions would be laughed to scorn as hopelessly inadequate.

The Guild then would supplant the present capitalist class on the one hand; on the other, it would assume, instead of the State, complete responsibility for the material welfare of its members.

Inheriting the direction of industry from the present private employer and capitalist, the Guild must be able more efficiently to produce wealth and more economically to distribute it. This involves the closest intimacy and coöperation with all the other Guilds. The work of the community could not be done by the Guilds in isolation; each must be in constant and sympathetic touch with the Guilds that supply them and the Guilds that distribute their products. There is no room here for any policy of dog in the manger. The Guild must never be allowed to say: "These things are ours." They must say and think: "We hold this machinery and these products in trust." They must not exist to accumulate property; their moral and legal status must be that of trustee. Thus there must spring out of the Guilds some form of joint management, not only with the other Guilds but with the State.

The abolition of the competitive wage system implied in the organisation of the Guild necessarily carries with it the abolition of all distinctions between the administrative and working departments. It therefore follows that every type and grade of worker, mental or manual, must be a member of the Guild. The technical man, for example, must look to the Guild to give effect to his inventions and improvements, whereas formerly he looked to his employer or even to some outside capitalist. It will be to the interest of all his fellow-members to insist that whatever improvements he may suggest for the increase of production or the decrease of manual toil shall be given a thorough trial. No longer will he be regarded as dangerous to the employees who, as competitive wage slaves, feared that his inventions might mean dismissal and starvation. The essence of Guild life is in its unification of economic interest and purpose.

There can be no doubt that the tendency inside the existing wage system is to level wages. The old distinction between skilled and unskilled is rapidly being dissipated, both by the development of machinery and the economic pressure exerted by foreign competition, and the increased price of money. With this tendency we have no quarrel—on the contrary, we welcome it. But this wage approximation has as yet hardly touched the rent of ability still more or less willingly paid to those in the upper reaches of the administrative hierarchy. That they will finally find their true economic level is certain. Meantime their services are rightly in demand and their remuneration is assured. Even if the process of wage approximation goes much further than we now foresee, it is nevertheless inevitable that graduations of position and pay will be found necessary to efficient Guild administration. We do not shrink from graduated pay; we are not certain that it is not desirable. There will be no inequitable distribution of Guild resources, we may rest assured; democratically controlled organisations seldom err on the side of generosity. But experience will speedily teach the Guilds that they must encourage technical skill by freely offering whatever inducements may at the time most powerfully attract competent men. There are many ways by which invention, organising capacity, statistical aptitude or what not may be suitably rewarded. It is certain that rewarded these qualities must be.

Broadly, then, this is an outline of the Guild as we conceive it. . . .

Occupations Not Suited to Guildism.[1] It is clear, then, that the Guild must be the instrument of emancipation and continuing liberty, and not a new tyranny supplanting the old. Before we can provide for those occupations not amenable to Guild routine let us see what they are.

(i) The profession of ideas, as distinct from the actual production and distribution of concrete wealth. Priests and preachers, artists, craftsmen, journalists, authors would come into this category.

(ii) Inventors.

(iii) Groups devoted to the initiation of new ideas and inventions not yet accepted by their appropriate Guilds.

(iv) Pure scientists and all those who are devoted to original research.

(v) Remaining groups in which the wage system may persist.

We deliberately omit from the foregoing the professions of law and medicine, because these occupations are already Guilds in embryo if not in fact. At a recent medical congress, Dr. R. Rentoul, of Manchester, actually sketched out a Medical Guild on principles precisely similar to those advocated by us, and his proposals appeared to meet with the approval of his colleagues.

(i) Nothing could be more fatal to intellectual liberty and progress than to subject intellectual life to the routine of any human machine. The spirit, like the wind, bloweth where it listeth; to capture it and cage it would be the maddest conceivable enterprise. But we have already transferred from the State to the Guild sick and unemployed benefits as well as old-age pensions. It follows, therefore, that those standing out of Guild organisation are barred from these and other benefits. A man, therefore, who deliberately leaves his Guild to become a priest, preacher, artist, craftsman, or journalist must depend upon voluntary support of some sort for his maintenance. But his appeal is obviously to a much more opulent circle than is possible to-day, when the vast mass of the population is living at the bare subsistence standard. The increase in consumptive capacity of the Guild workers

[1] Pp. 163–165.

means presumably that they may purchase those things they need, amongst which, of course, would be access to ideas, to literature, and to such religious observances as they most desire. They can have, in reason, what they want, because they can give economic effect to their demands. Thus the continuance of the religious congregation is rendered more secure, provided the religious principles enunciated appeal to sufficiently large numbers. The dominance of the prosperous deacon or rich church subscriber gives way to the dominance of an enriched congregation. In like manner, there must certainly be an increased demand for works of art, either the originals or fine reproductions, whilst craftsmanship will be at a premium because improved good taste will call for good work, either in architecture, furniture, fabrics, or what not. It is true that, in this sense, the craftsman may find it advantageous to remain inside his Guild because the demand for his work will be greater inside than outside. But being debarred from the economy of large production, and having only one pair of hands, he may prefer an independent life, relying upon his reputation and skill to secure his financial requirements. Nor do we see any reason why he should not combine independence with affiliation to his Guild. Suppose a young carpenter to develop into a carver of high ability. In his early years he has carved for pleasure or experience, but earning his pay by obedience to the call of his Guild. Gradually his name and fame spread and men give him special commissions—to carve a mantel-shelf, or a chair, or a staircase. What is there to prevent him getting leave of absence from his Guild for a year at a time, but maintaining his membership by paying to the Guild whatever dues may be required for sickness, unemployment, and old age? Such an amount is actuarially easily ascertained. If he finally prefer to go back to the Guild, his vogue having passed, he goes back a valuable man with a valuable experience. In like manner, the preacher may be temporarily released from mission work, in which those interested in the mission maintain him, in due course returning to his Guild and resuming his ordinary occupation. This would probably apply to many Nonconformist sects, but Roman and Anglican priests would probably build up their own voluntary organisations for their maintenance. . . .

Motives under the Guild.[1] Any proposed change in the economic life of a nation inevitably raises a whole category of questions

[1] Pp. 209, 211–215.

as to the motives that move men, particularly in material affairs. It is a rooted belief amongst the generality of people that our human nature and our economic system are chemically combined and incapable of precipitation. It is asserted, with varying degrees of emphasis, that our existing economy is precisely what it is because it is the product of human nature; because it responds with delicate certainty to the motives that vitalise human nature. . . .

Even if human nature does not change, if it persists in all its essentials through the vicissitudes of material and moral upheavals, it by no means follows that as yet we know it in all its fulness. In the stress of physical hunger it may manifest itself in one direction, in the plenitude of wealth in quite another. When we realise the possibilities of human motive, the heights it has reached in adversity, may we not assume that it will blossom into even richer colouring when removed from the strain, the anxiety, of material cares? Shall we not then discover that mankind is only a little lower than the angels, and crowned with glory and honour? The question, then, is not whether human nature changes, but whether under a more humane and economically sounder rearrangement of society, human nature may not develop into a greatness beyond all present anticipation. The case for Guild Socialism is based upon an unchanging faith that man's motives and hopes, freed from the contamination of poverty, will replenish the world with unsuspected richness and variety of wealth and life. . . .

Unless we can be assured that the mass of Guild membership will *con amore* give its utmost skill to the production of Guild wealth, the moral, and therefore the economic, foundation of the Guild will sink. Can we then rely upon the general membership to do its work honestly? Is there a strong and enduring motive to put real value into its products? We answer unhesitatingly in the affirmative. We affirm that there is no such motive under private capitalism, and that the motive of honest production can only be found in coöperative production, from which the labour commodity theory of the wage system has been eliminated. We affirm that the wage system kills the motive inherent in honest production because it dehumanises the human element in labour, reducing it to wage slavery.

Those who have intimate dealings with the workers of Great Britain (doubtless the remark is equally applicable to other countries) know how deeply rooted is the passion to do good work if opportunity serves. It is a miracle and a mercy that modern industrialism has not killed it outright. Kill the craftsmanship of an industrial country, and what remains? Yet to-day, difficult though it be to believe, the vast majority of the manufacturers of Western Europe and America seem to be in a gigantic conspiracy to crush out that very craftsmanship that is the life-blood of their occupation. The reason is simple: mechanical production necessitates intense specialisation, so that to-day a man no longer learns a trade—he is put to a section of it, and there he sticks for the rest of his life. But the workers are by nature gregarious and companionable, so that by exchange of experiences the tradition of each trade is maintained—a tradition that will bloom into human reality when labour ceases to be a non-human commodity and becomes as richly human as it was under the mediæval Guild. Motive! What workman is there who would not sell his soul to become a craftsman? Even to-day the labourer starves himself that he may put his son to some so-called skilled trade.

There are, however, many other motives and aspirations. There is the motive or ambition of the Guild member to rise in the Guild hierarchy and become an administrator. This form of motive to-day has two branches: one man gradually attains foremanship, and graduates into the commercial side of his trade; another man becomes absorbed in trades unionism, and finally plays a more or less prominent part as an official, a delegate, or what not. The organisation of the Guilds will not be complete unless full scope be given to both these types to achieve their appropriate careers. In this connection we see the technical associations indefinitely extending their membership by the admission into their ranks of the actual workers, now their inferiors, but, under the Guilds, their equals and their comrades. Under private capitalism most men are precluded from the satisfaction of these motives; their rightful positions are seized by the blood relations of their employers. But under Guild organisation every private carries a marshal's baton.

It is doubtful, however, whether the majority of mankind regard their means of livelihood as the main concern of life. They would fain work that they may live; wagery compels them to live that they may work. The preoccupations, practical and spiritual, of bare subsistence, benumb faculties and aspirations which are of incalculable value. It is impossible to move amongst even the most poorly paid wage slaves without encountering innumerable signs of genius, of thought, of artistic or literary or religious cravings. We have written it before, but it bears constant repetition: the case for democracy is that it is the inexhaustible well from which the nation draws its resources, human, economic, social, spiritual. All these are comprehended in democracy, and only in democracy. It is the ground out of which fructifies the seed of national life. The case against the wage system is that it starves the ground—"lets it run down," to use an agricultural term. If this be so, does it not follow that any economic reformation of society that gives ample scope to the endlessly varied and kaleidoscopic motives, ambitions and cravings of the mass rather than of the favoured few will best harmonise with motive, enriching that democracy which is the fountain of national life?

It is often contended that the wage slave is almost as lazy and shiftless as the chattel slave; that to maintain wealth production it is therefore necessary to keep the wage slave at the spur point of starvation. "Give them money, and they instantly ease off," we are constantly told in varying terms of contempt. We merely mention the point to show that it has not escaped us; we shall certainly not argue such a foolish proposition. It is not an argument; it is an excuse for sweated wages. It is, of course, true that a man's face may be so ground that he may lose all heart, all resilience, and sink into utter indifference and inertia. But if this be true of the majority of the wage-earners—the majority of the nation—how about the glories of the British Empire? Is it built up on the basis of a thriftless and shiftless proletariat—a proletariat that starts work at six o'clock in the morning, and treads the corn for nine, ten, or eleven hours? The more far-sighted employers, alive to the essential falsity of this conception, have discovered that there is an economy of high wages so scientifically accurate that it destroys the wage-fund theory and resists the law of diminishing returns. It is universally true that acquisition stimulates accumulation—the appetite grows by what it feeds upon. Place a man and his family beyond the reach of urgent want, give him some scope for his faculties, some ease of movement, he instantly becomes a source of national wealth. How often do we hear it said: "If only I were in some measure free from the cursed grind, I could do something worth while." And we implicitly believe it. One of the most appalling aspects of private capitalism is its callous disregard for any kind of genius, skill, or ability which it cannot exploit. Worse! It kills out even the wealth-producing capacities of the workers. . . .

Inter-Guild Relations.[1] As the Guilds gradually shape themselves into their natural economic forms and groupings, it is certain

[1] Pp. 226, 227–228, 230–231.

that many vexed controversies will call for patient and statesmanlike discussion and settlement. . . . Now we do not suggest that these Guilds are all of equal economic strength, and accordingly we may expect dissatisfaction amongst the weaker Guilds when the stronger from time to time impose their wills—that is, in the last resort, exercise their "pull." In what direction, then, can we reasonably anticipate dissatisfaction, followed by strenuous agitation for rectification?

Primarily, we imagine in the value each Guild sets upon its own labour, which may be disputed by the other Guilds. . . . In the earlier stages the more highly skilled industries would insist upon a higher value being attached to their labour than to the labour of the so-called "unskilled" groups. . . .

Fortunately, private capitalism has already evolved a plan which would largely meet the difficulties here cited. When groups of companies have mutual interests as buyers and sellers to each other, to avoid these very complications they take financial holdings in each other and exchange directors. They recognise their inter-dependence and take precautions against disturbing it. In like manner, the Guilds will probably exchange representation upon their several governing bodies, so that each Guild authority may understand, and sympathetically enter into, the difficulties and problems of the others. Nor is there any reason why these Guild ambassadors should not be clothed with large authority to commit their Guilds to proposals that vary existing contracts or understandings. If large changes were proposed, the assent of the other Guilds, through their ambassadors, would be as deliberate as the changes were important. We here hit upon a valuable truth: When bodies between which there is no economic harmony disagree (labour and capital under modern industrialism) such disagreement tends towards disintegration; but disagreements between two or more bodies whose economic interests are fundamentally harmonious, tend towards closer economic integration. Thus dissensions amongst the Guilds would almost certainly create a movement to reduce all such friction to its smallest area, and by good-will on all sides finally to eliminate it. And probably the way to achieve this end would be by closer relations reached through the interchange of Guild ambassadors, whose functions would be precisely those of a national ambassador, who must not only watch the interests of his country but promote closer relations, and, if required, help to smooth out difficulties when they arise elsewhere. The position of Guild representative would obviously be very important—a position to which the best men in the Guild might aspire.

But whilst nine out of every ten disputes between the Guilds would probably be solved by a system of inter-representation, it is quite conceivable that a dissatisfied Guild would carry its discontent considerably further. We have already postulated a supreme governing body of the united Guilds; to this body, in which is vested plenary power, every Guild would have the right to appeal. In the last resort, too, every Guild would have the right to strike, although why they should strike, and against whom, at the moment passes our comprehension. . . .

The Approach to the Guild.[1] We are aware that we have written so explicitly, so confidently, of future developments that we are open to a charge of Utopianism. But there is nothing Utopian in this: it is as certain as a proposition in Euclid. We should, however, prove ourselves pure-blooded Utopians did we conceive it probable, or even possible, that the change from wage slavery to State partnership would be achieved without an intervening period of some form of partnership with existing capitalism. There is no magician's wand to transform at a word wagery into Guild organisation. The process will inevitably be slow: the movement will necessarily be step by step. The obstacles to a swift development are many and great. They are to be found in the subtle strength of capitalism and the inherent weaknesses and inadequacy of labour organisation.

When Labour, finally convinced that the wage system spells perpetual servitude, wills to determine it; when, instead of a multiplicity of sectional strikes aiming at a modification of wagery—higher wages, shorter working days, and the like—Labour organises the industrial struggle on the basis of wage abolition, it is certain that capitalism will strive to save itself by more or less spurious proposals to share profits. But profits can only spring out of the margin between the price paid for labour as a commodity and the exchange value of the finished product, such value being dependent (*a*) upon other industries also maintaining wagery, and (*b*) upon a gold standard imposed by the banks. Therefore, capitalism will seek to bribe Labour to maintain, or at least to continue, the wage system, undertaking as a *quid pro quo* to share such profits as may be made out of the existing commercial methods. It is very doubtful if capitalism will fight upon any

[1] Pp. 236–239.

claim to a fundamental right to engage labour in the competitive wage market, and so keep it permanently enmeshed in wage servitude. The case for Labour's increased share in wealth production is admitted. But the private capitalist has another shot in his locker. He can say to the trade unions that as yet their organisation is imperfect in two important directions. Firstly, they exclude the technical men, the experts, the scientists, all of whom are vitally important factors in wealth production. Secondly, by faulty organisation they also exclude the actual majority of the wage-earners in every trade. How then can the capitalist take into partnership the trade unionists who after all are but a minority, and exclude the other two sections, who form the majority? Nothing easier; he can do it on the principle of "divide and conquer." He can let in the trade unionists by offering special advantages to the trade unionists. But any such advantages are illusory, if the others are kept out. For it is obvious that the excluded wage-earners, the non-unionists, must either be maintained by the triumphant unionists, or, in the alternative, the non-unionists will bear down real wages. Not only so, but the technical men will continue the faithful henchmen of the private capitalist. Thus, unless it is careful, Labour will be lured into a vicious circle—a pretence of partnership, a continuance of disguised wages, rent, interest and profits hardly impaired.

Labour, having grasped the meaning and significance of the wage system, has only learnt its first lesson. When it has mastered its second lesson it will see its way more clearly out of the vicious circle with which capitalism would surround it. This second lesson is that economic emancipation can only come through the elimination of rent, interest and profits. A mere change in the form of remuneration which did not bring in its train a greatly enhanced standard of life would be a mockery and a snare. There is, however, literally no fund from which to draw this increased means of livelihood except from rent, interest and profits. An increase in the cost of production (the inevitable result of extended profit-sharing) would only exacerbate the existing problem of the fall in real wages. There is now no room in modern economy for rent-mongers and profiteers as well as a well-disciplined and self-respecting industrial democracy. Profiteering can only exist by maintaining the wage system. It is also important to remember that economy calls for a decrease and not an increase in the cost of production and distribution. Labour, therefore, is compelled to say to the exploiter: "Friend, either thou or I must go, and I intend to stay. The world can do without thee; it cannot do without me." The admission of Labour, or any section of Labour, into a profit-sharing scheme, which does not at the same time cut deeply into rent, or interest, or profit, would increase the cost of production and solve no problem. But if capitalism can play the game of "divide and conquer," so also can Labour. If the profiteer finds himself squeezed by Labour, will he not, so far as is possible, save his own skin by squeezing rent and the other forms of unearned increment? But the profiteer's natural affiliations are with rent and interest. If, therefore, he can divide and conquer Labour, he will protect his economic associates; if, however, Labour presents an unbroken front, the profiteer, in a *sauve qui peut*, will sacrifice his sleeping partners. After all, they sleep and he is awake; he is industrially more useful than they.

When Labour has thoroughly mastered the first and second lessons of the new economy, its plan of campaign becomes clarified. In accordance with the first lesson, it will strike at the wage system by declining to work for wages—*i.e.*, to sell itself as a commodity. In accordance with its second lesson, it will unitedly proceed to acquire for itself all that surplus value which is at present conveyed ("convey," the wise it call) into the pockets of those who sleep and toil not. To achieve this, it must first reorganise itself. It must call into its councils, by sound material inducements, the brains of the trades—the experts, chemists, managers, salesmen, clerks. It must also bring into its ranks that vast army of unorganised labour that at present drags it down to the bare subsistence level. As in the parable of the wedding feast, it must go out into the highways and hedges and compel them to come in.

In its campaigns for the abolition of the wage system and its ensuing absorption of rent, interest and profits, Labour's first desideratum is an unbroken front—unbroken in its intellectual left flank, unbroken in its disorganised and unskilled right flank. If, however, it can bring its brain and muscle into one organisation, or, to be more precise, into one federation of trade organisations, it will have achieved the form if not the substance of a Guild. In negotiation with the profiteers, it is essential that this unbroken front should be rigidly and at all costs maintained. That is to say, the incipient Guild must not only carry out all negotiations, but *as an organisation* it must receive from the profiteers every penny of value extracted from rent and sleeping capital. *This is supremely important, because the wage system will continue until organised labour receives the share of rent and sleeping capital, not through its individual members, but as an organisation.* The partnership must not be between private capitalism and its individual employees, but between private capitalism and the incipient Guild. . . .

The State and the Guilds.[1] The economies effected in the production and distribution of wealth by the elimination of rent, interest and profits are obviously of incalculable social value, but that value must express itself in citizenship even more than in Guild membership. We have now reached the point where we discover that these two functions may diverge in the affections and person of the worker. As a citizen he may prefer this or that policy; as a Guildsman his business is to concentrate upon wealth production and distribution. For the first time in the history of mankind he will clearly understand that nations, like men, do not live by bread alone. The intermixture of spiritual with economic considerations which now paralyses every State action will be, in form certainly and largely in substance, ended. By transferring the conduct of material affairs to the Guilds (not only wealth production but the responsibility for maintenance in sickness, accident and old age) statesmanship is left free to grapple with its own problems, undisturbed and undeterred by class considerations and unworthy economic pressure. This statement does not invalidate our oft-repeated dictum that economic power dominates political power. No nation will continuously weaken itself economically in the pursuit of a purely political policy—that is, so far as industrial policy can be differentiated from political—but in providing the State exchequer with the equivalent of economic rent (the annual charge for the Guild charters) we secure its independence so far as it can rely upon the support of the working population, acting not as Guildsmen but as citizens. As the Guildsman on due occasion remembers that he is a citizen and has duties apart from his Guild, so also on such occasion will the Guilds also realise that the State has functions and duties that cut clean across all lines of industrial organisation. . . .

The problem, then, of the modern State is to give free play in their appropriate environment to the economic and political forces respectively. We have seen that they do not coalesce; that where they are intermixed, they not only tend to nullify each other, but to adul-

[1] Pp. 255–256, 258–263.

terate those finer passions and ambitions of mankind that ought properly to find expression and satisfaction in the political sphere. It is a quality inherent in private capitalism to dominate and mould State policy to its own ends, precisely as it exploits labour. If the interests of private capitalism were synonymous with those of the community as a whole this danger might be theoretical rather than real. But we know that the assumption of unity of interest between private capitalism and the State degrades the standard of national life and stifles all aspirations towards that spiritual influence which is the true mark of national greatness. But, whilst the separation of the political and economic functions gives equipoise and stability to the State, nevertheless the policy and destiny of the State, in the final analysis, depend upon its economic processes being healthy and equitable. For this reason amongst others, the State, acting in the interests of citizenship as distinct from Guild membership, must be adequately represented upon the governing bodies of the Guilds.

With the achievement of a healthy national economy, the problem of statesmanship will be to transmute the economic power thus obtained into the highest possible social and spiritual voltage. Before we can understand this we must distinguish the two sets of functions. There are those who take a tragically short view of statesmanship. They assert that the organisation of the Guilds (or some similar bodies not as yet defined) suffices: that, once the workers are in complete command of the economic processes, they can manage affairs of State, as though these were a mere item in the activities of the Guild Congress. Let us, then, after allocating every economic activity to the Guilds, consider what remains in the political sphere. Its problems will hinge upon one or other of the following: (i) Law; (ii) Medicine; (iii) The Army, Navy and Police; (iv) Foreign relations; (v) Education; (vi) Central and Local Government and Administration. To these we might add the Church, which, by the way, is a Guild.

(i) Probably no man living can forecast the future of law and the legal profession. It is common knowledge that lawyers are the most securely entrenched trade union in the world. But the most remunerative legal practice is in the protection and administration of private property—chancery work, conveyancing, joint-stock law, patents. In short, wherever the law gives sanction to private exploitation, there will the lawyers be gathered together. The abolition of wagery *ipso facto* abolishes exploitation and so renders nugatory all that vast body of law relating to rent, interest, and profits. In addition, we are surely not romantic in assuming that a large part of criminal practice will also go. We may reasonably assume that crime that springs out of poverty will largely become a memory. Further, such criminality as remains will be treated far more scientifically than to-day. Still more difficult is it to foresee how far the Guilds will govern themselves by standing orders, internal rules and regulations without legal registration. Industrial law to-day mainly relates to master and servant (abolished obviously with wagery), factory laws relating to sanitation, hours of labour, employment of women and young persons, fencing of machinery, and the like (clearly the affair of each Guild), sickness, accident and old age (by hypothesis transferred to the Guilds). It may or may not be that the rights of individual members of the Guild are given legal sanction; on such a point it would be futile to speculate. It is evident, however, that a considerable proportion of existing legal occupations would lapse. But against this we may fairly set the fact that the legal mind has its value in any community, and whilst the demand for it would necessarily change, the legal habit would prove its usefulness. It is to-day customary for large corporations, notably the railways, to keep their own lawyers on the premises, so to speak. Perhaps in this may be seen the germ of the lawyer's future employment. But so far as the State is concerned, it is certain that it will still be concerned with law—law-making and law-administering.

(ii) The practice of medicine differs in many ways from that of the law. It pervades the individual and family life from birth to death. It is true that so also does law, but not in the same intimate sense. It does not depend upon any particular legal interpretation of property; its interests are not bound up with property, but rather with the person. Probably the doctors will be among the first to constitute themselves into a Guild; but as preventive medicine depends for its success both upon law and administration, the Medical Guild will become responsible to the State, and not to the Guild Congress.

(iii) Without discussing the tangled problem of militarism, this at least may be affirmed: the strength and organisation of our military and naval forces are necessarily dependent upon State policy. We may further assume that our wars of aggression in the interests of the profiteers will automatically cease. But there is always the danger that the profiteering elements in States not developed to the Guild stage may force war upon us in their own protection. We do not expect this, because we believe that the way out for other nations threatened by our superior Guild organisation (from which the handicap of rent, interest and profits has been removed), will be to follow our example. Superior economic methods have inevitably won in the long run, whether in civilisation or savagery. It is inherent in human association. So long then as the maintenance of an army and navy be deemed (rightly or wrongly) necessary, and bearing in mind that it is finally determined by State policy, it follows that the State, acting for its citizens, must be the instrument by which that policy is declared.

(iv) Nor can it be doubted that our relations with other nations will become more intimate, more complex, perhaps more difficult than under existing dynastic conditions. In a previous chapter [1] ("International Economy and the Wage System") we have outlined the future of the Consular Service under the Guild organisation of society. Problems of international exchange, backed by State credit, must become the daily work of the consuls, who would be the representatives of the State and through the State of the Guilds. In every consular office, Guild representatives would buy and sell, transforming the value of the labour units (the guilder) into whatever may be the currency of the country in which they are situated. When we remember that our foreign trade exceeds £1,000,000,000 annually we may glimpse the future of our national economic diplomacy. It is not improbable that the Consular Service may be transferred to the existing Board of Trade, whose functions would be so enlarged as to make it the channel of communications between the State and the Guilds. But we must not assume that international exchange will be the only duty of our diplomatic machinery. Endless problems loom up before us even as we write—subject races, tropical medicine, the monstrous problem of the white and yellow races, race intermixture, tribal government, spheres of influence, there is literally no end to them. Again, then, we find in diplomacy one of the most important of State functions. And upon right and informed diplomacy depends in large degree our influence upon the comity of the nations.

(v) The subject of education is too large to be discussed cursorily. A chapter must be devoted to it.

(vi) The administration of central and local government is obviously State business, because it is common not only to all the Guilds as corporations, but to their members as citizens. Central and local policy must be conditioned by the liberality of the budget and the

[1] Omitted here. (Editor.)

spiritual insight of statesmen. We have already argued that the State must be maintained by levying precepts upon the Guilds for the annual amount budgeted. This amount is what we have roughly described as the equivalent of economic rent. Not the least of State duties will be the care of those remnants of the human wastage now thrown upon the scrap-heap by our present industrial system. These unemployable members of society must be regarded as victims and not as criminals. We make no doubt that they will be so regarded by a community socially so cultured as to form Guilds. In regard to local government, it is certain that it must play a large part in providing for the comfort and the amenities of an economically emancipated people. It must be finally subject, not to the Guild Congress, but to Parliament.

It would be easy, of course, to enlarge the list of the functions and duties of the State as distinct from the Guilds. It is only necessary here to mention enough to prove how disastrous it would be to rely only upon the Guilds in the making and administering of the law. We do not forget that many duties are on the borderland between State and Guild. There is, for example, the Postal and Telegraph Service. Are the postal workers properly members of the Civil Service, or are they more naturally in fellowship with the Guilds? Do they really belong to the Transit Guild, or ought they to be kept as a separate service under the command of the Postmaster-General? We would certainly argue that they are civil servants. But if they possess a monopoly of the labor required for this service, it is they and not the Government who will dictate their status.

Broadly stated, these are the reasons for our belief that the State, with its Government, its Parliament, and its civil and military machinery must remain independent of the Guild Congress. Certainly independent; probably even supreme. That will ultimately depend upon the moral powers and cultural capacity of the nation's citizens. Having solved the problem of wealth production, exchange and distribution, we may rest assured that a people thus materially emancipated will move up the spiral of human progress, and that out of that part of this movement will grow a purified political system, in which great statesmanship will play its part. . . .

XXVIII

LEO XIII
1810–1903

There was a hint of romantic radicalism in Leo XIII's ancestry: his mother descended from Cola di Rienzi, a fourteenth-century revolutionist who set up a Roman republic. The republic lasted only for a moment, however, and other experiences of revolution among Leo's ancestors were scarcely more encouraging. During the sixteenth century his father's family were driven out of their native Siena by civil strife. But they took refuge in the states of the Church, and under the protection of the popes found safety and promotion. An uncle of Leo XIII rose to the dignity of Commissary of the Apostolic Chamber and became the confidant of Pius VI. Leo's father held a colonelcy in the army, although he was more occupied with his duties as a magistrate and a paternal lord. Thus Giacchino Pecci (the future Leo XIII) was born at Carpineto in 1810 with all the prestige that rank and official connection could give him. His talents do not seem to have been below his opportunities. At Jesuit schools in Viterbo and Rome he showed great promise in philosophy, chemistry, and mathematics and turned out Latin prose and verse at the age of twelve. He was destined for the priesthood, however, and after taking his doctor's degree in theology at twenty-two, went on to the Academy of Nobles where prospective clergymen of good family were trained for the diplomatic and administrative services of the pope. There he studied Roman and canon law.

A brilliant career for a Pecci seemed assured. His uncle, the papal commissary, had already provided the capital to found a "family prelacy" and the ability of Giacchino himself had won the protection of a cardinal. In 1838, two months after entering the priesthood, Pecci was appointed apostolic delegate at Benevento. He quickly demonstrated that he was a man of action by clearing Benevento of the brigands who infested it in spite of the fact that they were protected by the nobility of the district. In this enterprise his diplomacy was backed by papal troops. Similar posts at Perugia and Spoleto followed and in 1843 Gregory XVI promoted him to the nunciature at Brussels; he picked up French on the way to Belgium.

In Brussels a conflict between the Liberals and the Church over control of education was what chiefly concerned Pecci as a churchman, but he also evinced an interest in the development of railways and gas lighting. In fact the rise of Pecci illustrated the speed of a new age. After three years in Brussels he became, at the age of thirty-six, Archbishop of Perugia, where he remained until his election to the papacy in 1878. Meanwhile, however, he had received the cardinal's hat (1853) and become chamberlain to Pius IX (1877).

Nothing unexpected in the way of social thought or action is discoverable in Pecci's career until a year or so before he became pope. As Archbishop of Perugia he showed zeal in founding colleges, schools, hospitals, and charitable institutions, but a pastoral letter of 1877 in which he criticized child labor and excessive working hours and attacked the current economic doctrine as destructive of morality and human values is the first intimation that he also grasped the newer problems of industrial society.

The practice not only of Pecci but of the papacy itself was reversed when he arrived in Rome. He still showed solicitude for the poor, the orphaned, and the unlettered, but he spoke much more frequently on modern social and political questions. In the twenty-five years of his pontificate (1878–1903) no less than eight encyclicals are enumerated which bore, directly or indirectly and with varying degrees of thoroughness, on such matters. In *Quod Apostolici Muneris* (1878), also known as *Socialism, Communism, Nihilism,* he laid down the general lines of his social-reform policy, denouncing what he considered the destructive aspects of those faiths and looking to religion and labor associations as the cure for social distress. But a more thoroughgoing treatment of the labor question occurred in *Immortale Dei* (1885, *The Christian Constitution of States*) and especially in *Rerum Novarum* (1891, *The Condition of the Working Classes*). The latter appeared four years after the pilgrimage of a group of French workers to Rome with an appeal for a pronouncement in behalf of labor. The document is looked upon as the capstone of Leo's achievement in this field.

For much of his social philosophy Leo XIII went directly to St. Thomas Aquinas. Leo's encyclical *Æterni Patris* (1879) enjoining the study of scholastic philosophy emphasized the importance of St. Thomas, one of whose precepts was that private property is not an absolute right. But Leo was also in touch with the contemporary social Catholic movement in France, Germany, Austria, and Switzerland, and with Catholic action elsewhere. He approved of the American Cardinal Gibbons's defense of the Knights of Labor, a trade union of great influence during the 1880's and '90's which reactionaries had attempted to discredit. He also supported Cardinal Lavigerie's campaign against the African slave trade, contributing 300,000 francs to the cause.

Leo's championship of reform gave the Catholic social movement in all countries a direction, a unity, and most important of all, a sanction which it had lacked up to that time. While he did not revolutionize Catholic thought he at least made it clear that the head as well as the members of Catholicism could adjust and apply the principles of Christianity to the needs of a new age. The negative result of his efforts was only less important. "If to-day," says a recent admirer (with some exaggeration), "the entire world of labor is not socialist, it is the fruit and effect of Leo's action."

REFERENCES

Leo's chief utterances are translated in *The Great Encyclical Letters of Leo XIII* (ed. J. J. Wynn, 1903), and his philosophy is minutely analyzed in Vincenzo Mangano's *Il Pensiero sociale e politico di Leone XIII* (1931). Joseph Husslein's *The Christian Social Manifesto* (1931) is an "interpretative study" of *Rerum Novarum* and of Pius XI's encyclical *Quadragesimo Anno* which restated the papal attitude in social matters.

The fullest biography (professedly an apology) is that of Charles de T'Serclaes (French, 1907). In English the short life by Justin McCarthy (1899) is a temperate account.

Among the works on the Social Catholic movement in general are P. T. Moon's *The Labor Problem and the Social Catholic Movement in France* (1921); G. P. McEntee's *The Social Catholic Movement in England* (1927); and F. Nitti's *Catholic Socialism* (1895).

READINGS FROM

THE CONDITION OF THE WORKING CLASSES[1]

Seriousness of the Labor Question.[2] That the spirit of revolutionary change, which has long been disturbing the nations of the world, should have passed beyond the sphere of politics and made its influence felt in the cognate sphere of practical economics is not sur-

[1] The Latin title is *Rerum Novarum*. This encyclical was issued in 1891.

[2] *The Great Encyclical Letters of Pope Leo XIII*, preface by J. J. Wynn (1903), pp. 208, 209. Copyright by Benziger Brothers, New York.

prising. The elements of the conflict now raging are unmistakable in the vast expansion of industrial pursuits and the marvellous discoveries of science; in the changed relations between masters and workmen; in the enormous fortunes of some few individuals, and the utter poverty of the masses; in the increased self-reliance and closer mutual combination of the working classes; as also, finally, in the prevailing moral degeneracy. The momentous gravity of the state of things now obtaining fills every mind with painful apprehension; wise men are discussing it; practical men are proposing schemes; popular meetings, legislatures, and rulers of nations are all busied with it—and actually there is no question which has taken a deeper hold on the public mind.

Therefore, Venerable Brethren, as on former occasions when it seemed opportune to refute false teaching, We have addressed you in the interests of the Church and of the commonweal, and have issued Letters bearing on "Political Power," "Human Liberty," "The Christian Constitution of the State," and like matters, so have We thought it expedient now to speak on THE CONDITION OF THE WORKING CLASSES. . . .

It is no easy matter to define the relative rights and mutual duties of the rich and of the poor, of capital and of labor. And the danger lies in this, that crafty agitators are intent on making use of these differences of opinion to pervert men's judgments and to stir up the people to revolt.

But all agree, and there can be no question whatever, that some remedy must be found, and found quickly, for the misery and wretchedness pressing so heavily and unjustly at this moment on the vast majority of the working classes.

For the ancient workingmen's guilds were abolished in the last century, and no other organization took their place. Public institutions and the very laws have set aside the ancient religion. Hence by degrees it has come to pass that workingmen have been surrendered, all isolated and helpless, to the hard-heartedness of employers and the greed of unchecked competition. The mischief has been increased by rapacious usury, which, although more than once condemned by the Church, is nevertheless, under a different guise, but with the like injustice, still practised by covetous and grasping men. To this must be added the custom of working by contract, and the concentration of so many branches of trade in the hands of a few individuals; so that a small number of very rich men have been able to lay upon the teeming masses of the laboring poor a yoke little better than that of slavery itself.

Defects of Socialism.[1] To remedy these wrongs the Socialists, working on the poor man's envy of the rich, are striving to do away with private property, and contend that individual possessions should become the common property of all, to be administered by the State or by municipal bodies. They hold that by thus transferring property from private individuals to the community, the present mischievous state of things will be set to rights, inasmuch as each citizen will then get his fair share of whatever there is to enjoy. But their contentions are so clearly powerless to end the controversy that were they carried into effect the workingman himself would be among the first to suffer. They are moreover, emphatically unjust, because they would rob the lawful possessor, bring State action into a sphere not within its competence, and create utter confusion in the community.

It is surely undeniable that, when a man engages in remunerative labor, the impelling reason and motive of his work is to obtain property, and thereafter to hold it as his very own. If one man hires out to another his strength or skill, he does so for the purpose of receiving in return what is necessary for sustenance and education; he therefore expressly intends to acquire a right full and real, not only to the remuneration, but also to the disposal of such remuneration, just as he pleases. Thus, if he lives sparingly, saves money, and, for greater security, invests his savings in land, the land, in such case, is only his wages under another form; and, consequently, a workingman's little estate thus purchased should be as completely at his full disposal as are the wages he receives for his labor. But it is precisely in such power of disposal that ownership obtains, whether the property consist of land or chattels. Socialists, therefore, by endeavoring to transfer the possessions of individuals to the community at large, strike at the interests of every wage-earner, since they would deprive him of the liberty of disposing of his wages, and thereby of all hope and possibility of increasing his stock and of bettering his condition in life.

What is of far greater moment, however, is the fact that the remedy they propose is manifestly against justice. For every man has by nature the right to possess property as his own. This is one of the chief points of distinction between man and the animal creation, for the brute has no power of self-direction, but is governed by two main instincts, which keep his powers on the alert, impel him to develop them in a fitting manner, and stimulate and determine him to

[1] *Ibid.*, pp. 209–216.

action without any power of choice. One of these instincts is self-preservation, the other the propagation of the species. Both can attain their purpose by means of things which lie within range; beyond their verge the brute creation cannot go, for they are moved to action by their senses only, and in the special direction which these suggest. But with man it is wholly different. He possesses, on the one hand, the full perfection of the animal being, and hence enjoys, at least as much as the rest of the animal kind, the fruition of things material. But animal nature, however perfect, is far from representing the human being in its completeness, and is in truth but humanity's humble handmaid, made to serve and to obey. It is the mind, or reason, which is the predominant element in us who are human creatures; it is this which renders a human being human, and distinguishes him essentially and generically from the brute. And on this very account—that man alone among the animal creation is endowed with reason—it must be within his right to possess things not merely for temporary and momentary use, as other living things do, but to have and to hold them in stable and permanent possession; he must have not only things that perish in the use of them, but those also which, though they have been reduced into use, remain his own for further use.

This becomes still more clearly evident if man's nature be considered a little more deeply. For man, fathoming by his faculty of reason matters without number, and linking the future with the present, becoming, furthermore, by taking enlightened forethought, master of his own acts, guides his ways under the eternal law and the power of God, whose providence governs all things. Wherefore it is in his power to exercise his choice not only as to matters that regard his present welfare, but also about those which he deems may be for his advantage in time yet to come. Hence man not only can possess the fruits of the earth, but also the very soil, inasmuch as from the produce of the earth he has to lay by provision for the future. Man's needs do not die out, but recur; although satisfied to-day they demand fresh supplies for to-morrow. Nature accordingly owes to man a storehouse that shall never fail, affording the daily supply for his daily wants. And this he finds solely in the inexhaustible fertility of the earth.

Neither do we, at this stage, need to bring into action the interference of the State. Man precedes the State, and possesses, prior to the formation of any State, the right of providing for the sustenance of his body. Now to affirm that God has given the earth for the use and enjoyment of the whole human race is not to deny that private property is lawful. For God has granted the earth to mankind in general, not in the sense that all without distinction can deal with it as they like, but rather that no part of it has been assigned to any one in particular, and that the limits of private possession have been left to be fixed by man's own industry, and by the laws of individual races. Moreover, the earth, even though apportioned among private owners, ceases not thereby to minister to the needs of all, inasmuch as there is no one who does not sustain life from what the land produces. Those who do not possess the soil, contribute their labor; hence it may truly be said that all human subsistence is derived either from labor on one's own land, or from some toil, some calling which is paid for either in the produce of the land itself, or in that which is exchanged for what the land brings forth.

Here, again, we have further proof that private ownership is in accordance with the law of nature. Truly, that which is required for the preservation of life, and for life's well-being, is produced in great abundance from the soil, but not until man has brought it into cultivation and expended upon it his solicitude and skill. Now, when man thus turns the activity of his mind and the strength of his body towards procuring the fruits of nature, by such act he makes his own that portion of nature's field which he cultivates—that portion on which he leaves, as it were, the impress of his individuality; and it cannot but be just that he should possess that portion as his very own, and have a right to hold it without any one being justified in violating that right.

So strong and convincing are these arguments, that it seems amazing that some should now be setting up anew certain obsolete opinions in opposition to what is here laid down. They assert that it is right for private persons to have the use of the soil and its various fruits, but that it is unjust for any one to possess outright either the land on which he has built, or the estate which he has brought under cultivation. But those who deny these rights do not perceive that they are defrauding man of what his own labor has produced. For the soil which is tilled and cultivated with toil and skill utterly changes its conditions: it was wild before, now it is fruitful; was barren, but now brings forth in abundance. That which has thus altered and improved the land becomes so truly part of itself as to be in great measure indistinguishable and inseparable from it. Is it just that the fruit of a man's own sweat and labor should be possessed and enjoyed by any one else? As effects follow their cause, so is it just and right that the results of labor should belong to those who have bestowed their labor.

With reason, then, the common opinion of mankind, little affected by the few dissentients who have contended for the opposite view, has found in the careful study of nature, and in the laws of nature, the foundations of the division of property, and the practice of all ages has consecrated the principle of private ownership, as being preeminently in conformity with human nature, and as conducing in the most unmistakable manner to the peace and tranquillity of human existence. The same principle is confirmed and enforced by the civil laws—laws which, so long as they are just, derive from the law of nature their binding force. The authority of the divine law adds its sanction, forbidding us in severest terms even to covet that which is another's:—*Thou shalt not covet thy neighbor's wife; nor his house, nor his field, nor his man-servant, nor his maid-servant, nor his ox, nor his ass, nor anything which is his.*

The rights here spoken of, belonging to each individual man, are seen in much stronger light when considered in relation to man's social and domestic obligations. In choosing a state of life, it is indisputable that all are at full liberty to follow the counsel of Jesus Christ as to observing virginity, or to bind themselves by the marriage tie. No human law can abolish the natural and original right of marriage, nor in any way limit the chief and principal purpose of marriage, ordained by God's authority from the beginning: *Increase and multiply.* Hence we have the family; the "society" of a man's house—a society limited indeed in numbers, but no less a true "society," anterior to every kind of State or nation, invested with rights and duties of its own, totally independent of the civil community.

That right of property, therefore, which has been proved to belong naturally to individual persons, must in like wise belong to a man in his capacity of head of a family; nay, such person must possess this right so much the more clearly in proportion as his position multiplies his duties. For it is a most sacred law of nature that a father should provide food and all necessaries for those whom he has begotten; and, similarly, nature dictates that a man's children, who carry on, so to speak, and continue his own personality, should be by him provided with all that is needful to enable them to keep themselves honorably from want and misery amid the uncertainties of this mortal life. Now in no other way can a father effect this except by the ownership of lucrative property, which he can transmit to his children by inheritance. A family, no less than a State, is, as we have said, a true society, governed by a power within its sphere, that is to say, by the father. Provided, therefore, the limits which are prescribed by the very purposes for which it exists be not transgressed, the family has at least equal rights with the State in the choice and pursuit of the things needful to its preservation and its just liberty.

We say, at least equal rights; for inasmuch as the domestic household is antecedent, as well in idea as in fact, to the gathering of men into a community, the family must necessarily have rights and duties which are prior to those of the Community, and founded more immediately in nature. If the citizens of a State—in other words the families—on entering into association and fellowship, were to experience at the hands of the State hindrance instead of help, and were to find their rights attacked instead of being upheld, such association should be held in detestation, rather than be an object of desire.

The contention, then, that the civil government should at its option intrude into and exercise intimate control over the family and the household, is a great and pernicious error. True, if a family finds itself in exceeding distress, utterly deprived of the counsel of friends, and without any prospect of extricating itself, it is right that extreme necessity be met by public aid, since each family is a part of the commonwealth. In like manner, if within the precincts of the household there occur grave disturbance of mutual rights, public authority should intervene to force each party to yield to the other its proper due; for this is not to deprive citizens of their rights, but justly and properly to safeguard and strengthen them. But the rulers of the State must go no further: here nature bids them stop. Paternal authority can be neither abolished nor absorbed by the State; for it has the same source as human life itself. "The child belongs to the father," and is, as it were, the continuation of the father's personality; and, speaking strictly, the child takes its place in civil society, not of its own right, but in its quality as member of the family in which it is born. And for the very reason that "the child belongs to the father," it is, as St. Thomas of Aquin says, "before it attains the use of free-will, under power and charge of its parents." The Socialists, therefore, in setting aside the parent and setting up a State supervision, act *against natural justice*, and break into pieces the stability of all family life.

And not only is such interference unjust, but it is quite certain to harass and worry all classes of citizens, and subject them to odious and intolerable bondage. It would throw open the door to envy, to mutual invective, and to discord; the sources of wealth themselves would run dry, for no one would have any interest in exerting his talents or his industry; and that ideal equality about which they entertain pleasant dreams would be in reality the levelling down of all to a like condition of misery and degradation.

Social Principles of the Church.[1] Hence it is clear that the main tenet of Socialism, community of goods, must be utterly rejected, since it only injures those whom it would seem meant to benefit, is directly contrary to the natural rights of mankind, and would introduce confusion and disorder into the commonweal. The first and most fundamental principle, therefore, if one would undertake to alleviate the condition of the masses, must be the inviolability of private property. This being established, we proceed to show where the remedy sought for must be found.

We approach the subject with confidence, and in the exercise of the rights which manifestly appertain to us, for no practical solution of this question will be found apart from the intervention of Religion and of the Church. It is We who are the chief guardian of Religion and the chief dispenser of what pertains to the Church, and We must not by silence neglect the duty incumbent on Us. Doubtless this most serious question demands the attention and the efforts of others besides ourselves—to wit, of the rulers of States, of employers of labor, of the wealthy, aye, of the working classes themselves, for whom We are pleading. But We affirm without hesitation that all the striving of men will be vain if they leave out the Church. It is the Church that insists, on the authority of the Gospel, upon those teachings whereby the conflict can be brought to an end, or rendered, at least, far less bitter; the Church uses her efforts not only to enlighten the mind but to direct by her precepts the life and conduct of each and all; the Church improves and betters the condition of the workingman by means of numerous useful organizations; does her best to enlist the services of all ranks in discussing and endeavoring to meet, in the most practical way, the claims of the working classes; and acts from the positive view that for these purposes recourse should be had, in due measure and degree, to the intervention of the law and of State authority.

Let it, then, be taken as granted, in the first place, that the condition of things human must be endured, for it is impossible to reduce

[1] *Ibid.*, pp. 216–223.

civil society to one dead level. Socialists may in that intent do their utmost, but all striving against nature is in vain. There naturally exist among mankind manifold differences of the most important kind; people differ in capacity, skill, health, strength; and unequal fortune is a necessary result of unequal condition. Such inequality is far from being disadvantageous either to individuals or to the community. Social and public life can only be maintained by means of various kinds of capacity for business and the playing of many parts; and each man, as a rule, chooses the part which suits his own peculiar domestic condition. As regards bodily labor, even had man never fallen from *the state of innocence*, he would not have remained wholly unoccupied; but that which would then have been his free choice and his delight became afterwards compulsory, and the painful expiation for his disobedience. *Cursed be the earth in thy work; in thy labor thou shalt eat of it all the days of thy life.* In like manner, the other pains and hardships of life will have no end or cessation on earth; for the consequences of sin are bitter and hard to bear, and they must accompany man so long as life lasts. To suffer and to endure, therefore, is the lot of humanity; let them strive as they may, no strength and no artifice will ever succeed in banishing from human life the ills and troubles which beset it. If any there are who pretend differently—who hold out to a hard-pressed people the boon of freedom from pain and trouble, an undisturbed repose, and constant enjoyment—they delude the people and impose upon them, and their lying promises will only one day bring forth evils worse than the present. Nothing is more useful than to look upon the world as it really is—and at the same time to seek elsewhere, as we have said, for the solace to its troubles.

The great mistake made in regard to the matter now under consideration is to take up with the notion that class is naturally hostile to class, and that the wealthy and the workingmen are intended by nature to live in mutual conflict. So irrational and so false is this view, that the direct contrary is the truth. Just as the symmetry of the human frame is the resultant of the disposition of the bodily members, so in a State is it ordained by nature that these two classes should dwell in harmony and agreement, and should, as it were, groove into one another, so as to maintain the balance of the body politic. Each needs the other: Capital cannot do without Labor, nor Labor without Capital. Mutual agreement results in pleasantness of life and the beauty of good order; while perpetual conflict necessarily produces confusion and savage barbarity. Now, in preventing such strife as this, and in uprooting it, the efficacy of Christian institutions is marvellous and manifold. First of all, there is no intermediary more powerful than Religion (whereof the Church is the interpreter and guardian) in drawing the rich, and the poor bread-winners, together, by reminding each class of its duties to the other, and especially of the obligations of justice. Thus Religion teaches the laboring man and the artisan to carry out honestly and fairly all equitable agreements freely entered into; never to injure the property, nor to outrage the person, of an employer; never to resort to violence in defending their own cause, nor to engage in riot or disorder; and to have nothing to do with men of evil principles, who work upon the people with artful promises, and excite foolish hopes which usually end in useless regrets, followed by insolvency. Religion teaches the wealthy owner and the employer that their work-people are not to be accounted their bondsmen; that in every man they must respect his dignity and worth as a man and as a Christian; that labor is not a thing to be ashamed of, if we lend ear to right reason and to Christian philosophy, but is an honorable calling, enabling a man to sustain his life in a way upright and creditable; and that it is shameful and inhuman to treat men like chattels to make money by, or to look upon them merely as so much muscle or physical power. Again, therefore, the Church teaches that, as Religion and things spiritual and mental are among the workingman's main concerns, the employer is bound to see that the worker has time for his religious duties; that he be not exposed to corrupting influences and dangerous occasions; and that he be not led away to neglect his home and family, or to squander his earnings. Furthermore, the employer must never tax his work-people beyond their strength, or employ them in work unsuited to their sex or age. His great and principal duty is to give every one a fair wage. Doubtless, before deciding whether wages are adequate, many things have to be considered; but wealthy owners and all masters of labor should be mindful of this—that to exercise pressure upon the indigent and the destitute for the sake of gain, and to gather one's profit out of the need of another, is condemned by all laws, human and divine. To defraud any one of wages that are his due is a crime which cries to the avenging anger of Heaven. *Behold, the hire of the laborers . . . which by fraud hath been kept back by you, crieth aloud; and the cry of them hath entered into the ears of the Lord of Sabaoth.* Lastly, the rich must religiously refrain from cutting down the workmen's earnings, whether by force, by fraud, or by usurious dealing; and with all the greater reason because the laboring man is, as a rule, weak and unprotected, and because his slender means should in proportion to their scantiness be accounted sacred.

Were these precepts carefully obeyed and followed out, would they not be sufficient of themselves to keep under all strife and all its causes?

But the Church, with Jesus Christ as her Master and Guide, aims higher still. She lays down precepts yet more perfect, and tries to bind class to class in friendliness and good feeling. The things of earth cannot be understood or valued aright without taking into consideration the life to come, the life that will know no death. Exclude the idea of futurity, and forthwith the very notion of what is good and right would perish; nay, the whole scheme of the universe would become a dark and unfathomable mystery. The great truth which we learn from Nature herself is also the grand Christian dogma on which Religion rests as on its foundation—that when we have given up this present life, then shall we really begin to live. God has not created us for the perishable and transitory things of earth, but for things heavenly and everlasting; He has given us this world as a place of exile, and not as our abiding-place. As for riches and the other things which men call good and desirable, whether we have them in abundance, or lack them altogether—so far as eternal happiness is concerned—it matters little; the only important thing is to use them aright. Jesus Christ, when He redeemed us with *plentiful redemption*, took not away the pains and sorrows which in such large proportion are woven together in the web of our mortal life. He transformed them into motives of virtue and occasions of merit: and no man can hope for eternal reward unless he follow in the blood-stained footprints of his Saviour. *If we suffer with Him, we shall also reign with Him.* Christ's labors and sufferings, accepted of His own free-will, have marvellously sweetened all suffering and all labor. And not only by His example, but by His grace and by the hope held forth of everlasting recompense, has He made pain and grief more easy to endure; *for that which is at present momentary and light of our tribulation, worketh for us above measure exceedingly an eternal weight of glory.*

Therefore those whom fortune favors are warned that freedom from sorrow and abundance of earthly riches are no warrant for the bliss that shall never end, but rather are obstacles; that the rich should tremble at the threatenings of Jesus Christ—threatenings so unwonted in the mouth of Our Lord—and that a most strict account must be given to the Supreme Judge for all we possess. The chief and most excellent rule for the right use of money is one which the heathen philosophers hinted at, but which the Church has traced out clearly, and has not only made known to men's minds, but has impressed upon their lives. It rests on the principle that it is one thing to have a right to the possession of money, and another to have a right to use money as one wills. Private ownership, as we have seen, is the natural right of man; and to exercise that right, especially as members of society, is not only lawful, but absolutely necessary. "It is lawful," says St. Thomas of Aquin, "for a man to hold private property; and it is also necessary for the carrying on of human existence." But if the question be asked, How must one's possessions be used? the Church replies without hesitation in the words of the same holy Doctor: "Man should not consider his outward possessions as his own, but as common to all, so as to share them without hesitation when others are in need. Whence the Apostle saith, Command the rich of this world . . . to offer with no stint, to apportion largely." True, no one is commanded to distribute to others that which is required for his own needs and those of his household; nor even to give away what is reasonably required to keep up becomingly his condition in life; "for no one ought to live other than becomingly." But when what necessity demands has been supplied, and one's standing fairly taken thought for, it becomes a duty to give to the indigent out of what remains over. *Of that which remaineth, give alms.* It is a duty, not of justice (save in extreme cases), but of Christian charity—a duty not enforced by human law. But the laws and judgments of men must yield place to the laws and judgments of Christ the true God, who in many ways urges on His followers the practice of alms-giving—*It is more blessed to give than to receive;* and who will count a kindness done or refused to the poor as done or refused to Himself—*As long as you did it to one of My least brethren, you did it to Me.* To sum up, then, what has been said: Whoever has received from the divine bounty a large share of temporal blessings, whether they be external and corporeal, or gifts of the mind, has received them for the purpose of using them for the perfecting of his own nature, and, at the same time, that he may employ them, as the steward of God's providence, for the benefit of others. "He that hath a talent," says St. Gregory the Great, "let him see that he hide it not; he that hath abundance, let him quicken himself to mercy and generosity; he that hath art and skill, let him do his best to share the use and the utility thereof with his neighbor.". . .

Practical Contributions of the Church.[1] But the Church, not content with pointing out the remedy, also applies it. For the Church does her utmost to teach and to train men, and to educate them; and by the intermediary of her bishops and clergy diffuses her salutary teachings far and wide. She strives to influence the mind and the heart so that all may willingly yield themselves to be formed and guided by the commandments of God. It is precisely in this fundamental and momentous matter, on which everything depends, that the Church possesses a power peculiarly her own. The agencies which she employs are given to her by Jesus Christ Himself for the very purpose of reaching the hearts of men, and derive their efficiency from God. They alone can reach the innermost heart and conscience, and bring men to act from a motive of duty, to resist their passions and appetites, to love God and their fellow-men with a love that is singular and supreme, and to break down courageously every barrier which impedes the way of a life of virtue. . . .

The Church, moreover, intervenes directly in behalf of the poor by setting on foot and maintaining many associations which she knows to be efficient for the relief of poverty. Herein again she has always succeeded so well as to have even extorted the praise of her enemies. Such was the ardor of brotherly love among the earliest Christians that numbers of those who were in better circumstances despoiled themselves of their possessions in order to relieve their brethren; whence *neither was there any one needy among them.* To the order of Deacons, instituted in that very intent, was committed by the apostles the charge of the daily doles; and the Apostle Paul, though burdened with the solicitude of all the churches, hesitated not to undertake laborious journeys in order to carry the alms of the faithful to the poorer Christians. Tertullian calls these contributions, given voluntarily by Christians in their assemblies, deposits of piety; because, to cite his own words, they were employed "in feeding the needy, in burying them, in the support of youths and maidens destitute of means and deprived of their parents, in the care of the aged, and the relief of the shipwrecked."

Thus by degrees came into existence the patrimony which the Church has guarded with religious care as the inheritance of the poor. Nay, to spare them the shame of begging, the common mother of rich and poor has exerted herself to gather together funds for the support of the needy. The Church has aroused everywhere the hero-

[1] *Ibid.*, pp. 224, 226–227.

ism of charity, and has established congregations of religious and many other useful institutions for help and mercy, so that hardly any kind of suffering could exist which was not afforded relief. At the present day many there are who, like the heathen of old, seek to blame and condemn the Church for such eminent charity. They would substitute in its stead a system of relief organized by the State. But no human expedients will ever make up for the devotedness and self-sacrifice of Christian charity. Charity, as a virtue, pertains to the Church; for virtue it is not, unless it be drawn from the Sacred Heart of Jesus Christ; and whosoever turns his back on the Church cannot be near to Christ.

The Function of the State.[1] It cannot, however, be doubted that to attain the purpose we are treating of, not only the Church but all human agencies must concur. All who are concerned in the matter should be of one mind and according to their ability act together. It is with this, as with the Providence that governs the world: the results of causes do not usually take place save where all the causes coöperate.

It is sufficient, therefore, to inquire what part the State should play in the work of remedy and relief. . . .

As regards the State, the interests of all, whether high or low, are equal. The poor are members of the national community equally with the rich; they are real component living members which constitute, through the family, the living body; and it need hardly be said that they are in every State very largely in the majority. It would be irrational to neglect one portion of the citizens and favor another; and, therefore, the public administration must duly and solicitously provide for the welfare and the comfort of the working classes; otherwise that law of justice will be violated which ordains that each man shall have his due. To cite the wise words of St. Thomas of Aquin: "As the part and the whole are in a certain sense identical, the part may in some sense claim what belongs to the whole." Among the many and grave duties of rulers who would do their best for the people, the first and chief is to act with strict justice—with that justice which is called by the schoolmen *distributive*—towards each and every class alike.

But although all citizens, without exception, can and ought to contribute to that common good in which individuals share so advantageously to themselves, yet it should not be supposed that all

[1] *Ibid.*, pp. 227, 228–231, 234–235, 235–237.

can contribute in the like way and to the same extent. No matter what changes may occur in forms of government, there will ever be differences and inequalities of condition in the State. Society cannot exist or be conceived of without them. Some there must be who devote themselves to the work of the commonwealth, who make the laws or administer justice, or whose advice and authority govern the nation in times of peace and defend it in war. Such men clearly occupy the foremost place in the State, and should be held in highest estimation, for their work concerns most nearly and effectively the general interests of the community. Those who labor at a trade or calling do not promote the general welfare in such measure as this; but they benefit the nation, if less directly, in a most important manner. Still we have insisted that, since the end of society is to make men better, the chief good that society can possess is virtue. Nevertheless, in all well-constituted States it is in no wise a matter of small moment to provide those bodily and external commodities *the use of which is necessary to virtuous action.* And in order to provide such material well-being, the labor of the poor—the exercise of their skill, and the employment of their strength, in the culture of the land and in the workshops of trade—is of great account and quite indispensable. Indeed, their coöperation is in this respect so important that it may be truly said that it is only by the labor of workingmen that States grow rich. Justice, therefore, demands that the interests of the poorer classes should be carefully watched over by the administration, so that they who contribute so largely to the advantage of the community may themselves share in the benefits which they create—that being housed, clothed, and enabled to sustain life, they may find their existence less hard and more endurable. It follows that whatever shall appear to prove conducive to the well-being of those who work should obtain favorable consideration. Let it not be feared that solicitude of this kind will be harmful to any interest; on the contrary, it will be to the advantage of all; for it cannot but be good for the commonwealth to shield from misery those on whom it so largely depends.

We have said that the State must not absorb the individual or the family; both should be allowed free and untrammelled action so far as is consistent with the common good and the interests of others. Rulers should, nevertheless, anxiously safeguard the community and all its members: the community, because the conservation thereof is so emphatically the business of the supreme power that the safety of the commonwealth is not only the first law, but it is a government's whole reason of existence; and the members, because both philosophy and the Gospel concur in laying down that the object of the government of the State should be, not the advantage of the ruler, but the benefit of those over whom he is placed. The gift of authority derives from God, and is, as it were, a participation in the highest of all sovereignties; and should be exercised as the power of God is exercised—with a fatherly solicitude which not only guides the whole but reaches also to details.

Whenever the general interest or any particular class suffers, or is threatened with mischief which can in no other way be met or prevented, the public authority must step in to deal with it. Now, it interests the public, as well as the individual, that peace and good order should be maintained; that family life should be carried on in accordance with God's laws and those of nature; that religion should be reverenced and obeyed; that a high standard of morality should prevail, both in public and private life; that the sanctity of justice should be respected, and that no one should injure another with impunity; that the members of the commonwealth should grow up to man's estate strong and robust, and capable, if need be, of guarding and defending their country. If by a strike, or other combination of workmen, there should be imminent danger of disturbance to the public peace; or if circumstances were such as that among the laboring population the ties of family life were relaxed; if religion were found to suffer through the operatives not having time and opportunity afforded them to practise its duties; if in workshops and factories there were danger to morals through the mixing of the sexes or from other harmful occasions of evil; or if employers laid burdens upon their workmen which were unjust, or degraded them with conditions repugnant to their dignity as human beings; finally, if health were endangered by excessive labor, or by work unsuited to sex or age—in such cases, there can be no question but that, within certain limits, it would be right to invoke the aid and authority of the law. The limits must be determined by the nature of the occasion which calls for the law's interference—the principle being that the law must not undertake more, nor proceed further, than is required for the remedy of the evil or the removal of the mischief.

Rights must be religiously respected wherever they exist; and it is the duty of the public authority to prevent and to punish injury, and to protect every one in the possession of his own. Still, when there is a question of defending the rights of individuals, the poor and helpless have a claim to especial consideration. The richer class have many ways of shielding themselves, and stand less in need of help from the State; whereas those who are badly off have no resources of their own to fall back upon, and must chiefly depend upon the assistance of the State. And it is for this reason that wage-earners, who are undoubtedly among the weak and necessitous, should be specially cared for and protected by the Government. . . .

It is neither just nor human so to grind men down with excessive labor as to stupefy their minds and wear out their bodies. Man's powers, like his general nature, are limited, and beyond these limits he cannot go. His strength is developed and increased by use and exercise, but only on condition of due intermission and proper rest. Daily labor, therefore, should be so regulated as not to be protracted over longer hours than strength admits. How many and how long the intervals of rest should be must depend on the nature of the work, on circumstances of time and place, and on the health and strength of the workmen. Those who work in mines and quarries, and extract coal, stone, and metals from the bowels of the earth, should have shorter hours in proportion as their labor is more severe and trying to health. Then, again, the season of the year should be taken into account; for not infrequently a kind of labor is easy at one time which at another is intolerable or exceedingly difficult. Finally, work which is quite suitable for a strong man cannot reasonably be required from a woman or a child. And, in regard to children, great care should be taken not to place them in workshops and factories until their bodies and minds are sufficiently developed. For just as very rough weather destroys the buds of spring, so does too early an experience of life's hard toil blight the young promise of a child's faculties, and render any true education impossible. Women, again, are not suited for certain occupations; a woman is by nature fitted for home work, and it is that which is best adapted at once to preserve her modesty and to promote the good bringing up of children and the well-being of the family. As a general principle it may be laid down that a workman ought to have leisure and rest proportionate to the wear and tear of his strength; for waste of strength must be repaired by cessation from hard work. . . .

We now approach a subject of great and urgent importance, and one in respect of which, if extremes are to be avoided, right notions are absolutely necessary. Wages, as we are told, are regulated by free consent, and therefore the employer, when he pays what was agreed upon, has done his part and seemingly is not called upon to do anything beyond. . . .

This mode of reasoning is, to a fair-minded man, by no means convincing, for there are important considerations which it leaves out of account altogether. To labor is to exert one's self for the sake of procuring what is necessary for the purposes of life, and chief of all for self-preservation. *In the sweat of thy brow thou shalt eat thy bread.* Hence a man's labor bears two notes or characters. First of all, it is *personal*, inasmuch as the exertion of individual strength belongs to the individual who puts it forth, employing such strength to procure that personal advantage on account of which it was bestowed. Secondly, man's labor is *necessary;* for without the result of labor a man cannot live; and self-preservation is a law of nature, which it is wrong to disobey. Now, were we to consider labor so far as it is *personal* merely, doubtless it would be within the workman's right to accept any rate of wages whatsoever; for in the same way as he is free to work or not, so is he free to accept a small remuneration or even none at all. But this is a mere abstract supposition; the labor of the workingman is not only his personal attribute, but it is *necessary;* and this makes all the difference. The preservation of life is the bounden duty of one and all, and to be wanting therein is a crime. It follows that each one has a right to procure what is required in order to live; and the poor can procure it in no other way than through work and wages.

Let it be then taken for granted that workman and employer should, as a rule, make free agreements, and in particular should agree freely as to the wages; nevertheless, there underlies a dictate of natural justice more imperious and ancient than any bargain between man and man, namely, that remuneration ought to be sufficient to support a frugal and well-behaved wage-earner. If through necessity or fear of a worse evil the workman accept harder conditions because an employer or contractor will afford him no better, he is made the victim of force and injustice. In these and similar questions, however—such as, for example, the hours of labor in different trades, the sanitary precautions to be observed in factories and workshops, etc.—in order to supersede undue interference on the part of the State, especially as circumstances, times, and localities differ so widely, it is advisable that recourse be had to societies or boards such as We shall mention presently, or to some other mode of safeguarding the interests of the wage-earners; the State being appealed to, should circumstances require, for its sanction and protection.

If a workman's wages be sufficient to enable him to maintain himself, his wife, and his children in reasonable comfort, he will not find it difficult, if he be a sensible man, to study economy; and he will not fail, by cutting down expenses, to put by some little savings and thus secure a small income. Nature and reason alike would urge him to this. We have seen that this great labor question cannot be solved save by assuming as a principle that private ownership must be held sacred and inviolable. The law, therefore, should favor ownership, and its policy should be to induce as many as possible of the humbler class to become owners.

Many excellent results will follow from this; and first of all, property will certainly become more equitably divided. For the result of civil change and revolution has been to divide society into two widely differing castes. On the one side there is the party which holds power because it holds wealth; which has in its grasp the whole of labor and trade; which manipulates for its own benefit and its own purposes all the sources of supply, and which is even represented in the councils of the State itself. On the other side there is the needy and powerless multitude, broken down and suffering, and ever ready for disturbance. If working-people can be encouraged to look forward to obtaining a share in the land, the consequence will be that the gulf between vast wealth and sheer poverty will be bridged over, and the respective classes will be brought nearer to one another. . . .

Associations for Mutual Help.[1] In the last place — employers and workmen may of themselves effect much in the matter we are treating, by means of such associations and organizations as afford opportune aid to those who are in distress, and which draw the two classes more closely together. Among these may be enumerated societies for mutual help; various benevolent foundations established by private persons to provide for the workman, and for his widow or his orphans, in case of sudden calamity, in sickness, and in the event of death; and what are called "patronages," or institutions for the care of boys and girls, for young people, as well as homes for the aged.

The most important of all are workingmen's unions; for these virtually include all the rest. History attests what excellent results

[1] *Ibid.*, pp. 238–239, 241–242, 243–244, 244–245, 247.

were brought about by the artificers' guilds of olden times. They were the means of affording not only many advantages to the workmen, but in no small degree of promoting the advancement of art, as numerous monuments remain to bear witness. Such unions should be suited to the requirements of this our age—an age of wider education, of different habits, and of far more numerous requirements in daily life. It is gratifying to know that there are actually in existence not a few associations of this nature, consisting either of workmen alone, or of workmen and employers together; but it were greatly to be desired that they should become more numerous and more efficient. . . .

Associations of every kind, and especially those of workingmen, are now far more common than heretofore. As regards many of these there is no need at present to inquire whence they spring, what are their objects, or what the means they employ. There is a good deal of evidence, however, which goes to prove that many of these societies are in the hands of secret leaders, and are managed on principles ill-according with Christianity and the public well-being; and that they do their utmost to get within their grasp the whole field of labor, and force workingmen either to join them or to starve. Under these circumstances Christian workingmen must do one of two things: either join associations in which their religion will be exposed to peril, or form associations among themselves—unite their forces and shake off courageously the yoke of so unrighteous and intolerable an oppression. No one who does not wish to expose man's chief good to extreme risk will for a moment hesitate to say that the second alternative should by all means be adopted. . . .

To sum up, then, We may lay it down as a general and lasting law, that workingmen's associations should be so organized and governed as to furnish the best and most suitable means of attaining what is aimed at; that is to say, for helping each individual member to better his condition to the utmost in body, mind, and property. It is clear that they must pay special and chief attention to the duties of religion and morality, and that their internal discipline must be guided very strictly by these weighty considerations; otherwise they would lose wholly their special character, and end by becoming little better than those societies which take no account whatever of religion. . . .

The foundations of the organization being thus laid in religion, We next proceed to make clear the relations of the members one to another, in order that they may live together in concord and go forward prosperously and with good results. The offices and charges of the society should be apportioned for the good of the society itself, and in such mode that difference in degree or standing should not interfere with unanimity and good-will. Office-bearers should be appointed with due prudence and discretion, and each one's charge should be carefully mapped out. Hereby no member will suffer injury. Let the common funds be administered with strict honesty, in such a way that a member may receive assistance in proportion to his necessities. The rights and duties of the employers, as compared with the rights and duties of the employed, ought to be the subject of careful consideration. Should it happen that either a master or a workman believe himself injured, nothing would be more desirable than that a committee should be appointed composed of reliable and capable members of the association, whose duty would be, conformably with the rules of the association, to settle the dispute. Among the several purposes of a society one should be to try to arrange for a continuous supply of work at all times and seasons, as well as to create a fund out of which the members may be effectually helped in their needs, not only in cases of accident but also in sickness, old age, and distress. . . .

We have now laid before you, Venerable Brethren, both who are the persons and what are the means whereby this most arduous question must be solved. Every one should put his hand to the work which falls to his share, and that at once and straightway, lest the evil which is already so great become through delay absolutely beyond remedy. Those who rule the State should avail them of the laws and institutions of the country; masters and wealthy owners must be mindful of their duty; the poor, whose interests are at stake, should make every lawful and proper effort; and since religion alone, as We said at the beginning, can avail to destroy the evil at its root, all men should rest persuaded that the main thing needful is to return to real Christianity, apart from which all the plans and devices of the wisest will prove of little avail. . . .

PART VIII

FASCISM

XXIX

ALFREDO ROCCO

1875–

The figure of Mussolini so dominates the Italian scene that his colleagues in the establishment of fascism have gone into more or less complete eclipse. It is easily forgotten that fascism is the outcome of movements in Italian politics which were under way long before Mussolini assumed his commanding rôle and that some of their leaders are now largely responsible for carrying the new scheme into execution. Yet when one seeks a concise and reasoned statement of fascist theory and aims, one finds it, not in the pronunciamentos of the Duce, but in the works of these less glittering colleagues. Undoubtedly one of the most influential of them is Alfredo Rocco.

Rocco was born at Naples in 1875. He chose an academic career and at the age of twenty-four became a member of the faculty of the University of Urbino where he taught commercial law. In the following years he occupied posts successively at the universities of Macerata, Palermo, Padua, and Rome, teaching various legal subjects and for a time specializing in labor legislation.

Rocco entered the journalistic field while still very young and shortly before the World War became an outstanding propagandist of nationalism. In a series of articles published in 1913 he scrutinized the condition of public life and the state of the leading Italian parties. The same year he officially joined the nationalist movement. In 1914 at the Nationalist Congress held in Milan he presented an economic program which ran directly counter to the Liberal doctrine. Rocco, in fact, became largely responsible for the party's policy of nationalism in economics and finance.

In 1914 a conflict raged in Italy over the question of entering the war. At Padua Rocco founded *National Duty*, an organ of militant nationalism and an advocate of intervention. When the country finally gave in to the interventionists in 1915, Rocco volunteered for war service and was attached to the First Army. A war cross was bestowed upon him for meritorious conduct in the field.

After the armistice of 1918 Rocco again took up the struggle against socialism and assisted in founding *Politics*, which was designed to stimulate public interest in foreign affairs. Three years later he was elected to the Chamber of Deputies. His speeches were extremely nationalistic in tone and he opposed "every kind of democratic régime and every subversive movement leading to disunion." Rocco, like others of the nationalist group, was influenced by the doctrines of Charles Maurras and Georges Sorel.

After Mussolini's famous march on Rome in 1922, Rocco worked for a fusion between the nationalists and fascists; he was rewarded by being appointed under-secretary of the Treasury and then of Pensions. In 1924 he was elected president of the Chamber of Deputies, but the next year he returned to the government as Minister of Justice. The appointment was an appropriate one: as a teacher of law and author of numerous legal treatises he was recognized as an authority on the subject.

His function since then has been to translate fascist doctrines into juridical forms. Thus his hand is seen in many of the great statutes of the corporate state, especially those governing the organization of industry, and Mussolini has entrusted him with the supervision of a general reform of the legal codes. It has been said that of all the fascist politicians Rocco is "perhaps the most intimately connected with the supposedly constructive reforms of the fascist state." One of the most interesting of these is the system of syndicates, corporations, and confederations of industry and the professions, in which workers and employers, separately or in concert, endeavor to promote their respective interests and to reconcile their differences. Over all the state presides as a final arbiter. The syndicates also have a political function, being charged with nominating candidates for parliament. It is claimed that a representation more in harmony with modern economic arrangements is thus secured.

REFERENCES

Rocco's scholarly and propagandist writings are voluminous but it is believed that his speech at Perugia, almost all of which is printed below, is the only fragment translated into English.

Rocco's writings are briefly examined in Ennio Ronchi's *Alfredo Rocco* (Italian, 1931) which also contains a few details as to his career. Other biographical facts are given in the Italian *Who's Who* (*Chi è*).

On fascism in general see J. S. Barnes, *Fascism* (1931); H. W. Schneider, *Making the Fascist State* (1928) and *Making Fascists* (1929); G. S. Counts, Luigi Villari, and M. C. Rorty, *Bolshevism, Fascism and Capitalism* (1932). A study of the new industrial régime is given in "The Italian Corporate State," by Carmen Haider (*Political Science Quarterly*, June, 1931).

READINGS FROM

THE POLITICAL DOCTRINE OF FASCISM[1]

Fascism as Action, as Feeling, and as Thought

Much has been said, and is now being said for or against this complex political and social phenomenon which in the brief period of six years has taken complete hold of Italian life and, spreading beyond the borders of the Kingdom, has made itself felt in varying degrees of intensity throughout the world. But people have been much more eager to extol or to deplore than to understand—which is natural enough in a period of tumultuous fervor and of political passion. The time has not yet arrived for a dispassionate judgment. For even I, who noticed the very first manifestations of this great development, saw its significance from the start and participated directly in its first doings, carefully watching all its early uncertain and changing developments, even I do not feel competent to pass definite judgment. Fascism is so large a part of myself that it would be both arbitrary and absurd for me to try to dissociate my personality from it, to submit it to impartial scrutiny in order to evaluate it coldly and accurately. What can be done, however, and it seldom is attempted, is to make inquiry into the phenomenon which shall not merely consider its fragmentary and adventitious aspects, but strive to get at its inner essence. . . .

First of all let us ask ourselves if there is a political doctrine of Fascism; if there is any ideal content in the Fascist state. For in order to link Fascism, both as concept and system, with the history of Italian thought and find therein a place for it, we must first show that it is thought; that it is a doctrine. Many persons are not quite convinced that it is either the one or the other; and I am not referring solely to those men, cultured or uncultured, as the case may be and very numerous everywhere, who can discern in this political innovation nothing except its local and personal aspects, and who know Fascism only as the particular manner of behavior of this or that well-known Fascist, of this or that group of a certain town; who therefore like or dislike the movement on the basis of their likes and dislikes for the individuals who represent it. Nor do I refer to those intelligent and cultivated persons, very intelligent indeed and very

[1] A speech delivered at Perugia, 30 August, 1925, and endorsed by Mussolini. Translated by Dino Bigongiari and reprinted from International Conciliation Pamphlet No. 223 published by the Carnegie Endowment for International Peace.

cultivated, who because of their direct or indirect allegiance to the parties that have been dispossessed by the advent of Fascism, have a natural cause of resentment against it and are therefore unable to see, in the blindness of hatred, anything good in it. I am referring rather to those—and there are many in our ranks too—who know Fascism as action and feeling but not yet as thought, who therefore have an intuition but no comprehension of it.

It is true that Fascism is, above all, action and sentiment and that such it must continue to be. Were it otherwise, it could not keep up that immense driving force, that renovating power which it now possesses and would merely be the solitary meditation of a chosen few. Only because it is feeling and sentiment, only because it is the unconscious reawakening of our profound racial instinct, has it the force to stir the soul of the people, and to set free an irresistible current of national will. Only because it is action, and as such actualizes itself in a vast organization and in a huge movement, has it the conditions for determining the historical course of contemporary Italy.

But Fascism is thought as well and it has a theory, which is an essential part of this historical phenomenon, and which is responsible in a great measure for the successes that have been achieved. To the existence of this ideal content of Fascism, to the truth of this Fascist logic we ascribe the fact that though we commit many errors of detail, we very seldom go astray on fundamentals, whereas all the parties of the opposition, deprived as they are of an informing, animating principle, of a unique directing concept, do very often wage their war faultlessly in minor tactics, better trained as they are in parliamentary and journalistic manoeuvres, but they constantly break down on the important issues. Fascism, moreover, considered as action, is a typically Italian phenomenon and acquires a universal validity because of the existence of this coherent and organic doctrine. The originality of Fascism is due in great part to the autonomy of its theoretical principles. For even when, in its external behavior and in its conclusions, it seems identical with other political creeds, in reality it possesses an inner originality due to the new spirit which animates it and to an entirely different theoretical approach.

Common Origins and Common Background of Modern Political Doctrines; from Liberalism to Socialism

Modern political thought remained, until recently, both in Italy and outside of Italy under the absolute control of those doctrines which, proceeding from the Protestant Reformation and developed by the adepts of natural law in the 17th and 18th centuries, were firmly grounded in the institutions and customs of the English, of the American, and of the French Revolutions. Under different and sometimes clashing forms these doctrines have left a determining imprint upon all theories and actions both social and political, of the 19th and 20th centuries down to the rise of Fascism. The common basis of all these doctrines, which stretch from Languet, from Buchanan, and from Althusius down to Karl Marx, to Wilson and to Lenin is a social and state concept which I shall call mechanical or atomistic.

Society according to this concept is merely a sum total of individuals, a plurality which breaks up into its single components. Therefore the ends of a society, so considered, are nothing more than the ends of the individuals which compose it and for whose sake it exists. An atomistic view of this kind is also necessarily anti-historical, inasmuch as it considers society in its spatial attributes and not in its temporal ones; and because it reduces social life to the existence of a single generation. Society becomes thus a sum of determined individuals, viz., the generation living at a given moment. This doctrine which I call atomistic and which appears to be anti-historical, reveals from under a concealing cloak a strongly materialistic nature. For in its endeavors to isolate the present from the past and the future, it rejects the spiritual inheritance of ideas and sentiments which each generation receives from those preceding and hands down to the following generation thus destroying the unity and the spiritual life itself of human society.

This common basis shows the close logical connection existing between all political doctrines; the substantial solidarity, which unites all the political movements, from Liberalism to Socialism, that until recently have dominated Europe. For these political schools differ from one another in their methods, but all agree as to the ends to be achieved. All of them consider the welfare and happiness of individuals to be the goal of society, itself considered as composed of individuals of the present generation. All of them see in society and in its juridical organization, the state, the mere instrument and means whereby individuals can attain their ends. They differ only in that the methods pursued for the attainment of these ends vary considerably one from the other.

Thus the Liberals insist that the best manner to secure the welfare of the citizens as individuals is to interfere as little as possible with the free development of their activities and that therefore the essential task of the state is merely to coördinate these several liberties in such a way as to guarantee their coexistence. Kant, who was without doubt the most powerful and thorough philosopher of liberalism, said, "man, who is the end, cannot be assumed to have the value of an instrument." And again "justice, of which the state is the specific organ, is the condition whereby the freedom of each is conditioned upon the freedom of others, according to the general law of liberty."

Having thus defined the task of the state, Liberalism confines itself to the demand of certain guarantees which are to keep the state from overstepping its functions as general coördinator of liberties and from sacrificing the freedom of individuals more than is absolutely necessary for the accomplishment of its purpose. All the efforts are therefore directed to see to it that the ruler, mandatory of all and entrusted with the realization, through and by liberty, of the harmonious happiness of everybody, should never be clothed with undue power. Hence the creation of a system of checks and limitations designed to keep the rulers within bounds; and among these, first and foremost, the principle of the division of powers, contrived as a means for weakening the state in its relation to the individual, by making it impossible for the state ever to appear, in its dealings with citizens, in the full plenitude of sovereign powers; also the principle of the participation of citizens in the lawmaking power, as a means for securing, in behalf of the individual, a direct check on this, the strongest branch, and an indirect check on the entire government of the state. This system of checks and limitations, which goes by the name of constitutional government resulted in a moderate and measured liberalism. The checking power was exercised only by those citizens who were deemed worthy and capable, with the result that a small élite was made to represent legally the entire body politic for whose benefit this régime was instituted.

It was evident, however, that this moderate system, being fundamentally illogical and in contradiction with the very principles from which it proceeded, would soon become the object of serious criticism. For if the object of society and of the state is the welfare of individuals, severally considered, how is it possible to admit that this welfare can be secured by the individuals themselves only through the possibilities of such a liberal régime? The inequalities brought about both by nature and by social organizations are so numerous and so serious, that, for the greater part, individuals abandoned to themselves not only would fail to attain happiness, but would also contribute to the perpetuation of their condition of misery and dejection. The state therefore cannot limit itself to the merely negative function of the defense of liberty. It must become active, in behalf of everybody, for the welfare of the people. It must intervene, when necessary, in order to improve the material, intellectual, and moral conditions of the masses; it must find work for the unemployed, instruct and educate the people, and care for health and hygiene. For if the purpose of society and of the state is the welfare of individuals, and if it is just that these individuals themselves control the attainment of their ends, it becomes difficult to understand why Liberalism should not go the whole distance, why it should see fit to distinguish certain individuals from the rest of the mass, and why the functions of the people should be restricted to the exercise of a mere check. Therefore the state, if it exists for all, must be governed by all, and not by a small minority: if the state is for the people, sovereignty must reside in the people: if all individuals have the right to govern the state, liberty is no longer sufficient; equality must be added: and if sovereignty is vested in the people, the people must wield all sovereignty and not merely a part of it. The power to check and curb the government is not sufficient. The people must be the government. Thus, logically developed, Liberalism leads to Democracy, for Democracy contains the promises of Liberalism but oversteps its limitations in that it makes the action of the state positive, proclaims the equality of all citizens through the dogma of popular sovereignty. Democracy therefore necessarily implies a republican form of government even though at times, for reasons of expediency, it temporarily adjusts itself to a monarchical régime.

Once started on this downward grade of logical deductions it was inevitable that this atomistic theory of state and society should pass on to a more advanced position. Great industrial developments and the existence of a huge mass of working men, as yet badly treated and in a condition of semi-servitude, pushed the labor problem violently to the fore. Social inequalities, possibly endurable in a régime of domestic industry, became intolerable after the industrial revolution. Hence a state of affairs which towards the middle of the last century appeared to be both cruel and threatening. It was therefore natural that the following question should be raised: "If the state is created for the welfare of its citizens, severally considered, how can it tolerate an economic system which divides the population into a small minority of exploiters, the capitalists, on one side, and an immense multitude of exploited, the working people, on the other?" No! The state must again intervene and give rise to a different and less iniquitous economic organization, by abolishing private property, by assuming direct control of all production, and by organizing it in such a way that the products of labor be distributed solely among those who create them, viz., the working classes. Hence we find Socialism, with its new economic organization of society, abolishing private ownership of capital and of the instruments and means of production, socializing the product, suppressing the extra profit of capital, and turning over to the working class the entire output of the productive processes. It is evident that Socialism contains and surpasses Democracy in the same way that Democracy comprises and surpasses Liberalism, being a more advanced development of the same fundamental concept. Socialism in its turn generates the still more extreme doctrine of Bolshevism which demands the violent suppression of the holders of capital, the dictatorship of the proletariat, as means for a fairer economic organization of society and for the rescue of the laboring classes from capitalistic exploitation.

Thus Liberalism, Democracy, and Socialism, appear to be, as they are in reality, not only the offspring of one and the same theory of government, but also logical derivations one of the other. Logically developed Liberalism leads to Democracy; the logical development of Democracy issues into Socialism. It is true that for many years, and with some justification, Socialism was looked upon as antithetical to Liberalism. But the antithesis is purely relative and breaks down as we approach the common origin and foundation of the two doctrines, for we find that the opposition is one of method, not of purpose. The end is the same for both, viz., the welfare of the individual members of society. The difference lies in the fact that Liberalism would be guided to its goal by liberty, whereas Socialism strives to attain it by the collective organization of production. There is therefore no antithesis nor even a divergence as to the nature and scope of the state and the relation of individuals to society. There is only a difference of evaluation of the means for bringing about these ends and establishing these relations, which difference depends entirely on the different economic conditions which prevailed at the time when the various doctrines were formulated. Liberalism arose and began to thrive in the period of small industry; Socialism grew with the rise of industrialism and of world-wide capitalism. The dissension therefore between these two points of view, or the antithesis, if we wish so to call it, is limited to the economic field. Socialism is at odds with Liberalism only on the question of the organization of production and of the division of wealth. In religious, intellectual, and moral matters it is liberal, as it is liberal and democratic in its politics. Even the anti-liberalism and anti-democracy of Bolshevism are in themselves purely contingent. For Bolshevism is opposed to Liberalism only in so far as the former is revolutionary, not in its socialistic aspect. For if the opposition of the Bolsheviki to liberal and democratic doctrines were to continue, as now seems more and more probable, the result might be a complete break between Bolshevism and Socialism notwithstanding the fact that the ultimate aims of both are identical.

Fascism as an Integral Doctrine of Sociality Antithetical to the Atomism of Liberal, Democratic, and Socialistic Theories

The true antithesis, not to this or that manifestation of the liberal-democratic-socialistic conception of the state but to the concept itself, is to be found in the doctrine of Fascism. For while the disagreement between Liberalism and Democracy, and between Liberalism and Socialism lies in a difference of method, as we have said, the rift between Socialism, Democracy, and Liberalism on one side and Fascism on the other is caused by a difference in concept. As a matter of fact, Fascism never raises the question of methods, using in its political praxis now liberal ways, now democratic means and at times even socialistic devices. This indifference to method often exposes Fascism to the charge of incoherence on the part of superficial observers, who do not see that what counts with us is the end and that therefore even when we employ the same means we act with a radically different spiritual attitude and strive for entirely different results. The Fascist concept then of the nation, of the scope of the state, and of the relations obtaining between society and its individual components, rejects entirely the doctrine which I said proceeded from the theories of natural law developed in the course of the 16th, 17th, and 18th centuries and which form the basis of the liberal, democratic, and socialistic ideology.

I shall not try here to expound this doctrine but shall limit myself to a brief résumé of its fundamental concepts.

Man—the political animal—according to the definition of Aristotle, lives and must live in society. A human being outside the pale of society is an inconceivable thing—a non-man. Humankind in its entirety lives in social groups that are still, today, very numerous and diverse, varying in importance and organization from the tribes of Central Africa to the great Western Empires. These various societies are fractions of the human species each one of them endowed with a unified organization. And as there is no unique organization of the human species, there is not "one" but there are "several" human societies. Humanity therefore exists solely as a biological concept not as a social one.

Each society on the other hand exists in the unity of both its biological and its social contents. Socially considered it is a fraction of the human species endowed with unity of organization for the attainment of the peculiar ends of the species.

This definition brings out all the elements of the social phenomenon and not merely those relating to the preservation and perpetuation of the species. For man is not solely matter; and the ends of the human species, far from being the materialistic ones we have in common with other animals, are, rather, and predominantly, the spiritual finalities which are peculiar to man and which every form of society strives to attain as well as its stage of social development allows. Thus the organization of every social group is more or less pervaded by the spiritual influxes of: unity of language, of culture, of religion, of tradition, of customs, and in general of feeling and of volition, which are as essential as the material elements: unity of economic interests, of living conditions, and of territory. The definition given above demonstrates another truth, which has been ignored by the political doctrines that for the last four centuries have been the foundations of political systems, viz., that the social concept has a biological aspect, because social groups are fractions of the human species, each one possessing a peculiar organization, a particular rank in the development of civilization with certain needs and appropriate ends, in short, a life which is really its own. If social groups are then fractions of the human species, they must possess the same fundamental traits of the human species, which means that they must be considered as a succession of generations and not as a collection of individuals.

It is evident therefore that as the human species is not the total of the living human beings of the world, so the various social groups which compose it are not the sum of the several individuals which at a given moment belong to it, but rather the infinite series of the past, present, and future generations constituting it. And as the ends of the human species are not those of the several individuals living at a certain moment, being occasionally in direct opposition to them, so the ends of the various social groups are not necessarily those of the individuals that belong to the groups but may even possibly be in conflict with such ends, as one sees clearly whenever the preservation and the development of the species demand the sacrifice of the individual, to wit, in times of war.

Fascism replaces therefore the old atomistic and mechanical state theory which was at the basis of the liberal and democratic doctrines with an organic and historic concept. When I say organic I do not wish to convey the impression that I consider society as an organism after the manner of the so-called "organic theories of the state"; but rather to indicate that the social groups as fractions of the species receive thereby a life and scope which transcend the scope and life of the individuals identifying themselves with the history and finalities of the uninterrupted series of generations. It is irrelevant in this connection to determine whether social groups, considered as fractions of the species, constitute organisms. The important thing is to ascertain that this organic concept of the state gives to society a continuous life over and beyond the existence of the several individuals.

The relations therefore between state and citizens are completely reversed by the Fascist doctrine. Instead of the liberal-democratic formula, "society for the individual," we have, "individuals for society" with this difference however: that while the liberal doctrines eliminated society, Fascism does not submerge the individual in the social group. It subordinates him, but does not eliminate him; the individual as a part of his generation ever remaining an element of society however transient and insignificant he may be. Moreover the development of individuals in each generation, when coördinated and harmonized, conditions the development and prosperity of the entire social unit.

At this juncture the antithesis between the two theories must appear complete and absolute. Liberalism, Democracy, and Socialism look upon social groups as aggregates of living individuals; for Fascism they are the recapitulating unity of the indefinite series of generations. For Liberalism, society has no purposes other than those of the members living at a given moment. For Fascism, society has historical and immanent ends of preservation, expansion, improvement, quite distinct from those of the individuals which at a given moment compose it; so distinct in fact that they may even be in opposition. Hence the necessity, for which the older doctrines make little allowance, of sacrifice, even up to the total immolation of individuals, in behalf of society; hence the true explanation of war, eternal law of mankind, interpreted by the liberal-democratic doctrines as a degenerate absurdity or as a maddened monstrosity.

For Liberalism, society has no life distinct from the life of the individuals, or as the phrase goes: solvitur in singularitates. For Fascism, the life of society overlaps the existence of individuals and projects itself into the succeeding generations through centuries and millennia. Individuals come into being, grow, and die, followed by others, unceasingly; social unity remains always identical to itself. For Liberalism, the individual is the end and society the means; nor is it conceivable that the individual, considered in the dignity of an ultimate finality, be lowered to mere instrumentality. For Fascism, society is the end, individuals the means, and its whole life consists in using individuals as instruments for its social ends. The state therefore guards and protects the welfare and development of individuals not for their exclusive interest, but because of the identity of the needs of individuals with those of society as a whole. We can thus accept and explain institutions and practices, which like the death penalty, are condemned by Liberalism in the name of the preëminence of individualism.

The fundamental problem of society in the old doctrines is the question of the rights of individuals. It may be the right to freedom as the Liberals would have it; or the right to the government of the commonwealth as the Democrats claim it, or the right to economic justice as the Socialists contend; but in every case it is the right of individuals, or groups of individuals (classes). Fascism on the other hand faces squarely the problem of the right of the state and of the duty of individuals. Individual rights are only recognized in so far as they are implied in the rights of the state. In this preëminence of duty we find the highest ethical value of Fascism.

The Problems of Liberty, of Government, and of Social Justice in the Political Doctrine of Fascism

This, however, does not mean that the problems raised by the other schools are ignored by Fascism. It means simply that it faces them and solves them differently, as, for example, the problem of liberty.

There is a Liberal theory of freedom, and there is a Fascist concept of liberty. For we, too, maintain the necessity of safeguarding the conditions that make for the free development of the individual; we, too, believe that the oppression of individual personality can find no place in the modern state. We do not, however, accept a bill of rights which tends to make the individual superior to the state and to empower him to act in opposition to society. Our concept of liberty is that the individual must be allowed to develop his personality in behalf of the state, for these ephemeral and infinitesimal elements of the complex and permanent life of society determine by their normal growth the development of the state. But this individual growth must be normal. A huge and disproportionate development of the individual, of classes, would prove as fatal to society as abnormal growths are to living organisms. Freedom therefore is due to the citizen and to classes on condition that they exercise it in the interest of society as a whole and within the limits set by social exigencies, liberty being, like any other individual right, a concession of the state. What I say concerning civil liberties applies to economic freedom as well. Fascism does not look upon the doctrine of economic liberty as an absolute dogma. It does not refer economic problems to individual needs, to individual interest, to individual solutions. On the contrary it considers the economic development, and especially the production of wealth, as an eminently social concern, wealth being for society an essential element of power and prosperity. But Fascism maintains that in the ordinary run of events economic liberty serves the social purposes best; that it is profitable to entrust to individual initiative the task of economic development both as to production and as to distribution; that in the economic world individual ambition is the most effective means for obtaining the best social results with the least effort. Therefore, on the question also of economic liberty the Fascists differ fundamentally from the Liberals; the latter see in liberty a principle, the Fascists accept it as a method. By the Liberals, freedom is recognized in the interest of the citizens; the Fascists grant it in the interest of society. In other terms, Fascists make of the individual an economic instrument for the advancement of society, an instrument which they use so long as it functions and which they subordinate when no longer serviceable. In this guise Fascism solves the eternal problem of economic freedom and of state interference, considering both as mere methods which may or may not be employed in accordance with the social needs of the moment.

What I have said concerning political and economic Liberalism applies also to Democracy. The latter envisages fundamentally the problem of sovereignty; Fascism does also, but in an entirely different manner. Democracy vests sovereignty in the people, that is to say, in the mass of human beings. Fascism discovers sovereignty to be inherent in society when it is juridically organized as a state. Democracy therefore turns over the government of the state to the multitude of living men that they may use it to further their own interests; Fascism insists that the government be entrusted to men capable of rising above their own private interests and of realizing the aspirations of the social collectivity, considered in its unity and in its relation to the past and future. Fascism therefore not only rejects the dogma of popular sovereignty and substitutes for it that of state sovereignty, but it also proclaims that the great mass of citizens is not a suitable advocate of social interests for the reason that the capacity to ignore individual private interests in favor of the higher demands of society and of history is a very rare gift and the privilege of the chosen few. Natural intelligence and cultural preparation are of great service in such tasks. Still more valuable perhaps is the intuitiveness of rare great minds, their traditionalism and their inherited qualities. This must not however be construed to mean that the masses are not to be allowed to exercise any influence on the life of the state. On the contrary, among peoples with a great history and with noble traditions, even the lowest elements of society possess an instinctive discernment of what is necessary for the welfare of the race, which in moments of great historical crises reveals itself to be almost infallible. It is therefore as wise to afford to this instinct the means of declaring itself as it is judicious to entrust the normal control of the commonwealth to a selected élite.

As for Socialism, the Fascist doctrine frankly recognizes that the problem raised by it as to the relations between capital and labor is a very serious one, perhaps the central one of modern life. What Fascism does not countenance is the collectivistic solution proposed by the Socialists. The chief defect of the socialistic method has been clearly demonstrated by the experience of the last few years. It does not take into account human nature, it is therefore outside of reality, in that it will not recognize that the most powerful spring of human activities lies in individual self-interest and that therefore the elimination from the economic field of this interest results in complete paralysis. The suppression of private ownership of capital carries with it the suppression of capital itself, for capital is formed by savings and no one will want to save, but will rather consume all he makes if he knows he cannot keep and hand down to his heirs the results of his labors. The dispersion of capital means the end of production since capital, no matter who owns it, is always an indispensable tool of production. Collective organization of production is followed therefore by the paralysis of production since, by eliminating from the productive mechanism the incentive of individual interest, the product becomes rarer and more costly. Socialism then, as experience has shown, leads to increase in consumption, to the dispersion of capital and therefore to poverty. Of what avail is it, then, to build a social machine which will more justly distribute wealth if this very wealth is destroyed by the construction of this machine? Socialism committed an irreparable error when it made of private property a matter of justice while in truth it is a problem of social utility. The recognition of individual property rights, then, is a part of the Fascist doctrine not because of its individual bearing but because of its social utility.

We must reject, therefore, the socialistic solution but we cannot allow the problem raised by the Socialists to remain unsolved, not only because justice demands a solution but also because the persistence of this problem in liberal and democratic régimes has been a menace to public order and to the authority of the state. Unlimited and unrestrained class self-defense, evinced by strikes and lockouts, by boycotts and sabotage, leads inevitably to anarchy. The Fascist doctrine, enacting justice among the classes in compliance with a fundamental necessity of modern life, does away with class self-defense, which, like individual self-defense in the days of barbarism, is a source of disorder and of civil war.

Having reduced the problem to these terms, only one solution is possible, the realization of justice among the classes by and through the state. Centuries ago the state, as the specific organ of justice, abolished personal self-defense in individual controversies and substituted for it state justice. The time has now come when class self-defense also must be replaced by state justice. To facilitate the change Fascism has created its own syndicalism. The suppression of class self-defense does not mean the suppression of class defense which is an inalienable necessity of modern economic life. Class organization is a fact which cannot be ignored but it must be controlled, disciplined, and subordinated by the state. The syndicate, instead of being, as formerly, an organ of extra-legal defense, must be turned into an organ of legal defense which will become judicial defense as soon as labor conflicts become a matter of judicial settlement. Fascism therefore has transformed the syndicate, that old revolutionary instrument of syndicalistic socialists, into an instrument of legal defense of the classes both within and without the law courts. This solution may encounter obstacles in its development; the obstacles of malevolence, of suspicion of the untried, of erroneous calculation, etc., but it is destined to triumph even though it must advance through progressive stages.

Historical Value of the Doctrine of Fascism

I might carry this analysis farther but what I have already said is sufficient to show that the rise of a Fascist ideology already gives evidence of an upheaval in the intellectual field as powerful as the change that was brought about in the 17th and 18th centuries by the rise and diffusion of those doctrines of ius naturale which go under the name of "Philosophy of the French Revolution." The philosophy of the French Revolution formulated certain principles, the authority of which, unquestioned for a century and a half, seemed so final that they were given the attribute of immortality. The influence of these principles was so great that they determined the formation of a new culture, of a new civilization. Likewise the fervor of the ideas that go to make up the Fascist doctrine, now in its inception but destined to spread rapidly, will determine the course of a new culture and of a new conception of civil life. The deliverance of the individual from the state carried out in the 18th century will be followed in the 20th century by the rescue of the state from the individual. The period of authority, of social obligations, of "hierarchical" subordination will succeed the period of individualism, of state feebleness, of insubordination.

This innovating trend is not and cannot be a return to the Middle Ages. It is a common but an erroneous belief that the movement, started by the Reformation and heightened by the French Revolution, was directed against mediaeval ideas and institutions. Rather than as a negation, this movement should be looked upon as the development and fulfillment of the doctrines and practices of the Middle Ages. Socially and politically considered the Middle Ages wrought disintegration and anarchy; they were characterized by the gradual weakening and ultimate extinction of the state, embodied in the Roman Empire, driven first to the East, then back to France, thence to Germany, a shadow of its former self; they were marked by the steady advance of the forces of usurpation, destructive of the state and reciprocally obnoxious; they bore the imprints of a triumphant particularism. Therefore the individualistic and anti-social movement of the 17th and 18th centuries was not directed against the Middle Ages, but rather against the restoration of the state by great national monarchies. If this movement destroyed mediaeval institutions that had survived the Middle Ages and had been grafted upon the new states, it was in consequence of the struggle primarily waged against the state. The spirit of the movement was decidedly mediaeval. The novelty consisted in the social surroundings in which it operated and in its relation to new economic developments. The individualism of the feudal lords, the particularism of the cities and of the corporations had been replaced by the individualism and the particularism of the bourgeoisie and of the popular classes.

The Fascist ideology cannot therefore look back to the Middle Ages, of which it is a complete negation. The Middle Ages spell disintegration; Fascism is nothing if not sociality. It is if anything the beginning of the end of the Middle Ages prolonged four centuries beyond the end ordinarily set for them and revived by the social democratic anarchy of the past thirty years. If Fascism can be said to look back at all it is rather in the direction of ancient Rome whose social and political traditions at the distance of fifteen centuries are being revived by Fascist Italy.

I am fully aware that the value of Fascism, as an intellectual movement, baffles the minds of many of its followers and supporters and is denied outright by its enemies. There is no malice in this denial, as I see it, but rather an incapacity to comprehend. The liberal-democratic-socialistic ideology has so completely and for so long a time dominated Italian culture that in the minds of the majority of people trained by it, it has assumed the value of an absolute truth, almost the authority of a natural law. Every faculty of self-criticism is suppressed in the minds and this suppression entails an incapacity for understanding that time alone can change. It will be advisable therefore to rely mainly upon the new generations and in general upon persons whose culture is not already fixed. This difficulty to comprehend on the part of those who have been thoroughly grounded by a different preparation in the political and social sciences explains in part why Fascism has not been wholly successful with the intellectual classes and with mature minds, and why on the other hand it has been very successful with young people, with women, in rural districts, and among men of action unencumbered by a fixed and set social and political education. Fascism moreover, as a cultural movement, is just now taking its first steps. As is the case with all great movements, action regularly outstrips thought. It was thus at the time of the Protestant Reformation and of the individualistic reaction of the 17th and 18th centuries. The English revolution occurred when the doctrines of natural law were coming into being and the theoretical development of the liberal and democratic theories followed the French Revolution.

At this point it will not be very difficult to assign a fitting place in history to this great trend of thought which is called Fascism and which, in spite of the initial difficulties, already gives clear indication of the magnitude of its developments.

The liberal-democratic speculation both in its origin and in the manner of its development appears to be essentially a non-Italian formation. Its connection with the Middle Ages already shows it to be foreign to the Latin mind, the mediaeval disintegration being the result of the triumph of Germanic individualism over the political mentality of the Romans. The barbarians, boring from within and hacking from without, pulled down the great political structure raised by Latin genius and put nothing in its place. Anarchy lasted eight centuries during which time only one institution survived and that a Roman one—the Catholic Church. But, as soon as the laborious process of reconstruction was started with the constitution of the great national states backed by the Roman Church the Protestant Reformation set in followed by the individualistic currents of the 17th and 18th centuries, and the process of disintegration was started anew. This anti-state tendency was the expression of the Germanic spirit and it therefore became predominant among the Germanic peoples and wherever Germanism had left a deep imprint even if afterward superficially covered by a veneer of Latin culture. It is true that Marsilius of Padua is an Italian writing for Ludwig the Bavarian, but the other writers who in the 14th century appear as forerunners of the liberal doctrines are not Italians: Occam and Wycliff are English; Oresme is French. Among the advocates of individualism in the 16th century who prepared the way for the triumph of the doctrines of natural law in the subsequent centuries, Hotman and

Languet are French, Buchanan is Scotch. Of the great authorities of natural law, Grotius and Spinoza are Dutch; Locke is English; l'Abbé de St. Pierre, Montesquieu, d'Argenson, Voltaire, Rousseau, Diderot and the encyclopaedists are French; Althusius, Pufendorf, Kant, Fichte are German.

Italy took no part in the rise and development of the doctrines of natural law. Only in the 19th century did she evince a tardy interest in these doctrines, just as she tardily contributed to them at the close of the 18th century through the works of Beccaria and Filangieri.

While therefore in other countries such as France, England, Germany, and Holland, the general tradition in the social and political sciences worked in behalf of anti-state individualism, and therefore of liberal and democratic doctrines, Italy, on the other hand, clung to the powerful legacy of its past in virtue of which she proclaims the rights of the state, the preëminence of its authority, and the superiority of its ends. The very fact that the Italian political doctrine in the Middle Ages linked itself with the great political writers of antiquity, Plato and Aristotle, who in a different manner but with an equal firmness advocated a strong state and the subordination of individuals to it, is a sufficient index of the orientation of political philosophy in Italy. We all know how thorough and crushing the authority of Aristotle was in the Middle Ages. But for Aristotle the spiritual cement of the state is "virtue," not absolute virtue but political virtue, which is social devotion. His state is made up solely of its citizens, the citizens being either those who defend it with their arms or who govern it as magistrates. All others who provide it with the materials and services it needs are not citizens. They become such only in the corrupt forms of certain democracies. Society is therefore divided into two classes, the free men or citizens who give their time to noble and virtuous occupations and who profess their subjection to the state, and the laborers and slaves who work for the maintenance of the former. No man in this scheme is his own master. The slaves belong to the freemen, and the freemen belong to the state.

It was therefore natural that St. Thomas Aquinas the greatest political writer of the Middle Ages should emphasize the necessity of unity in the political field, the harm of plurality of rulers, the dangers and damaging effects of demagogy. . . .

Italy in the Middle Ages presented a curious phenomenon: while in practice the authority of the state was being dissolved into a multiplicity of competing sovereignties, the theory of state unity and authority was kept alive in the minds of thinkers by the memories of the Roman Imperial tradition. It was this memory that supported for centuries the fiction of the universal Roman Empire when in reality it existed no longer. . . .

The Roman tradition, which was one of practice but not of theories —for Rome constructed the most solid state known to history with extraordinary statesmanship but with hardly any political writings—influenced considerably the founder of modern political science, Nicolo Machiavelli, who was himself in truth not a creator of doctrines but a keen observer of human nature who derived from the study of history practical maxims of political import. He freed the science of politics from the formalism of the scholastics and brought it close to concrete reality. His writings, an inexhaustible mine of practical remarks and precious observations, reveal dominant in him the state idea, no longer abstract but in the full historical concreteness of the national unity of Italy. Machiavelli therefore is not only the greatest of modern political writers, he is also the greatest of our countrymen in full possession of a national Italian consciousness. To liberate Italy, which was in his day "enslaved, torn and pillaged," and to make her more powerful, he would use any means, for to his mind the holiness of the end justified them completely. In this he was sharply rebuked by foreigners who were not as hostile to his means as they were fearful of the end which he propounded. He advocated therefore the constitution of a strong Italian state, supported by the sacrifices and by the blood of the citizens, not defended by mercenary troops; well-ordered internally, aggressive and bent on expansion. . . . Machiavelli was not only a great political authority, he taught the mastery of energy and will. Fascism learns from him not only its doctrines but its action as well.

Different from Machiavelli's, in mental attitude, in cultural preparation, and in manner of presentation, G. B. Vico must yet be connected with the great Florentine from whom in a certain way he seems to proceed. In the heyday of "natural law" Vico is decidedly opposed to ius naturale and in his attacks against its advocates, Grotius, Selden and Pufendorf, he systematically assails the abstract, rationalistic, and utilitarian principles of the 18th century. As Montemayor justly says: "While the 'natural jurists', basing justice and state on utility and interest and grounding human certitude on reason, were striving to draft permanent codes and construct the perfect state, Vico strongly asserted the social nature of man, the ethical character of the juridical consciousness and its growth through the history of humanity rather than in sacred history. Vico therefore maintains that doctrines must begin with those subjects which take up and explain the entire course of civilization. Experience and not ratiocination, history and not reason must help human wisdom to understand the civil and political régimes which were the result not of reason or philosophy, but rather of common sense, or if you will of the social consciousness of man" and farther on, "to Vico we owe the conception of history in its fullest sense as magistra vitae, the search after the humanity of history, the principle which makes the truth progress with time, the discovery of the political 'course' of nations. It is Vico who uttered the eulogy of the patrician 'heroic hearts' of the 'patres patriae', first founders of states, magnanimous defenders of the commonwealth and wise counsellors of politics. To Vico we owe the criticism of democracies, the affirmation of their brief existence, of their rapid disintegration at the hands of factions and demagogues, of their lapse first into anarchy, then into monarchy, when their degradation does not make them a prey of foreign oppressors. Vico conceived of civil liberty as subjection to law, as just subordination of the private to the public interests, to the sway of the state. It was Vico who sketched modern society as a world of nations each one guarding its own imperium, fighting just and not inhuman wars. In Vico therefore we find the condemnation of pacifism, the assertion that right is actualized by bodily force, that without force, right is of no avail, and that therefore 'qui ab iniuriis se tueri non potest servus est.'" [He who cannot protect himself from injuries is a slave.]

It is not difficult to discern the analogies between these affirmations and the fundamental views and the spirit of Fascism. Nor should we marvel at this similarity. Fascism, a strictly Italian phenomenon, has its roots in the Risorgimento and the Risorgimento was influenced undoubtedly by Vico.

It would be inexact to affirm that the philosophy of Vico dominated the Risorgimento. Too many elements of German, French, and English civilizations had been added to our culture during the first half of the 19th century to make this possible, so much so that perhaps Vico might have remained unknown to the makers of Italian unity if another powerful mind from Southern Italy, Vincenzo Cuoco, had not taken it upon himself to expound the philosophy of Vico in those very days in which the intellectual preparation of the Risorgimento was being carried on. . . .

The influence of Cuoco, an exile at Milan, exerted through his writings, his newspaper articles, and Vichian propaganda, on the Italian patriots is universally recognized. Among the regular readers of his *Giornale Italiano* we find Monti and Foscolo. Clippings of his articles were treasured by Mazzini and Manzoni, who often acted as his secretary, called him his "master in politics."

The influence of the Italian tradition summed up and handed down by Cuoco was felt by Mazzini whose interpretation of the function of the citizen as duty and mission is to be connected with Vico's doctrine rather than with the philosophic and political doctrines of the French Revolution.

"Training for social duty," said Mazzini, "is essentially and logically unitarian. Life for it is but a duty, a mission. The norm and definition of such mission can only be found in a collective term superior to all the individuals of the country—in the people, in the nation. If there is a collective mission, a communion of duty . . . it can only be represented in the national unity." And farther on: "The declaration of rights, which all constitutions insist in copying slavishly from the French, express only those of the period . . . which considered the individual as the end and pointed out only one half of the problem" and again, "assume the existence of one of those crises that threaten the life of the nation, and demand the active sacrifice of all its sons . . . will you ask the citizens to face martyrdom in virtue of their rights? You have taught men that society was solely constituted to guarantee their rights and now you ask them to sacrifice one and all, to suffer and die for the safety of the 'nation?'"

In Mazzini's conception of the citizen as instrument for the attainment of the nation's ends and therefore submissive to a higher mission, to the duty of supreme sacrifice, we see the anticipation of one of the fundamental points of the Fascist doctrine.

Unfortunately, the autonomy of the political thought of Italy, vigorously established in the works of Vico, nobly reclaimed by Vincenzo Cuoco, kept up during the struggles of the Risorgimento in spite of the many foreign influences of that period, seemed to exhaust itself immediately after the unification. Italian political thought which had been original in times of servitude, became enslaved in the days of freedom.

A powerful innovating movement, issuing from the war and of which Fascism is the purest expression, was to restore Italian thought in the sphere of political doctrine to its own traditions which are the traditions of Rome.

This task of intellectual liberation, now slowly being accomplished, is no less important than the political deliverance brought about by the Fascist Revolution. It is a great task which continues and integrates the Risorgimento; it is now bringing to an end, after the cessation of our political servitude, the intellectual dependence of Italy.

Thanks to it, Italy again speaks to the world and the world listens to Italy. It is a great task and a great deed and it demands great efforts. To carry it through, we must, each one of us, free ourselves of the dross of ideas and mental habits which two centuries of foreign intellectualistic tradition have heaped upon us; we must not only take on a new culture but create for ourselves a new soul. We must methodically and patiently contribute something towards the organic and complete elaboration of our doctrine, at the same time supporting it both at home and abroad with untiring devotion. We ask this effort of renovation and collaboration of all Fascists, as well as of all who feel themselves to be Italians. After the hour of sacrifice comes the hour of unyielding efforts. To our work, then, fellow countrymen, for the glory of Italy!

PART IX

CRITICS AND INTERPRETERS OF MODERN SOCIETY

XXX

LEO TOLSTOY

1828–1910

Count Leo Tolstoy was born in 1828 on his father's estate of Yasnaya Polyana ("Clear Glade") about 130 miles southeast of Moscow. Tolstoy later inherited the property and lived there most of his life. His father after dissipating his fortune had repaired it by a wealthy marriage which gave the Tolstoys a connection with many of the leading aristocratic families. The elder Tolstoy was a lenient landlord with perhaps some inclinations toward liberalism—at any rate, although he had fought in the Napoleonic wars and later on occupied civil office, he refused to serve Alexander I when the latter turned reactionary.

Tolstoy's mother died when he was two years old; his father, when he was nine. Some time afterward he was placed in the care of an aunt and taken to Kazan. As a child he was susceptible to music, sensitive about the defects of his personal appearance, but on the whole of a happy though somewhat erratic disposition. A number of religious fanatics lived in the neighborhood; he was taught to respect them and to admire the loftiness of their aims. The contrasting qualities of his brothers and sisters seemed to be summed up in Tolstoy: religious fanaticism and humility struggled with paganism and sensuality.

In 1844 he entered the University of Kazan intending to fit himself for a diplomatic career. But his record at the university was not impressive—he spent much time in social activities and professed a contempt for academic learning. It was at this time, however, that he read the eighteenth-century French philosophers and was especially moved by the ideas of Rousseau. In 1847 he left Kazan; having come into his estate he tried to lead the life of a benevolent landowner at Yasnaya Polyana. The attempt was a failure and he returned to the dissipations of Moscow society. But idleness troubled his conscience. He therefore entered the army, and when the Crimean War broke out shortly afterward had the fortune to be present at the famous siege of Sebastopol. In 1858 he gave up army life. But the experience had been fruitful—during the interval he had written several short stories and published *Sebastopol,* an account of the horrors of war. The latter work was praised by Turgenief. Tolstoy had also sketched out the plan of a new humanitarian religion.

After a couple of years spent in foreign travel, dissipation, and further literary work, Tolstoy again settled down on his estate. Along with writing he gave much time to a school for peasants, conducted along Rousseauist lines. This undertaking aroused the interest of the police who suspected a lurking revolution, but his status as an aristocrat sheltered him from too much official interference. In 1862 he married, having threatened to shoot himself if he was refused.

The first fourteen years of Tolstoy's marriage were the happiest of his life. He had given up his school and seemed content to lose himself in study, writing, and the pleasures of family life. *War and Peace,* his most ambitious novel, and part of *Anna Karenina* are the fruit of this period.

In 1876, however, the old disquietude returned. The conflict between his worldly appetites and his desire for spiritual redemption drove him first to the Church, which he soon deserted as cruel and reactionary, and then back to the ethical, pacifist beliefs that he had evolved many years before. The new religion gradually took on a more social complexion; as a census-taker in the slums Tolstoy had discovered conditions which convinced him that the economic basis of society was "morally indefensible." The outcome was *What Is to Be Done?* (1886).

Meanwhile Tolstoy's teachings drew flocks of converts to Yasnaya who tried to support themselves by the manual labor he recommended. Colonies of his disciples sprang up in other places. The stream of his writings continued, but now always the moral theme was uppermost. He used it to create a theory of art (*What Is Art?* 1898) and to denounce the sensual side of marriage (*The Kreutzer Sonata,* 1889). *The Kingdom of God* (1893) was only one of a number of works in which he continued to advocate pacifism and nonresistance. The government viewed these transactions with disapproval and after 1881 most of his theological and moral works were suppressed in Russia. But the authorities did not dare to go further—his fame had now become worldwide. Perhaps they drew some consolation from Tolstoy's refusal to support the revolution of 1905. But his coolness was natural for, after all, he called himself a "Christian anarchist."

It was easier for Tolstoy to attract disciples than to practice what he preached. He had to contend not only with his wife but with the weaknesses of his own flesh. He might valiantly chop wood, plough, and make boots, but he could not deny himself the luxuries of an aristocrat. If he must obey Christ's mandate to give up all his worldly goods, his wife demanded that he at least provide for his numerous children. He did so and thus, although technically a pauper, continued to live surrounded by most of the comforts of former times. The spiritual unrest, however, did not subside. Continual bickerings with his wife and mental conflicts between his ideals and the obligations to his family are said to have preserved the vitality of his genius; but they could lead only to a tragic end. In 1910 the situation at last became so intolerable that he decided to leave Russia. He set out accompanied by one daughter but fell ill on the way and died after a week's illness.

Tolstoy, says Bernard Shaw "was a man of genius in the very first flight of that rare species. He had the penetrating common sense of that first flight." The incongruities of his actions neither reduce his stature as an artist nor detract from his social message.

REFERENCES

There are several collected editions of Tolstoy's works in English. The most recent one, published by the Oxford Press, is now in progress.

The social side of Tolstoy's teaching is dealt with in a pamphlet by M. S. Stanoyevich, *Tolstoy's Theory of Social Reform* (1926).

The fullest biography in English is by Aylmer Maude (1929–30). Edward Garnett's *Tolstoy* (1914) is a short sketch.

READINGS FROM

WHAT IS TO BE DONE?

AND

THE KINGDOM OF GOD IS WITHIN YOU

Quotations.[1]

"And the people asked him, saying, What shall we do then?

"He answereth and saith unto them, He that hath two coats, let him impart to him that hath none; and he that hath meat, let him do likewise."—Luke iii. 10, 11.

[1] *What Is to Be Done?* Isabel F. Hapgood, ed. (1899), p. 3. Copyright by the T. Y. Crowell Co., New York.

"Lay not up for yourselves treasurers upon earth, where moth and rust doth corrupt, and where thieves break through and steal:

"But lay up for yourselves treasures in Heaven where neither moth nor rust doth corrupt, and where thieves do not break through nor steal:

"For where your treasure is, there will your heart be also.

"The light of the body is the eye: if therefore thine eye be single, thy whole body shall be full of light.

"But if thine eye be evil, thy whole body shall be full of darkness. If therefore the light that is in thee be darkness, how great is that darkness!

"No man can serve two masters: for either he will hate the one, and love the other; or else he will hold to the one, and despise the other. Ye cannot serve God and mammon.

"Therefore I say unto you, Take no thought for your life, what ye shall eat, or what ye shall drink; nor yet for your body, what ye shall put on. Is not the life more than meat, and the body than raiment?"—Matt. vi. 19–25.

"Therefore take no thought, saying, What shall we eat? or, What shall we drink? or, Wherewithal shall we be clothed?

"(For after all these things do the Gentiles seek:) for your heavenly Father knoweth that ye have need of all these things.

"But seek ye first the kingdom of God, and his righteousness; and all these things shall be added unto you."—Matt. vi. 31–33.

"For it is easier for a camel to go through a needle's eye, than for a rich man to enter into the kingdom of God."—Luke xviii. 25. . . .

Some Contrasts.[1] There was a great ball in Moscow. On the same night I left home after eight o'clock. I live in a locality surrounded by factories; and I left home after the factory whistle had sounded, and when, after a week of incessant work, people were freed for their holiday. Factory men passed by me, and I by them, all turning their steps to the public houses and inns. Many were already tipsy; many more were with women.

Every morning at five I hear each of the whistles, which means that the labor of women, children, and old people has begun. At eight o'clock another whistle,—this means half an hour's rest; at twelve the third whistle,—this means an hour for dinner. At eight o'clock the fourth whistle, indicating cessation from work. By a

[1] *Ibid.*, pp. 150–151, 151–152, 153–154.

strange coincidence, all the three factories in my neighborhood produce only the articles necessary for balls.

In one factory—the one nearest to me—they make nothing but stockings; in the other opposite, silk stuffs; in the third, perfumes and pomades.

One may, on hearing these whistles, attach to them no other meaning than that of the indication of time. "There, the whistle has sounded: it is time to go out for a walk."

But one may associate with them also the meaning they in reality have,—that at the first whistle at five o'clock in the morning, men and women, who have slept side by side in a damp cellar, get up in the dark, and hurry away into the noisy building, and take their part in a work of which they see neither cessation nor utility for themselves, and work often so in the heat, in suffocating exhalations, with very rare intervals of rest, for one, two, or three, or even twelve and more hours. They fall asleep, and get up again, and again do this work, meaningless for themselves, to which they are compelled exclusively by want. And so it goes on from one week to another, interrupted only by holidays.

And now I saw these working-people freed for one of these holidays. They go out into the street; everywhere there are inns, public houses, and gay women. And they, in a drunken state, pull each other by the arms, and carry along with them girls like the one whom I saw conducted to the police station; they hire hackney-coaches, and ride and walk from one inn to another, and abuse each other, and totter about, and say they know not what. . . .

Thus I walked on, looking at these men, observing how they went about the streets till eleven o'clock. Then their movements became quieter; there remained here and there a few tipsy people, and I met some men and women who were being conducted to the police station. And now, from every side, carriages appeared, all going in one direction. On the coach-box sat a coachman, sometimes in a sheepskin coat; and a footman—a dandy with a cockade. Well-fed trotters, covered with cloth, ran at the rate of fifteen miles an hour; in the carriages sat ladies wrapped in shawls, and taking great care not to spoil their flowers and their toilets. All, beginning with the harness on the horses, carriages, gutta-percha wheels, the cloth of the coachman's coat, down to the stockings, shoes, flowers, velvet, gloves, scents,—all these articles have been made by those men, some of whom fell asleep on their own pallets in their mean rooms, some in night-houses with prostitutes, and others in the police station.

The ball-goers drive past these men, in and with things made by them; and it does not even enter into their minds that there could possibly be any connection between the ball they are going to and these tipsy people, to whom their coachmen shout out so angrily. . . .

We know that each woman at this ball whose dress costs a hundred and fifty rubles was not born at the ball, but she has lived also in the country, has seen peasants, knows her own nurse and maid, whose fathers and brothers are poor, for whom earning one hundred and fifty rubles to build a cottage with is the end and aim of a long, laborious life; she knows this; how can she, then, enjoy herself, knowing that on her half-naked body she is wearing the cottage which is the dream of her housemaid's brother? . . .

If these young women and girls, from the hypnotic influence of the ball, fail to see all this, we cannot judge them. Poor things! they consider all to be good which is pronounced so by their elders. How do these elders explain their cruelty? They, indeed, always answer in the same way: "I compel no one; what I have, I have bought; footmen, chambermaids, coachman, I hire. There is no harm in engaging and in buying. I compel none; I hire; what wrong is there in that?" . . .

The Justification of Living without Working.[1] If I came among savages who gave me chops which I thought delicious, but the next day I learned (perhaps saw, myself) that these delicious chops were made of a human prisoner who had been slain in order to make them; and if I think it bad to eat men, however delicious the cutlets may be, and however general the custom to eat men among the persons with whom I live, and however small the utility to the prisoners who have been prepared for food my refusal to eat them may be, I shall not and will not eat them.

Maybe I shall eat human flesh when urged by hunger; but I shall not make a feast of it, and shall not take part in feasts with human flesh, and shall not seek such feasts, and be proud of my partaking of them. . . .

Men in this world are like those on a dismantled or water-logged ship, with a short allowance of food; all are put by God, or by nature, in such a position that they must husband their food, and unceasingly war with want.

Each interruption in this work of every one of us, each absorption

[1] *Ibid.*, pp. 156, 167–170, 172–173, 173–178, 206, 207, 209, 210, 214–216.

of the labor of others useless for the common welfare, is ruinous, alike for us and them.

How is it that the majority of educated people, without laboring, are quietly absorbing the labors of others, necessary for their own lives, and are considering such an existence quite natural and reasonable?

If we are to free ourselves from the labor proper and natural to all, and lay it on others, at the same time not considering ourselves to be traitors and thieves, we can do so only by two suppositions,—first, that we (the men who take no part in common labor) are different beings from working men, and have a peculiar destiny to fulfil in society (like drone bees, which have a different function from the working bees); or secondly, that the business which we (men freed from the struggle for existence) are doing for other men is so useful for all that it undoubtedly compensates for that harm which we do to others in overburdening them.

In olden times, men who utilized the labor of others asserted, first, that they belonged to a different race; and secondly, that they had from God a peculiar mission,—caring for the welfare of others; in other words, to govern and teach them: and therefore they assured others, and partly believed themselves, that the business they did was more useful and more important for the people than those labors by which they profit. This justification was sufficient so long as the direct interference of God in human affairs, and the inequality of human races, was undoubted.

But with Christianity, and the consciousness of the equality and unity of all men proceeding from it, this justification could no longer be expressed in its previous form.

It was no longer possible to assert that men are born of different kind and quality, and having a different destiny; and the old justification, though still held by some, has been little by little destroyed, and has now almost entirely disappeared.

But though the justification disappeared, the fact itself, of the freeing of some men from labor, and the appropriation by them of other men's labor, remained the same for those who had the power of enforcing it. For this existing fact, new excuses have constantly been invented, in order that, without asserting the difference of human beings, men might be able to free themselves from personal labor with apparent justice. A great many such justifications have been invented.

However strange it may seem, the main object of all that has been called science, and the ruling tendency of science, has been the seeking out of such excuse.

This has been the object of the theological sciences and of the science of law; this was the object of so-called philosophy, and this became lately the object of modern rationalistic science. All the theological subtleties which aimed at proving that a certain church is the only true successor of Christ, and that, therefore, she alone has full and uncontrolled power over the souls and bodies of men, had in view this very object.

All the legal sciences—those of state law, penal law, civil law, and international law—have this sole aim; the majority of philosophical theories, especially that of Hegel, which reigned over the minds of men for such a long time, and maintained the assertion that everything which exists is reasonable, and that the state is a necessary form of the development of human personality, had only this one object in view.

Comte's positive philosophy and its outcome, the doctrine that mankind is an organism; Darwin's doctrine of the struggle for existence, directing life and its conclusion, the teaching of diversity of human races, the now so popular anthropology, biology, and sociology,—all have the same aim. These sciences have become favorites, because they all serve for the justification of the existing fact of some men being able to free themselves from the human duty of labor, and to consume other men's labor.

All these theories, as is always the case, are worked out in the mysterious sanctums of augurs, and in vague, unintelligible expressions are spread abroad among the masses, and adopted by them.

As in olden times, the subtleties of theology, which justified violence in church and state, were the special property of priests; and in the masses of the people, the conclusions, taken by faith, and ready made for them, were circulated, that the power of kings, clergy, and nobility was sacred; so afterward, the philosophical and legal subtleties of so-called science became the property of the priests of science; and through the masses only the ready-made conclusion, accepted by faith, that social order (the organization of society) must be such as it is, and cannot be otherwise, was diffused. . . .

The theory by which men who have freed themselves from personal labor justify themselves, in its simplest and most exact form, is this: We men, having freed ourselves from work, and having by violence appropriated the labor of others, find ourselves better able to benefit them; in other words, certain men, for doing the people a palpable and comprehensible harm,—utilizing by violence their labor, and thereby increasing the difficulty of their struggles with nature,—do to them an impalpable and incomprehensible good.

This proposition is a very strange one; but men, as well of former as also of modern times, who have lived on the labors of working-men, believe it, and calm their conscience by it. Let us see in what way it is justified in different classes of men, who have freed themselves from labor in our own days. . . .

There are only two indications of the usefulness of any activity of one man for another: an exterior indication,—the acknowledgment of the utility of activity by those to whom it is produced; and an interior indication,—the desire to be of use to others lying at the root of the activity of the one who is trying to be of use.

Statesmen (I include the Church dignitaries appointed by the government in the category of statesmen) are of use to those whom they govern. The emperor, the king, the president of a republic, the prime minister, the minister of justice, the minister of war, the minister of public instruction, the bishop, and all under them, who serve the state, all live, having freed themselves from the struggle of mankind for existence, and having laid all the burden of this struggle upon other men, upon the ground that their non-activity compensates for this.

Let us apply the first indication to those for whose welfare the activity of statesmen is bestowed. Do they, I ask, recognize the usefulness of this activity?

Yes, it is recognized: most men consider statesmanship necessary to them; the majority recognize the usefulness of this activity in principle; but in all its manifestations as known to us, in all particular cases as known to us, the usefulness of each of the institutions and of each of the manifestations of this activity is not only denied by those for whose advantage it is performed, but they assert that this activity is even pernicious and hurtful. There is no state function or social activity which is not considered by many men to be hurtful; there is no institution which is not considered pernicious,—courts of justice, banks, local self-government, police, clergy. Every state activity, from the minister down to the policeman, from the bishop to the sexton, is considered by some men to be useful, and by others to be pernicious. And this is the case, not only in Russia, but throughout the world, in France as well as in America.

All the activity of the republican party is considered pernicious by the radical party, and *vice versa:* all the activity of the radical party, if the power is in their hands, is considered bad by the republican and other parties. But not only is it a fact that the activity of statesmen is never considered by all men to be useful: their activity has, besides, this peculiarity, that it must always be carried on by violence, and that, in order to attain this end, there are necessary, murders, executions, prisons, taxes raised by force, and so on.

It therefore appears that, besides the fact that the usefulness of state activity is not recognized by all men, and is always denied by one portion of men, this usefulness has the peculiarity of vindicating itself always by violence.

And therefore the usefulness of state activity cannot be confirmed by the fact that it is recognized by those men for whom it is performed.

Let us apply the second test: let us ask statesmen themselves, from the tsar down to the policeman, from the president to the secretary, from the patriarch to the sexton, begging for a sincere answer, whether in occupying their respective positions, they have in view the good which they wish to do for men, or something else. In their desire to fill the situation of a tsar, a president, a minister, a police-sergeant, a sexton, a teacher, are they moved by the desire of being useful to men, or for their own personal advantage? And the answer of sincere men would be that the chief motive is their own personal advantage.

And so it appears that one class of men, who utilize the labor of others who perish by their labors, compensate for such an undoubted evil by an activity which is always considered by a great many men to be not only useless, but pernicious; which cannot be voluntarily accepted by men, but to which they must always be compelled, and the aim of which is not the benefit of others, but the personal advantage of those men who perform it.

What is it, then, that confirms the theory that state activity is useful for men? Only the fact that those men who perform it, firmly believe it to be useful, and that it has been always in existence; but so have always been not only useless institutions, but very pernicious ones, like slavery, prostitution, and wars.

Business people (merchants, manufacturers, railway proprietors, bankers, landowners) believe in the fact that they do a good which undoubtedly compensates for the harm done by them. Upon what grounds do they believe it? To the question by whom the usefulness of their activity is recognized, men in church and in state are able to point to the thousands and millions of working-people who in principle recognize the usefulness of state and church activity; but to whom will bankers, distillers, manufacturers of velvet, of bronzes, of looking-glasses, to say nothing of guns,—to whom will they point when we ask them is their usefulness recognized by the majority?

If there can be found men who recognize the usefulness of manufacturing chintzes, rails, beer, and such like things, there will be found also a still greater number of men who consider the manufacture of these articles pernicious.

And as for the activity of merchants who raise the prices of all articles, and that of landowners, nobody would even attempt to justify it.

Besides, this activity is always associated with the harm done to working-people and with violence, if less direct than that of the state, yet just as cruel in its consequences; for the activities displayed in industry and in trade are entirely based upon taking advantage of the wants of working-people in every form, in order to compel working-men to hard and hated labor; to buy all goods cheap, and to sell to the people the articles necessary for them at the highest possible price, and to raise the interest on money. From whatever point we consider their activity, we see that the usefulness of business-men is not recognized by those for whom it is expended, neither in principle nor in particular cases; and by the majority their activity is considered to be directly pernicious. If we were to apply the second test, and to ask, What is the chief motive of the activity of business-men? we should receive a still more determinate answer than that on the activity of statesmen.

If a statesman says that besides a personal advantage he has in view the common benefit, we cannot help believing him, and each of us knows such men; but a business-man, from the very nature of his occupations, cannot have in view a common advantage, and would be ridiculous in the eyes of his fellows if he were in his business aiming at something besides the increasing of his own wealth and the keeping of it. And, therefore, working-people do not consider the activity of business-men of any help to them. Their activity is associated with violence toward such people; and its object is not their good, but always and only personal advantage; and lo! strange to say, these business-men are so assured of their own usefulness that they boldly, for the sake of this imaginary good, do an undoubted obvious harm to working-men by extricating themselves from laboring, and consuming the labor of the working-classes. Men of science and of art have freed themselves from laboring by putting this labor on others, and live with a quiet conscience, thinking they bring a sufficient advantage to other men to compensate for it.

On what is their assurance based? Let us ask them as we have done statesmen and business-men.

Is the utility of the arts and sciences recognized by all, or even by the majority of working-people?

We shall receive a very deplorable answer. The activity of men in church and state is recognized to be useful in theory by almost all, and in application by the majority of those for whom it is performed; the activity of business-men is recognized as useful by a small number of working-people; but the activity of men of science and of art is not recognized to be useful by any of the working-class. The usefulness of their activity is recognized only by those who are engaged in it, or who desire to practise it. Those who bear upon their shoulders all the labor of life, and who feed and clothe the men of science and art, cannot recognize the usefulness of the activity of these men, because they cannot even form any idea about an activity which always appears to working-men useless and even depraving.

Thus, without any exception, working-people think the same of universities, libraries, conservatories, picture and statue galleries, and theaters, which are built at their expense.

A working-man considers this activity to be so decidedly pernicious that he does not send his children to be taught; and in order to compel people to accept this activity, it has been everywhere found necessary to introduce a law compelling parents to send the children to school.

A working-man always looks at this activity with ill-will, and only ceases to look at it so when he ceases to be a working-man, and having saved money, and been educated, he passes out of the class of working-people into the class of men who live upon the necks of others.

And notwithstanding the fact that the usefulness of the activity of men of science and art is not recognized, and even cannot be recognized, by any workman, these men are all the same compelled to make a sacrifice for such an activity.

A statesman simply sends another to the guillotine or to prison; a business-man, utilizing the labor of another, takes away from him his last resource, leaving him the alternative of starvation, or labor destructive of his health and life; but a man of science or of art seemingly compels nobody to do anything: he merely offers the good he has done to those who are willing to take it; but, in order to be able to make his productions, undesirable to the working-people, he takes away from the people, by violence, through the statesmen, the greatest part of their labor for the building and keeping open of academies, universities, colleges, schools, museums, libraries, conservatories, and for the wages for himself and his fellows. . . .

The division of labor in human society has always existed, and I dare say always will exist; but the question for us is, not whether or not it has been and will still continue, but what should guide us to arrange that this division may be a right one. . . .

Division of labor!

Some are occupied with mental and spiritual, others with muscular and physical, labor.

With what an assurance do men express this! They wish to think so, and that seems to them in reality a correct exchange of services which is only the very apparent ancient violence.

Thou, or rather you (because it is always many who have to feed one),—you feed me, dress me, do for me all this rough labor, which I require of you, to which you are accustomed from your infancy, and I do for you that mental work to which I have already become accustomed. Give me bodily food, and I will give you in return the spiritual.

The statement seems to be a correct one; and it would really be so if only such exchange of services were free, if those who supply the bodily food were not obliged to supply it before they get the spiritual. . . .

We agree that spiritual food is as necessary to man as bodily. The learned man, the artist, says, Before we can begin to serve men by giving them spiritual food, we want men to provide us with bodily food.

But why should not the producers of this latter say, Before we begin to serve you with bodily food, we want spiritual food; and until we receive it, we cannot labor? . . .

What, then, should we, men of intellectual labor, answer, if such simple and lawful claims were made upon us? How should we satisfy these claims? Should we satisfy the religious wants of the people by the catechism of Philaret, by sacred histories of Sokolof, by the literature sent out by various monasteries and St. Isaak's cathedral? And should we satisfy their demand for order by the Code of Laws, and cassation verdicts of different departments, or by statutes of committees and commissions? And should we satisfy their want of knowledge by giving them spectrum analysis, a survey of the Milky Way, speculative geometry, microscopic investigations, controversies concerning spiritualism and mediumism, the activity of academies of science? How should we satisfy their artistic wants? By Pushkin, Dostoyevsky, Turgenief, L. Tolstoy, by pictures of French *salons*, and of those of our artists who represent naked women, satin, velvet, and landscapes, and pictures of domestic life, by the music of Wagner, and that of our own musicians?

All this is of no use, and cannot be of any use, because we, with our right to utilize the labor of the people, and absence of all duties in our preparation of their spiritual food, have quite lost from sight the single destination our activity should have.

We do not even know what is required by the working-man; we have even forgotten his mode of life, his views of things, his language; we have even lost sight of the very working-people themselves, and we study them like some ethnographical rarity or newly discovered continent. . . .

We have taken upon ourselves a peculiar department: we have a peculiar functional activity of our own. We are the brain of the people. They feed us, and we have undertaken to teach them. Only for the sake of this have we freed ourselves from labor. What, then, have we been teaching them? They have waited years, tens of years, hundreds of years. And we are still conversing among ourselves, and teaching each other, and amusing ourselves, and have quite forgotten them; we have so totally forgotten them, that others have taken upon themselves to teach and amuse them, and we have not even become aware of this in our flippant talk about division of labor: and it is very obvious that all our talk about the utility we offer to the people was only a shameful excuse. . . .

"But it is," you say, "this very division of labor, the freeing men of science and of art from the necessity of earning their bread, that has rendered possible that extraordinary success in science which we see in our days.

"If everybody were to plow, these enormous results would not be attained; there would not be those astonishing successes which have so enlarged man's power over nature; there would not be those discoveries in astronomy which so strike the minds of men and promote navigation; there would be no steamers, railways, wonderful bridges, tunnels, steam-engines, and telegraphs, photographs, telephones, sewing-machines, phonographs, electricity, telescopes, spectroscopes, microscopes, chloroform, Lister bandages, carbolic acid."

I will not attempt to enumerate all the things of which our century is so proud. This enumeration, and the ecstasy of contemplation of ourselves and of our great deeds, you may find in almost every newspaper and popular book.

These raptures of self-contemplation are so often repeated, and we are so seldom tired of praising ourselves, that we really come to believe, with Jules Verne, that science and art have never made such progress as in our time. And all this is rendered possible only by division of labor: how can we, then, avoid countenancing it?

Let us suppose that the progress of our century is indeed striking, astonishing, extraordinary; let us suppose that we, too, are particularly lucky in living at such an extraordinary time: but let us try to ascertain the value of these successes, not by our own self-contentment, but by the very principle of the division of labor; that is, by that intellectual labor of men of science for the advantage of the people which has to compensate for the freeing men of science and art from labor.

All this progress is very striking indeed; but owing to some unlucky chance, recognized, too, by men of science, this progress has not as yet ameliorated, but it has rather deteriorated, the condition of working-men.

Though a working-man, instead of walking, can use the railway, it is this very railway which has caused his forest to be burned, and has carried away his bread from under his very nose, and put him into a condition which is next door to slavery to the railway proprietor.

If, thanks to the engines and steam-machines, a working-man can buy cheap, and poor calico, it will be these very engines and machines which have deprived him of his wages, and brought him to a state of entire slavery to the manufacturer.

If there are telegraphs, which he is not forbidden to use, but which he does not use because he cannot afford it, then each of his productions, the value of which fluctuates, is bought up from under his very eyes by capitalists at low prices, thanks to the telegraph, before the working-man even becomes aware that the article is in demand.

Though there are telephones and telescopes, novels, operas, picture-galleries, and so on, the life of the working-man is not at all improved by any of them, because all, owing to the same unlucky chance, are beyond his reach. So that, after all, these wonderful discoveries and productions of art, if they have not made the life of working-people worse, have by no means improved it: on this the men of science are agreed.

So that, if to the question as to the reality of the successes attained by the sciences and arts, we apply, not our rapture of self-contemplation, but the very standard on which the ground of the division of labor is defended,—utility to the working world,—we shall see that we have not yet any sound reason for the self-contentment to which we consign ourselves so willingly.

A peasant uses the railway; a peasant's wife buys calico; in the cottage a lamp, and not a pine-knot, burns; and the peasant lights his pipe with a match,—this is comfortable; but what right have I from this to say that railways and factories have done good to the people?

If a peasant uses the railway, and buys a lamp, calico, and matches, he does it only because we cannot forbid his doing so: we all know very well that railways and factories have never been built for the use of the people; why, then, should the casual comfort a working-man obtains by chance be brought forward as a proof of the usefulness of these institutions to the people?

We all know very well that if those engineers and capitalists who build a railway or a factory have been thinking about working-people, they have been thinking only how to make the best possible use of them. And we see they have fully succeeded in doing so as well in Russia as in Europe and America.

In every hurtful thing there is something useful. After a house has been burned down, we may sit and warm ourselves, and light our pipes with one of the firebrands; but should we therefore say that a conflagration is beneficial? . . .

What Is to Be Done.[1] What is to be done? What must we do? This question, which includes the acknowledgment of the fact that our life is bad and unrighteous, and at the same time hints that there is no possibility of changing it,—this question I hear everywhere, and therefore I chose it for the title of my work. . . .

I am a man, like all others; and if I distinguish myself from an average man of my own circle in anything, it is chiefly in the fact that I, more than this average man, have served and indulged the false teaching of our world, that I have been praised by the men of the prevalent school of teaching, and that therefore I must be more depraved, and have gone farther astray, than most of my fellows.

[1] *Ibid.*, pp. 240, 241, 243–245, 245–246, 248–249, 260.

Therefore I think that the answer to this question which I have found for myself will do for all sincere persons who will put the same question to themselves. First of all, to the question, "What is to be done?" I answer that we must neither deceive other men nor ourselves; that we must not be afraid of the truth, whatever the result may be.

We all know what it is to deceive other men; and notwithstanding this we do deceive from morning to evening,—"Not at home," when I am in; "Very glad," when I am not at all glad; "Esteemed," when I do not esteem; "I have no money," when I have it, and so on.

We consider the deception of others, particularly a certain kind of deception, to be evil; but we are not afraid to deceive ourselves: but the worst direct lie to men, seeing its result, is nothing in comparison with that lie to ourselves according to which we shape our lives. . . .

Besides avoiding lying to myself, I had moreover to *repent*, because, though the one results from the other, the wrong idea about my great importance was so much a part of my own nature, that until I had sincerely repented, and had put aside that wrong estimate of myself which I had, I did not see the enormity of the lie of which I had been guilty.

It was only when I repented,—that is, left off considering myself to be a peculiar man, and began to consider myself to be like *all* other men,—it was then that my way became clear to me. Before this, I was not able to answer the question, "What is to be done?" because the very question itself was put incorrectly.

Before I repented, I had put the question thus: "What activity should I choose, I, the man with the education I have acquired? How can I compensate by this education and these talents for what I have been taking away from the people?"

This question was a false one, because it included a wrong idea as to my not being like other men, but a peculiar man, called to serve other men with those talents and that education which I had acquired in forty years.

I had put the question to myself, but in reality I had already answered it in advance by having determined beforehand the kind of activity agreeable to myself by which I was called upon to serve men. I really asked myself, "How have I, so fine a writer, one so very well informed, and with such talents, how can I utilize them for the benefit of mankind?"

But the question ought to have been put thus, as it would have to be put to a learned rabbi who had studied all the Talmud, and knew the exact number of the letters in the Holy Scripture, and all the subtleties of his science: "What have I to do, who, from unlucky circumstances, have lost my best years in study instead of accustoming myself to labor, in learning the French language, the piano, grammar, geography, law, poetry; in reading novels, romances, philosophical theories, and in performing military exercises? what have I to do, who have passed the best years of my life in idle occupations, depraving the soul? what have I to do, notwithstanding these unlucky conditions of the past, in order to requite those men, who, during all this time, have fed and clothed me, and who still continue to feed and to clothe me?"

If the question had been put thus, after I had repented, "What have I, so ruined a man, to do?" the answer would have been easy: First of all, I must try to get my living honestly,—that is, learn not to live upon the shoulders of others; and while learning this, and after I have learned it, to try on every occasion to be of use to men with my hands and with my feet, as well as with my brain and my heart, and with all of me that is wanted by men. . . .

Very often good young people, who sympathize with the negative part of my writings, put to me the question, "What must I then do? What have I, who have finished my study in the university or in some other high establishment,—what have I to do in order to be useful?"

These young people ask the question; but in the depths of their souls they have already decided that that education which they have received is their great advantage, and that they wish to serve the people by this very advantage.

And therefore there is one thing which they do not do,—honestly and critically examine what they call their education, by asking themselves whether it is a good or a bad thing.

But if they do this, they will be unavoidably led to deny their education, and to begin to learn anew; and this is alone what is wanted. They never will be able to answer the question as to what there is to be done, because they put it wrongly. The question should be put thus: "How can I, a helpless, useless man, seeing now the misfortune of having lost my best years in studying the scientific Talmud, pernicious for soul and body, how can I rectify this mistake, and learn to serve men?" But the question is always put thus: "How can I, who have acquired so much fine information, how can I be useful to men with this my information?"

And, therefore, a man will never answer the question, "What is to be done?" until he leaves off deceiving himself, and repents. And repentance is not dreadful, even as truth is not dreadful, but it is equally beneficent and fruitful of good. We need only accept the whole truth and fully repent in order to understand that in life no one has any rights or privileges, and that there is no end of duties, and no limits to them, and that the first and unquestionable duty of a man is to take a part in the struggle with nature for his own life, and for the lives of other men. And this acknowledgment of men's duty forms the essence of the third answer to the question, "What is to be done?"

I have tried to avoid deceiving myself. I have endeavored to extirpate the remainders of the false estimate of the importance of my education and talents, and to repent; but before answering the question, *What is to be done?* stands a new difficulty.

There are so many things to be done that one requires to know what is to be done in particular. And the answer to this question has been given me by the sincere repentance of the evil in which I have been living.

What is to be done? What is there exactly to be done? everybody keeps asking; and I, too, kept asking this, while, under the influence of a high opinion of my own calling, I had not seen that my first and unquestionable business is to earn my living, clothing, heating, building, and so forth, and in doing this to serve others as well as myself, because, since the world has existed, the first and unquestionable duty of every man has been comprised in this. . . .

To the question, "What have we to do?" I received a very plain answer: Do first what is necessary for yourself; arrange all you can do by yourself,—your tea-urn, stove, water, and clothes.

To the question, "Would not this seem strange to those who had been accustomed to do all this for me?" it appeared that it was strange only during a week, and after a week it seemed more strange for me to return to my former condition.

In answer to the question, "Is it necessary to organize this physical labor, to establish a society in a village upon this basis?" it appeared that it was not at all necessary to do all this; that if the labor does not aim at rendering idleness possible, and at utilizing other men's labor, as is the case with men who save up money, but merely the satisfying of necessities, then such labor will naturally induce people to leave towns for the country, where this labor is most agreeable and productive.

There was also no need to establish a society, because a workingman will naturally associate with other working people. In answer to the question, "Would not this labor take up all my time, and would it not deprive me of the possibility of that mental activity which I am so fond of, and to which I have become accustomed, and which in moments of self-conceit I consider to be useful to others?" the answer will be quite an unexpected one. In proportion to bodily exercise the energy of my mental activity increased, having freed itself from all that was superfluous.

In fact, having spent eight hours in physical labor,—half a day,—which formerly I used to spend in endeavoring to struggle with dullness, there still remained for me eight hours, out of which in my circumstances I required five for mental labor; and if I, a very prolific writer, who had been doing nothing during forty years but writing, and who had written three hundred printed sheets, that if during these forty years I had been doing ordinary work along with working people, then, not taking into consideration winter evenings and holidays, if I had been reading and learning during the five hours a day, and written only on holidays two pages a day (and I have sometimes written sixteen pages a day), I should have written the same three hundred printed sheets in fourteen years. . . .

These are, then, the answers to the question, "What is to be done?" which I have found for myself.

First, To avoid deceiving myself. However far I have gone astray from that road of life which my reason shows to me, I must not be afraid of the truth.

Secondly, To renounce my own righteousness, my own advantages, peculiarities, distinguishing me from others, and to confess the guilt of such.

Thirdly, To fulfil that eternal, unquestionable law of man,—by laboring with all my being to struggle with nature, to sustain my own life, and the lives of others. . . .

The State and Violence.[1] The efforts which the educated men of the upper classes are making to silence the growing consciousness that the present system of life must be changed, are constantly on the increase, while life itself, continuing to develop and to become more complex without changing its direction, as it increases the incongruities and suffering of human existence, brings men to the

[1] *The Kingdom of God Is within You*, Aline Delano, trans. (1899), pp. 153, 154, 166–168, 171, 174–175, 177. Copyright by the T. Y. Crowell Co., New York.

extreme limit of this contradiction. An example of this uttermost limit is found in the general military conscription.

It is usually supposed that this conscription, together with the increasing armaments and the consequent increase of the taxes and national debts of all countries, are the accidental results of a certain crisis in European affairs, which might be obviated by certain political combinations, without change of the interior life.

This is utterly erroneous. The general conscription is nothing but an internal contradiction which has crept into the social life-conception, and which has only become evident because it has arrived at its utmost limits at a period when men have attained a certain degree of material development.

The social life-conception transfers the significance of life from the individual to mankind in general, through the unbroken continuity of the family, the tribe, and the State. . . .

The advocates of the social life-conception usually attempt to combine the idea of authority, otherwise violence, with that of moral influence; but such a union is utterly impossible.

The result of moral influence upon man is to change his desires, so that he willingly complies with what is required of him. A man who yields to moral influence takes pleasure in conforming his actions to its laws; whereas authority, as the word is commonly understood, is a means of coercion, by which a man is forced to act in opposition to his wishes. A man who submits to authority does not do as he pleases, he yields to compulsion, and in order to force a man to do something for which he has an aversion, the threat of physical violence, or violence itself, must be employed: he may be deprived of his liberty, flogged, mutilated, or he may be threatened with these punishments. And this is what constitutes power both in the past and in the present. . . .

"Were it not for the State," we are told, "we should be subjected to violence and to the attacks of evil men in our own land."

But who are these evil men from whose violence and attacks the government and the army saves us? If such men existed three or four centuries ago, when men prided themselves on their military skill and strength of arm, when a man proved his valor by killing his fellow-men, we find none such at the present time: men of our time neither use nor carry weapons, and, believing in the precepts of humanity and pity for their neighbors, they are as desirous for peace and a quiet life as we are ourselves. Hence this extraordinary class of marauders, against whom the State might defend us, no longer exists. But if, when they speak of the men from whose attacks the government defends us, we understand that they mean the criminal classes, in that case we know that they are not extraordinary beings, like beasts of prey among sheep, but are men very much like ourselves, who are naturally just as reluctant to commit crimes as those against whom they commit them. We know now that threats and punishments are powerless to decrease the numbers of such men, but that their numbers may be decreased by change of environment and by moral influence. Hence the theory of the necessity of State violence in order to protect mankind against evil-doers, if it had any foundation three or four centuries ago, has none whatever at the present time. One might say quite the reverse nowadays, for the activity of governments, with their antiquated and merciless methods of punishment, their galleys, prisons, gallows, and guillotines, so far below the general plane of morality, tends rather to lower the standard of morals than to elevate it, and therefore rather to increase than to lessen the number of criminals.

It is said that "without the State there would be no institutions, educational, moral, religious, or international; there would be no means of communication. Were it not for the State, we should be without organizations necessary to all of us."

An argument like this could only have had a basis several centuries ago. If there ever was a time when men had so little international communication, and were so unused to intercourse or interchange of thought that they could not come to an agreement on matters of general interest—commercial, industrial, or economical—without the assistance of the State, such is not the case at present. The widely diffused means of communication and transmission of thought have achieved this result,—that when the modern man desires to found societies, assemblies, corporations, congresses, scientific, economical, or political institutions, not only can he easily dispense with the assistance of governments, but in the majority of cases governments are more of a hindrance than a help in the pursuit of such objects.

Since the end of the last century almost every progressive movement on the part of mankind has been not only discouraged, but invariably hampered, by governments. Such was the case with the abolition of corporal punishment, torture, and slavery; with the establishment of freedom of the press and liberty of meeting. Furthermore, State authorities and governments nowadays not only do not coöperate, but they directly hinder the activity by means of which men work out new forms of life. The solution of labor and land questions, of political and religious problems, is not only unencouraged, but distinctly opposed, by the government authority. . . .

But the question concerning the State, whether its continued existence is a necessity, or whether it would be wiser to abolish it, cannot be decided by discussion on its usefulness for the men who are required to support it by taking part in the military service, and still less by weighing the comparative advantages and disadvantages of submission or non-submission for the individual himself. It is decided irrevocably and without appeal by the religious consciousness, by the conscience of each individual, to whom no sooner does military conscription become a question than it is followed by that of the necessity or non-necessity of the State. . . .

The question of resistance or non-resistance of evil by violence arose with the first contest among men, for every contest is simply the resistance by violence of something which each combatant believes to be an evil. But before the time of Christ men did not understand that resistance by violence of whatever the individual believed to be evil—only the same action which seems evil to one man may seem good to another—is simply one mode of settling the difficulty, and that the other method consists in not resisting evil by violence.

Before the appearance of the doctrine of Christ men believed that there could be but one way of deciding the contest, that of resisting evil by violence, and acted accordingly, while each combatant strove to persuade himself and others that what he regarded as evil was in fact the actual and absolute evil. For this purpose, dating from the oldest times, men began to invent certain definitions of evil which should be obligatory for all, and for the purpose of establishing definitions which should be thus binding, were issued, either certain laws supposed to have been received in a supernatural manner, or commands of individuals or of bodies of men to whom an infallible wisdom was ascribed. Men used violence against their fellow-men and assured themselves and others that they were but using such violence against an evil acknowledged by all.

This was the custom from the most ancient times, particularly among men who had usurped authority, and men have been long in seeing its baselessness.

But the longer mankind existed the more complex grew its mutual relations, and the more evident it became that to resist by violence everything that is considered evil is unwise; that the struggle is not diminished thereby, and that no human wisdom can ever define an infallible standard of evil. . . .

Thus matters went on for eighteen centuries, and at last arrived at their present condition, which is, that no man can dispute the fact that an infallible definition of evil will never be made. We have reached the point when men have ceased not only to believe in the possibility of finding a universal definition which all men will admit, but they have even ceased to believe in the necessity of such a definition. We have reached the point when men in authority no longer seek to prove that that which they consider evil is evil, but candidly acknowledge that they consider that to be evil which does not please them, and those who are subject to authority obey, not because they believe that the definitions of evil made by authority are just, but only because they have no power to resist. . . .

Christianity and Non-Resistance.[1] A man needs but to realize that the object of his life is the fulfilment of God's law; then the pre-eminence of that law, claiming as it does his entire allegiance, will of necessity invalidate the authority and restrictions of all human laws.

The Christian who contemplates that law of love implanted in every human soul, and quickened by Christ, the only guide for all mankind, is set free from human authority.

A Christian may suffer from external violence, may be deprived of his personal freedom, may be a slave to his passions,—the man who commits sin is the slave of the sin,—but he cannot be controlled or coerced by threats into committing an act contrary to his consciousness. He cannot be forced to this, because the privations and sufferings that are so powerful an influence over men who hold the social life-conception have no influence whatever over him. The privations and sufferings that destroy the material welfare which is the object of the social life-conception produce no effect upon the welfare of the Christian's life, which rests on the consciousness that he is doing God's will—nay, they may even serve to promote that welfare when they are visited upon him for fulfilling that will. . . .

A Christian enters into no dispute with his neighbor, he neither attacks nor uses violence; on the contrary, he suffers violence himself without resistance, and by his very attitude toward evil not only sets himself free, but helps to free the world at large from all outward authority.

[1] *Ibid.*, pp. 196–197, 199–200.

"And ye shall know the truth, and the truth shall make you free." If there were any doubt of the truth of Christianity there could be no more indubitable proof of its authenticity than the complete freedom, recognizing no fetters, which a man feels as soon as he assimilates the Christian life-conception.

Human beings in their present condition may be likened to bees in the act of swarming, as we see them clinging in a mass to a single bough. Their position is a temporary one, and must inevitably be changed. They must rise and find themselves a new abode. Every bee knows this, and is eager to shift its own position, as well as that of the others, but not one of them will do so until the whole swarm rises. The swarm cannot rise, because one bee clings to the other and prevents it from separating itself from the swarm, and so they all continue to hang. It might seem as if there were no deliverance from this position, precisely as it seems to men of the world who have become entangled in the social net. Indeed, there would be no outlet for the bees if each one were not a living creature possessed of a pair of wings. Neither would there be any issue for men if each one were not a living individual, being gifted with a capacity for assimilating the Christian life-conception.

If among these bees who are able to fly not one could be found willing to start, the swarm would never change its position. And it is the same among men. If the man who has assimilated the Christian life-conception waits for others before he proceeds to live in accordance with it, mankind will never change its attitude. And as all that is needed to change a solid mass of bees into a flying swarm is for one bee to spread its wings and fly away, when the second, the third, the tenth, and the hundredth will follow suit; so all that is needed to break through the magic circle of social life, deliverance from which seems so hopeless, is, that one man should view life from a Christian standpoint and begin to frame his own life accordingly, whereupon others will follow in his footsteps.

But men think that the deliverance of mankind by this method is too slow a process, and that a simultaneous deliverance might be effected by some other method. Just as if bees, when the swarm was ready to rise, were to decide that it would be too long a process if they waited for each bee to spread its wings and rise separately, and that some means must be devised whereby the swarm may rise all at once, whenever it pleases. But that is impossible. Not until the first, second, third, and hundredth bee has unfolded its wings and flown away can the swarm take flight and find for itself a new home. Not until each individual man adopts the Christian life-conception, and begins to live in conformity with its precepts, will the contradictions of human life be solved, and new forms of life become established. . . .

XXXI

THORSTEIN VEBLEN

1857–1929

The parents of Veblen migrated from Norway to America in 1847. The father was a workingman—a carpenter and builder—who, possessing little money, travelled to Wisconsin and then to Minnesota, taking up land in both states and ultimately becoming a prosperous farmer. The future economist, Thorstein Bunde Veblen, the sixth of twelve children, was born in Manitowoc County, Wisconsin, in 1857. The only other member of the family to attain prominence was Thorstein's nephew, Oswald Veblen, at present a well-known mathematician.

Like the normal country boy, Thorstein helped with farm work; but he had a curiosity about plants and animals that was perhaps unusual. His talents were shown in other ways: he astonished the countryside by writing anathemas in Greek against a neighbor whose dog had worried his father's cattle. Most of his early education was obtained at home. He read much and took part in family discussions, in which he was usually the leader. Thorstein had an abundant respect for his father—the finest mind, he said afterward, that he had ever known. His mother too was a woman of unusual character. Possessed of a keen intelligence, she was a first-rate physician although without professional training, and her home was always open to the needy and unfortunate.

The Veblen children were sent to Carleton College at Northfield, Minnesota. John Bates Clark was then teaching at Carleton, and Thorstein became a close friend of the economist. This may have determined Thorstein's future line of interest. Perhaps the ethical trend of Clark's theory and its historical, sociological texture may have had their effect as well. It is also true that Clark was given to the kind of abstract speculation that Veblen later on came to abhor.

Leaving Carleton with a B.A. degree in 1880, Veblen proceeded to Johns Hopkins for graduate study. Johns Hopkins, however, disappointed him; he deserted it for Yale. There he won a prize for a study of the panic of 1837, but his interest temporarily shifting to philosophy he took his Ph.D. degree in 1884 with a dissertation on *Kant's Critique of Judgment.* There followed a period of years during which Veblen, unable to obtain a teaching position on account of his agnostic views in religion, led a somewhat aimless life, supported largely by his relatives.

In 1891 Veblen arrived at Cornell again as a student. This time he so impressed J. L. Laughlin, the economist, that the latter obtained a teaching fellowship for him and in 1892 took him to the newly organized University of Chicago. From a fellowship Veblen passed through successive grades of the faculty to an assistant professorship in 1900. In 1899 he published *The Theory of the Leisure Class.*

The book gave evidence of wide and rather miscellaneous learning. Veblen's interest in fact had ranged from Norse literature to Cretan archaeology, with large draughts of Herbert Spencer on the way. Into the making of his economic viewpoint had gone not only the influences already mentioned but the stimulus of his Chicago environment. Contact with other members of the economics department, discussions with his colleagues John Dewey and the biologist Jacques Loeb, last and perhaps as important as anything else, the rushing life of Chicago itself—"pressing its bulk and growth and tinsel wealth into his consciousness"—all this underlay his original if unorthodox economics.

The Theory of the Leisure Class inaugurated a series of works in which Veblen analyzed contemporary and especially American institutions in terms of his leading concept, the friction between advancing culture and an exaggerated profit motive. One after another, business enterprise, international politics, higher learning, passed under review. No less than twelve books, developments of the main theme, were published between 1899 and 1923. During this time Veblen's academic career had been somewhat checkered. Careless of the dignities and dignitaries of college life and unconventional as to morality, he nevertheless often wounded himself on these angularities—experiences which perhaps sharpened the satirical tone of his writing. Nor was he a success with undergraduates; their impenetrability exhausted his patience. He left Chicago in 1906, changing his base to Leland Stanford (1906–09), then to the University of Missouri (1911–18), and finally, after an interval of government service in 1918, to the New School for Social Research. Here he remained until failing health obliged him to give up scholastic work altogether. He retired to California in 1926 and died there three years later.

The effect of Veblen's writing has been considerable in spite of its repetitious, polysyllabic style, a fault which deceived H. L. Mencken into describing Veblen as a "geyser of pishposh." His strictures on the classical method in economics—its out-of-date assumptions as to competition and business organization, the principles it deduced from them and the way it deduced them—failed to move the older group of economists. But younger scholars were attracted by his evolutionary and psychological approach to economic problems. In time something of a school developed about his doctrines: it became known as "institutionalism." The result has been that if Veblenism is at present "not yet orthodox," says one of his interpreters, it is "at least a respectable heresy." Such popular writers as Stuart Chase and Sinclair Lewis are exemplars of the heresy.

Veblen was primarily a critic; nevertheless he laid down a few specifications for a better society. In *The Engineers and the Price System* (1921) he suggested putting technicians and engineers in supreme control of industry in place of the bankers and profit-seeking business men who now dominate it. The idea (of which Veblen was not the sole originator) has gained some acceptance. It was dramatized in a now almost forgotten movement called "Technocracy" which flourished in 1932–33.

REFERENCES

Some of Veblen's more important works (besides those mentioned) are *The Theory of Business Enterprise* (1904), *The Instinct of Workmanship* (1914), *An Inquiry into the Nature of Peace and the Terms of Its Perpetuation* (1917), *The Higher Learning in America* (1918), *The Vested Interests* (1919), *The Place of Science in Modern Civilization* (1920), and *Absentee Ownership and Business Enterprise* (1923).

Critical estimates of Veblen's work are given in P. T. Homan's *Contemporary Economic Thought* (1928) and Max Lerner's "Veblen and the Waste Land" (*The New Freeman*, 1931, pp. 565–567). An interesting interpretation of Veblen's *Leisure Class* as an inversion of Spencer's sociology is offered by Joseph Dorfman in the *Political Science Quarterly* for September, 1932, pp. 363–409. H. L. Mencken's amusing essay occurs in *Prejudices, First Series*.

Homan's study (above) contains biographical matter. See also for this purpose Florence Veblen's "Thorstein Veblen: Reminiscences of his Brother Orson" (*Social Forces*, Vol. X, pp. 187–195).

READINGS FROM

THE THEORY OF THE LEISURE CLASS

The Desire for Distinction as a Motive for Ownership.[1] Wherever the institution of private property is found, even in a slightly developed form, the economic process bears the character of a struggle between men for the possession of goods. It has been customary in economic theory, and especially among those economists who adhere with least faltering to the body of modernised classical doctrines, to construe this struggle for wealth as being substantially a struggle for subsistence. Such is, no doubt, its character in large part during the earlier and less efficient phases of industry. Such is also its character in all cases where the "niggardliness of nature" is so strict as to afford but a scanty livelihood to the community in return for strenuous and unremitting application to the business of getting the means of subsistence. But in all progressing communities an advance is presently made beyond this early stage of technological development. Industrial efficiency is presently carried to such a pitch as to afford something appreciably more than a bare livelihood to those engaged in the industrial process. It has not been unusual for economic theory to speak of the further struggle for wealth on this new industrial basis as a competition for an increase of the comforts of life,—primarily for an increase of the physical comforts which the consumption of goods affords.

The end of acquisition and accumulation is conventionally held to be the consumption of the goods accumulated—whether it is consumption directly by the owner of the goods or by the household attached to him and for this purpose identified with him in theory. This is at least felt to be the economically legitimate end of acquisition, which alone it is incumbent on the theory to take account of. Such consumption may of course be conceived to serve the consumer's physical wants—his physical comfort—or his so-called higher wants—spiritual, æsthetic, intellectual or what not; the latter class of wants being served indirectly by an expenditure of goods, after the fashion familiar to all economic readers.

But it is only when taken in a sense far removed from its naïve meaning that consumption of goods can be said to afford the incentive from which accumulation invariably proceeds. The motive that

[1] Published by The Viking Press, Inc., New York. Pp. 24–29, 32.

lies at the root of ownership is emulation; and the same motive of emulation continues active in the further development of the institution to which it has given rise and in the development of all those features of the social structure which this institution of ownership touches. The possession of wealth confers honour; it is an invidious distinction. Nothing equally cogent can be said for the consumption of goods, nor for any other conceivable incentive to acquisition, and especially not for any incentive to the accumulation of wealth.

It is of course not to be overlooked that in a community where nearly all goods are private property the necessity of earning a livelihood is a powerful and ever-present incentive for the poorer members of the community. The need of subsistence and of an increase of physical comfort may for a time be the dominant motive of acquisition for those classes who are habitually employed at manual labour, whose subsistence is on a precarious footing, who possess little and ordinarily accumulate little; but it will appear in the course of the discussion that even in the case of these impecunious classes the predominance of the motive of physical want is not so decided as has sometimes been assumed. On the other hand, so far as regards those members and classes of the community who are chiefly concerned in the accumulation of wealth, the incentive of subsistence or of physical comfort never plays a considerable part. Ownership began and grew into a human institution on grounds unrelated to the subsistence minimum. The dominant incentive was from the outset the invidious distinction attaching to wealth, and, save temporarily and by exception, no other motive has usurped the primacy at any later stage of the development.

Property set out with being booty held as trophies of the successful raid. So long as the group had departed but little from the primitive communal organisation, and so long as it still stood in close contact with other hostile groups, the utility of things or persons owned lay chiefly in an invidious comparison between their possessor and the enemy from whom they were taken. The habit of distinguishing between the interests of the individual and those of the group to which he belongs is apparently a later growth. Invidious comparison between the possessor of the honorific booty and his less successful neighbours within the group was no doubt present early as an element of the utility of the things possessed, though this was not at the outset the chief element of their value. The man's prowess was still primarily the group's prowess, and the possessor of the booty felt himself to be primarily the keeper of the honour of his group. This appreciation of exploit from the communal point of view is met with also at later stages of social growth, especially as regards the laurels of war.

But so soon as the custom of individual ownership begins to gain consistency, the point of view taken in making the invidious comparison on which private property rests will begin to change. Indeed, the one change is but the reflex of the other. The initial phase of ownership, the phase of acquisition by naïve seizure and conversion, begins to pass into the subsequent stage of an incipient organisation of industry on the basis of private property (in slaves); the horde develops into a more or less self-sufficing industrial community; possessions then come to be valued not so much as evidence of successful foray, but rather as evidence of the prepotence of the possessor of these goods over other individuals within the community. The invidious comparison now becomes primarily a comparison of the owner with the other members of the group. Property is still of the nature of trophy, but, with the cultural advance, it becomes more and more a trophy of successes scored in the game of ownership carried on between the members of the group under the quasi-peaceable methods of nomadic life.

Gradually, as industrial activity further displaces predatory activity in the community's everyday life and in men's habits of thought, accumulated property more and more replaces trophies of predatory exploit as the conventional exponent of prepotence and success. With the growth of settled industry, therefore, the possession of wealth gains in relative importance and effectiveness as a customary basis of repute and esteem. Not that esteem ceases to be awarded on the basis of other, more direct evidence of prowess; not that successful predatory aggression or warlike exploit ceases to call out the approval and admiration of the crowd, or to stir the envy of the less successful competitors; but the opportunities for gaining distinction by means of this direct manifestation of superior force grow less available both in scope and frequency. At the same time opportunities for industrial aggression, and for the accumulation of property by the quasi-peaceable methods of nomadic industry, increase in scope and availability. And it is even more to the point that property now becomes the most easily recognised evidence of a reputable degree of success as distinguished from heroic or signal achievement. It therefore becomes the conventional basis of esteem. Its possession in some amount becomes necessary in order to any reputable standing in the community. It becomes indispensable to accumulate, to acquire property, in order to retain one's good name. When accumulated goods have in this way once become the accepted badge of efficiency, the possession of wealth presently assumes the character of an independent and definitive basis of esteem. The possession of goods, whether acquired aggressively by one's own exertion or passively by transmission through inheritance from others, becomes a conventional basis of reputability. The possession of wealth, which was at the outset valued simply as an evidence of efficiency, becomes, in popular apprehension, itself a meritorious act. Wealth is now itself intrinsically honourable and confers honour on its possessor. By a further refinement, wealth acquired passively by transmission from ancestors or other antecedents presently becomes even more honorific than wealth acquired by the possessor's own effort; but this distinction belongs at a later stage in the evolution of the pecuniary culture and will be spoken of in its place. . . .

In the nature of the case, the desire for wealth can scarcely be satiated in any individual instance, and evidently a satiation of the average or general desire for wealth is out of the question. However widely, or equally, or "fairly," it may be distributed, no general increase of the community's wealth can make any approach to satiating this need, the ground of which is the desire of every one to excel every one else in the accumulation of goods. If, as is sometimes assumed, the incentive to accumulation were the want of subsistence or of physical comfort, then the aggregate economic wants of a community might conceivably be satisfied at some point in the advance of industrial efficiency; but since the struggle is substantially a race for reputability on the basis of an invidious comparison, no approach to a definitive attainment is possible. . . .

Conspicuous Consumption.[1] During the earlier stages of economic development, consumption of goods without stint, especially consumption of the better grades of goods,—ideally all consumption in excess of the subsistence minimum,—pertains normally to the leisure class. This restriction tends to disappear, at least formally, after the later peaceable stage has been reached, with private ownership of goods and an industrial system based on wage labour or on the petty household economy. But during the earlier quasi-peaceable stage, when so many of the traditions through which the institution of a

[1] Pp. 73–85.

leisure class has affected the economic life of later times were taking form and consistency, this principle has had the force of a conventional law. It has served as the norm to which consumption has tended to conform, and any appreciable departure from it is to be regarded as an aberrant form, sure to be eliminated sooner or later in the further course of development.

The quasi-peaceable gentleman of leisure, then, not only consumes of the staff of life beyond the minimum required for subsistence and physical efficiency, but his consumption also undergoes a specialisation as regards the quality of the goods consumed. He consumes freely and of the best, in food, drink, narcotics, shelter, services, ornaments, apparel, weapons and accoutrements, amusements, amulets, and idols or divinities. In the process of gradual amelioration which takes place in the articles of his consumption, the motive principle and the proximate aim of innovation is no doubt the higher efficiency of the improved and more elaborate products for personal comfort and well-being. But that does not remain the sole purpose of their consumption. The canon of reputability is at hand and seizes upon such innovations as are, according to its standard, fit to survive. Since the consumption of these more excellent goods is an evidence of wealth, it becomes honorific; and conversely, the failure to consume in due quantity and quality becomes a mark of inferiority and demerit.

This growth of punctilious discrimination as to qualitative excellence in eating, drinking, etc., presently affects not only the manner of life, but also the training and intellectual activity of the gentleman of leisure. He is no longer simply the successful, aggressive male,—the man of strength, resource, and intrepidity. In order to avoid stultification he must also cultivate his tastes, for it now becomes incumbent on him to discriminate with some nicety between the noble and the ignoble in consumable goods. He becomes a connoisseur in creditable viands of various degrees of merit, in manly beverages and trinkets, in seemly apparel and architecture, in weapons, games, dancers, and the narcotics. This cultivation of the æsthetic faculty requires time and application, and the demands made upon the gentleman in this direction therefore tend to change his life of leisure into a more or less arduous application to the business of learning how to live a life of ostensible leisure in a becoming way. Closely related to the requirement that the gentleman must consume freely and of the right kind of goods, there is the requirement that he must know how to consume them in a seemly manner. His life of leisure must be conducted in due form. Hence arise good manners in the way pointed out in an earlier chapter. High-bred manners and ways of living are items of conformity to the norm of conspicuous leisure and conspicuous consumption.

Conspicuous consumption of valuable goods is a means of reputability to the gentleman of leisure. As wealth accumulates on his hands, his own unaided effort will not avail to sufficiently put his opulence in evidence by this method. The aid of friends and competitors is therefore brought in by resorting to the giving of valuable presents and expensive feasts and entertainments. Presents and feasts had probably another origin than that of naïve ostentation, but they acquired their utility for this purpose very early, and they have retained that character to the present; so that their utility in this respect has now long been the substantial ground on which these usages rest. Costly entertainments, such as the potlatch or the ball, are peculiarly adapted to serve this end. The competitor with whom the entertainer wishes to institute a comparison is, by this method, made to serve as a means to the end. He consumes vicariously for his host at the same time that he is a witness to the consumption of that excess of good things which his host is unable to dispose of single-handed, and he is also made to witness his host's facility in etiquette.

In the giving of costly entertainments other motives, of a more genial kind, are of course also present. The custom of festive gatherings probably originated in motives of conviviality and religion; these motives are also present in the later development, but they do not continue to be the sole motives. The latter-day leisure-class festivities and entertainments may continue in some slight degree to serve the religious need and in a higher degree the needs of recreation and conviviality, but they also serve an invidious purpose; and they serve it none the less effectually for having a colourable non-invidious ground in these more avowable motives. But the economic effect of these social amenities is not therefore lessened, either in the vicarious consumption of goods or in the exhibition of difficult and costly achievements in etiquette.

As wealth accumulates, the leisure class develops further in function and structure, and there arises a differentiation within the class. There is a more or less elaborate system of rank and grades. This differentiation is furthered by the inheritance of wealth and the consequent inheritance of gentility. With the inheritance of gentility goes the inheritance of obligatory leisure; and gentility of a sufficient potency to entail a life of leisure may be inherited without the complement of wealth required to maintain a dignified leisure. Gentle blood may be transmitted without goods enough to afford a reputably free consumption at one's ease. Hence results a class of impecunious gentlemen of leisure, incidentally referred to already. These half-caste gentlemen of leisure fall into a system of hierarchical gradations. Those who stand near the higher and the highest grades of the wealthy leisure class, in point of birth, or in point of wealth, or both, outrank the remoter-born and the pecuniarily weaker. These lower grades, especially the impecunious, or marginal, gentlemen of leisure, affiliate themselves by a system of dependence or fealty to the great ones; by so doing they gain an increment of repute, or of the means with which to lead a life of leisure, from their patron. They become his courtiers or retainers, servants; and being fed and countenanced by their patron they are indices of his rank and vicarious consumers of his superfluous wealth. Many of these affiliated gentlemen of leisure are at the same time lesser men of substance in their own right; so that some of them are scarcely at all, others only partially, to be rated as vicarious consumers. So many of them, however, as make up the retainers and hangers-on of the patron may be classed as vicarious consumers without qualification. Many of these again, and also many of the other aristocracy of less degree, have in turn attached to their persons a more or less comprehensive group of vicarious consumers in the persons of their wives and children, their servants, retainers, etc.

Throughout this graduated scheme of vicarious leisure and vicarious consumption the rule holds that these offices must be performed in some such manner, or under some such circumstance or insignia, as shall point plainly to the master to whom this leisure or consumption pertains, and to whom therefore the resulting increment of good repute of right inures. The consumption and leisure executed by these persons for their master or patron represents an investment on his part with a view to an increase of good fame. As regards feasts and largesses this is obvious enough, and the imputation of repute to the host or patron here takes place immediately, on the ground of common notoriety. Where leisure and consumption is performed vicariously by henchmen and retainers, imputation of the resulting repute to the patron is effected by their residing near his person so that it may be plain to all men from what source they draw. As the group whose good esteem is to be secured in this way grows larger, more patent means are required to indicate the imputation of merit for the leisure performed, and to this end uniforms, badges, and liveries come into vogue. The wearing of uniforms or liveries implies a considerable degree of dependence, and may even be said to be a mark of servitude, real or ostensible. The wearers of uniforms and liveries may be roughly divided into two classes—the free and the servile, or the noble and the ignoble. The services performed by them are likewise divisible into noble and ignoble. Of course the distinction is not observed with strict consistency in practice; the less debasing of the base services and the less honorific of the noble functions are not infrequently merged in the same person. But the general distinction is not on that account to be overlooked. What may add some perplexity is the fact that this fundamental distinction between noble and ignoble, which rests on the nature of the ostensible service performed, is traversed by a secondary distinction into honorific and humiliating, resting on the rank of the person for whom the service is performed or whose livery is worn. So, those offices which are by right the proper employment of the leisure class are noble; such are government, fighting, hunting, the care of arms and accoutrements, and the like,—in short, those which may be classed as ostensibly predatory employments. On the other hand, those employments which properly fall to the industrious class are ignoble; such as handicraft or other productive labour, menial services, and the like. But a base service performed for a person of very high degree may become a very honorific office; as for instance the office of a Maid of Honour or of a Lady in Waiting to the Queen, or the King's Master of the Horse or his Keeper of the Hounds. The two offices last named suggest a principle of some general bearing. Whenever, as in these cases, the menial service in question has to do directly with the primary leisure employments of fighting and hunting, it easily acquires a reflected honorific character. In this way great honour may come to attach to an employment which in its own nature belongs to the baser sort.

In the later development of peaceable industry, the usage of employing an idle corps of uniformed men-at-arms gradually lapses. Vicarious consumption by dependents bearing the insignia of their patron or master narrows down to a corps of liveried menials. In a heightened degree, therefore, the livery comes to be a badge of servitude, or rather of servility. Something of an honorific character always attached to the livery of the armed retainer, but this honorific character disappears when the livery becomes the exclusive badge of the menial. The livery becomes obnoxious to nearly all who are required to wear it. We are yet so little removed from a state of effective slavery as still to be fully sensitive to the sting of any imputation of servility. This antipathy asserts itself even in the case of the liveries or uniforms which some corporations prescribe as the distinctive dress of their employees. In this country the aversion even goes the length of discrediting—in a mild and uncertain way—those government employments, military and civil, which require the wearing of a livery or uniform.

With the disappearance of servitude, the number of vicarious consumers attached to any one gentleman tends, on the whole, to decrease. The like is of course true, and perhaps in a still higher degree, of the number of dependents who perform vicarious leisure for him. In a general way, though not wholly nor consistently, these two groups coincide. The dependent who was first delegated for these duties was the wife, or the chief wife; and, as would be expected, in the later development of the institution, when the number of persons by whom these duties are customarily performed gradually narrows, the wife remains the last. In the higher grades of society a large volume of both these kinds of service is required; and here the wife is of course still assisted in the work by a more or less numerous corps of menials. But as we descend the social scale, the point is presently reached where the duties of vicarious leisure and consumption devolve upon the wife alone. In the communities of the Western culture, this point is at present found among the lower middle class.

And here occurs a curious inversion. It is a fact of common observation that in this lower middle class there is no pretence of leisure on the part of the head of the household. Through force of circumstances it has fallen into disuse. But the middle-class wife still carries on the business of vicarious leisure, for the good name of the household and its master. In descending the social scale in any modern industrial community, the primary fact—the conspicuous leisure of the master of the household—disappears at a relatively high point. The head of the middle-class household has been reduced by economic circumstances to turn his hand to gaining a livelihood by occupations which often partake largely of the character of industry, as in the case of the ordinary business man of to-day. But the derivative fact—the vicarious leisure and consumption rendered by the wife, and the auxiliary vicarious performance of leisure by menials—remains in vogue as a conventionality which the demands of reputability will not suffer to be slighted. It is by no means an uncommon spectacle to find a man applying himself to work with the utmost assiduity, in order that his wife may in due form render for him that degree of vicarious leisure which the common sense of the time demands.

The leisure rendered by the wife in such cases is, of course, not a simple manifestation of idleness or indolence. It almost invariably occurs disguised under some form of work or household duties or social amenities, which prove on analysis to serve little or no ulterior end beyond showing that she does not and need not occupy herself with anything that is gainful or that is of substantial use. As has already been noticed under the head of manners, the greater part of the customary round of domestic cares to which the middle-class housewife gives her time and effort is of this character. Not that the results of her attention to household matters, of a decorative and mundificatory character, are not pleasing to the sense of men trained in middle-class proprieties; but the taste to which these effects of household adornment and tidiness appeal is a taste which has been formed under the selective guidance of a canon of propriety that demands just these evidences of wasted effort. The effects are pleasing to us chiefly because we have been taught to find them pleasing. There goes into these domestic duties much solicitude for a proper combination of form and colour, and for other ends that are to be classed as æsthetic in the proper sense of the term; and it is not denied that effects having some substantial æsthetic value are sometimes attained. Pretty much all that is here insisted on is that, as regards these amenities of life, the housewife's efforts are under the guidance of traditions that have been shaped by the law of conspicuously wasteful expenditure of time and substance. If beauty or comfort is achieved,—and it is a more or less fortuitous circumstance if they are,—they must be achieved by means and methods that commend themselves to the great economic law of wasted effort. The more reputable, "presentable" portion of middle-class household paraphernalia are, on the one hand, items of conspicuous consumption, and on the other hand, apparatus for putting in evidence the vicarious leisure rendered by the housewife.

The requirement of vicarious consumption at the hands of the wife continues in force even at a lower point in the pecuniary scale than the requirement of vicarious leisure. At a point below which little if any pretence of wasted effort, in ceremonial cleanness and the like, is observable, and where there is assuredly no conscious attempt at ostensible leisure, decency still requires the wife to consume some goods conspicuously for the reputability of the household and its head. So that, as the latter-day outcome of this evolution of an archaic institution, the wife, who was at the outset the drudge and chattel of the man, both in fact and in theory,—the producer of goods for him to consume,—has become the ceremonial consumer of goods which he produces. But she still quite unmistakably remains his chattel in theory; for the habitual rendering of vicarious leisure and consumption is the abiding mark of the unfree servant.

This vicarious consumption practised by the household of the middle and lower classes can not be counted as a direct expression of the leisure-class scheme of life, since the household of this pecuniary grade does not belong within the leisure class. It is rather that the leisure-class scheme of life here comes to an expression at the second remove. The leisure class stands at the head of the social structure in point of reputability; and its manner of life and its standards of worth therefore afford the norm of reputability for the community. The observance of these standards, in some degree of approximation, becomes incumbent upon all classes lower in the scale. In modern civilized communities the lines of demarcation between social classes have grown vague and transient, and wherever this happens the norm of reputability imposed by the upper class extends its coercive influence with but slight hindrance down through the social structure to the lowest strata. The result is that the members of each stratum accept as their ideal of decency the scheme of life in vogue in the next higher stratum, and bend their energies to live up to that ideal. On pain of forfeiting their good name and their self-respect in case of failure, they must conform to the accepted code, at least in appearance.

The basis on which good repute in any highly organised industrial community ultimately rests is pecuniary strength; and the means of showing pecuniary strength, and so of gaining or retaining a good name, are leisure and a conspicuous consumption of goods. According, both of these methods are in vogue as far down the scale as it remains possible; and in the lower strata in which the two methods are employed, both offices are in great part delegated to the wife and children of the household. Lower still, where any degree of leisure, even ostensible, has become impracticable for the wife, the conspicuous consumption of goods remains and is carried on by the wife and children. The man of the household also can do something in this direction, and, indeed, he commonly does; but with a still lower descent into the levels of indigence—along the margin of the slums—the man, and presently also the children, virtually cease to consume valuable goods for appearances, and the woman remains virtually the sole exponent of the household's pecuniary decency. No class of society, not even the most abjectly poor, foregoes all customary conspicuous consumption. The last items of this category of consumption are not given up except under stress of the direst necessity. Very much of squalor and discomfort will be endured before the last trinket or the last pretence of pecuniary decency is put away. There is no class and no country that has yielded so abjectly before the pressure of physical want as to deny themselves all gratification of this higher or spiritual need. . . .

The Reputability of Waste.[1] Throughout the entire evolution of conspicuous expenditure, whether of goods or of services or human life runs the obvious implication that in order to effectually mend the consumer's good fame it must be an expenditure of superfluities. In order to be reputable it must be wasteful. No merit would accrue from the consumption of the bare necessaries of life, except by comparison with the abjectly poor who fall short even of the subsistence minimum; and no standard of expenditure could result from such a comparison, except the most prosaic and unattractive level of decency. A standard of life would still be possible which should admit of invidious comparison in other respects than that of opulence; as, for instance, a comparison in various directions in the manifestation of moral, physical, intellectual, or æsthetic force. Comparison in all these directions is in vogue to-day; and the comparison made in these respects is commonly so inextricably bound up with the pecuniary comparison as to be scarcely distinguishable from the latter. This is especially true as regards the current rating of expressions of intellectual and æsthetic force or proficiency; so that we frequently interpret as æsthetic or intellectual a difference which in substance is pecuniary only.

The use of the term "waste" is in one respect an unfortunate one. As used in the speech of everyday life the word carries an undertone of deprecation. It is here used for want of a better term that will adequately describe the same range of motives and of phenomena, and it is not to be taken in an odious sense, as implying an illegitimate expenditure of human products or of human life. In the view of economic theory the expenditure in question is no more and no less legitimate than any other expenditure. It is here called "waste" because

[1] Pp. 96–98.

this expenditure does not serve human life or human well-being on the whole, not because it is waste or misdirection of effort or expenditure as viewed from the standpoint of the individual consumer who chooses it. If he chooses it, that disposes of the question of its relative utility to him, as compared with other forms of consumption that would not be deprecated on account of their wastefulness. Whatever form of expenditure the consumer chooses, or whatever end he seeks in making his choice, has utility to him by virtue of his preference. As seen from the point of view of the individual consumer, the question of wastefulness does not arise within the scope of economic theory proper. The use of the word "waste" as a technical term, therefore, implies no deprecation of the motives or of the ends sought by the consumer under this canon of conspicuous waste.

But it is, on other grounds, worth noting that the term "waste" in the language of everyday life implies deprecation of what is characterised as wasteful. This common-sense implication is itself an outcropping of the instinct of workmanship. The popular reprobation of waste goes to say that in order to be at peace with himself the common man must be able to see in any and all human effort and human enjoyment an enhancement of life and well-being on the whole. In order to meet with unqualified approval, any economic fact must approve itself under the test of impersonal usefulness—usefulness as seen from the point of view of the generically human. Relative or competitive advantage of one individual in comparison with another does not satisfy the economic conscience, and therefore competitive expenditure has not the approval of this conscience. . . .

XXXII

RICHARD HENRY TAWNEY

1880–

Tawney, it has been said, is in the long tradition of the English governing class—"university education and Established Church affiliation." His father, educated at Rugby and Trinity College, Cambridge, served the government of Bengal, India, for twenty-six years as an official in the Educational Department, meriting a C. I. E. Richard Henry Tawney was born at Calcutta in 1880. In 1893 his father returned to England to become librarian of the India Office, the son going to Rugby and then to Balliol College, Oxford.

Since leaving the university as a student, Tawney's social activity, aside from his writing, has been mainly concerned with adult education and with investigations, governmental and other, of industry. He early became a member of the executive committee of the Workers' Educational Association (1905). After two years as an assistant lecturer in economics at the University of Glasgow (1906–08) he was chosen as the first teacher under the tutorial class system, his stipend being paid by New College, Oxford. This was a development of the older practice of university extension, with the difference that instead of lecturing to large audiences in a more or less popular vein the tutor pursued a regular course of instruction with a small group of adults. Tawney understood working-class conditions, having observed them in poverty-stricken East London; he also proved to be a first-rate teacher. His engagement therefore was a distinct success and he continued to labor in this field until 1914. In 1917 when the Lloyd-George government named a committee to consider adult education, Tawney was appointed to it and his hand is seen in the committee's final report, issued in 1918. During the war he saw service in France, being wounded in action.

For some time Tawney had been investigating labor conditions and industrial organization at close range. His scholarly treatise on *The Agrarian Problem in the Sixteenth Century* appeared in 1912. A year or two afterward he was appointed director of the Ratan Tata Foundation whose object was "to promote the study and further the knowledge of methods of preventing poverty and destitution." To this enterprise he contributed studies of minimum wage rates in the tailoring and chain-making trades (1914 and 1915). Accordingly when the well-known but somewhat ill-fated Royal Commission to investigate the coal industry was set up in 1919, Tawney was chosen by the Miners' Federation as one of the experts (the others being Sidney Webb and Sir L. Chiozza-Money) to represent the miners' interests. He next served for three years (1919–22) as a member of the Chain-Trade Board. In 1918 he was elected to a fellowship at Balliol College, Oxford, which he held until 1921.

Meanwhile Tawney was acquiring a definite, and socialistic, point of view in economic matters and when the National Guilds League was organized in 1915 he became one of its most effective propagandists. *The Acquisitive Society* (1920) is of course a guild-socialist document. But it is likewise an acute criticism of modern society, and this in fact is what gives the book its more permanent value. The socialism of Tawney has a distinctly religious cast. He was a friend of the late Bishop Charles Gore, one of the leaders of Christian Socialism and a protagonist of the moderate Anglo-Catholic party in the Church of England. In 1918 when the Anglican archbishops appointed a committee of clergy and laity to consider the relation of Christianity to industrial problems, Tawney received a place on it. The committee's report, which was surprisingly advanced considering its origin, undoubtedly owed some of its radicalism to Tawney. While all of the committee except Tawney "jibbed at socialism," says George Lansbury (another member), the document still remains one of the most comprehensive semi-official pronouncements of the Church on social matters. Tawney has since published two books dealing with the historic social functions of the Church: *Religion and the Rise of Capitalism* (1926), and an edition of Thomas Wilson's *Discourse on Usury* (1925).

Tawney has lectured in America at the Williamstown Institute of Politics. At present he is professor of economic history in the University of London and a member of the executive committee of the Fabian Society.

REFERENCES

Other works of Tawney include *The British Labor Movement* (1925), *Tudor Economic Documents* (with E. Power, 1924), *Equality* (1931), and *Land and Labor in China* (1932).

Biographical data has to be collected from a variety of sources, none of which, except the British *Who's Who*, contains enough to warrant individual mention.

READINGS FROM

THE ACQUISITIVE SOCIETY

First Principles.[1] An appeal to principles is the condition of any considerable reconstruction of society, because social institutions are the visible expression of the scale of moral values which rules the minds of individuals, and it is impossible to alter institutions without altering that moral valuation. Parliament, industrial organizations, the whole complex machinery through which society expresses itself, is a mill which grinds only what is put into it, and when nothing is put into it grinds air. There are many, of course, who desire no alteration, and who, when it is attempted, will oppose it. They have found the existing economic order profitable in the past. They desire only such changes as will insure that it is equally profitable in the future. *Quand le Roi avait bu, la Pologne était ivre.* They are genuinely unable to understand why their countrymen cannot bask happily by the fire which warms themselves, and ask, like the French farmer-general:—"When everything goes so happily, why trouble to change it?" Such persons are to be pitied, for they lack the social quality which is proper to man. But they do not need argument; for Heaven has denied them one of the faculties required to apprehend it.

There are others, however, who are conscious of the desire for a new social order, but who yet do not grasp the implications of their own desire. Men may genuinely sympathize with the demand for a radical change. They may be conscious of social evils and sincerely anxious to remove them. They may set up a new department, and appoint new officials, and invent a new name to express their resolution to effect something more drastic than reform, and less disturbing than revolution. But unless they will take the pains, not only to act, but to reflect, they end by effecting nothing. For they deliver themselves bound to those who think they are practical, because they take their philosophy so much for granted as to be unconscious of its implications, and directly they try to act, that philosophy reasserts itself, and serves as an over-ruling force which presses their action more deeply into the old channels. . . .

Yet all the time the principles upon which industry should be based are simple, however difficult it may be to apply them; and if

[1] *The Acquisitive Society* (1920), pp. 3–4, 6–7. Copyright by Harcourt, Brace and Co., New York.

they are overlooked it is not because they are difficult, but because they are elementary. They are simple because industry is simple. An industry, when all is said, is, in its essence, nothing more mysterious than a body of men associated, in various degrees of competition and co-operation, to win their living by providing the community with some service which it requires. Organize it as you will, let it be a group of craftsmen laboring with hammer and chisel, or peasants plowing their own fields, or armies of mechanics of a hundred different trades constructing ships which are miracles of complexity with machines which are the climax of centuries of invention, its function is service, its method is association. Because its function is service, an industry as a whole has rights and duties towards the community, the abrogation of which involves privilege. Because its method is association, the different parties within it have rights and duties towards each other; and the neglect or perversion of these involves oppression.

The conditions of a right organization of industry are, therefore, permanent, unchanging, and capable of being apprehended by the most elementary intelligence, provided it will read the nature of its countrymen in the large outlines of history, not in the bloodless abstractions of experts. The first is that it should be subordinated to the community in such a way as to render the best service technically possible, that those who render no service should not be paid at all, because it is of the essence of a function that it should find its meaning in the satisfaction, not of itself, but of the end which it serves. The second is that its direction and government should be in the hands of persons who are responsible to those who are directed and governed, because it is the condition of economic freedom that men should not be ruled by an authority which they cannot control. The industrial problem, in fact, is a problem of right, not merely of material misery, and because it is a problem of right it is most acute among those sections of the working classes whose material misery is least. It is a question, first of Function, and secondly of Freedom. . . .

A Functional versus an Acquisitive Society.[1] A function may be defined as an activity which embodies and expresses the idea of social purpose. The essence of it is that the agent does not perform it merely for personal gain or to gratify himself, but recognizes that he is responsible for its discharge to some higher authority. The

[1] *Ibid.*, pp. 8–9, 20–21, 28–32.

purpose of industry is obvious. It is to supply man with things which are necessary, useful or beautiful, and thus to bring life to body or spirit. In so far as it is governed by this end, it is among the most important of human activities. In so far as it is diverted from it, it may be harmless, amusing, or even exhilarating to those who carry it on, but it possesses no more social significance than the orderly business of ants and bees, the strutting of peacocks, or the struggles of carnivorous animals over carrion.

Men have normally appreciated this fact, however unwilling or unable they may have been to act upon it; and therefore from time to time, in so far as they have been able to control the forces of violence and greed, they have adopted various expedients for emphasizing the social quality of economic activity. It is not easy, however, to emphasize it effectively, because to do so requires a constant effort of will, against which egotistical instincts are in rebellion, and because, if that will is to prevail, it must be embodied in some social and political organization, which may itself become so arbitrary, tyrannical and corrupt as to thwart the performance of function instead of promoting it. When this process of degeneration has gone far, as in most European countries it had by the middle of the eighteenth century, the indispensable thing is to break the dead organization up and to clear the ground. In the course of doing so, the individual is emancipated and his rights are enlarged; but the idea of social purpose is discredited by the discredit justly attaching to the obsolete order in which it is embodied.

It is not surprising, therefore, that in the new industrial societies which arose on the ruins of the old régime the dominant note should have been the insistence upon individual rights, irrespective of any social purpose to which their exercise contributed. . . .

This doctrine has been qualified in practice by particular limitations to avert particular evils and to meet exceptional emergencies. But it is limited in special cases precisely because its general validity is regarded as beyond controversy, and, up to the eve of the present war, it was the working faith of modern economic civilization. What it implies is, that the foundation of society is found, not in functions, but in rights; that rights are not deducible from the discharge of functions, so that the acquisition of wealth and the enjoyment of property are contingent upon the performances of services, but that the individual enters the world equipped with rights to the free disposal of his property and the pursuit of his economic self-interest, and that these rights are anterior to, and independent of, any service which he may render. True, the service of society will, in fact, it is assumed, result from their exercise. But it is not the primary motive and criterion of industry, but a secondary consequence, which emerges incidentally through the exercise of rights, a consequence which is attained, indeed, in practice, but which is attained without being sought. It is not the end at which economic activity aims, or the standard by which it is judged, but a by-product, as coal-tar is a by-product of the manufacture of gas; whether that by-product appears or not, it is not proposed that the rights themselves should be abdicated. For they are regarded, not as a conditional trust, but as a property, which may, indeed, give way to the special exigencies of extraordinary emergencies, but which resumes its sway when the emergency is over, and in normal times is above discussion. . . .

A society which aimed at making the acquisition of wealth contingent upon the discharge of social obligations, which sought to proportion remuneration to service and denied it to those by whom no service was performed, which inquired first not what men possess but what they can make or create or achieve, might be called a Functional Society, because in such a society the main subject of social emphasis would be the performance of functions. But such a society does not exist, even as a remote ideal, in the modern world, though something like it has hung, an unrealized theory, before men's minds in the past. Modern societies aim at protecting economic rights, while leaving economic functions, except in moments of abnormal emergency, to fulfil themselves. The motive which gives color and quality to their public institutions, to their policy and political thought, is not the attempt to secure the fulfillment of tasks undertaken for the public service, but to increase the opportunities open to individuals of attaining the objects which they conceive to be advantageous to themselves. If asked the end or criterion of social organization, they would give an answer reminiscent of the formula the greatest happiness of the greatest number. But to say that the end of social institutions is happiness, is to say that they have no common end at all. For happiness is individual, and to make happiness the object of society is to resolve society itself into the ambitions of numberless individuals, each directed towards the attainment of some personal purpose.

Such societies may be called Acquisitive Societies, because their whole tendency and interest and preoccupation is to promote the acquisition of wealth. The appeal of this conception must be powerful, for it has laid the whole modern world under its spell. Since England first revealed the possibilities of industrialism, it has gone from strength to strength, and as industrial civilization invades countries hitherto remote from it, as Russia and Japan and India and China are drawn into its orbit, each decade sees a fresh extension of its influence. The secret of its triumph is obvious. It is an invitation to men to use the powers with which they have been endowed by nature or society, by skill or energy or relentless egotism or mere good fortune, without inquiring whether there is any principle by which their exercise should be limited. It assumes the social organization which determines the opportunities which different classes shall in fact possess, and concentrates attention upon the right of those who possess or can acquire power to make the fullest use of it for their own self-advancement. By fixing men's minds, not upon the discharge of social obligations, which restricts their energy, because it defines the goal to which it should be directed, but upon the exercise of the right to pursue their own self-interest, it offers unlimited scope for the acquisition of riches, and therefore gives free play to one of the most powerful of human instincts. To the strong it promises unfettered freedom for the exercise of their strength; to the weak the hope that they too one day may be strong. Before the eyes of both it suspends a golden prize, which not all can attain, but for which each may strive, the enchanting vision of infinite expansion. It assures men that there are no ends other than their ends, no law other than their desires, no limit other than that which they think advisable. Thus it makes the individual the center of his own universe, and dissolves moral principles into a choice of expediences. And it immensely simplifies the problems of social life in complex communities. For it relieves them of the necessity of discriminating between different types of economic activity and different sources of wealth, between enterprise and avarice, energy and unscrupulous greed, property which is legitimate and property which is theft, the just enjoyment of the fruits of labor and the idle parasitism of birth or fortune, because it treats all economic activities as standing upon the same level, and suggests that excess or defect, waste or superfluity, require no conscious effort of the social will to avert them, but are corrected almost automatically by the mechanical play of economic forces.

Under the impulse of such ideas men do not become religious or wise or artistic; for religion and wisdom and art imply the acceptance of limitations. But they become powerful and rich. They inherit the earth and change the face of nature, if they do not possess their own souls; and they have that appearance of freedom which consists in the absence of obstacles between opportunities for self-advancement and those whom birth or wealth or talent or good fortune has placed in a position to seize them. It is not difficult either for individuals or for societies to achieve their object, if that object be sufficiently limited and immediate, and if they are not distracted from its pursuit by other considerations. The temper which dedicates itself to the cultivation of opportunities, and leaves obligations to take care of themselves, is set upon an object which is at once simple and practicable. The eighteenth century defined it. The twentieth century has very largely attained it. Or, if it has not attained it, it has at least grasped the possibilities of its attainment. The national output of wealth per head of population is estimated to have been approximately $200 in 1914. Unless mankind chooses to continue the sacrifice of prosperity to the ambitions and terrors of nationalism, it is possible that by the year 2000 it may be doubled.

The Evils of an Acquisitive Society.[1] Such happiness is not remote from achievement. In the course of achieving it, however, the world has been confronted by a group of unexpected consequences, which are the cause of its *malaise,* as the obstruction of economic opportunity was the cause of social *malaise* in the eighteenth century. And these consequences are not, as is often suggested, accidental mal-adjustments, but flow naturally from its dominant principle: so that there is a sense in which the cause of its perplexity is not its failure, but the quality of its success, and its light itself a kind of darkness. The will to economic power, if it is sufficiently single-minded, brings riches. But if it is single-minded it destroys the moral restraints which ought to condition the pursuit of riches, and therefore also makes the pursuit of riches meaningless. For what gives meaning to economic activity, as to any other activity is, as we have said, the purpose to which it is directed. But the faith upon which our economic civilization reposes, the faith that riches are not a means but an end, implies that all economic activity is equally estimable, whether it is subordinated to a social purpose or not. Hence it divorces gain from service, and justifies rewards for which no function is performed, or which are out of all proportion to it. Wealth in mod-

[1] *Ibid.*, pp. 33–39, 40–41.

ern societies is distributed according to opportunity; and while opportunity depends partly upon talent and energy, it depends still more upon birth, social position, access to education and inherited wealth; in a word, upon property. For talent and energy can create opportunity. But property need only wait for it. It is the sleeping partner who draws the dividends which the firm produces, the residuary legatee who always claims his share in the estate.

Because rewards are divorced from services, so that what is prized most is not riches obtained in return for labor but riches the economic origin of which, being regarded as sordid, is concealed, two results follow. The first is the creation of a class of pensioners upon industry, who levy toll upon its product, but contribute nothing to its increase, and who are not merely tolerated, but applauded and admired and protected with assiduous care, as though the secret of prosperity resided in them. They are admired because in the absence of any principle of discrimination between incomes which are payment for functions and incomes which are not, all incomes, merely because they represent wealth, stand on the same level of appreciation, and are estimated solely by their magnitude, so that in all societies which have accepted industrialism there is an upper layer which claims the enjoyment of social life, while it repudiates its responsibilities. The *rentier* and his ways, how familiar they were in England before the war! A public school and then club life in Oxford and Cambridge, and then another club in town; London in June, when London is pleasant, the moors in August, and pheasants in October, Cannes in December and hunting in February and March; and a whole world of rising bourgeoisie eager to imitate them, sedulous to make their expensive watches keep time with their preposterous calendar!

The second consequence is the degradation of those who labor, but who do not by their labor command large rewards; that is of the great majority of mankind. And this degradation follows inevitably from the refusal of men to give the purpose of industry the first place in their thought about it. When they do that, when their minds are set upon the fact that the meaning of industry is the service of man, all who labor appear to them honorable, because all who labor serve, and the distinction which separates those who serve from those who merely spend is so crucial and fundamental as to obliterate all minor distinctions based on differences of income. But when the criterion of function is forgotten, the only criterion which remains is that of wealth, and an Acquisitive Society reverences the possession of wealth, as a Functional Society would honor, even in the person of the humblest and most laborious craftsman, the arts of creation.

So wealth becomes the foundation of public esteem, and the mass of men who labor, but who do not acquire wealth are thought to be vulgar and meaningless and insignificant compared with the few who acquire wealth by good fortune, or by the skilful use of economic opportunities. They come to be regarded, not as the ends for which alone it is worth while to produce wealth at all, but as the instruments of its acquisition by a world that declines to be soiled by contact with what is thought to be the dull and sordid business of labor. They are not happy, for the reward of all but the very mean is not merely money, but the esteem of their fellow-men, and they know they are not esteemed, as soldiers, for example, are esteemed, though it is because they give their lives to making civilization that there is a civilization which it is worth while for soldiers to defend. They are not esteemed, because the admiration of society is directed towards those who get, not towards those who give; and though workmen give much they get little. And the *rentiers* whom they support are not happy; for in discarding the idea of function, which sets a limit to the acquisition of riches, they have also discarded the principle which alone give riches their meaning. Hence unless they can persuade themselves that to be rich is in itself meritorious, they may bask in social admiration, but they are unable to esteem themselves. For they have abolished the principle which makes activity significant, and therefore estimable. They are, indeed, more truly pitiable than some of those who envy them. For like the spirits in the Inferno, they are punished by the attainment of their desires.

A society ruled by these notions is necessarily the victim of an irrational inequality. To escape such inequality it is necessary to recognize that there is some principle which ought to limit the gains of particular classes and particular individuals, because gains drawn from certain sources or exceeding certain amounts are illegitimate. But such a limitation implies a standard of discrimination, which is inconsistent with the assumption that each man has a right to what he can get, irrespective of any service rendered for it. Thus privilege, which was to have been exorcised by the gospel of 1789, returns in a new guise, the creature no longer of unequal legal rights thwarting the natural exercise of equal powers of hand and brain, but of unequal powers springing from the exercise of equal rights in a world where property and inherited wealth and the apparatus of class institutions have made opportunities unequal. Inequality, again, leads to the mis-direction of production. For, since the demand of one income of £50,000 is as powerful a magnet as the demand of 500 incomes of £100, it diverts energy from the creation of wealth to the multiplication of luxuries, so that, for example, while one-tenth of the people of England are overcrowded, a considerable part of them are engaged, not in supplying that deficiency, but in making rich men's hotels, luxurious yachts, and motor-cars like that used by the Secretary of State for War, "with an interior inlaid with silver in quartered mahogany, and upholstered in fawn suede and morocco," which was recently bought by a suburban capitalist, by way of encouraging useful industries and rebuking public extravagance with an example of private economy, for the trifling sum of $14,000.

Thus part of the goods which are annually produced, and which are called wealth, is, strictly speaking, waste, because it consists of articles which, though reckoned as part of the income of the nation, either should not have been produced until other articles had already been produced in sufficient abundance, or should not have been produced at all. And some part of the population is employed in making goods which no man can make with happiness, or indeed without loss of self-respect, because he knows that they had much better not be made, and that his life is wasted in making them. Everybody recognizes that the army contractor who, in time of war, set several hundred navvies to dig an artificial lake in his grounds, was not adding to, but subtracting from, the wealth of the nation. But in time of peace many hundred thousand workmen, if they are not digging ponds, are doing work which is equally foolish and wasteful; though, in peace, as in war, there is important work, which is waiting to be done, and which is neglected. It is neglected because, while the effective demand of the mass of men is only too small, there is a small class which wears several men's clothes, eats several men's dinners, occupies several families' houses, and lives several men's lives. As long as a minority has so large an income that part of it, if spent at all, must be spent on trivialities, so long will part of the human energy and mechanical equipment of the nation be diverted from serious work, which enriches it, to making trivialities, which impoverishes it, since they can only be made at the cost of not making other things. And if the peers and millionaires who are now preaching the duty of production to miners and dock laborers desire that more wealth, not more waste, should be produced, the simplest way in which they can achieve their aim is to transfer to the public their whole incomes over (say) $5,000 a year, in order that it may be spent in setting to work, not gardeners, chauffeurs, domestic servants and shopkeepers in the West End of London, but builders, mechanics, and teachers. . . .

The rejection of the idea of purpose involves another consequence which every one laments, but which no one can prevent, except by abandoning the belief that the free exercise of rights is the main interest of society and the discharge of obligations a secondary and incidental consequence which may be left to take care of itself. It is that social life is turned into a scene of fierce antagonisms and that a considerable part of industry is carried on in the intervals of a disguised social war. The idea that industrial peace can be secured merely by the exercise of tact and forbearance is based on the idea that there is a fundamental identity of interest between the different groups engaged in it, which is occasionally interrupted by regrettable misunderstandings. Both the one idea and the other are an illusion. The disputes which matter are not caused by a misunderstanding of identity of interests, but by a better understanding of diversity of interests. Though a formal declaration of war is an episode, the conditions which issue in a declaration of war are permanent; and what makes them permanent is the conception of industry which also makes inequality and functionless incomes permanent. It is the denial that industry has any end or purpose other than the satisfaction of those engaged in it.

That motive produces industrial warfare, not as a regrettable incident, but as an inevitable result. It produces industrial war, because its teaching is that each individual or group has a right to what they can get, and denies that there is any principle, other than the mechanism of the market, which determines what they ought to get. For, since the income available for distribution is limited, and since, therefore, when certain limits have been passed, what one group gains another group must lose, it is evident that if the relative incomes of different groups are not to be determined by their functions, there is no method other than mutual self-assertion which is left to determine them. Self-interest, indeed, may cause them to refrain from using their full strength to enforce their claims, and, in so far as this happens, peace is secured in industry, as men have attempted to secure it in international affairs, by a balance of power. But the maintenance of such a peace is contingent upon the estimate of the parties to it that they have more to lose than to gain by an overt struggle, and is not the result of their acceptance of any standard of remuneration as an equitable settlement of their claims. Hence it is precarious, insincere and short. It is without finality, because there can be no finality in the mere addition of increments of income, any more than in the gratification of any other desire for material goods. When demands are conceded the old struggle recommences upon a new level, and will always recommence as long as men seek to end it merely by increasing remuneration, not by finding a principle upon which all remuneration, whether large or small, should be based. . . .

Property Rights Proportioned to Work.[1] The application of the principle that society should be organized upon the basis of functions, is not recondite, but simple and direct. It offers in the first place, a standard for discriminating between those types of private property which are legitimate and those which are not. During the last century and a half, political thought has oscillated between two conceptions of property, both of which, in their different ways, are extravagant. On the one hand, the practical foundation of social organization has been the doctrine that the particular forms of private property which exist at any moment are a thing sacred and inviolable, that anything may properly become the object of property rights, and that, when it does, the title to it is absolute and unconditioned. . . .

On the other hand, the attack has been almost as undiscriminating as the defense. "Private property" has been the central position against which the social movement of the last hundred years has directed its forces. The criticism of it has ranged from an imaginative communism in the most elementary and personal of necessaries, to prosaic and partially realized proposals to transfer certain kinds of property from private to public ownership, or to limit their exploitation by restrictions imposed by the State. But, however varying in emphasis and in method, the general note of what may conveniently be called the Socialist criticism of property is what the word Socialism itself implies. Its essence is the statement that the economic evils of society are primarily due to the unregulated operation, under modern conditions of industrial organization, of the institution of private property. . . .

The characteristic fact, which differentiates most modern property

[1] *Ibid.*, pp. 52, 53, 61–64.

from that of the pre-industrial age, and which turns against it the very reasoning by which formerly it was supported, is that in modern economic conditions ownership is not active, but passive, that to most of those who own property to-day it is not a means of work but an instrument for the acquisition of gain or the exercise of power, and that there is no guarantee that gain bears any relation to service, or power to responsibility. For property which can be regarded as a condition of the performance of function, like the tools of the craftsman, or the holding of the peasant, or the personal possessions which contribute to a life of health and efficiency, forms an insignificant proportion, as far as its value is concerned, of the property rights existing at present. In modern industrial societies the great mass of property consists, as the annual review of wealth passing at death reveals, neither of personal acquisitions such as household furniture, nor of the owner's stock-in-trade, but of rights of various kinds, such as royalties, ground-rents, and, above all, of course shares in industrial undertakings which yield an income irrespective of any personal service rendered by their owners. Ownership and use are normally divorced. The greater part of modern property has been attenuated to a pecuniary lien or bond on the product of industry which carries with it a right to payment, but which is normally valued precisely because it relieves the owner from any obligation to perform a positive or constructive function.

Such property may be called passive property, or property for acquisition, for exploitation, or for power, to distinguish it from the property which is actively used by its owner for the conduct of his profession or the upkeep of his household. To the lawyer the first is, of course, as fully property as the second. It is questionable, however, whether economists shall call it "Property" at all, and not rather, as Mr. Hobson has suggested, "Improperty," since it is not identical with the rights which secure the owner the produce of his toil, but is opposite of them. A classification of proprietary rights based upon this difference would be instructive. If they were arranged according to the closeness with which they approximate to one or other of these two extremes, it would be found that they were spread along a line stretching from property which is obviously the payment for, and condition of, personal services, to property which is merely a right to payment from the services rendered by others, in fact a private tax. The rough order which would emerge, if all details and qualification were omitted, might be something as follows:—

1. Property in payment made for personal services.
2. Property in personal possessions necessary to health and comfort.
3. Property in land and tools used by their owners.
4. Property in copyright and patent rights owned by authors and inventors.
5. Property in pure interest, including much agricultural rent.
6. Property in profits of luck and good fortune: "quasi-rents."
7. Property in monopoly profits.
8. Property in urban ground-rents.
9. Property in royalties.[1]

The first four kinds of property obviously accompany, and in some sense condition, the performance of work. The last four obviously do not. Pure interest has some affinities with both. It represents a necessary economic cost, the equivalent of which must be borne, whatever the legal arrangements under which property is held, and is thus unlike the property represented by profits (other than the equivalent of salaries and payment for necessary risk), urban ground-rents and royalties. It relieves the recipient from personal services, and thus resembles them. . . .

Organization of a Functional Society.[2] The first step, then, towards the organization of economic life for the performance of function is to abolish those types of private property in return for which no function is performed. The man who lives by owning without working is necessarily supported by the industry of some one else, and is, therefore, too expensive a luxury to be encouraged. Though he deserves to be treated with the leniency which ought to be, and usually is not, shown to those who have been brought up from infancy to any other disreputable trade, indulgence to individuals must not condone the institution of which both they and their neighbors are the victims.

The application to industry of the principle of purpose is simple, however difficult it may be to give effect to it. It is to turn it into a Profession. A Profession may be defined most simply as a trade which is organized, incompletely, no doubt, but genuinely, for the performance of function. It is not simply a collection of individuals who get a living for themselves by the same kind of work. Nor is it merely a group which is organized exclusively for the economic protection of its members, though that is normally among its purposes. It is a body of

[1] *I.e.*, payments to landowners for the right to extract minerals. (Editor.)
[2] *Ibid.*, pp. 87–88, 92, 94–96, 126–128.

men who carry on their work in accordance with rules designed to enforce certain standards both for the better protection of its members and for the better service of the public. . . .

The difference between industry as it exists to-day and a profession is, then, simple and unmistakable. The essence of the former is that its only criterion is the financial return which it offers to its shareholders. The essence of the latter, is that, though men enter it for the sake of livelihood, the measure of their success is the service which they perform, not the gains which they amass. They may, as in the case of a successful doctor, grow rich; but the meaning of their profession, both for themselves and for the public, is not that they make money but that they make health, or safety, or knowledge, or good government or good law. They depend on it for their income, but they do not consider that any conduct which increases their income is on that account good. And while a boot-manufacturer who retires with half a million is counted to have achieved success, whether the boots which he made were of leather or brown paper, a civil servant who did the same would be impeached.

So, if they are doctors, they recognize that there are certain kinds of conduct which cannot be practised, however large the fee offered for them, because they are unprofessional; if scholars and teachers, that it is wrong to make money by deliberately deceiving the public, as is done by makers of patent medicines, however much the public may clamor to be deceived; if judges or public servants, that they must not increase their incomes by selling justice for money; if soldiers, that the service comes first, and their private inclinations, even the reasonable preference of life to death, second. Every country has its traitors, every army its deserters, and every profession its blacklegs. To idealize the professional spirit would be very absurd; it has its sordid side, and, if it is to be fostered in industry, safeguards will be needed to check its excesses. But there is all the difference between maintaining a standard which is occasionally abandoned, and affirming as the central truth of existence that there is no standard to maintain. The meaning of a profession is that it makes the traitors the exception, not as they are in industry, the rule. It makes them the exception by upholding as the criterion of success the end for which the profession, whatever it may be, is carried on, and subordinating the inclination, appetites and ambitions of individuals to the rules of an organization which has as its object to promote the performance of function.

There is no sharp line between the professions and the industries. A hundred years ago the trade of teaching, which to-day is on the whole an honorable public service, was rather a vulgar speculation upon public credulity; if Mr. Squeers was a caricature, the Oxford of Gibbon and Adam Smith was a solid port-fed reality; no local authority could have performed one-tenth of the duties which are carried out by a modern municipal corporation every day, because there was no body of public servants to perform them, and such as there were took bribes. It is conceivable, at least, that some branches of medicine might have developed on the lines of industrial capitalism, with hospitals as factories, doctors hired at competitive wages as their "hands," large dividends paid to shareholders by catering for the rich, and the poor, who do not offer a profitable market, supplied with an inferior service or with no service at all. . . .

The work of making boots or building a house is in itself no more degrading than that of curing the sick or teaching the ignorant. It is as necessary and therefore as honorable. It should be at least equally bound by rules which have as their object to maintain the standards of professional service. It should be at least equally free from the vulgar subordination of moral standards to financial interests. . . .

The organization of industry as a profession does not involve only the abolition of functionless property, and the maintenance of publicity as the indispensable condition of a standard of professional honor. It implies also that those who perform its work should undertake that its work is performed effectively. It means that they should not merely be held to the service of the public by fear of personal inconvenience or penalties, but that they should treat the discharge of professional responsibilities as an obligation attaching not only to a small *élite* of intellectuals, managers or "bosses," who perform the technical work of "business management," but as implied by the mere entry into the industry and as resting on the corporate consent and initiative of the rank and file of workers. It is precisely, indeed, in the degree to which that obligation is interpreted as attaching to all workers, and not merely to a select class, that the difference between the existing industrial order, collectivism and the organization of industry as a profession resides. The first involves the utilization of human beings for the purpose of private gain; the second their utilization for the purpose of public service; the third the association in the service of the public of their professional pride, solidarity and organization.

The difference in administrative machinery between the second and third might not be considerable. Both involve the drastic limitation or transference to the public of the proprietary rights of the existing owners of industrial capital. Both would necessitate machinery for bringing the opinion of the consumers to bear upon the service supplied them by the industry. The difference consists in the manner in which the obligations of the producer to the public are conceived. He may either be the executant of orders transmitted to him by its agents; or he may, through his organization, himself take a positive part in determining what those orders should be. In the former case he is responsible for his own work, but not for anything else. If he hews his stint of coal, it is no business of his whether the pit is a failure; if he puts in the normal number of rivets, he disclaims all further interest in the price or the seaworthiness of the ship. In the latter his function embraces something more than the performance of the specialized piece of work allotted to him. It includes also a responsibility for the success of the undertaking as a whole. And since responsibility is impossible without power, his position would involve at least so much power as is needed to secure that he can affect in practice the conduct of the industry. It is this collective liability for the maintenance of a certain quality of service which is, indeed, the distinguishing feature of a profession. It is compatible with several different kinds of government, or indeed, when the unit of production is not a group, but an individual, with hardly any government at all. What it does involve is that the individual, merely by entering the profession should have committed himself to certain obligations in respect of its conduct, and that the professional organization, whatever it may be, should have sufficient power to enable it to maintain them. . . .

The Inefficiency of an Acquisitive Society.[1] During the greater part of the nineteenth century industry was driven by two forces, hunger and fear, and the employer commanded them both. He could grant or withhold employment as he pleased. If men revolted against his terms he could dismiss them, and if they were dismissed what confronted them was starvation or the workhouse. Authority was centralized; its instruments were passive; the one thing which they dreaded was unemployment. And since they could neither prevent its occurrence nor do more than a little to mitigate its horrors when it occurred, they submitted to a discipline which they could

[1] *Ibid.*, pp. 140, 141, 144.

not resist, and industry pursued its course through their passive acquiescence in a power which could crush them individually if they attempted to oppose it.

That system might be lauded as efficient or denounced as inhuman. But, at least, as its admirers were never tired of pointing out, it worked. And, like the Prussian State, which alike in its virtues and deficiencies it not a little resembled, as long as it worked it survived denunciations of its methods, as a strong man will throw off a disease. But to-day it is ceasing to have even the qualities of its defects. It is ceasing to be efficient. It no longer secures the ever-increasing output of wealth which it offered in its golden prime, and which enabled it to silence criticism by an imposing spectacle of material success. . . .

For the instruments through which Capitalism exercised discipline are one by one being taken from it. It cannot pay what wages it likes or work what hours it likes. In well-organized industries the power of arbitrary dismissal, the very center of its authority, is being shaken, because men will no longer tolerate a system which makes their livelihood dependent on the caprices of an individual. In all industries alike the time is not far distant when the dread of starvation can no longer be used to cow dissatisfied workers into submission, because the public will no longer allow involuntary unemployment to result in starvation. . . .

Thus the time has come when absolutism in industry may still win its battles, but loses the campaign, and loses it on the very ground of economic efficiency which was of its own selection. In the period of transition, while economic activity is distracted by the struggle between those who have the name and habit of power, but no longer the full reality of it, and those who are daily winning more of the reality of power but are not yet its recognized repositories, it is the consumer who suffers. He has neither the service of docile obedience, nor the service of intelligent coöperation. For slavery will work—as long as the slaves will let it; and freedom will work when men have learned to be free; but what will not work is a combination of the two. So the public goes short of coal not only because of the technical deficiencies of the system under which it is raised and distributed, but because the system itself has lost its driving force—because the coal owners can no longer persuade the miners into producing more dividends for them and more royalties for the owners of minerals, while the public cannot appeal to them to put their whole power into serving itself, because it has chosen that they should be the servants, not of itself, but of shareholders. . . .

XXXIII

JOHN DEWEY

1859–

John Dewey was born in 1859 at Burlington, Vermont, "one of the high, cold pinnacles of Culture." He escaped the chilling influence without foregoing the intellectual advantages of the climate. "My ancestry, particularly on my father's side," he says, "is free from all blemish. All my forefathers earned an honest living as farmers, wheelwrights, coopers." He attended the University of Vermont. After receiving his B. A. degree he was uncertain whether to follow a bent toward philosophy, being doubtful of his ability along that line. He therefore submitted an article to the *Journal of Speculative Philosophy*, asking the editor, W. T. Harris, for advice as to his future career. Harris reassured him on that point and he went on to take a Ph. D. degree at Johns Hopkins in 1884. In 1886 he married Alice Chapman; four children were born to them, another was adopted.

Meanwhile Dewey had invaded the Middle West where he was to make his reputation. His first post was an instructorship in the University of Michigan; he was later promoted to assistant professor. While at Michigan he published his *Psychology* (1886), treating the subject more as a natural science than as a branch of metaphysics, although the latter was the prevailing tendency at the time. In 1888 he was called to the University of Minnesota as professor of philosophy but returned to Michigan the next year with the same rank.

Dewey had also been working out a theory of education. The laboratory school of the University of Chicago, where he went as professor of philosophy in 1894, gave him an opportunity of testing it out. Mrs. Dewey worked with him, says a commentator, in attempting "to utilize instead of to suppress the four-fold impulses of childhood: the interest in conversation, the interest in inquiry, the interest in construction, and the interest in artistic expression." He explained the project in *School and Society* (1899), a book which is said to have marked the beginning of an era in education.

Acceptance of a chair of philosophy at Columbia in 1904 permitted Dewey to concentrate his attention on other aspects of the problem of knowledge, although he continued to contribute frequently to educational theory. His doctrine of cognition, "instrumentalism," was the result. This was put into plain language in *How We Think* (1909). He had already written a book on ethics (1894) and one on logic (1903). In spite of his dislike of neat classifications he became identified with the pragmatists in philosophy, especially with the left-wing group.

Dr. Dewey's interest has also ranged over the field of politics and government both in a theoretical and of late in a very practical way—in fact he has usually been the first to put his ideas in any field to the test of practice. A believer in democracy although admitting that it is still on trial, he has traced its psychological basis and advocated its extension to industry. In 1929 he accepted the presidency of the League for Independent Political Action, a group which carried on an active propaganda and gained considerable publicity especially during the presidential campaign of 1932. This is designed to be the nucleus of a third (or fourth) party movement.

Although Dewey is still relatively unknown to most citizens, it is very likely that he has had more to do with molding their careers than any other living American. Even an occasionally tortuous literary style (caused, it is said, by over-anxiety to express himself exactly) and a rather difficult, hesitant method of lecturing have not noticeably restricted his influence. Indeed, his educational principles more and more tend to dominate the school system, while a host of disciples carry the Deweyite philosophy into religion, politics, journalism, and the social sciences. "Croly, Kallen, Lippmann, Robinson, van Loon, La Follette, Eastman, Baker, Howe, John Haynes Holmes, Rabbi Wise, Clarence Darrow—such, with scores of others, are the men who have colored the very action of our world with the thought of this man."

REFERENCES

John Dewey is a very prolific writer—an incomplete bibliography of his books and articles covers more than a hundred pages. A useful epitome of his work (up to 1928) is given in *The Philosophy of John Dewey*, selected and edited by Joseph Ratner (1928).

Biographical material is very scanty; there are brief sketches in *Six Major Prophets*, by E. E. Slosson (1917) and in *Time Exposures*, by "Search-Light" (Waldo D. Frank, 1926).

READINGS FROM

INDIVIDUALISM OLD AND NEW

Contradictions of American Life.[1] It was not long ago that it was fashionable for both American and foreign observers of our national scene to sum up the phenomena of our social life under the title of "individualism." Some treated this alleged individualism as our distinctive achievement; some critics held that it was the source of our backwardness, the mark of a relatively uncivilized estate. Today both interpretations seem equally inept and outmoded. Individualism is still carried on our banners and attempts are made to use it as a war cry, especially when it is desired to defeat governmental regulation of any form of industry previously exempt from legal control. Even in high quarters, rugged individualism is praised as the glory of American life. But such words have little relation to the moving facts of that life.

There is no word which adequately expresses what is taking place. "Socialism" has too specific political and economic associations to be appropriate. "Collectivism" is more neutral, but it, too, is a party-word rather than a descriptive term. Perhaps the constantly increasing rôle of corporations in our economic life gives a clue to a fitting name. The word may be used in a wider sense than is conveyed by its technical legal meaning. We may then say that the United States has steadily moved from an earlier pioneer individualism to a condition of dominant corporateness. The influence business corporations exercise in determining present industrial and economic activities is both a cause and a symbol of the tendency to combination in all phases of life. Associations tightly or loosely organized more and more define the opportunities, the choices, and the actions of individuals.

I have said that the growth of legal corporations in manufacturing, transportation, distribution, and finance is symbolic of the development of corporateness in all phases of life. The era of trust-busting is an almost forgotten age. Not only are big mergers the order of the day, but popular sentiment now looks upon them with pride rather than with fear. Size is our current measure of greatness in this as in other matters. It is not necessary to ask whether the opportunity for speculative manipulation for the sake of private gain, or increased

[1] Pp. 35–37, 74–80. Copyright by John Dewey (1932), and published by Minton, Balch and Co., New York.

public service at a lower cost, is the dominant motive. Personal motives hardly count as productive causes in comparison with impersonal forces. Mass production and mass distribution inevitably follow in the wake of an epoch of steam and electricity. These have created a common market, the parts of which are held together by intercommunication and interdependence; distance is eliminated and the tempo of action enormously accelerated. Aggregated capital and concentrated control are the contemporary responses. . . .

Our material culture, as anthropologists would call it, is verging upon the collective and corporate. Our moral culture, along with our ideology, is, on the other hand, still saturated with ideals and values of an individualism derived from the prescientific, pretechnological age. Its spiritual roots are found in medieval religion, which asserted the ultimate nature of the individual soul and centered the drama of life about the destiny of that soul. Its institutional and legal concepts were framed in the feudal period.

This moral and philosophical individualism anteceded the rise of modern industry and the era of the machine. It was the context in which the latter operated. The apparent subordination of the individual to established institutions often conceals from recognition the vital existence of a deep-seated individualism. But the fact that the controlling institution was the Church should remind us that in ultimate intent it existed to secure the salvation of the individual. That this individual was conceived as a soul, and that the end served by the institution was deferred to another and everlasting life conceal from contemporary realization the underlying individualism. In its own time, its substance consisted in just this eternal spiritual character of the personal soul; the power of the established institutions proceeded from their being the necessary means of accomplishing the supreme end of the individual.

The early phase of the industrial revolution wrought a great transformation. It gave a secular and worldly turn to the career of the individual, and it liquefied the static property concepts of feudalism by the shift of emphasis from agriculture to manufacturing. Still, the idea persisted that property and reward were intrinsically individual. There were, it is true, incompatible elements in the earlier and later versions of individualism. But a fusion of individual capitalism, of natural rights, and of morals founded in strictly individual traits and values remained, under the influence of Protestantism, the dominant intellectual synthesis.

The basis of this synthesis was destroyed, however, by the later development of the industrial system, which brought about the merging of personal capacity, effort, and work into collective wholes. Meanwhile, the control of natural energies eliminated time and distance, so that action once adapted to local conditions was swallowed up in complex undertakings of indefinite extent. Yet the older mental equipment remained after its causes and foundations had disappeared. This, fundamentally, is the inner division out of which spring our present confusion and insincerities.

The earlier economic individualism had a definite creed and function. It sought to release from legal restrictions man's wants and his efforts to satisfy those wants. It believed that such emancipation would stimulate latent energy into action, would automatically assign individual ability to the work for which it was suited, would cause it to perform that work under stimulus of the advantage to be gained, and would secure for capacity and enterprise the reward and position to which they were entitled. At the same time, individual energy and savings would be serving the needs of others, and thus promoting the general welfare and effecting a general harmony of interests.

We have gone a long way since this philosophy was formulated. To-day, the most stalwart defenders of this type of individualism do not venture to repeat its optimistic assertions. At most, they are content to proclaim its consistency with unchanging human nature—which is said to be moved to effort only by the hope of personal gain—and to paint dire pictures of the inevitable consequences of change to any other régime. They ascribe all the material benefits of our present civilization to this individualism—as if machines were made by the desire for money profit, not by impersonal science; and as if they were driven by money alone, and not by electricity and steam under the direction of a collective technology.

In America, the older individualism assumed a romantic form. It was hardly necessary to elaborate a theory which equated personal gain with social advance. The demands of the practical situation called for the initiative, enterprise and vigor of individuals in all immediate work that urgently asked for doing, and their operation furthered the national life. The spirit of the time is expressed by Dr. Crothers, whose words Mr. Sims has appropriately taken for part of the text of his "Adventurous America":

"If you would understand the driving power of America, you must understand 'the divers discontented and impatient young men' who in each generation have found an outlet for their energy. . . . The noises which disturb you are not the cries of an angry proletariat, but are the shouts of eager young people who are finding new opportunities. . . . They represent to-day the enthusiasm of a new generation. They represent the Oregons and Californias toward which sturdy pioneers are moving undisturbed by obstacles. This is what the social unrest means in America."

If that is not an echo of a voice of long ago, I do not know what it is. I do not, indeed, hear the noises of an angry proletariat; but I should suppose the sounds heard are the murmurs of lost opportunities, along with the din of machinery, motor cars, and speakeasies, by which the murmurs of discontent are drowned, rather than shouts of eagerness for adventurous opportunity.

The European version of the older individualism had its value and temporal justification because the new technology needed liberation from vexatious legal restrictions. Machine industry was itself in a pioneer condition, and those who carried it forward against obstacles of lethargy, skepticism and political obstruction were deserving of special reward. Moreover, accumulation of capital was thought of in terms of enterprises that to-day would be petty; there was no dream of the time when it would reach such a mass that it would determine the legal and political order. Poverty had previously been accepted as a dispensation of nature that was inevitable. The new industry promised a way out, at least to those possessed of energy and will to save and accumulate. But there was no anticipation of a time when the development of machine technology would afford the material basis for reasonable ease and comfort and of extensive leisure for all.

The shift that makes the older individualism a dying echo is more marked as well as more rapid in this country. Where is the wilderness which now beckons creative energy and affords untold opportunity to initiative and vigor? Where is the pioneer who goes forth rejoicing, even in the midst of privation, to its conquest? The wilderness exists in the movie and the novel; and the children of the pioneers, who live in the midst of surroundings artificially made over by the machine, enjoy pioneer life idly in the vicarious film. I see little social unrest which is the straining of energy for outlet in action; I find rather the protest against a weakening of vigor and a sapping of energy that emanate from the absence of constructive opportunity; and I see a confusion that is an expression of the inability to find a secure and morally rewarding place in a troubled and tangled economic scene.

A New Individualism Required.[1] Because of the bankruptcy of the older individualism, those who are aware of the breakdown often speak and argue as if individualism were itself done and over with. I do not suppose that those who regard socialism and individualism as antithetical really mean that individuality is going to die out or that it is not something intrinsically precious. But in speaking as if the only individualism were the local episode of the last two centuries, they play into the hands of those who would keep it alive in order to serve their own ends, and they slur over the chief problem—that of remaking society to serve the growth of a new type of individual. There are many who believe that socialism of some form is needed to realize individual initiative and security on a wide scale. They are concerned about the restriction of power and freedom to a few in the present régime, and they think that collective social control is necessary, at least for a time, in order to achieve its advantages for all. But they too often seem to assume that the result will be merely an extension of the earlier individualism to the many.

Such thinking treats individualism as if it were something static, having a uniform content. It ignores the fact that the mental and moral structure of individuals, the pattern of their desires and purposes, change with every great change in social constitution. Individuals who are not bound together in associations, whether domestic, economic, religious, political, artistic or educational, are monstrosities. It is absurd to suppose that the ties which hold them together are merely external and do not react into mentality and character, producing the framework of personal disposition.

The tragedy of the "lost individual" is due to the fact that while individuals are now caught up into a vast complex of associations, there is no harmonious and coherent reflection of the import of these connections into the imaginative and emotional outlook on life. This fact is of course due in turn to the absence of harmony within the state of society. There is an undoubted circle. But it is a vicious circle only as far as men decline to accept—in the intellectual, observing and inquiring spirit defined in the previous chapter [2]—the realities of the social estate, and because of this refusal either surrender to the division or seek to save their individuality by escape or sheer emotional revolt. The habit of opposing the corporate and collective to the individual tends to the persistent continuation of the

[1] Pp. 80–84, 89–90.
[2] Not printed here. (Editor.)

confusion and uncertainty. It distracts attention from the crucial issue: How shall the individual refind himself in an unprecedentedly new social situation, and what qualities will the new individualism exhibit?

That the problem is not merely one of extending to all individuals the traits of economic initiative, opportunity and enterprise; that it is one of forming a new psychological and moral type, is suggested by the great pressure now brought to bear to effect conformity and standardization of American opinion. Why should regimentation, the erection of an average struck from the opinions of large masses into regulative norms, and in general the domination of quantity over quality, be so characteristic of present American life? I see but one fundamental explanation. The individual cannot remain intellectually a vacuum. If his ideas and beliefs are not the spontaneous function of a communal life in which he shares, a seeming consensus will be secured as a substitute by artificial and mechanical means. In the absence of mentality that is congruous with the new social corporateness that is coming into being, there is a desperate effort to fill the void by external agencies which obtain a factitious agreement. . . .

The chief obstacle to the creation of a type of individual whose pattern of thought and desire is enduringly marked by consensus with others, and in whom sociability is one with coöperation in all regular human associations, is the persistence of that feature of the earlier individualism which defines industry and commerce by ideas of private pecuniary profit. Why, once more, is there such zeal for standardized likeness? It is not, I imagine, because conformity for its own sake appears to be a great boon. It is rather because a certain kind of conformity gives defense and protection to the pecuniary features of our present régime. The foreground may be filled with depiction of the horror of change, and with clamor for law and order and the support of the Constitution. But behind there is desire for perpetuation of that régime which defines individual initiative and ability by success in conducting business so as to make money. . . .

The Approach to a New Individualism.[1] I have attempted to portray the split between the idea of the individual inherited from the past and the realities of a situation that is becoming increasingly corporate. Some of the effects produced on living individuality by

[1] Pp. 146–152, 153–154, 164–165, 169–170.

this division have been indicated. I have urged that individuality will again become integral and vital when it creates a frame for itself by attention to the scene in which it must perforce exist and develop. It is likely that many persons will regard my statement of the problem as a commonplace. Others will deplore my failure to offer a detailed solution and a definite picture of just what an individual would be if he were in harmony with the realities of American civilization. Still others will think that a disease has been described as a remedy; that the articles are an indiscriminate praise of technological science and of a corporate industrial civilization; that they are an effort to boost upon the bandwagon those reluctant to climb.

I have indeed attempted analysis, rather than either a condemnation of the evils of present society or a recommendation of fixed ends and ideals for their cure. For I think that serious minds are pretty well agreed as to both evils and ideals—as long as both are taken in general terms. Condemnation is too often only a way of displaying superiority; it speaks from outside the scene; it discloses symptoms but not causes. It is impotent to produce; it can only reproduce its own kind. As for ideals, all agree that we want the good life, and that the good life involves freedom and a taste that is trained to appreciate the honorable, the true and the beautiful. But as long as we limit ourselves to generalities, the phrases that express ideals may be transferred from conservative to radical or vice versa, and nobody will be the wiser. For, without analysis, they do not descend into the actual scene nor concern themselves with the generative conditions of realization of ideals.

There is danger in the reiteration of eternal verities and ultimate spiritualities. Our sense of the actual is dulled, and we are led to think that in dwelling upon ideal goals we have somehow transcended existing evils. Ideals express possibilities; but they are genuine ideals only in so far as they are possibilities of what is now moving. Imagination can set them free from their encumbrances and project them as a guide in attention to what now exists. But, save as they are related to actualities, they are pictures in a dream.

I have, then, ventured to suppose that analysis of present conditions is of primary importance. Analysis of even a casual kind discloses that these conditions are not fixed. To accept them intellectually is to perceive that they are in flux. Their movement is not destined to a single end. Many outcomes may be projected, and the movement may be directed by many courses to many chosen goals, once conditions have been recognized for what they are. By becoming conscious of their movements and by active participation in their currents, we may guide them to some preferred possibility. In this interaction, individuals attain an integrated being. The individual who intelligently and actively partakes in a perception that is a first step in conscious choice is never so isolated as to be lost nor so quiescent as to be suppressed.

One of the main difficulties in understanding the present and apprehending its human possibilities is the persistence of stereotypes of spiritual life which were formed in old and alien cultures. In static societies—those which the industrial revolution has doomed—acquiescence had a meaning, and so had the projection of fixed ideals. Things were so relatively settled that there was something to acquiesce in, and goals and ideals could be imagined that were as fixed in their way as existing conditions in theirs. The medieval legal system could define "just" prices and wages, for the definition was a formulation of what was customary in the local community; it operated merely to prevent exorbitant deviations. It could prescribe a system of definite duties for all relations, for there was a hierarchical order, and occasions for the exercise of duty fell within an established and hence known order. Communities were local; they did not merge, overlap, and interact in all kinds of subtle and hidden ways. A common church was the guardian and administrator of spiritual and ideal truth, and its theoretical authority had direct channels for making itself felt in the practical details of life. Spiritual realities might have their locus in the next world, but this afterworld was intimately tied into all the affairs of this world by an institution existing here and now.

To-day there are no patterns sufficiently enduring to provide anything stable in which to acquiesce, and there is no material out of which to frame final and all-inclusive ends. There is, on the other hand, such constant change that acquiescence is but a series of interrupted spasms, and the outcome is mere drifting. In such a situation, fixed and comprehensive goals are but irrelevant dreams, while acquiescence is not a policy but its abnegation.

Again, the machine is condemned wholesale because it is seen through the eyes of a spirituality that belonged to another state of culture. Present evil consequences are treated as if they were eternally necessary, because they cannot be made consistent with the ideals of another age. In reality, a machine age is a challenge to generate new conceptions of the ideal and the spiritual. Ferrero has said that machines "are the barbarians of modern times, which have destroyed the fairest works of ancient civilization." But even the barbarians were not immutably barbarous; they, too, were bearers of directive movement, and in time they wrought out a civilization that had its own measure of fairness and beauty.

Most attacks on the mechanistic character of science are caused by the survival of philosophies and religions formed when nature was the grim foe of man. The possibility of the present, and therefore its problem, is that through and by science, nature may become the friend and ally of man. I have rarely seen an attack on science as hostile to humanism which did not rest upon a conception of nature formed long before there was any science. That there is much at any time in environing nature which is indifferent and hostile to human values is obvious to any serious mind. When natural knowledge was hardly existent, control of nature was impossible. Without power of control, there was no recourse save to build places of refuge in which man could live in imagination, although not in fact. There is no need to deny the grace and beauty of some of these constructions. But when their imaginary character is once made apparent, it is futile to suppose that men can go on living and sustaining life by them. When they are appealed to for support, the possibilities of the present are not perceived, and its constructive potentialities remain unutilized. . . .

There are those who welcome science provided it remain "pure"; they see that as a pursuit and contemplated object it is an addition to the enjoyed meaning of life. But they feel that its applications in mechanical inventions are the cause of many of the troubles of modern society. Undoubtedly these applications have brought new modes of unloveliness and suffering. I shall not attempt the impossible task of trying to strike a net balance of ills and enjoyments between the days before and after the practical use of science. The significant point is that application is still restricted. It touches our dealings with things but not with one another. We use scientific method in directing physical but not human energies. Consideration of the full application of science must accordingly be prophetic rather than a record of what has already taken place. Such prophecy is not however without foundation. Even as things are there is a movement in science which foreshadows, if its inherent promise be carried out, a more humane age. For it looks forward to a time when all individuals may share in the discoveries and thoughts of others, to the liberation and enrichment of their own experience. . . .

Because science starts with questions and inquiries it is fatal to all social system-making and programs of fixed ends. In spite of the bankruptcy of past systems of belief, it is hard to surrender our faith in system and in some wholesale belief. We continually reason as if the difficulty were in the particular system that has failed and as if we were on the point of now finally hitting upon one that is true as all the others were false. The real trouble is with the attitude of dependence upon any of them. Scientific method would teach us to break up, to inquire definitely and with particularity, to seek solutions in the terms of concrete problems as they arise. It is not easy to imagine the difference which would follow from the shift of thought to discrimination and analysis. Wholesale creeds and all-inclusive ideals are impotent in the face of actual situations; for doing always means the doing of something in particular. They are worse than impotent. They conduce to blind and vague emotional states in which credulity is at home, and where action, following the lead of overpowering emotion, is easily manipulated by the self-seekers who have kept their heads and wits. Nothing would conduce more, for example, to the elimination of war than the substitution of specific analysis of its causes for the wholesale love of "liberty, humanity, justice and civilization." . . .

The future is always unpredictable. Ideals, including that of a new and effective individuality, must themselves be framed out of the possibilities of existing conditions, even if these be the conditions that constitute a corporate and industrial age. The ideals take shape and gain a content as they operate in remaking conditions. We may, in order to have continuity of direction, plan a program of action in anticipation of occasions as they emerge. But a program of ends and ideals if kept apart from sensitive and flexible method becomes an encumbrance. For its hard and rigid character assumes a fixed world and a static individual; and neither of these things exists. It implies that we can prophesy the future—an attempt which terminates, as someone has said, in prophesying the past or in its reduplication. . . .

INDEX